THE
ACKERMAN
CHARLES HEIDSIECK
GUIDE

to the best
hotels and restaurants
in Great Britain and Ireland

Contents

First published 1993 by Leading Guides Ltd
73 Uverdale Road, London SW10 0SW

© Leading Guides Limited, 1993
73 Uverdale Road, London SW10 0SW

Illustrations, cover illustration and cover design by Chris Ackerman-Eveleigh
Design by Elizabeth Ayer
Photography by Leigh Simpson
Front cover photography by Leigh Simpson
Front cover from left to right: Roy Ackerman, Sally Clarke, Richard Shepherd
Back cover from left to right: Roy Ackerman, Antony Worrall Thompson, Sally Clarke,
Brian Turner, Richard Shepherd

CHAMPAGNE
Charles Heidsieck
In the FOOTSTEPS *of*
CHAMPAGNE CHARLIE

In 1992, an ambitious notion came to Trevor Bell, the Directeur Général of Champagne Charles Heidsieck in Reims. In an age when most travellers are reliant on the aeroplane, what if he recreated the pioneer spirit and classic adventurism of his company's founder, Charles Camille Heidsieck, with an international challenge to travel around the surface of the globe? The contestants should follow as closely as possible 'In the Footsteps of Champagne Charlie', (as Charles Camille became known) not just in the places where he introduced the joys of his champagne, but also to emulate his debonair style as one of the great philanthropists of the mid-19th century. He travelled with dash and brio; he relished every challenge. His journeys were marked by his continual quest for excitement, often peppered with intrigue.

The idea took shape, and the first challenge of what has now become an annual event was firmly established. Six international teams took up the gauntlet to visit 20 specified cities around the world, all within 100 days. To keep it within the true spirit of classic travel, there were to be no aeroplanes.

Inexhaustible in his enthusiasm, his resourcefulness, and his unwitting adoration of champagne, Nicholas Courtney, a member of the British team, here recounts some of his more memorable moments in his victorious journey around the world.

'Do you know of a writer and a photographer couple,' Countess Alexander of Tunis inquired, 'who would be free to go round the world?'

'Whatever for?' I asked.

'Charles Heidsieck, the *grande marque* champagne house, who I advise,' the Countess continued, 'have this wonderful challenge for six international teams, to visit 20 cities, within 100 days, following in the footsteps of Champagne Charlie.'

'So who's Champagne Charlie?' The music hall character, I supposed.

'Charles Camille Heidsieck who travelled the world selling his fine champagnes in the mid-1800s. This challenge is to show how Charles Heidsieck are still making a truly international champagne that is now better than ever. By the way, Charles Camille died in 1893, so no aeroplanes are allowed this time round either.'

It all sounded most exciting. 'How about us?' I asked. Three weeks later, my wife, Vanessa, and I were selected as the British team. The other teams came from France, Germany, the United States, Singapore and another from England.

Appropriately, the launch on September 7th 1992 of 'In the Footsteps of Champagne Charlie' challenge was a champagne breakfast in the Explorers' Room at the National Portrait Gallery. Robin Knox-Johnston, the yachtsman, popped a magnum of Charles Heidsieck in Trafalgar Square, a battery of cameras popped at us, and we were off driving a Morgan Plus 8 - an appropriate car as Vanessa's grandfather had started the company. We felt like proper travellers.

Our first stop was Dublin and the Shelbourne Hotel. The next morning, we had yet another champagne breakfast, a habit that would be difficult to break. This one was truly Irish and quite vast. We stayed our statutory 24 hours in Dublin, which fitted neatly with the ferry to Holyhead. We then drove through the night, the rain, Snowdonia, and a thousand hairpin bends to arrive in Shrewsbury at 3.30 am. Thereafter, we had a municipal wake-up call every half hour from the dustmen, milkman, postman, and telephone engineers!

We had planned everything minutely, but before we even left, disaster struck in the form of an uncharted rock that ripped out the bottom of the *Queen Elizabeth II*, the liner that was to take us across the Atlantic. Fortunately, we found another ship, the *Seabourn Pride,* which is like a large, luxurious private yacht rather than the small cruise ship she is. We fell all too easily into the life, not least under the spell of their wonderful Austrian chef, Johannes Bacher, who had our weight and gastric juices equally in mind. For lunch and dinner, there were two menus, 'Simplicity' and the main menu, with the chef's dinner and lunch recommendations to ease the considerable choice of seriously good food. The portions were small, the courses many. There were surprises too, like white of egg omelette or bay scallops with rosemary *jus* and wilted endive.

The night before we arrived in Boston, the Captain told us that we had consumed 35 lb. of caviar (between all of us!), about 1/2lb. a head.

As we boarded the train for New York, we knew that this was the end of our soft travel. Ahead lay a total of 12 days in a train around America and Canada. However, it did not take long to get into 'train mode' aboard such romantically named trains as Yankee Clipper or Desert Wind. We became used to the motion, so much so that after a long journey we found it difficult to sleep in a stationary bed. There were train buffs, and there were eccentrics, like the Nomad Ski Team from Chicago who, in evening dress and top hats, were going to New Orleans to check out the skiing conditions.

We spent our twenty four hours in New York, then onto Montreal, which we loved, and Toronto which did not have quite the same charm. Toronto is full of amazing modern architecture, multi-

cultural taxi drivers, and clean streets. No wonder Peter Ustinov described the city as being like New York, only run by the Swiss!

It had long been an ambition to visit Niagara Falls, the scene of many stories remembered from childhood. There was Captain Webb, who conquered the English Channel but not his finances, and perished trying to swim the Rapids. There was Blondin, the tight-rope walker, who carried his manager on his back, then told him to dismount half way. Unlike the manager, who broke out into a cold sweat at the mention of the Falls, we were greatly impressed.

New Orleans, predictably, was a definite high point of our journey. Champagne Charlie himself had been there often - at the height of his success, New Orleans was drinking 70,000 bottles of his champagne a year. He was even imprisoned there for four months as a spy during the Civil War. We cased the bars and jazz halls of Bourbon Street as unashamed tourists, and dined at the 'N'arleans Cajun Cookin'. Cajun cooking is unlike any other. During the 18th century, French settlers forced out of Newfoundland moved south to Louisiana where their cuisine became confused with that of the earlier Spanish settlers and the spicy food of the African slaves. We tried a little of everything - soft-shelled crabs with a pecan sauce, followed by jambalaya, a wonderful mixture of rice, shrimps, ham, chicken and Cajun spices. Best of all was the blackened catfish, a dish recently invented by the masterchef Paul Prudhomme.

It seems that every circumnavigator has to go by balloon, a mode apparently started by the film version of *Around the World in Eighty Days* where Passepartout stylishly leans out of the balloon as they cross the Alps to grab an armful of snow to chill Phileas Fogg's champagne. Our balloon trip over the vineyards of Napa Valley very early one morning was less adventurous, and the only frost that day hung between Vanessa and me, as we had fallen out (our only quarrel on the whole trip) over the directions (what else?). After such an exhilarating experience, champagne was the order of the day.

A whole new experience unfolded as we boarded our first container ship, the *Neptune Amber*, owned by the Neptune Orient Lines, bound for Tokyo. I cannot think what we did for the twelve days, but those improving books were largely unread, the needlepoint canvas remained almost bare. Captain Ong regaled us throughout the day with tales of the sea, of pirates and ghost ships, or, as we called them, 'Ongoing sagas'. Zarak, the Malay chef, was a marvel. For our first dinner, he left out the spices in the chicken and overcooked the potatoes and vegetables. We preferred his curried cuttlefish, so when one of the crew came in late, he ate our food. We heard him choke, spit, and leave - 'disgusted, Singapore'! On our last night, the Captain gave us a 'steam-boat'. This consisted of raw fish, dumplings, squid balls, prawns, and noodles, which we cooked ourselves in pans filled with spicy, boiling stock. We soon discovered that it was essential to guard your own prawns jealously on a spoon. When we arrived in Tokyo, we were truly sorry to say good-bye to Captain Ong and his crew.

Our trip was hugely enjoyable, not least that it was one of contrasts, from a fairly basic container ship to the majestic splendour of the Imperial Hotel, Tokyo. We were given a reception to meet the press, but the only problem was that the six who turned up were film critics and nothing to do with wine or travel. The dinner, however, was quite wonderful. The first course of lobster and caviar was so beautifully presented that it seemed a crime to eat it. The next, a consommé with a short-crust pastry top, was novel, and that was followed by steak served with *julienne* vegetables. We drank the Charles Heidsieck Brut Réserve most of the way through dinner (the only wine that truly goes with every course), ending up with the Rosé Vintage. If the food was perfection itself, the conversation was difficult in the extreme as I struggled, through an interpreter, to be amusing. Later, I was informed that the translator had no idea what I was talking about, but the guests should laugh when she stopped speaking!

With five whole days in Japan, our pace slowed a little, except for the 160 mph bullet train that took us to Kyoto. This city was everything that we had ever dreamed about in Japan - the gilded temples and shrines, the gardens that exuded peace and tranquillity. We stayed in a charming *ryokan* where we slept on the floor, put on special slippers marked WC to go to the lavatory, and ate raw fish for breakfast which was foul. However, dinner at the Hokusai Restaurant the night before was most palatable and entertaining. In the 12th century, a nobleman of the district demanded a peasant cook the game that he had killed that day out hunting. As the peasant did not have a stove, the resourceful farmer had the idea to cook on the blade of his broad hoe over the fire. The nobleman was delighted with the result, and a new culinary form was created. Hokusai is the only restaurant in the world that still uses this method of cooking, although this particular hoe was gas-fired. A geisha look-alike prepared delicious pieces of duck, chicken and a miscellany of vegetables for us, kneeling by our table. We toasted Champagne Charlie for our fortune in finding this restaurant and enjoying such an unusual dinner.

No sooner had we become used to Japan than we were off again by the P & O container ship, *Peninsular Bay*. For nearly seven days, we steamed down to Singapore. As we crossed the Tropic of Cancer, we opened yet another bottle of Charles Heidsieck to Hillaire Belloc's *The Modern Traveller* :

And yet I really can't complain,   *Presumably the latter*
About this company's champagne.   *While stern, indomitable men,*
This most expensive kind of wine,   *Have told me time and time again*
In England is a matter,   *The nuisance of the Tropics is*
Of pride or habit when we dine,   *The sheer necessity of Fizz!*

Singapore was 'our kind of town' as their national pastime is eating! There are dozens of small parks with hundreds of separate food stalls, serving the most exquisite food, day and night, all for a very few dollars. At the other end of the scale, we had a Singapore Sling in Raffles Hotel and we drank champagne in the Compass Bar on top of the Westin Stamford, the tallest hotel in the world. Our culinary highpoint came when we were treated to a *rijstaffel* dinner at the Alkaff Mansion, a sugar broker's house built solely to entertain his friends. Our *rijstaffel* was a collection of ten, beautiful Malay dishes, (mostly rice and chicken) served by ten beautiful girls, all wearing kebayas (long wrap-around skirts). They formed up behind the head girl in size order like a line-up of Bisto-kids, while a rather fierce chaperon poured the Charles Heidsieck Blanc des Millénaires.

Part of our incredible good fortune was that all our sea passages worked so well. Two days after we arrived in Singapore, another P & O ship, the *Jervis Bay*, sailed with us (and 4,000 containers) to Hong Kong. From Hong Kong, we took the train to Canton, where the new Canton of Mercedes cars and 5 star hotels jostled alongside old Canton, with its market selling a menagerie of birds and animals for the table - dogs, cats, tortoises, frogs, snakes, even foxes and badgers. After that, Vanessa suggested that we ate at the White Swan Hotel that night!

The train journey of two nights and a day between Canton and Peking was most amusing and interesting. For the first night, we shared our compartment with two men, who left at dawn. When we returned from breakfast, we found our compartment open with four Chinese men firmly ensconced. They were supposed to leave at the next stop, only the next stop turned out to be 10.30 that night! As I became exasperated, the only thing to do was to crack open a bottle of champagne. To my lasting shame, I was heard to say 'what a pity none of you has a glass!' ...Champagne is certainly a cure for those little frustrations of travel.

With only twenty four hours in Peking, we 'did' the Great Wall, the only man-made structure (apart from the M25!) to be seen by the naked eye from the Moon, and the Forbidden City: we saw Tiananmen Square, bought Vanessa an army private's coat for $5, and ate Peking duck for dinner, although it has to be admitted that it is far better at home.

Ever mindful of our stomachs, we had chosen a Chinese train for the 5,000 mile journey from Peking to Moscow on the TransMongolian Express. We did not realise that the Chinese restaurant car was replaced by a Mongolian car at the border, where, whatever we ordered from the exotic menu, we were given *boeuf Stroganoff* and beetroot. The Russian restaurant car, too, was basic, although it did have its compensations. Each evening, we met up with a psychiatrist and his sex-therapist wife, for bridge and dinner that included two pots of caviar at $3 each.

The whole journey was quite fascinating - we followed the Great Wall for hundreds of miles, we crossed the Gobi Desert where Tartars caught wild horses before our very eyes. It began to snow when we reached Siberia, which made it even more romantic. It also made it very cold inside in our compartment. Nothing would make our attendant stoke the boilers, so we froze until I taped up the gaps in the ill-fitting windows with sticky tape traded with a Chinese merchant for two Charles Heidsieck pin badges! On the last night, the restaurant car attendant, a bear of a Russian called Gregory, opened our last bottle of Charles Heidsieck by slicing the neck off with a meat cleaver - not quite as romantic as a *sabrage* with a curved sword, but every bit as effective.

For our two days in Moscow, we stayed at the Metropol Hotel, a marvellous monument to Art Nouveau. The dining room had been the scene of many an historic event - a speech from Lenin, a song from Shalyapin. That night, our own historic event was to present a bottle of Charles Heidsieck to Madame Anna Sakharov. Champagne is such a marvellous present. You can give a lady flowers, you can give her champagne, but try giving her something like a bottle of whisky, and you give offence.

The lowest point of our journey was the train to Berlin, where the restaurant car remained in Russia. Undaunted, I made lightning raids on trolleys during the two minute stops at stations, grabbing food and showering dollar bills in return, regardless of the dollar/zloti black market exchange rate. From Berlin, we visited Sans Souci, Frederic the Great's wonderful creation. The rococo palace is a perfect confection, verifying the maxim that there are three forms of art - painting, music and ornamental pastry-making, with architecture being a sub-division of the third.

The next city was Copenhagen. We took in the royal Rosenborg Palace, a little gem that at least two Americans a year offer to buy to ship home, brick by brick. There, we bought a pair of silver beakers, facsimiles of Christian IV's christening mugs, which we christened with a bottle of Brut Réserve. Some think that champagne tastes better out of a silver tankard, and I now agree. That night we dined in 'The Ship', a splendid restaurant in Nyhavns Foergekro, an attractive area with a canal, filled with old sailing boats, built in the 18th century. A salad, a rare steak and a sticky pudding with a bottle of house red, and we were in our element and well content.

From there we went to Amsterdam, not too exciting in the rain on a Monday. We dined that night in an Indonesian restaurant, but despite the interesting decor (red lacquer and tartan!) the menu was disappointing with interminable courses of glutinous food. We thought fondly of Zarak, the cook aboard the *Neptune Amber*.

Moving on to Brussels we were good and patriotic British and visited the battlefield of Waterloo. Brussels is not only the home of the European Parliament, but also to of some of the best cuisine in Europe. We went off in search of a restaurant which, after whittling down the multiple choice to just two, we settled on Le Calalou. The live-long memory of their *bisque de homard*, scallops, and the steak béarnaise is vivid. The chocolate cake, large, sticky and gooey, must have been the inspiration of the line 'a blissful moment on the lips is a lifetime on the hips'! Quite the best dinner we had eaten so far.

By then, we were moving fast, staying for 24 hours in each city and travelling by train at night. We arrived in Vienna on the same day as the *Beaujolais Nouveau*, cause for a double celebration at the Restaurant Daniel. Originally the restaurant to the opera house, it has been cleverly restored losing none of its theatrical feel. The dinner they had prepared for us was truly wonderful. The wild mushrooms were sublime, the *Erdäpfelzahne* soup perfection. This was followed by boiled beef and dumplings (which sounded dull, but was quite delicious) served with an interesting combination of apple and horseradish sauce. We ended with a 'senior' *Apfelstrudel*. We drank Charles Heidsieck Brut Réserve followed by an Argentinian Cabernet Sauvignon. Then the *Beaujolais Nouveau est arrivé* - full of fruit and body, with a great nose.

Zurich was our next city, and it rained all day. That night we dined at a Swiss restaurant called Kindli. At first glance, it appeared very touristy, but, as our eyes became used to the dimly lit room, we found we were in a local haunt. Our host steered us through a Swiss dinner starting with *raclette* cheese, followed by a fillet of seared venison, served with another Swiss dish, *rösti*, a kind of potato pancake. We drank a crisp white wine from Vallée, our host's home town. The Swiss band struck up, then the trumpeter, switching to an enormous mountain horn, produced a tune of haunting beauty.

In Milan, we were thoroughly spoilt by staying in the Hotel Principe di Savoia, our room quite the grandest of the whole trip with its marble halls and bathroom. As it happened, we were on the same floor as Mario Cuomo, Governor of New York, whom I reminded of our last meeting on the Island of Mustique in the West Indies. When he had been shown a particularly fine beach, I had told him that the Queen had swum there in 1962. 'And we have not changed the water since!' I had added.

Our penultimate city was Madrid, made specially memorable by a visit to the Thyssen-Bornemisza art collection. We had floated all round the world with comparative ease, with never a hint of train or boat fever. In Madrid, we came close to losing everything after visiting a charity event where the Queen of Spain was serving tea, and I had my fortune told by the Princess Romanov. Short of time, all I wanted to know was if we would catch our train to Paris that night, as our luggage was in the Hotel Palace downtown, the station was in the opposite direction, and there was a solid traffic jam between. Thankfully, the Princess was right about one thing. An hour later, we were on our way to Paris.

It was fitting that Paris should be our last city, and we had planned that it should be so. It was a curious sensation. We half wanted to get back to England, but at the same time, we did not want our dream of a journey to end. We were taken to the opera, then to dinner at the Café de Madrid with the editor of a champagne and gourmet magazine. Seeing him savour the Charles Heidsieck Blanc des Millénaires, taste the lobster, then the pyramid of the richest nougat served with a Cointreau sauce, certainly belied the fact that he had started his journalist life as a reporter on a Communist newspaper. The good life had obviously got to him, as indeed it had to us.

On our final morning, we left our hotel knowing that night we would be in our own bed. We had stayed in 22 different hotels, travelled on five ships, with 24 separate train journeys, and, when we returned to England, we would have done it all in 80 days. When we touched the lion in Trafalgar Square to mark the end of our travels, it was dark and raining. But the weather did nothing to dampen our delight of winning - as it turned out, we had won by 14 days, the American team just beating the French into second place.

After such an epic journey around the world, with so much excitement, the high points and the low ebbs, the luxury hotels and the draughty station waiting rooms, the gourmet meals and the snatched platform sandwiches, we are invariably asked if we never tired of drinking Charles Heidsieck Champagne? How easy (and truthful) it is to reply, No, not ever, ever, ever ....!

Nicholas Courtney is a writer, gourmet, and traveller in the true sense of the word. In circumnavigating the world 'In the Footsteps of Champagne Charlie', he re-created that spirit of adventure which has immortalised Charles Camille Heidsieck. With his wife, Vanessa, they completed the epic journey in just 80 days, so winning the challenge handsomely.

Charles Heidsieck

CHAMPAGNE

Introduction
by ROY ACKERMAN

1993 admittedly had its full crop of failures in the hotel and restaurant sector, but hopefully we will remember significantly more of the dramatic new bunch of openings. I personally cannot remember a better year for seeing people put their money where the knives and forks are.

Following hard on the heels of Le Pont de la Tour came Sir Terence Conran's La Cantina del Ponte, also at Butlers Wharf, and the much-hyped Quaglino's, of which I've heard more than one restaurateur remark ". . . it's full of people you don't normally see in West End restaurants . . ." and without doubt it has found its own niche – it's extremely busy and has a vibrant buzzy atmosphere. As we go to press, news from the Conran stable is of another restaurant opening in October 1993 and rumours of more to come during 1994.

Marco Pierre White has proved his critics wrong at the Canteen in Chelsea Harbour and continues with his partners and team to turn out some consistently good and interesting food at reasonable prices. What's more, this lively friendly restaurant seems at last to have brought Chelsea Harbour to life. His addition to the Hyde Park Hotel team is another brilliant strategic move for Forte, for Marco himself and for the restaurant-going public in general – in my opinion, every-body wins.

Richard Shepherd opened Shepherd's in 1993 and has firmly put his stamp on Westminster, once more making this site a favourite meeting place for MPs and increasingly local and showbiz clientele, offering some straightforward and reasonably-priced, mainly British dishes.

Of the many more new openings, especially worth a mention are Daphne's, Mogens Tholstrup's revamped restaurant in Walton Street; Martin Lam at Ransome's Dock; Albero & Grana which is packing them in at Chelsea Cloisters; L'Escargot in Soho which returns with Hollihead and Cavalier at the stoves; the 309-bedroomed Regent Hotel in Marylebone adding another significant venue to the London hotel scene and Harvey Nichols' imaginative and well-thought-out food hall. Visit for the Julyan Wyckham-inspired decor, the bar for lighter meals or indeed, the restaurant itself.

Outside London, Andrew Radford's Atrium in Edinburgh looks set for a busy 1994, as does Phillipe Roy's Clos de Roy in Bath and the excellent Harvey's restaurant in Bristol. At the latter they've at last got the team to produce the food and service that match this unusual cellar restaurant with its outstanding wine list. Also in Bristol, the Swallow Royal Hotel deserves a special mention for its imaginative restoration, magnificent decor and stylish restaurant. All of the above have clearly identified their own market and offer value for money in their own class.

There are many more I hope you'll enjoy reading about in this book or better still, visiting. So open up a bottle of Charles Heidsieck, sit back and enjoy!

SERVE 2000

AMONG the entries in this book, you will find a couple of unusual ones – On The Town in London (see Page 102) and Kiddington Manor (Page 312). I cannot urge you strongly enough to telephone these entries and ask for details.

Calls cost 36p per minute at cheap rates and 48p per minute at all other times.

Any revenue earned on these telephone numbers will be going to "Serve 2000" – an appeal that has been launched by the hotel and catering industry, under the patronage of Viscount Montgomery of Alamein, in conjunction with the Academy of Food and Wine Service, to raise £200,000 to produce a professional food service training programme.

This will be based on the successful format of the Professional Wine Service Pack, which includes a 27-minute video as well as a step-by-step learning guide, illustrated reference book and easy to use work book. The ultimate aim of this training pack is to improve quality of service, profitability and customer satisfaction within the industry. Your support will ensure this is achieved.

!STOP PRESS!

As we went to press the following restaurants had just opened:

Restaurant Aubergine
11 Park Walk, London SW10   Tel: 071-352 3449

Chef/Patron Gordon Ramsay brings Robuchon-style food to SW10. Amazing value menus at £14 for 2 courses and £18 for 3 courses. Emily Green of The Independent was there at the same time as I was and we both chose the only dish on the menu that was not available! However, there are some exceptional dishes including risotto of crab with clams or tranche of cod Viennoise. Good ravioli of goat's cheese on a hazelnut dressing and stuffed with tapenade – the oxtail 'en crepinette' with puréed potatoes was superb. The decor is not exciting, but when the restaurant is full – which it deserves to be – this should be of little importance.

The Restaurant at the Hyde Park Hotel
66 Knightsbridge, SW1X 7LA   Tel: 071-259 5380

No shrinking violet is Marco Pierre White – from the canopied entrance through to the well-ordered restaurant he leaves you in no doubt as to the star of the show. Even down to the menu, where under each dish is noted its year of creation – and why not? This chef has undoubted talent and his cooking is on top form. From the evening menu try the excellent '87 vinai-grette of leeks and langoustines with caviar followed by the '88 vintage roast sea bass served with boulangère potatoes and a subtle sauce a nti-boise, one of 14 main courses on offer, each one tempting in its description and execution. Make sure you take a guest and opt for the excellent tarte tatin of pears for 2 persons. At £60 for 3 courses, you do get what you pay for – something very special. Lunchtime is a relative bargain at £22.50 for 3 courses. This will be *the* place to beat in 1994.

The Four-Leaf Clover

The four-leaf clover has been chosen because it is a symbol of luck and also a rare find. There is always a degree of luck involved when good ambience, excellent food, wine and service and the response of the customer combine to make a perfect occasion. A White Clover means that in my opinion, this is a very special place for many reasons, and made for a memorable experience. A Black Clover represents excellence in all aspects of food, service and decor, and these are the very best in Great Britain and the Republic of Ireland. With new clovers (58) for this year marked [N], The Ackerman Charles Heidsieck Guide Clover Leaf Awards for 1994 are given to:

LONDON

Alistair Little
The Berkeley [N]
Bibendum
Bistrot Bruno [N]
Blakes Hotel [N]
Bistrot 190 [N]
Bombay Brasserie [N]
Boulestin [N]
Café Royal Grill Room [N]
Cantina del Ponte [N]
The Canteen
The Capital Hotel
Le Caprice
Chez Nico at Ninety
Churchill Inter-Continental
    Hotel [N]
Chutney Mary [N]
Claridge's
Clarke's
The Connaught
dell'Ugo
The Dorchester
Four Seasons Hotel
Frederick's [N]
Le Gavroche
Gay Hussar
Greenhouse
The Halkin Hotel
Hilaire
Hyatt Carlton Tower [N]
L'Incontro
Inter-Continental
    (Le Soufflé)
The Ivy
Kalamaras
Kensington Place
The Lanesborough
Langan's Brasserie
Leith's
Le Meridien (Oak Room)
Mijanou [N]

Mirabelle
Mosimann's
Neal Street Restaurant [N]
Odette's [N]
Odin's Restaurant [N]
Osteria Antica Bologna [N]
Pied à Terre [N]
Le Pont de la Tour
Ransome's Dock [N]
The Ritz
River Café
San Lorenzo [N]
Les Saveurs
The Savoy
Simply Nico [N]
Soho Soho [N]
The Square
Stephen Bull
Le Suquet
La Tante Claire
Turner's

ENGLAND

Amberley, Amberley Castle
Aston Clinton, Bell Inn
Aylesbury, Hartwell House
Baslow, Fischer's
Bath, Bath Spa Hotel
Bath, Queensberry Hotel [N]
Bath, Clos du Roy [N]
Bath, Royal Crescent [N]
Bibury, The Swan [N]
Birmingham, Sloans
Birmingham, Swallow
Bradford, Restaurant
    Nineteen
Bradford-on-Avon,
    Woolley Grange [N]
Bray-on-Thames,
    Waterside Inn
Brimfield, Poppies
    at the Roebuck Inn [N]

Bristol, Restaurant Lettonie [N]

Bristol, Swallow Royal Hotel [N]

Broadway, Lygon Arms[N]

Brockenhurst, Le Poussin

Bury, Normandie Hotel

Cambridge, Midsummer House [N]

Castle Coombe, Manor House [N]

Chagford, Gidleigh Park

Cheltenham, Le Champignon Sauvage [N]

Cheltenham, Epicurean

Cheltenham, Redmond's

Chester, Chester Grosvenor Hotel [N]

Colerne, Lucknam Park

Corse Lawn, Corse Lawn House

Dartmouth, Carved Angel

Dedham, Le Talbooth

East Grinstead, Gravetye Manor

Emsworth, 36 On Th Quay [N]

Evershot, Summer Lodge [N]

Faversham, Read's

Fressingfield, Fox & Goose [N]

Gillingham, Stock Hill House

Goring on Thames, Leatherne Bottel

Grasmere, Michael's Nook

Great Milton, Le Manoir aux Quat'Saisons

Grimston, Congham Hall

Gulworthy, Horn of Plenty

Haslemere, Morel's

Hastings, Röser's

Herstmonceux, Sundial

Hetton, Angel Inn

Hintlesham, Hintlesham Hall

Ledbury, Hope End

Longridge, Paul Heathcote's

Lower Slaughter, Lower Slaughter Manor [N]

Malvern, Croque-en-Bouche

Melbourn, Pink Geranium [N]

Moulsford-on-Thames, Beetle & Wedge

New Milton, Chewton Glen

Newcastle, 21 Queen Street

Northleach, Old Woolhouse

Norwich, Adlard's

Oakham, Hambleton Hall

Oxford, Gee's [N]

Padstow, Seafood Restaurant

Plymouth, Chez Nous

Pool-in-Wharfedale, Pool Court

Pulborough, Stane Street Hollow

Ridgeway, Old Vicarage

Romsey, Old Manor House

Shinfield, L'Ortolan

South Molton, Whitechapel Manor

Speen, The Old Plow

Staddle Bridge, McCoy's

Stapleford, Stapleford Park

Ston Easton, Ston EastonPark

Storrington, Manley's

Stroud, Oakes

Stuckton, Three Lions [N]

Taplow, Cliveden

Taunton, The Castle Hotel

Thornbury, Thornbury Castle

Tunbridge Wells, Thackeray's House [N]

Twickenham, McClements [N]

Uckfield, Horsted Place [N]

Ullswater, Sharrow Bay

Warminster, Bishopstrow House

Waterhouses, Old Beams

Windermere, Miller Howe

Windermere, Roger's Restaurant

Winteringham, Winteringham Fields [N]

Woburn, Paris House

Worcester, Brown's

York, Melton's

York, Middlethorpe Hall

SCOTLAND

Auchterarder,
  Gleneagles Hotel
Crinan, Crinan Hotel [N]
Edinburgh, Martin's
Fort William, Inverlochry
  Castle
Glasgow, One Devonshire
  Gardens [N]
Gullane, La Potinière
Kingussie, The Cross
Linlithgow, Champanay Inn
Peat Inn, Peat Inn
Port Appin, Airds Hotel [N]
Turnberry,
  Turnberry Hotel [N]
Ullapool, Altnaharrie Inn

WALES

Abergavenny, Walnut Tree
Llandudno, Bodysgallen Hall

Llyswen, Llangoed Hall [N]
Portmerion, Hotel
Portmerion [N]
Pwllheli, Plas Bodegroes [N]

NORTHERN IRELAND

Belfast, Roscoff
Portrush, Ramore

REPUBLIC OF IRELAND

Adare, Adare Manor [N]
Dingle, Doyle's
  Seafood Bar [N]
Dublin, Le Coq Hardi [N]
Dublin, Patrick Guilbaud
Kenmare, Park Hotel
Mallow, Longueville
  House [N]
Shanagarry, Ballymaloe

How to Use this Guide

Main reviews

Following our established successful formula, the main reviews are set out very simply: London is arranged alphabetically by establishment name. Reviews in England, Scotland, Wales, Northern Ireland and the Republic of Ireland are arranged alphabetically by location, then by establishment name.

Some reviews are longer than others. The length of a review does not necessarily indicate the relative importance of an establishment - some have been covered more fully in previous editions of the Guide, which are available from Leading Guides.

I have used a small team of reviewers who have worked with me for some years and whose judgement I trust, and who understand what I am seeking in standards of cuisine, atmosphere and service.

Clover Award Winners

The Clover Award Winners are featured on the previous two pages, and Clovers are also indicated alongside the text entries for the winners.

Listings

Where we are unsure about an establishment, or have visited it only once, or where there has been a change of some significance since our last visit, we list it without a full review. These listings appear at their correct geographical point amidst the main reviews.

Vital Statistics

These have been compiled from information supplied to us by the establishments themselves, in response to our questionnaires. They have been checked and we have done our best to ensure that all information contained in this book is accurate. However, it is perfectly feasible that a restaurant or hotel may choose to change its last order times, or the days of the week that it is closed. Similarly, an owner, manager or chef may well move on. Even the style of food might be changed. We assume that in most cases you will book before going to a restaurant or hotel, and if you feel that any detail is especially important, we suggest you check it at the time of booking. When we have quoted particular dishes in a review, we cannot guarantee that they will be available on your visit - this is obviously true if you visit in a different season. In most cases, menus will be more comprehensive than the extracts we have chosen.

Price

The price shown is the average cost of dinner for two people, without wine but including coffee, service and VAT. Where possible, we have quoted a set price dinner menu, which in some cases might be four or even five or more courses; otherwise the figure relates to a typical three-course meal.

Vests

As before, I have used the "vested interest" symbol to indicate restaurants in which I have a personal investment:

Cercle des Ambassadeurs

This symbol ✐ indicates that an establishment is host to a member of the Cercle. A full list can be found on page 19.

Academy of Food and Wine Service

This symbol ❖ indicates that an establishment is host to a member of the Academy. More details can be found on page 21.

CERCLE DES AMBASSADEURS DE L'EXCELLENCE

The Cercle des Ambassadeurs de l'Excellence was created by Champagne Charles Heidsieck to celebrate the 140th anniversary of this 'grande marque' champagne. This unique circle has approximately 140 founder members who represent the very best of gastronomic excellence in this country. Listed below are the members (and the host restaurant/hotel, applicable at the time of the award) of the Cercle des Ambassadeurs de L'Excellence. Throughout this guide members are identified by a champagne bottle symbol next to their entry.

Member	Host restaurant/hotel	Member	Host restaurant/hotel
LONDON		Mr Keith Podmore	Boodles
Mr Roy Ackerman, OBE	(Leading Guides)	Mr Silvano Giraldin	Le Gavroche
Mr Paul Gayler	The Lanesborough	Simone Green	Odette's
Mr Raymond André	Le Meridien Hotel	Mr Ramon Pajares	Four Seasons Hotel
Mr George Goring	Goring Hotel	Mr Jean-Pierre Durantet	La Tante Claire
Frances Bissell	(Food Writer)	Mr Bev Puxley	(Westminster Coll)
Mr Patrick Gwynn-Jones	Pomegranates	Mr Gary Rhodes	The Greenhouse
Mr Neville Blech	Mijanou	Jancis Robinson	(Writer/
Sonia Blech	Mijanou		Broadcaster)
Mr Eduard Hari	(Freelance)	The Hon. Rocco Forte	Forte plc
Mr Vaughan Archer	London Hilton	Mr Richard Shepherd	Langan's Brasserie
Mr Gary Hollihead	L'Escargot	Mr Egon Ronay	(Consultant)
Mr Don Hewitson	Cork & Bottle	Monsieur Albert Roux	Le Gavroche
Mr Simon Hopkinson	Bibendum	Mr Duncan Rutter	(HCTC)
Mr Philip Britten	The Capital Hotel	Mr Giles Shepherd	The Savoy Group
Mr Laszlo Holecz	Gay Hussar	Mr Herbert Striessnig	The Savoy
Mr Michael Broadbent	(Christie's)	Mr Brian Turner	Turner's
Mr Terry Holmes	The Ritz	Mr Bryan Webb	Hilaire
Mr Antonio Carluccio	Neal Street Rest.	Mr Marco Pierre White	The Canteen
Mr Ronald Jones, OBE	Claridges	Carla Tomasi	(Freelance)
Mr Kevin Kennedy	Boulestin	Mr Peter Webber	My Kinda Town
Mr David Chambers	Le Meridien Hotel	Dagmar Woodward	May Fair
Mr John Kinges	Les Ambassadeurs		Inter-Continental
Mr Malcolm Broadbent	Cadogan Hotel	Mr Paolo Zago	The Connaught
Mr Peter Kromberg	Inter-Continental	Mr Antony Worrall	
Mr Stephen Bull	Stephen Bull Rest.	Thompson,	dell'Ugo
Mr David Cavalier	L'Escargot	MOGB	
Susan Cavalier	L'Escargot	Doreen Boulding	Hotel Conrad
Mr Robin Lees, CB, MBE	(Brit Hospitality)		
Mr Gian Chiandetti	Forte plc		
Mr David Levin	The Capital Hotel	**ENGLAND**	
Miss Prudence Leith	Leith's		
Mr Michael Coaker	MayFair Inter- Cont	Mr Douglas Barrington,	
Mr Brian Cotterill	(Chefs & Cooks Circle)	OBE	The Lygon Arms
Mr Eddie Khoo	Beauchamp Place	Monsieur Jean Quero	Angel, Guildford
Mr Peter Davies	Le Gavroche	Mr David Adlard	Adlard's
Mr Pierre Koffman	La Tante Claire	Mr Willy Bauer	Wentworth Club
Mr Nico Ladenis	Chez Nico	Mr Raymond Blanc	LeManoirAux
Mr Rowley Leigh	Kensington Place		Quat'Saisons
Mr Marjan Lesnik	Claridge's	Mr Mauro Bregoli	Old Manor House
Mr Alastair Little	Alastair Little Rest.	Mr John Burton-Race	L'Ortolan
Mr Pierre Martin	Le Suquet	Mr Kit Chapman, MBE	The Castle Hotel
Mr Christian Delteil	(Freelance)	Mr Kevin Cape	(Overseas)
Mr Robert Mey	Hyatt Carlton	Mr Victor Ceserani	(Consultant)
	Tower	Mr Peter Chandler	Paris House
Sally Clarke	Clarke's	Mr Pierre Chevillard	Chewton Glen
Monsieur Bruno Loubet	Four Seasons Hotel	Mr John Dicken	Dicken's Restaurant
Mr Philip Corrick	RAC Club	Mr Christopher Cole	(Consultant)
Mr Eric Deblonde	Four Seasons Hotel	Mr Francis Coulson	Sharrow Bay
Mr Eoin Dillon	Freelance)	Mr Alain Desenclos	LeManoirAux
Mr Anton Mosimann	Mosimann's		Quat'Saisons
Mr David Dorricott	SAS Portman	Mr Clive Fretwell	LeManoirAux
Mr Michael Nadell	Nadell Patisserie		Quat'Saisons
Mr Anton Edelmann	The Savoy	Mr Peter Herbert	Gravetye Manor
Mr Ricci Obertelli	The Dorchester	Mr Hugh Johnson	Writer/
Lord Forte	Forte plc		Broadcaster)
Mr David Foskett	Ealing College	Mr Tim Hart	Hambleton Hall
Mr Nicholas Picolet	Au Jardin des	Mr Shaun Hill	Gidleigh Park Hotel
	Gourmets	Mr John Huber	(Thames Val Coll)
Mr Bernard Gaume	Hyatt Carlton	Mr Murdo MacSween	Oakley Court Hotel
	Tower		

Member	Host restaurant/hotel	Member	Host restaurant/hotel
Kathryn McWhirter	(Wine writer)	Mr Rick Stein	The Seafood Rest.
Joyce Molyneux	The Carved Angel	Mr Auberon Waugh	(Writer)
Mr Guy Mouilleron	(Chef/Consultant)		
Sir Colin Marshall	(British Airways)	**SCOTLAND**	
Mr Gerald Milsom, OBE	Le Talbooth	Mr Alan Hill	Gleneagles Hotel
Mr Harry Murray	The Imperial Hotel	Mrs Grete Hobbs	Inverlochy Castle
Mr Bob Payton	Stapleford Park	Mr Peter J Lederer,	Gleneagles Hotel
Mr Martyn Pearn	Buckland Manor	MI, FHCIMA	
Monsieur Michel Perraud,	(Freelance)	Mr David Wilson	The Peat Inn
MOGB			
Mr David Pitchford	Read's Restaurant	**WALES**	
Monsieur Michel Roux	The Waterside Inn	Mr Franco Taruschio	Walnut Tree Inn
Mr Brian Sack	Sharrow Bay		
Mr Martin Skan	Chewton Glen		
Mr Peter Smedley	Ston Easton Park		
The Hon John Sinclair	E Sussex National		
	Golf Club		
Mr Jonathan W Slater	Chester Grosvenor		
Kate Smith	Beetle & Wedge		
Mr Richard Smith	Beetle & Wedge		
Mr C Jonathan Thompson	Hartwell House		
Mr Michael Womersley	Lucknam Park		
	Hotel		

THE ACADEMY OF FOOD AND WINE SERVICE

The Academy of Food and Wine Service was formed six years ago as a joint initiative by the Hotel and Restaurant Industry and the Wine and Spirit Trade.

The objective of the Academy is to increase the level of knowledge and, in particular, service skills, of those waiting staff employed in restaurants throughout the United Kingdom to benefit both the Industry and, more importantly, the Customer, by ensuring that there develops a network of waiting staff throughout the country who have been trained to National Vocational Qualifications Standards, initially at levels One and Two, and ultimately to even higher levels.

The Academy first set about this task by producing an open learning programme for Wine Waiters, which is available as a complete self-study pack, including a skills video, knowledge competence book and work book. This programme has been greeted by the Industry with much enthusiasm, and has encouraged the Academy to pursue further research into a similar open learning programme on Food Service. Development of this new pack is well advanced and will be available to the Industry in early 1994.

This edition of The Ackerman Charles Heidsieck Guide to the Best Hotels and Restaurants in Great Britain and Ireland sees another step forward for the Academy. Readers will notice that certain entries are marked with a new symbol, ❖. This denotes that the establishment employs a current member of the Academy or has worked closely with the organisation and supports its aims and objectives.

You will be able to identify our members by a small uniform lapel badge - green and gold for food service associate members, burgundy and gold for wine service associate members and a combined burgundy, green and gold badge for a full member. Membership is only available to those members of the waiting profession who have been trained and assessed to a National Standard and on whom you should be able to rely for professional service when you are dining out. Please look out for these badges recognising competence and skills and start to demand that your favourite restaurant employs these dedicated professional staff.

If you would like to obtain further information on the work of the Academy of Food and Wine Service, or as an employer wish to involve your own staff in the training programmes, please contact the Academy at the following address:

> The Academy of Food and Wine Service
> Chelsea Chambers
> 262a Fulham Road
> London SW10 9EL
> Telephone: 071-352 6997
> Fax: 071-351 9678

London Establishment Reviews

ABBEY COURT   W2

20 Pembridge Gardens, W2 4DU
Telephone: 071-221 7518 Fax: 071-792 0858
Twenty-two rooms with brass or 4-poster beds. London's most up-market bed and breakfast establishment. This hotel has no restaurant but serves light dishes and drinks at any time.

L'ACCENTO ITALIANO   W2

16 Garway Road, W2 4NH
Telephone: 071-243 2201   £35
Open: lunch + dinner daily
Meals served: lunch 12.30-2.30, dinner 6.30-11.30 (Sun to 10.30)

New Italian cooking at its best - cheap and friendly with strong use of flavours. The decor is rustic, with an elevated, stylish bar and one wall plain metal grey, while the others are sandblasted rust, yellow and gold. Minimal yet bold also describes the set menu of 2-courses with pumpkin risotto, polenta dumplings in an intense tomato and lentil broth, deep-fried squid with aubergines or pan-fried kidneys with parsley and garlic.

ADAM'S CAFÉ   W12

77 Askew Road, W12
Telephone: 081-743 0572   £30
Open: lunch + dinner Mon-Sat (closed Bank Holidays)
Meals served: lunch English café: 7.15am-6.30pm, Sat 8-2,
dinner Tunisian restaurant: 7.30-10.30

An English café by day, so it should really be called Eve's by night, when it turns into a fashionable Tunisian restaurant, doubled in size to keep up with demand. Couscous is the speciality and is very good. There are other Tunisian, and some Mediterranean dishes. Wines are mostly Tunisian or Moroccan.

AL SAN VINCENZO   W2

30 Connaught Street, W2 2AS
Telephone: 071-262 9623   **£50**
Open: lunch Mon-fri, dinner Mon-Sat (closed 2 wks Xmas)
Meals served: lunch 12.30-2, dinner 7-10.30

Vincenzo Borgonzolo's cooking pulls no punches and doesn't bow to trends since he cooks what is good, what has always been good and will continue to be so. Starters could be fresh oreciette with black olive pesto, capers, chilli and parmesan, or mussels and squid pan-fried with olive oil, parsley and a dash of tomato sauce; whereas main courses bring out hot tongue with Italian pickles, haunch of venison with juniper and a sweet and sour sauce or pan-fried calves' liver with coarse grain mustard. A hot baked apple is a good excuse for a grappa, and panettone italianises the bread and butter pudding. Concise Italian wine list.

ALASTAIR LITTLE   W1

49 Frith Street, W1V 5TE
Telephone: 071-734 5183   **£70**
Open: lunch Mon-Fri, dinner Mon-Sat (closed Bank Holidays)
Meals served: lunch 12-3, dinner 6-11.30

On a street fast becoming a haven for the Soho foodie you can find Alastair's small and unpretentious restaurant. Monochromatic decor looks back to the '80s, but the cooking is very much up to the minute, with well presented dishes, designed to surprise by the low-key descriptions they are given on a hand-written menu. Alastair has an natural talent and knack with ingredients which is apparent in salad of sliced salt beef, beetroot and horseradish or pacific oysters with shallot relish and spicy sausages. They demonstrate his originality and depth of experience in combining flavours and textures. Simple things are done to perfection, such as asparagus risotto and fish soup with rouille bound to be a winner, but then so are all the remaining dishes that make up this innovative and eclectic menu. Good bread, butter and staff.

ALBA   EC1

107 Whitecross Street, EC1Y 8JD
Telephone: 071-588 1798   **£50**
Open: lunch + dinner Mon-Fri (closed Bank Holidays, 2 wks Xmas)
Meals served: lunch 12-3, dinner 7-11

Alba is great for Barbican dwellers and seekers alike. A warm welcome always meets you at the door, and is extended to your guests by
the enthusiastic owners. It's named after the Piedmontese town at the
centre of the wine-making region, so you will appreciate their wide
(yet concise), entirely Italian wine list. A couple of half bottles exist
(rare on Italian lists) and pleasing dessert wines by the glass are sensibly priced. Some say the pink and grey interior needs warming up, but
for this you can rely on the crowd who come to absorb everything
about this North Italian cooking. Traditional favourites abound here,
such as bresaola served with ricotta, but the plate will contain both
beef and deer meat, and just a grind of black pepper is all it needs.
Prosciutto is bathed in three nectar-like fruits - the usual melon but
also mango and kiwi. Minestrone with a touch of pesto is hard to
choose when it's that or a thick Tuscan soup with buckwheat and borlotti beans, and then there is a whole host of pastas. Porcini and truffles when in season, anchovies, olives and artichokes are also used lib-
erally. Braised rabbit with olives, pan-fried chicken deglazed with balsamic vinegar and a touch of rosemary, or thinly sliced fillet of beef,
just lightly grilled to retain its juiciness and seared with radicchio and
a sprinkling of aromatic olive oil make up typical main courses. After a
breather comes a daily selection of sweets in true trattoria-style from
the trolley, or taleggio, gorgonzola, pecorino and parmigiano cheese
eaten with a juicy ripe pear. All that is now required is a really good
cup of coffee served with cantuccini.

ALBERO & GRANA   SW3

Chelsea Cloisters, 39 Sloane Avenue, SW3 3DW
Telephone: 071-225 1048/9 Fax: 071-581 3259   **£55**
Open: lunch + dinner daily
Meals served: lunch (tapas 12.30-3.30), dinner 7.30-12 (tapas 6-12)

Loud background music makes this place vibrate when filled to capacity. There is perhaps an excess of style but the cooking is good and long overdue in the aftermath of tapas-fever and the run of unsuccessful restaurants on this site. At the top end of Sloane Avenue, a few doors down from the high trend stores and Michelin Building, this little corner of Chelsea Cloisters now has a spacious bar in front offering 30 traditional tapas dishes, while behind is a brash pink dining room with futuristic sculpture of wire and mantilla combs, and a glass-brick wall and tented ceiling. Heavily-fashioned with black and white accessories - the floor length tablecloths, the checkerboard floor, and the denim-like waistcoats worn by the waiters - this isn't a place for home cooking or simple traditional dishes, but is set to wow. This is full-blown restaurant stuff, with little to nothing of the old but plenty of the new. Chef Angel Garcia's has done his homework and brings in his knowledge of what is happening in the kitchens across Europe. Artistic licence beefs up the menu, what you and I would call a soufflé is obviously lost in translation. A short choice is arranged in entradas (starters), pescados (fish), carnes (meat) and postres (puddings). Eclectic options push the menu further - lasagne of black pudding with a green pepper sauce, warm tartlet of cauliflower, crab and scallops, stuffed squid pan-fried with a Jerez sauce; scallops with cocido of olives and capers; veal kidneys with endives and Jerez sauce. Puddings are Spanish but mirror Europe with apple and cinnamon mille-feuille, rice cream with a brûlée crust, puff pastry tart of pears and light custard, and lemon and sweet tomato tart. A totally OTT place, where you come to be entertained from every aspect. Entirely Spanish wine list.

L'ALTRO   W11

210 Kensington Park Road, W11
Telephone: 071-792 1066   **£55**
Open: lunch + dinner Mon-Sat (closed lunch Bank Holidays)
Meals served: lunch 12-2.30 (Sat 12-3), dinner 7-11 (Fri+Sat 7-11.30)

A patio is transformed into a Romanesque courtyard complete with classical statues, trompe l'oeil walls, wooden tables and chairs and a menu that specialises in seafood prepared with a vibrant modern approach. Sister of Cibo, the menu is uncomplicated and might include briefly deep-fried baby squid and cuttlefish, or a stew of baby octopus with spinach and tomatoes, baked sea bass with balsamic vinegar and grilled radicchio and endives, and grilled sardines in a light basil and lemon sauce. Assorted clams, mussels, baby scallops and razor clams come in a light tomato and spicy sauce while lobster and prawns are wrapped in foil with basil and pine kernels.

Busy, popular & fun restaurant.

VICOLO
L'ALTRO

ANNA'S PLACE   N1

90 Mildmay Park, Newington Green, N1 4PR
Telephone: 071-249 9379   £45
Open: lunch + dinner Tue-Sat (closed 2 wks Xmas, 2 wks
Easter, 2 wks Aug)
Meals served: lunch 12.15-2.15, dinner 7.15-10.45

Everyone is welcome at this open house run by the greatly enthusiastic Anna Hegarty. With a popularity almost equalling that of IKEA on a
Bank Holiday Monday, Anna's Place is another of the best things yet
to have yet reached us from Sweden. With a sole aim to make everyone happy and with a team of highly-efficient staff, the restaurant is
busy but runs smoothly. Coloured vinyl tablecloths support an informal and friendly air, a "let's just pop round the corner to Anna's" kind
of place. But a word of warning - don't even consider just turning up
without booking, because you won't even get a standing place at the
bar. Book first and don't bring credit cards. Close-set tables make this
a bustling bistro-type place with mementos of the restaurant's past life
as a tobacconist still evident and the big warming Aga behind the bar,
atmospheric in summer and useful in winter. The menu changes 3
times a year to reflect the seasons. The dishes are approachable, with
Swedish specialities - gravadlax with dill and mustard sauce, marinated herrings or mixed game tartlet, lapped up in particular in winter
with a swig of ice cold snaps to kickstart the old ticker, or a more slow-
to-come-round Swedish beer. The spread between fish and meat is
even - roast turbot with onion marmalade or a Dutch calves' liver with
a cider glaze, hearty meat hotpots are common in winter. Puddings
must not be missed with svenska wafflor and choklad tarta (which
proves that this is an easy language for the English to learn): Swedish
waffles with blueberry compote and chocolate truffle cake.

THE ARGYLL   SW3

316 King's Road, SW3
Telephone: 071-352 0025   £55
Open: lunch Tue-Sat, dinner Mon-Sat (closed Bank Holidays)
Meals served: lunch 12-2.30, dinner 7-11

Anand Sastry said he had something up his sleeve, and no-one
doubted the tenacity of this young chef who has worked in his time
with some of the best in the trade. Last year he made his dream a reality in a simply decorated and bright restaurant on the middle part of
King's Road. With co-patron Christian Arden (ex-Sutherlands, as was)
he makes an eclectic team. In summer the front of the restaurant
opens to the pavement and with bare walls, wooden floors and high
backed leather chairs made for maximum comfort all your attention is
focused on the food. The cooking has the sure Sastry touch, with a
carte that includes ravioli of foie gras with lentils and sauternes, baked
cod with a shallot confit and tomato bouillon, a braise of oxtail with
woodland mushrooms and black peppered tuna with fondant potato
and olives. There is nothing quiet or sedate about his dishes, a serious
mix of terroir cooking with fine tuned edges - pleasing both on the
plate and to the palate. Very good local restaurant.

THE ARK   W8

122 Palace Gardens Terrace, Notting Hill W8
Telephone: 071-229 4024   £35
Open: lunch Mon-Sat, dinner daily (closed 3 days Xmas)
Meals served: lunch 12-3, dinner 6.30-11.15
Something of an institution, this neighbourhood restaurant is true to early '70s bistro
origins. Loyal following, so go early or book.

L'ARTISTE ASSOIFFÉ   W11

122 Kensington Park Road, W11 2EP
Tel: 071-727 4712   £50
Open: dinner daily (closed Xmas, Easter)
Meals served: 7.30-11
Local French restaurant with friendly service.

ARTS THEATRE CAFÉ   WC2

6 Great Newport Street, WC2
Telephone: 071-497 8014   £30
Open: all day Mon-Fri, dinner Sat (closed Bank Holidays,
1 wk Xmas/New Year)
Meals served: 12-11, dinner Sat 6-11

In the hubbub between Covent Garden and Leicester Square you
wouldn't be to blame for missing the stairs going down from the pavement as you rush past The Photographers Gallery and Arts Theatre.
Unassuming is the understatement, but don't let that discredit chef
and owner Phillip Owens. It is quite simply a find, and one many of us
would rather keep quiet, since at lunchtime it is nearly impossible to
get a table after 12.30 for the entourage who flock here from the
offices of WC2. A mix of legal minds, media execs and all-day shoppers
congregate, bringing their clients as well as their mothers, because of
its food. Relaxed, but sort of off-beat New York basement feel, inter-
spersed by oohs and aahs towards the end of lunchtime service, as a
crocodile of matching jumpers of around age 9 size troops tightly-hud-
dled together through the small room, on their way to the theatre. But
don't let that put you off, it's a wonderful place offering freshly-cooked
Italian based dishes. Daily specials from the blackboard are extensive,
such as tomato and basil tart or crostini of chicken liver pâté and pickled vegetables, grilled scallops with spicy puy lentils and rocket, for
starters. To follow, try chicken and pork meatballs with lemon and
parmesan, grilled and served with cannellini beans and sautéed tomatoes and herbs, stewed monkfish, mussels and squid with vegetables
and wine or couscous with vegetables and beans and aubergine
polportone. As you would expect, the wine list is Italian.

THE ATHENAEUM   W1

116 Piccadilly, W1V 0BJ
Telephone: 071-499 3464 Fax: 071-493 1860   **£45**
Open: lunch Sun-Fri, dinner daily
Meals served: lunch 12.30-2, dinner 6-10 (Tea 3-6)   ❖

Overlooking Green Park, this 112-bedroomed hotel offers attentive
service throughout, including its 34 stylish apartments in Down Street.
As we went to press The Athenaeum, under the direction of the affable
and capable James Brown, was about to commence the refurbishment
of many of the suites, lounges and the restaurant and also the addition
of a health and leisure club, due to open during 1994.

AU BON ACCUEIL   SW3

19 Elystan Street, SW3 3NT
Tel: 071-589 3718£40
Open: lunch Mon-Fri, dinner Mon-Sat (closed Bank Holidays)
Meals served: lunch 12.30-2.30, dinner 7-11.30
French restaurant with an English accent, well patronised by the Chelsea set.

AU JARDIN DES GOURMETS   W1

5 Greek Street, W1V 5LA
Telephone: 071-437 1816 Fax: 071-437 0043   **£40**
Open: lunch Mon-Fri, dinner Mon-Sat (closed Bank Holidays)
Meals served: lunch 12.15-2.30, dinner 6.15-11.15

Since last year this favourite of the glitterati set has had a change of
face. Downstairs there is now a brasserie called the salle à manger
while above (on the first floor) the restaurant has a more serious
appeal. The cooking for both remains predominantly French with coq
au vin and steak frites, but a brochette of assorted meats served with
risotto incorporates the modern Mediterranean influences that have
swept over the rest of Soho.

L'AVENTURE   NW8

3 Blenheim Terrace, NW8 0EH   *good local restaurant makes you*
Telephone: 071-624 6232   **£55**
Open: lunch Sun-Fri, dinner daily (closed Xmas, Easter) *want nearby!*
Meals served: lunch 12.30-2.30, dinner 7.30-11 (Sun 7.30-10) *to live*

Just as they do in provincial French towns, the menus here change
daily and offer a good concise assortment. The tables break out on to
the patio alfresco-style in fine weather, reinforcing the European
flavour. Evenings are the busier and Sunday lunch most of all sees
Catherine Parisot and her staff with their work cut out, moving back
and forth with plates of coquilles St Jacques, pork with morilles, char-
grilled beef with black pepper sauce, grilled turbot with mussels and
lashings of saffron sauce, and tarte fine au citron.

BASIL STREET HOTEL SW3

Basil Street, SW3 1AH
Telephone: 071-581 3311 Fax: 071-581 3693 **£45**
Open: lunch Sun-Fri, dinner daily

Meals served: lunch 12.30-2.30, dinner 6.30-10 (Sat+Sun 6.30-9.30)
This is a very special place, a small, friendly hotel with 92 rooms,
tucked in behind Sloane Street just before you reach Harrods. The
style is chintz - long polished corridors, Turkish rugs, palms and
antiques - and consistent. The dining room offers traditional English
cooking. The hotel also caters well for women guests - its Parrot Club
is a bar exclusively for women.

BELGO NW1

72 Chalk Farm Road, NW1 8AN
Telephone: 071-267 0718 **£45**
Open: lunch + dinner daily (closed 25 Dec, 1 Jan)
Meals served: lunch 12-3, dinner 6-11.30 (all day Sat+Sun 12-11.30)

Blonde, fruity or pale - no that isn't the clientèle, but the large variety
of beers available at this alternative restaurant where the waiters are
dressed as trappist monks. With a menu that lists asparagus 4 ways,
moules from pan-fried with lemon to flavoured with fennel and pastis
and lobster specials from à l'escargot with butter and garlic or froid
with mayonnaise, this is a different style of eating from a sort of ad hoc
and unstructured menu which is why it proves to be so popular with
the young and trendy. Belgian specialities include stoemp and wild
boar sausages, stuffed butternut squash and a hochepot of salmon. An
extraordinary and lively place to come and drink Belgian beer and
walk the gang-plank on the way out.

BELVEDERE IN HOLLAND PARK W8

Holland Park, off Abbotsbury Road, W8 6LU
Tel: 071-602 1238 **£55**
Open: lunch daily, dinner Mon-Sat (closed 3 days Xmas)
Meals served: lunch 12-3, dinner 7-11

The Belvedere is located in what was originally the summer ballroom
of Holland House and is surrounded by the beautiful grounds of the
park. The contemporary elegance of the interior is matched by the
dishes to be found on the menus, which change every 2 months. You
might like to start with warm tartlet of caramelised onions with sun
dried tomatoes, or smoked salmon on an olive brioche with crème
fraîche, followed by char-grilled breast of chicken with polenta and
lentil and thyme vinaigrette, or perhaps roast saddle of rabbit wrap
in bayonne ham served with rosemary potatoes and leeks. If pudd
aren't your fancy, try the selection of farmhouse cheeses served
toasted walnut and raison bread; otherwise choose between the
of apple croustade with cinnamon sauce and a cinnamon ice crea
rhubarb and blackberry crumble with vanilla anglaise. Reaso
priced wine list. This venue is especially worth a visit in summe
terrace seating is available.

BENTLEY'S   W1

11 Swallow Street, W1R 7HD
Telephone: 071-287 5025   £65
Open: lunch + dinner Mon-Sat (closed some Bank Holidays)
Meals served: lunch 12-3, dinner 6-10.45
Tucked into a side street between Piccadilly and Regent Street is this elegant dining
room serving classical seafood dishes.

THE BERKELEY   SW1

Wilton Place, SW1X 7RL   🐾
Telephone: 071-235 6000 Fax: 071-235 4330   **£45**
Open: lunch + dinner Sun-Fri (closed 2 wks Aug)
Meals served: lunch 12.30-2.30 (Sun 12.30-2.15),
dinner 6.30-10.45 (Sun 7-10)   ❖

A youthful hotel, belied by its grandiose setting, antique furniture and
tail-coated staff. The Berkeley soaks up the Knightsbridge set and
executive crowd for lunch at its Perroquet restaurant, which is an
excellent place to try the current style of food. Choose from a collection of carpaccio, risotto and pasta or soup to start, and main courses
of salmon with tomatoes, capers and olives or simply grilled chicken.
This is a lighter style of lunch than that provided by the Restaurant
which lies beyond the foyer, with its more formal setting and fixed-
price menu of quenelles of sole, parfait of foie gras and noisettes of
lamb with herbs and red wine sauce. Traditional or contemporary -
both are well presented and offer a diversity of dishes. The service
throughout the hotel is polished and correct, and standards from the
bedrooms to marbled-floored bathrooms are in keeping with their 21
years of exacting and pleasurable service, made all the more memorable by the adjoining Minema cinema and café and the roof-top health
spa. A very personal, 160-bedroomed hotel.

BERKSHIRE HOTEL **W1**

350 Oxford Street, W1N 0BY
Telephone: 071-629 7474 Fax: 071-629 8156   £55
Open: lunch Sun-Fri, dinner daily
Meals served: lunch 12.30-2.30, dinner 6-10.30 (Sun 6.30-10.30)
Edwardian Hotels' country house atmosphere in the heart of the city. Chintzy drawing
rooms and 147 bedrooms. Dining room with vegetarian and low calorie options.

BERTORELLI'S **WC2**

44a Floral Street, WC2E 9DA
Telephone: 071-836 3969   **£55**
Open: lunch + dinner Mon-Sat (closed 26 Dec)
Meals served: lunch 12-3, dinner 5.45-11.30

A comfortable, friendly yet stylish restaurant, right by the stage-door
of the Royal Opera House. A favourite for pre- and after-theatre-goers
who nip in for a bowl of torchietti with mussels and cherry tomatoes,
or pizza of oyster mushrooms, leeks and dolcelatte. Bertorelli's has
found strength in new chef Maddalena Bonnino who brings a modern
approach to the old Bertorelli stable. Eat in the wine bar/café in the
basement or the ground floor, two- level restaurant. Laurence Isaacson
and Neville Abraham, the owners of Bertorelli's, are also the creative
brains behind the annual Covent Garden Festival. If you missed '93,
make sure you get information ASAP for '94, as it is one of the most
innovative festivals of its kind, and not to be missed.

BIBENDUM   SW3

81 Fulham Road, SW3 6RD
Telephone: 071-581 5817 Fax: 071-823 7925   £75
Open: lunch + dinner daily (closed 4 dys Xmas, Easter Monday)
Meals served: lunch 12.30-2.30 (Sat+Sun 12.30-3) dinner 7-11.30
(Sun 7-10.30)

For the best value come here at lunch time when you can enjoy a
selection of Simon Hopkinson's food for a mere £25 for 3 courses - a
plateful of thick, gleaming slices of rare beef with an anchovy cream
dressing and some good little capers, deep-fried courgettes with a garlic mayonnaise or grilled squid with gremolata. His fish and chips are
famous and having on repeated visits sampled the plaice, monkfish
and lemon sole, with tartare sauce and chips, I can say that each time
the food is better than the last! Desserts further demonstrate his skill
with Pithiviers au chocolat and tarte fine aux pommes, both requiring
20 minutes to prepare and cook. The wait is an added bonus as it gives
you time to finish at leisure the last glass of wine, take in the magnifi-
cence of the room, and sit back and watch the place in smooth
operation. *Simon is on top form here - cooking as well as ever!*

BIBENDUM OYSTER BAR   SW3

Michelin House, 81 Fulham Road, SW3 6RD
Telephone: 071-589 1480 Fax: 071-823 7925   £40
Open: all day Mon-Sat, lunch + dinner Sun
Meals served: lunch Sun 12-2, dinner Sun 7-10.30 (light meals Mon-Sat 12-
10.30pm)

Below the main restaurant and just before you enter the Conran store
is this stylish oyster bar with etched Michelin windows and tiled walls
and floors. Choose to sit in the small bar area or branch out into the
foyer of the main building, decorated with a whimsical frieze of
Michelin's travels. Take a table and order a jug of house white wine
and a selection of natives. They come with the best red wine vinegar
and shallot mix (good for dipping your bread in while you wait) lemon
wedges or a bottle of Tabasco. Other items to savour are clams and
prawns, or dressed crab with mayonnaise, grilled salmon or squid, and
a good Szechuan chicken salad.

BILLBOARD CAFÉ   NW6

222 Kilburn High Road, NW6 4JP
Telephone: 071-328 1374   £40
Open: lunch Sat+Sun, dinner Mon-Sat (closed Bank Holidays)
Meals served: lunch 12-3, dinner 6.30-12.45am

Here you'll find a fashionable menu of Italian and Californian influences with occasional Oriental overtones. Low lighting ensures intimate conversation and a relaxing atmosphere for the local community
and others seeking unpretentious food.

BISTROT BRUNO   W1

63 Frith Street, W1V 5TA
Telephone: 071-734 4545 Fax: 071-287 1027   **£50**
Open: lunch Mon-Fri, dinner Mon-Sat (closed 3-4 days Xmas)
Meals served: lunch 12.15-2.30, dinner 6.15-11.30

On the site formerly occupied by L'Hippocampe, there is now the new joint venture of Pierre and Kathleen Condou and Bruno Loubet. The menu is unmistakably Bruno although his role is more that of an associated consultant, leaving the day-to-day running of the kitchen to chef Desmond Yare. The food is gutsy and strong with dishes originating from south-west France - snails stewed in tomato with a polenta base and parsley and cream, sardine and roast pepper tart, and smoked fish cannelloni in a horseradish sauce. Main courses include the likes of cassoulet, fresh salt cod on minestrone vegetables, and sautéed rabbit, swiss chard, olives and rosemary. Where else would you be able to choose braised ox cheeks with macaroni gratin? At long last you can dine on cuisine terroir without having to wear a tie or endure a grand hotel setting.

BISTROT 190   SW7

190 Queen's Gate, SW7 5EU
Telephone: 071-581 5666   **£45**
Open: lunch + dinner daily (closed 24-26 Dec)
Meals served: 7am-12.30am (Sun 7am-11.30pm)

To get to the Bistro, you go through Club 190's bar (its own restaurant/brasserie is downstairs and across the hall of the Gore Hotel. Once installed, enjoy good cooking from head chef, Chris Millar, on an Antony Worrall Thompson-influenced menu. It's packed to the seams with locals, off-duty chefs and those in the know. On Sundays get there early since no bookings are taken (unless you're a member), and take your time over a leisurely fixed-price Sunday lunch at £13.50 for 2-courses or £16.50 for 3. The food has a strong Californian flavour - try country bread with tapenade and olives, pan-fried razor clams with garlic and thyme, the AWT lamb shank with flageolet beans and pan-roasted hare with tolosa beans and deep-fried polenta. These are just some of the highlights on an extensive menu. It's the type of place you need to return to at least a couple of times to try out all the options. Service is fashionable and reasonably swift, the decor bistro-style with a bare wooden floor and marble tables.

BLAH! BLAH! BLAH!   W12

78 Goldhawk Road, W12 8HA
Telephone: 081-746 1337   **£35**
Open: lunch + dinner Mon-Sat (closed Bank Holidays)
Meals served: lunch 12-3, dinner 7.30-11

A full and fun evening is to be had at this eclectic, totally vegetarian
dining establishment in Shepherds Bush. It's not for the faint hearted -
you will immediately mix in with the crowd if you wear a bandanna and
tight, brightly coloured shorts! There certainly won't be a dull moment
in vaguely surreal decor, with gargoyle heads as candle-holders and
dead vine branches as wall-hangings. The menu for both upstairs and
ground floor restaurants is fashionable, a medley of Italian, Middle
Eastern, Thai and Indian influences on a collection of vegetables,
grains, nuts and yoghurts. Warm goat's cheese on griddled vegetables
with a sun-dried tomato dressing is not out of place alongside toasted
mushroom cup on rye with artichokes and sunflower seeds. Main
courses are more substantial, such as a complex layering of gorgonzola, walnuts and spinach in a galette, eaten with a pepperonata,
parmesan and spinach sauce, while the house pasta is redolent of a
rich tomato and courgette sauce with olive paste, pesto and aioli. Since
this place is unlicensed, bring your own bottle (50p corkage) and
remember, no credit cards.

BLAKES HOTEL   SW7

33 Roland Gardens, SW7 3PF   ✿
Telephone: 071-370 6701 Fax: 071-373 0442   **£120**
Open: lunch + dinner daily
Meals served: lunch 12.30-2.30, dinner 7.30-12

Highly designed, highly beautiful and highly priced this town-house
hotel and restaurant might be, but there are not many places of this calibre in London, let alone the rest of England. Exquisite with a dark green
exterior, it is sheer fancy and one that will live on in your memory. It
comes as no surprise that each room was designed by Anouska Hempel
(Lady Weinberg) whose couturier showroom is only a skip and a jump
away in Fulham Road. Oriental elements influence the foyer and continue into the bar and restaurant. Luxurious, but not bland or ostentatious-
ly flashy, the rooms are highlighted by blocks of strong colour. Green
and black predominate in the public rooms, but they are not subdued in
any way, in fact completely the opposite. The 50 bedrooms vary widely
in decor from a pristine all-white room to masses of swagged fabrics,
rare silks, tapestries and woods. The same high standards of comfort
and style will be found in the restaurant, the new domain of Peter
Thornley who took over from David Wilson. Appealing to the eye, his
dishes are not overdone and are usually preceded by complimentary
crisp wonton crescents of spiced chicken. The evening carte menu is
spiced with the flavours of the orient and sashays through French and
Italian adaptations - blini of golden beluga, salmon carpaccio with
capers, sashimi, langoustine satay followed by lava seared calves' liver
with Meaux and Dijon sauces, Szechuan duck with roasted salt and pepper, or lamb enclosed in a mint wrap. Needless to say the wine list offers
equally expensive wines - only the house wines are under £20. For the
resident there is a 24-hour room service, so there is no real need to leave
the confines of your own Shangri-la!

BLOOM'S	E1

90 Whitechapel High Street, E1 7RA
Tel: 071-247 6001 £45
Open: all day Sun-Fri (closed Xmas, Jewish holidays)
Meals served: 11.30-9.30 (Fri 11.30-3)
Popular Jewish restaurant with branch in Golder's Green. Close to Brick Lane market and Whitechapel Art Gallery.

BLOOM'S	NW11

130 Golder's Green Road, NW11 8HB
Tel: 081-455 1338 £45
Open: all day Sun-Thu, lunch Fri, dinner Sat (closed Good Friday, Xmas, Jewish Holidays)
Meals served: 11.30-11 (Fri 11.30-sunset, Sat sunset-3am)
Sister restaurant to Bloom's in Whitechapel serving kosher food.

BLUE PRINT CAFÉ SE1

Design Museum, Shad Thames, Butlers Wharf, SE1 2YD
Telephone: 071-378 7031 **£45**
Open: lunch daily, dinner Mon-Sat
Meals served: lunch 12-3, dinner 7-11

On the first floor of the Design Museum is this stylish café, where you can have snackettes of squid salad with avocado and watercress or grilled goat's cheese with roquette and roasted peppers, or a more substantial bouillabaisse, roast cod with parsley mash and tapenade, or lamb-burger with cracked wheat, garlic and tomato. Chef Lucy Crabb heads the operation and creates dishes that have made this a fine place in which to while away a few hours within the Conran temple of design. The terrace offers alfresco dining with a view of the river.

BOMBAY BRASSERIE SW7

Courtfield Close, Courtfield Road, SW7 4UH
Telephone: 071-370 4040 Fax: 071-835 1669 **£60**
Open: lunch + dinner daily (closed 26+27 Dec)
Meals served: lunch 12.30-3, dinner 7.30-12 (Sun 7.30-11.30)

The jewel in the Taj Hotel's crown is this affluent restaurant offering a mixture of dishes gathered from all over India. Book a table in the conservatory, which adds to the colonial ambience with palms and greenery, or choose one of the tables running the length of the left hand wall. At lunchtime buffet-style service allows sampling of at least 8 dishes from mild through to hot or otherwise. Try jhinga masala - sweet-water shrimps tossed with peppers, tomatoes and onions, or sev batata puri - small biscuit-type puris topped with cubed boiled potatoes. Then move along to Parsi fare like the badami margi - a light and aromatic chicken dish made with yoghurt and almonds, or from Goa chicken xakuti - a fiery dry chicken curry made with coconut and a blend of spices. Ask the advice of the well-informed staff if you're unfamiliar with any of the dishes. Order a cobra coffee at the end of dinner - it's worth it for the spectacle of the flaming orange rind! Sunday lunch is popular, and in the evening a pianist tinkles the ivories.

Still the most stylish of Indian restaurants.

LA BOUCHÉE   SW7

56 Old Brompton Road, SW7
Telephone: 071-589 1929   **£35**
Open: all day (closed 25+26 Dec, 1 Jan)
Meals served: 9am-11pm

Dark, atmospheric and slightly cramped, this place lives up to the
stereotype of the real down-to-earth French bistro - plain wooden
tables and dripping candles. The menu mixes salads with classics like
fish and thick onion soups - this is as close as you are currently going
to get in London to a real left-bank bistro. A shellfish stand is set up
outside on the pavement and with such simple and approachable food
inside, it is hardly surprising that you will need to book, especially at
weekends. The food is outstandingly good value on both the à la carte
and set menus - two of the latter, at £4.95 and £5.95. The day's specials
are on the blackboard - cassoulet, roasted wood pigeon with lentils,
rabbit with rich mustard sauce, salmon with sorrel sauce and thickly
sliced ham with white beans accompany the more predictable but
always favoured steak-frites. The staff are typically French and
bubbling with enthusiasm.

BOULESTIN   WC2

Garden Entrance, 1a Henrietta Street, WC2E 8PS
Telephone: 071-836 7061 Fax: 071-836 1283   **£60**
Open: lunch Mon-Fri, dinner Mon-Sat (closed Bank Holidays,
1 wk Xmas, 3 wks Aug)
Meals served: lunch 12-2.30, dinner 7.30-11.15

For the diner, now is the most advantageous time to sample Kevin
Kennedy's sound classical cooking - it is going for a song and knowing
Kevin, he will be in fine voice! In the heart of Covent Garden, across
the piazza on the south side, is a small glass entrance. Despite a basement location it is one of the classiest rooms in town, having been
founded in the '20s by Marcel Boulestin. Service is exceptional and
attentive. Romantic and timeless in decor and elegance, this grand and
traditional dining room has always offered some of the best cooking of
its type in London. Kevin is a master and at the moment is offering set
menus for lunch and dinner at massively deflated prices. A 3-course
dinner will cost only £25.50 and might include coddled eggs with sea
urchin coral and caviar, or queen scallops on the half-shell with a delicate garlic butter, followed by strips of red snapper poached with a
champagne sauce. And on the last lap you have two directions to go -
tour de france of cheese or a puff pastry layered with praline! In
Kevin's own words the set prices 'are likely to yo-yo' depending on
what is in the market that day. This is an excellent venue for an after-
theatre dinner. The à la carte is still faithful to its former style - 7 types
of fish and shellfish, marinated, smoked, grilled and poached, pheasant with chestnut and cranberry and a calvados sauce, or grilled rib of
Scotch beef with a 3-pepper sauce.

BOYD'S   W8

135 Kensington Church Street, W8 7LP
Telephone: 071-727 5452 Fax: 071-221 0615   **£55**
Open: lunch + dinner Mon-Sat (closed 2 wks Xmas)
Meals served: lunch 12.30-2.30, dinner 7-11

In a road well known for its eating establishments Boyd's maintains its
position well. Green-stained table tops, rattan chairs, plenty of plants,
stripped floors and ceiling fans combine to make this a pleasant neighbourhood restaurant. Self-taught chef Boyd Gilmour operates a good
value menu, but no longer opens on Sundays, so instead make for the
sunny conservatory on Saturdays, having shopped-till-you-drop in High
Street Ken or Knightsbridge. For £14 the set menu offers a soup or
other typical starter like an onion tart with sage, and then on to chick-
en with sun-dried tomatoes and coriander or stir-fried squid with red
pepper tagliatelle. Pudding could be chocolate mousse with raspberry
coulis or lemon parfait. In the evening the talented Boyd brings his à la
carte menu to the fore - try crab ravioli with spring onions, ginger and
mangetout, char-grilled turbot with basil beurre blanc (there are
always a couple of daily fish specials), or baked chicken with Thai
spices and fresh egg noodles. Attractive presentation sets off these
carefully crafted dishes.

THE BRACKENBURY   W6

129-131 Brackenbury Road, W6   *Good local*
Telephone: 081-748 0107   *restaurant.*   **£35**
Open: lunch Tue-Fri + Sun, dinner Mon-Sat (closed Xmas, Easter)
Meals served: lunch 12.30-2.45, dinner 7-10.45

Hugely affordable and popular, the Brackenbury achieves the
Robinsons' objectives. Sensible pricing and straightforward cooking is
what we all want, and that's exactly what we get here. What was once
an uninteresting wine bar (itself the result of 2 shops knocked together) has metamorphosed into an inviting restaurant in salmon pink and
green. The eating areas are functional with school benches and tightly
packed tables - the locals love it and Adam and Katie Robinson, with
children of their own, welcome young families. Adam is adept at
utilising low-cost ingredients to the full to make imaginative dishes,
and succeeds where so many others fail in the current simple, modern
cooking style. He's particularly renowned for his soups. Good wholesome food is scattered throughout the menu, with roast pork, buckwheat noodles and black bean dressing, roast rib of beef, chips and
béarnaise (enough for two) and fish stew, rouille and saffron potatoes -
all exceedingly good value. Unusual European cheeses will surprise as
well as a difficult choice between puddings such as saffron ice cream,
iced praline terrine, and Seville orange curd tart.

LE BRACONNIER   SW14

467 Upper Richmond Road West, SW14 7PU
Telephone: 081-878 2853   **£35**
Open: lunch Sun in winter, dinner daily (closed Bank
Holidays, 5 days Xmas)
Meals served: lunch 12.30-2.30 (Sun Oct-Mar only), dinner 7-11

With Terry Speers at the wheel, tour France from the comfort of this
little pink and green restaurant in East Sheen, specialising in French
regional cooking. The different regions are featured on a monthly
basis - on one visit to the Loire, starters were soupe solognote au lapin,
or omelette with potato, bacon and sorrel, while pointe de culotte
(pan-fried steak with shallots and a red wine sauce) or quenelles de
poisson completed the extremely reasonably priced 2-course menu.
Other dishes featured included porc en chemise, carré d'agneau, and
of course some well chosen wines.

LA BRASSERIE   SW3

272 Brompton Road, SW3 2AW
Telephone: 071-581 3089 Fax: 071-823 8553   **£40**
Open: all day daily (closed 25+26 Dec)
Meals served: 8am-midnight, (Sun 10am-11.30pm)

On what is known locally as the Brompton Cross, almost opposite the
Michelin Building, stands this authentic French brasserie where the
young gather late on a Saturday night. It is exactly as the name suggests - styled in the Parisian way with doors that open onto the pavement and opening hours from first thing Monday until last thing
Sunday. Freshly-imported French waiters, complete with long aprons
and waistcoats, serve breakfast with the papers for a leisurely start or
pit-stop for early shoppers. The pace picks up with les snacks - well-
filled baguettes, niçoise and roquefort salads, croques and BLT toasted
sandwiches from lunchtime. The evening brings out the full-blown
brasserie classics such as lamb with haricot beans, medallions of veal
with roquefort and skate with black butter. Plats du jour can include
boeuf daube and frites or oxtail.

BRASSERIE DU MARCHÉ AUX PUCES   **W10**

349 Portobello Road, W10 5SA
Telephone: 081-968 5828   **£45**
Open: all day Mon-Sat, Sun lunch only (closed Bank Holidays)
Meals served: 12-11 (Sun 11-4), (coffee from 10am)

There's the distinct air of a French market town at this little corner of
the street, where there is pavement dining. You could easily believe
you've crossed the Channel when you see the large windows, plain
wooden tables, mahogany bar, plateau of cheeses and lots of pavement
strollers. Coffee is available from 10 until 12, when the menu takes on
the colours of Portobello. Owner/chef Robert Price allows the eclectic
local mood to evoke his cooking - haggis in filo with quince purée and
crab apple jelly, aubergine and yoghurt charlotte, French bean and
scallop salad with saffron potatoes, and jerk chicken with street rice
rub shoulders with brandade of cod, seafood sausages with cider and
savoy cabbage, lamb with flageolets and fricassée of mussels. Desserts
are more French in origin - prune and armagnac ice cream, white
chocolate torte, pumpkin and mincemeat tart.

BROWN'S HOTEL   **W1**

Albemarle Street, W1A 4SW
Telephone: 071-493 6020 Fax: 071-493 9381   **£55**
Open: lunch + dinner daily
Meals served: lunch 12-2.30, dinner 6.30-10 (Sat 6-10), (light
meals Tea 3.15-6, High Tea 4.15-5.45)   ❖

Brown's was originally several separate but terraced 19th-century
houses, now combined to make one of the first town-house hotels
where old fashioned service and standards have been retained, which
also means that a jacket, collar and tie are requested as part of normal
attire for gentlemen. It remains on the list of places to visit for
American tourists who want to experience that typical English charm
in good old traditional surroundings. Brown's is after all a shining
example of all that is British, including that great institution, afternoon
tea. Sip your Earl Grey with cucumber sandwiches, brown bread and
butter with jams and preserves, scones and clotted cream, cakes and
pastries. Or go instead for high tea which is afternoon tea plus the
additional fishcakes, ham with chutney and bubble and squeak. Lunch
and dinner can of course also be enjoyed in this resplendent atmosphere with the emphasis once again on tradition - roasts and English
daily specials being favourites. It's also a great place for a traditional
English breakfast.

BUBB'S   EC1

329 Central Markets, EC1A 9NB
Telephone: 071-236 2435   **£55**
Open: lunch + dinner Mon-Fri (closed Bank Holidays)
Meals served: lunch 12-2, dinner 6.30-9.30

Just a stone's throw from Smithfield is this more-typical-than-typical
French restaurant. It is reminiscent of those found in any French market town with its lace curtains, prints and posters, music, and predominantly male clientèle. Evenings are quieter and candle-lit with the
interconnecting rooms giving a degree of intimacy. Booking is essential. The cooking is friendly and well-planned, contributing to a memorable and enjoyable evening. A concise menu includes fish and onion
soups with all the trimmings, snails and grilled sardines, pheasant with
chestnuts, beef with wild mushrooms and béarnaise.

LE CADRE   N8

10 Priory Road, Crouch End, N8 7RD
Telephone: 081-348 0606   **£35**
Open: lunch Mon-Fri, dinner Mon-Sat (closed Bank Holidays,
2 wks Aug/Sep)
Meals served: lunch 12-2.30, dinner 7-11

In the shadow of Ally Pally, this simple and stylish good neighbourhood restaurant was opened in 1987 under David Misselbrook and
Marie Fedyk and, ably assisted by young chef Daniel Delagarde from
Touraine, they continue to attract acclaim. Daniel's craft is well practised and his mousses are seventh-heaven stuff - delicate yet softly textured. The fish soup was good, as was poussin with good garlicky new
potatoes. Excellent tarte tatin and vacherin with strawberries, cassis
sorbet and dense blackcurrant coulis completed a delicious menu. The
set menus are good value and cleverly change price according to what
time of the week you go - on Monday and Tuesday it's £10.50 while
Friday and Saturday evenings see a jump to £15.50 - good marketing
practice, and it evens out the orders. Some outside tables in fair
weather.

CAFÉ DELANCEY   NW1

3 Delancey Street, NW1 7NN
Telephone: 071-387 1985 Fax: 071-383 5314   **£40**
Open: all day daily (closed 25+26 Dec, 1 Jan)
Meals served: 8am-midnight

Continuing successfully with its original formula of brasserie, bar and
café serving good food from croissants to baguettes, croque monsieurs
and steak sandwiches to calves' liver with bacon and onions served
with rösti, or saucisses du café. You don't have to eat, as the full
licence allows customers to drink there during pub hours.

CAFÉ DES AMIS DU VIN   WC2

11-14 Hanover Place, WC2
Telephone: 071-379 3444   **£30**
Open: lunch + dinner Mon-Sat (closed 1 wk Xmas)
Meals served: lunch 12-3, dinner 7-11.30

In a tiny alley running between Long Acre and Floral Street is this faithfully French wine bar, café and restaurant. Its proximity to the Royal Opera House makes it popular for pre- and post-theatre goers, and on occasions the stars themselves pop in for a quick bite. The basement houses the wine bar which serves over 20 different wines by the glass and a good selection of 30 French cheeses. The ground floor is the brasserie which spills over onto the pavement in summer. It has the usual steadfast menu choices and offers a more relaxed setting than the first floor Salon Restaurant. The Salon, with a separate menu, offers the diner the likes of seafood in puff pastry or galantine of duck with pistachios followed by a choice of fish, vegetarian or meat main courses including the likes of king prawns pan-fried in butter and then flambéed with Ricard and finished with cream or pan-fried calves' liver with a squeeze of lemon. All main courses come with vegetables. 60 French wines to choose from, as well as some from the New World.

CAFÉ DU MARCHE   EC1

22 Charterhouse Square, Charterhouse Mews, EC1M 6AH
Telephone: 071-608 1609   **£50**
Open: lunch Mon-Fri, dinner Mon-Sat, (closed Bank Holidays,
Xmas/New Year)
Meals served: lunch 12-2.30, dinner 6-10   *good local restaurant*

This quaint restaurant is near Smithfield and not far from the Barbican. Unsurprisingly perhaps, it was originally a meat warehouse and the decor, stripped to the bare essentials (exposed brick, wooden floor, cane furniture and large beams), enhances the barn-like feeling of this splendid place. The upstairs attic is also open at lunchtime, adding to the feeling of spaciousness. Hand-written, gutsy menus make this a favourite with the locals and city types. The prix fixe dinner at £19 gives a choice of 7 starters from duck and foie gras terrine to fish soup, and then main courses such as prune stuffed pork, goulash, cassoulet and côté du boeuf. The meat undoubtedly is excellent, and so it should be considering location! Cheese or dessert round off the menu with crème caramel, bavois and coffee torte with Grand Marnier among the more popular choices.

jazz in the evenings piano + double bass

— cluttered fun interior of Café du Marché

CAFÉ FLO N1

334 Upper Street, N1 8EA
Telephone: 071-226 7916 Fax: 071-704 2965
Open: all day daily (closed 25+26 Dec)
Meals served: 9am-11.30pm (Sun 9am-10.30pm)

There are also "Flo's" in Hampstead & Kew.

£35

It's sometimes hard to find a space in this bustling, French-style bistro, the perfect place for a rendezvous both at lunchtime and in the evening. You can either linger, or just grab a quick tasty steak frites or poisson frites before the theatre or another appointment.

CAFÉ FLO SW6

676 Fulham Road, SW6 5RS
Telephone: 071-371 9673 Fax: 071-731 5178
Open: all day daily (closed 25+26 Dec, 1 Jan)
Meals served: 9am-11.30pm (Sun 9am-10.30pm)

£35

The success of Café Flo is evident in the number of outlets that have sprung up since the first opening. All are of the French bistro/brasserie ilk, offering good food and wine - it seems to be just what the Fulhamites are looking for in the way of a quick snack, good coffee and a fun atmosphere.

CAFÉ FLO W8

127/129 Kensington Church Street, W8 7LP
Telephone: 071-727 8142 Fax: 071-243 2935
Open: all day daily (closed 25+26 Dec)
Meals served: 9am-11.30pm

£35

The Café Flo theme continues in this branch, which remains popular and thriving and has created a little piece of France in this corner of London. It's a welcome relief to come here after shopping and enjoy a coffee or good brasserie fare. Choose from the specials which usually include a soup, poisson du jour, plat du jour and a dessert du jour. Good coffee and excellent fresh bread.

CAFÉ FLO WC2

51 St Martins Lane, WC2N 4EA
Telephone: 071-836 8289 Fax: 071-379 0314
Open: all day daily (closed Bank Holidays, 5 days Xmas)
Meals served: lunch 12-3 (Sat+Sun 12-4), dinner 5.30-11.45
(Sun 5.30-10.30), (light meals 9am-11.30, Sun 10-10.30pm)

£30

The French formula is proving successful for owner Russell Joffe. A quick turnover eaterie bang in the centre of theatre-land, it caters for both hungry office-workers and pre- or after-theatre goers. Affordable bistro classics, soundly cooked. The wine draws heavily on the New World. The service and crowd are young and bustling. A good place to meet for a coffee and snack.

CAFÉ ROYAL GRILL ROOM   W1

68 Regent Street, W1R 6EL
Telephone: 071-439 6320 Fax: 071-439 7672   **£65**
Open: lunch Mon-Fri, dinner Mon-Sat (closed Bank Holidays)
Meals served: lunch 12.30-3, dinner 6-10.30

In my opinion this - being one of the oldest dining rooms in London,
established in 1865 - has always been worth a visit, if only for the
extravagance of the original decor: over-the-top rococo, and the very
sense of history that the place pervades. But now there is the added
pleasure of eating from the menu devised by Herbert Berger, a man
with undoubted talent, who seems to have settled in and found himself
a worthy dining room. His menu includes an excellent pressed terrine
of calves' sweetbreads served with a spicy broad-bean coulis from the
carte, or an equally exciting feuilleteé of smoked haddock and quail's
eggs with a light English mustard sauce, a good fillet of sea bass,
roasted with saffron oil, fennel and the natural juices from the pan; or
from the meat section, medallions of veal with foie gras, savoy cabbage
and a sauternes sauce. The popular grilled meat and fish dishes are
very sensibly retained, and at lunch and dinner there is a set menu. An
extensive wine list and formal but pleasant service are helping to put
the Café Royal Grill Room back on the map as one of the better dining
rooms in London.

CAMDEN BRASSERIE   NW1

216 Camden High Street, Camden Town, NW1 8QR
Telephone: 071-482 2114   **£55**
Open: lunch + dinner daily (closed 24-26 + 31 Dec)
Meals served: lunch 12-3 (Sun 12.30-3.30), dinner 6-11.30 (Sun 5-10.30)

Right at the centre of busy Camden life is this bustling brasserie. It
opened a decade before brasserie-fever hit London and has catered to
the high trend crowd ever since. The surroundings are sparse with
lots of wood and white walls, and the atmosphere mediterranean.
Mexican ceramics decorate the bar, and the crowd adds the final
splash of colour. During the day large skylights give the unusual feeling of eating alfresco (as do open doors in the summer), and at night
the brasserie is warmly lit. Chef Blaise Vasseur concentrates on char-
grilled meats and fish with plentiful amounts of roasted peppers, potato
mash and great frites as accompaniments. Salads are good with rocket,
cherry tomato, roasted peppers and avocado making a delicious
starter, as does warm salad of eel with chorizo and aged vinegar or
tuna tataki with sesame and soya.

CANAL BRASSERIE   W10

Canalot Studios, 222 Kensal Road, W10 5BN
Telephone: 081-960 2732   £40
Open: lunch Mon-Fri (closed Bank Holidays)
Meals served: lunch 12.30-3.30

The canal side location is an added bonus at this brasserie, converted from
a Victorian chocolate factory in Kensal Docks. The interior is spacious,
washed with earthy tones and completed by a glass-covered atrium. It is a
modern brasserie, and has a showing of eye-catching sculptures and temporary exhibitions by modern European artists. The short and simple
menu continues the contemporary theme - tomato and basil soup, duck
galantine, avocado and melon salad followed by chicken curry or a cod and
salmon strudel. Pudding is typified by syrup sponge, crème brûlée or
chocolate mousse with coffee sauce. This is a place in which to relax as you
watch the Regent's Canal through porthole windows.

CANNIZARO HOUSE   SW19

West Side, Wimbledon Common, SW19 4UF
Telephone: 081-879 1464 Fax: 081-879 7338   £50
Open: lunch + dinner daily
Meals served: lunch 12-2, dinner 7-10.30

Stately lawns run down to an ornamental lake and the sunken gardens
at this magnificent and unique Georgian hotel, self-styled as London's
first country house hotel. Set on the edge of Wimbledon Common,
Cannizaro House is pitched at the business and conference side of the
market and is ideally suited to June and crowds who flock to the All-
England Tennis Championships. Offers of well-planned packages exist
for the tournament fortnight and a limousine service is available, useful also for travelling to the airport. The house is decorated with grand
antique furniture, oil paintings and sumptuous seating - elegance is the
key. The 46 bedrooms are divided between the main house and a new
wing. The beautiful 60-seater restaurant and the Queen Elizabeth
Room with cream, green and pink colouring, crystal chandelier, gilt
and draped windows are superbly appointed. Dinner is as carefully
arranged, with ample French classics and fine wines.

THE CANTEEN   SW10

Harbour Yard, Chelsea Harbour, SW10
Telephone: 071-351 7330
Open: lunch + dinner daily
Meals served: lunch 12-3 (Sun 12-3.30), dinner 6.30-12 (Sun 7-11)

£50

The Marco Pierre White touch has come to Chelsea Harbour and whereas other restaurants have floundered in this complex, the Canteen doesn't seem to be able to fail. Service is now accomplished and attentive, and the place is busy every night of the week. The menu in harlequin colours - a suggestion of the entertainment you will find inside - is relatively concise, offering watercress soup with poached egg, escabèche of red mullet with saffron, or bang bang salad. Main courses are a mix of fish, shellfish, meat and poultry - fillet of salmon with a crab crust and shellfish sauce, guinea fowl with creamed cabbage and pommes anna - some imaginative and satisfying cooking. All starters and main courses are a standard price. A brilliant bargain and Marco food for the masses, with the added bonus of those coveted marina views. Without doubt, a restaurant with modern style that will continue to grow in stature.

CANTINA DEL PONTE   SE1

36C Shad Thames, Butlers Wharf, SE1 2YE
Telephone: 071-403 5403
Open: lunch daily, dinner Mon-Sat
Meals served: lunch 12-3, dinner 6-11

£45

In the same building as big brother, Le Pont de la Tour, this is the newcomer to the Conran empire of London's finest and extends the range to include a New-Med designer restaurant. Here there are no tablecloths but instead maple-topped tables and a floor of large terracotta tiles. A vast mural by Timna Woollard painted in warm browns, creams and rust reds runs the length of the back wall. So Sir Terence Conran has managed it again - a stylish, informal restaurant enjoying that exclusive view of the bridge. In summer the large double windows open back to reveal the terrace giving an extra 35 places - and they will be much needed - for this is one of the best alfresco eating places in London. Chef Louis Loizia (ex-Zuma) has thought out and designed his menu well and at a good price. Served from bright white, slightly bowl-shaped plates the choices are strong, vivid and more often than not superb - stuffed zucchini flowers, pumpkin and ricotta ravioli, ossobucco with gremolata, Savoy cabbage and polenta and a side order of garlic and rosemary bread followed by poached pear, fresh dates and cinnamon bavarois. A short wine list (all under £20) provides a good choice.

THE CAPITAL   SW3

22-24 Basil Street, SW3 1AT
Telephone: 071-589 5171 Fax: 071-225 0011
Open: lunch + dinner daily
Meals served: lunch 12-2.30, dinner 7-11

Extravagant attention to detail prevails through David Levin's 48-bed-roomed hotel, from rugs and fabrics to flower arrangements and the dishes on Philip Britten's menus. 'Sedate and beautifully under control' - sums up the atmosphere in the Nina Campbell refitted dining room, which is big on striped curtains but in an arresting peach tone. From behind the glass screen that allows you to observe but not feel too involved, Philip cooks a 3-course menu of dishes such as boudin of guinea fowl and leeks, sauced with girolles, followed by deep fried sweetbreads in goose fat with pancetta on a purée of celery, rounded off by tarte tatin served with vanilla custard and calvados sorbet. These are interesting dishes showing an admirable depth of flavour - master-pieces in their own right.

LE CAPRICE   SW1

Arlington House, Arlington Street, SW1A 1RT
Telephone: 071-629 2239   **£60**
Open: lunch + dinner daily (closed 24 Dec-2 Jan)
Meals served: lunch 12-3 (Sun 12-3.30), dinner 6-12

The place to go to be seen, but you need to book days if not weeks
ahead to guarantee a table at a certain time. A sleek and highly fashionable restaurant in black and white with David Bailey classics adorning the wall, this is still the watering hole of the young élite and show-
biz glitterati. If you can squeeze in unannounced, find a space for yourself at the long gleaming bar by the door and take in a quick snack of
risotto, either nero (made with squid ink) or alternatively with butternut squash, or opt for a fresh tuna niçoise. Executive head chef Mark
Hix has made some changes to the menu to keep up with ever-chang-
ing trends but happily the popular salmon fishcake remains, on its bed
of spinach and sorrel. Appetizers are predominately Med-influenced
with focaccia of roasted baby artichokes, rocket, chorizo and mozzarella salad or a tomato and basil galette; while main courses could be cat-
alonian fish stew with aioli, deep-fried cod with pea purée and chips, or
grilled spring chicken with sweetcorn fritters. With Jesus Adorno at
the helm, service continues to be courteous and the customers themselves provide as captivating viewing as the Bailey prints.

CASA COMINETTI   SE6

129 Rushey Green, SE6 4AA
Telephone: 081-697 2314   £40
Open: lunch Mon-Fri, dinner Mon-Sat (closed 25+26 Dec)
Meals served: lunch 12-2.30, dinner 6.30-11
An Italian faithful - the restaurant has been serving usual dishes since 1916.

CASALE FRANCO   N1

134 Upper Street, N1 1PQ
Telephone: 071-226 8994   **£40**
Open: lunch Fri-Sun, dinner Tue-Sun (closed Bank Holidays, 1 wk Dec)
Meals served: lunch 12.30-2.30, dinner 6.30-11.30

A family affair, but nevertheless very designerish - modernist interior,
with brick walls and visible piping. The fast turnover of tables has kept
prices to a reasonable level. Pizzas, pastas and house specialities make
for an interesting Italian evening.

CHAPTER 11 SW10

47 Hollywood Road, SW10 9HX
Telephone: 071-351 1683   Fax: 071-376 5083   **£50**
Open: dinner Mon-Sat (closed some Bank Holidays, 3 days Xmas)
Meals served: dinner 6.45-12

Chapter 11 is an informal, but extremely busy local brasserie. On hearing the name you might think it is a meet for bikers and their groupies, or a hang-out for the heavyweight legal profession, but how far removed could it be? The clientele is Sloanie and the restaurant a delight, with a fusion of modern and traditional elements. The menu reads well with choices such as smoked haddock fishcake, baby squid with a scallop mousse and citrus beurre blanc, or tiger prawns in a light herb batter and raita. Main courses range from braised ham hock with spicy green lentils and celeriac purée to fresh pasta with aubergine, tomato, red onion, basil and garlic, with side-orders of sautéed potatoes, courgettes, spinach and leeks. The wine list travels the world, with some reasonably priced options.

CHARLOTTE'S PLACE W5

16 St Matthew's Road, W5 3JT
Telephone: 081-567 7541   **£45**
Open: lunch Mon-Fri, dinner Mon-Sat (closed Bank Holidays,
1 wk Xmas/New Year)
Meals served: lunch 12.30-2, dinner 7.30-10

Intimate, predominantly pink with a touch of green, this family-run restaurant has been in business for 10 years and has a set of loyal customers who have grown with it from its early origins as a bistro. Home-cooked English fare is on offer with haddock baked in a cream sauce under a lid of puff pastry, home-made chicken liver pâté with herbs and garlic, or a seafood crêpe with a parsley sauce. Mains include rainbow trout is simply cooked, or sole in a delicate sauce of mushrooms and cream, beef wellington or duck roasted rare, sliced thinly and with Cumberland sauce.

CHELSEA HOTEL SW1

17-25 Sloane Street, SW1X 9NU
Telephone: 071-235 4377 Fax: 071-235 3705   £40
Open: lunch + dinner daily
Meals served: lunch 12.30-2, dinner 6.30-10.30
Modern hotel with 225 rooms, close to Knightsbridge tube. Excellent shopping. Restaurant offers a modern eclectic menu with an international flavour and reasonable prices.

CHESTERFIELD HOTEL　　　　　　　**W1**

35 Charles Street, W1X 8LX
Telephone: 071-491 2622 Fax: 071-491 4793　　　　　**£60**
Open: lunch + dinner daily
Meals served: lunch 12.30-2, dinner 6.30-10.30 (Sun 7-10)

'I'll be wearing a red carnation' - it sounds like a line from a thriller, but
in fact it could be the concierge, the porter or any other member of
staff you meet at this very charming hotel just off Berkeley Square, for
they will all be wearing a fresh red carnation. The epitome of
Englishness, this place has the aura of an exclusive club. High button-
backed chairs and leather Chesterfields are very much in evidence.
Dining in the restaurant is formal, with choices such as smoked quail
and hare, or mussels, scallops and langoustine scented with lemon
grass, followed by monkfish and parma ham niçoise or corn-fed guinea
fowl with spinach and morrels. On a lighter note is the Terrace in the
conservatory which is ideal for a late breakfast, or pre-theatre supper.

CHEZ GERARD　　　　　　　　　　**W1**

8 Charlotte Street, W1P 1HE　　　　　*The new modern bistro*
Telephone: 071-636 4975　　　　　　　*style decor* **£40**
Open: lunch Sun-Fri, dinner daily (closed Bank Holidays) *works well.*
Meals served: lunch 12-2.45, dinner 6.30-11　　　　　❖

Bang in the centre of theatreland, the atmosphere here is warm and
very much the French bistro-style. The steaks, like the frites, are
splendid and really are best followed up by cheese. Other dishes
include moules marinières, grilled salmon and daily specials, plus a
fixed-price menu. As you would expect from this group, a very reasonably priced French wine list is offered.

CHEZ GERARD　　　　　　　　　　**W1**

31 Dover Street, W1
Telephone: 071-499 8171　　　　　　　　　£40
Open: lunch daily, dinner Mon-Sat (closed Bank Holidays)
Meals served: lunch 12-2.45, dinner 6-11.30

The formula continues with frites and a fun evening being part of the
menu. For those liking their beef rare the French cut onglet fits the
bill or maybe the steak tartare mixed with spice. Wooden floor, panelling and French artefacts ensure a pleasant ambience.

CHEZ GERARD   WC2

119 Chancery Lane, WC2A 1BB
Telephone: 071-405 0290   **£40**
Open: lunch + dinner Mon-Fri (closed Bank Holidays)
Meals served: lunch 12-2.45, dinner 5.30-10

The garlic and Gallic charm come hand-in-hand in this good value brasserie. Old pine panelling, French paintings and rustic collection of ceramics make this a good lunchtime haunt for the legal brains of the city who also return after 5.30, when the 4-course fixed-price menu joins the carte with soup, salads or moules followed by fish of the day, grilled brochette of lamb or French cut steak. The upstairs bar also opens for business, offering a selection of snacks - warm goat's cheese, moules, scrambled eggs with salmon and a plate of French cheeses. Specialities of the house include a wide selection of charcoal grills - côtes de boeuf, châteaubriand and the ubiquitous steak-frites. Good range wine list with many at reasonable prices.

CHEZ LILINE   N4

101 Stroud Green Road, Finsbury Park, N4 3PX
Telephone: 071-263 6550   **£30**
Open: lunch + dinner daily (closed Bank Holidays)
Meals served: lunch 12.30-3, dinner 6.30-11

Younger sister to La Gaulette, this family-owned Mauritian fish restaurant is minimal in decor, but then you are here for the fish. The menu is long and extensive and warns the customer that the wait might be longer than expected since to retain the freshness of the fish it is only cut and cooked to order - an honest practise, worth waiting for. The atmosphere is predominantly provincial French with poster-clad walls and lino floor. The portions are generous and the Mauritian element comes from the variety of fresh fish flown in - bourgeoise, parrot fish, vacoa, red snapper. Pascal Doudrich cooks in a gutsy French/Mauritian way with plenty of ginger, garlic, chilli, tomatoes, mango, coconut, spring onions and herbs but creamy sauces are also available. Favourites are parrot fish with mustard and king prawns with lemon juice. The menu is exotic and it's hard to pinpoint what you might enjoy most - vindaye de poisson (slices of tropical fish with saffron and mustard seed sauce), scallops with brandy and garlic, tropical fish curry, assiette de crustace (cold shellfish including half a lobster) or shelled prawns with onions and tomatoes.

CHEZ MOI   W11

1 Addison Avenue, Holland Park, W11 4QS
Telephone: 071-603 8267   **£55**
Open: lunch Mon-Fri, dinner Mon-Sat (closed Bank Holidays, 1 wk Xmas)
Meals served: lunch 12.30-2, dinner 7-11

Little has changed at this haunt of the late `60s and if you haven't been back since your youth you won't feel out of place. No discredit meant to owners Colin Smith and Richard Walton, in fact quite the reverse; it confirms that they had it right from the beginning and the rest of London has only just caught up! The menu is in tune with tradition, with hot and cold hors d'oeuvres from spinach salad with chicken livers to seafood rolled in angel hair noodles and deep-fried, plus main courses of poached salmon sausages with a lobster sauce and rack of lamb with garlic and mint. Set lunches are good value and show a leaning towards modern interpretation with sautéed pigeon in a sesame oil vinaigrette or slowly braised boned rolled hare leg, served with a mushroom and white wine sauce. The hot pancake filled with an almond and orange flavoured cream cheese, and with sultanas and maple syrup, is a popular dessert.

CHEZ NICO AT NINETY PARK LANE   W1

90 Park Lane, W1A 3AA
Telephone: 071-409 1290 Fax: 071-355 4877   **£115**
Open: lunch Mon-Fri, dinner Mon-Sat (closed Bank Holidays,
10 days Xmas/New Year)
Meals served: lunch 12-2, dinner 7-11

Nico Ladenis has spent the last year settling into his new position at 90 Park Lane and has now renamed the restaurant Chez Nico at Ninety Park Lane. The style is the old Nico but heightened and, could it be possible, even better? In head chef Paul Flynn and 13-strong brigade he has loyal disciples and the effort and judgement is paying dividend. Nico is quite delighted with his new operation, they say, and so are his customers who enjoy a set menu that brings skill and stunning presentation to the plate with creations such as crisp salmon fingers teriyaki with plum sauce, or a ravioli of langoustines with ginger and chives. A typical fish main course is brill studded with tiny croutons on a bed of sweet shallots. Such is the tenacity of the man, in good spirits and cooking like a wonder in this stylish and well-appointed restaurant. To save you from an agonising decision, try the selection of all the menu's desserts, truly to experience the extent of his mastery.

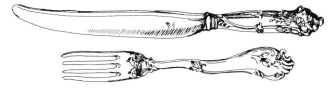

CHINON   W14

23 Richmond Way, W14 0AS
Telephone: 071-602 5968   **£65**
Open: dinner Tue-Sat (closed some Bank Holidays, 1 wk Aug)
Meals served: (lunch 12.30-2.30 wine bar only), dinner 7-11
(wine bar 6.30-10.30)

The restaurant has moved one place up the street and acquired a wine
bar and a garden in the process. Otherwise very little has changed.
Jonathan Hayes is still cooking with imagination to produce a short
menu and uses ingredients of the best and freshest quality. Scallops
remain one of his favoured ingredients, just cooked and served on a
cabbage cushion filled with leeks. Good wine list, mostly French, but
including others.

CHRISTIAN'S   W4

Station Parade, Burlington Lane, W4 3HD
Telephone: 081-995 0382   **£50**
Open: lunch Sun, dinner Tue-Sat (closed Bank Holidays)
Meals served: lunch 12.30-3, dinner 7.30-10.30

This is a simple neighbourhood restaurant with an attractive decor of
light blue striped wallpaper, hung with prints, and with the open
kitchen very much part of the show. A hand written menu speaks volumes for this French chef who, unpretentiously and with good taste
and skill creates simple and spot-on dishes - black bean soup with
tomato salsa, vegetable navarin with a mixed leaf salad and poached
corn-fed chicken with tarragon cream. The dishes may sound elementary but there's nothing wrong with cooking like this. The choice is
short but sound, the menu approachable and reliable. A nice relaxed
place with a few tables outside.

CHRISTOPHER'S   WC2

18 Wellington Street, WC2E 7DD
Telephone: 071-240 4222   **£60**
Open: lunch Sun-Fri, dinner Mon-Sat (closed Bank Holidays)
Meals served: lunch 12-3 (Sun brunch 11.30-2.30), dinner 6-11.30

High '90s fashion in decor, menu and clientele, this place has been a
winner from day one with an eclectic mix of the American and the
Mediterranean with appetizers of carpaccio, Peking duck salad and
smoked tomato soup. Main dishes include sausages of chicken and
veal with a mustard sauce, pig's trotter with sweetbreads and a New
York strip steak, or grilled chicken with red pepper salad and shoe-
strings! Whatever you finally choose, always get a side order of their
fries - skinny and crisp - and celeriac mash. The staff are young and the
place is perpetually packed, so booking is a must. Good for Sunday
brunch.

CHURCHILL INTER-CONTINENTAL HOTEL   W1

30 Seymour Street, Portman Square, W1A 4ZX
Telephone: 071-486 5800 Fax: 071-486 1255
Open: lunch + dinner daily
Meals served: lunch 12-3, dinner 6-11 (Sun 7.30-11)

Idris Caldora's cooking is as good as ever. ✿ **£65** ❖

The restaurant has been renamed Clementines which is a natural reflection of the large bowls of citrus fruits which are used to decorate the room - acid lemon, orange and lime green all piled on top of one another as if fine art. This is a contemporary design with a menu to match. Executive chef Idris Caldora continues with the dishes he introduced when he arrived last autumn, a mix of British cooking with influences from the East - chicken tikka with raita sauce, or steamed salmon with ginger and limes on a bed of Chinese greens and sea bass with puréed potatoes, braised fennel and a star anise sauce.

CHUTNEY MARY   SW10

535 King's Road, SW10 0SZ
Telephone: 071-351 3113 Fax: 071-351 7694
Open: lunch + dinner daily (closed Sun for bar food)
Meals served: lunch 12.30-2.30 (Sun 12.30-3), dinner 7-11.30 (Sun 7-10)

✿ **£50**

Namita Punjabi has brought new life to Indian restaurants. The Verandah bar upstairs offers freshly squeezed and blended nectar-like fruit juices, colonial beers and tiffin snacks, while downstairs is the cool, striped restaurant with a conservatory to one side. The menu brings into the open anglicised recipes from the days of the Raj, from salmon kedgeree with crisp fried onions and served with dal, to masala roast lamb - a Bombay version of lamb first braised with spice and ground sesame seeds. The menu is augmented by more straightforward Indian dishes such as almond chicken korma which is perfect with mango chutney - infinitely better than any other normally served - and a particularly spicy green chicken curry from Goa. The wine list is helpfully annotated by a chilli symbol, to indicated which choices are best with spicy food.

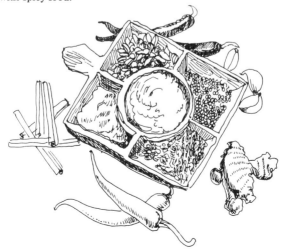

CIBO   W14

3 Russell Gardens, W14 8EZ
Telephone: 071-371 6271   **£60**
Open: lunch + dinner daily (closed 24, 25 Dec, 1 Jan, Bank Holidays)
Meals served: lunch 12-2.30, dinner 7-11

Contemporary in expression, Cibo is Italian and very much a high-style restaurant - one of the first. Vivid and bright, the food is served in a dramatic way on huge colourful plates which echo the paintings on the walls. It's now also open on Sundays, which means you can take lunch at a more leisurely pace and enjoy the modern translations - asparagus wrapped in prosciutto with melted fontina cheese, sautéed radicchio, endives and rocket with mozzarella - and then move on to pasta made with chestnut flour and filled with venison and served with a wild mushroom sauce or fresh pappardelle noodles with rocket in a scallop and red mullet sauce. Other main course options include stewed baby octopus and squid in tomatoes and spinach, whole sea bass baked with fresh herbs or grilled with olive oil and grilled beef fillet in balsamic vinegar sauce.

CLARIDGE'S   W1

Brook Street, W1A 2JQ
Telephone: 071-629 8860 Fax: 071-499 2210
Restaurant: **£85**
Open: lunch + dinner daily
Meals served: lunch 12.30-3, dinner 7-11.15
Causerie:
Open: lunch + dinner Sun-Fri
Meals served: lunch 12-3, dinner 5.30-11 (Sun 7-11)   **£65**

Going to Claridge's is an event and a treat, for during its 100-year reign as one of London's top hotels it has consistently waved the flag for Britain. Footmen wear breeches and gold braid. Within these historic walls (where the Empress Eugenie once stayed), no two rooms are alike and many are decorated in Art Deco style. The black and white tiled foyer opens out to a genteel lounge which is used by those in the know as a perfect meeting place for tea or an early evening drink, while being entertained by the Hungarian Quartet. To the right is the restaurant decorated in pale tones. Dining at Claridge's is another event in itself and the cooking is some of the best a grand hotel can offer. The Causerie may hold a few surprises with its Scandinavian flavours, such as a smörgasbord at lunchtimes from which you help yourself. Marjan Lesnik's cuisine is also available in the rather more formal main restaurant, equally beautifully decorated in keeping with Basil Ionides' 1926 design and featuring a new mirrored mural by Christopher Ironside. Here the cooking is at its best: classical French with an emphasis on modern interpretation and presentation. The à la carte and 3-course set menus offer well-tuned dishes such as mousseline of smoked salmon with pink champagne, pot-roast guinea fowl with black pudding ballotine, or scallops with herbs, crisp pastry and young spinach. For those staying in one of the 190 beautiful bedrooms there is the Bath and Racquets Club adjoining the hotel.

CLARKE'S   **W8**

124 Kensington Church Street, W8 4BH
Telephone: 071-221 9225 Fax: 071-229 4564
Open: lunch + dinner Mon-Fri (closed Bank Holidays,
2 wks Aug, 1 wk Xm, 4 days Easter)
Meals served: lunch 12.30-2, dinner 7-10

Sally Clarke deserves her success for her talent & dedication & hard work! **£75**

Sally Clarke has a definite style of her own and her restaurant is a joy -
light and breezy, with wooden floor and plain decor. The menu is a
colourful array of grilled meats, fish, mozzarella, plenty of fresh crisp
vegetables, salad leaves, lentils and good, good bread. Char-grilling is
widely used, as are marinades, the freshness of herbs complementing
the sunny cooking. This is a singularly special place to eat, but also
take time to visit the shop next door - cheeses, breads, oat cakes and
preserves are all there to tempt you.

COFFEE GALLERY   **WC1**

23 Museum Street, WC1A 1JT
Telephone: 071-436 0455   £25
Open: all day daily (closed 25+26 Dec, 1 Jan, Easter Sunday)
Meals served: 8-5.30 Mon-Fri, 10-5.30 Sat, 12-6.30 Sun
Close to British museum. Menus change daily at this anglo-Italian café. No smoking,
but 2 pavement tables!

CONDOTTI   **W1**

4 Mill Street, W1R 9TE
Telephone: 071-499 1308   **£30**
Open: lunch + dinner Mon-Sat (closed Bank Holidays)
Meals served: 11.30am-12 midnight

A very reasonably priced pizzeria, with a good fun menu that's not
short on choice. American-style salads - on the large side of generous -
include niçoise, potatoe, avocado and olive salad. The other choice is
pizza - adequately topped with numerous combinations.

Hotel Conrad

THE CONNAUGHT W1

Carlos Place, W1Y 6AL
Telephone: 071-499 7070 Fax: 071-495 3262
Open: lunch + dinner daily (Grill Room Mon-Fri, closed
Bank Holidays)
Meals served: lunch 12.30-2, dinner 6.30-10.30 (Grill Room from 6)

£90

This hotel has great character and offers some of the most courteous service in London. Despite the predominantly French classic cuisine, a few British greats have also been allowed prominence with either Irish stew, steak and kidney pie, oxtail or boiled silverside scheduled as the special luncheon dish on specific days of the week. There are in fact 2 restaurants although both serve similar menus and both are longtime favourites. The Restaurant, embellished with ornate plasterwork, oak panelling and mirrors, fine white linen, china, cutlery and crystal is in contrast to the Grill Room, resplendent in green with a less serious atmosphere. Michel Bourdin continues to direct his brigade commanding endless respect, and presents hors d'oeuvres, potages, grills and roasts all cooked and served in typical French manner, appropriately accompanied and sauced - classicism at its best.

HOTEL CONRAD SW10

Chelsea Harbour, SW10 OXG
Telephone: 071-823 3000 Fax: 071-351 6525
Open: lunch + dinner daily
Meals served: lunch 12-3, (Sun Brunch 12-3.30), dinner 7-10.30

£55

A monument to hotel design in the '90s, this member of the Conrad chain is modelled to give the best of everything - a traffic-free location, riverside and marina view, standards of the highest order and a restaurant that takes in world-wide influences. Designed by David Hicks, the brasserie-style restaurant offers particularly good value at lunchtime when Andrew Bennett's cooking offers Mediterranean soups, oriental style duck, and jumbo prawns in a Thai dressing. Most of the menu is English/continental and on Fridays and Saturdays a buffet barbecue is also available. Desserts are from the sweet trolley.

CORK & BOTTLE WC2

44-46 Cranbourn Street, WC2H 4AN
Telephone: 071-734 7807 Fax: 071-483 2230
Open: all day daily (closed 25 Dec)
Meals served: 11-midnight, Sun 12-10.30

£35

Having been in the business for over 21 years Don Hewitson is a fount of knowledge and enthusiasm. Don is the only person in the UK to receive both the Diplôme d'Honneur and Grande Medaille d'Argent by the Corporation des Vignerons de Champagne. With longer opening hours, food is now becoming even more important in drinking establishments and in this legendary bar the client is well looked after from both sides of the counter. No formal menu exists but a daily selection written on the blackboard lists specials such as their well-loved raised ham and cheese pie, tartare de loup (chopped sea bass with tartare and parsley wrapped in smoked salmon) or Hungarian meat loaf.

CORNEY & BARROW   EC2

109 Old Broad Street, EC2N 1AP
Telephone: 071-638 9308   **£60**
Open: lunch Mon-Fri (closed Bank Holidays)
Meals served: lunch 11.30-3.30

The oldest of the chain, this one has a distinctive club-like atmosphere.
The room is small and rectangular with muted bottle-green walls and
carpet. A complimentary copy of the Financial Times comes as no surprise, since we are only a stone's throw from the Stock Exchange.
Geared to the city with city prices and a suggested 15% discretionary
service charge, the cooking is safe. There's a choice of 5 starters ranging from a platter of smoked salmon with a shallot and chablis dressing to a red and yellow bavarois on frisée lettuce and a tarragon and
shallot dressing. Typical main courses come at about £17.95 with a
mixed grill of salmon, halibut and haddock with a lime and ginger butter or roasted breast of duck with almonds and apple.

CORNEY & BARROW   EC4

44 Cannon Street, EC4N 6JJ
Telephone: 071-248 1700   **£50**
Open: lunch Mon-Fri (closed Bank Holidays)
Meals served: lunch 11.30-3

Still catering for city slickers, this branch has a lighter and brighter art
deco interior. State-of-the-art technology keeps the dealers up-to-date
while they try to relax. A lively ground floor houses the bar. The menu
here is set, with a choice between 2- (at £16.95) and 3- courses (at
£21.95) and provides a mixture of traditional and modern brasserie
cooking - artichoke and fennel soup, tagliatelle with fresh basil and
black olive sauce, fillet of red mullet with coriander and tomato dressing, crab fishcakes with dill and Pernod sauce, steak and kidney pie
and rhubarb and strawberry fool. Concessions for healthy eating are
very much in mind.

LA CROISETTE   SW10

168 Ifield Road, SW10 9AF
Telephone: 071-373 3694   **£65**
Open: dinner Tue-Sat
Meals served: dinner 7-11.30

The formula here has always been a great success: a fixed-price menu,
which includes kir and coffee and a menu that sees a selection of
seafood from plateau de fruits de mer, moules prepared in 3 ways,
coquilles St Jacques with saffron, provençale, nage, bordelaise or with
a hint of curry. Pierre Martin's original restaurant imports its wine, raw
ingredients and staff from France and is an ideal place to sample a
mollusc or two on a lazy Friday evening.

CROWTHERS   SW14

481 Upper Richmond Road West, SW14 7PU
Telephone: 081-876 6372   £50
Open: lunch Tue-Fri, dinner Mon-Sat (closed Bank Holidays)
Meals served: lunch 12-2, dinner 7-10.45

Safe and well priced, this good neighbourhood restaurant is at its best
in the evening - it offers value for money and a simple style of cooking.
Philip Crowther is in charge of the kitchen with a 2- or 3-course set
menu while wife Shirley runs the front. Dishes include a feuilletée of
scallops, leeks, oyster mushrooms in a light curry sauce and confit of
duck with lime and ginger. Pork comes with prunes, and guinea fowl
with pine nuts while puddings remain faithful to tradition - sticky toffee
pudding with butterscotch sauce and tarte au citron are sometimes on
offer.

DAN'S   SW3

119 Sydney Street, SW3 6NR
Telephone: 071-352 2718 Fax: 071-352 3265   £45
Open: lunch Mon-Fri, dinner daily (closed Bank Holidays, 1 wk Xmas)
Meals served: lunch 12.30-2.30, dinner 7.30-10.45 (Sat 7.30-10.30)

New chef Thierry Rousseau adds further depth to this local Chelsea
restaurant with a light and concise menu that changes weekly. He
cooks in a direct and modern style, unadorned by flounces and frills
with strong, flavourful combinations. Make a bee-line for the conservatory or garden and choose the set dinner menu which is constantly
changing but recently offered an asparagus and sweet pepper quiche,
then a moist baked chicken breast with cucumber sauce followed by a
tangy mango and strawberry parfait.

DAPHNE'S   SW3

110-112 Draycott Avenue, SW3 3AE
Telephone: 071-589 4257 Fax: 071-581 2232   *Glamourous*
Open: lunch + dinner daily (closed Bank Holidays) *& stylish* £50
Meals served: lunch 12-3 (Sun 11-4), dinner 7-11.30 *restaurant.*

The old Daphne's has gone and new owners Mogens Tholstrup and
chef Eddie Baines (ex-Est) have installed a resplendent Italian villa in
her place - a trio of rooms linked together on different levels, rejuve-
nated in warm terracotta tones and inlaid with squares of gold. A tree
in the second room and creeping plants at the back give an alfresco
feel, completed by the conservatory whose glass roof slides open in
good weather. The cooking is modern and simple, with deep- fried
crab or carpaccio with shavings of parmesan and artichoke to open the
proceedings, swiftly followed by char-grilled fish, or breast of chicken
with a lemon and sage crust. Desserts include poached pears in chocolate and panacotta with strawberries. Booking is required, particularly
on warm evenings when the conservatory is the place to be.

DEALS WEST RESTAURANT DINER W1

14/16 Fouberts Place, W1V 1HH
Telephone: 071-287 1001 £40
Open: all day daily
Meals served: 12-11 (Sun 12-3)
No Big Deals, Raw Deals, Hot Deals and Side Deals are all part of what is in store at
this up-town spin-off of the successful Eddie Lim, Viscount Linley and Lord Lichfield-
owned Chelsea restaurant and bar.

DE CECCO SW6

189 New King's Road, Parsons Green, SW6
Telephone: 071-736 1145 £35
Open: lunch + dinner Mon-Sat (closed Bank Holidays)
Meals served: lunch 12.30-2.30, dinner 6.45-11.15

A rather ordinary exterior hides a lively, sparkling interior. Rich blues,
bright yellows and a mirrored bar area with prints and posters cram-
ming the walls - all this makes a good back-drop to a busy restaurant
with a loyal local clientele and charming owners, Mr and Mrs Piccirilli.
Booking is essential. The menu reads as standard Italian but the food
is good and well presented on large plates. Interesting pasta combinations might be something like fettucini with lamb's kidneys, spinach,
cream and parmesan. The daily specials are typified by ossobucco,
squid with garlic, and beef in calvados and wine sauce on a bed of
pappardelle.

DEL BUONGUSTAIO SW15

283 Putney Bridge Road, SW15 2PY
Telephone: 081-780 9361 £45
Open: lunch + dinner Mon-Sat (closed Sun, Bank Holidays, 2 wks Xmas)
Meals served: lunch 12-3, dinner 6.30-11.30

This comparatively recently opened younger sister of Osteria Antica
Bologna in Battersea, is located at the bridge end of the road, just
opposite Café Rouge. The food is gutsy and good, with simple country
flavours and an emphasis on North Italian dishes. The atmosphere is
both lively and relaxing and the meal starts off well with a basket of
home-made bread and brilliant black olives with orange zest. Try their
fresh artichoke, spinach, rice and parmesan torta, or then hearty country soup garnished with grilled radicchio and followed by Calabrian
meatballs with chillies, garlic and chestnuts served on soft polenta, or
squid stuffed with bread, fresh herbs, garlic and capers and served
with a basil sauce. Equally enticing is cotechino sausage with spicy
lentils and potato purée. Puddings complete the meal - try fresh figs
baked with zabaglione cream or a rice torta served with Moscato de
Pantelleria. The wine list is mostly Italian and Australian, as befits the
nationalities and heritages of the owners.

DELL'UGO   W1

56 Frith Street, W1V 5TA
Telephone: 071-734 8300 Fax: 071-734 8784   **£40**
Open: lunch + dinner Mon-Sat (closed lunch Sat 1st+2nd floors)
Meals served:
1st Floor: lunch 12.30-3, dinner 7-11.45
2nd floor: lunch 12.30-3, dinner 5.30-11
Ground Floor café: all day 11am-12.30am

Antony Worrall Thompson at his most creative. Such is the success of
the place that it continues to thrive every night of the week giving the
media and the stylish of Soho somewhere close at hand and busy in
which to meet, eat and stay late. With 3-tier dining, each floor has a different style and pace, yet the fashion overall remains the same - young
and European high style. The bustling café downstairs with Warhol-
style wall hangings of Saxa salt tubs and Rowntrees jelly packets spills
out onto the pavement and offers vibrant snacks of crostini, bruschetta
and Tuscan soups, in a style rarely seen before this place came along.
A selection of interesting beers from Duvel to Framboise, as well as
wines and juices, are presented by trendy young things in bright AWT
waistcoats with the dell'Ugo logo on the back. The first floor is lively
with a mural and close-packed tables - then it's up to the more sedate
`gentleman's club' room on the top floor, with central viewing to
observe the noise and bustle of the colourful crowd below. All floors
share menus in the same vein - bright, lively, with hints of the exotic
and big on Italian influence. This may be a trendy place but the food
tastes good too, so the atmosphere continues to buzz and booking
remains necessary for the two upper floors. That still leaves the bar
area, which operates one a first come, first served basis, so it pays to
get there early.

DON PEPE   NW8

99 Frampton Street, NW8 8NA
Telephone: 071-262 3834 Fax: 071-724 8305   **£35**
Open: lunch daily, dinner Mon-Sat (closed 24+25 Dec)
Meals served: lunch 12-3, dinner 7-1

The bar is the place to take a crowd, since you then get to sample a little of everything! There's clams, prawns in garlic, octopus, grilled sardines, small squid, pickled and fried anchovies, meatballs, tortilla, fried
aubergine, mussels, stuffed peppers and fillet of cod in batter. In the
more formal restaurant you can enjoy tapas in comfort, along with the
specials of paella, escalopes in a cream sauce and plenty of prawn and
hake dishes, or the good value set menus. A well-travelled wine list
concentrates on Spain with a wine map on the back for quick indentifi-
cation of area.

THE DORCHESTER W1

Park Lane, W1A 2HJ
Telephone: 071-629 8888 Fax: 071-409 0114
Grill: £90
Open: lunch + dinner daily
Meals served: lunch 12.30-2.30, dinner 6-11 (Sun 7-10.30)
Oriental Room: £65
Open: lunch Mon-Fri, dinner Mon-Sat
Meals served: lunch 12-2.30, dinner 7-11
Terrace Restaurant: £90
Open: Tue-Sat (closed Bank Holidays)
Meals served: dinner 7-1

Executive chef Willi Elsener has his work cut out with the highest standards to maintain and 3 restaurants to watch over as well as private dining, banquets and room service. The Terrace offers dinner and dancing, and dishes from far and wide - a result of the chef's extensive travels. He makes clever use of spices and aromatic ingredients, shown in duck stuffed with peaches, apple and cinnamon, or a 3-pepper terrine with pan-fried king prawns in a lemon-grass infused sesame oil. The Grill Room is the most traditional of the trio and offers English cooking at its most original, for example poached salmon and warm Jersey potatoes, horseradish and elderberry vinaigrette. Finally, there's the Oriental Room, with shark's fin soup, abalone and dishes such as pan-fried roast duck with celery and bean sprouts, deep-fried spare ribs in chilli pepper and herbal salt or jelly-fish and mixed seafood marinated in sesame oil and chilli bean sauce, cooked by Simon Yang. It's rated as one of the top oriental restaurants in London. This year sees a new dim sum menu for £20, and an Italian menu has been introduced in the Dorchester Bar. All the ground floor areas are ornately decorated and standards here and in the 197 bedrooms are under the watchful eye of general manager Ricky Obertelli.

LA DORDOGNE W4

5 Devonshire Road, W4 2EU
Telephone: 081-747 1836 Fax: 081-994 9144 £50
Open: lunch Mon-fri, dinner daily (closed Bank Holidays)
Meals served: lunch 12-2.30, dinner 7-11

Book a table or just pop into the oyster bar for 6 or so natives or rocks and soak up the Frenchness of the place. Provincial and classical, this local restaurant brings together a myriad of dishes from the 4 corners of France. The staff are freshly imported along with the wine which is well-balanced and reasonably priced. For an all-round indulgent starter try the salad of quail's egg, foie gras and smoked duck or a salmon terrine served with a light mustard sauce. Dover sole with saffron sauce or lamb cooked with honey make good mains, but I can think of nothing nicer than a bowl of moules and a salad!

DOWNSTAIRS AT 190   SW7

190 Queen's Gate, SW7 5EU
Telephone: 071-581 5666   **£45**
Open: dinner Mon-Fri (closed Bank Holidays, 2 wks Aug)
Meals served: dinner 7-12

It's sometimes hard to move with the times when those times move on
so quickly, and nowhere is this more true than in the restaurant world.
Antony Worrall Thompson, however, not only sets trends but predicts
fashions. Below stairs at 190, the '90s less-meat palate is catered for in
AWT's inimitable Mediterranean style. The menu moves through
snacking food - crostini of fish: mussels, clams, smoked salmon, brandade, taramasalata and deep-fried whitebait - to appetizers - spicy crab
blinis, steamed mussels with coriander, greens and lentil broth - and
on to salads, stews and soups. From the pan come fish cakes, creole
blackened fish, and fish and chips. Not that meat-eaters are forgotten,
for 5 or 6 meat dishes are normally available daily. The opulent
entrance perhaps belies the lighter, more informal style of 190's
restaurant, but not the quality of food - it's still pure AWT!

DOWNTOWN SULEMAN'S   SE1

1 Cathedral Street, SE1
Telephone: 071-407 0337   **£40**
Open: lunch Mon-Fri, dinner Tue-Fri
Meals served: lunch 12-2.45, dinner 5.30-10.30

At the heart of London Bridge, chef David Hill runs a transcontinental
kitchen with a short but tempting menu of starters from chooky fungi,
galloping snails and egg sulemans. Main courses are no tamer with
nanny's soufflé, vegetarian jungawali and pork scrumpy to think about.
A set Thai menu of 9 dishes (minimum of 2) takes in all the flavours of
the east. Desserts are more easily recognisable with pecan crêpe
stack, rhubarb strudel and lemon pancakes on offer.

DRONES RESTAURANT   SW1

1 Pont Street, SW1X 9EJ
Telephone: 071-235 9638   **£50**
Open: lunch + dinner daily (closed Bank Holidays)
Meals served: lunch 12.30-4.45, dinner 7-11

Drones has been here since the early '70s and continues to be the
haunt of the young fashionable and trendy of Belgravia. Owner Nicky
Kerman has kept this restaurant up to the minute and with chef Nigel
Kent provides a light and bright Californian menu littered with seafood
and grilled meats and fish - from gigot steak with coriander butter,
calves' liver with red onions and mashed potatoes, grilled dover sole
and smoked bacon and cheeseburger with the lightest pommes
allumettes to steak tartare seared and served with lamb's lettuce. The
selection of vegetables is good, with carrot and parsnip purée, buttered
savoy cabbage and minted potatoes. Juanita Kerman has introduced a
cabaret on certain evenings - it is worth telephoning to find out who is
appearing and when.

DUKES HOTEL   SW1

35 St James's Place, SW1A 1NY
Telephone: 071-491 4840 Fax: 071-493 1264   £65
Open: lunch Sun-Fri, dinner daily
Meals served: lunch 12.30-2, dinner 6-10 (Sun-10)
Smart staff, fine antiques and traditional dishes make this an attractive 64-bedroomed
hotel, hidden away off St James's.

THE EAGLE   EC1

159 Farringdon Road, EC1R 3AL
Telephone: 071-837 1353   £40
Open: lunch + dinner daily (closed Bank Holidays, 3 wks Xmas)
Meals served: lunch 12.30-2.30, dinner 6.30-10.30

From the outside it looks like any normal boozer, but inside it is
stripped to the bare boards, with widely spaced tables and - for those
that get there early - a leather sofa and chairs. Here they serve voguish
food in the Italian sense from noon until night and it's good stuff too -
caldo verde soup, focaccia bread sandwich with grilled mixed vegetables and taleggio cheese, risotto of radicchio and parmesan and, best
of all, grilled mackerel with coriander and lime salsa, tomato salad and
cornbread. And if you thought that was adventurous for this corner
pub how do you feel about strawberries and parmesan with a balsamic
vinegar dressing? Full range of desserts, of which the lively clientele
take full advantage.

ENGLISH GARDEN   SW3

10 Lincoln Street, SW3 2TS
Telephone: 071-584 7272 Fax: 071-581 2848   *consistent value*
Open: lunch + dinner daily (closed 25+26 Dec)   *since 1979 & so*   £55
Meals served: lunch 12.30-2.30 (Sun 12.30-2), dinner   *deserve*
7.30-11.30 (Sun 7.30-10)   *their loyal following)*

In the midst of Chelsea stands this town-house restaurant offering
English cooking from the 18th Century brought gently up to date.
Wallow in the Englishness of it all, from wallpapers and curtains to
flower arrangements. Try for a window table, or one as close as possible to the conservatory at the back. The menu changes with the seasons but a typical spring offering might be sweetbreads and pickled
walnut pâté or grilled green vegetables topped with toasted spring
onion, steamed salmon roulade with crab and ginger or Glamorgan
sausages with creamed spring cabbage. Puddings are as quaint as the
place itself - sweet Yorkshire pudding with apricot preserve, honey
brittle ice cream, or apple syllabub with cinnamon shortbread.

ENGLISH HOUSE   SW3

3 Milner Street, SW3 2QA
Telephone: 071-584 3002 Fax: 071-581 2848   **£45**
Open: lunch + dinner daily (closed 26 Dec)
Meals served: lunch 12.30-2.30, dinner 7.30-11.30 (Sun 7.30-10)

Sibling to the English Garden, and located just off King's Road, this
Victorian terraced English home has small flower-print wallpaper,
chintz and dried flowers, and epitomises the kind of place Americans
drool over and want to take back with them! English tastes are catered
for by Andy Bailey - you might like to try his galantine of chicken and a
vegetable preserve, or baked egg with asparagus and cheese, followed
by braised beef and ale pie or roast leg of lamb with leeks, red wine
and mint sauce. Regional cheeses, chilled raspberry custard pudding
or a baked apple in pastry with caramel sauce finish the evening. For
guests and those London-bound, the restaurant is open for lunch on
the biggest day of the year with all the Christmas trimmings. Good
wine selection with some reasonable prices.

ENOTECA   SW15

28 Putney High Street, SW15 1SQ
Telephone: 081-785 4449   **£45**
Open: lunch Mon-Fri, dinner Mon-Sat (closed Bank Holidays, 1 wk Xmas)
Meals served: lunch 12.30-3, dinner 7-11.30

On a corner location just south of Putney Bridge, Enoteca sells good
Italian cooking to thirtysomething professionals. Lunchtime offers the
luncher quick bistro-like meals with bruschetta, mussels, plenty of
pasta and Tuscan sausages. Haddock baked with potatoes and courgettes or lamb with a lambrusco sauce make more of a 2-course meal
for the more serious eater. The evening brings an unpretentious menu
- parcels of aubergine with mozzarella and fresh basil, spinach
gnocchi with a walnut sauce, a couple of pastas and risotto dishes.
Main courses bring the grill and kitchen into action with roasted fish,
or meat such as fillet of pork stuffed with apple and raisins and served
with savoy cabbage and pancetta, or swordfish grilled with pine
kernels and fresh herbs. Home-made puddings and good coffee.

THE ENTERPRISE   SW3

35 Walton Street, SW3
Telephone: 071-584 1060
Good local restaurant
£45
Open: lunch daily, dinner Mon-Sat (closed 25 Dec)
Meals served: lunch 12.30-2.30, dinner 7.30-10.30

The grey painted pub front hides an unexpected interior, which has undergone a metamorphosis into a restaurant and bar. The decor retains the charm of the former drinking place but with the added elegance of recent additions - heavy golden moiré curtains and beautiful floral arrangements on a highly polished central isle. Old books add a touch of lived-in appeal, and, with the open plan kitchen with its hanging lanterns and baskets, lend a country feel. The tables are simple with paper tops and napkins yet the menu is smart with fashionable dishes like quesadillas served with guacamole and salsa, crab hollandaise tart, Lincolnshire sausages turned in mustard and honey and supreme of chicken stuffed with spinach, pesto and sun-dried tomatoes. Hazelnut and apple strudel, served in generous portions, is warm and soft. Cooking is unpretentious and the dishes are put together with care. Some good reasonably priced selections on the wine list.

L'ESCARGOT   W1

48 Greek Street, W1V 5LR
Telephone: 071-437 2679 Fax: 071-437 0790
£70
Open: lunch Mon-Fri, dinner Mon-Sat (closed Bank Holidays)
Meals served: lunch 12-2.30, dinner 7-11.30

L'Escargot has returned but this time with Jimmy Lahoud as owner and David Cavalier (ex-Cavaliers) and Garry Hollihead (ex-Sutherlands) sharing the kitchen. Abstract art hangs on the walls and although the room has been refurbished it retains its old style, just as classic dishes now appear in reworked forms. L'Escargot boasts Jonathan Ross amongst its backers - the hope is that the glitterati will hang out here. In the brasserie downstairs the menu offers roast goat's cheese with provençale vegetables, snails in chablis, pot au feu for 2 and cassoulet toulousain. The main restaurant is more elegant and serious but has a menu that continues in the same vein - baked sea bass with fennel, shallots and garlic and risotto milanese with fried squid. It's nice to see the restaurant out of its shell again, and much interest will no doubt be focused on the emergence of the various differing styles of food that these talented young chefs produce.

48 GREEK STREET LONDON W.1.

EST   W1

54 Frith Street, W1V 5TE
Telephone: 071-437 0666   **£40**
Open: lunch Mon-Fri, dinner Mon-Sat (closed Bank Holidays)
Meals served: lunch 12-3, dinner 6-11 (Fri+Sat 6-11.30)

Large front windows take the restaurant atmosphere out on to the
pavement, in full view of those sauntering down Frith Street. At night
the place can be seen humming with the fashionable and Soho trendy
who pile into this Scandinavian, stripped wood-panelled bar and restaurant. The menu is modern with bruschetta and crostini rating high,
whilst those dining at the tables might sample the char-grilled lamb,
seafood and salads topped with parmesan. It will be packed towards
the end of the week and has a lively and friendly atmosphere, so be
warned, it's not a place for a quiet drink.

L'ESTAMINET   WC2

14 Garrick Street, WC2
Telephone: 071-379 1432   **£55**
Open: lunch + dinner Mon-Sat (closed Bank Holidays)
Meals served: lunch 12-2.30, dinner 6.30-11.30

In the heart of the Covent Garden scene is this attractive French
brasserie at the site of the old Inigo Jones. Just off Floral Street it's
always busy and the basement wine bar La Tartine especially is packed
at lunchtimes and on Fridays, with a lookalike René (*Allo, Allo*) bar-
man adding to the mood. The brasserie serves a concise menu of 12
hors d'oeuvres from crêpes aux fruits de mer, and assiette de charcuterie to brochettes of mussels with rice. Main courses are covered by a
selection of fish from monkfish or roasted cod to dover sole; and the
meat from a good coq au vin, lamb cutlets, or pheasant to grilled or
roast cuts of beef with a choice of sauce. Desserts range from tartes,
sorbets and the ubiquitous crème caramel to chocolate mousse.
Adequate French and New World wine list.

LA FAMIGLIA   SW10

7 Langton Street, SW10
Tel: 071-351 0761 Fax: 071-351 2409   £70
Open: lunch + dinner daily (closed 25+26 Dec)
Meals served: lunch 12-3, dinner 7-12
Bright, modern Italian restaurant with traditional menu and one of London's largest
outdoor seating area.

THE FENJA   SW3

69 Cadogan Gardens, SW3 2RB
Telephone: 071-589 7333 Fax: 071-581 4958
High-quality town house hotel with exquisite decor and good antiques. Comfortable
furnishings and welcoming staff combine to create its homely appeal. 13 bedrooms,
no restaurant but breakfast served until 2pm in your room. A member of Small
Luxury Hotels of the World - so you'll know the quality.

FIFTH FLOOR AT HARVEY NICHOLS   SW1

Knightsbridge, SW1
Telephone: 071-235 5250   **£65**
Open: lunch daily, dinner Mon-Sat (closed 25+26 Dec)
Meals served: lunch 12-3 (Sat+Sun 12-3.30), dinner 6.30-11.30

We have all heard about the new floor added to Harvey Nichols, the expense, and the eye-catching `food' windows down on Sloane Street reminding all passers by when it was finally completed. An express lift shoots you to the top of the building. The food store and restaurant, by day run side by side separated only by glass. A modern, pale grey restaurant with a hangar-like appearance has a very busy bar at one end but is in fact very relaxing. From the bustle of the café and the store it draws you in to its enticing serenity. The menu encompasses the current fashions as much as the rest of the store - chef Henry Harris cooks black bean soup, grilled vegetable bruschetta, crab salad with coriander and lime dressing or leek and parmesan tart with truffle oil as starters, followed by poached salmon with horseradish chantilly, roast rack of lamb with aubergine baked with pesto or baked salt cod provençale and polenta. A stylish place at stylish prices. Desserts are enticing but then you might not get into that little Jasper Conran number afterwards - rhubarb and raisin bread pudding with honey anglaise, or plum fool with cinnamon snaps.

FLORIANS   N8

4 Topsfield Parade, Middle Lane, N8 8RP
Telephone: 081-348 8348   **£45**
Open: lunch + dinner daily (closed Bank Holidays)
Meals served: lunch 12-3, dinner 7-11 (Sun 7-10.30),(wine bar 12-11)

Busy and buzzy, wine bar at the front, simple and unfussy food in the relaxed café-style brasserie at the rear. Bottles of olive oil grace the table along with paper napkins.

FORMULA VENETA   SW10

14 Hollywood Road, SW10 9HY
Telephone: 071-352 7612   **£40**
Open: lunch daily, dinner Mon-Sat (closed Bank Holidays)
Meals served: lunch 12.30-2.45, dinner 7-11.15

At this restaurant on the Chelsea/Fulham border there's ample alfresco dining. Typical modern Italian cooking, with specials like proscuitto with olives and rocket, ravioli filled with ricotta and spinach with a tomato and basil sauce, charcoal grilled cuttlefish with only a hint of garlic and roasted rabbit with polenta. The food is simply cooked, but well presented and flavourful. A good local restaurant.

FOUR SEASONS HOTEL   W1

Hamilton Place, Park Lane, W1A 1AZ
Telephone: 071-499 0888 Fax: 071-493 1895
Open: lunch + dinner daily
Meals served: lunch 12.30-3, dinner 7-11 (lounge: 9am-2am,
Sun 9am-1am)

£80

Formerly the Inn on the Park, renamed after its better known restaurant, the 227-bedroomed Four Seasons Hotel itself continues in grand style, but changes are afoot in the kitchens. As we went to press Bruno Loubet left and was replaced by Jean-Christophe Novelli (ex-Gordleton Mill). Judging by the respected Ramon Pajares' previous choices of chef, and Jean-Christophe's own reputation, expect some exciting innovations here.

47 PARK STREET   W1

47 Park Street, W1Y 4EB
Telephone: 071-491 7282 Fax: 071-491 7281

This Edwardian town house in the heart of Mayfair offers a rather grand, special category of accommodation. The rooms are exemplary and spacious and have been designed by Monique Roux (wife of Albert). Keeping things well and truly in the family, the 24-hour room service is provided by the downstairs kitchens of Albert's restaurant Le Gavroche which runs like clockwork, headed by son Michel.

FREDERICK'S   N1

Camden Passage, N1 8EG
Telephone: 071-359 2888 Fax: 071-359 5173
Open: lunch + dinner Mon-Sat (closed Bank Holidays)
Meals served: lunch 12-2.30 dinner 6-11.30

£35

Good local restaurant, 3 minutes from the Angel tube, with a leafy conservatory (brilliant for parties), a beautiful courtyard garden for drinks and alfresco dining, and a chef with a passion for variety that rarely leaves you bored with the menu. Regis Patte doesn't just rotate his menus but renews his classical dishes every fortnight. Popular dishes in the past have been grilled rib steak with Provence herbs and béarnaise sauce, sole with smoked salmon and a dill and prawn sauce and creamy crab soup laced with cognac. The set menu of £16.95 offers 3 courses with coffee, and all the extras including service. Excellent value. The wine list is outstanding with some very good buys and the addition of Thierry Dumont (ex 190 Queen's Gate) adds another dimension to this long standing restaurant of style.

FRENCH HOUSE DINING ROOM
49 Dean Street, Soho W1V 5HL
Tel. 071 437 2477

Small dining room - above
the pub - offers good, interesting
& mainly English food.

LA GAULETTE   W1

53 Cleveland Street, W1P 5PQ
Telephone: 071-580 7608   **£60**
Open: lunch Sun-Fri, dinner Mon-Sat (closed Bank Holidays)
Meals served: lunch 12-2.30, dinner 6.30-11

A simple, dark decor with blue ceiling and walls does little to prepare you for the wonderful, robust cooking you are about to encounter. Sister to Chez Liline this place has a strong Mauritian influence with fish flown in from the crystal waters, varying according to what is best that day. Parrot fish, vacqua, tuna and merou are popular and come cooked with plenty of herbs, garlic and ginger. The style is strong and gutsy but the fish is always in tip-top condition. Tiger prawns with ginger and salad onions might be your starter, followed by a fillet of parrot fish in a creamy aioli sauce.

LE GAVROCHE   W1

43 Upper Brook Street, W1Y 1PF
Telephone: 071-408 0881 Fax: 071-409 0939   **£150**
Open: lunch + dinner Mon-Fri (closed Bank Holidays,
23 Dec-2 Jan)
Meals served: lunch 12-2, dinner 7-11

To say it is set in its ways would be an injustice to Le Gavroche, for despite the philosophy of offering classical French dishes, created from ancient recipes, Albert's son Michel continues to impress and delight with his own creations such as soufflé suissesse, bavaroise de piments doux et tartare de St Jacques, suprême de volaille fermière paline or pigeonneau de Bresse en vessie aux deux céléris. The menu exceptionnel, a fixed-price, set menu, may help those more indecisive amongst us to choose a perfectly balanced meal, such as marnière de coquillages, paupiette de saumon beauvilliers, sorbet à la rhubarbe, mignonette de boeuf poêlée rossini, then plateau de fromage and finally a gelée d'orange et pamplemousse au champagne to finish. The wine list compromises neither quality nor variety as it takes you on a tour of some of France's finest vineyards. Another family concern, adjacent to the restaurant, overseen by Albert's wife Monique, is 47 Park Street .

GAVVER'S SW1

61 Lower Sloane Street, SW1W 8DH
Telephone: 071-730 5983 £55
Open: lunch Mon-Fri, dinner Mon-Sat (closed Bank Holidays)
Meals served: lunch 12-2.30, dinner 6.30-11

The Roux brothers' Chelsea dining room is handy for the Knightsbridge set. This is where the up-and-coming prodigies perfect their repertoire before moving on, although the turnover is on-going, standards are stable and still exceptional. The undeniable mark of the Rouxs is evident in the presentation and perfection of the set and à la carte menus, currently cooked by Bruno Valette, giving us a chance to sample terrine of grilled vegetables, fillet of red mullet with a sauce vierge and basil oil or quenellles of brandade with leek vinaigrette and roast leg of rabbit in parma ham and a mustard seed sauce at a fraction of the usual up-town establishment prices.

GAY HUSSAR W1

2 Greek Street, W1V 6NB
Telephone: 071-437 0973 £50
Open: lunch + dinner Mon-Sat (closed Bank Holidays)
Meals served: lunch 12.30-2.30, dinner 5.30-11

Eat well, drink well and live well is the name of the game at this Soho institution with its gentlemen's club atmosphere of red plush seating, oak-panelling and hearty Hungarian portions. This is not the place to go thinking about your waistline, as Laszlo Holecz's portions are more than just generous. Choose from the old Soho faithfuls of wild cherry soup, pressed boar's head and cold pike with beetroot sauce and cucumber and then move down to more robust dishes like creamed chicken paprikash with thimble egg dumplings or roast duck with red cabbage, Hungarian potatoes and apple sauce. Desserts shouldn't be missed - try their sweet cheese pancakes or rum, cream and walnut delicacy or the poppyseed strudel. The wine list encompasses Hungarian, Bulgarian and French wines.

Bela Molnar now heads the front of house - bringing yet more Hungarian charm.

- with the legendary Elena Salvoni on the first floor

GEALES   W8

2 Farmer Street, W8 7SN
Telephone: 071-727 7969 Fax: 071-229 8632   **£40**
Open: lunch + dinner Tue-Sat (closed Bank Holidays + following Tue,
2 wks Xmas, 3 days Easter, 2 wks Aug)
Meals served: lunch 12-3, dinner 6-11

No ordinary fish and chip shop but a monument to the great British
tradition - this is the place to come for the best crisp, light batter on
your cod and perfect chips cooked in the best oil. The secret of its success is, believe it or not, that they fry their fish in beef dripping - and it
works! I would suggest you take a table promptly, as it can fill up
quickly, and dine like a king on deep-fried clams as a taster, followed
by your favourite type of fish.

GILBERT'S   SW7

2 Exhibition Road, SW7 2HF
Telephone: 071-589 8947   **£40**
Open: lunch Mon-Fri, dinner Mon-Sat (closed Bank Holidays,
1 wk Xmas/New Year)
Meals served: lunch 12.30-2, dinner 7-10.15

Red ochre-painted walls, crisp white linen and a few prints make up the
simple decor to this small dining room. Julia Chalkley prepares the
dishes with personal care while Ann Wregg, American, chatty and
pleasant, welcomes you warmly, with good herby marinated olives.
The prix fixe menu changes every two weeks, and some additional
dishes attract a small supplement. Choose carrot soup with coriander
or buckwheat crêpes with an amazing leek and cheese filling, followed
by a grilled entrecôte with herb butter or as a vegetarian option -
stuffed braised cabbage with a rich tomato sauce. Unpasteurised
cheeses come from Neal's Yard and an impressive list of Californian
wines completes the evening.

GLAISTER'S GARDEN BISTRO   SW10

4 Hollywood Road, SW10 9HW
Telephone: 071-352 0352   **£40**
Open: lunch + dinner daily (closed Bank Holidays, 2 wks Xmas)
Meals served: lunch 12.30-3, (Sun 12.30-4) dinner 7-11.30 (Sun 7-10.30)

In a side road opposite the new Chelsea and Westminster hospital is
this restaurant-cum-café-bar which welcomes families and entertains
the youngsters in the registered Nipper Snippers Crèche for a cost of
£2.50 - a welcome extra for parents wanting a relaxed Sunday lunch. A
bistro-style menu offers smoked salmon muffin with sour cream and
chives, deep-fried camembert with an onion and redcurrant marmalade or a selection of good sized salads. Traditional roast sirloin is
served on Sunday and there are other daily specials such as steak,
Guinness and mushroom pie with prunes, char-grilled chicken with
honey and herbs or angel-hair pasta with lobster.

THE GORE   SW7

189 Queen's Gate, SW7 5EX
Telephone: 071-584 6601 Fax: 071-589 8127

The Gore offers something a little different in terms of hospitality, it's more like the type of exclusive small hotel you'll find in Paris or New York. There is a relaxed yet grand and personable atmosphere, with smart and efficient staff. Decorated with antiques and with individually furnished bedrooms and suites, this place proves popular with clients from the music and film industry. Enter the front door and there is Bistrot 190 on the right, the lounge-bar with comfortable sofas and seating on the left and the fish restaurant, Downstairs at 190, where else but in the basement. A laid-back, almost club-like style makes this a charming hotel which is ideally placed for business customers or pleasure seekers alike.

THE GORING   SW1

17 Beeston Place, Grosvenor Gardens, SW1W 0JW
Telephone: 071-936 9000 Fax: 071-834 4393   **£60**
Open: lunch Sun-Fri, dinner daily
Meals served: lunch 12.30-2.30, dinner 6-10 (Tea 3.30-5)   ❖

Leather sofas, a uniformed door man and cream teas; this is the scene for the Goring, a family hotel and probably one of the few of its type left in London. Built in 1910 it has remained in caring hands ever since and maintains its reputation for service. Traditional and elegant, it is ideally suited to the business traveller or those searching for a quiet place in which to park their bags but still want to be in the heart of the action. The dining room offers precise and polished set menus. Lemon sole comes with a nut butter and capers, grilled veal with tarragon mustard and herb pancake with ratatouille and mozzarella.

GRAHAME'S SEAFARE   W1

38 Poland Street, W1V 3DA
Telephone: 071-437 3788   £25
Open: lunch + dinner Mon-Sat (closed Bank Holidays, Jewish New Year)
Meals served: lunch 12-2.45, dinner 5.30-9 (Fri+Sat 5.30-8)
Fish is served deep-fried, grilled, steamed or cooked in milk or butter. Guaranteed kosher.

window detail

terracotta head on dark green trellis

A decorative display of a Basket man + glazed pottery in the entrance to the Greenhouse

THE GREENHOUSE • PAGE 74

GRANITA   N1

127 Upper Street, N1
Telephone: 071-226 3222   **£40**
Open: lunch Wed-Sun, dinner Tues-Sat (closed 10 days Xmas,
1 wk Easter, 10 days Aug)
Meals served: lunch 12.30-2.30, dinner 6.30-10.30

Vikki Leffman and Ahmed Kharshoum must be delighted with the
reception their new restaurant - startlingly modern with zinc bar and
simple tables and chairs - has received, for they've had to turn customers away! The modern menu owes a lot to the Med with artichoke,
tomatoes and mozzarella all taking their turn while California has influenced Ahmed's menu to produce char-grilled organic salmon with a
tomato and courgette gratin. Cheeses are from Neal's Yard and the
puddings are an anglicised mixture of apple crumble, chocolate and
whisky ice cream and chocolate torte.

Simple clean lines of
the cool interior of
GRANITA

GREEN'S RESTAURANT & OYSTER BAR   SW1

36 Duke Street, St James's, SW1Y 6DF
Telephone: 071-930 4566 Fax: 071-930 1383   **£65**
Open: lunch daily, dinner Mon-Sat (closed 25 Dec)
Meals served: lunch 11.30-3 (Sun 12-2.30), dinner 5.30-11

Tucked down the side of Jermyn Street is this oyster bar, with booths
of dark wood to the left hand side and a fully fledged restaurant to the
right. Green's high standards are evident in the dishes of smoked eel,
potted shrimps, dressed crab or salmon cakes with parsley and tomato
sauce. Grills include lamb cutlets and bangers and mash which prove
popular with the largely male clientele, as does the daily special which
is always shepherd's pie on Monday and braised oxtail on Thursdays.
Gooseberry fool is the lightest pudding but not the least calorific, but
the cheese platter from Paxton & Whitfield is far more appealing. Beth
Coventry has moved on and Carolyn Marshall is now at the stove.

GREENHOUSE   W1

27a Hays Mews, W1X 7RJ
Telephone: 071-499 3331   **£65**
Open: lunch Sun-Fri, dinner daily (closed Bank Holidays)
Meals served: lunch 12-2.30 (Sun 12-3), dinner 7-11 (Sun 6-10)

Gary Rhodes' cooking career has been dedicated to putting English
food back on the map, and due praise has been heaped on him, combining as he does the roles of chef and breakfast TV host. His faggots
in a rich gravy and his modern interpretation of oxtail have become
signature dishes. Enter the conservatory-style restaurant reception
and the mood is green with topiary-type art forms. Attractive prints and
dried flowers continue the traditional theme but none of it is twee -
there is a strong masculinity to the place, matched by the predominantly male clientèle. On the dot of 12.15 the kitchen is a flurry of
activity, serving the likes of pan-fried cod with cabbage and wild mushrooms, mackerel croquettes with lemon butter sauce and stewed pork
with vegetables, butter beans and dumplings. English cooking has
rarely tastes so good and with puds like hot apple fritters with apricot
sauce, steamed lemon sponge with custard and jam tart with clotted
cream, you can see why the faithful customers tend to be men.

ALISTAIR GREIG'S GRILL   W1

26 Bruton Place, W1X 7AA
Telephone: 071-629 5613   **£55**
Open: lunch Mon-Fri, dinner Mon-Sat (closed Bank Holidays)
Meals served: lunch 12.30-2.30, dinner 6.30-11

A long story lies behind the instructions you are given when you telephone to make your booking - that is to remember it is a red door and
number 26. There will be no menu to meet you but an array of fresh
steaks and prime sirloins are the speciality. Everything here is simply
handled. Starters are smoked salmon, asparagus, avocado and melon.
Main courses are veal, lamb, fillet steaks and poussin all simply
adorned with grilled tomatoes and button mushrooms.

GRILL ST QUENTIN   SW3

2 Yeoman's Row, SW3 2AL
Telephone: 071-581 8377 Fax: 071-584 6064   **£60**
Open: lunch + dinner daily (closed 1 wk Xmas)
Meals served: lunch 12-3 (Sun 12-3.30) dinner 6.30-11.30 (Sun 6.30-10.30)

Step through the little entrance just behind Brompton Road and you're
in France. Grill St. Quentin is in the style of a parisian brasserie, decorated with fresh flowers and pastel colours it has a wonderful feeling of
space. Grills are `les pièces de résistance', fish, steaks and lamb
cooked to order and served with frites, of course. Save room for the
pâtisserie and desserts from Specialités St Quentin. A relaxed, con-
vivial and authentic taste of France.

GROSVENOR HOUSE   W1

90 Park Lane, W1A 3AA
Telephone: 071-499 6363 Fax: 071-493 3341   **£40**
Open: lunch Mon-Fri, dinner Mon-Sat (closed Bank Holidays)
Meals served: lunch 12.30-2.30, dinner 6-10 (Pasta Vino 12.30-2.30,
7.30-11.30)   ❖

After serious investment by Forte plc in this their flagship, the hotel is
resplendent and flying full colours. The two restaurants are good alternatives in style and price, as well as the top-rated Chez Nico at 90 Park
Lane which is still an integral part of Grosvenor House. The Pavilion
offers meals all day from breakfast through to dinner, in a colonial-
style setting of teak floor and cherry wood mouldings. Sean Davies'
cooking is contemporary and can be seen at first hand in the open
kitchen. Soups of sorrel and ricotta, pork rillette with a prune chutney,
cod cooked with grain mustard or skate with broad beans are his forte.
Meat dishes bring fillet of beef with green tomato and apple chutney,
or braised oxtail with green lentils. The second restaurant is called
Pasta Vino, and is in the care of Pino Longorso. In a restful, earthy-
toned setting the menu offers penne ai quattro formaggi, veal escalope
with lemon and white wine, or fresh tuna with onions and peppers and
capers. There's a different speciality each day of the week, so find out
when ossobucco or lasagna pasticciata are scheduled and make it a
date. There is also a fixed-price menu that is set to increase by only
one penny each year (it's £19.93 at the moment!). For a fuller description of this 454-bedroomed hotel, see the special feature in the *1993
Ackerman Charles Heidsieck Guide.*

GUMBO YA YA   W11

184a Kensington Park Road, W11 2GS
Telephone: 071-221 2649   **£25**
Open: lunch + dinner daily
Meals served: 11.30-11.30

Cajun-Creole cooking with a large Jamaican influence is to be found in
this vibrant, fun restaurant. Design LSM have once more been
involved in the concept and decor, theming the place on New Orleans,
Mardi Gras, and carnival colours. Purples and musty yellows, voodoo-
style lighting, masks, bric-a-brac and an interlinking of all 3 levels by
knocking holes through the floors works well. Recommendations - the
gumbo spicy fish soup, jazzy wings (chicken cooked to a secret recipe)
salmon rolled in cajun spices and blackened on a hot skillet and served
with exotic vegetables. Save room for sweet potato pudding and key
lime cake. Sunday brunch is served till 4pm and set lunch is an
unbelievable £4.95 for 2 courses!

THE HALCYON   W11

81 Holland Park, W11 3RZ
Telephone: 071-727 7288 Fax: 071-229 8516   **£60**
Open: lunch + dinner daily
Meals served: lunch 12-2.30 (Sun 12-4), dinner 7-11   ❖

Halcyon days start with a large breakfast which attracts the power
executives to this otherwise peaceful 43-bedroomed hotel, but on a
good day you can always escape to the tranquillity of alfresco eating on
the patio and leave them to it. Chef Martin Wadden has created a contemporary menu which at dinner and lunch includes dishes like mixed
leaves with balsamic vinegar and extra virgin olive oil, bruschetta of
tomatoes and a potato cake with smoked salmon, sour cream and
chives. A main course could be chicken wrapped in pancetta with
braised lentils or grilled calves' livers with roasted onions and sage.
Martin has worked with Nico Ladenis and Shaun Hill and won the
Roux Brothers' Scholarship in 1989. He is definitely a chef worth
noting.

HALKIN HOTEL   SW1

5 Halkin Street, SW1X 7DT   ✿
Telephone: 071-333 1000 Fax: 071-333 1100   **£75**
Open: lunch Mon-Fri, dinner daily
Meals served: lunch 12.30-2.30, dinner 7.30-10.30   ❖

A small and personal hotel with 41 bedrooms, run along the lines of a
very modern town house except that here there are really no public
rooms to speak of except the dining room. Sleek and swish, this has a
romanesque feel and is fashionably dressed with strategically placed
single blooms, clever use of lighting, drapes and frosted glass screens
- a theatrical set for glamorous people. It has been renamed simply the
Halkin Restaurant since the association with Milan master Gualtiero
Marchesi has ended. His style, however, is to continue in the hands of
disciple Stefano Cavallini who came from the Marchesi kitchen and
has now been head chef here for 3 years.

HAMPSHIRE HOTEL   WC2

31 Leicester Square, WC2 7LH
Telephone: 071-839 9399 Fax: 071-930 8122   **£65**
Open: lunch + dinner daily
Meals served: lunch 12-3, dinner 6-10.45

Enjoying a central location in Leicester Square, the Hampshire Hotel
has not undergone major surgery but has enjoyed a facelift. The decor
is busy, chintzy and floral. Some of the suites enjoy a view over
Leicester Square, while other bedrooms tend to vary in size. The dining room offers an international-flavoured menu with oriental,
Mediterranean and middle eastern influences creeping in. Starters
include polenta, green salad and parma ham, or mushroom crumble,
or soups of lettuce with caraway cheese snippets, or langoustine minestrone. There's grilled saddle of rabbit, chorizo, red pepper and chick
pea salad or crab fish cake and cockle dressing, as main courses.
Lunch menus are good value and Oscar's wine bar offers more
informal eating.

HARVEYS   SW17

2 Bellevue Road, SW17 7EG
Telephone: 081-672 0114   **£120**
Open: lunch Tue-Sat, dinner Tue-Sat (closed Bank Holidays, 2 wks Xmas,
2 wks Aug/Sept)
Meals served: lunch 12.30-2.15, dinner 7.30-11.15

Marco Pierre White's Harveys as we knew it, moved to the Hyde Park
Hotel in September 1993. The Wandsworth restaurant will be known
as Harveys the Bistro with a similar form at the Canteen - real quality
at affordable prices.

HARVEYS CAFÉ & BAR   SW10

The Black Bull, 358 Fulham Road, SW10 9UU
Telephone: 071-352 0625   £35
Open: lunch Tues-Sun, dinner Mon-Sat (closed Bank Holidays
 2 wks Aug, 1 wk Xmas)
Meals served: lunch 12-3, dinner 7.30-11

Harvey Sambrook's place used to be just on the first floor above the
Black Bull pub but he's now expanded to take over the entire premises. Downstairs is a lively bar selling wines, beers and a few of the
snacks from the upstairs café, whose presence is still pinpointed by a
blue chair precariously hanging from the corner of the building. With
light sea-blue decor, extensive use of pine and a regularly changing
menu it is highly popular with the Fulham set. The dishes are bright
and Mediterranean-based and you must try their excellent olives and
bread and then possibly roasted peppers with feta cheese or mixed
leaves with parmesan. Main courses are simple enough: gnocchi with
tomato, roast peppers and pine nuts and a cassoulet of duck are typical
dishes.

HILAIRE   SW7

68 Old Brompton Road, SW7 3LQ
Telephone: 071-584 8993 Fax: 071-581 2949
Open: lunch Mon-Fri, dinner Mon-Sat (closed Bank Holidays, 1 wk Xmas, 1 wk Easter, 2 wks Aug)
Meals served: lunch 12.30-2.30, dinner 7-11.30

A talented & creative chef who keeps & his place keen £65

How green is your valley? In the case of Bryan Webb's restaurant, his Welsh origins are perfectly reflected in the tones of the walls and the foliage. His cooking is naturally punctuated with Welsh ingredients - lamb, cheese and laverbread for his oyster au gratin - and bursts with flavours at every mouthful. This place is a true bastion of fine cooking, Bryan's unpretentious style influenced by the relaxed Italian trend - baked lemon sole with a herb crust comes with a broad bean purée, with his famed scallops quickly seared on both sides and gilded in a herb vinaigrette. Try the combination of avocado, broccoli and anchovies with shavings of parmesan and, if dining à deux, ask to be seated at the back of the restaurant, as the tables here are more intimate.

L'HOTEL   SW3

28 Basil Street, SW3 1AT
Telephone: 071-589 6286 Fax: 071-225 0011
Open: all day Mon-Sat (closed 25+26 Dec)
Meals served: 12-10.30 (coffee & breakfast 8am-11am)

£60

This small informal hotel with only 12 bedrooms makes a nice change from some of the larger hotels of the area, and it's an ideal spot for guests who like to shop until they drop. The basement houses Le Metro, the place that locals in the know flock to for lunch after a nip around Harvey Nichols or the boutiques of Sloane Street. One of you should get there early, for the word has spread about the risotto and other bistro favourites and after 12.30 you can't get a table. Wine is available by the glass and the service prompt and friendly.

HYATT CARLTON TOWER   SW1

2 Cadogan Place, SW1X 9PY
Telephone: 071-235 5411 Fax: 071-245 6570
Open: lunch + dinner daily
Meals served: lunch 12.30-2.45, dinner 7-10.45 (Sun 7-10)

£70

In the Chelsea Room restaurant overlooking Cadogan Gardens, Bernard Gaume continues his reign with a notorious classic skill and dishes that are executed with exacting precision and flair. A typical evening menu might be crab sausages with a mustard and chervil sauce, sautéed fillet of beef with a beef marrow sauce and a selection of cheese or dessert from the trolley. In the evening a pianist completes the scene. By contrast to this light limed-oak room and the greenery through the conservatory style windows, the Rib Room is dark but glowing with a clubby atmosphere and specialises in beef and seafood. In both the restaurants, attention to detail and service is impeccable. This 224-bedroomed hotel offers a stylish place to stay, and has a health club on the 9th floor.

HYDE PARK HOTEL   SW1

66 Knightsbridge, SW1Y 7LA
Telephone: 071-235 2000 Fax: 071-235 4552
Open: lunch + dinner daily
Meals served: lunch 12.30-2.30, dinner 7-11

see Press stop page 14 £70

Traditions are upheld, the service continues to be of a high standard and the decor retains that luxurious feel in this 185-bedroomed hotel. There has been some refurbishment over the last few years but this has improved rather than drastically changed the feel of the place. Food in the Terrace Room comes in a variety of Italian/Mediterranean styles, or traditional English, depending on your mood and choice. A sound wine list is available both here and throughout the hotel. The big change, however, is the addition of Marco Pierre White as chef in what was formerly the Cavalry Grill. I did not have time to eat in the restaurant before we went to press, but I have no hesitation in recommending it. Based on the description of the style of the place, and of the dishes that this indisputably talented chef has in mind, this will be one of the destination restaurants in London. What an excellent move for Marco Pierre White, for Forte (who are to be congratulated on repeating the successful formula under which Nico Ladenis was installed within Grosvenor House - see Chez Nico) and most importantly, for the general public, who will have easier access to Marco in this West End location.

L'INCONTRO   SW1

87 Pimlico Road, SW1 8PH   ✿
Telephone: 071-730 3663 Fax: 071-730 5062   **£85**
Open: lunch Mon-Fri, dinner daily (closed Bank Holidays)
Meals served: lunch 12.30-2.30, dinner 7-11.30 (Sun 7-10.30)

In keeping with the fashion for Italian food, this restaurant is bound to
be popular. All the pastas are made on the premises and include tagliatelle al Montello, tagliatelle in a wild mushroom sauce, and also worth
trying is Incontro di pasta, a selection of all their homemade pastas.
Move along from antipasta and pasta to fish: salmon Incontro or baked
monkfish in garlic butter sauce, meats, maize fed chicken with fresh
tomato and herbs or roast quail with polenta and wild mushrooms. The
wine list, of course, is heavily in favour of Italian wines, and you'll find
some very fine ones. L'Incontro is not cheap, but you get what you pay
for in this stylish restaurant.

INTER-CONTINENTAL   W1

1 Hamilton Place, Hyde Park Corner, W1V 1QY   ✿
Telephone: 071-409 3131 Fax: 071-409 7460   **£95**
Open: lunch Sun-Fri, dinner daily (closed 26 Dec, Good Friday)   🍾
Meals served: lunch 12.30-3, dinner 7-10.30

The American dream! Situated in the prime location of Hyde Park
Corner, this luxury hotel appeals to business and pleasure travellers
alike. It is elegant, stylish and discreet in decor and will soon have a
new-look lobby and huge ballroom, which unusually will benefit from
natural daylight. Le Soufflé restaurant is more of the same - a grand
dining room, it is the showcase for Peter Kromberg's classic cooking
which has kept abreast of modern trends for the past 18 years. You
really should try one of Peter's renowned soufflés, perhaps the oven-
baked scallop soufflé in its shell with diced vegetables, shallot sauce
and baby spinach to start, followed by braised fillet of turbot with basil
and light Riesling cream sauce served with lime scented ribbon noodles, or sautéed fillets of spring lamb with rosemary scented cream
served with crisp potato cake layered with celeriac, tomato petals,
baby turnips and snow peas. This is one of the best hotel restaurants in
London.

THE IVY   WC2

Painter Peter Blake's favourite restaurant & I've never been disappointed.

1 West Street, WC2H 9NE
Telephone: 071-836 4751 Fax: 071-497 3644
Open: lunch + dinner daily (closed 25+26 Dec, 1 Jan)
Meals served: lunch 12-3, dinner 5.30-12   **£60**

The show-biz and arty set love it here, all sitting chatting and nodding
to one another. You will find on the menu a friendly mix of traditional
dishes elevated to trendy, such as the steak and kidney pudding with
mashed neeps and dishes with modern influences such as focaccia of
avocado and crostini of lamb's brains with sweetbreads plus a mix of
grills, sauced, fried or kedgereed fish and plenty of pasta or hors
d'oeuvres to start you off. Old favourites from sister restaurant Le
Caprice are also there, from the salmon fishcakes with sorrel to bang
bang chicken. Mark Hix is the executive chef but it is Des McDonald
who is the chef in charge when in full swing. A good place to eat, drink
and be seen in this discreet and stylish restaurant.

JOE ALLEN   WC2

13 Exeter Street, WC2E 7DT
Telephone: 071-836 0651 Fax: 071-497 2148
Open: all day daily (closed 25 Dec)   **£40**
Meals served: 12pm-1am (Sun 12-12)

This basement restaurant is still fast, noisy and fun and remains one of
the most popular venues in Covent Garden, so be sure to book. Style
has shifted to main-stream American and Californian to make plenty of
room for ideas from sister restaurant Orso. Choose from a range of
starters like smoked trout with green beans, horseradish and radicchio, and grilled spicy chicken wings or roast fennel and tomato soup.
Main courses can be a giant caesar salad, Mexican sausage and
shrimp, or a mixture of hot options from vegetable and cheese que-
sadilla with sour cream and guacamole to true American-style ribs with
spinach, black-eyed peas and a corn muffin. Desserts are predictable
and sweet with pecan pie, brownies, carrot cake and cheesecake. Two
sittings in the evening accommodate theatre goers. No credit cards.

Joe Allen's JukeBox. Fast, noisy, fun!

JOE'S CAFÉ   SW3

126 Draycott Avenue, SW3 3AH
Telephone: 071-225 2217   **£65**
Open: lunch daily, dinner Mon-Sat (closed 25+26 Dec)
Meals served: lunch 12-4 (Sat 9.30-4 Sun 9.30-3.30), dinner 7-11.30

Very much part of the London scene, this is still, for many, the place to
hang out. With monochromatic design, the style is undeniably chic
and up to the minute, offering mainstream Mediterranean cooking
ranging from carpaccio with a side salad to risotto of veal with saffron
and a seafood gazpacho with more than just a hint of basil. Mains are
characteristic with the famous Porkinson bangers and mash and a
prime piece of entrecôte with slim golden fries. Tarte tatin is cooked
the way it should be, with sharp apples and a good caramel and nice
thin crust. It opens from 9.30am these days to offer croissants and
coffee.

JULIE'S   W11

A unique place atmosphere, with a clubby food good value & a wine list to match

135 Portland Road, W11 4LW
Telephone: 071-229 8331   **£77**
Open: lunch Sun-Fri, dinner daily (closed Xmas, Easter)
Meals served: lunch 12-2.45 (Sun 12.30-3), dinner 7.30-11 (Sun 7.30-10)

Julie's is an institution where the best of British cooking has been
upheld since 1969. The first decision to make on entering is which
atmosphere or room to choose, from flowery champagne bar, to fairy-
pink room, smart white-themed conservatory or ruby-red gothic room.
And why not match the food to suit the theme? Smoked salmon with
lemon, horseradish and juniper berry mousse in the conservatory,
whilst aubergine and sour cream mousse with toasted pumpkin seeds
may go well in the gothic room. Mains of fillets of sole with pawpaw
and lime butter sauce, field mushroom stroganoff with wild rice or
steak and kidney pie demonstrate the diversity of food. Innes' goat's
cheese and a good selection of other English cheeses should be
enjoyed with a glass of port. A perfect place, too, for Sunday lunches.

KALAMARAS

still the best & most authentic Greek restaurant in town.

W2

76-78 Inverness Mews, Bayswater, W2 3JQ
Telephone: 071-727 9122   **£35**
Open: dinner Mon-Sat (closed Bank Holidays)
Meals served: dinner 6.30-12

At the end of a quiet mews running parallel with Queensway is Stelios
Platanos' excellent taverna. This is one of the most authentic totally
Greek (not a vestige of Cypriot) restaurants in town and extends
beyond the customary tarama and moussaka to include spiced Greek
sausages, spliced langoustines, deep-fried baby squid, baked dry haricot beans with fresh tomatoes, onions and parsley plus a range of
grilled, roasted and pounded meats like casseroled lamb with spinach
and lemon juice or chicken with avgolemono sauce. The best sign is
that it is loyally frequented by extended Greek families and has been
so successful that many years ago Stelios opened a second premises in
the same mews called Micro Kalamaras. Here menus are at a fixed-
price of £12 for a minimum of 2. This sibling establishment is unlicensed but you can take your own wine which makes it an ideal place
for value when eating in a crowd.

KASPIA

W1

18/18a Bruton Place, W1X 7AH
Telephone: 071-493 2612   £60
Open: lunch + dinner Mon-Sat (closed Bank Holidays)
Meals served: lunch 12-2.30, dinner 7.30-11.30

We have oyster and seafood bars but how about a caviar restaurant? A
cousin of the distinguished restaurant and shop in Paris, Kaspia is
decked out with sea-blue tablecloths and offers a choice of salmon,
sevruga, osietra and beluga caviar in 30g, 50g and 125g servings. The
main menu includes a range of Russian dishes such as salads of
smoked fish and lobster and potatoes, with 30g of your favourite
caviar. The fixed-price Kaspia Sanka menu offers bortsch and pirojki,
pressed caviar and blinis, cheese or patisserie and coffee. New chef
Annabelle Job (ex-Leiths and Royal Oak, Yattendon) has added some
daily specials to the menu amongst which could be fishcakes with
sorrel and fresh vegetables, or salmon mousse wrapped in smoked
salmon with salmon caviar. The adjoining shop offers caviar, vodka
and Russian conserves. Kaspia has certainly found a niche, offering not
only caviar to the discerning but also a stylish venue with chic clientele
for anyone interested. What better place to drink a chilled glass of
Charles Heidsieck champagne?

KENNY'S   NW3

70 Heath Street, Hampstead, NW3 1DN
Telephone: 071-435 6972 Fax: 071-431 5694   **£45**
Open: all day daily (closed 25+26 Dec)
Meals served: 12-11.45

Fast, furious and authentically cajun, Ken Miller's restaurants bring
cajun-creole cooking to the streets of London. Black bean soup with
jalapeno sour cream, dirty rice, catfish lafayette (the fish is shipped in
from the Mississippi) and jambalaya are just a sampler. The staff are
extrovert and explain the ingredients in the dishes, the degree of hot-
ness (there's a bottle of chilli sauce on each table if you like it extra
hot) plus the best drinks to go with them. A fun night out and reasonably priced.

KENNY'S   SW3

2a Pond Place, SW3 6QJ
Telephone: 071-225 2916   **£45**
Open: all day daily
Meals served: 12-11.45

Cajun-creole food in the same style as the Hampstead restaurant. A
good venue for Sunday brunch with some mean Bloody Marys. Happy,
informal staff and some genuinely good Cajun cooking. Try their
lighter jambalaya. Fun, friendly and worth a visit.

KENSINGTON PLACE   W8

205 Kensington Church Street, W8 7LX
Telephone: 071-727 3184 Fax: 071-229 2025   **£60**
Open: lunch + dinner daily (closed 3 days Xmas, 3 days Aug)
Meals served: lunch 12-3 (Sat+Sun 12-3.45), dinner 6.30-11.45
(Sun 6.30-10.15)

At the top of the street as you come round the one way system, there,
in all its splendour, shining at night like a beacon, is the place where
Rowley Leigh continues to cook for the famous and stylish. Seemingly
recession-proof, it continues to pack them in, which is no wonder with
a menu that's modern and seems to improve with each passing year,
covering all the favourites from a light omelette, moist and herby, to
that wonderful combination of herring and beetroot salad. Griddled
scallops are graced with a pea purée and main courses consist of
Chinese five spice with duck and a breast of chicken with snails. The
vegetables are as interesting as the main dishes, so don't miss out on
the braised fennel or spring greens with garlic. Nick Smallwood and
Simon Slater were ahead of the field when they started Kensington
Place, and they continue to hold that position.

THE LANESBOROUGH

This hotel deserves its success & the management are dedicated to see it continues.

SW1

1 Lanesborough Place, Hyde Park Corner, SW1X 7TA
Telephone: 071-259 5599 Fax: 071-259 5606

The Dining Room: £90
Open: lunch + dinner daily
Meals served: lunch 12.30-2.30, dinner 7-10.30

The Conservatory: £70
Open: lunch + dinner daily
Meals served: lunch 12.30-2.30, dinner 7-10.30

It was to here that Paul Gayler moved from the Halkin to practise his modern British cooking and in the eccentricity of this larger-than-life hotel (somewhat reminiscent of an overgrown doll's house) he has found his niche. The Conservatory is open all day from breakfast to dinner and it is here that Paul's imagination is allowed free flight and where he displays his love affair with spices in dishes of cumin noodles with a Chinese-style duck and salad of tempura shrimps with avocado, fennel and chilli tartare. The Dining Room is on a far grander scale with chateaubriand and sirloin with horseradish béarnaise heading up the grills, and specialities such as pan-fried Dover sole with rosemary, artichoke and wild mushrooms allowing him space to experiment. This is undeniably a find, as the style of the dining room combined with excellent service is a fitting accompaniment to Paul's accomplished and inspired cooking.

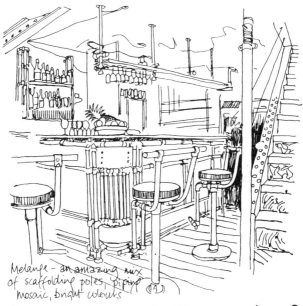

Melange – an amazing mix of scaffolding poles, piping, mosaic, bright colours (?!)

The quirky Interior of Mélange see page 91.

LANGAN'S BISTRO   W1

26 Devonshire Street, W1N 1RJ
Telephone: 071-935 4531   **£55**
Open: lunch Mon-Fri, dinner Mon-Sat (closed Bank Holidays)
Meals served: lunch 12.30-2.30, dinner 7-11.30

This is a charming, warm bistro, comfortingly similar to its big brother
in Mayfair, and you'll miss none of the style or the straightforward
good food of the other, but possibly just the glitterati. The menu is far
smaller and concise but still has that certain style. Starters include
smoked chicken with a hot potato salad and baked snails with plenty of
garlic as well as a wild boar terrine. For main course there is always a
dish of the day, or favourites of baked trout with prawns, mushrooms
and capers and a char-grilled chicken breast with a red pepper sauce
and chives. The wine list is small but reasonably priced.

LANGAN'S BRASSERIE   W1

Stratton Street, W1X 5FD   ❦
Telephone: 071-491 8822   **£70**
Open: lunch Mon-Fri, dinner Mon-Sat (closed Bank Holidays)
Meals served: lunch 12.30-3, dinner 7-11.45 (Sat 8-12.45)

This legendary brasserie is larger than life in all respects, from the
buzz of the atmosphere to the size of the menu. Bustling with celebrities and the classy set, food is served by clued-up staff who will talk
you through your choice with interest. The menu might take some
time to read unless you have been here before, since the choice is gargantuan - baked egg, cabbage and bacon hash, smoked pink trout,
Langan's seafood salad - and that's just for starters. Main courses are
no less impressive, with braised knuckle of gammon with butter
beans, and black pudding with kidney and bacon. Puddings bring out
all the old favourites from plum and almond crumble, or treacle tart, to
simple strawberries and clotted cream. A civilised, but fun place to eat.
Langan's continues to delight, and has defeated the recession and the
rush of new openings with disdain and not a little mirth. In the past
some critics have gone out of their way to try to rubbish Langan's, and
whilst I respected the late Peter Langan's ability and talent as a restaurateur, to suggest that he influenced the menu or even actually cooked
is far from the truth. It must be very rewarding for Richard Shepherd,
therefore, to have been awarded Personality of the Year 1993 (voted by
his piers) after all his efforts over the last 13 years in the kitchen and
out front.

THE LANGHAM   W1

Portland Place, W1N 3AA
Telephone: 071-636 1000 Fax: 071-323 2340   **£75**
Open: lunch + dinner Mon-Sat
Meals served: lunch 12.30-3, dinner 6.30-10.30 (Palm Court: Tea 3-5.30)

The Hilton flagship, the Langham offers the sparkle and grandeur of a
grand hotel. It has 3 restaurants, the Palm Court for afternoon tea
accompanied, naturally, by a pianist, and 383 bedrooms. The refurbishment programme continues so that the rooms remain in top-notch condition. Additionally, a health club is planned. The Memories of the
Empire restaurant with consultant chef Ken Hom offers a blend of east
and west in authentic Victorian surroundings with wicker chairs and
crisp linen. The à la carte menu offers an interesting mix of English
and oriental dishes with some Californian elements - grilled tiger
prawns with a pesto sauce, steamed salmon in Chinese cabbage with a
spiced butter tea sauce and duck with a damson and blueberry sauce.
Across the hall is the King's Room restaurant which continues under
the direction of Kees Stavenuiter and executive chef Anthony
Marshall, with dishes that remain firmly French-based but with once
again touches of the Orient. A small intimate room of 20 tables or so,
the surroundings are resplendent with fine stencilled walls and painted
ceiling and a menu that continues to uphold healthier lighter cooking.
Dishes arrive under cloches and are formally unveiled to reveal crab
and langoustine with rice wine vinegar and chervil, or pan-fried salmon
and sea bass on a bed of chicory with sesame seed oil and balsamic
vinegar. A fine list of vodka and caviar is served in the Tsars' Bar.
Other specialities here include turbot with a champagne and caviar
sauce, oyster and thyme chowder and Baltic salmon.

LAUNCESTON PLACE   W8

1a Launceston Place, W8 5RL
Telephone: 071-937 6912 Fax: 071-938 2412   **£35**
Open: lunch Sun-fri, dinner Mon-Sat (closed Bank Holidays)
Meals served: lunch 12.30-2.30 (Sun 12.30-3), dinner 7-11.30

The quieter of Nick Smallwood and Simon Slater's 'Places', the cooking here is modern British with distinctly European touches, although
Sundays are more traditional. Being more comfortable, unintimidating
and one step back from the restaurant hype, it attracts a diverse
clientele who come to enjoy the specials cooked by Cathy Gradwell
from Kensington Place - it remains to be seen how much the menu will
change, but at present it rests on such dishes as roast monkfish with
thyme, roast chicken with bread sauce and tarragon gravy, and chump
of lamb with tomato and basil. This is a relaxed and friendly
restaurant, well worth a visit.

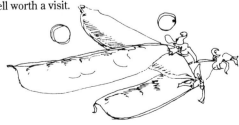

LAURENT   NW2

428 Finchley Road, NW2 2HY
Telephone: 071-794 3603   £30
Open: lunch + dinner Mon-Sat (closed Bank Holidays, 3 wks Aug)
Meals served: lunch 12-2, dinner 6-11
Lamb and vegetable couscous eaten in house or take-away. Algerian and Moroccan
wine.

LEITH'S   W11

Sparkling new decor in yellow - colourful shades of triptych by Dene Matthews

92 Kensington Park Road, W11 2PN
Telephone: 071-229 4481   £85
Open: dinner daily (closed Bank Holidays, 2 days Aug,
4 days Xmas)
Meals served: dinner 7.30-11.30   ❖

Leith's has come into its own at the ripe old age of 25. It has matured
nicely and earned itself a position as one of the foremost locations at
which to dine. Alex Floyd has been cooking with the Leith's light
touch for a while, producing creations that always fulfil their promise.
Try the mushroom, tomato and courgette gateau which is served on a
pesto dressing, or a salad of wood pigeon and quail's eggs with an
interesting cabernet sauvignon vinaigrette. Poussin is boned out and
served with morels and spring vegetables, while monkfish gets a roasting with spice and is added to with spring onions and sweet yellow
peppers. Desserts are also fine - a hot pineapple soufflé with rum and
coconut ice cream or a semolina flummery with a compote of rhubarb
being two examples. The house wines are outstanding. It is interesting
to note that wherever possible the ingredients that are used are supplied by Leith's own farm - is there no stopping this lady!

THE LEXINGTON   W1

45 Lexington Street, W1R 3LG
Telephone: 071-434 3401 Fax: 071-287 2997   £60
Open: lunch + dinner Mon-Sat (closed Bank Holidays)
Meals served: lunch 12-3, dinner 6-11.30

The Lexington is slightly more than just a café, inhabited though it
may be by trendy members of the café society. The menu reflects
today's fashions, with its Mediterranean influences and light and simple combinations. Starters could include a salad of goat's cheese and
roast pepper followed by tagliatelle, smoked tomato, olives and
pancetta, fricassée of chicken, white wine and mushrooms or galette of
roast peppers and aubergine.

LINDSAY HOUSE

very special restaurant with original decor & some inventive food.

W1

21 Romilly Street, W1V 5TG
Telephone: 071-439 0450 Fax: 071-581 2848
Open: lunch + dinner daily (closed 25+26 Dec)
Meals served: lunch 12.30-2, dinner 6-12 (Sun 7-10)

£60

One of London's venues that will always feel like your own private dis-covery, the 17th-century Lindsay House offers English cooking in an English period setting. Perfect for theatre-goers, or for pretending you're not really in London at all! Try the creamed Jerusalem Artichoke soup, hot or chilled, or pan-fried scallops with cullen skink, followed by a plainly-grilled supreme of salmon, or the more gutsy medallions of beef served with baby vegetables and a port sauce. Desserts are the likes of rice pudding studded with fresh fruit and served with a spiced custard, chocolate teardrop filled with a white chocolate mousse on a passion fruit sauce, and of course stilton cheese served with celery, grapes and homemade biscuits.

LONDON HILTON ON PARK LANE

W1

22 Park Lane, W1A 2HH
Telephone: 071-493 8000 Fax: 071-493 4957
Open: lunch Sun-Fri, dinner daily
Meals served: lunch 12.30-2.30, dinner 7-2am (Sun 7-1am)

£110

Race to the top and enjoy the panoramic views from the Windows of the World and then race back down to Trader Vic's restaurant in the basement for Polynesian eats and drinks. 448 bedrooms.

LOU PESCADOU

SW5

241 Old Brompton Road, SW5 9HP
Telephone: 071-370 1057
Open: lunch + dinner daily (closed 25+26 Dec)
Meals served: lunch 12-3, dinner 7-12

£50

A nautical theme runs through this bustling restaurant. Maritime para-phernalia hangs from the walls and there's a porthole at the front. Considering the decor, it will probably come as no surprise that the speciality is fish – the menu boasts a nice catch – soup, red mullet, shellfish, moules, skate, mullet and daily specials fresh from the market. The wine list, although short, has a good selection. Be forewarned and book a table to avoid a tiresome queue.

LUC'S RESTAURANT & BRASSERIE EC3

A no-nonsense that brasserie has been busy since day one. £50

17-22 Leadenhall Market, EC3V 1LR
Telephone: 071-621 0666
Open: lunch Mon-Fri (closed Bank Holidays, 5 days Xmas)
Meals served: lunch 11.30-3

In the centre of Leadenhall Market (so the meat and fish couldn't be better) and right in the city, Luc's proves popular with the brokers and lawyers of the area who pop in for a quick steak and glass of red wine. The menu is a classic with a Victorian scene of the market on the front and a tempting array of soups - clear chicken with vermicelli or soupe de poisson with rouille and croutons - and hors d'oeuvres: pâtés, salads, or seafood in a raspberry dressing and quail with foie gras for the connoisseur. Main courses are especially renowned with speciality fish from prawns, brochettes of scallops, and monkfish in a vermouth sauce to grills of steak cooked 3 ways.

MAGNO'S BRASSERIE WC2

65a Long Acre, WC2E 9JH
Tel: 071-727 3062
Open: lunch Mon-Fri, dinner Mon-Sat (closed Xmas, New Year, Easter)
Meals served: lunch 12-2.30, dinner 6-11.30
Typical brasserie fare, popular with pre- and post-theatre goers.

£60

MANZARA W11

24 Pembridge Road, W11 3HG
Telephone: 071-727 3062
Open: all day daily
Meals served: 8am-midnight (Sun 10am-midnight)

£30

This is a Turkish restaurant that obviously takes pride in its food rather than treating it as a gimmick. Sip a raki with your mezzes (Turkish appetizers). Its best to get a selection – when in Turkey do as the Turkish humus (chick peas with tahini, chillis, olive oil, lemon juice and a hint of garlic) biber dolma: (green peppers, served cold with a generous filling of nuts, raisins and rice), taramasalata; and aubergine served cold with a delicious stuffing of onions, green peppers, tomatoes, parsley and a hint of garlic. Hot hors d'oeuvres are also worth trying – boreks, pastirma, hellim, cyprus cheese fresh or grilled. Main courses are numerous and range from well-known dishes such as moussaka and chicken shish to more unusual incik - a large knuckle of lamb on the bone, cooked in rosemary.

MANZI'S   E14

Turnberry Quay, off Pepper Street, E14 9TS
Telephone: 071-538 9615   £45
Open: lunch + dinner Mon-Fri (closed Bank Holidays)
Meals served: lunch 12-3 dinner 6-11
A glass-fronted room overlooking Millwall Docks. Mixed Italian and French menu -
busy at lunchtime.

MANZI'S   WC2

1 Leicester Square, WC2H 7BL
Telephone: 071-734 0224 Fax: 071-437 4864   £60
Open: lunch + dinner Mon-Sat (closed Xmas)
Meals served: lunch 12-3, dinner 5.30-11.30
One of London's oldest seafood restaurants, serving straightforward fish dishes in
trail-net setting.

MARTIN'S   NW1

239 Baker Street, NW1 6XE
Telephone: 071-935 3130   £50
Open: Lunch Mon-Fri, Dinner Mon-Sat (closed bank holidays)
Meals served: 12-2.30, dinner 6.30-10
Major changes afoot as we went to press.

MAY FAIR INTER-CONTINENTAL   W1

Stratton Street, W1A 2AN
Telephone: 071-629 7777 Fax: 071-629 1459   **£65**
Open: lunch Sun-Fri, dinner daily (closed 25 Dec after lunch to 4 Jan)
Meals served: lunch 12.30-2.30, dinner 7-11   ❖

In mid-refurbishment at the time of going to press, the May Fair café
was due to change but the stylish Le Chateau restaurant continues to
offer a mix of modern and classic dishes under the guidance of executive chef Michael Coaker. First courses of artichoke and leek with
woodland mushrooms, or glazed medallions of monkfish with mozzarella and tomatoes could be followed by grilled trout with marinated
courgettes and peppers and baked haddock with herbs and tomato
mash. This 322-bedroomed hotel with its own swimming pool has a
clubby atmosphere and many regulars.

MÉLANGE RESTAURANT   WC2

59 Endell Street, WC2H 9AJ
Telephone: 071-240 8077 Fax: 071-379 9129   £40
Open: lunch Tue-Fri dinner Mon-Sat (closed Bank Holidays, 10 days Xmas)
Meals served: 11.30-11.30

The food here is definitely a mélange, described best as modern
British and international. The mezze bar (which resembles a designer
building site) makes a good place to drop in for a snack - vegetarian
spring rolls, baked potato skins, marinated olives, or Cajun chicken
wings of fire. Starters on the main menu include Indonesian style
gado-gado salad, rocket and wild garlic salad with parmesan shavings
and olive croutons or avocado papaya and prawns. Move on to the
steamed snapper, char-grilled poussin sausages of the week or
Chinese noodles. There's a large selection for vegetarians, nicely
balanced with fish and meat dishes. Worth remembering if you want to
escape the Covent Garden hordes. *- see sketch on page 85*

LE MERIDIEN   W1

Undoubtedly some of the finest food in town.

Piccadilly, W1V 0BH
Telephone: 071-734 8000 Fax: 071-437 3574
Oak Room   £105
Terrace   £55
Open: lunch Mon-Fri, dinner Mon-Sat (closed Bank Holidays)
Meals served: lunch 12-2, dinner 7-10.30

Almost on Piccadilly Circus, this is a polished hotel with red-caped doormen who usher you through the swing doors and into a lavish reception area. Le Meridien is home to the modern French cooking of David Chambers, and the extent of his skill is evident. A jolly chap, he shares his culinary throne in the ornate Oak Room with Michel Lorain from Côtes St Jacques at Joigny. They harmonise beautifully and create à la carte and gourmand menus that are punctuated with goose liver, puy lentils, olive oil and bites of aromatic spice like star anise, lemon grass and coriander. The Oak Room continues to grow in reputation, for there is no denying the brilliance and verve of this team. On the second floor is the Terrace restaurant which provides an informal place to eat croque monsieur or a club sandwich while watching the hustle and bustle on the streets below. This 263-bedroomed hotel is very professionally managed and has its own health spa.

MESON DON FELIPE   SE1
53 The Cut, SE1 8LF
Telephone: 071-928 3237 Fax: 071-386 0337   £35
Open: all day Mon-Sat (closed Bank Holidays)
Meals served: 12-11
The original of the trio, this Spanish tapas bar is busy with IPC journos at lunchtime and pre-theatre drinkers of the Old and New Vic in the evening - it seems to throb with life at all times. Perhaps the nearest you can get to the real thing without travelling to Spain.

MESON DON JULIAN   SW6
125-127 Dawes Road, SW6 7EA
Telephone: 071-386 5901   £35
Open: all day daily (closed Bank Holidays)
Meals served: 12-11
The third of Philip and Ana Diment's tapas bars. In the heart of residential Fulham, the tables at the windows fill up as the evening progresses and the locals return home.

MESON DOÑA ANA   W11
37 Kensington Park Road, W11 2EU
Telephone: 071-243 0666 Fax: 071-386 0337   £35
Open: all day daily (closed Bank Holidays)
Meals served: 12-11.30
Middle sister of the trio - a wide selection of tapas and Spanish wines, served as they should be, in a friendly and relaxed atmosphere.

LE MESURIER   EC1

113 Old Street, EC1V 9JR
Telephone: 071-251 8117 Fax: 071-608 3504   **£65**
Open: lunch Mon-Fri (closed Bank Holidays, 10 days Xmas/New Year)
Meals served: lunch 12-3, dinner 6-11 (parties only)

A small and intimate restaurant, close enough to the city to attract
those types. The lunch menu offers a choice of 3 starters, mains and
desserts and may feature provençal fish soup, herb brioche filled with
chicken livers and bacon, mains of sea bass with ratatouille and red
peppers or chicken with oranges and lemons. Desserts are substantial:
pancakes stuffed with candied fruit and coated in chocolate sauce, and
lemon and almond roulade.

LE MIDI   SW6

488 Fulham Road, SW6
Telephone: 071-386 0657   £55
Open: lunch Sun-Fri, dinner Mon-Sat (closed Bank Holidays, lunch Sun Jul/Aug)
Meals served: lunch 12-2.30 (Sun 12-3), dinner 7-10.30
Close to Fulham Broadway, this small restaurant offers a good mix of Mediterranean
style cooking. Very popular with locals.

MIJANOU   SW1

143 Ebury Street, SW1W 9QN
Telephone: 071-730 4099 Fax: 071-823 6402   **£80**
Open: lunch + dinner Mon-Fri (closed Bank Holidays, 3wks
Aug, 2wks Xm, 1wk Easter)
Meals served: lunch 12.15-2, dinner 7.15-11

A well respected restaurant run by Neville and Sonia Blech, where the
clients are long-standing and loyal. Sonia's cooking is French and well
executed with a menu that offers you the difficult choice between
mille-feuille of puréed vegetables with a watercress and basil sauce or
a poached terrine of capon stuffed with truffles and foie gras. The
pièce de résistance is the gateau montelimar made with honey and
roasted praline of cashew and pistachio. Selecting from Neville's wine
list is made a little easier by the winematch suggestions listed under
each dish.

MILBURNS NEW RESTAURANT   SW7

Victoria and Albert Museum, SW7 2RL
Telephone: 071-581 2159   **£20**
Open: lunch daily (closed religious Holidays)
Meals served: lunch 12-5 Mon, 10-5 Tue-Sun,

Long gone are the days of curling, soggy sandwiches, limp lettuce and
unappealing snacks that used to be the fare available in museums.
Milburns certainly comes up to the higher standards demanded by
today's discerning museum visitors. For coffee time there's a good
selection of croissants, biscuits and cakes and sandwiches, while
lunchtime dishes include soup of the day, hot dishes with vegetables,
cold meats, mousses and terrines and salads. It's a great place to meet
friends and certainly enhances a trip to the V&A.

THE MILESTONE W8

1-2 Kensington Court, W8 5DL
Telephone: 071-917 1000 Fax: 071-917 1010   **£40**
Open: lunch + dinner daily
Meals served: lunch 12.30-2.30, dinner 7-11

This must be one of the best addresses in London, even if you only use it for one night. This exquisite town house it has 57 luxury suites. Some look out over Kensington Gardens while others enjoy a peek into the ground of the royal palace itself. Restoration has been extensive and carefully observed by English Heritage since the buildings date from the late 19th-century and still have many original features like carved panelling, fireplaces and the oratory. With its own health spa, it lacks none of the facilities of larger hotels. Dine in Chenistons Restaurant, which continues the elegant theme of the Milestone.

MIMMO D'ISCHIA SW1

61 Elizabeth Street, Eaton Square, SW1 9PP
Telephone: 071-730 5406   **£65**
Open: lunch + dinner Mon-Sat (closed Bank Holidays)
Meals served: lunch 12.30-2.15, dinner 7.30-11.15

A reminder of how good Italian cooking can be (in this day and age of everyone jumping on the Italian bandwagon), this is a well established restaurant popular with English and American tourists alike. While you're waiting for your meal glance around at the patron's celebrity photos adorning the walls. The menu definitely has some of Mamma's old favourites - fritto misto, scampi aragonese, grilled lobster tails, petto di pollo rosa, breast of chicken in wine sauce and mushrooms, osso bucco and pizzas, pastas and spare ribs (a speciality). What would a good Italian meal be without ice cream? Gelati al gusto may go down well before a steaming cup of espresso. This bustling restaurant is always busy, so book. Buon appetito!

MIRABELLE W1

56 Curzon Street, W1   ✿
Telephone: 071-499 4636 Fax: 071-499 5449   **£65**
Open: lunch Mon-Fri, dinner Mon-Sat (closed Bank
Holidays, 3 wks Aug, 1 wk Xmas)
Meals served: lunch 12-2, dinner 6.30-10.30

This London institution of the '30s continues under Japanese owners. Most of the operation remains in keeping with the Mirabelle's tradition of French cuisine but 2 teppanyaki rooms cater for the owners, city bond dealers and financial executives. The main restaurant and private dining rooms are orchestrated by chef Michael Croft whose French repertoire has a few new influences. Confit de canard is given a novel twist when served as an hors d'oeuvres with pickled vegetables in a coriander oil, as is lobster with vegetable cous-cous and sauce americaine. The remainder of the menu continues in the more traditional vein with foie gras, osso bucco and a petite marmite of chicken and vegetables.

MON PETIT PLAISIR   W8

33 Holland Street, W8 4LX
Telephone: 071-937 3224   **£30**
Open: lunch + dinner Mon-Fri (closed Bank Holidays, Xmas/New Year)
Meals served: lunch 12-2.30, dinner 7-10.30

Mon Petit Plaisir is an old favourite, boasting a strong local following
who come to enjoy its old-fashioned dishes and traditional bistro
atmosphere. The food's never dissapointing and guaranteed to fill the
gap. The menu is in French and but no translation is needed for dishes
such as crevettes du pacifique au Ricard, or raviolis aux noix et fines
herbs for starters, while for main courses try entrecôte grillée béarnaise - one of the specialities - coquilles St. Jaques persillées and escalope de saumon et shiitake. The vegetables come well prepared and
nicely seasoned. The French cheese board always proves tempting, as
does the tarte tatin.

MON PLAISIR   WC2

21 Monmouth Street, WC2H 9DD   *warm, friendly local*
Telephone: 071-240 3757 Fax: 071-379 0121   *— a good* **£55**
Open: lunch Mon-Fri, dinner Mon-Sat (closed Bank Holidays) *restaurant*
Meals served: lunch 12-2.15, dinner 6-11.15

The flagship of the small chain of French bistro-cum-restaurants with
its excellent selection of meat and fish dishes. Now over 50 years old,
it is still keeping up with trends like brioche with wild mushrooms in a
light cream sauce, or skate removed from the bone in a garlic and
chilli dressing. The cassoulet, confit, entrecôte and fillet of lamb en
croute still remain firm favourites with the thin and perfectly fried
allumettes and cooked but crisp vegetables. An enjoyable place to relish a leisurely meal in comfort with pleasing bistro-style surroundings
after the theatre. Excellent cheese board and attentive service, good
selection of French wines. The third outlet is Mon Plaisir du Nord, in
Islington.

MONKEYS   SW3

1 Cale Street, SW3 3QT
Telephone: 071-352 4711   **£55**
Open: lunch + dinner Mon-Fri (closed Bank Holidays, 2 wks Easter,
3 wks Aug)
Meals served: lunch 12.30-2.30, dinner 7.30-11

Monkeys is the ideal place for a light lunch, preferably taken in the
brighter, newly decorated back section of the restaurant. The menu is
unpretentious and concentrates on good home-made food. Start with
the smoked salmon mousse or a soupe du jour, and follow with the
fish pie, the fried trout (they really know how to cook fish here) or
black pudding and apples, followed by an exquisite mango mousse or
raspberry sorbet.

MOSIMANN'S   SW1

11b West Halkin Street, SW1X 8JL
Telephone: 071-235 9625 Fax: 071-245 6354
Open: lunch + dinner Mon-Sat (closed Bank Holidays)
Meals served: lunch 12-3, dinner 6-11

£100

Built in 1830 as a church, later to become a spiritualist venue, this former belfry is a dining club, the religion is food, and membership of the
·institution much sought after. Anton Mosimann has excelled in his
execution of decor, menu and atmosphere. Sponsors have funded the
decoration of the 4 dining rooms so there are now the Harvey Nichols,
the Wedgwood, the Alfa Romeo, and the Bulthaup rooms. To preserve
the inimitable atmosphere of the building, Anton left the wooden
church floor in the main restaurant and arranged for the wallpaper to
match the original that hung there in Mrs Oakley Maund's day (she
was the lady who converted the church into a private home). In fact
there's no end of things to look at, from the wine cellar on display
behind glass in the bar to the kitchen staff at work behind a specially
designed window in the Bulthaup room. The food is excellent, as can
only be expected of Anton Mosimann and head chef Ray Neve, with
dishes such as salmon and sorrel soup, char-grilled red bream with
tomato and pickled ginger salsa or piccata of veal with basil and spätzli. The clientele are as stylish as the Club itself and range from talented and chic ladies-at-lunch to suave and sophisticated international
travellers.

MOTCOMB'S   SW1

26 Motcomb Street, SW1X 8JU
Telephone: 071-235 9170 Fax: 071-245 6351
Open: lunch Mon-Fri, dinner Mon-Sat (closed Bank Holidays)
Meals served: lunch 12-3, dinner 7-11

£55

In the part of Belgravia that they call the Village is this upstairs wine
bar and basement restaurant. Phillip Lawless' watering hole is as much
a part of the community as Harrods and Sloane Street. The wine bar
has a short-and-sweet menu of the usual salads, sardines and soup
while downstairs the choice expands to include oyster mushrooms
sautéed with garlic and pinot blanc, oysters mornay, mussel and
chablis soup as well as smoked trout and salmon mousse. There is a
selection of fish courses from fishcakes to baked seabass with coriander and a finishing of mint and olive oil to a wide selection of roast
game, steak tartar, calves' liver, crispy duck and rack of lamb (to serve
2) coated with crushed peppercorns and dijon mustard. A selection of
vintage wines, some by the half bottle and per glass. No credit cards.
Good local restaurant and bar.

MULLIGANS OF MAYFAIR   W1

13-14 Cork Street, W1X 1PF
Telephone: 071-409 1370   **£50**
Open: lunch Mon-Fri, dinner Mon-Sat (closed Bank Holidays)
Meals served: lunch 12-2.30, dinner 6.15-11

An Irish institution in the heart of an English one, Mulligans boasts
traditional decor with mahogany wood panelling and pictures of distinguished Irish artists on the walls. Baked ham with colcannon and a
mustard grain sauce, hearty Irish stew and braised beef with Guinness
are a few of the productions of Martin Lynch. Starters blend the more
contemporary wild mushrooms and asparagus with basil along side
the sweet home-cured Irish salmon which is served with pickled
cucumber and a herb dressing. A selection of farmhouse cheese has
more affinity with the Emerald Isle than the range of predominantly
French puddings, but a tumbler of Bushmills wouldn't go amiss on a
cold winter's evening!

LE MUSCADET   W1

25 Paddington Street, W1M 3RF
Telephone: 071-935 2883   **£55**
Open: lunch Mon-Fri, dinner Mon-Sat (closed Bank Holidays,
3 wks Aug)
Meals served: lunch 12.30-2.30, dinner 7.30-10.45 (Sat 7.30-10)

The hand written menu is in French and presents an opportunity to
practise your pronunciation - croustade de champignons, bisque de
homard, coquille Saint Jacques and saumon sauce hollandaise should
take little guessing, but if you are not fully fledged in français take a
dictionary or call over one of the amiable staff who will happily help
out. The cooking is good and the clientele loyal. The wine list is equally traditional and French. Owner and general man-about-restaurant,
François Bessonard, once threatened to retire, but I hope and suspect
that he will be around for a lot longer.

MUSEUM STREET CAFÉ   WC1

47 Museum Street, WC1A 1LY
Telephone: 071-405 3211   **£45**
Open: lunch + dinner Mon-Fri (closed Bank Holidays, 1 wk summer)
Meals served: lunch 12.30-2.30, dinner 7.30-9.15

What a pity there aren't more bring-your-own restaurants in London,
especially in times of recession when it would encourage more people
to eat out more often. So firstly, a pat on the back to Museum Street
Café for that, and for not charging corkage. It's a simply decorated
place but it feeds a part of London that is otherwise gastronomically
hungry. The char-grill is the centrepiece of the lunch menu preceded
perhaps by a rocket salad with sliced fennel, mushrooms, pine nuts
and parmesan shavings. The selection of seasonal Neal's Yard cheeses
is also rather special.

NEAL STREET RESTAURANT *still stylish* WC2
& successful after twenty odd years.

26 Neal Street, WC2H 9PH
Telephone: 071-836 8368 Fax: 071-497 1361
Open: lunch + dinner Mon-Sat (closed Bank Holidays,
1 wk Xmas/New Year)
Meals served: lunch 12.30-2.30, dinner 7.30-11

£70

Famous mushroom connoisseur and owner of this Covent Garden restaurant, Antonio Carluccio is here most lunch times circulating the room offering mushroom stories and samplings of rare specimens to old friends and customers. The room's look retains its familiarity of recent years, with modern paintings, painted brick walls and a basket of mushrooms from the morning's pickings by the door. The menu is a feast for the eyes: wild garlic soup with dumplings, nettle gnocchi with dolcelatte, and his warm mushroom salad that occasionally includes finely chopped chilli, then main courses of fresh eel roman-style or crusted ragout of sweetbreads and morelles. They are all watched over carefully by Antonio who is the kitchen's greatest critic. Be sure to nip into the delicatessen next door which he runs with wife Priscilla (Terence Conran's sister) for the array of Italian produce is equally good for presents and the kitchen cupboard.

NEWTONS SW4

73 Abbeville Road, SW4 9LA
Telephone: 081-673 0977
Open: lunch + dinner daily (closed 25+26 Dec, Easter Sat+Sun)
Meals served: lunch 12.30-2.30, (Sat 12.30-4) dinner 7-11.30,
(light meals Sun 12.30-11.30)

£40

Where so many have failed before, Zue Newton continues to light up the Abbeville Road, aided by a loyal core of clients who love the bistro-style rooms with simple furnishings and red brick walls. The 2-course lunch at £9.95 is going down well. Simple starters crafted by Sebastian Tyson could be a rich dark French onion soup or a warm goat's cheese salad with a herb dressing; followed by chicken, char-grilled and served with a flavoursome hoisin sauce, or a large Thai vegetable curry which comes with a bamboo steamer of jasmine-scented rice. Children get a good deal on Saturdays, with balloons and clowns thrown in with the bangers and beans. The wine list encourages you to try some wines by the glass and offers some 14 choices. Although they no longer have a 'Toy Boy of an Italian chardonnay' listed, they do offer a South African chardonnay, 'soft and seducingly smooth', instead!

NICO CENTRAL   W1

35 Great Portland Street, W1N 5DD
Telephone: 071-436 8846 Fax: 071-436 0134   **£60**
Open: lunch Mon-Fri (except Bank Holidays), dinner Mon-Sat (closed 10
days Xmas)
Meals served: lunch 12-2.15, dinner 7-11

Since Nico has moved to Park Lane, his former flagship has become a
very good up-market brasserie, with cooking by the capable and
skilled Andrew Jeffs. There's no mistaking that Nico glances more
than just an eye over the operation for such is the level of service and
quality of the menu, but that isn't meant to undermine Andrew in any
way. At a snip of a price you can sample a few of the old Nico
favourites like his pièce de resistance chocolate tart. The handwritten
menu offers the diner a profusion of Mediterranean-influenced dishes
including rillette of smoked and marinated salmon with cucumber and
a chive cream plus a good ravioli of goat's cheese with a tomato sauce.
Boudin blanc with caramelised apples and essence of truffle has to be
tried as does grilled guinea fowl with white coco beans. Puddings keep
up the standard and bring a more traditional French element, with
tarte tatin and armagnac parfait among the choices.

NIKITA'S   SW10

65 Ifield Road, SW10 9AU
Telephone: 071-352 6326 Fax: 081-993 3680   **£55**
Open: dinner Mon-Sat (closed Bank Holidays, 2 wks Aug)
Meals served: dinner 7.30-11.30

What else could Nikita's be but Russian, and Russian it is in the most
hospitable sense of the word. Enjoy a candlelit dinner as many diners
have done for years now, under the watchful eye of owner, Silvano
Borsi. Tuck into hearty Russian food caviar, borscht, blinis, chicken
kiev, steak tartare, while knocking back one of the many flavoured
vodkas - pepper, honey, tarragon - and sit back and enjoy the sumptuous atmosphere to the strains of Russian music.

NOW AND ZEN   WC2

Orion House, 48 Upper St Martin's Lane, WC2
Telephone: 071-497 0376   £50
Open: lunch + dinner daily (closed 25+26 Dec)
Meals served: lunch 12-3, dinner 6-11.30 (Sun 6-11)
Stylish and in vogue, this is the most up-to-date of the Zen chain. Run by Lawrence
Leung, designed by Rick Mather.

ODETTE'S NW1

Simone green odette* is the (not inspiration behind this gem.)

130 Regent's Park Road, NW1 8XL
Telephone: 071-586 5486
Open: lunch Mon-Fri, dinner Mon-Sat (closed Bank Holidays,
1 wk Xmas)
Meals served: lunch 12.30-2.30 (Sun 12-3), dinner 7-11

£60

A little local restaurant in Primrose Hill that has a daily-changing menu
and a relaxed and charming manner. The decor is green on green with
gilded mirrors and a balcony overlooking a conservatory. Odette*
(possibly the lady on the menu cover?) introduces a modern hand-
written menu with dishes that are gutsy and simple but big on impact,
with good textures and flavours. Paul Holmes cooks squid with pesto
mash and a skate, scallop and oyster terrine with a cucumber coriander and lime relish. The main courses are no less adventurous: lamb
meatballs with garlic potatoes and rosemary, and grilled sea bass with
fresh peas, rocket and salsa verde.

ODIN'S RESTAURANT W1

27 Devonshire Street, W1N 1RJ
Telephone: 071-935 7296
Open: lunch Mon-Fri, dinner Mon-Sat (closed Bank Holidays)
Meals served: lunch 12.30-2.30, dinner 7-11.30

£65

The subtle refurbishment that took place in 1993 has lifted Odin's, the
fourth of the Langan quartet, to new heights. Situated in a street that is
fast becoming the connoisseurs' half-mile, the whole place buzzes and
the staff try hard to help you enjoy yourself. The walls are crammed
with pictures and paintings and the place has a comforting similarity to
its little sister, Langan's Bistro next door, yet the menus differ consid-
erably. This menu is more hearty yet still refined and typically British:
with medallions of venison with wild mushrooms and a madeira sauce,
halibut braised in cider and a saffron sauce, rabbit braised with mustard and served with fresh pasta. Desserts win hands down here - regular favourites are Mrs Langan's chocolate pudding, a date and ginger
creation with lashings of butterscotch sauce, while Odin's bread-and-
butter stands out in the crowd and has to be tasted, so take along a few
friends and try them all out.

O'KEEFE'S   SW1

19 Dering Street, off Oxford Street, W1R 9AA
Telephone: 071-495 0878   £35
Open: lunch Mon-Sat, dinner Thu (closed Bank Holidays,
4 days Easter, 2 wks Aug)
Meals served: lunch 12-3, dinner 7.30-11 (light meals 8am-3pm)

The chef has changed at O'Keefe's but the spirit remains the same.
Caroline Brett joins this fashionable deli-restaurant with its airy and
bright room with high ceilings and white walls. Large windows open on
to the pavement and welcome you in. The menu changes daily and
offers soups, charcuterie or cheese plates and a choice of 3 hot dishes
always including one vegetarian option. The theme is strongly
Mediterranean and emphasises pure quality products and healthy eating. Service is efficient and relaxed and it proves popular at lunchtime.
Open daily for free-range breakfasts and intimate, candlelit dining on
Thursdays.

OLIVER'S   W14

10 Russell Gardens, W14 8EZ
Telephone: 071-603 7645   £35
Open: lunch + dinner daily (closed 25+26 Dec)
Meals served: lunch + dinner 12-11.30

A small and friendly restaurant, located close to the Olympia exhibition
halls. Although it's licensed you can still bring-your-own. Choose, if you
can, from 20 starters and an even more extensive list of main courses.
Good choices are calamari provençale, prawns and chilli, turkey pâté
and toast for starters; braised pheasant, venison au poivre, and grilled
salmon steak to follow, or perhaps just a light salad. Service from smiling waiters, a patio at the rear for sunny days and walls adorned with
bric-a-brac all combine to give Oliver's a friendly feel.

OLIVO   SW1

21 Eccleston Street, SW1W 9LX
Telephone: 071-730 2505   £50
Open: lunch Mon-Fri, dinner Mon-Sat (closed Bank Holidays, 3 wks Aug/Sep)
Meals served: lunch 12-2.30, dinner 7-11
Modern cooking with an Italian bias. A handwritten menu features lamb with apricots
and a chicken and roquefort strudel.

ON THE TOWN SW6

1 Very Close, SW69 0IL
Telephone: 0891 334 330 – see Page 14 **£20**
Open: all day daily
Meals served: on a plate

An innocuous large faded blue door in a high brick wall marks the entrance to this delightful courtyard restaurant seating about sixty outside under an amazing electronically-operated sliding glass roof. Floodlit at night, the flagstoned courtyard is surrounded by orange trees groaning under the weight of ripe fruits, other tropical plants and the intoxicating smells of lavender. To gain access to the inside restaurant, you enter the house via the kitchen, passing on either side lines of chefs beavering away preparing that day's dishes, into the tasting room where 20 wines, selected by Joseph Berkmann, can be sampled from the giant cruvinet machine. Once you've chosen your wine(s) to accompany the meal the young sommeliers in their blue aprons take it and you through to your table, where you are almost immediately served with a basket of assorted breads, or a small, crusty, brown home-baked loaf. This is accompanied by 2 Kilner jars containing Greek and Spanish olives. The bistro-style dining room, which though seating about 100 seems smaller since tables are situated in one of the ten dining areas, each with paintings by different artists who include Peter Blake, Martin Fuller, Patrick Hughes, Patrick Propter and Val Archer. Bevelled glass partitions glitter in the reflection of the candle chandeliers. Choose from starters of chargrilled vegetables served with couscous; terrine of foie gras with brioche toast or a classic, rich bouillabaise and amongst the 10 main courses, my favourites are fresh calves' liver thinly sliced and served pink with fresh bacon and glazed button mushrooms; simply char-grilled sea bream with braised fennel and new potatoes or traditional steak frites. Don't miss out on the puddings which include crisp tarte tatin; steamed rich marmalade pud at lunchtimes and an original dark chocolate pot. The warm welcome and greeting you receive make this an especially friendly place, with well-informed and trained staff. Who can blame the owners for showing the red card to some rather pretentious customers, who were silly enough to present a voucher from a Sunday newspaper, demanding they receive good food and service! They are apparently considering introducing Fothergill's habit of charging face money! When you ring I'll tell you about it. Calls cost 36p per minute cheap rate and 48p per minute at all other times.

192 W11

192 Kensington Park Road, W11 2JF
Telephone: 071-229 0482 **£45**
Open: lunch + dinner daily (closed Bank Holidays)
Meals served: lunch 12.30-3 (Sun 1-1.30), dinner 7.30-11.30 (Sun 7.30-11)

Expansion has led to a revamp of this informal restaurant, creating a much larger bar area, kitchen and restaurant. Despite the casual approach and informality, 192 works well and the food produced by Josh Hampton delights. Lunch menus are good with seasonal salads, marinated salt cod, artichoke hearts, green olives and basil, Toulouse sausages with mash and red onions, or roast red-legged partridge, polenta, bubble and squeak and truffle sauce, followed by a small selection of desserts or cheese plate.

ORSO   WC2

27 Wellington Street, WC2E 7DA
Telephone: 071-240 5269 Fax: 071-497 2148   **£55**
Open: all day daily (closed 24+25 Dec)
Meals served: 12-12

A large glass and wood door are all that announce this New York-style basement restaurant. Beautifully designed, it remains a favourite lunchtime place and is equally popular with pre-theatre goers. The walls are hung with arty mono photographs and the tables are graced with the rustic Tuscan pottery famed in well-heeled cookshops. The menu looks enormous but in fact is only half the size: dishes appear twice - once in Italian, the second in translation. Take your time. The charcuterie and rocket salads which form the appetizers are good, as are the mini pizzas and risotto which are substantial for a first or second course. Next courses, if you can accommodate them as well, are pasta-based, with seafood, rabbit and vegetables. Entrées include grilled and roast fish and meats from veal shank with baby vegetables and grilled spinach polenta, venison steaks with green peppercorns to roast sea bass with wild garlic and new potatoes. No credit cards. An all Italian wine list offers some not unreasonable prices.

OSTERIA ANTICA BOLOGNA   SW11

23 Northcote Road, SW11 1NG
Telephone: 071-978 4771   **£45**
Open: all day Wed-Sat, dinner only Mon+Tue (closed Bank Holidays,
2 wks Xmas)
Meals served: 12-11 (Sun 12.30-10.30, Mon+Tue 6-11)

The Osteria has been the talk of Clapham for quite some time but now the rest of London has caught on and it is becoming full to overflowing. A true osteria in style, with wood panelling in every direction, it offers a tasteful selection of rustic dishes but before you start the meal proper, order some of their little olives marinated in garlic as appetisers, a bottle of wine and take in the atmosphere. Peruse the menu from polpettine di ricotta (deep-fried ricotta balls) with a fresh basil salsa, freshly boiled octopus with rocket, herbs, olive oil and spices, although the boned cod and salmon with a spicy garlic sauce is also too good to miss. Main courses could be a salad or bowl of pasta or pananonda a Neapolitan, a dish of liver, heart and meats cooked with peppers and chillies and served on a giant crostini. It's well worth crossing the river for this real Italian home cooking with a modern twist.

LA PAESANA   W8

30 Uxbridge Street, W8 7TR
Telephone: 071-229 4332   £35
Open: lunch + dinner Mon-Sat (closed Bank Holidays)
Meals served: lunch 12-2.45, dinner 6.30-11.45
An old favourite from the '60s serving sound Italian cooking behind the Coronet cinema in Notting Hill. Set lunch £9.95.

LE PALAIS DU JARDIN   WC2

136 Long Acre, WC2E 9AD
Telephone: 071-379 5353   **£50**
Open: all day daily
Meals served: 12-12, Sun 12-10.50

It's hard to pass by Le Palais du Jardin, so inviting does it look with its huge windows and very French atmosphere which seeps out and shouts "bien-venue". Breakfast is available from 10 in the morning for only £2. For lunches on a sunny day it's a perfect venue, as the glass roof towards the rear of the restaurant slides back. The menu is also typically French with hors d'oeuvres, grillades, traditional dishes such as boeuf bourgignon, coq au vin and moules. The service is professional and it's already a welcome addition to the scene for some of the more jaded Covent Garden palates.

PELHAM HOTEL   SW7

15 Cromwell Place, SW7 2LA
Telephone: 071-589 8288 Fax: 071-584 8444   **£45**
Open: all day daily
Meals served: 12-10.30

The epitome of Englishness with swags and drapes, masses of rugs

PELICAN   WC2

45 St Martin's Lane, WC2N 4EJ
Telephone: 071-379 0309 Fax: 071-379 0782   **£40**
Open: all day daily (closed 24-26 Dec)
Meals served: 12-12 (Sun 12-11)

This large café (part of the Café Rouge group) is worthy of note for its late opening and reasonably priced dishes. With a bar at the front, it makes a good rendezvous before the theatre for a glass of wine and a snack, or pop in after the show for a quick supper. Choose from a typical brasserie menu, from assiette de charcuterie through to French onion soup, salads and grills. Roast duck comes with kumquat and orange sauce and pan-fried pork with spinach gratin and coarse-grained mustard.

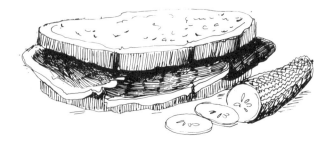

PETER'S   NW6

65 Fairfax Road, NW6 4EE
Telephone: 071-624 5804   £35
Open: lunch Sun-Fri, dinner Mon-Sat (closed 26 Dec, 1 Jan)
Meals served: lunch 12-3, dinner 6.30-11.30

Scallops of veal with mushrooms and madeira, and duck roasted and
served with Calvados and ginger sauce are chef Jean Charles' speciality. A French '20s style decor with resident pianist brings a fun air to
this local restaurant where the cooking is traditional and based on
market specials. The menu is fixed-price, so all the main courses cost
the same, as do the hors d'oeuvres and desserts. The wine list is true
to form, but also branches out to include Germany, Italy and Australia.

LE P'TIT NORMAND   SW18

185 Merton Road, SW18 5EF
Telephone: 081-871 0233   £45
Open: lunch Sun-Fri, dinner daily
Meals served: lunch 12-1.30, dinner 7-10

Phillippe Herrard originates from Normandy and his good rustic cooking proves his allegiance, with boudin noir aux pommmes and a
casserole of snails holding court amongst the hors d'oeuvres, while
entrées may be short on number but not in authentic value; magret of
duck, entrecôte with pepper and veal normandy. A good selection of
cheese and a wine list that spells out the characteristics - in English
thankfully! A lovely restaurant which is kind to the purse as well as the
stomach.

PIED À TERRE   W1

Last year this appeared only as a listing - our mistake. I enjoyed one of the best meals here of '93 It continues to excite.

34 Charlotte Street, W1P 1HJ
Telephone: 071-636 1178   £85
Open: lunch Mon-Fri, dinner Mon-Sat (closed Bank
Holidays, Xmas/New Year, 2 wks Aug)
Meals served: lunch 12.15-2, dinner 7.15-10

Another addition to the top end of the restaurant market, this is a
serious venture from chef Richard Neat and his partner David Moore.
Clever use of peach and apricot tablecloths and artwork by Warhol and
Richard Hamilton add splashes of colour to otherwise plain rough plaster walls, glass panels and comfortable metal chairs. The hard-working
pedigree partnership is obviously paying off with a fixed-price lunch
menu for £19, which reads hare fillet with wild mushrooms, fillet of
whiting and smoked salmon sauce and chocolate tart or cheese. In the
evening a set menu at £36 offers more choice at each course with sensible and well-thought out alternatives like pan-fried foie gras with
endive and honey, salad of skate, broccoli purée and fondant potato or
pan-fried red mullet with almond sauce. A second course of roasted
sweetbreads with caramelised apple and black trumpets shows
Richard's continued dedication to offal. Also try the cod and roasted
scallop with red wine juice, or roasted pigeon, turnip confit and garlic.
All is just as it reads, handsomely cooked and presented and brings to
this street a high level of skill and sophistication.

PINOCCHIO'S   NW1

160 Eversholt Street, NW1 1BL
Telephone: 071-388 7482   **£50**
Open: lunch Mon-Fri, dinner Mon-Sat (closed Bank Holidays, 24-31 Dec)
Meals served: lunch 12-3, dinner 6.30-11

A light, attractively decorated restaurant with large modern paintings
on the walls that's especially popular for lunch. Some dishes are traditional Italian. Choose from a selection of pastas, fish (monkfish, king-
prawns and fresh salmon on skewers) and meats (sautéed duck breast
with orange and frangelica sauce). Desserts are good, so save room
for the tiramisu, zabaglione or Italian cheeses.

PJ'S BAR & GRILL   SW10

52 Fulham Road, SW10
Tel: 071-589 0025   £45
Open: all day daily
Meals served: 11am-11.30pm
American-style bar and grill with branch in Covent Garden.

POISSONNERIE DE L'AVENUE   SW3

82 Sloane Avenue, SW3 3DZ
Telephone: 071-589 2457   **£55**
Open: lunch + dinner Mon-Sat (closed Bank Holidays,
23 Dec-3 Jan, 4 days Easter)
Meals served: lunch 12-3, dinner 7-11.45

The Poissonnerie has been around for over 30 years and has seen off
many of its new-wave competitors. There's something very comforting
about the solidarity of the place, and Peter Rosignoli makes old and
new customers most welcome. A fish restaurant and oyster bar that
offers a relaxed ambience and a perfect place to rest your feet after
heavy shopping at Conran's emporium just round the corner. The
service is professional and the menu classical with dishes carefully
prepared. Crab soup, oysters and lobsters remain favourites with the
loyal customers.

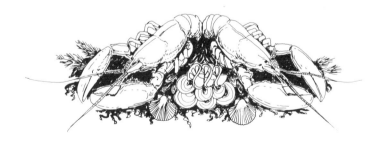

LE PONT DE LA TOUR   SE1

Butlers Wharf Building, 36D Shad Thames, Butlers Wharf, SE1
Telephone: 071-403 8403
£75
Open: lunch Sun-Fri, dinner daily (closed 3 days Xmas)
Meals served: lunch 12-3, dinner 6-12 (Sun 6-11) (Bar + Grill
12-12 Mon-Sat, Sun 12-11))

Although is in full Tower Bridge view

For Conran fanatics this restaurant deserves full praise for its design, desirable food and location. Housed in the self-styled Gastrodrome with wine shop, bakery and food store all under the same roof, the main restaurant is reached by traversing the crustacea bar and grill which is brimming with plateaux de fruits de mer and snacks in similar style to those on offer at the Bibendum oyster bar - Caesar salads, grills and starters of Bayonne ham and the like. The restaurant proper is resplendent with buff yellow walls, mounted pictures and a left-hand run of windows which look across to the north side of the Thames, and of course that magnificent bridge. Book early and try and reserve a table by the window where you can watch the river by night. Dine on squid ink risotto with scallops and gremolata or jambon persillé - a slice of the most tender ham and parsley bound in aspic with crunchy cocktail gherkins, or grilled polenta with roasted tomato sauce, basil and parmesan. It's nice to see oxtail in vogue, and here it's served with haricot beans and spiced celeriac, while braised lamb shank comes with rosemary mash. The menu is memorable and with David Burke (once sous at Bibendum) at the helm, the strong mix of dishes is set to run successfully. Look out for Conran's next venture here, the Chop House. *—somehow you're in Paris, sitting outside on a balmy summer evening*

PORTERS ENGLISH RESTAURANT   WC2

17 Henrietta Street, Covent Garden, WC2E 8QH
Telephone: 071-836 6466 Fax: 071-379 4296
£35
Open: all day daily (closed 25+26 Dec)
Meals served: 12-11.30 (Sun 12-10.30)

Try a slice of England in Porters restaurant, famous for its pies, salmon and bangers and mash. It's a favourite with Americans as you would expect, but the food remains stylishly done and is very good. Popular are the faggots with a Guinness and onion gravy, beef with herb dumplings, steak and mushroom pie and old English fish pie. Not forgetting, of course, the sticky toffee pudding, bread and butter pudding and strawberry jam roly poly - if there's room that is, as portions are generous.

LA POULE AU POT   SW1

231 Ebury Street, SW1W 8UT
Telephone: 071-730 7763   £55
Open: lunch + dinner daily (closed 24-28 Dec)
Meals served: lunch 12.30-2.30, dinner 7-11.15

After a bit of a hiccup in '92, this restaurant still offers good old home
cooking in a rustic and cosy atmophere. Khaki walls and bare wooden
floorboards are complemented by wicker baskets filled with dried
flowers. The menu has a flavour of France à la campagne. You might
opt for hot tomato soup or terrine du chef for starters, steak bearnaise
or boeuf bourgignon or gigot d'agneau to follow; and crème brûlée to
finish, all served by friendly waiters in a relaxing atmosphere.

'La Poule au Pot in Ebury St.'

QUAGLINO'S   SW1

16 Bury Street, St James's, SW1Y 6AL
Telephone: 071-930 6767   £55
Open: lunch daily, dinner Mon-Sat
Meals served: lunch 12-3, dinner 5.30-12
(Fri+Sat 5.30-1.45am) (bar 11.30am-midnight, Sun 12-11)

Opened to much hype and publicity, Sir Terence Conran is on to
another winner, it seems. Still on the site just off Jermyn Street that
was so famous in the '20s, it was impossible in the early days to book a
table sooner than 3 months ahead. It wasn't without its teething
problems, though these are hopefully ironed out now. The food's good
considering the size of the place, but it's not a place to linger as the
tables are re-booked 2 or sometimes 3 times per session and not
suprisingly, service can sometimes be under pressure. Martin Webb
has devised a fashionable menu of dishes that are on everyone's lips
these days – mozzarella and roast tomato bruschetta or rocket and
parmesan salad for starters, or his own more inventive dishes of
Toulouse sausage and potato salad, or seafood bisque with tarragon
and cream. There's a good selection of crustacea (crab, lobster and
langoustine), grills and rôtisserie, and other main courses could be
skate with capers and mash, or roast duck with coriander and ginger.
Vegetables are extra and if you haven't had to vacate your table, stay
for crème brûlée, or dark chocolate mousse and a palmier. For older
gourmets, don't go expecting the Quags of yesteryear this is a noisy,
bustling, highly stylised restaurant and bar - the latter where the
young definitely rule, OK!

LE QUAI ST PIERRE   W8

7 Stratford Road, W8 3JS
Telephone: 071-937 6388   £55
Open: lunch Tue-Sat, dinner Mon-Sat
Meals served: lunch 12.30-2.30, dinner 7-11.30

The plats du jour and wine list have had a shake up and the prices are
now more competitive, but otherwise all remains the same at this
highly likeable seafood restaurant in Kensington. The decor and menu
are evocative of France, with lobsters in a tank waiting to be selected,
scallops, mussels and clams being the popular choices. The fruits de
mer continues to appear in gargantuan quantities.

QUALITY CHOP HOUSE   EC1

94 Farringdon Road, EC1R 3EA
Telephone: 071-837 5093   £45
Open: lunch Sun-Fri, dinner daily
Meals served: lunch 12-3 (Sun 12-4), dinner 6.30-12 (Sun 7-11.30)
(light meals from 7.30am Mon-Fri)

'Progressive working class caterer' Charles Fontaine re-opened this
Victorian chop house in 1989 to London's delight. His aim to provide
straightforward no-nonsense fodder, well cooked and in very friendly
surroundings very much in keeping with the original aim, and one that
succeeds in surviving the test of time. We love it and hope it continues
(without a break) for another 100 years. Good plain food served in
ample portions is characterised by the matter-of-fact menu card
offering corned beef hash with fried egg, lamb chops, toulouse
sausages with mash and onion gravy and avocado and prawn cocktail.
But in between this plethora of down-to-earthness the influences of the
London scene and Charles' own Caprice history have crept in - bang
bang chicken, carpaccio, grilled swordfish, omelette with mixed forest
mushrooms and confit of duck - but who minds? There's something
here for everyone. Friendly staff and atmosphere, pared down furnishings - good value.

QUINCY'S   NW2

675 Finchley Road, NW2 2JP   *Friendly, charming*
Telephone: 071-794 8499   *staff in a*   £50
Open: dinner Tue-Sat (closed 1 wk Xmas, 2 wks Sep) *good restaurant*
Meals served: dinner 7-11   *local restaurant*

Chicken mousseline in field mushrooms with tarragon, smoked haddock and horseradish cream on a potato blini and roast Barbary duck
with chestnuts and apricots are all well-flavoured and balanced dishes,
served in ample portions and cooked by David Philpott. Gratin of sat-
sumas with fruit ices in brandy snaps and a lemon tart with crème
fraîche round off the meal with Britain and France standing firmly in
place on the cheese board, neither needing to give way to the other.
This is the best kind of anglicised French restaurant, rustic in appeal
with scrubbed tables, wooden floors, and window-boxes.

RANSOME'S DOCK   SW11

35-37 Parkgate Road, Battersea Wharf, SW11
Telephone: 071-223 1611
Open: all day Mon-Sat, lunch Sun (closed Bank Holidays,
2 wks summer, 1 wk Xmas)
Meals served: 11-11 (Sat 12-12, Sun 12-3.30)

£50

Ransome's Dock is tucked away between Battersea and Albert Bridges
in the new Battersea dockland's ice-factory conversion. Martin Lam,
previous head chef of L'Escargot, has created a relaxed, colourful and
extremely welcoming restaurant, with cobalt blue and eau-de-nil walls
punctuated with colourful paintings. Martin Lam could be described as
the Christopher Columbus of New English cooking - his eclectic menu
is influenced by many cuisines, using the best of produce available
here. Each dish is carefully prepared, the seasoning, spices and textures artistically complementing each other. There's mussel and saffron soup, pasta with crab and coriander, rabbit done with broad beans
in a cream sauce, parsnip mash (excellent), char-grilled quails with
couscous and lemon sauce and on the brunch menu on Sundays, the
smoothest kedgeree in town. The extensive wine list reflects Lam's
love of wine and features some specially selected wines. The restaurant has already built up a loyal custom, family-oriented on Sundays,
and boasts keen prices and excellent service to boot. A winning team.

THE REGENT LONDON   NW1

222 Marylebone Road, NW1 6JQ
Telephone: 071-631 8000 Fax: 071-631 8080
Open: lunch + dinner daily
Meals served: lunch 12-3 (Sun 12.30-3), dinner 7-11

£70

The lavish restoration work is complete and £75 million later the grand
old hotel is resplendent again, offering health spa, classy public rooms
and 309 of the largest bedrooms in town. A sophisticated hotel, the
architecture is Victorian-gothic with an entrance hall panelled in oak and
a staircase that leads to the glorious Winter Garden restaurant with its 8-
storey atrium and 25-ft palm trees. Across the street from Marylebone
station, this hotel is a most exciting addition to the London scene and
has the experienced General Manager, Wolfgang Nitschke (ex-
Dorchester) at the helm. The restaurant offers light snacks and has
become the chic, new meeting place for cocktails and afternoon teas.
The Dining Room, where executive chef Ralf Kutzner has created a
Mediterranean-based menu, is in keeping with the style of the hotel -
huge chandeliers, ornate plaster ceiling and large French windows.
Decorated in tones of light pink and burnt orange, it offers a selection of
traditional and modern Italian dishes from roast fillet of rabbit with basil
sauce to monkfish with green olives and a saffron sauce and somewhat
incongruously, beef from the trolley. Down in the basement is the health
club with swimming pool and a traditional pub-cum-bar called the
Cellars which has retained many of its original features of wood panelling, Adam fireplaces and intricate plaster work. On one of my visits
there was also some rather loud pop music, but I suspect it was only
temporary! The Regent is a good rendezvous point for business people
waiting for a train, but if you're fortunate to experience an overnight stay
at the Regent, opt for one of the rooms overlooking the atrium.

LOS REMOS   W2

38a Southwick Street, W2 1JQ
Telephone: 071-723 5056   **£30**
Open: lunch + dinner Mon-Sat
Meals served: lunch 12-3, dinner 7-12

Still a popular haunt despite the slight lull in tapas mania after the '80s boom. The usual tapas fare is available: tortilla, patatas bravas, baked peppers, jamon serrano but there's also a wonderful selection of fish dishes: calamares, sardines a la plancha, langostinos, merluza a la romano (hake fried in butter), halibut, monkfish, octopus, witch fish fillets. In fact the à la carte menu also offers a huge selection of dishes – not a place for the indecisive. Good honest Spanish food, reasonably priced.

THE RITZ   W1

150 Piccadilly, W1V 9DG   **£100**
Telephone: 071-493 8181 Fax: 071-493 2687
Open: lunch + dinner daily
Meals served: lunch 12.30-2.30, dinner 6.30-11

Of all the places in the world, the Ritz is still synonymous with fine English afternoon tea, an inheritance from the turn of the century when soon after the hotel had opened the Palm Court became the only establishment deemed suitable for unchaperoned young ladies to come and partake of refreshment. Tea at the Ritz is still fundamental to this lavish and refined hotel, and lunch or dinner could not be more pleasurable either, when taken on the Terrace in summer overlooking the park or in the sumptuous and glistening rococo restaurant with its painted ceilings and ornate work that constantly draws the attention of the eye. The fixed-priced menu is cooked amiably by David Nicholls and is a gentle translation of classic dishes, such as a starter of chilled fillet of red mullet with tomato and artichoke and basil, cream of fresh pea soup with smoked duck breast and sugar snap peas, followed by beef cooked in herb bread with madeira sauce and a dessert as lavish as the room itself: peach Ritz with strawberries in an almond basket. A hotel worth visiting for the aura, the 129 rooms and also now for the lighter and more intuitive cooking.

see page 110

RIVA   SW13

169 Church Road, SW13 9HR
Telephone: 081-748 0434   £60
Open: lunch Sun-Fri, dinner daily (closed Bank Holidays, 2 wks Aug)
Meals served: lunch 12-2.30, dinner 7-11

This is new wave Italian cooking at its best – robust flavours, regularly
changing dishes and already boasting a large and loyal following in the
3 years since its opening. The decor is sparse and modern, creating a
suitable atmosphere in which to enjoy good honest food. Try the
grilled seasonal vegetables or insalata al formaggio – rocket and
spinach salad with parmesan shavings - to lead the way into a risotto
valtellinese with borlotti beans and speck, or the stracotto di cinghiale
wild boar braised in red wine with polenta. Finish with a tiramisu and a
grappa! Good local restaurant.

Ochre ragged walls
soft greens in the
paintwork
+ tiny flying
spotlight

the glass cube
of tableereflected
in the top
mirrored wall

Hard wooden
school-type chairs

deep golden
ohiv oil on
table + flat
moist Italian breads

RIVER CAFÉ   W6

This restaurant remains a favourite with locals & tourists alike.

Thames Wharf Studios, Rainville Road, W6 9HA
Telephone: 071-381 8824   £80
Open: lunch daily, dinner Mon-Sat (closed 10 days Xmas,
4 days Easter, Bank Holidays)
Meals served: lunch 12.30-3, dinner 7.30-9.45

The River Café remains a favourite of modern Italian cum
Mediterranean cookery. Rose Gray and Ruth Rogers despite their non-
Italian backgrounds deliver the goods in an artistic, stylish and inventive way. Look out towards the river (though it's not exactly on the
waterfront), through the large glass paned floor-to-ceiling windows. It's
stark inside, and you eat off plain, unclothed tables and simple glass-
ware – a plain stage for decorative food. The first act may be pappa
pomodoro, a soup of plum tomatoes, basil and Tuscan bread, or fresh
asparagus with parmesan slivers and extra virgin olive oil, to set the
scene for cape sante, grilled scallops with pancetta and balsamic vinegar and braised spinach, or spring lamb with fennel, parmigiano and
salsa verde. And the final curtain – lemon and mascarpone tart, and
bitter chocolate and almond torte. The cooking reflects the
proprietors' love of regional Italian food.

ROBBIE'S RESTAURANT   **W4**

Burlington Lane, (Chiswick BR station), W4 3HB
Telephone: 081-742 3620   **£40**
Open: lunch Sun-Fri, dinner Mon-Sat (closed Bank Holidays)
Meals served: lunch 12-3, dinner 6-11.30

To say that this restaurant is a trifle unusual is an understatement. It occupies what was once a railway café and Robbie Simon, who trained under the Roux brothers, cooks an eclectic menu which varies by the week and is short on choice but long on imagination. Main courses are a mix of the hearty and the unusual, such as black spotted rubberlip fish, steak and kidney sausages with caramelised red onions, or black-feathered chicken. A choice of starters from prawns, cockles and mussels, or quail with chicken liver pâté precede and the main course is followed by a savoury course of spinach tart topped with smoked onions. This restaurant is for the bold and those who like a novel night out.

ROYAL GARDEN HOTEL   **W8**

Kensington High Street, W8 4PT
Telephone: 071-937 8000 Fax: 071-938 4532   **£75**
Open: lunch + dinner Mon-Sat (closed Bank Holidays)
Meals served: lunch 12.30-2.30, dinner 7.30-10.30 (Fri+Sat to 11)

Adjacent to Kensington Palace and Gardens, this hotel offers a pleasant location and professional and polished service. It's a modern high-rise, so the top rooms overlook Hyde Park, and the Garden Café overlooks Kensington Gardens. Here you can enjoy a buffet-style lunch of cold meats, prawns, salads or hot dishes (on a cold dreary London day!). Try the stroganoff, or spare ribs in a sweet and sour sauce. Also boasting a stunning view over London is the Royal Roof restaurant, where chef Gunther Schlender puts his attractive ideas into practice. Each evening you can choose from the Menu du Chef which changes weekly, or from the à la carte menu. Whichever you choose, you'll be recipient of dishes such as quail consommé flavoured with port, soufflé d'avocat et saumon fumé au poivre vert followed by fish: red mullet with scallops and truffle, or meat: chicken breast filled with morel and chicken mousse. The dessert menu is equally extensive and imaginative. Choose a hot raspberry soufflé or be decadent - only apt in these surroundings - and go for the fondant et moelleux et glace au chocolat – 3 different chocolate desserts.

ROYAL LANCASTER HOTEL   W2

Lancaster Terrace, W2 2TY
Telephone: 071-262 6737 Fax: 071-724 3191   **£60**
Open: lunch Mon-Fri, dinner Mon-Sat
Meals served: lunch 12.30-3, dinner 6.30-10.45

Conveniently close to Hyde Park for walks and views and just above
Lancaster Gate tube station, this well-placed hotel offers excellent facilities for meetings and conferences as well as tourists. Its restaurants,
the Pavement Café and La Rosette restaurant, cater for all tastes, more
formally in the latter. Dinner in La Rosette could consist of a selection
of seafood appetisers, fan of seasonal melon with Parma ham and fresh
figs, grilled fillet or sirloin steak with a choice of sauces or whole dover
sole, grilled or pan fried and a selection of desserts from the trolley.
Recent investment in the latest state of the art equipment for the
conference and banqueting rooms looks set to make the Royal
Lancaster one of London's top venues.

RSJ   SE1

13a Coin Street, SE1 8YQ
Telephone: 071-928 4554   **£45**
Open: lunch Mon-Fri, dinner Mon-Sat (closed Bank Holidays)
Meals served: lunch 12-2, dinner 6-11

Down on the South Bank, on the sometimes barren stretch of
Stamford Street, is this little corner of civilisation - well worth remembering if you're ever down that way visiting the theatre or art galleries
of the Festival Hall and complex. Both first-floor restaurant and lower
ground floor brasserie are frequented heavily at lunchtime by executives from surrounding offices, but at night they take on a more sedate
mood. The fixed-price menu offers a choice of dishes such as fillet of
halibut pan-fried and served with asparagus and langoustine tails,
while pork receives a sauce of cream, morels and apples and is served
with braised rice. The wines from the Loire are worth seeking out. A
pleasant and well-run establishment.

RULES   WC2

35 Maiden Lane, WC2E 7LB
Telephone: 071-836 5314 Fax: 071-497 1081   £55
Open: all day daily (closed 3/4 days Xmas)
Meals served: 12-11.30 (Sun 12-10.15)
One of the oldest eating houses in London, this is the first stop-off point for many
Americans wanting to sample steak and kidney pudding, game pie and the like, in a
choice of clubby rooms that retain their style and atmosphere.

ST JAMES COURT HOTEL   SW1

41 Buckingham Gate, SW1E 6AF
Telephone: 071-834 6655 Fax: 071-630 7587   **£70**
Open: lunch Mon-Fri, dinner Mon-Sat (closed Bank Holidays,
2 wks Aug, Xmas/New Year)
Meals served: lunch 12.30-2.30, dinner 7.30-11

Down by Petit France is this grand Edwardian hotel with ornamental
courtyard, business centre and plentiful accommodation. The menu in
the Auberge de Provence is presided over by master chef Jean-André
Charial from his own restaurant L'Oustau de Baumanière in Provence.
Chef Bernard Brique is entrusted to cook the well-tuned dishes such
as soupe au pistou, sautéed scallops and light mousse with a citrus
sauce, or Burgundy snails with a truffle and leek cream. Salmon is
supremely dressed with a black olive sauce and pan-fried lamb
noisettes take to a light anchovy gravy. This 390-bedroomed hotel also
has an oriental restaurant, call the Inn of Happiness, where Michael
Fung cooks, while the Café Mediterranée offers a brasserie-style
menu.

ST QUENTIN   SW3

243 Brompton Road, SW3 2EP
Telephone: 071-581 5131 Fax: 071-584 6064   **£45**
Open: lunch + dinner daily
Meals served: lunch 12-3 (Sat+Sun 12-4), dinner 7-11.30 (Sat 6.30-11.30)

In much the same tempo as Grill St Quentin and under the same direction of Didier Garnier, St Quentin in the Brompton Road offers
Frenchness on a plate. The staff are dressed for the part, in long black
aprons and white shirts and black waistcoats, and offer the same good
service. The menu retains lots of old favourites but that's clearly what
the folks who dine here want, as they confidently order pâté de campagne, terrine de canard, goat's cheese salad, cassoulet, and dover
sole or chicken fricassée with wild mushrooms.

Classic French decor that transports you back to Paris

SAMBUCA   SW3

6 Symons Street, SW3
Telephone: 071-730 6571   **£50**
Open: lunch + dinner Mon-Sat (closed Bank Holidays)
Meals served: lunch 12.30-2.30, dinner 7-11.30

When you want to take a break from shopping at Peter Jones, nip just
behind the shop and you'll find Sambuca. It's a great place for lunch or
dinner and offers good Italian fare. The menu is relatively straightforward and features home-made pâté, prawns with a hot sauce, Parma
ham and melon, wonderful peppers in oil and garlic roasted in the
oven, chicken, lamb and steaks cooked in various styles, sole trout and
mixed fried fresh seafood.

SAN FREDIANO   SW3

62 Fulham Road, SW3 6HH
Telephone: 071-584 8375 Fax: 071-589 8860   **£65**
Open: lunch + dinner Mon-Sat (closed Bank Holidays)
Meals served: lunch 12-2.45, dinner 7-11.30

San Frediano is no longer a youngster as it reaches its 25th birthday
this year, but there's buzz and life in the old chap yet. A terrific atmosphere, it bustles with chatting and laughing and charms the ladies in
that old Latin way. The cooking is good and honest with simple plates
of grilled herrings and beans, or chicken served with asparagus. The
prices are very reasonable for both food and wine with a relaxed yet
prompt service - the way it has always been.

SAN LORENZO   SW3

22 Beauchamp Place, SW3 1NL   ❀
Telephone: 071-584 1074   £75
Open: lunch + dinner Mon-Sat (closed Bank Holidays)
Meals served: lunch 12.30-3, dinner 7.30-11.30

After many years, San Lorenzo still remains one that stands out in a
crowd. Its loyal and star-studded clientele, which can include royalty,
love it here and come for the attention and the Italian food. So, as you
can imagine, booking is a necessity and something you need to plan
well ahead. Well-heeled young ladies lunch together here and royal
mothers have been known to introduce their children to the delights of
their favourites, be it the braised rabbit with polenta, oxtail and plenty
of penne, or simply cooked fish.

- Still an all time favourite for many.

SAN MARTINO   SW3

103 Walton Street, SW3 2HP
Telephone: 071-589 3833   **£60**
Open: lunch + dinner daily (closed 10 days Xmas, 4 days Easter)
Meals served: lunch 12-3, dinner 6.30-11.30

Long established, this busy trattoria is run by Costanzo Martinucci and
family. Some of the herbs, vegetables and other ingredients are home-
grown by the owner himself. Out of the kitchen comes food that is
billed as Tuscan: there's a large selection of prosciutto ham served in
various ways, fantastic fish soup, spaghetti San Martino (fine spaghetti
cooked in a paper bag with fish and some secret ingredients – a house
speciality), and linguine al salmone. If choosing is hard there's usually
a `chef recommends' section such as wild boar sausages or fresh
papaya filled with white crab meat.

SANDRINI   SW3

260 Brompton Road, SW3 2AS
Telephone: 071-584 1724   £55
Open: lunch + dinner daily
Meals served: lunch 12-3, dinner 7-11.30
An affable menu and restaurant complete with risotto, grilled and sauced meats and
fish with garlic and tomatoes. Modern and traditional dishes for a diverse clientele.

SANTINI   SW1

29 Ebury Street, SW1W 0NZ
Telephone: 071-730 4094 Fax: 071-730 0544   **£100**
Open: lunch Mon-Fri, dinner daily (closed Bank Holidays)
Meals served: lunch 12.30-2.30, dinner 7-11.30 (Sun 7-11)

Without a doubt, Santini is a classy restaurant and remains a favourite
with business people for lunchtime têtes-à-têtes and the theatre-goers
in the evenings. Service bustles along nicely, it's friendly and
courteous and there's always a good buzzy atmosphere here. The
menu has some old favourites - insalata di mare, grilled vegetable platter, osso bucco Milanese and pastas - punctuated with some more
unusual dishes: stuffed courgette flowers, squid cooked Venetian-style
with polenta, or spicy Italian sausages with cannellini beans.

SAS PORTMAN HOTEL   W1

22 Portman Square, W1H 9FL
Telephone: 071-486 5844 Fax: 071-935 0537   **£60**
Open: lunch Sun-Fri, dinner Mon-Sat (closed
some Bank Holidays, Xmas/New Year)
Meals served: lunch 12.30-2.30 (Sun 12.30-3.30) dinner 7-11

Under SAS management, this is a 272-bedroomed hotel for the corporate businessman and traveller who has little time to spare, but who
appreciates high standards of service. All the mod cons, laundry service, air-conditioning, stereo and remote TV control. In fact, all that
you come to expect from a modern hotel.

LES SAVEURS   W1

37a Curzon Street, W1Y 8EY
Telephone: 071-491 8919 Fax: 071-491 3658   £70
Open: lunch + dinner Mon-Fri (closed 10 days Xmas/NY, 2 wks Aug)
Meals served: lunch 12-2.30, dinner 7-10.30   ❖

In a restaurant right next to the Curzon Cinema, chef Joël Antunès
amalgamates a firm foundation of French classicism with accents of
spice picked up from his stint at the Bangkok Hilton. The restaurant is
big on style and chic and Joël uses strong bold colours to heighten an
otherwise cream-coloured sedate restaurant. He's up amongst the elite
of London's chefs, with his immaculate presentation of dishes that are
innovative and use flavours that complement each other well. His 5-
course set dinner menu is finely executed and might include terrine of
foie gras served with confit of eggplant, followed by risotto of Dublin
Bay prawns redolent with just a hint of truffle oil, then ravioli of pigeon
breast served with mushrooms, and a fine selection of cheese that
come before clafoutis of red fruits flavoured with kirsch. But it is his
£18 lunchtime menu that is one of the best bargains in town. A young
and talented team that thoroughly deserve continued success.

THE SAVOY   WC2

The Strand, WC2R OEU
Telephone: 071-836 4343 Fax: 071-240 6040   £68
Open: lunch + dinner daily
Meals served: lunch 12.30-2.30, dinner 7.30-11.30 (Sun 7-10.30)

To walk into the Savoy is like stepping back in time, with tea in the
piano lounge and service and politeness from a bygone era. It houses 3
restaurants: the yew-panelled Grill Room under David Sharland's
direction, which caters for the traditional palate offering les specialités
such as eggs Arnold Bennett, grills of sirloin steak and lamb cutlets,
entrées of tournedos and rabbit, and plats du jour of beef wellington on
Wednesdays, Norfolk goose on Fridays. The River Room which boasts
some of the finest views of the Thames is where executive chef Anton
Edelmann shows his proficiency with both à la carte and fixed menus
of consistently good dishes such as thinly-sliced marinated
langoustines with caviar, fillets of veal, kidney and brains in a
coriander flavoured sauce with vegetable tagliatelle and crepes
suzette. Anton continues to amaze, for even with restaurants of this
calibre and a hotel of this size, his banqueting remains some of the
best in town. A new evening fixed-price menu includes a well chosen
glass of wine at each course and is well worth sampling. Moving on up
to Upstairs at the Savoy, the mood is more informal and set in a wonderful position to watch the comings and goings of the courtyard. The
menu here offers seafood in all manner of ways from roe with sour
cream, blinis and red onion, shellfish platters and fish soups with sour-
dough bread. This year sees the addition to the hotel of the stunning
new Fitness Gallery at the top of the historic Savoy theatre, making it
the first hotel in London to boast a rooftop swimming pool.

The Melba toast served here is like no
other - the Savoy assure us that theirs
is the right one!

SCALINI   SW3

loyal lunch trade with a glitzy show-biz crowd in the evening.

1-3 Walton Street, SW3 2JD
Telephone: 071-225 2301
Open: lunch + dinner daily (closed 3 days Xmas, 2 days Easter)
Meals served: lunch 12.30-3, dinner 7-12

£60

This is a smart, informal and jolly restaurant where the waiters are keen to please and aren't short of recommendations. A dish of giant green olives and chopped tomatoes flavoured with fresh basil and olive oil (served with toasted baguette) might be offered while you peruse the menu. The conservatory at the back of the restaurant lends a summery atmosphere to the place. Also recommended is wide tagliatelle with artichoke sauce, and sea bass with cream and chopped herbs, artfully filleted and served with fried cubed potatoes, green beans and broccoli al dente. The desserts are limited but offer a tempting and airy tiramisu, chocolate cake, or oranges in caramel. Finish with an excellent espresso.

SCOTT'S RESTAURANT   W1

20 Mount Street, W1Y 6HE
Telephone: 071-629 5248 Fax: 071-491 2477
Open: lunch Mon-Fri, dinner Mon-Sat (closed Bank\
Holidays, Xmas-New Year)
Meals served: lunch 12-2.45, dinner 6-10.45

£70

Scott's is classy and clubby, with a well-respected history. Adjoining the main restaurant, there is a quick-service oyster bar, frequented by a slightly younger crowd or those wanting a lighter or quicker meal. It has built up a loyal clientele, admirers of the traditional British fish dishes in which it specialises. It's a hard choice between oysters – Imperials or Scott's specials - mussels in champagne, lobster and langoustine bisque, papaya and crab salad, smoked eel, avocado and bacon salad, caviar with smoked salmon, blinis and sour cream, to name but a few of the starters. There are some alternatives to fish but dishes such as spiced curry of fruits de mer, roast king scallop, red mullet, turbot and sea bass, lobster, grilled or thermidor are what this place knows how to prepare best.

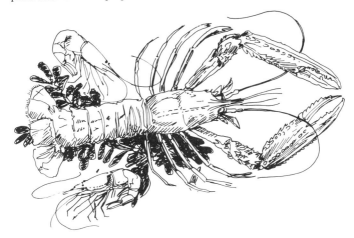

SHEEKEY'S RESTAURANT WC2

28-32 St Martins Court, Leicester Square, WC2N 4AL
Telephone: 071-240 2565 Fax: 071-379 1417 **£40**
Open: lunch Mon-Fri, dinner Mon-Sat (closed Bank Holidays,
24 Dec-2 Jan)
Meals served: lunch 12.30-2.45, dinner 6-11.15

It's hard to miss Sheekey's with its extravagant, if somewhat faded, painted facade. Inside it is full of theatre-goers, it's busy and it's buzzing. And the walls play host to celebrity photos collected over the 100 years it has been open. The speciality is fish, from jellied eels and crispy fried whitebait, to salad vaudeville - langoustine, crispy bacon, chives and virgin oil dressing and grilled queen scallops. A lunch or pre-theatre set menu is offered for £16.50. It's traditionally run and certainly knows how to serve the good old British classics.

SHEPHERD'S SW1

Marsham Court, Marsham Street, SW1P 4LA
Telephone: 071-834 9552 Fax: 071-233 6047 **£40**
Open: lunch + dinner Mon-Fri (closed Bank Holidays)
Meals served: lunch 12.30-3, dinner 6.30-11.30 (bar 5.30-8)

The chef and actor team spirit once again comes into action at Richard Shepherd's and Michael Caine's new joint venture. Resplendent with green walls, wall seats and low partitions between the tables, this is a traditional place to lunch or dine. The menu is a cornucopia of British classics from jellied eels, poached eggs with haddock, fish cakes made of fresh salmon coated with caraway seed, to a roast rib of Scotch beef with Yorkshire pudding from the trolley. Not forgetting the vegetarian, there is a mushroom terrine with tomato chutney, or vegetable crumble. Dessert brings out the faithful bread and butter pud, bakewell tart and burnt Cambridge cream. My early doubts about location in the evening have proved totally unfounded and it's interesting to see so many MPs eating here. Some of them obviously do care about food, and Shepherd's is quickly establishing itself as the Commons' canteen. Hear! Hear!

SHERATON PARK TOWER SW1

101 Knightsbridge, SW1X 7RN
Telephone: 071-235 8050 Fax: 071-235 8231 £60
Open: lunch + dinner daily
Meals served: lunch 12-3 (Sun 12-4), dinner 6.30-11 ❖
The Restaurant 101 is directed at the business expense account diner and was receiving a major change in image and direction to a modern English menu as we went to press.

SIGNOR SASSI SW1

14 Knightsbridge Green, SW1X 7QL
Telephone: 071-584 2277 £60
Open: lunch + dinner Mon-Sat (closed 3 days Xmas)
Meals served: lunch 12-2.30 (Sat 12-2.45), dinner 7-11.30
Fashionable, Italian and sassy! This restaurant has a loyal clientele who return for all those old favourites. Extremely busy at the weekend.

SIMPLY NICO SW1

48A Rochester Row, SW1P 1JU
Telephone: 071-630 8061
Open: lunch Mon-Fri (except Bank Holidays), dinner
Mon-Sat (closed 10 dys Xmas, Easter)
Meals served: lunch 12-2.15, dinner 6.45-11.15

£60

In a part of town virtually devoid of decent restaurants, Simply Nico is
a haven and offers an excellent lunch menu of 3-courses with an all-in-
price which includes extras right down to service. Andrew Barber
cooks the thoroughly Nico-inspired and guided menu with skill, and
might offer fresh pork sausages with herbs and spices with an onion
compote, alongside bouchons of fresh salmon deep-fried in batter and
eaten with aïoli and escarole leaves. This is modern English cooking at
its best, remaining true to the foundations of classicism, but pushing
out the frontiers by clever use of sauces and dressings. This is highlighted by braised oxtail on a bed of shredded cabbage or sautéed
lamb's kidneys served with sage blinis. Pudding are similar to those at
Nico Central, with sherry trifle and chocolate tart being at the top of
the list.

SIMPSON'S-IN-THE-STRAND WC2

100 Strand, WC2R 0EW
Telephone: 071-836 9112 Fax: 071-836 1381
Open: lunch daily, dinner Mon-Sat (closed Bank Holidays)
Meals served: lunch 12-2.30, dinner 6-10.45

£55

You step back in time as you step through the doors into Simpson's-in-
the-Strand, not fuddy duddy but classical and conservative, where the
waiters treat you as an old friend but with the right sense of formality
and humour. Although ladies are now admitted, Simpson's retains its
gentlemen's club atmosphere in the dark-panelled dining room
upstairs. Roast beef is really the order of the day, which usually comes
on a plate groaning with Yorkshire puddings, roasted potatoes,
steamed cabbage and a piquant horseradish sauce. Starters are in the
same ilk with Scotch broth and Brown Windsor soups, Dublin Bay
prawns, oysters and smoked eel fillets. If there's still a space afterwards, spotted dick or bread and butter pudding are there to fill it. I
still prefer the downstairs restaurant, where you're seated in stalls and
feel as if you're part of London's history.

ESTABLISHED

1828

S I M P S O N ' S
IN · THE · STRAND

SNOWS ON THE GREEN   W6

166 Shepherds Bush Road, W6 7PB
Telephone: 071-603 2142   £55
Open: lunch Sun-Fri, dinner Mon-Sat (closed Bank Holidays)
Meals served: lunch 12-3, dinner 7-11

Sebastian Snow, chef and owner of Snows on the Green, has now settled in and his influences remain rustic and Mediterranean. So it's no
surprise to find such dishes on the menu as crostinis, Toulouse
sausages, mountain ham, rocket and parmesan salads featuring alongside more inventive terrines, salads of warm rabbit, provençale and
vegetable pistou. Main courses range from daube of ox cheeks with
bacon, gremolata, red wine and mash, goat's cheese, potato and tomato tapenade feuilleté, to chartreuse of Bresse pigeon and black pudding and savoy cabbage with steak frites. Desserts are more simple
and include rhubarb and apple charlotte or crème caramel. The setting
is simple and relaxed with photographs of the French countryside on
the walls. The young staff work hard to make you feel welcome.

SOHO SOHO   W1

Favourite Soho establishment, with good choice, by a well managed & friendly young & friendly team ✿

11-13 Frith Street, W1
Telephone: 071-494 3491   £55
Open: lunch Mon-Fri, dinner Mon-Sat (closed Bank Holidays)
Meals served: lunch 12-3, dinner 6-12

Soho Soho has been a resounding success, the feather in the cap of
the Chez Gérard group. The ground floor offers a place to drink and
snack on Mediterranean eats like soups, salads, pâtés and grilled specialities such as squid with a spicy pepper and nut salsa and French
spiced sausage with Lyonnaise sauce. In the first floor dining room
things are more restrained and the accent is strong - a room designed
with modern panache that has even played host to the likes of Robert
Carrier. Tony Howarth cooks a modern menu which includes pissaladière and pan-fired sardines and main courses of young pheasant
served with a turnip compote and a game jus and estocoficada of salt
cod with tomatoes, garlic and potatoes. Good wine list with some
fairly priced choices.

SONNY'S   SW13

very good local restaurant with buzzy & relaxed atmosphere

94 Church Road, SW13 0DQ
Telephone: 081-748 0393
Open: lunch daily, dinner Mon-Sat (closed Bank Holidays)
Meals served: lunch 12.30-3, dinner 7.30-11 (light meals all day)

£55

Not that it needed it, but this friendly local restaurant received a boost
in June 1993 when a new chef was recruited, Alec Howard (directly
from the Bath Spa, but with a respectable pedigree before that). His
style of cooking, although performed within the framework of owner
Rebecca Mascarenhas' menu concept, is more direct and gutsy than
had previously been seen here, full of intense flavours and drawing
inspiration from all over the world. Contrast the light and delicious rillettes of salmon with cucumber salad and lemon crème fraiche with
the very filling tomato, lentil and coriander soup (almost a meal in
itself). Or very fresh cod, roasted, served on a square of crispy pan-
fried polenta set in a pool of brilliant red roasted pepper sauce, set
against the black bean chilli with corn bread and guacamole. Puddings
might include an excellent deep-flavoured dark chocolate tart served
with Jersey cream, or straightforward Kent strawberries, delivered
that afternoon, if you're very lucky! All the elements that made Sonny's
such a joy in the past are still there - great atmosphere, friendly service, good value for money. Now with a new twist to the cooking, it
looks set to become even more popular.

THE SQUARE   SW1

32 King Street, St James's, SW1 6RJ
Telephone: 071-839 8787
Open: lunch Sun-Fri, dinner daily (closed most Bank Holidays)
Meals served: lunch 12-2, dinner 6-11.45

£80

Cream walls, minimalist decor, and deep blue, ochre, amber and
orange fabrics, create a warm, if stark atmosphere in which to enjoy
Philip Howard's daily changing menus. Dishes are light and uncomplicated yet show a flair for artistic combinations and extraordinarily
good results. A mixed seafood hors d'oeuvres might include queen
scallops, set on a crab and tomato salsa, served in a scallop shell with
miniature smoked salmon cornets filled with cream cheese, smoked
eel fillet on a bed of boulangère potatoes and a wedge of raw tuna, one
side seared and coarsely peppered, and so it goes on. It's a hard act to
follow but the mains are equally well designed and include roast
Bresse pigeon and crisp guinea fowl salad for 2, or roast cod with
black truffles and a range of tempting desserts: tarte tatin, passion fruit
soufflé or an assiette des desserts. The wine list is stylish and arranged
by country, region and grape variety.

THE STAFFORD   SW1

16 St James's Place, SW1A 1NJ
Telephone: 071-493 0111 Fax: 071-493 7121   £70
Open: lunch + dinner daily
Meals served: lunch 12.30-2.30, dinner 6-10.30 (Sun 6-9.30)

Once a gentleman's club, it hardly seems to have changed with its low-key antique decor and predominantly male clientele. It is now a hotel however, with a hushed and sedate atmosphere. The staff are amiable and some have been serving for as long as the oldest customers have been coming. The standard of fare doesn't break with tradition, offering hors d'oeuvres of salmon, oysters and lobster and specialities of the house meaning doused in brandy and flambéed as is the case of a veal brownie, steak Diane and cerises Jubilé. This rather special hotel has 74 bedrooms and suites and its regular customers would not dream of staying anywhere else.

STAKIS ST ERMINS   SW1

Caxton Street, SW1H OQW
Telephone: 071-222 7888 Fax: 071-222 6914   £35
Open: lunch Sun-Fri, dinner daily (closed most Bank Holidays)
Meals served: lunch 12.30-2.30, dinner 6-9.30
Set in its own courtyard near Westminster Abbey. Reception rooms with antiques and ornate staircase seen in many film sets. 290 well-appointed bedrooms.

STEPHEN BULL   W1

5-7 Blandford Street, W1H 3AA
Telephone: 071-486 9696   £80
Open: lunch Mon-Fri, dinner Mon-Sat (closed
Bank Holidays, 10 days Xmas/New Year)
Meals served: lunch 12.15-2.30, dinner 6.30-10.30

Stephen Bull's cooking is refreshingly different and innovative, inspired in its choice of ingredients and combinations and staying one step ahead in terms of experimental cooking. A recommended starter is the twice-cooked goat's cheese soufflé, simple yet executed with precision, beautifuly risen, and full of fine flavour and seasoning. There are fresh pastas with mussels, spinach and aïöli, and jellied terrine of monkfish with provençale sauce. The main courses are no less creative – escalope of salmon, with preserved lemons, pistachios and Sauternes, holds the complexities of sweet and sour, and the contrasting textures very well. Roast monkfish with ratatouille and basil oil, roast quail with sweet raisins, grilled polenta and pine nuts are just a few of the stars in a star studded menu. Desserts include crema fritta, with banana and passion fruit salsa, lemon and pistachio roulade, with coffee sauce, or rhubarb cheesecake and are also typical of his adventurous style. Modern cooking in a modern and minimalist interior - enjoy it!

STEPHEN BULL'S BISTRO & BAR   EC1

71 St John Street, EC1M 4AN
Tel: 071-490 1750   £60
Open: lunch Mon-Fri, dinner Mon-Sat (closed
Bank Holidays, 10 days Xmas)
Meals served: lunch 12-2.30, dinner 6-10.45

Stephen Bull's Bistro & Bar has been popular since its opening in
1992, due not only to its city location (close to Smithfield market) but
also to the contemporary cooking on offer. The black and white, minimalist decor enables you to concentrate more on what the daily-changing, hand-written menu has to offer. As a starter you might choose
celeriac, spring onion and ginger soup, followed by a main course of
tagine of guinea-fowl with cous-cous, dates and walnuts. Then perhaps
round off your meal with iced ceylon tea parfait served with mango
sauce, or try the cheeseboard of British and Irish farmhouse cheeses
with home-made oatcakes. Concise, reasonably-priced wine list.

LE SUQUET   SW3

104 Draycott Avenue, SW3 3AE
Telephone: 071-581 1785   **£60**
Open: lunch + dinner daily
Meals served: lunch 12.30-3, dinner 7-11.30

A little corner of France can be found on the boarders of Chelsea and
Knightsbridge – the staff are charming and the food so typically
French with a saffron-dominated petite bouillabaisse or grilled sole.
But what you come here for is the shellfish, a sight to behold piled up
on a bark trough with plenty of seaweed and ice. Perch yourself up by
the bar with a friend and a bottle of wine and expect at least an hour to
go by for you to crack the crab, pick the winkles out of their shells
with the pins provided and eat your way through the oysters, shrimps
and mussels, or alternatively eat at one of the closely spaced tables.
The conversation will be thick with French and the customers all
seems to know one another but that doesn't matter - it might encourage you to become a regular.

SWEETINGS   EC4

39 Queen Victoria Street, EC4N 4SA
Telephone: 071-248 3062   £50
Open: lunch Mon-Fri (closed Bank Holidays, Xmas/New Year)
Meals served: lunch 12-3
Thankfully, this restaurant remains as always, a City institution for the seafood and
pudding lover in a typical English setting. Remember, no credit cards.

SYDNEY BRASSERIE & BAR   SW11

31-32 Battersea Square, SW11 3JB
Telephone: 071-978 5395 Fax: 071-738 1460   **£25**
Open: lunch + dinner daily (closed Bank Holidays)
Meals served: lunch 12-3 (Sun 12-4), dinner 6-11
(open all day for light meals)

This is the sort of place the Clapham yuppies would go for a wild night
out! This brasserie with an Australian theme actually serves brasserie-
style food, not very Australian, except perhaps in the names. No guess-
es as to what roo skins may be – potato skins with melted cheese and
bacon. Port Jackson seafood (fried calamari and whitebait with seafood
sauce), fair dinkum fromage (crumbed and fried brie with redcurrant
preserve) continue the theme as do Ned Kelly's pasta in a sauce of
garlic cream, spinach and mushrooms, Skippy's omelette and Bondi
bangers. To be fair, the food is good, it's set in a pretty square (some
tables outside) and it's fun.

TALL HOUSE RESTAURANT   SE1

134 Southwark Street, SE1 0SW
Telephone: 071-401 2929 Fax: 071-401 3780   **£40**
Open: lunch Mon-Fri, (closed Bank Holidays)
Meals served: lunch 12-3

In an area short of good lunchtime places, the Tall House comes as
welcome relief. Pasta with a tomato tuna and basil sauce, beef and
Guinness casserole, chicken stroganoff and mushroom bourgignonne
demonstrate the restaurant's market. It's a good place to remember
when you're looking for good honest food and a quick, unfussy lunch.

LA TANTE CLAIRE   SW3

68 Royal Hospital Road, SW3 4HP
Telephone: 071-352 6045 Fax: 071-352 3257   **£130**
Open: lunch + dinner Mon-Fri (closed Bank Holidays, 1 wk Xmas)
Meals served: lunch 12.30-2, dinner 7-11

Stuffed pig's trotters with morels is the signature dish, the original,
and is what you come to expect at La Tante Claire: good honest, robust
cooking, a credit to Pierre Koffmann's undoubted talent. From the
moment you walk in the love affair starts. The dishes are inventive and
strong on technique with a kiss of colour. After the ameuse-geules try
the millefeuille d'escargots et coulis de champignons or the consommé de homard aux épices et raviolis, before the filet de chevreuil au
chocolat amer et vinaigre de framboise or assiette de canardière aux
deux sauces. Tantalising desserts are too tempting to resist: try the
gratin of red fruits under a warm sabayon with ice cream in a crisp
tuile, before the French cheeses and excellent coffee. Service, super-
vised by Jean-Pierre Durantet, is professional and attentive.

THIERRY'S   SW3

342 King's Road, SW3 5UR
Telephone: 071-352 3365   **£35**
Open: lunch + dinner daily (closed Bank Holidays)
Meals served: lunch 12-2.30 (Sun 12-3), dinner 7.30-11 (Sun 7.30-10.30)

Popular with the residents of Chelsea, this French bistro is complete
with red-checked tablecloths and booths in the window, all amiably
orchestrated by Hervé Salez. It's an enjoyable small restaurant that
serves a characteristic menu of petit soufflé, snails in garlic butter and
or a full-blown bouillabaisse. Main courses include roasted poussin, a
rich beef bourguignon or juicy fillet with béarnaise and for lighter
options a warm salad of scallops with bacon. The plateau de fromages
brings a selection of 5 cheeses or, if you feel like being a little more
indulgent, try the good tarte tatin or Paris brest (hazelnut choux pastry
gateau).

THISTELLS   SE22

65 Lordship Lane, SE22
Telephone: 081-299 1921   **£45**
Open: lunch Tue-Fri + Sun, dinner Mon-Sat
Meals served: lunch 12-3, dinner 7-10.30

The south of the river is reputedly short of good restaurants, or that's
what they say north of it! It's when you discover places like this you
realise south London has some hidden jewels in her crown too. Set in
an ornately tiled former grocer's shop, it's atmospheric and not short
on style. Sami Youssef's Egyptian background is apparent from the
menu with falafel and taboulah salad, sitting alongside more western
and classic French-style foods - soups, pan-fried duck's liver and
moules marinières. Main courses follow a similar theme, with horora,
a main course of 3-bean soup with coriander and country bread, lamb
sweetbreads, or ful medemes - Egyptian brown beans, cooked in herbs
with mixed salad, egg and olive oil.

TIBERIO   W1

22 Queen Street, W1
Telephone: 071-629 3561 Fax: 071-409 3397   **£65**
Open: lunch Mon-Fri, dinner Mon-Sat (closed Bank Holidays)
Meals served: lunch 12-2.30, dinner 7-11.30
Basement restaurant complete with pianist and loyal customers who come here for
good Italian cooking.

LE TIRE BOUCHON   W1

6 Upper James Street, W1R 3HF
Telephone: 071-437 5348
Open: all day Mon-Fri (closed Bank Holidays)   **£40**
Meals served: 12-9.30

This is a comfortable French restauaurant in the old tradition. No-one
would get lost in the menu of soupe de legumes, salade du chef,
moules marinières, truite rotie, sauce moutarde, or confit du canard à
l'ail. Prices are reasonable and the food is good.

Grill St-Quentin
—see page 75

TURNER'S   SW3

87-89 Walton Street, SW3 2HP
Telephone: 071-584 6711 Fax: 071-584 9337   **£64**
Open: lunch Sun-Fri, dinner daily (closed Bank Holidays, 1 wk Xmas)
Meals served: lunch 12.30-2.30, dinner 7.30-11.15 (Sun 7.30-10)

Offering good old Yorkshire hospitality and excellent food, Brian
Turner has created a winning restaurant. The menu combines French,
English, Italian and other Mediterranean influences. Cream of smoked
haddock and garlic with dill-flavoured cucumber, a light salad of langoustines and young rabbit terrine with aubergine chutney are encour-
aging starters, followed by roasted monkfish with a crust of olives on a
bed of green noodles, breast of English duck with savoy cabbage, or
poached fillet of Scottish beef with a light horseradish and ginger
sauce. Brian is more often to be found at front of house than in the
kitchen, allowing his bubbly personality to add to the charm of the
place.

TWENTY TRINITY GARDENS   SW9

20 Trinity Gardens, SW9 8DP
Telephone: 071-733 8838   **£45**
Open: lunch + dinner daily (closed 25 Dec, 1 Jan)
Meals served: lunch 12.30-2.30, dinner 7-10.30 (wine bar 10am-2am)

A bright plant-filled conservatory by day brings light flooding into this
restaurant, whereas by night it is cosy and lit by candles. A change in
management has brought some changes, with a new bar found on the
ground level at the rear of the restaurant, and a menu that offers a profusion of dishes from many different influences. You might now see
the likes of goat curry with plantain and rice, a traditional English
cheese pudding with a hint of mustard, classic chicken with tarragon,
or stir-fried pork with saffron rice and a sweet and sour sauce.
Puddings are more traditional, such as treacle tart and ginger ice
cream.

VERONICA'S   W2

3 Hereford Road, W2 4AB
Telephone: 071-229 5079 Fax: 071-229 1210   **£50**
Open: lunch Mon-Fri, dinner Mon-Sat (closed Bank Holidays)
Meals served: lunch 12-3, dinner 7-12

Veronica Shaw is a live wire and runs this restaurant with her husband
as if it was all just done for fun. The menus change from month to
month and normally follow run along a theme which may be historic
but will always tend to be British. In the Scottish month Veronica
rounded up tweed kettle - salmon, mushrooms and prawns, Scottish
collops of veal (1783 recipe), sweet haggis and bacon and an Orkney
hard cheese coated in granary crumbs, deep-fried and served with an
elderflower syrup. Having doubled the size of the restaurant and
redecorated, and in celebration of their 10th birthday they are present-
ing, menus entitled 'The very best of Veronica's'. Acclaimed for their
awareness of vegetarians and the needs of those looking for a healthier diet there will always be interesting options. The selection of cheese
is also worth trying.

VILLAGE TAVERNA   SW10

196-198 Fulham Road, SW10 9TW
Tel: 071-351 3799   £50
Open: lunch + dinner daily (closed 4 days Xmas)
Meals served: 12 noon-1am
Local Greek restaurant that remains one of my personal favourites. Fantastic kleftiko!
Ask for their rosé wine in a jug with ice – then ask where it comes from.

VILLANDRY DINING ROOM   W1

89 Marylebone High Street, W1M 3DE
Telephone: 071-224 3799   **£50**
Open: lunch Mon-Sat (closed Bank Holidays, 10 days Xmas)
Meals served: lunch 12.30-3 (light meals 9.30-5.30)

Walk through the deli and mentally make a note of the cheese and
charcuterie they have on sale so you can buy a few items on the way
out. Move on into the restaurant and take a table, and skip down the
menu, noting the dishes as you go - lemon grass, ginger and sweetcorn soup served with a spicy tomato sauce and coriander to stir in,
fish and vegetable terrine with a tomato vinaigrette, grilled salmon
with blanched cucumbers and sorrel sauce, potato and goat's cheese
tatin with a rich red wine gravy. Decisions, decisions, it all sounds so
good. Whatever you do eventually choose, don't miss out on the
chocolate and strawberry tart, for I am told it is quite an experience!

WAGAMAMA   WC1

4 Streatham Street, WC1
Telephone: 071-323 9223   **£15**
Open: lunch + dinner Mon-Sat
Meals served: lunch 12-2.30 (Sat 1-3.30), dinner 6-11

It's speedy and stylish and it's cheap, and so popular no one seems to
mind queuing to get in. By 6 the queue stretches right around the corner! This is Japanese-style eating in a stark, clean, communal atmosphere. Long wooden tables run the length of the room and everyone
crams in, side-by-side with strangers. As soon as you've sat down
things start rolling fast. Friendly and fun staff order on electronic note
pads and before you blink your order arrives - grilled dumplings
served with chilli sauce, and steaming bowls of ramen noodles, brimming with vegetables, fish, chicken or beef. Three set menus are available - Pure Wagamama, the vegetarian - dumplings, ramen noodles
and raw juice; Absolute Wagamama with meat; and Almost
Wagamama with seafood. Wash it all down with raw juices made to
order, or a designer beer like Sapporo. London needs more places
where the food is this good and at such a reasonable price.

THE WALDORF   WC2

Aldwych, WC2B 4DD
Telephone: 071-836 2400 Fax: 071-836 7244   **£55**
Open: lunch Mon-Fri, dinner Mon-Sat (closed
Bank Holidays, 4 wks Jul/Aug)
Meals served: lunch 12.30-2.30, dinner 6-11 (Sun 7-10)

As an 85th birthday present the Waldorf was completely refurbished in
keeping with its original Edwardian elegance. It opened in 1908 and
very little has changed, from the famous palm court lounge that tingles
with the sight and sound of tea dances in the afternoons to the club
bar, Footlights bar and restaurant. In the latter the lighting is excellent, with high ceiling and corinthian columns and extremely comfortable chairs in which to recline and soak up the atmosphere. You may
decide to order a salmon steak, turbot steak or chateaubriand for two
from the à la carte menu which is strong on grills or medallions of
monkfish with avocado and chablis sauce or the mignon of beef fillet,
wild mushrooms and artichoke. The menu and hotel both offer good
traditional values.

WALSH'S SEAFOOD & SHELLFISH RESTAURANT W1

5 Charlotte Street, W1P 1HD
Telephone: 071-637 0222   £60
Open: lunch Mon-Fri, dinner Mon-Sat
Meals served: lunch 12-2.30, dinner 6-11

The original Wheelers owners, the Emmanuels, are back in business
doing what they obviously do best - creating and managing a superior
seafood restaurant. This year saw the opening of the aptly named
Walsh's (Bernard Walsh was the founder of Wheelers), with chef
Christopher German (ex-Odins) as driving force in the kitchen.
Oysters, dover sole, plaice, scallops, turbot and wild Scotch salmon are
each cooked in a number of ways and are priced with service included.
The aim is to create a mix of classic and modern dishes and present
them in a warm and friendly setting at affordable prices. The oyster
bar out front caters to the mollusc and champagne- or chablis- downer
whereas the restaurant is more traditional and sedate. Front-of-house
is in the capable hands of Elaine Emmanuel, Bernard Walsh's grand-
daughter.

WALTON'S   SW3

121 Walton Street, SW3 2PH
Telephone: 071-584 0204 Fax: 071-581 2848   **£90**
Open: lunch + dinner daily (closed 26 Dec)
Meals served: lunch 12.30-2.30 (Sun 12-2), dinner 7.30-11.30 (Sun 7-10)

Walton's fits the Knightsbridge chic and glossy image well. The service is polished and slick, the food, British-cum-international, shines. If
you have a few pounds to spare between Joseph and Harrods, pop in
and luxuriate in a salmon and brill terrine, home-smoked duck breast,
a traditional sirloin of beef or steamed fillet of salmon with a spring
onion and tomato vinaigrette. The Simply Walton's Lunch is very good
value at £10 for two courses, perhaps soup, salmon terrine, quail and
sweet pepper pie, pan-fried grey mullet, home-made ribbons of herb
pasta; or £14.75 for 3-courses, to include the home-made fruit ices.
Comprehensive and international wine list, strong on clarets and bur-
gandies.

THE WESTBURY   W1

Conduit Street, W1A 4UH
Telephone: 071-629 7755 Fax: 071-495 1163   £55
Open: lunch daily, dinner Mon-Sat
Meals served: lunch 12.30-3 (Sun 6.30-11
A 244-bedroomed Forte hotel, the Westbury has been comfortably designed and fur-
nished and remains one of the best places in town for afternoon tea. New chef Gary
Chappell joins The Grill Restaurant.

WHITE TOWER   W1

1 Percy Street, W1P 0ET
Telephone: 071-636 8141   £55
Open: lunch + dinner Mon-Fri (closed Bank Holidays, 1 wk Xmas)
Meals served: lunch 12.30-2.15, dinner 6.45-10.15
Up-market Greek restaurant with fine examples of traditional cooking and customers.
Not the type of place in which you would smash your plate, but you can order a good
moussaka.

WHITTINGTON'S   EC4

21 College Hill, EC4 2RP
Telephone: 071-248 5855   **£55**
Open: lunch Mon-Fri (closed Bank Holidays)
Meals served: lunch 11.45-2.15

Believe it or not they say Dick Whittington once owned the building
which now houses this basement restaurant. The 14th-century wine
cellar has a wide selection of champagne, French, New World, Spanish
and Italian wines to offer and a limited menu of simple wine bar-style
food from filo parcels of sweet and sour pork, home-made fish cakes
served with creamed spinach, sauté of chicken with a ginger, lime and
spring onion sauce to boneless quail stuffed with orange and nuts.
Check the blackboard for a list of daily specials.

THE WILDS   SW10

376 Fulham Road, SW10
Telephone: 071-376 5553   **£55**
Open: lunch Fri-Sun, dinner Mon-Sat (closed Bank Holidays)
Meals served: lunch 12.30-2.30 (Sun 12.30-4), dinner 7-11.30

The Wilds is perhaps an inappropriate name for a restaurant so obviously exact in quality and service. The menu, however, breaks a few
boundaries and remains innovative and well prepared. The menu has a
somewhat New World feel to it, reflecting the experimental cooking of
chef, Roy Stott, with corn and asparagus soup, oyster and button
mushrooms with mascarpone and grilled polenta, tataki of beef with
Japanese brown sauce as starters, linguine with crispy aubergine and
pesto, rack of lamb with spinach and feta with a tomato salsa and
home-made farm sausage with mash and salsa verde. The South
African owner Corinne Young also lends a New World influence to the
wine list that boasts some reasonable prices.

WILLOUGHBY'S   N1

26 Penton Street, N1 9PS
Telephone: 071-833 1380   **£40**
Open: lunch Mon-Fri, dinner Mon-Sat (closed Bank Holidays)
Meals served: lunch 12-3, dinner 6.30-10.30

An accomplished menu featuring some of the best English food.
Starters include devilled kidneys, split pea soup and Glamorgan
sausages, mains might be parsnip and leek pie, plaice baked in cider,
beef casseroled in red wine and walnuts, or salmon fishcakes.
Puddings are also hearty and uplifting - apple tart, cinnamon custard
and treacle tart are all prime examples.

WILTON'S   SW1

55 Jermyn Street, SW1Y 6LX
Telephone: 071-629 9955 Fax: 071-495 6233   **£80**
Open: lunch Mon-Fri, dinner Mon-Sat (closed Bank Holidays)
Meals served: lunch 12.30-2.30, dinner 6.30-10.30

A long-established institution off St James's, this restaurant has a
strong gentleman's club atmosphere and obviously has a very serious
and loyal set of customers. Good savouries should, according to tradition, be left to last, but I have a friend who always opts for angels on
horseback before dinner! The menu draws heavily on seafood from
oysters, and potted shrimps to halibut or dover sole cooked in a variety
of ways. Otherwise grills of steak, lamb or kidneys are on offer with
vegetables of the season an added extra. This is not a cheap place, but
the quality is unsurpassable if it's traditional and the old school tie you
seek.

WODKA   W8

12 St Alban's Grove, W8 5PN
Telephone: 071-937 6513   **£55**
Open: lunch Sun-Fri, dinner daily (closed Bank Holidays)
Meals served: lunch 12.30-2.30, dinner 7-11

Good solid Polish cooking is invigorated with new influences like sun-dried tomatoes in the cheese and herb dumplings, while venison and wild boar sausages come with an olive oil and parsley mash. A few other Franglais derivations have crept in on the periphery of the menu but otherwise it stays true to form: veal goulash with khuski, zrazy (beef olives filled with dill cucumber, bacon and onion) and golabki (cabbage stuffed with pork and wild rice). Vodka is the drink of the house and comes in at least 14 versions, but if fire water is not to your liking, at least sample a bottle of eastern European wine.

ZIANI   SW3

45/47 Radnor Walk, SW3 4BT
Telephone: 071-352 2698   **£50**
Open: lunch + dinner daily (closed Bank Holidays)
Meals served: lunch 12.30-2.45 (Sun 12.30-3.15), dinner 7-11.30
(Sun 7-10.30)

Find space if you can in this bright, cheerful and colourful Italian restaurant, where the pastas are reliable, from home-made lasagne to fettucine with a seafood sauce; and the fish is popular, char-grilled, baked and pan-fried, preceded, of course, by one of a good selection of antipasti.

ZOE   W1

St Christopher's Place, W1M 5HH
Telephone: 071-224 1122   **£55**
Open: lunch daily, dinner Mon-Sat (closed Bank Holidays)
Meals served: lunch 12.30-3, dinner 6.30-11.30

Zoe continues Antony Worrall Thompson's Mediterranean restaurant theme. It's divided between 2 floors: downstairs for intimacy and upstairs, the hectic café bar for snacks, where the after-work crowd gather. Dulcet Mediterranean colours are soothing and so is the food. Choose from the country, city or café menus: country breads, Mediterranean crostini, roast chilli-rubbed chicken, garlic potatoes and deep-fried okra, available in the café; smoked duck broth with mushroom ravioli, seared scallops, smoked chipotle lentils and wild greens on the city and covered tart of asparagus, potatoes, spinach and artichokes, risotto of spinach with grilled field mushrooms and pigs' trotter with Toulouse sausage and sweetbread ravioli on the country.

EVEN NON-VINTAGE
CHAMPAGNE
CHARLES HEIDSIECK
CONTAINS THIS
MUCH VINTAGE

Traditionally, the best
champagne makers always
like to include some older,
reserve stocks from good
years with a non-vintage,
to bring the blend a much
greater depth and maturity.

Champagne
Charles Heidsieck is no
exception. Except that, in
their case, the proportion
included is astoundingly
generous.

Nearly 40% in fact.

Brut Réserve

Charles Heidsieck

CHAMPAGNE

FOR THE RARELY IMPRESSED

Cantina del Ponte
36C Shad Thames, Butlers Wharf, London SE1.

IT TAKES 105 VINEYARDS TO PRODUCE THIS BOTTLE OF CHAMPAGNE CHARLES HEIDSIECK

Every year, up to 105 carefully selected 'crus' contribute to the making of Champagne Charles Heidsieck. And in an exceptional year, a champagne will be made solely from the grapes of that year.

The declaration of a vintage year on the label - such as the excellent 1985 - is your assurance that only grapes from that year are used. A mere 105 vineyards' worth of them.

Brut Vintage 1985

Charles Heidsieck

CHAMPAGNE

FOR THE RARELY IMPRESSED

Quaglino's
16 Bury Street, London SW1

Le Pont de la Tour
36D Shad Thames, Butlers Wharf, London SE1

Brut Rosé Vintage

TO PRODUCE AN OUTSTANDING CHAMPAGNE, WE ONLY EVER USE THE FIRST PRESSING

Even the strictest rules of the Champagne region allow grapes to be pressed twice, or even three times, to extract the most from the precious juices.

At Champagne Charles Heidsieck, however, we use the first and finest pressing and no other, having no desire to increase the quantity of our output at even the slightest cost to our quality. Whether the bottle in question is a Brut Réserve or a vintage such as our unique Brut Rosé Vintage.

Charles Heidsieck

CHAMPAGNE

FOR THE RARELY IMPRESSED

Le Pont de la Tour,
36D Shad Thames, Butlers Wharf, London SE1

The Halkin Hotel
5 Halkin Street, London SW1

ALL CHAMPAGNE CHARLES HEIDSIECK IS WELL-AGED, IN A CELLAR THAT IS ABSOLUTELY ANCIENT

We have the ancient Romans (or rather their slaves) to thank for digging the deep chalk cellars in which every bottle of Champagne Charles Heidsieck spends at least three years.

The cellars are over 2,000 years old (double 'millénaires') and house many of our greatest treasures, including examples of our pure Chardonnay vintage, Charles Heidsieck Blanc des Millénaires.

Blanc des Millénaires

Charles Heidsieck

CHAMPAGNE

FOR THE RARELY IMPRESSED

The Argyll
316 King's Road, London SW1

The Argyll
316 King's Road, London SW3

Osteria Antica Bologna
23 Northcote Road, London SW11

Osteria Antica Bologna
23 Northcote Road, London SW11

The Faustino Guide to fine Rioja.

Faustino I, a magnificent Gran Reserva Rioja, aged in cask at least 2½ years and another 3 years in bottle. Excellent with all meat dishes as well as fish served with strong sauces.

Faustino V, an elegant Reserva Rioja aged up to 1½ years in cask and almost 2 years in bottle. Its smoothness makes it a perfect partner to pastas, red meats and any smoked meat or fish.

Faustino

FOR THOSE WHO KNOW THEIR RIOJA.

The Square
32 King Street, London SW1

The Square
32 King Street, London SW1

COINTREAU ON ICE...

...VOULEZ-VOUS ?

Les Saveurs
37A Curzon Street, London W1

Les Saveurs
37A Curzon Street, London W1

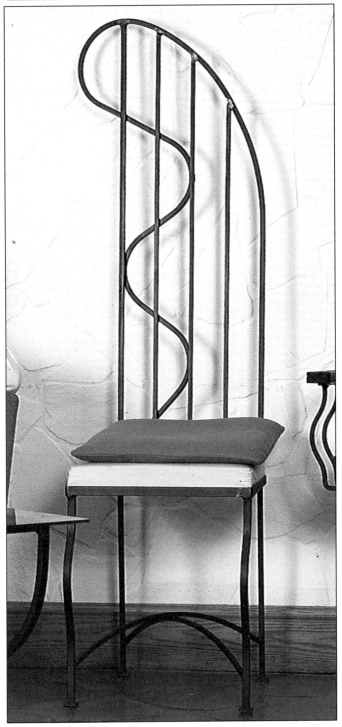

La Sémillante, 3 Mill Street, London W1 .
This restaurant closed as the Guide was going to press

La Sémillante
3 Mill Street, London W1

Pied à Terre
34 Charlotte Street, London W1

England Establishment Reviews

ABBERLEY   Elms Hotel

Stockton Road, Abberley, Nr Worcester, Hereford & Worcester WR6 6AT
Telephone: (0299) 896666 Fax: (0299) 896804   **£50**
Open: lunch + dinner daily
Meals served: lunch 12.30-2, dinner 7.30-9.30

A splendid and gracious setting in the Teme valley makes this a good choice when visiting Shakespeare country. A majestic Queen Anne mansion, set in its own parkland, offers 25 bedrooms enhanced by fine antiques and a welcoming entrance.

ABINGDON   Thame Lane House

1 Thame Lane, Culham, Abingdon, Oxon OX14 3DS
Telephone: (0235) 524177   **£50**
Open: lunch Tue-Sun, dinner Mon-Sat (closed 2-9 Jan)
Meals served: lunch 12.30-1, dinner 7-8.30

Thame Lane House is a restaurant and guest-house with 5 bedrooms and a secluded garden, and Marie-Claude Beech offers some good cooking from her hand-written, daily changing menu. The terrine de campagne au pigeon is a choice from the 5 or so starters, followed by a cassoulet or a confit d'oie, or lotte à l'americaine. Puddings in a traditional French fashion, some with modern interpretations.

ALDERLEY EDGE   Alderley Edge Hotel

Macclesfield Road, Alderley Edge, Cheshire, SK9 7BJ
Telephone: (0625) 583033 Fax: (0625) 586343   **£50**
Open: lunch + dinner daily
Meals served: lunch 12-2, dinner 7-10

A well-informed and knowledgeable team run this 32-bedroomed Victorian hotel, which has been completely renovated, with much money lavished upon it. They know and like their wines in this part of the world, and a lot of time has been spent compiling a good list to accompany the menu, which offers some good modern cooking in the French style, served with very good home-made breads.

ALDERNEY   Georgian House

Victoria Street, St Anne, Alderney
Telephone: (0481) 822 471   **£40**
Open: lunch daily, dinner Wed-Mon
Meals served: lunch 12-2.30, dinner 7-10

A country pub that oozes charm and offers light lunches that are by no means your average pub grub. Alderney Crab, priced by weight, is always popular, as are moules à la creme. If you prefer something meatier there are also lamb chops with rosemary gravy. The dinner menu is larger and includes a platter of fruits de mer. Desserts are special, including a very good summer pudding. Cosy and warm in those winter months, fresh and alfresco in the summer.

ALDERNEY — Inchalla Hotel

The Val, St Anne, Alderney, Channel Islands
Telephone: (0481) 823220 Fax: (0481) 823551   **£35**
Open: lunch Sun, dinner Mon-Sat (closed 1 wk Xmas/New Year)
Meals served: lunch 1-1.45, dinner 7-8.30

As you step off the plane there will be a taxi waiting for you, such is the charm and thoughtfulness that awaits you at Valerie Willis' small hotel, set in its own grounds. Each of the 10 bedrooms has a different view; the ones at the front overlook the sea and the ones at the back look out onto a peaceful and well-stocked garden where Alm the drake and Wellington the duck roam freely. Duck is on the menu but rest assured that neither of these characters will find their way into the pot. The cooking is perfect and simple, with fillet of skate poached in white wine, lemon and a hint of ginger or fillet of poached lamb with a marsala and cream sauce. You could opt for the crab and lobster salad, or the day's catch, cooked which ever way you like.

ALDERNEY — Nellie Gray's Restaurant
Victoria Street, St Anne, Alderney, Channel Islands
Telephone: (0481) 823333   £40
Open: lunch + dinner daily
Meals served: lunch 12-3, dinner 7-12
New chef, Peter Charles joins this popular local restaurant. Some interesting dishes on offer and in summer look out for a good selection of fish and local seafood.

ALNWICK — John Blackmore's Restaurant
1 Dorothy Forster Court, Narrowgate, Alnwick, Northumberland NE66 1NL
Telephone: (0665) 604465   £45
Open: dinner Tue-Sat (closed Jan)
Meals served: dinner 7-9
Small friendly restaurant almost in the shadow of the castle, pleasant selection of dishes.

ALSTON — Lovelady Shield

Nenthead Road, Alston, Cumbria CA9 3LF
Telephone: (0434) 381203 Fax: (0434) 381515   **£50**
Open: dinner daily (closed Jan-mid Feb)
Meals served: dinner 7.30-8.30 (bar lunches available)

Start the day the Lovelady way with freshly squeezed orange juice, croissants, kedgeree, home-made marmalade and mixed grills. In the fells of the High Pennines dinner is candle-lit with a short 4-course menu, simple in style and changing daily. It is sure to keep the wolf from the door with a mélange of pork, apple and crunchy cashews with a light chive mayo followed by cream of carrot and sweet potato soup before a roast quail with a minted plum stuffing or English veal with root vegetables and herbs and oyster mushrooms. A wedge of treacle tart could complete the meal. 12 bedrooms, golf and leisure pursuits are all available at this country house.

ALTRINCHAM — Francs
2 Goose Green, Altrincham, Cheshire, WA14 1DW
Telephone: (061) 941 3954   £30
Open: lunch + dinner daily (closed Bank Holidays)
Meals served: lunch 12-3, dinner 5-11 (Sun 12-5)
Good French bistro set in this well-known conservation area. Sunday lunch is always busy. Try the bourride served with spicy mayonnaise, gruyère and croutons to start, followed by gigot d'agneau with a good garlic and basil gravy.

ALTRINCHAM   **The French Brasserie**

---

24 The Downs, Altrincham, South Manchester, Cheshire
Telephone: (061) 928 0808   **£25**
Open: all day daily
Meals served: 12-11

Fun, lively and popular. The Paris-style brasserie with blackboard, bar and small informal tables is as reminiscent of France as the menu: black pudding sautéed with onions and thyme or a warm salad with bacon, mangetout and blue cheese. Lots of grilling and pan-frying mean spicy green peppercorn butter to accompany beef or tomato hollandaise for salmon and a peach purée with lamb steaks. Desserts feature brûlée, chocolate mousse and crème caramel. A complete vegetarian menu offers 4 starters and 4 main courses.

ALTRINCHAM   **The French Restaurant**

---

25 The Downs, Altrincham, South Manchester, Cheshire
Telephone: (061) 941 3355   **£40**
Open: lunch + dinner daily
Meals served: lunch 12-2.30 dinner 6-10.30

Standing side-by-side with its sister, the Brasserie, the French offers a popular set Sunday lunch for £8.95. It might include a choice of entrées varying from the ubiquitous salade aux lardons to mousse au saumon laced with cognac, strawberries, lime and fresh cream. The selection for the main course accommodates slices of prime sirloin with a rich red wine gravy, shoulder of lamb braised in a pesto, red wine and tomato sauce or cured ham poached in a juniper and honey stock, sliced and served with a wild mushroom and tarragon sauce. Desserts, all at £3.50, are reliably predictable with crème brûlée and crêpes among those on offer.

AMBERLEY   **Amberley Castle**

Amberley, Nr Arundel, West Sussex BN18 9ND
Telephone: (0798) 831992 Fax: (0798) 831998   *A very special*   **£55**
Open: lunch + dinner daily   *place to visit.*
Meals served: lunch 12-2, dinner 7-9.30

With its massive gatehouse, oak portcullus and legends to match, this hotel, set within the walls of the old castle, retains everything historic and typically British, right down to the finest English woven linen, Dartington crystal and Wedgwood china. The transformation from castle to hotel fulfills Joy and Martin Cummings' greatest dream and the addition of Rye and Hastings brings the total of dramatic bedrooms (each named after a Sussex castle) to 14. With much research under his belt chef Nigel Boschetti has created Castle Cuisine. Peppered with Saxon and Roman influences, the menu shows glimpses of the past - pan-fried zander on braised cabbage and garlic, elderflower wine jelly with caramelised oranges and a scattering of pine kernels, and a salad of tender southdown lamb with mustard, spices and mushrooms cooked in honey.

AMBLESIDE   Rothay Manor Hotel

Rothay Bridge, Ambleside, Cumbria LA22 0EH
Telephone: (053 94) 33605 Fax: (053 94) 33607   **£50**
Open: lunch + dinner daily (closed early Jan-mid Feb)
Meals served: lunch 12.30-2 (Sun 12.30-1.30, buffet only Mon-Sat), dinner 8-9

Maybe what makes this place different from other hotels is the Nixons'
philosophy that 'if it is worth doing, it is worth doing properly'. 15 bedrooms have a restful, cool decor with a couple of suites for the more
reclusive of guests. Artists from all spheres - painting, music and the
written word - come here to soak up the special atmosphere, and also
for the range of specialised courses which run through the winter
months. The 5- or 3-course dinner menu is typified by goujons of turbot with tartare sauce or wood pigeon braised in red wine with fresh
herbs and bay leaves. Pudding might be bakewell tart or coffee and
walnut gateau. Extensive wine list with some reasonable prices.

AMBLESIDE   Sheila's Cottage

The Slack, Ambleside, Cumbria LA22 9DQ
Telephone: (053 94) 33079   £45
Open: lunch + dinner Mon-Sat (closed Jan)
Meals served: lunch 12-2.30 dinner 7-9.30
Cottage adjoining former coaching stables offers predominantly English cooking with
all the baking done on the premises. Several varieties of breads and tea breads on
offer. In addition to lunch and dinner, afternoon tea also available from 2.30pm to
5pm.

AMBLESIDE   Wateredge Hotel

Waterhead Bay, Ambleside, Cumbria LA22 0EP
Telephone: (053 94) 32332   **£55**
Open: lunch + dinner daily (closed mid Dec-end Jan)
Meals served: lunch 12-2, dinner 7-8.30

At the tip of Lake Windermere is picturesque Ambleside and this 17th-
century hotel comprises of former fishermen's cottages with roses
round the doors and the lake just immediately beyond. With a jetty and
its own rowing boat, the Wateredge is in an idyllic spot, with fine views
and a cosy atmosphere. A candle-lit dining room is a friendly place for
the 6-course evening menus which might include crab soufflé fritters,
carrot and lentil soup and poussin in a herb butter with a lemon and
mushroom sauce. The golden walnut tart should be tried.

APPLEBY-IN-WESTMORLAND   Appleby Manor

Roman Road, Appleby-in-Westmorland, Cumbria CA16 6JD
Telephone: (07683) 51571 Fax: (07683) 52888   **£45**
Open: lunch + dinner (closed 3 days Xmas)
Meals served: lunch 12-1.45, dinner 7-9

A friendly, family-owned hotel surrounded by the mountains and fells
of the Lake District, North Pennines and Yorkshire Dales, suitable for
lovers of the great outdoors and anyone whose appetite needs sharp-
ening! Golf and fishing are to hand for the energetic or for those
wanting more of a stroll, the charms of Appleby Castle and numerous
local pubs await. The oak-panelled restaurant offers good portions of
reliably cooked food. Expect to see dishes such as Gressingham duck,
and manor house beefsteak and oyster suet pudding. 30 bedrooms are
shared between the main house, coach house and modern wing.
Everything is provided, from sauna, spa bath swimming pool to hair-
dryers. A separate menu for children is available.

APPLEBY-IN-WESTMORLAND   Tufton Arms

Market Square, Appleby-in-Westmorland, Cumbria CA16 6XA
Telephone: (07683) 51593 Fax: (07683) 52761   **£35**
Open: lunch + dinner daily
Meals served: lunch 12-2, dinner 7-9.30

A well-restored Victorian coaching inn carefully nurtured back to high
standards under the auspices of the Milsom family. The 17 bedrooms
are evocative of the 19th Century with period prints and authentic
pieces. They try to use local fresh produce from the Vale of Eden in
the kitchen, and the restaurant menu offers dishes such as a straightforward sirloin of beef from the trolley to salmon en croûte with hollandaise sauce. Puddings include home-made rhubarb crumble,
Mississippi pie and steamed chocolate pudding.

APPLETHWAITE   Underscar Manor

Applethwaite, Keswick, Cumbria CA12 4PH
Telephone: (076 87) 75000 Fax: (076 87) 74904   **£55**
Open: lunch + dinner daily
Meals served: lunch 12-1.30, dinner 7-8.30

One year on this italianate, Victorian house with 11 bedrooms is pros-
pering after the recent restorations – and hasn't it been worth it? Set
against the slopes of Skiddaw, overlooking tranquil Derwentwater, it is
a million miles away from the traffic jams of urban life. Pauline and
Derek Harrison's 18 years of experience at their Manchester restaurant Moss Nook have proved an exceptional advantage here and
together with the notable cooking of Robert Thornton and Steven
Yare, Underscar cannot fail to refresh body and mind. The dinner
menu offers dishes such as chicken and morel mousse wrapped in puff
pastry, or a plate of tempura-style king prawns to start, followed by of
chicken marinated in Thai spices and char-grilled, or pan-fried lamb
with garden herbs.

ASCOT   Royal Berkshire

London Road, Sunninghill, Ascot, Berkshire SL5 0PP
Telephone: (0344) 23322 Fax: (0344) 874240   **£65**
Open: lunch + dinner daily
Meals served: lunch 12.30-2, dinner 7.30-9.30

A fine Queen Anne, 63-bedroomed mansion set in 15 acres of woodlands and gardens makes an ideal base during the nearby races. An
elegant and relaxed dining room looks out over the lawns and gardens.
Chef Andy Richardson creates à la carte and fixed-price menus which
offer good value dishes cooked with great skill - loin of venison with
peppered noodles and mulled pear, pan-fried foie gras with plum and
venison chutney accompanied by warm brioche, and a ginger and
praline mousse with candied orange marmalade.

ASHBOURNE   Callow Hill

Mappleton Road, Ashbourne, Derbyshire DE6 2AA
Telephone: (0335) 343403 Fax: (0335) 343624   **£60**
Open: lunch + dinner daily (closed Xmas)
Meals served: lunch 12.30-2, dinner 7.30-9.15

Ideally situated for touring the Peak District, this family-run hotel overlooks the valleys of Bentley Brook and the River Dove, a majestic
building set in Victorian gardens. The 12 rooms have been sympathetically restored by the resident proprietors David and Dorothy Spencer.
This year sees a new, small, intimate dining room to complement the
existing one - a light and warm atmosphere, decorated in pale lemon,
apricot and rust with Chinese silk prints. From the kitchen comes an
array of home-cured wares such as bacon, salmon and sausages, fresh
bread and traditional puddings and pastries. Sunday lunch is typical of
good English cooking and could offer cream of asparagus and celeriac
soup with toasted almonds, roast Aylesbury duck with bramley apples
rounded off by Callow flan – sweet pastry, an almond, apple and mincemeat filling, glazed with apricot.

ASHBURTON   Holne Chase Hotel

Ashburton, Devon TQ13 7NS
Telephone: (036 43) 471 Fax: (036 43) 453   **£45**
Open: lunch + dinner daily
Meals served: lunch 12.30-1.45, dinner 7.15-9

The best and freshest of raw ingredients are the backbone to the cooking at this 14-bedroomed country house hotel. The ambience is completed by fishing on the river Dart and croquet when in season.
Edward Nuttall is the chef who combines daily menus with flair and
imagination. Whether dinner for 2, a buffet for 6 or a banquet for 60,
it's freshly prepared and stylishly served. Some unusual wines at reasonable prices on the list.

ASHFORD   Eastwell Manor

Eastwell Park, Boughton Aluph, Ashford, Kent TN25 4HR
Telephone: (0233) 635751 Fax: (0233) 635530   **£55**
Open: lunch + dinner daily
Meals served: lunch 12.30-2, dinner 7-9.30 (Sat 7-9.45)

In the garden of England is this Jacobean manor, whose guest book (if
they had kept one from the start) would have included a couple of
queens, a king and a prince. It has been restored over the years, but
always in the same style. The 28 bedrooms and public rooms remain
sumptuous and overlook the estate. The cooking continues in a majestic way, offering beef with a horseradish and chive mousse, duck with
spiced red cabbage and brill with sea bream, served with cous-cous,
olive oil and tomatoes. Good wine list, with helpful tasting notes.

ASHINGTON   The Willows

London Road, Ashington, West Sussex RH20 3JR
Telephone: (0903) 892575   **£40**
Open: lunch Sun-Fri, dinner Tue-Sat
Meals served: lunch 12-2, dinner 7-10

This is a family affair, with Carl Illes cooking and Julie in charge of the
intimate 25-seat restaurant in this originally 15th-century farmhouse.
Some traditional puddings, which might include floating islands and
summer pudding, or a very good chocolate and rum mousse, might be
preceded by simple pan-fried calves' liver with grilled bacon or
caramelised apples, or a supreme of salmon, pan-fried and served with
a vermouth cream sauce, sprinkled with some salmon caviar, and a
turned cucumber garnish.

ASPLEY GUISE   Moore Place

The Square, Aspley Guise, Nr Woburn, Bedfordshire MK17 8DW
Telephone: (0908) 282000 Fax: (0908) 281888   £45
Open: lunch Sun-Fri, dinner daily
Meals served: lunch 12.30-2.30, dinner 7.30-9.45
Francis Moore's handsome 1786 country house. Courtyard extension provides 54 bed-
rooms.

ASTON CLINTON — Bell Inn

London Road, Aston Clinton, Buckinghamshire HP22 5HP
Telephone: (0296) 630252   £80
Open: lunch + dinner daily
Meals served: lunch 12.30-1.45, dinner 7.30-9.45

A simple façade with roses round the door and red brick walls epitomises the manner in which the Harris family run the former coaching
inn. Home to a tradition of good cooking, it has nevertheless had its
share of unsettling times with the departure of David Cavalier and the
advent of Jean-Claude McFarlane. But the latter is now firmly in position having taken to this stove like a duck to water, and is continuing
with short set menus. Foie gras terrine with a muscat jelly or seared
tiger prawns in a citrus dressing with main courses well accompanied
by single-flavour assertive sauces, such as corn-fed chicken with woodland mushroom sauce or fillet of red mullet with basil and black olives.
The Bell Bistro, launched last year, offers a more informal setting for a
lunch or dinner of salads, confit of duck, charcuterie and fish soup.
This former inn with its flagstone floor has 21 rooms in the hotel or
courtyard annex, just across the road.

AUSTWICK — The Traddock

Austwick, Nr Settle, N. Yorkshire LA2 8BY
Telephone: (05242) 51224   £35
Open: all day daily
Meals served: lunch 12-2, dinner 7-8.30
Frances and Richard Michaelis offer good terms for 3-day breaks at this 12-bed-
roomed Georgian hotel with dining-room, situated in the Yorkshire Dales' National
Park.

AVEBURY — Stones Restaurant

Avebury, Nr Marlborough, Wiltshire SN8 1RF
Telephone: (067 23) 514   £25
Open: all day daily (closed Jan also Mon-Fri Nov-Mar)
Meals served: 10-6

A restaurant with a mission, Stones cooks solely for vegetarians. The
self-serve restaurant is open all day offering a selection of wholesome
things from Stonesoups, made from seasonal ingredients and served
with their specially baked bread, to a selection of freshly cooked
savoury dishes. The butter is from a local farm as is the Guernsey
cream. Alcoholic drinks are only available with food but the selection
available makes it worth having an accompanying snack, so you can
try Bunce's Best - a local ale, Dunkerton's cider or Hugh Rock's range
of country wines from gooseberry to plum or strawberry.

AYLESBURY   Hartwell House

Oxford Road, Aylesbury, Buckinghamshire HP17 8NL
Telephone: (0296) 747444 Fax: (0296) 747450
Open: lunch + dinner daily
Meals served: lunch 12.30-2, dinner 7.30-9.45

£85

Set in landscaped gardens, Hartwell has 2 façades, one Jacobean, the
other Georgian. The standards here are exceptionally high and the
house itself of such interest you could spend the weekend just soaking
it all in. Alan Maw joined as chef in June '93 and continues to serve
beef from the royal estate at Highgrove and fish from all around
Britain. He has inherited a finely tuned and excellent team who hand-
craft everything, even down to the petits fours. A typical menu might
include tartare of smoked haddock with gravadlax, cucumber and avocado, john dory grilled with a brioche crust and a Trinity College burnt
cream. Such is the stuff of a great country house – relaxed surroundings, attentive staff, an extensive wine list and excellent leisure
facilities, thoughtfully housed in a separate building.

BAGSHOT   Pennyhill Park

London Road, Bagshot, Surrey GU19 5ET
Telephone: (0276) 471774 Fax: (0276) 473217   £70
Open: lunch + dinner daily
Meals served: lunch 12.30-2, dinner 7.30-10
A 76-bedroomed hotel and country club, including a 9-hole golf course and trout lake.
19th-century house with stained glass windows, slate floors, panelling and beamed
gallery also offers full range of executive and health spa facilities.

BARHAM   Old Coach House

Dover Road, Barham, Nr Canterbury CT4 6SA *This is a place*
Tel: (0227) 831218 Fax: (0227) 831932 *friendly reminescent of £35 in*
Open: lunch Tue-Sun, dinner Mon-Sat (closed 25 Dec, 1 Jan) *many France*
Meals served: lunch 12-2, dinner 7.30-9

Originally a coaching inn, the Old Coach House now welcomes travellers to enjoy good food, drink and comfortable rooms. Jean-Claude
and Angela Rozard run their hotel along the lines of a French auberge,
and with only 5 bedrooms you will be well looked after. This year sees
a refreshed and upgraded dining room from which to enjoy the excellent home-cooked dishes.

BARNSLEY   Armstrongs

6 Shambles Street, Barnsley, South Yorkshire S70 2SQ
Telephone: (0226) 240113   **£30**
Open: lunch Tue-Fri, dinner Tue-Sat (closed Bank Holidays)
Meals served: lunch 12-2, dinner 7-10

Nick Pound has extended his range from small beginnings as a bistro-
cum-bar to a fully-fledged restaurant with a reasonably priced wine list
that gives prominence to good-value, individual growers and estates.
In the kitchen he uses compound butters, salsas, relishes and purées
in rustic cooking with a deference to herbs and touches of soft spices
as typified by fried lemon sole with buttered spinach and lemon nutmeg sauce, or shin of venison with cumin, coriander and celeriac rel-

BARNSLEY   Restaurant Peano

102 Dodworth Road, Barnsley, South Yorkshire S70 6HL
Telephone: (0226) 244990   **£35**
Open: lunch + dinner Tue-Sat (closed 2 wks Sep)
Meals served: lunch 12-2, dinner 7-9.30

This restaurant has made a great impact in the surrounding area and
hopefully will continue to do so. Michael Peano creates no-nonsense
food - pigs' trotter with braised lentils, Tuscan bean soup and terrine of
bacon and potato, saddle of lamb with braised cous-cous, pine kernels
and raisins, chicken with hazelnut tagliatelle or sea bream with roasted
courgette, olive oil and balsamic vinegar all hint at the heritage of
Michael's cooking. Desserts are always interesting with Italian confec-
tions creating the core – iced mirabelle plum parfait and caramel
pears, orange sformato and gateau marjolaine.

BARNSTAPLE   Lynwood House

Bishop's Tawton Road, Barnstaple, Devon EX32 9DZ
Telephone: (0271) 43695 Fax: (0271) 79340   **£40**
Open: lunch + dinner Mon-Sat
Meals served: lunch 12-2, dinner 7-10 (winter 7-9.30)

An all-out family affair with Ruth Roberts taking care of the kitchen
with No.2 son Matthew, while No.3 son Christian and father John take
care of you. Seafood is what you come for, with mussels grilled under
a crust of garlicky breadcrumbs or a chunky fish soup to begin, followed by fresh scallops pan-cooked with lime, soy and ginger or gou-
jonettes of turbot with shellfish in a creamy white wine sauce for main
courses. Try out the melting vodka sorbet or double helping of crème
brûlée to finish. 5 bedrooms are available with full English breakfast.

BASINGSTOKE — Audleys Wood

Alton Road, Basingstoke, Hampshire RG25 2JT
Telephone: (0256) 817555 Fax: (0256) 817500   **£50**
Open: lunch Sun-Fri, dinner daily (closed Bank Holidays)
Meals served: lunch 12-1.45 (Sun 12-2.15), dinner 7-9.45 (Fri+Sat 7-10.15, Sun 7-9.15)

Once home to one of the greatest train spotters of our time, Sir George Bradshaw (the original creator of the railways timetable), Audleys Wood is rich in ornate carved wood-panelling, fireplaces and arches, creating a masterful impression. The lounges are large and quiet considering the size of the hotel, with the 71 guest rooms overlooking lawns and woods. Situated in the original palm house is the striking restaurant. Main course dishes range from guinea-hen and pheasant breast with woodland mushroom stuffing to Scottish beef speared with tarragon and horseradish, saturated with sherry and shallot jus. Terence Greenhouse has established a sound reputation here and the fixed-price menu offers some imaginative dishes at a reasonable price. The restaurant is capably overseen by Horst Stenzel. An extensive international wine list is available with some good prices.

BASLOW — Cavendish Hotel

Baslow, Derbyshire DE4 1SP
Telephone: (0246) 582311 Fax: (0246) 582312   **£60**
Open: lunch + dinner daily
Meals served: lunch 12.30-2, dinner 7-10 (light meals 11-11)

If you had passed by here on the way to the turnpike a mere 200 years ago you could have nipped into an inn for a jar or two of ale and a crusty pie. Today the tastefully modernised oasis for travellers offers a more hospitable welcome, with smoked fillet of eel and quail's eggs, ham hock with mustard and honey and creamed broad beans and a few toasted fresh strawberries with elderflower sabayon to whet your appetite. With the restaurant and Garden Room conservatory to choose between, you shouldn't be disappointed with the variety and style of food available. Good wine list, with many interesting choices. Why not rest your weary head in a 4-poster in one of the 24 well-appointed rooms. Eric Marsh and his team work hard to make your stay enjoyable at this hotel, with some lovely views over the Chatsworth Estate.

BASLOW   FISCHER'S BASLOW HALL

Calver Road, Baslow, Derbyshire DE4 1RR
Telephone: (0246) 583259   **£75**
Open: lunch Tue-Sun, dinner Mon-Sat (closed 25+26 Dec)
Meals served: lunch 12-2 (Sun 12-2.30), dinner 7-9.30 (Sat to 7-10), light
meals Café Max open 10-10

This impressive turn-of-the-century Hall enjoys fine views and distinctive cooking. Max Fischer presides in the kitchen and cooks in an
assured European style using the best seasonal produce. Fish and
game are a speciality on the hand-written menus and can be enjoyed in
the comfort of any of the 3 dining rooms that make up the main restaurant. Expect to see dishes such as home-made ravioli filled with duck
confit and sage or millefeuilles of smoked salmon with salmon eggs,
pesto and watercress. Main courses might include a fillet of beef with a
fricassée of wild mushrooms or duck with oriental spices. The overtones of the orient continue with desserts of jasmine tea crème brûlée
or a rhubarb tartlet with stem ginger meringue and a yoghurt sorbet.
Service is unobtrusive. Café Max offers an informal setting for simpler
dishes of goat's cheese salad, Alsace onion tart or omelette and fish
cakes. The 6 bedrooms are warm and characterful, making this a
lovely and quaint place to stay. A unique and very pleasant experience.

BASSENTHWAITE   Armathwaite Hall

Bassenthwaite Lake, Nr Keswick, Cumbria CA12 4RE
Telephone: (076 87) 76551 Fax: (076 87) 76220   **£60**
Open: lunch + dinner daily
Meals served: lunch 12.30-1.45, dinner 7.30-9.30   ❖

Developed in the late 1800s, but with much earlier origins, this stately
home in baronial style is set in secluded parkland at the heart of the
Lake District and has gardens and lawns which lead down to
Bassenthwaite lake. Enjoy tennis, croquet and riding, the rare breeds
animal farm or, if it should rain, there's the indoor pool and leisure
centre.

BASSENTHWAITE   Lake Pheasant Inn

Bassenthwaite Lake, Nr Cockermouth, Cumbria CA13 9YE
Telephone: (07687) 76234 Fax: (07687) 76002   **£40**
Open: lunch + dinner daily (closed 25 Dec)
Meals served: lunch 12-1.30, dinner 7.30-8.15   ❖

This traditional Victorian roadside inn, set in an unspoilt corner of the
Lake District region, is very well kept - with polished wood, and rambling flowers in the gardens and in welcoming pots before the rustic
porch and front door. The 20 bedrooms are tastefully decorated with
the minimum of frills. Warming in the winter with log fires blazing, it
is also attractive in the summer when the garden's in full bloom. A typical dinner is a mix of traditional and modern tastes.

BATH — Bath Spa Hotel

Sydney Road, Bath, Avon BA2 6JF
Telephone: (0225) 444424 Fax: (0225) 444006
Open: lunch Sun, dinner daily
Meals served: lunch 12.30-2, dinner 7-10 (Sat 7-10.30) (light meals Alfresco:
12-2, 6.30-9.30, Mon-Sat)

£80

One of Forte's finest, a superb looking hotel surrounded by cedar
trees, this Georgian house with a Grecian façade has a mass of grandly
decorated rooms with oriental rugs covering tiled or slate floors,
except in the conservatory where the floors are polished wood. With
Robin Shepherd at the helm, the service is well marshalled and further
strengthened by newcomer to the Vellore restaurant, chef Jonathan
Fraser (ex-Hilton). His skills are best displayed in a pesto-crusted halibut with a beurre blanc reduction, pot-roasted farmhouse chicken
with broad beans, bacon and thyme, charred chicken and exotic herb
soup, and desserts that each deserve tasting from strawberry indul-
gence to warm St Clements soufflé. Some good suites have interconnecting rooms for families with children, and there's a swimming pool
and gym.

BATH — Circus Restaurant

34 Brock Street, Bath, Avon AB1 2LN
Telephone: (0225) 330208
Open: lunch daily, dinner Mon-Sat (closed Bank Holidays)
Meals served: light meals 10-5, dinner 7-10 (Fri+Sat 7-11)

£40

Lunch is now an all-day affair with about 10 dishes to choose from. The
menu is in the typical French café-style – grilled goat's cheese with
roasted peppers, rack of lamb with rosemary and garlic. Lively atmosphere and good value.

BATH — Clos du Roy

1 Seven Dials, Saw Close, Bath, Avon BA1 1EN
Telephone: (0225) 444450
Open: lunch + dinner daily
Meals served: lunch 12-2.30, dinner 6-11.30

£45

Phillipe Roy gained a wealth of experience in top restaurants in Paris,
Monte Carlo, and London, before opening his first restaurant in Bath in
1984. Since then the acclaim has followed him around and the restaurant. A new site under the prominent wrought-iron dome of the Seven
Dials centre (next to Theatre Royal and overlooking Kingsmead
Square) has given Phillipe the chance to return to the city. The first
floor setting provides a spacious, curved dining room that opens out
onto a balcony, and has an elegant, modern decor. A white grand piano
in the centre of the room is in use several nights of the week. Phillipe's
food has taken on a more earthy flavour, enjoyable and inspiring – john
dory with onion confit, stuffed breast of pheasant with Noilly Prat
sauce, artichoke and mushroom casserole with saffron sauce – and
leave room for some excellent puddings! Pre- and post-theatre goers
are also catered for here and there's a good, reasonably priced wine list.

BATH   Lansdown Grove Hotel

Lansdown Road, Bath, Avon BA1 5EH
Telephone: (0225) 315891 Fax: (0225) 448092   £40
Open: lunch Sun, dinner daily
Meals served: lunch 12.30-2, dinner 7-9.30 (Sun 7-9)
Well-kept hotel and gardens, cheerful and comfortable. Set high up above the city.

BATH   The New Moon

Seven Dials, Sawcross, Bath, Avon BA1 1ES
Telephone: (0225) 444407   **£40**
Open: all day (closed 25 Dec)
Meals served: 9-11pm

The Seven Dials is fast becoming a haunt for foodies who enjoy a
smart, modern brasserie with an additional courtyard development.
Start the day with continental-style breakfast and move onto lunch
time with Michel Lemoine's eclectic cooking - rillettes of duck, teriyaki
of chicken wings and grilled sardines. The evening changes pace again
to a fixed-price menu. Extensive, reasonably priced wine list.

BATH   Priory Hotel

Weston Road, Bath, Avon BA1 2XT
Telephone: (0225) 331922 Fax: (0225) 448276   **£80**
Open: lunch + dinner daily
Meals served: lunch 12-2.30, dinner 7-9

This Georgian house built of Bath stone in 1835 stands in 2 acres of
private gardens. Each of the 21 bedrooms is individually decorated,
and there's a civilized, relaxing feel to the public rooms. Michael
Collom is still at the stove producing reliable and sound cooking to be
served in the 3 contrasting dining rooms. The cooking is mainly
French but does draw on some local traditional dishes. It is well worth
a journey to enjoy Collom's food and good service by some knowledgeable young staff.

BATH   Queensberry Hotel

Russel Street, Bath, Avon BA1 2QT   ✤
Telephone: (0225) 447928 Fax: (0225) 446065   **£40**
Open: lunch Tue-Sat, dinner Mon-Sat (closed 1 wk Xmas/New Year)
Meals served: lunch 12-2, dinner 7-10.30

In one of the quieter back streets of the city you will find this haven of
tranquillity. Stephen and Penny Ross, formerly of Homewood Park,
have created this stylish and comfortable 22-bedroomed hotel.
Stephen remains in the kitchen where he continues to turn out his
sophisticated and well executed dishes. As the restaurant name suggests, the Olive Tree is a refreshing informal restaurant, modestly
priced. Oriental rugs over white ceramic tiles, rag-rolled walls and the
crispest linen set the scene for the contemporary menu – scallops
grilled with apple, sweet onion torte baked in spinach and saffron,
aubergine galette with tomatoes and mozzarella, beef braised in red
wine and prunes and guinea fowl with sauce of pears, tarragon and
cream.

BATH — Royal Crescent Hotel

16 Royal Crescent, Bath, Avon BA1 2LS
Telephone: (0225) 319090 Fax: (0225) 339401
Open: lunch + dinner daily
Meals served: lunch 12.30-2, dinner 7-9.30 (Fri+Sat 7-10)

£60

❖

John Wood's magnificent Royal Crescent has retained its 18th-century
elegance and this hotel, set at the very centre, is a first-class establishment in unashamedly luxurious surroundings. The Royal Crescent is
one of the city's greatest architectural masterpieces and undoubtedly
is one of the most prestigious addresses in Bath. Steven Blake's cooking lives up to the ambience. The Dower House restaurant is set in a
separate building across the garden. It is a relaxed, civilized and pleasant place in which to enjoy his traditional skills. The food is executed
beautifully and he has an excellent eye for presentation – try the soup
of seafish poached in Ricard cream, brill with an olive and pimento
sauce scented with herbs, or game with wood mushrooms and
lardons.

BATH — Woods

9-13 Alfred Street, Bath, Avon BA1 2QX
Telephone: (0225) 314812 Fax: (0225) 443146
Open: lunch + dinner Mon-Sat (closed Xmas/New Year)
Meals served: lunch 12-2.30, dinner 6.30-11

£25

Popular brasserie-style restaurant, seating 100+ and is run by horse-racing enthusiast
David Price in relaxed surroundings. Menu changes daily; some outside seating is
arranged in summer.

BATTLE — Netherfield Place

Battle, East Sussex TN33 9PP
Telephone: (0424) 774455 Fax: (0424) 774024
Open: lunch + dinner daily (closed 2 wks Xmas/New Year)
Meals served: lunch 12-2, dinner 7-9.30 (Sun 7-9)

£50

A Georgian-style retreat in 30 acres of parkland. A very peaceful setting with the large gardens providing all the flowers for the house.
Dishes from proprietor/chef Michael Collier's menu include spinach
and snowpea soup, boudin of chicken with tarragon, steamed seabass
on a bed of vegetables with a fennel butter, pan-fried beef with two
mustard sauces. Vegetarians can choose from deep-fried chabicho
goat's cheese, mangetout and fine bean pancake, rosemary and tomato
risotto, stir-fried vegetables with wild rice and a sweet and sour sauce.
14 bedrooms, and children stay free when in parents' room.

BEAULIEU   Montagu Arms

Palace Lane, Beaulieu, Hampshire SO42 7ZL
Telephone: (0590) 612324 Fax:(0590) 612188   **£55**
Open: lunch + dinner daily
Meals served: lunch 12.30-2, dinner 7.30-9.30

Beautifully dressed in ivy and creepers, this is a place for relaxation.
Attractively decorated throughout, choose between the conservatory
or garden where you can sip your aperitif before moving into the
restaurant (overlooking the terraced gardens) to enjoy traditional and
modern cuisine, attractively presented. Decor in the bedrooms ranges
from the ruched to the plain, but all is colour coordinated.

BECKINGHAM   Black Swan

Hillside, Beckingham, Lincolnshire LN5 0RF
Telephone: (0636) 626474   **£50**
Open: lunch Tue-Sun, dinner Tue-Sat
Meals served: dinner 7-10

The riverside garden and old village pub atmosphere of this 17th-cen-
tury coaching inn, set on the banks of the River Witham, make this an
exceptionally popular place for Sunday lunch. A garden menu makes
an appearance in summer with crab and sorrel soup, seafood lasagne
or sirloin with mustard seed sauce. Dinner is à la carte with the likes of
pigeon pie in brown beer with baked vegetables, or home-made venison sausages with red cabbage, apple and a caraway seed sauce. Book
early.

BERWICK-UPON-TWEED Funnywayt'mekalivin'

41 Bridge Street, Berwick-upon-Tweed, Northumberland TD15 1ES
Telephone: (0289) 308827   **£37**
Open: lunch Mon-Fri, dinner Wed-Sat (closed 25+26 Dec, 1 Jan)
Meals served: lunch 11.30-2.30, dinner 7.30 for 8

Trading up and gaining a drinks licence has obviously made all the dif-
ference to Elizabeth Middlemiss, and as a way of a celebration she
offers a complimentary white port or pineau des charentes to begin
her set dinner menu – the rest of the evening unfolds naturally from
this relaxing start, capably cooked dishes succeeding one another
smoothly. By next year Elizabeth hopes also to have rooms to let and
by all accounts this will make her hospitality even more irresistible.

BIBURY

There is some seriously good cooking to be had here.

The Swan

Bibury, Gloucestershire GL7 5NW
Telephone: (0285) 740695 Fax: (0285) 740473 **£70**
Open: lunch Sun, dinner daily (closed 24 Dec-8 Jan)
Meals served: lunch 12.30-2, dinner 7.30-9.30 (Fri+Sat 7.30-10)

Immediately adjacent to the Swan Bridge in Bibury is this romantic, ivy-clad hotel, with 18 bedrooms individually furnished – a picture-postcard setting. Chef Alain Pochciol rises to the challenge that everything you eat is made from start to finish in the kitchen. Even the trout are caught fresh from the river opposite and kept in a holding pen until the diners are ready. You can't get much fresher than that! The set dinner menu could typically read: cream of scallop and garlic soup or poached quail's eggs served in puff pastry with creamed leeks; steamed shellfish with citrus sauce and chive couscous or braised oxtail with prunes and baby vegetables followed by apple tart with caramel sauce and honey ice cream. This young French chef can certainly cook well. There is also Jankowski's Brasserie, where chef Ian Lavering rules the roost. Aided by the young and charming staff in the stylish dining rooms, the Swan is set to make culinary waves in the Cotswolds.

BIGBURY-ON-SEA

Burgh Island Hotel

Burgh Island, Bigbury-on-Sea, Devon TQ7 4AU
Telephone: (0548) 810514 Fax: (0548) 810243 **£60**
Open: lunch + dinner daily (closed Sun-Thu in Jan+Feb)
Meals served: lunch 12-2.30, dinner 7.30-9

Location and surroundings rate high on Beatrice and Tony Porter's Art Deco hotel, unique in that at high tide it is completely cut off from the mainland and can only be reached by sea tractor. It was to this 26-acre private island that the jet set of the '30s reputedly came to play and where Agatha Christie wrote *And Then There Were None* and *Evil Under The Sun*. Noel Coward, Mountbatten, Edward and Mrs Simpson were also guests, a fact of which you're reminded by the names of the 14 suites comprising this famous hotel. It's a wonderful place for week-end parties or for those who just love the sea and everything Art Deco. Dinner dances are on Saturdays so bring your black tie, or for an alternative evening, pull on a woolly jumper and head for the Pilchard Inn (also on the island) for a well-pulled pint.

BILBROUGH   Bilbrough Manor

Bilbrough, York, North Yorkshire YO2 3PH
Telephone: (0937) 834002 Fax: (0937) 834724   **£55**
Open: lunch + dinner daily (closed 25-29 Dec)
Closed (in week)
Meals served: lunch 12-2, dinner 7-9.30 (Sun 7-9)

The oak-panelled dining room, leaded windows and warm colours
throughout, make this is a special place, lovingly restored by Sue and
Colin Bell. The 12 prettily decorated rooms are light and airy with soft
furnishings and everything here is taken care of by attentive staff.
Andrew Pressley cooks in a classical way but adds his own ingenious
twists to steamed sea bass with purée of nettles and rocket and crab
sauce, stir-fry of rabbit with sesame and honey sauce and deep-fried
celeriac, or calves' liver with a crust of brioche crumbs and a sweet
pepper sauce.

BIRDLIP   Kingshead House

Birdlip, Nr Gloucester, Gloucestershire GL4 8JH
Telephone: (0452) 862299   **£55**
Open: lunch Tue-Fri+Sun, dinner Tue-Sat (closed 25+26 Dec, 1 Jan)
Meals served: lunch 12.30-2.15 (Sun 12.30-2), dinner 7.30-10

Just 8 miles from both Gloucester and Cheltenham, on the Cotswold
Way, you'll find this relaxed country restaurant, which started life as a
17th-century coaching inn known as The King's Head. Today, it's an
elegant restaurant owned by Judy and Warren Knock. Judy is the master in the kitchen and draws inspiration from 18th-century recipes,
reflected in menus featuring rack of lamb with a purée of peas and peppercorns and a tomato and mint sauce, casseroled pheasant with walnuts and port, salmon fillet with ginger in pastry with a butter sauce
and a mushroom feast on a buckwheat pancake. One en-suite room is
available for over-indulgent guests!

BIRMINGHAM   Sloans

27 Chad Square, Hawthorne Road, Edgbaston, Birmingham,
West Midlands B15 3TQ
Telephone: 021-455 6697 Fax: 021-454 4335   **£55**
Open: lunch Mon-Fri, dinner Mon-Sat (closed Bank Holidays (open 25
Dec), 1 wk from 26 Dec)
Meals served: lunch 12-2, dinner 7-10

This smart, pale-green, split-level restaurant is a surprise find in a
small, suburban shopping centre. Owner John Narbett's emphasis
over the last year has been to provide his customers with an opportunity for more affordable dining and a broader choice of dishes. The
prices are now more competitive but that doesn't mean the standards
of food or service have been compromised. Simon Booth still woos the
clients with crisp legs of duck with deep fried cabbage and plum sauce,
grilled tuna with prawns, capers and nut butter and provençal soup
with rouille.

BIRMINGHAM   Swallow Hotel

12 Hagley Road, Five Ways, Birmingham, West Midlands B16 8SJ
Telephone: 021-452 1144 Fax: 021-456 3442   **£65**
Open: lunch Sun-Fri, dinner daily
Meals served: lunch 12.30-2.30, dinner 7.30-10.30

Unashamedly luxurious, this 98-bedroomed hotel is the epitome of
Edwardian elegance and is a first-class place to stay, with comprehensive leisure facilities including a swimming pool, spa bath and gym.
Having earned a noteworthy position for the excellence of its cooking
all is not lost in the kitchen now that chef Idris Caldora has been
drawn by the magnet of the London scene. Senior sous chef, Jonathan
Harrison, has risen to take his place. Providence is behind him, since
he has just won the Roux scholarship and spent part of the summer in
France with Alain Ducasse. Expect to see some strong Ducasse-style
cooking in 1994.

BISHOP'S TAWTON   Halmpstone Manor

Bishop's Tawton, Barnstaple, Devon EX32 0EA
Telephone: (0271) 830321 Fax: (0271) 830826   **£60**
Open: dinner daily (closed Jan)
Meals served: dinner 7-9.30

Only first-rate local produce makes it into Jane Stanbury's kitchen,
while husband Charles (who was born at the manor) looks after everything else. Small, with only 5 bedrooms, it has a lovely homely feel
with family mementos and pictures dotted about the place. Still part of
a working farm, it enjoys lovely views of the valley and rolling hills.

BLACKPOOL · September Brasserie

15-17 Queen Street, Blackpool, Lancashire FY1 1PU
Telephone: (0253) 23282   **£45**
Open: lunch + dinner Tue-Sat (closed 26 Dec, 2 wks summer, 2 wks winter)
Meals served: lunch 12-2.30, dinner 7-9.30

Located above a hairdresser's shop this is most certainly an unexpected find. On glancing at the hand-written menu, the words `creative eclectic cooking' spring to mind, and you can be sure of an unusual and entertaining evening. Michael Golowicz's aim is to use the greenest, and as many green ingredients as possible - and that is not just limited to the vegetables but wine too! Lentils, garlic, smoked trout broth, gratin of squid, crab and monkfish with vermouth, duck with lemon sauce and kumquats, fillet of beef with tapenade of basil and grain mustard all have the brain going into overdrive and make immediate choice very difficult. The puddings are nostalgic - bramley apple crumble with crème anglaise and marmalade, red wine and port-poached pears with pistachio ice cream.

BLANDFORD FORUM · La Belle Alliance

Whitecliff Mill Street, Blandford Forum, Dorset DT11 7BP
Telephone: (0258) 452842 Fax: (0258) 480053   **£50**
Open: dinner Tue-Sat (closed 3 wks Jan)
Meals served: dinner 7-9.30 (Sat 7-10)

Good food finds its complement in the best ingredients and here at Philip and Lauren Davison's Victorian house with 6 bedrooms, the two live side-by-side. With a network of local suppliers, Philip's cooking is discernably fresh and can not fail to impress - soufflé of goat's cheese with calvados and fried apple and celery, roasted guinea fowl, the leg meat casseroled with mushrooms and leeks are typical of his sound touch.

BOLLINGTON · Mauro's

88 Palmerston Street, Bollington, Nr Macclesfield, Cheshire SK10 5PW
Telephone: (0625) 573898   **£45**
Open: lunch Tue-Fri, dinner Tue-Sat (closed 25+26 Dec)
Meals served: lunch 12.15-2, dinner 7-10 (Sat 7-10.30)

This is an authentic southern Italian restaurant run by the Mauro family. Home-made ravioli stuffed with salmon, chicken consommé with pastina, mushrooms stuffed with home-made pâté and topped with garlic butter and rolled stuffed loin of pork with tomato and garlic sauce are examples of the simple cooking with strong flavours, and a Neapolitan influence. The decor consists of fresh white walls and pink tablecloths. It is worth noting that on the first Sunday of every month they will also open for lunch, offering a set Italian menu.

BOLLINGTON   **Randalls Restaurant**

22 High Street, Bollington, Cheshire SK10 5PH
Telephone: (0625) 575058   **£30**
Open: lunch Sun, dinner Tue-Sat
Meals served: lunch 12-2.30, dinner 7-10 (Fri+Sat 7-10.30)

Home-made salmon, scallop and herb sausage or mild cajun fillet steak with pimento coulis set the scene for Mark Zambelli's menu at this friendly neighbourhood restaurant. Puddings include classic renditions of fruits topped with a champagne and mint sabayon, or apple and mincemeat strudel with calvados ice cream.

BOLTON ABBEY   **Devonshire Arms**

Bolton Abbey, Nr Skipton, North Yorkshire BD23 6AJ
Telephone: (0756) 710441 Fax: (0756) 710564   **£55**
Open: lunch + dinner daily
Meals served: lunch 12-2, dinner 7-10 (Sun 7-9.30)

A much restored 18th-century former coaching inn, owned by the Duke of Devonshire since 1753. Imaginative cooking from Gavin Beedham - Chinese paper cooked chicken, lamb topped with mint and apple mousse, king prawns fried in cinnamon batter and a warm samosa filled with duck livers, shallot and thyme. Take time to enjoy the surroundings and appreciate the family paintings in the public rooms. Bedrooms in the main house are more in keeping with the style - regal but relaxed, with switched-on management.

BONCHURCH   **Winterbourne Hotel**

Bonchurch, Isle of Wight PO38 1RQ
Telephone: (0983) 852535 Fax: (0983) 853056   **£30**
Open: dinner daily (closed mid Nov-early Mar)
Meals served: dinner 6.30-10

Set in an almost bygone age, Winterbourne is a country house of great charm and historical value. It was to here that Charles Dickens retreated to write *David Copperfield* and delighted in the peace and happiness he experienced within it, with family and friends. In fact many of the characters' names came from his Bonchurch neighbours and still live on in the names of the hotel rooms.

BOTLEY   *Well worth a visit*   Cobbett's

15 The Square, Botley, Southampton, Hampshire SO3 2EA
Telephone: (0489) 782068   **£50**
Open: lunch Tue-Fri, dinner Mon-Sat (closed Bank Holidays, 2 wks summer, 2 wks winter)
Meals served: lunch 12-2, dinner 7.30-10 (Sat 7-10), (Bistro 12-2)

This village restaurant, situated in the main street, is complete with log fires, low beams and tapestry-type curtains. The timber-framed building looks very much like an old English establishment until you get inside and sample Lucie Skipwith's cooking. Delightful, it is very much based on her Bordeaux origins - sauté of St Jacques with Pernod, coarse game pâté, tournedos of beef with shallots, parsley, mustard and balsamic vinegar. House wine is available by the glass or you may bring your own, but there is a charge for corkage.

BOUGHTON MONCHELSEA   Tanyard Hotel

Wierton Hill, Boughton Monchelsea, Nr Maidstone, Kent ME17 4JT
Telephone: (0622) 744705 Fax: (0622) 741998   **£50**
Open: dinner daily (closed Dec-Jan)
Meals served: dinner at 8

Guests are actively encouraged to get to know one another here, and with only 6 rooms it should hardly be difficult to at least say hello to everyone. With uneven floors and beamed ceilings, this is a place of great enchantment. The menu is short and sweet and makes you feel like Jan Davies' personal, weekend house guest.

BOURNEMOUTH   Royal Bath Hotel

Bath Road, Bournemouth, Dorset BH1 2EW
Telephone: (0202) 555555 Fax: (0202) 554158   **£60**
Open: lunch + dinner Mon-Sat (closed Bank Holidays)
Meals served: lunch 12.30-2.15 (Garden: Sun only 12.45-2.15), dinner 6.30-10 (Garden: 7.30-9.30)

Boasting a sea view from its cliff-top position, space and elegance are key features in this Victorian hotel. An indoor swimming pool and two restaurants complete the facilities. New executive chef Wayne Charles Asson joins Steve Bredemear in the kitchen, and together they have improved the daily menu with an emphasis on a fresher style of cooking: try a ragôut of local seafood with forest mushrooms, lamb topped with apple galettes and basil sauce and layered terrine of leeks, potato and roquefort cheese. The food is well above what you would normally expect to find in a large seaside hotel. While this 131-bedroomed hotel clearly has to rely extensively on the conference market, it still retains its grand hotel feeling and individual guests are well cared for.

BOWNESS-ON-WINDERMERE   Gilpin Lodge

Crook Road, Bowness-on-Windermere, Cumbria LA23 3NE
Telephone: (053 94) 88818 Fax: (053 94) 88058   **£55**
Open: lunch + dinner daily
Meals served: lunch 12-2.30, dinner 7-8.45

Christine Cunliffe spent some time at Bath's famous Hole in the Wall
before branching out with husband John to create their own 9-bed-
roomed country house hotel. Here she demonstrates the good
classical foundations to which she has added a modern dimension –
celeriac, leek and chive soup, duo of smoked and fresh salmon on a
champagne sauce and a potato galette 'mille-feuille' of roast quail with
wild mushrooms.

BOWNESS-ON-WINDERMERE Linthwaite House

Bowness-on-Windermere, Cumbria LA23 3JA
Telephone: (053 94) 88600 Fax: (053 94) 88601   **£50**
Open: lunch Sun, dinner daily (closed 1 wk New Year)
Meals served: lunch 12-2, dinner 7.15-9

This warm Edwardian-style house is both romantic and hospitable,
with an unstuffy attitude, good food, scenery and fresh, fresh air. What
more could you want? This is the perfect base from which to visit the
breathtaking Lakes. Its commanding location, 18 well-furnished rooms
and interior make this a haven for anyone who loves the Lakes – or
just wants to fall in love! The restaurant is intimate, candle-lit yet casual. Dinner consists of 4 courses - warm Cheddar cheese beignets with
a creamy, white onion sauce, courgette and cucumber soup, steamed
brill with white wine and saffron sauce with pan-fried scallops, and iced
rosewater parfait with a compôte of fresh raspberries. Good wine list.
On a sunny day you might have breakfast outside, enjoying stunning
views of the lake and surrounding countryside.

BRADFIELD COMBUST   Bradfield House

Bradfield Combust, Bury St Edmonds, Suffolk IP30 OLR
Telephone: (0284386) 301   **£40**
Open: lunch Sun, dinner Tue-Sat (closed 1 wk from Xmas Eve)
Meals served: lunch 12-1.45, dinner 7-9 (Sat 7-9.30)

This is an unpretentious yet comfortable family run restaurant with
guest rooms. The cooking is described as English/French country
cooking and includes home-made soups, or hot prawn soufflé with a
creamy lobster sauce for starters, followed by guinea fowl pie or fillet
of beef pan-fried in garlic and served in slices with dijon mustard,
sliced mushrooms and creamy sauce as main courses.

A welcome find in Bradford - long

BRADFORD   Restaurant 19

may they continue

Belevedere Hotel, 19 North Park Road, Heaton, Bradford,
West Yorkshire BD9 4NT
Telephone: (0274) 492559   £60
Open: dinner Mon-Sat (closed 1 wk Xmas, 1 wk May, 1 wk Aug/Sep)
Meals served: dinner 7-9.30 (Sat 7-10.30)

Robert Barbour must be a fan of Sir Russell Flint for he has named the
4 bedrooms, which accompany this restaurant, after his works of art.
The name of the establishment is not easy to forget, nor are the dishes
that you will sample here. Immaculately set tables offset an array of
dishes like sautéed polenta with lamb's kidneys, pancetta and mushrooms, artichoke and ricotta tart, cucumber soup, ossobucco with saffron rice cakes and hake with spring vegetables and coriander. This is
the talent and style of partner Stephen Smith. Good wine list.

BRADFORD-ON-AVON   Leigh Park Hotel

Leigh Road West, Bradford-on-Avon, Wiltshire BA15 2RA
Telephone: (0225) 864885   £40
Open: lunch + dinner daily
Meals served: lunch 12-2, dinner 7-9.30
22-bedroomed Georgian country house hotel, 7 miles from Bath. A gift to the Earl of
Leicester from Elizabeth I in 1574. English and international menu.

BRADFORD-ON-AVON   Woolley Grange

Woolley Green, Bradford-on-Avon, Wiltshire BA15 1TX   ✵
Telephone: (0225) 864705 Fax: (0225) 864059   £55
Open: lunch + dinner daily
Meals served: lunch 12-2.30 (Sat+Sun 12-3), dinner 7-10

This is certainly a special country hotel, with a fast-growing reputation
for the excellent standard of food and genuine welcome to families that
it offers - deep sofas to relax in and plenty of countryside to explore,
fresh flowers, brass bedsteads, patchwork quilts, Victorian freestand-
ing baths, beamed-ceiling bedrooms and antiques. The young
Chapman family is very much in evidence, along with the springer
spaniels and cat, and when Nigel Chapman says that this is your place
to enjoy as much as they do, he certainly means it. Colin White is the
chef, attracting attention for his uncomplicated yet sophisticated way
of cooking - game pâté with spiced oranges, salmon cakes with coriander butter sauce, char-grilled red mullet, griddled polenta and roasted
peppers, sauté of guinea fowl with stir-fry vegetables and star anise.
Cheese is an excellent alternative to dessert considering the selection
which could include Mr Gould's Cheddar, Cerney, Gubbeens,
Duddleswell, Wensleydale Blue and Cooleeney. If you can't be
tempted by cheese then you can always succumb to pear and sultana
crumble tart or baked plums with praline mousse and almond milk. An
interesting wine list with some good prices.

BRAITHWAITE
Ivy House

Braithwaite, Nr Keswick, Cumbria CA12 5SY
Telephone: (076 87) 78338
Open: dinner daily (closed 1st wk Jan)
Meals served: dinner at 7.30
Nick and Wendy Shill's 12-bedroomed hotel at the foot of the Lakeland fells. Good food, wine and vegetarian options.

£40

BRAMLEY
Le Berger

4a High Street, Bramley, Nr Guildford, Surrey GU5 0HB
Telephone: (0483) 894037
Open: dinner Tue-Sat (closed Bank Holidays except Easter Sun, 2 wks Jan)
Meals served: dinner 7-9.30
Modern French cooking. Concise yet alluring menu.

£35

BRAMPTON
Farlam Hall

Hallbankgate, Brampton, Cumbria CA8 2NG
Telephone: (069 77) 46234 Fax: (069 77) 46683
Open: dinner daily (closed 25-30 Dec)
Meals served: dinner only at 8

£55

This mellow ivy-clad hall, set in lovely grounds complete with stream and ornamental lake, has 13 tastefully decorated Victorian-style bedrooms and offers half-board terms only. Dinner starts promptly at 8.00 and there is only one sitting, so don't be late. The menu (changed daily) is short and to the point, with good use of local produce - roulade of sole, salmon and herbs, medallions of pork with an apple and potato cake, boned quail with a mousseline of pheasant and a red wine and chestnut sauce. Concise, reasonably priced wine list.

Woolley Grange

BRAY-ON-THAMES   The Waterside Inn

Ferry Road, Bray-on-Thames, Berkshire SL6 2AT
Telephone: (0628) 20691 Fax: (0628) 784710   £130
Open: lunch Wed-Sun, dinner Tue-Sun (closed Bank
Holidays, Xmas-end Jan, also dinner Sun in winter)
Meals served: lunch 12-2 (Sun 12-3), dinner 7-10

The Waterside brings a new meaning to the phrase 'At Home with the
Roux Brothers'. There is only Michel here since Albert is in London,
but in Bray you can reside in sheer, unadulterated luxury surrounded
on all sides by everything that the Rouxs embody. Six bedrooms maintain exclusivity but for the more reclusive amongst us the River
Cottage would be ideal - sheer bliss, hidden from the rest of the world,
dining on pavé of sea bass brushed with tapenade and accompanied by
grilled vegetables or a tender, sweet lamb chop glazed with parmesan
and sage served with a gateau of ratatouille with a white wine and sage
sauce. However, the majority want - and have - the opportunity of
dining in the glorious peach coloured room with its terrace and views
of the Thames. Choose the `menu exceptionnel' which gives a greater
variety of dishes but in smaller portions, more courses and thus a good
chance to sample more but at about the same outlay. At the Waterside
you really get your just desserts, for Michel is an acclaimed pâtissier
and this course is always a highlight. International and comprehensive
wine list, well selected. The front of house magicians glide professionally around the room giving helpful and informative advice and when
they recommend a dish, you know they speak from first-hand experience, having been allowed to taste it themselves beforehand. The star
performer in the kitchen maintains the ability to be consistent but still
inspire with new dishes.

BRIDPORT   Riverside Restaurant

West Bay, Bridport, Dorset DT6 4EZ   *Table service is*
Telephone: (0308) 22011   *now the order of* £35
Open: lunch Tue-Sun, dinner Tue-Sat   *the day -*
Meals served: lunch 10.30-3 (Sat+Sun 10.30-4), dinner 6.30-8.30

At the height of the summer season, you are going to have to wait to
get in, so take a book if you are a serious fish lover. The menu is mostly fish and shellfish, fresher than fresh and simply cooked - stuffed
clams, local Dorset oysters, warm salad of scallops, grilled john dory
with onion and cream sauce, baked brill Greek-style, poached turbot,
hake with provençale sauce or skate in black butter, all in good-sized
portions. A far better option than fish and chips of the more conven-
tional kind, though some main courses do come with chips. New or
sautéed potatoes or a light salad are also available. Even the local fishermen come here to eat! Opening hours can extend in the high season
to accommodate everybody. Reasonably priced wine list with some
good New World choices.

*-see you in the summer
Arthur & Jan.*

BRIGHTLING   Jack Fuller's

Oxley's Green, Brightling, Nr Robertsbridge, East Sussex TN32 5HD
Telephone: (042 482) 212   **£25**
Open: lunch Wed-Sun, dinner Wed-Sat
Meals served: lunch 12-3 (Sun 12-4), dinner 7-11

Once you find this place (it's easy to miss), you'll be delighted by its
jolly atmosphere, exemplified and encouraged by the owners. A former pub, it has been turned into a country restaurant by Roger and
Shirl Berman. The menu majors on main courses and nostalgic puds,
served in serious portions. Flaky pies, savoury puddings and
casseroles are the backbone of the menu. There are some starters but
be warned, when you see the size of what is to come you may need to
think twice before ordering one!

BRIGHTON   Browns

3-4 Duke Street, Brighton, East Sussex BN1 1AH
Telephone: (0273) 323501 Fax: (0273) 327427   £35
Open: all day daily (closed 25 Dec)
Meals served: 11am-11.30pm (Sun + Bank Holidays 12-11.30)
Jeremy Mogford's original and ultra-busy, good-value brasserie near the Lanes.
Breakfast through to tea and dinner.

BRIGHTON   Grand Hotel

King's Road, Brighton, East Sussex BN1 2FW
Telephone: (0273) 321188 Fax: (0273) 202694   **£65**
Open: lunch + dinner daily
Meals served: lunch 12-2, dinner 7-10

With 200 bedrooms, the Grand has established itself in the leisure and
conference market and - a nice touch - has some rooms designated for
executive ladies. Enjoy early morning pastries in the hotel lounge or
rendezvous in the elegant Victoria bar before supper. If you're looking
for scones and tea at around 4pm, head for the conservatory which
overlooks the seafront. The elegant dining room offers mainly traditional style dishes with one or two surprises. Complete with its own
health club and night club, you can see why it rates highly with the
conference and business trade.

Brighton Pavilion

BRIGHTON   Le Grandgousier

---

15 Western Street, Brighton, East Sussex BN1 2PG
Telephone: (0273) 772005   **£30**
Open: lunch Sun-Fri, dinner Mon-Sat (closed 23 Dec-2 Jan)
Meals served: lunch 12.30-2 (Sun 12.30-4), dinner 7.30-9.30

At the Hove end of town, you will discover the kind of French restaurant you sometimes find in a rural French town, and this one has been
going strong in Britain for years. Lewis and Gaye Harris try personally
to greet every customer, in the same way that they have done for the
last 14 years. This is not a place for twosomes, tables are for 4 or more,
so couples will share tables. The set menu is the main point of coming
and it consists of a vast basket of crudités with just-made garlic mayonnaise, lentil salad and bread, and the plat-du-jour will be explained to
you or, if that isn't what you were looking for, you can have some fillets
of trout. Take your pick from 3 desserts, or the ripest brie. It's
amazingly good value and has to be sampled to be believed.

BRIGHTON   Langan's Bistro

---

1 Paston Place, Brighton, East Sussex BN2 1HA
Telephone: (0273) 606933   **£55**
Open: lunch Tue-Fri+Sun, dinner Tue-Sat (closed 26 Dec, 2 wks Jan, 2 wks Aug)
Meals served: lunch 12.30-2.15, dinner 7.30-10.15

Chef Mark Emmerson continues in charge and prepares a menu that
shames most bistro establishments - tranche of gigot with flageolet
beans, brill with sorrel and tomato butter and duck with honey and ginger are all cooked with skill. The Bistro itself, bedecked with paintings
and prints and the familiar Langan's style menu, make this a must in
the Brighton area.

BRIGHTON   La Marinade

---

77 St George's Road, Kemp Town, Brighton, East Sussex BN2 5QT
Telephone: (0273) 600992   **£35**
Open: lunch Tue-Fri + Sun, dinner Tue-Sat
Meals served: lunch 12-2, dinner 7-10

Under new ownership, there's still the same chef at this popular little
restaurant serving bistro food. Fixed-price menus only include a special
on Sunday. Expect to see coarse pâté, crudités, garlicky snails, lamb
with lots of garlic and entrecôte. There's always a fish special.

BRIGHTON   Topps Hotel

---

17 Regency Square, Brighton, East Sussex BN1 2FG
Telephone: (0273) 729334 Fax: (0273) 203679   **£45**
Open: dinner Mon+Tue Thu-Sat
Meals served: dinner 7-9.30

Paul Collins cooks up a mean English breakfast at this 14 bedroom
hotel overlooking a square near the seafront. Two Regency town houses create this amiable hotel complete with all the extra little touches;
armchairs or sofas, flowers, drinks trays and excellent bathrooms.
Dinner is fixed-price, unpretentious, English and usually cooked by
wife Pauline. Steak and kidney pie is always available in winter.

BRIMFIELD   Poppies Restaurant

The Roebuck Hotel, Brimfield, Nr Ludlow, Hereford & Worcester   ※
SY8 4NE
Telephone: (0584) 711230 Fax: (0584) 711654   **£60**
Open: lunch + dinner Tue-Sat (closed Xmas, 2 wks Feb, 1 wk Oct)
Meals served: lunch 12-2, dinner 7-10

A bright and cheerful place whose menu has similar characteristics. Carole Evans is a self-taught chef, but proves a lesson to us all with her intelligent use of ingredients, colours and textures. Totally spontaneous and original, she creates duck with a white port and Seville orange sauce, spinach soufflé with anchovy hollandaise and smoked pigeon with pickled pear. Puddings must not be missed - try poppy seed parfait with fresh dates and rum sauce, burnt cream with rhubarb and stem ginger or lemon pancakes with strawberries. Wherever possible organic produce is used, and honey from their own bees will turn up on the breakfast table for those lucky enough to be staying in one of the 3 cottage bedrooms. Some reasonably priced wines.

BRISTOL   Bistro Twenty One

21 Cotham Road South, Kingsdown, Bristol, Avon BS6 5TZ
Telephone: (0272) 421744   £35
Open: lunch Mon-Fri, dinner Mon-Sat (closed Bank Holidays)
Meals served: lunch 12-2.30, dinner 7-11.30
New linen and crockery at this popular place. Friendly service, good atmosphere, straightforward menu.

BRISTOL   Harveys Restaurant

12 Denmark Street, Bristol, Avon BS1 5DQ   ※
Telephone: (0272) 277665 Fax: (0272) 253378   **£60**
Open: lunch Mon-Fri, dinner Mon-Sat
Meals served: lunch 12-1.45, dinner 7-10

Cast:- A talented young chef - Ramon Farthing; a capable and personable general manager - Simon Bell (son of Kenneth Bell of Restaurant Elizabeth and Thornbury Castle fame); an agreeable sommelier - Chris Pollington; supporting cast - young staff, sprinkled with one or two older members for gravitas. Set the whole show in historic, vaulted cellars dating from 1796 then add an outstanding and reasonably priced wine list and you have one of the most exciting finds of 1993, that will hopefully run as long as one of Sir Andrew's musicals! You can choose from the 4-course set dinner menu or from the 8 choices of starter and main courses. I would gladly have tried all the starters, but settled for loin of rabbit in pastry, followed by the roast fillet of turbot, then an excellent British cheese board and to finish, Harvey's British dessert. However, as this is Harveys, perhaps those last two courses should be the other way round, considering the staggering array of ports on offer. A superb performance all round. Book now!

BRISTOL   Howard's

1A Avon Crescent, Bristol, Avon BS1 6XQ
Telephone: (0272) 262921   **£35**
Open: lunch Mon-Fri, dinner Mon-Sat (closed 25+26 Dec)
Meals served: lunch 12-2.30, dinner 7-11.30

This grade II listed Georgian building enjoys an enviable dockside
position from which to admire the SS Great Britain and Brunel's
Clifton Suspension Bridge. Howard's is run very much as a family business with a fierce pride about the freshness and honesty of the food.
Hot and cold smoked fish is always a popular choice to start, otherwise
try warm chicken liver salad with home-made bread. For a main
course choose breast of chicken with lobster and a lemon and dill
sauce, calves' liver with blueberry sauce or strips of lamb in a rosemary and whisky sauce. The blackboards declare the catch of the day.

BRISTOL   Hunt's

26 Broad Street, Bristol, Avon BS1 2HG
Telephone: (0272) 265580   **£45**
Open: lunch Tue-Fri, dinner Tue-Sat (closed Bank Holidays, 2 wks Aug)
Meals served: lunch 12-2, dinner 7-10.30 (pâtisserie + coffee from 8.30am)

Andy and Anne Hunt have a faithful following at their small establishment by St John's Gate. There are sensible fixed-price lunch and à la
carte dinner menus which demonstrate Andy's common sense cooking
- home-made saffron tagliatelle with smoked bacon, Barnstaple mussels with garlic butter and a herb and lemon crust, grilled duck with
honey, ginger and peppercorns, medallions of venison with sweet
gherkins and sour cream.

BRISTOL   Restaurant Lettonie

9 Druid Hill, Stoke Bishop, Bristol, Avon BS9 1EW
Telephone: (0272 686456   **£70**
Open: lunch + dinner Tue-Sat
Meals served: lunch 12.30-1.30, dinner 7-9.30

It is well worthwhile finding this tiny restaurant, situated in an unassuming parade on the outskirts of the town, for Martin Blunos' true talent in the kitchen. The attention to detail is stunning and extends to
the daily making of petit fours. A typical dinner menu can include
oyster, potato and leek soup scented with cumin or cabbage and wild
mushroom cannelloni with a creamed leek sauce followed by honey
roast stuffed quail on sauerkraut, its juices finished with white port. To
follow, a selection of fine cheeses or desserts such as apple croustade
with caramel ice cream. Lunch is a simpler affair. A well chosen,
predominantly French wine list.

BRISTOL   Markwick's

43 Corn Street, Bristol, Avon BS1 1HT
Telephone: (0272) 262658 Fax: (0272) 262658   **£45**
Open: lunch Mon-Fri, dinner Mon-Sat (closed Bank Holidays, 1 wk Xmas,
1 wk Easter, 1 wk Aug, 1 wk Sep)
Meals served: lunch 12-2, dinner 7-10

Not far from the Corn Exchange in the old town you will find Stephen
Markwick's elegant but busy restaurant. A set lunchtime menu helps
those business men in a hurry while at night things are more relaxed
and the à la carte comes into its own – sun-dried tomato risotto with
scallops and pesto, bourride of fish, roast guinea fowl with madeira,
hazelnut and apple soufflé pancakes.

BRISTOL   Michael's Restaurant

129 Hotwell Road, Bristol, Avon BS8 4RU
Telephone: (0272) 276190   £45
Open: lunch Tue-Fri, dinner Tue-Sat (closed 26 Dec + 1 Jan)
Meals served: lunch 12.30-2, dinner 7-11
Long-standing loyal following, informal Victorian/Edwardian atmosphere, reception
room on the first floor for private parties.

BRISTOL   Muset

12-16 Clifton Road, Bristol, Avon BS8 1AF
Telephone: (0272) 732920   **£35**
Open: dinner Mon-Sat
Meals served: dinner 7-10.30

A noisy haven, tucked round the back of sedate crescents. The exteri-
or belies the chaotic maze of interconnecting rooms, arches, plastic
tablecloths and candles. Fixed-price 2- or 3- course menus offer scrambled eggs and smoked salmon with Italian bread, cold salmon and sole
mousse with parsley and dill, prawn thermidor, pan-fried escalope of
pork coated in saged breadcrumbs with lemon butter and finally a
choice of chocolate and raspberry mousse, timbale of creamed rice
with blackcurrant coulis, or cheese, grapes, celery and biscuits, all
served by chatty, friendly waiters. You can bring your own wine (no
extra charge for corkage) and be set for a really good night out.

BRISTOL   Neil's Bistro

112 Princess Victoria Street, Clifton, Bristol   **£45**
Tel: (0272) 733669
Open: dinner daily (closed 1 wk Xmas)
Meals served: 7-11.30

Neil's Bistro offers a pleasant respite from the current trends towards Cal-Ital food, remaining as firmly entrenched in the bistro culture of yesteryear as it ever was. There's still a studenty-bistro atmosphere that doesn't seem to have changed in 25 years. Some good old favourites are available, and well worth trying is what they call their `bistro classic seafood soup' from one of the 6 printed starters (there might be another 3 or 4 on the blackboard menu). From one of the 6 main courses, try the lightly peppered fillet of beef which they serve with a cream and dijon mustard sauce. Again there might be 6 or 7 choices on the blackboard, and a choice of 6 puddings to follow that. The whole selection comes at a very reasonable price. It's good to see this restaurant still going strong, especially as Neil, (under whom I served part of my apprenticeship) originally started here with Keith Floyd more years ago than any of us care to remember! In between he tried other venues in Bristol but has now settled once again in his original stamping ground.

BRISTOL   Swallow Royal Hotel

College Green, Bristol, Avon BS1 5TA
Telephone: (0272) 255100 Fax: (0272) 251515   *Another*   **£45**
Open: lunch + dinner daily   *Swallow*
Meals served: lunch 12.30-2.30, dinner 6.30-10.30 *hotel with style*

Favoured by Churchill, admired by Victoria but perhaps more importantly, near to my own heart (I worked in the kitchen as a commis chef many years ago), the Royal continues in a grand and opulent manner having re-opened in 1991 after more than just the proverbial lick of paint. You can dine either on duck sausage and creamed parsnip with foie gras in the Palm Court, with its coloured glass dome and Bath stone balconies; or on risotto Milanese in the more relaxed Terrace restaurant, overlooking the cathedral square – both are sumptuous and stylish. The 242 bedrooms are luxuriously designed and furnished — 24-hour room service is available. The well-designed health spa includes a swimming pool, complete with hand-painted murals and mosaics, a sauna and steam and fitness rooms, use of all of which is free to residents.

BROADHEMBURY — Drewe Arms

Broadhembury, Devon EX14 0NE
Telephone: (040 484) 267   £40
Open: lunch daily, dinner Mon-Sat (closed 25 Dec)
Meals served: lunch 12-2, dinner 7-10

Nigel and Kirstin Burge have created a rustic paradise with a restaurant that incorporates stylish yet simple cooking that majors on fish. The menu for the day is written up on blackboards and may offer gravadlax with dill and mustard sauce, Scottish salmon with sorrel butter, turbot hollandaise or red mullet with garlic. Ploughmans lunches, soups of the day and various English puds are also available. The inglenook fireplaces, piles of old magazines, and artefacts are all in keeping with this 15th-century building.

BROADWAY — Collin House

Collin Lane, Broadway, Hereford & Worcester WR12 7PB
Telephone: (0386) 858354   £55
Open: lunch + dinner daily (closed)
Meals served: lunch 12-1.30, dinner 7-9

A characterful, 16th-century, 7-bedroomed Cotswold stone house set amongst banks of trees. Owners John and Judith Mills are intent on maintaining an easy-going and cheerful atmosphere in their candle-lit restaurant with beamed ceiling where they periodically host fine wine dinners. It's a perfect setting for their specialities such as duck, beef and venison pie and casserole of oxtail.

BROADWAY — Dormy House

Willersey Hill, Broadway, Hereford & Worcester WR12 7LF
Telephone: (0386) 852711 Fax: (0386) 858636   £50
Open: lunch Sun-Fri, dinner daily (closed 3 days Xmas)
Meals served: lunch 12.30-2 (Sun 12.30-2.30), dinner 7.30-9.30
(Fri+Sat 7-9.30, Sun 7.30-9)

Privately-owned, 50-bedroomed converted 17th-century farmhouse with beams, exposed stonework and tiled floors. Eat in the conservatory or dining room. Conference and banqueting facilities.

BROADWAY — Hunters Lodge

High Street, Broadway, Hereford & Worcester WR12 7DT
Telephone: (0386) 853247   **£35**
Open: lunch Sat+Sun, dinner Wed-Sat (closed 3 wks Aug)
Meals served: lunch 12.30-2, dinner 7.30-10

Repeat business is always a good sign and here it is more than likely the result of the welcome you receive from hosts Kurt and Dottie Friedli. The menu is short and unadorned but refreshing none-the-less: Vale of Evesham asparagus with melted butter, boned and roasted quail in a cider cream, pan-fried monkfish with herbs and courgettes and herb crusted lamb. A selection of half bottles is included on the principally French wine list. Take your pre-lunch drinks in the garden on a summer's day. This friendly restaurant seems to have been here for more years than I can remember.

BROADWAY — Lygon Arms

High Street, Broadway, Hereford & Worcester WR12 7DU
Telephone: (0386) 852255 Fax: (0386) 858611   **£70**
Open: lunch + dinner daily (closed 2 wks Jan)
Meals served: lunch 12.30-2, dinner 7-9.15

With a clientèle that spans the ages from Cromwell and Charles I, this is a very English hotel with 65 bedrooms and old-world charm, plenty of creaking floor boards and tales to tell. Steeped in history, the rooms are finished with wood panelling, vaulted ceilings and in some bedrooms, beams. The atmosphere in the Great Hall, with its 17th-century minstrels' gallery, is very traditional - roaring log fire, flickering candlelight and tables set with fine china and crystal. Clive Howe offers some of the best traditional cooking with touches of modernity such as braised faggots of venison with beetroot and onion sauce, beef glazed with horseradish and meat marrow crust, smoked oxtail broth with woodland mushrooms and a rack of lamb with minted cracked wheat and lentil sauce. Good wine list at reasonable prices. A new country club complete with gym and pool brings this 16th-century coaching inn bang up to date.

BROCKENHURST — Le Poussin

The Courtyard, Brookley Road, Brockenhurst, Hampshire
SO42 7RB
Telephone: (0590) 23063 Fax: (0590) 22912 **£75**
Open: lunch Wed-Sun, dinner Wed-Sat (closed 2 wks Jan)
Meals served: lunch 12-2, dinner 7-10.30

[handwritten: Alex Aitken has geared his cooking & menu just right for his market.]

Chef/patron Alex Aitken works single-handedly in the kitchen while
his wife Caroline runs front of house - and his cooking is better than
ever. The emphasis is on wild local produce so expect to see a plethora
of wild mushrooms in his dishes. A typical menu includes the likes of
pigeon char-grilled but left rare, lamb cooked in the French way and
served with aubergines and peppers or a rare haunch of venison with
creamed cheese potato. The pièce de résistance is his rendezvous of
seafood which is a fillet of bass and sea trout in olive oil, and fruits of
the forest which is wild forest rabbit, pigeon and venison in a rich port
sauce. Simple in presentation, his cooking allows all the natural
flavours to come forward and is complemented by a fine wine list.
Service is correct and formal in a courtyard setting at this elegant
country restaurant.

BROCKENHURST — Rhinefield House Hotel

Rhinefield Road, Brockenhurst, Hampshire SO42 7QB
Telephone: (0590) 22922 Fax: (0590) 22800 **£40**
Open: lunch Sun-Fri, dinner daily
Meals served: lunch 12.30-2, dinner 7.30-10

A jewel in the New Forest, this is a splendid neo-Elizabethan home
reached by a long ornamental drive bordered by rhododendrons and
redwood trees. Tranquillity presides over this 34-bedroomed Virgin-
owned hotel, with extravagant and fascinating architecture both inside
and out: a dramatic setting.

BROMSGROVE — Grafton Manor

Grafton Lane, Bromsgrove, Hereford & Worcester B61 7HA
Telephone: (0527) 579007 Fax: (0527) 575221 **£65**
Open: lunch Sun-Fri, dinner daily
Meals served: lunch 12.30-1.45, dinner 7.30-9 (Sat 7.30-9.30, Sun at 7.30)

Rich in history (it was apparently from here that the Gunpowder Plot
was hatched), this hotel is also rich in allure and surroundings.
Beautifully kept gardens produce many of the herbs that are to be
seen in Simon Morris's English style of cooking. Quite distinctive in
his approach, his menu is like a guided tour of his formal herb garden -
salmon infused with tarragon and a wild mushroom sauce, tomato and
rosemary terrine, lamb's liver cooked pink served with green peppercorn sauce and a tomato, thyme and sausage mousse. A small boardroom has recently been completed. A charming hotel with lived-in
appeal.

BROUGHTON   Broughton Park

418 Garstang Road, Broughton, Nr Preston, Lancashire PR3 5JB
Telephone: (0772) 864087 Fax: (0772) 861728   **£35**
Open: lunch Sun-Fri, dinner daily
Meals served: lunch 12-2, dinner 7-10 (Sun 7-9.30)

A mainstream business and conference hotel with 98 bedrooms, this is
conveniently located just off the M6 in a handsome red-brick manor
house. The interior is modern and functional but the facilities available
are extensive with squash courts, swimming pool, spa pool, fitness stu-
dio and sauna. Attentive service and competent cooking.

BROXTED   Whitehall

Church End, Broxted, Essex CM6 2BZ
Telephone: (0279) 850603 Fax: (0279) 850385   **£75**
Open: lunch Sun-Fri, dinner daily (closed 26-30 Dec)
Meals served: lunch 12.30-2, dinner 7.30-9.30 (Sun 7.30-8.30)

Care and attention to detail are certainly to be found throughout the
Keane family's East Anglian hotel. The wonderful walled Elizabethan
garden echoes the charm and tranquillity of the place, only overlooked
by the village church and lovingly restored throughout. The fabulous
timbered ceiling of the dining room sets the scene for Paul Flavell's
cooking - salad of poached egg, black pudding and smoked cheese,
steamed sea bass with spinach and tomato followed by a selection of
British and French cheese. An excellent wine list.

BRUTON   Claire de Lune Brasserie

2-4 High Street, Bruton, Somerset BA10 0EQ
Telephone: (0749) 813395   £40
Open: lunch Sun, dinner Tue-Sat (closed 2 wks Jan)
Meals served: lunch 12-2, dinner 7-10
Brasserie with 3 rooms, homely decor, straightforward rustic food, good portions.

BRUTON   Truffles Restaurant

95 High Street, Bruton, Somerset BA10 0AR
Telephone: (0749) 812255   **£45**
Open: lunch Tue-Sun, dinner Tue-Sat
Meals served: lunch 12-2.30, dinner 7-9.30

The small front room of a cottage is devoted to well presented, good
value French cooking - cassoulet, smoked fish, savoury tarts and
home-made soups. A loyal local following makes this a great find in the
middle of the countryside.

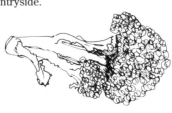

BUCKLAND   Buckland Manor

Buckland, Nr Broadway, Hereford & Worcester WR12 7LY
Telephone: (0386) 852626 Fax: (0386) 853557   **£70**
Open: lunch + dinner daily
Meals served: lunch 12.30-2, dinner 7.30-9

A delightful manor of Cotswold stone lies in a secluded and peaceful setting. The house with 11 bedrooms has real character with antiques and portraits throughout. Housekeeping under the eye of Nigel Power is friendly and willing while the restaurant offers Martyn Pearn's lavish array of well executed dishes such as pithiviers of scallops with chive and caviar sauce, galantine of foie gras, pistachio and truffle or chicken filled with purée of spring onions shrouded in puff pastry and complete with added zing when served with ginger juice. Very good wine list.

BURFORD   Bay Tree

Sheep Street, Burford, Oxfordshire OX8 4LW
Tel: (0993) 822791 Fax: (0993) 823008
Open: lunch + dinner daily
Meals served: lunch 12-2, dinner 6.30-9.30 (Sun 6.30-8.30)

This charming ivy-clad hotel, formerly home of Elizabeth I's Lord Chief Baron of the Exchequer Sir Lawrence Tanfield, is set in the picturesque Cotswold village of Burford. Recently refurbished, the Bay Tree retains much of its heritage - some of the original Tudor flagstones remain, along with exposed oak beams and even 4 of the original 4-poster beds, reputedly never moved from the building. All of the 23 bedrooms are comfortably furnished and successfully combine the old with the new. The terraced garden is a delightful place to enjoy a cool drink in the summer, surrounded as it is by ancient apple trees, plant pots and grey Cotswold stone. In the restaurant both à la carte and table d'hote menus are available created by chef Lionel McCartney and offer popular dishes such as Dublin Bay prawns cooked with fresh ginger, garlic and served with a lime dressing, followed by roast breast of Lunedale duckling with the leg 'confited' and placed on a Grand Marnier and kumquat spiked sauce, rounded off perhaps by banana and praline parcels with caramel sauce. A pleasant place to stay for its idyllic setting, historic interest and warm welcome.

BURFORD   Lamb Inn

Sheep Street, Burford OX18 4LR
Telephone: (0993) 823155 Fax: (0993) 822228   **£40**
Open: lunch Sun, dinner daily (closed 25+26 Dec)
Meals served: lunch 12-2, dinner 7.30-9

Entering this historic old hostelry in a picture-postcard Cotswold town
is like stepping back into the 14th Century. There are flagged floors,
gleaming copper, brass and silver, and antiques adorn the rooms. Log
fires blaze in the winter and candles flicker in the dining room. The
tables look pristine in their white linen cloths set with shiny cutlery. A
typical menu may feature cream of celery and Stilton soup, smoked
salmon parcel with avocado mousse, then half a roasted guinea fowl
with a mixed fruit sauce or pan-fried fillet steak with oyster mushrooms and port sauce. Delicious, relaxing and one of England's greatest assets.

BURGH LE MARSH   Windmill

46 High Street, Burgh-le-Marsh, Nr Skegness, Lincolnshire PE24 5JT
Telephone: (0754) 810281   £40
Open: lunch Sun, dinner Tue-Sat (closed 25 Dec)
Meals served: lunch 12-2, dinner 7-9.15
Good wholesome cooking by Tim Boskett. Wines selected by French chef André
Daguin.

BURY   Normandie Hotel & Restaurant

Elbut Lane, Birtle, Nr Bury, Greater Manchester BL9 6UT   ✿
Telephone: 061-764 3869 Fax: 061-764 4866   **£60**
Open: lunch Tue-Fri, dinner Mon-Sat (closed Bank Holidays)
Meals served: lunch 12-2, dinner 7-9.30 (Sat 7-10)

A standing ovation should end each evening's dining, for such is the
talent of chef Pascal Pommier. His dishes are rustic yet refined with
fish cooked just to that right degree. Sauces are assertive yet not over-
powering and venison, pigeon and beef are served juicy and pink.
Gillian and Max Moussa have found that one of their greatest assets is
their young Burgundian chef who continues to excel. Sample a few of
his delights and take a couple of friends so you can taste more than
one dish - red mullet in lemon and coriander, pork with smoked bacon
and prunes and crisp gratinated onion tart with olives. Extensive wine
list with reasonable prices. This 24-bedroomed hotel is a mixture of old
building with modern extensions and is very well run.

BURY ST EDMUNDS   Angel Hotel

Angel Hill, Bury St Edmunds, Suffolk IP33 1LT
Telephone: (0284) 753926 Fax: (0284) 750092   **£45**
Open: lunch + dinner daily
Meals served: lunch 12.30-2, dinner 7.30-10   ❖

This ivy-clad, 42-bedroomed hotel peeps out from behind its greenery
to offer friendly and welcoming service and atmosphere. In service
since 1452 this is a hotel well versed in the needs of the overnighter or
those who want to stay longer. Remember Dickens' Mr Pickwick, who
stayed here and enjoyed an excellent roast dinner? The room he called
his 'accommodation' was number 15, preserved today exactly as it was
more than a century ago.

BURY ST EDMUNDS   Mortimer's Seafood Restaurant

31 Churchgate Street, Bury St Edmunds, Suffolk IP33 1RG
Telephone: (0284) 760623 Fax: (0284) 752561   £30
Open: lunch Mon-Fri, dinner Mon-Sat (closed Bank Holidays + following day,
 2 wks Xmas/New Year, 2 wks Aug)
Meals served: lunch 12-2, dinner 7-9 (Mon 6.45-8.15)
Long-standing, much cherished and offering an extensive range of fresh fish and
seafood cooked in variety of ways and served in a straightforward manner.

CALSTOCK   Danescombe Valley Hotel

Lower Kelly, Calstock, Cornwall PL18 9RY
Telephone: (0822) 832414   **£60**
Open: dinner Fri-Tue (closed Nov-Easter but open Xmas)
Meals served: dinner 7.30 for 8

I don't think it would be entirely fair to say that the cooking is the sole
highlight here, since you also cannot fail to be impressed by this truly
spectacular setting on a wooded bend of the Tamar, in what is affectionately known as the hidden valley. You are in for a treat when
choosing to stay here. Anna Smith's cooking is beautiful, uncomplicated and tastes superb, drawing on Elizabeth David and Jane Grigson for
direction with dishes such as roast tomato soup, breast of chicken with
parmesan, baked radicchio with slices of smoked venison and fillet of
beef wrapped in parma ham and cooked in chianti. A reasonably priced
wine list.

CAMBRIDGE   Browns

---

23 Trumpington Street Cambridge, Cambridgeshire CB2 1QA
Telephone: (0223) 461655 Fax: (0233) 460426   **£30**
Open: all day daily (closed 25+26 Dec)
Meals served: 11am-11.30pm (Sun + Bank Holidays 12-11.30pm)

Opposite the Fitzwilliam Museum is this value-for-money restaurant.
The formula for this and its sister restaurants around the country is
spot-on for customers who want quick, reliable and good food at just
about any hour of the day. Relaxed and stylish surroundings.

CAMBRIDGE   Midsummer House

Midsummer Common, Cambridge, Cambridgeshire CB4 3AE   ✿
Telephone: (0223) 69299   **£70**
Open: lunch Mon-Fri, dinner Mon-Sat (closed 26 Dec, 1Jan)
Meals served: lunch 12.15-1.30, dinner 7.15-9.30

Expect to see mastery on the plate from chef patron Hans Schweitzer
in the blue room or plump for an alfresco table out in the conservatory,
under a large, colonial sun shade. The selection on the modern-style
menu will possibly include Cromer crab pâté, tea-smoked seafood brochette with avocado and papaya salsa, loin of lamb with boulangère
potatoes or spring lamb with a herb crust. The desserts are worth sampling and a walk across the common or down by the river Cam will
allow for it! A good wine list with some reasonable prices. This place
deserves to succeed and is well worth a visit.

CAMBRIDGE   RESTAURANT TWENTY TWO

22 Chesterton Road, Cambridge, Cambridgeshire CB4 3AX
Telephone: (0223) 351880   £40
Open: dinner Mon-Sat (closed 25+26 Dec)
Meals served: dinner 7-10
Juggling lecturing (at the catering college) and running this small Victorian restau-
rant, David Carter and Louise Crompton have invested in a short fixed-price menu
with some classically inspired dishes.

CAMPSEA ASHE   Old Rectory

Campsea Ashe, nr Woodbridge, Suffolk IP13 OPU
Telephone: (0728) 746524   **£45**
Open: dinner Mon-Sat (closed Xmas/New Year, 2 wks Feb, 1 wk Nov)
Meals served: dinner 7.30-8.30

At the Old Rectory you help yourself to drinks before dinner in the
drawing room, noting down your choice on a pad before moving into
one of the dining rooms to enjoy Stewart Bassett's works of art. These
might be salmon with spinach mousse baked in puff pastry with a lobster sauce, pork with a mild mustard, cream and gherkin and caper
sauce and guinea fowl with an oriental twist. A well thought out wine
list with some very reasonably prices. The 7 bedrooms are wonderfully
relaxing with a pleasant eccentric air and make this an establishment
worth a visit.

CANTERBURY   County Hotel

High Street, Canterbury, Kent CT1 2RX
Telephone: (0227) 766266 Fax: (0227) 451512   **£45**
Open: lunch + dinner daily
Meals served: lunch 12.30-2.30, dinner 7-10

The various ages that this historic establishment has seen since it was
built in 1588, are reflected in the 73 rooms of the old privately owned
city centre hotel. In Sully's restaurant the decor is more modern with
mirror-panelled walls, a style also reflected in the menu - warm tartlet
of 2 blue cheeses on a crisp walnut salad, pan-fried halibut with scallops and fresh herb sauce, braised paupiette of pork with olive oil and
sage sauce, cream beignets with dark chocolate and Tia Maria sauce,
roulade of strawberries with Cointreau and orange sauce.

CARTMEL FELL   Hodge Hill

Hodge Hill, Cartmel Fell, Grange Oversands, Cumbria
Telephone: (05395) 31480   £50
Open: lunch Sun, dinner daily (closed 25, 26 Dec)
Meals served: Sunday lunch from 1pm, dinner 7.30 for 8
Built in 1539, this manor-house restaurant has 3 bedrooms and an orchard.

CARTMEL   Uplands

Haggs Lane, Cartmel, Cumbria LA11 6HD
Telephone: (053 95) 36248   **£55**
Open: lunch + dinner Tue-Sun (closed Jan+Feb)
Meals served: lunch 12.30 for 1, dinner 7.30 for 8

Dinner `In the Miller Howe Manner' could run like this: oyster mush-
rooms in hot herb and garlic sauce with tagliatelle, courgette and rosemary soup, sea bass with fennel sauce and hot caramelised pear roll
with apricot. Diana and Tom Peter used to be with John Tovey before
moving here and now have their own charming 5-bedroomed
Edwardian country house hotel, which they run in the same style.

CASTLE CARY   Bond's Hotel & Restaurant

Ansford Hill, Castle Cary, Somerset BA7 7JP
Telephone: (0963) 350464   **£45**
Open: dinner daily (closed 1 wk Xmas)
Meals served: dinner 7-9.30

You will meet truly personal service from owners Kevin and Yvonne
Bond at their 7-bedroomed, listed Georgian house. Yvonne's cooking
gives plenty of choice, is nourishing and substantial - creamy curried
chicken livers, terrine of venison and pork with toasted cheese and
onion bread followed by daube of provençal beef, or fillet of pork
stuffed with cheddar and parsley, wrapped in cheese pastry with horseradish cream sauce. And as if you would need any more, there is an
excellent selection of artisan cheeses or indulgent puddings. The plate
of chocolate will please more than just the chocoholics amongst us -
chocolate chestnut torte, ice cream, marquise and eclair all rounded
off with another dose in the brandy and chocolate sauce! Reasonably
priced wine list. This year sees them serving light lunches and breakfasts - traditional, healthy, old-fashioned and continental - to the public
for the first time – but only if they're not too busy with residents. It's
probably best to ring first and book.

CASTLE COMBE   Manor House

Castle Combe, Nr Chippenham, Wiltshire SN14 7HR   ✿
Telephone: (0249) 782206 Fax: (0249) 782159   **£35**
Open: lunch + dinner daily
Meals served: lunch 12.30-2, dinner 7.30-9.30 (Sat 7.30-10)   ❖

A manor house at the heart of historic Castle Combe, the log fires here
burn all year round and together with the antiques and embellished
oak panelling give an unquestionably period appeal. Having been lovingly restored, many of the original features are only just now seeing
the light of day. 36 rooms are spread between the main house and
neighbouring cottages and all have up-to-date extras. Modern English-
style cooking graces the tables with seasonal lunch and dinner selections such as haddock and mustard soufflé, salmon on creamed leeks
coated with orange and lobster butter, sweet oak-smoked beef with
caramelised onions, foie gras and bacon. To round off the meal try
pear and date pudding with toffee sauce, queen of charlotte pudding
with apricot purée or croustade of warm cherries and a lemon parfait.
The wine list offers an extensive selection, and service is charming and
informed.

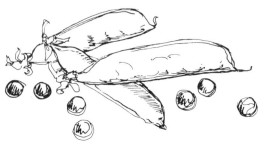

CHADDESLEY CORBETT   Brockencote Hall

Chaddesley Corbett, Nr Kidderminster, Hereford & Worcester DY10 4PY
Telephone: (0562) 777876 Fax: (0562) 777872   **£75**
Open: lunch Sun-Fri, dinner daily
Meals served: lunch 12.30-1.45, dinner 7.30-9.30

You could almost imagine yourself on the other side of the channel
when you stay in this classic white painted house run in exclusively
French run style by Alison and Joseph Petitjean. A recent extension
has doubled the number of bedrooms to 17. The elegant dining room
is very much at the centre of activity, enjoying fine views out across
the lawns to the lake. Chef Eric Bouchet cooks a variety of menus but
with the same French accent running through them all, occasionally
heightened with a little spice. Recent dishes have been pan-fried snails
in butter with quenelles of Stilton or a cold galantine of guinea fowl
served with vegetables cooked in coriander and white wine.

CHADLINGTON   The Manor

Chadlington, Oxfordshire OX7 3LX
Telephone: (0608) 76711   **£50**
Open: dinner daily
Meals served: dinner 7-9

Appealing to the culture-seeking traveller, this old Cotswold manor is
equidistant from Oxford, Stratford-upon-Avon and Cheltenham.
Chef/proprietor Chris Grant goes to great trouble in sourcing the
right ingredients while business partner David Grant runs the 7-bed-
roomed hotel and superb wine cellar. A short menu sees you spoilt for
choice with a home-made soup to start (on our visit broad bean and
hazelnut) followed by a choice of herb-stuffed mussels, pigeon salad or
grapefruit soufflé and then duck with orange, honey and ginger, pork
fillet with sage and mustard or baked salmon with hollandaise, a fine
choice of English puddings and finally cheese. A good, reasonably
priced wine-list. Well worth the stay.

CHAGFORD

Gidleigh is always a favourite for style, ambience & food.

Gidleigh Park

Chagford, Devon TQ13 8HH
Telephone: (0647) 432367 Fax: (0647) 432574
Open: lunch + dinner daily
Meals served: lunch 12.30-2, dinner 7-9

❀

£105

After a long and twisting drive up a narrow lane you eventually reach Gidleigh Park. Graceful in summer, with its lawns, streams and gardens, cosy in winter with log fires and comfortable sofas and arm chairs, Gidleigh to me is always worth the journey. And to cap it all, there's Shaun Hill's cooking, as brilliant as ever, a combination of quiet Irish wit and a steely command of his profession. His deep-fried lemon zest is intense and crisp and his basil mash has food critics and writers eating out of his hand for just one taste. His saffron risotto is how it should be - unctuous and creamy with such an intensity that the saffron must have been added right at the end of cooking to preserve its full effect. Sweet and succulent sautéed scallops with lentil and coriander sauce bring further recommendation, as does sautéed calves' liver with the aforementioned basil mash and lots of caramelised shallots. An extensive wine list has some very reasonable prices.

CHAPELTOWN

Greenhead House

84 Burncross Road, Chapeltown, Nr Sheffield, South Yorkshire
S30 4SF
Telephone: (0742) 469004
Open: dinner Tue-Sat (closed Bank Holidays, 2 wks Apr, 2 wks Aug)
Meals served: dinner 7-9

£55

A semi-fixed-price menu (the main course determines the overall price) doesn't make choosing any easier. The selection is concise but never meagre and extremely tempting. It offers the best of that month's produce, cooked in a lovingly robust way by Neil Allen. The popularity of this pretty, small restaurant just north of Sheffield is growing, hardly surprising when menu choices might include a terrine of venison layered with apples and prunes and served with walnut oil-dressed apples and french beans, followed by breast of wood-pigeon with a slice of foie gras mousse wrapped in cabbage and served on a puff pastry case, with a truffle and mandarin sauce.

CHARINGWORTH — Charingworth Manor

Charingworth, Nr Chipping Camden, Gloucestershire GL55 6NS
Telephone: (038 678) 555 Fax: (038 678) 353 **£60**
Open: lunch + dinner daily
Meals served: lunch 12.30-2, dinner 7.30-9.30 (Sat 7.30-10)

Beamed and bedecked in country splendour, this is an idyllic setting in winter or summer. The gardens are well kept and overlook the many private acres. Mullioned windows, rugs and polished floors are as pleasant as the willing yet unassuming staff. Bill Marmion's good classical cooking is fashionable yet, thankfully, not fussy - bourride of fish, onion tart, fricassée of game with wild mushrooms, nage of skate with grainy mustard sauce and seared fillet of brill and ratatouille to mention but a few. Don't go expecting a grand dining room; this is a series of 4 interconnecting rooms. A purpose-built spa has been recently added to the hotel, and bedrooms are either in the main house or the stable block conversion, which has been cleverly linked to allow direct access to the spa.

CHARLBURY — The Bull at Charlbury

Sheep Street, Charlbury, Oxfordshire OX7 3RR
Telephone: (0608) 810689 **£45**
Open: lunch daily, dinner Mon-Sat
Meals served: lunch 12-2, dinner 7-9.30

The food comes first at this small hotel where a pint of Speckled Hen is another highlight of the evening. Andrew Castle produces cooking that is simple in concept with fresh soups, the finest beef, corn-fed chicken and the freshest of trout cooked without fuss or frills. With a set up that has a bias towards quality dining, proprietors Peter and Lucy Wearing have found their man and the regulars show that they are in favour as well.

CHARTHAM — Thruxted Oast

Mystole, Chartham, Nr Canterbury, Kent CT4 7BX
Telephone: (0227) 730080 £70
Open: bed & breakfast only
Tim and Hilary Derouet have converted this former oast house into an unusual 3-roomed guest house. Conical roofs, pine furniture, patchwork quilts, farmhouse-style breakfasts served at a large, scrubbed pine table.

CHEDINGTON   Chedington Court

Chedington, Nr Beaminster, Dorset DT8 3HY
Telephone: (0935) 891265 Fax: (0935) 891442   **£60**
Open: dinner daily (closed Jan+Feb)
Meals served: dinner only 7-9

This Jacobean-style court has an elegant atmosphere and is set in 10 acres of gardens. The floral theme comes indoors with a passion-flower and mimosa-filled conservatory. In terms of accommodation and service the Chapmans have always sought to offer a fine country house and they are achieving just that. The spotlight remains on Hilary Chapman's cooking with a fixed-price dinner menu cooked with care and devotion - warm courgette charlotte with a chive butter sauce, red mullet with basil sauce and pork with apple and calvados are typical. Fairly priced and interesting wine list. A relaxing place to stay for the weekend.

CHELTENHAM   Bonnets Bistro at Staithes

12 Suffolk Road, Cheltenham, Gloucestershire GL50 2AQ
Telephone: (0242) 260666   **£50**
Open: lunch + dinner Tues-Sat
Meals served: lunch 12-2, dinner 7-9.45

Moving with the times, owner Paul Lucas has introduced a change of menu at this restaurant, though the decor remains the same. The price has lowered but the fare remains interesting - caramelised bacon salad dressed with vinegar, salmon en croute, chicken and leek tartlet and deep-fried parcel of apples and raisins served with calvados scented cream.

CHELTENHAM   Le Champignon Sauvage

24-26 Suffolk Road, Cheltenham, Gloucestershire GL50 2AQ
Telephone: (0242) 573449   **£70**
Open: lunch Mon-Fri, dinner Mon-Sat (closed Bank Holidays,
1 wk Xmas, 2 wks Jun)
Meals served: lunch 12.30-1.30, dinner 7.30-9.30

Mycologists will be disappointed because despite the name, mush-rooms do not dominate David Everitt-Matthias' cooking. His knack is for eclectic French cuisine with deference to a few new trends, and dishes on a 3- or 4-course dinner menu could include smoked haddock brandade bound with potato and served with red pepper fondue, home-made pasta with skate and watercress served with mussels, or boned salmon steak with a carrot butter sauce. Unobtrusive decor in pale grey and pink casts a cool background against which to hang modern prints. Good wine list with tasting notes.

CHELTENHAM · Epicurean & On The Park

Cleveland House, Evesham Road, Cheltenham, Gloucestershire ꗸ
GL52 2AH
Telephone: (0242) 222466   **£50**
Open: lunch Tue-Sun, dinner Tue-Sat
Meals served: lunch 12.30-2.30, dinner 7.30-9.30

Incorporated within the Regency hotel On The Park, but run as a completely separate concern by chef/patron Patrick MacDonald, the restaurant Epicurean is stylish and elegant with food described as neo-classical. It remains simple with full flavours allowed to take centre stage, while long standing dishes such as parsley soup, scallops and oysters, duck confit with foie gras still appear, I'm happy to say. Also featured are braised baby chicken, pigs' trotters with sage, onion and truffle and white stew of salmon and scallops. Patrick's puddings are always worth saving a place for, as are the stylishly prepared petits fours. An awareness of price barriers is reflected in the excellent value 4-course set lunch at £15, and dinner at £22.50. The wine list also offers some good choices at sensible prices.

CHELTENHAM · The Greenway

Shurdington, Cheltenham, Gloucestershire GL51 5UG
Telephone: (0242) 862352 Fax: (0242) 862780   **£55**
Open: lunch Sun-Fri, dinner daily (closed 2 wks Xmas)
Meals served: lunch 12.30-2, dinner 7-9.30

The outside terraces have been completed and a new herb garden added, so don't be surprised to see chef Chris Colmer out there harvesting his day's requirements. This is a stylish place to stay and looks as green as the proverbial valley with creeper clad walls. There's also a wealth of talent in the kitchen - salad of squid with marinated peppers, beef with woodland mushrooms and spinach followed by roasted apple pie were all enjoyable. With 19 rooms, the Greenway is a special sort of place and provides very comfortable and stylish surroundings.

CHELTENHAM · Redmond's

Cleeve Hill, Cheltenham, Gloucestershire GL52 3PR   ꗸ
Telephone: (0242) 672017   **£65**
Open: lunch Tue-Fri+Sun, dinner Tue-Sat (closed 24-26 Dec, 1 wk Jan)
Meals served: lunch 12.30-2, dinner 7.15-10

Scenery and food here are similarly captivating. Look out across the valley to the Malverns and wallow in the breath-taking beauty of it all, and if you stay overnight in one of the 5 bedrooms you'll have even longer to appreciate it. Redmond Hayward's capacity to enthral with his dishes is renowned. A meal here could include ravioli with roast peppers, grilled aubergine and fresh parmesan and ragôut of salmon, scallops, mussels together with monkfish, tomato and basil. Puddings shouldn't be missed with a hot rhubarb soufflé accompanied by a honey and cinnamon ice cream or baked vanilla egg custard with nutmeg crème fraîche. Good wine list with some reasonable prices.

CHELWOOD   Chelwood House

Chelwood, Bristol, Avon BS18 4NH
Telephone: (0761) 490730 Fax: (0761) 490730   **£35**
Open: lunch Sun, dinner Mon-Sat (closed 2 wks Xmas/New Year)
Meals served: lunch 12-1.15, dinner 7-9

A warm and welcome retreat some 10 miles from Bath. Good traditional breakfasts with good value for money cooking, peppered with Rudi
Birk's traditional specials of goulash, decent bolognaise and smoked
haddock with spätzle. Friday is put aside for a Bavarian evening when
Rudi creates even more of his specialities with herrentopf (beef with
gherkins, tomatoes and cream), wiener schnitzel and apfelstrudel. The
conservatory-style restaurant with its muralled walls only seats 24, so
book early. Chelwood House dates from 1680 and the bedrooms are
furnished in various styles, some with 4-poster beds.

CHESTER   Chester Grosvenor

This 86-bedroomed hotel has a welcoming & professional style

Eastgate Street, Chester, Cheshire CH1 1LT
Telephone: (0244) 324024 Fax: (0244) 313246   **£85**
Open: lunch Tue-Sat, dinner Mon-Sat (closed Bank Holidays)
Meals served: lunch 12-2.30, dinner 7-10.30

First class and never neglecting its unique heritage, this Grosvenor
Estates hotel is centrally located within the historic walled town. It
enjoys an international and business clientele and proves that large
hotels do not have to lack warmth and character. The Arkle Restaurant
– named after the Duchess of Westminster's steeplechaser – offers
modern cooking in elegant and stylish surroundings. Sophisticated
dishes are perfected by Paul Reed and Simon Radley, such as a collection of sweetbreads, trotters, foie gras and tongues, or carved venison
saddle with white cabbage and game sausage, or guinea-fowl with
charred peppers, crushed olives and basil. Fine cheeses and wine complement. For more modest eating La Brasserie has a distinctive
French decor and a more affordable menu. Historic, luxurious and
grand, this is definitely a destination hotel.

CHESTER   Crabwall Manor

Parkgate Road, Mollington, Chester, Cheshire CH1 6NE
Telephone: (0244) 851666 Fax: (0244) 851400   £75
Open: lunch + dinner daily
Meals served: lunch 12.30-2, dinner 7-9.45 (Sat 7-10, Sun 7-9)
Crabwall Manor dates from 1850. Well furnished and thought out with well equipped
bathrooms and efficient service.

CHESTER — Franc's

14 Cuppin Street, Chester, Cheshire CH1 2BN
Telephone: (0244) 317952 Fax: (0244) 340690   *Busy, popular restaurant* £50
Open: lunch + dinner daily
Meals served: lunch 12-3, dinner 6-11

French country cooking is served in this bustling brasserie to the sound of French rock music. Back to basics - the choice is wide and the food is what French people eat every day - moules bretagne, fruits de mer, crêpes filled with minced lamb, herbs and mild spices, cous-cous algerien, bouillabaisse, stuffed mushrooms with St Agur cheese, celery and breadcrumb topping, coq au vin.

CHICHESTER — Comme Ca

67 Broyle Road, Chichester, West Sussex
Telephone: (0243) 788724   £45
Open: lunch Tue-Sun, dinner Tue-Sat (closed Bank Holidays)
Meals served: lunch 12-2, dinner 7-10 (theatre nights 6-10.30)

Set in the heart of theatre land (just a few minutes' walk to Festival Theatre) this former pub has become a traditional French restaurant with bar. Chef-patron Michel Navet offers straightforward pre- and post-theatre menus - poached eggs served with red wine and mushrooms, deep-fried camembert with a gooseberry brandy sauce, lamb steak cooked in garlic and herbs, veal sautéed with wild mushrooms and madeira sauce and fillet of beef topped with dijon mustard, caramelized and flambéed. A French wine list offers some good prices, especially in the regional selection.

CHICHESTER — The Droveway

30a Southgate, Chichester, West Sussex PO19 1DR
Telephone: (0243) 528832   £45
Open: lunch Tue-Sun, dinner Tue-Sat (closed 2 wks Jan)
Meals served: lunch 12.30-2, dinner 7.30-10

Renamed and improved, the Thompsons' first floor restaurant remains stylish and smart but with a new section for smokers and another area in which to relax. Jonas remains the chef and cooks a complementary mix of French and British dishes.

CHILGROVE — White Horse Inn

Chilgrove, Nr Chichester, West Sussex PO18 9HX
Telephone: (0243) 59219 Fax: (0243) 59301   £50
Open: lunch Tue-Sun, dinner Tue-Sat (closed Feb, last wk Oct)
Meals served: lunch 12-1.45, dinner 7-9.30 (Sat 7-10)

Established in 1765 this famous inn has an award-winning wine selection. Cooking is confident and matches that fantastic wine cellar, which has been lovingly compiled over 20 years by acknowledged expert Barry Phillips. Neil Rusbridger brings his passion to the fore in the kitchen with fine, fresh ingredients featuring in appealing dishes - salad of lamb's kidneys with balsamic vinegar, sauté of rabbit, braised knuckle of lamb with chicory, ballotine of cabbage with chestnuts, wood pigeon with celeriac purée. To do justice to the wine list would take many pages, so my advice is just go there and enjoy it for yourself, even though you might be spoilt for choice!

CHIPPING CAMPDEN   Cotswold House

The Square, Chipping Campden, Gloucestershire GL55 6AN
Telephone: (0386) 840330 Fax: (0386) 840310   **£35**
Open: lunch Sun, dinner daily (closed 25+26 Dec)
Meals served: lunch 12.30-2, dinner 7.15-9.30 (light meals 9.30am-11pm in
Greenstocks)

This 12-bedroomed 17th-century hotel overlooks the town square. A
fine spiralling staircase meets you as you enter the stone-clad entrance
hall in this former wool merchant's house. The restaurant enjoys views
over the gardens and a reputation in the town for its food and cheerful
staff.

CHIPPING CAMPDEN   Seymour House

High Street, Chipping Campden, Gloucestershire GL55 6AH
Telephone: (0386) 840429 Fax: (0386) 840369   **£70**
Open: lunch + dinner daily
Meals served: lunch 12-2, dinner 7-10

With a 90-year old vine in the restaurant and a 500-year-old yew tree in
the small garden this 18th-century hotel is steeped in history. Now, in
the peak of condition after a recent overhaul, this 16-bedroomed hotel
has a lot to recommend it. The restaurant allows a choice of indoor or
alfresco (on the patio) eating and the dishes on offer, whilst mainly
English, occasionally dash around France and Italy.

CHOBHAM   Quails Restaurant

1 Bagshot Road, Chobham, Surrey GU24 8BP
Telephone: (0276) 858491   **£35**
Open: lunch Tue-Fri+Sun, dinner Tue-Sat (closed 26 Dec, 1 Jan)
Meals served: lunch 12-2, dinner 7-10

The Wale family runs this airy and light brasserie with aplomb. Every
month sees new menus which transport you to yet another region of
France. There is an à la carte menu or an exceptionally good value
prix-fixe menu which includes two glasses of regional wine. The entertaining wine list is well annotated and offers some fairly priced and
interesting selections, especially around the regions.

CHRISTCHURCH   Splinters Restaurant
11/12 Church Street, Christchurch, Dorset BH23 1BW
Telephone: (0202) 483454 Fax: (0202) 483454   £50
Open: lunch + dinner Mon-Sat (closed 26+27 Dec, 1 Jan, Mon in winter but open Sun)
Meals served: lunch 12-2.30, dinner 7-10.30
Small, informal French restaurant in the shadow of the priory. Country cooking and
warm atmosphere.

| CLANFIELD | **The Plough at Clanfield** |

Bourton Road, Clanfield, Oxfordshire OX8 2RB
Telephone: (036 781) 222 Fax: (036 781) 596   **£65**
Open: lunch + dinner daily
Meals served: lunch 12-2, dinner 7-10

Epicurian, Gourmand or Gastronome - whichever you are, Stephen Fischer has devised a menu for you, and if none of them take your fancy, there's still a house menu and a light lunch selection to keep you reading on and on. Perhaps chicken with forest mushroom sauce, steamed salmon with herb butter, a hot tartlet of Cornish crab and baby leek or a savoury croissant filled with ham and cheese. With English and French influences both vying for attention and puddings a speciality, this place offers something for most people's palates.

| CLAYGATE | **Les Alouettes** |

7 High Street, Claygate, Surrey KT10 0JW
Telephone: (0372) 464882 Fax: (0372) 65337   **£45**
Open: lunch + dinner Mon-Sat (closed Bank Holidays, 2 wks Aug)
Meals served: lunch 12.15-2, dinner 7-9.30 (Sat 7-10)

Pretty French restaurant with fine furnishings but now there's a simpler menu than in Michel Perraud's day. Thierry Obitz, former sous chef, has risen through the ranks to take over the helm and now offers a less expensive menu which is in no way a bad thing - braised monkfish with leeks and a tomato butter sauce, veal with tagliatelle. The wine list reflects the menu change with some reasonable options.

| CLITHEROE | **Browns Bistro** |

10 York Street, Clitheroe, Lancashire BB7 2DL
Telephone: (0200) 26928   **£50**
Open: lunch Mon-Fri, dinner Mon-Sat (closed Xmas/New Year)
Meals served: lunch 12-2, dinner 7-10

The fun, French atmosphere hits you as you enter – checked tablecloths, bare wooden floors and plenty of that bistro-style laid back charm. The menu is not entirely French with beef stroganoff and sea bass oriental alongside the likes of chicken chasseur, but no-one really minds as long as the food is cooked well, the menu is appetising and the wine is reasonably priced. Sit down, glance through the menu, order a glass of wine and enjoy the evening.

| COCKERMOUTH | **Quince & Medlar** |

13 Castlegate, Cockermouth, Cumbria CA13 9EU
Telephone: (0900) 823579   £35
Open: dinner Tue-Sun (closed Bank Holidays, 24-26 Dec, 3 wks Jan/ Feb,
 1 wk Oct/Nov, Sun Xmas-Easter)
Meals served: dinner 7-9.30
Informal, candle-lit vegetarian restaurant near Cockermouth castle.

COGGESHALL   Baumann's Brasserie

4-6 Stoneham Street, Coggeshall, Essex CO6 1TT
Telephone: (0376) 561453   **£50**
Open: lunch Tue-Fri+Sun, dinner Tue-Sat (closed Bank Holidays,
2 wks Jan)
Meals served: lunch 12.30-2, dinner 7.30-10

Rillettes of rabbit and guinea fowl with gherkin and olive oil dressing,
baked venison, cranberry and faggots with juniper berry sauce: there's
some good English cooking here with an imaginative touch. This
friendly restaurant with its young staff deserves continuing success.

COGGESHALL   White Hart

Market End, Coggeshall, Essex CO6 1NH
Telephone: (0376) 561654 Fax: (0376) 561789   £35
Open: lunch daily, dinner Mon-Sat
Meals served: lunch 12-2, dinner 7-10
With 2 resident ghosts you are never going to feel lonely here! Eighteen bedrooms in
this 14th-century meeting place, full of low beams, and pieces reflecting its history.
The restaurant to the rear of the building offers traditional-style Italian food with the
addition on Sundays of a fixed-price English menu - roast beef, lamb, and loin of pork.

COLERNE   Lucknam Park

Colerne, Wiltshire SN14 8AZ
Telephone: (0225) 742777 Fax: (0225) 743536   **£90**
Open: lunch + dinner daily
Meals served: lunch 12.30-2, dinner 7.30-9.30

Lucknam Park is an elegant Georgian house, approached by a long
straight avenue of beech trees. Polished wooden floors, rich colours
and a warming fire welcome you. Unstuffy in attitude as well as furnishings this is still one of the most elegant places to stay. The interior
is pretty but not twee, still striking and tasteful. Gastronomes have
been heading out this way (some via Paddington just for the joy of
lunch) for Michael Womersley's highly developed British cooking.
Regional produce is used wherever possible and graces the table in
the form of Cornish crab soup with herb chantilly or grilled salmis of
wood pigeon with baked aubergines and woodland mushrooms followed by pan-fried tenderloin of pork with lardons of pigs' trotter and
juices scented with lemon and caraway. For the vegetarian, the
lasagne of woodland mushrooms with coriander sauce, spiked with
vegetables and lentils makes a good tempting option which displays
equal care by the chef. Very good wine list. The housekeeping's
immaculate, the staff impeccable, and there are 42 luxury rooms and a
health spa.

CORFE CASTLE — Mortons House Hotel

45 East Street, Corfe Castle, Dorset BH20 5EE
Telephone: (0929) 480988 Fax: (0929) 480820 **£50**
Open: lunch + dinner daily
Meals served: lunch 12.30-2, dinner 7.30-9

Pierre Mathiot cooks at this patriotic house which in 1590 was designed in the shape of the letter E as a tribute to the then sovereign. Still appropriate today, I am sure the current incarnation also gets the royal seal of approval, for its renovations are in keeping with original features. A 17-bedroomed hotel, it accommodates business as well as leisure visitors and, like its walled garden, retains charm and history.

CORSE LAWN — Corse Lawn House

Corse Lawn, Nr Gloucester, Gloucestershire GL19 4LZ
Telephone: (0452) 780479 Fax: (0452) 780840 **£55**
Open: lunch + dinner daily
Meals served: lunch 12-2, dinner 7-10

Good value fixed-price lunch

Baba Hine heads the kitchen alone now since the departure of Tim Earley and is enjoying being back in sole command, having built up a good young team. Honest raw materials are very much to the fore, placing emphasis on value for money. A strong 'Englishness' and touch of the French (co-owner & husband Denis is French) envelopes the menu, and under her fastidious eye consistent and unpretentious dishes are continuously produced - artichoke and tarragon soup, chargrilled salmon with caper sauce and cucumber, calves' brains with black butter. Their son Giles now works at front of house - (a big plus point). A popular bistro extends the bar-snack operation and is proving successful. Be warned, the restaurant is becoming packed out at weekends, so book early. The wine list complements the menu and a huge choice is available. 19 rooms, some in the new wing sympathetically added to this listed Queen Anne house.

CORSHAM — Rudloe Park

Leafy Lane, Corsham, Wiltshire SN13 0PA
Telephone: (0225) 810555 Fax: (0225) 811412 **£35**
Open: lunch + dinner daily
Meals served: lunch 12-1.30, dinner 7-9.30

The drive leads directly from the A4 to this pleasing Bathstone manor standing in 10 acres of award-winning gardens and grounds. Popular with locals and travellers alike, the house has 11 bedrooms fitted out in a style worthy of the bygone era of the house. The Overends are proud of their almost pubby-feeling lounge bar with its enormous range of spirits and draught beers, and likewise their award-winning 400 bin-wine list which contains many bargains and much of interest. You can eat either in the bar for lunch and dinner, or in the 80-seater restaurant.

COSHAM   **Barnard's**

109 High Street, Cosham, Hampshire PO6 3BB
Telephone: (0705) 370226   £30
Open: lunch Tues-Fri, dinner Tues-Sat (closed 2 wks Aug, Dec 25-Jan 1)
Meals served: lunch 12-2, dinner 7.30-9.30
Fresh, wholesome French cooking with 3-course set menu and adequate choice.
Many wines under £15 on the 33-bin list.

COWAN BRIDGE   Cobwebs

Leck, Cowan Bridge, Nr Kirkby Lonsdale, Lancashire LA6 2HZ
Telephone: (052 42) 72141   **£55**
Open: dinner Tue-Sat (closed end Dec-mid Mar)
Meals served: dinner 7.30 for 8

Paul Kelly and Yvonne Thompson invite you into the Victorian parlour
for a pre-dinner aperitif. With only 16 covers the atmosphere is intimate and booking is essential. Paul chooses the wine while Yvonne
cooks dinner. Old-fashioned courtesies abound and with 5 bedrooms it
is worth an overnight stay on gourmet evenings.

CRANLEIGH   La Barbe Encore

High Street, Cranleigh, Surrey GU6 8AE
Telephone: (0483) 273889   **£45**
Open: lunch Tue-Fri + Sun, dinner Tue-Sat (closed Bank Holidays)
Meals served: lunch 12-2, dinner 7-10

The name has changed and the walls are now a warm orange with
cosy corners for twosomes but chef Jean-Pierre Bonnet continues to
produce satisfying dishes with particular flair. His new menu includes
supreme de volaille with tarragon, salmon fishcakes with watercress
and confit of duck with roasted shallots. Dessert is typified with îles
flotantes and fine apple tart with cinnamon ice cream. A good local
place with a true French flavour.

CROSBY-ON-EDEN   Crosby Lodge

High Crosby, Crosby-on-Eden, Nr Carlisle, Cumbria CA6 4QZ
Telephone: (0228) 573618 Fax: (0228) 573428   **£55**
Open: lunch + dinner daily (closed 24 Dec-end Jan)
Meals served: lunch 12.15-1.30, dinner 7.30-9 (Sun 7.30-8)

With 20 years of experience under their belt, the Sedgwick family continues to run this unusual 11-bedroomed Georgian country house with
style. Everyone mentions the fresh brown shrimps on garlic toast for a
good reason; it's a simple but tasty first course alongside grilled, open
mussels finished with herbs, garlic and breadcrumbs. These from a
choice of 16 or 17 starters, then a middle course of asparagus with hollandaise and then on to traditional roast farm duckling or escalopes of
venison with cranberries and port sauce. Very good house wines and
well annotated list of some 300 wines, many at affordable prices.
Bedrooms are shared between the main house and the stable block.

CROYDON   34 Surrey Street

34 Surrey Street, Croydon, Surrey, CRO 1RJ
Telephone: 081-686 0586   **£30**
Open: lunch + dinner Mon-Sat (closed Xmas day+Bank Holidays)
Meals served: lunch 12-3, dinner 7-11

An American seafood restaurant in the heart of Croydon's busiest market. It keeps busy delivering what people want in the way of blackened crab claws, Mexican mussels and baked prawns, char-grilled exotic fish steaks, a seafood platter and lobster. Surf 'n' Turf and chicken Orleans accommodate meat eaters. Service is provided by young and eager staff and the decor is a mix of high-backed, tapestry chairs and green plastic tablecloths.

CUCKFIELD   Murray's

Broad Street, Cuckfield, West Sussex RH17 5LJ
Telephone: (0444) 455826   **£45**
Open: lunch Mon-Fri, dinner Mon-Sat (closed Bank Holidays,
 2 wks Feb, 2 wks Sep)
Meals served: lunch 12-1.30, dinner 7.15-9.30

A collection of cottagey rooms make up Sue Murray's restaurant. It's pleasing to know that at least one room has been reserved for non-smokers. The short menu is designed around spices and herbs from all over the world - Scarborough pancakes with parsley, sage, rosemary and thyme, red pepper bavarois, and duck with baked banana demonstrate the individuality of the cooking here. There's a move away from heavier dishes to lighter fare, and the menu changes daily.

CUCKFIELD   Ockenden Manor

Ockenden Lane, Cuckfield, West Sussex RH17 5LD
Telephone: (0444) 416111 Fax: (0444) 415549   **£56**
Open: lunch + dinner daily
Meals served: lunch 12.30-2, dinner 7.30-9.30

Set in the centre of a largely Tudor village, this historic manor is ideally placed for avid horticulturists who come to the local stately gardens. An English rose itself, the 22-bedroomed house is somewhat rambling, each century having left its mark, the latest addition being a conservatory. A beamed entrance hall, 4-poster beds and an orchard conclude the scene that will greet you.

DARLINGTON   Sardis

196 Northgate, Darlington, Durham DL1 1QU
Telephone: (0325) 461222   **£40**
Open: lunch + dinner Mon-Sat (closed Bank Holidays)
Meals served: lunch 12-2, dinner 7-10

In the wake of recent Italian trends this restaurant appears very much
up to date with plenty of reliable Italian dishes, but then it has been
run by the Sardinian families, Pala and Obinu, for quite some years
now. Enjoy the largely traditional cooking with a fixed-price 3-course
dinner menu which includes half a bottle of house wine.

DARLINGTON   Victor's Restaurant

84 Victoria Road, Darlington, Durham DL1 5JW
Telephone: (0325) 480818   **£40**
Open: lunch + dinner Tue-Sat (closed 1 wk Xmas)
Meals served: lunch 12-2, dinner 7-10.30

With a strong local following Jayne and Peter Robinson continue to
serve their modern British menu using local produce wherever possible. A recent fixed-price dinner menu included galantine of pork with
pistachios, duck with cloves and fresh peaches or roast kid with garlic
and rosemary followed by treacle tart or Cotherstone cheese and a reasonably priced wine list, ensuring a pleasant meal.

DARTMOUTH   Carved Angel

2 South Embankment, Dartmouth, Devon TQ6 9BH
Telephone: (0803) 832465 Fax: **£85**
Open: lunch Tue-Sun, dinner Tue-Sat (closed Bank Holidays;
(open Good Friday), 6 wks Jan/Feb)
Meals served: lunch 12.30-2, dinner 7.30-9

The lady of the stove is Joyce Molyneux, for such is her perfectionism
and judgement that she is revered as one of the rare doyennes of
English cooking. Stir-fried cuttlefish with peppers and coriander, dover
sole with chervil butter, fennel and cucumber, char-grilled marinated
venison brochette on a bed of lentils with pears and red wine: such are
the combinations and that you can't really say you've enjoyed Devon
unless you have tasted her graceful cooking. To see her calmly glide
along in her open plan kitchen is a sight not to be missed. Neither are
her puddings or good house wines, part of an excellent wine list with
some very reasonable prices. A visit to this ornate and timeless building is a treat indeed.

DEDHAM   Dedham Vale Hotel

Stratford Road, Deedham, nr Colchester, Essex CO7 6HW
Telephone: (0206) 322273 Fax: (0206) 322752   £40
Open: lunch Sun-Fri, dinner Tue-Sat
Meals served: lunch 12-2, dinner 7-9.30
Terrace restaurant with a vast Edwardian conservatory mural, offers smorgasbörd
lunch, and the rotisserie cooks a mix of roasts and grills at evenings and weekends.

DEDHAM   Fountain House and Dedham Hall

Brook Street, Dedham, Essex CO7 6AD
Telephone: (0206) 323027   **£40**
Open: lunch Sun, dinner Tue-Sat (closed Bank Holidays)
Meals served: lunch 12.30-3, dinner 7.30-10   ❖

This 15th-century cottage looks out over a walled garden and is home
to Wendy Anne Sarton's restaurant and 12-bedroomed guest house.
She specialises in straightforward cooking with the emphasis on ingredients rather than clever and unnecessary saucing, so expect to see
fresh dressed crab or gazpacho followed by pan-fried skate with tartare
sauce, cold poached salmon salad and beef with a madeira sauce. The
wine collection is serious stuff with a particularly good New World section and array of half bottles at reasonable prices.

DEDHAM   Maison Talbooth

Stratford Road, Dedham, Nr Colchester, Essex CO7 6HN
Telephone: (0206) 322367 Fax: (0206) 322752   **£65**
Open: lunch + dinner daily
Meals served: lunch 12-2, dinner 7-9

A gem in the Milsom winning formula, this elegant timber-framed
house nestles by the River Stour. It is very much a John Constable setting, the gardens and house right on the river banks. The 10 bedroom
suites also enjoy tranquil treatments with canopied beds, sumptuous
bathrooms - some with the luxury of a sunken bath - and views out
across the river valley. Every attention to detail has been anticipated
from the large and thick bath towels to the abundance of fresh flowers
in the rooms. The standard of housekeeping is immaculate. The riverside restaurant is a short drive away in the courtesy car (see entry
below) but room service with breakfast and light dishes such as
omelettes, sandwiches and steaks are available up to 11pm.

DEDHAM   Le Talbooth

Gunhill, Dedham, Nr Colchester, Essex CO7 6HP   ✿
Telephone: (0206) 323150 Fax: (0206) 322752   **£50**
Open: lunch + dinner daily
Meals served: lunch 12-2, dinner 7-9   ❖   🍾

Gerald Milsom has re-arranged his restaurants to create a more
straightforward approach here. This Tudor building has been redecorated in soft shades of pink and blue with blackened oak beams,
Windsor chairs and oak tables. The dining room runs alongside a terrace where you can eat alfresco in fine weather. Even from indoors it's
a delightful place to dine, with its views out over the River Stour. New
chef Henrik Iversen is now in the kitchen producing approachable
food from a weekly changing menu. A fixed-price menu includes a tartlet of mushrooms with sliced smoked duck breast followed by panache
of seafood in the Basque style with saffron cous-cous followed by a
Pimms soufflé glacé with a strawberry and mint sauce. Sunday lunch
offers a good choice (including a traditional roast), and the wine cellar
has an excellent range of wines. The Weaver's Room on the first floor
is available for private dining.

DISS   Weavers

Market Hill, Diss, Norfolk IP22 3JZ
Telephone: (0379) 642411   **£80**
Open: lunch Mon-Fri, dinner Mon-Sat (closed Bank Holidays,
Xmas, 1 wk end Aug)
Meals served: lunch 12-2, dinner 7-9.30

William Bavin cooks reliably good food in generous portions in this
characterful restaurant complete with oak-beamed interior (formerly a
weavers' guild chapel). Depending on the season, you might be
offered pot-roasted pheasant cooked in red wine and juniper complete
with forcemeat balls and mushrooms; oxtail braised in red wine, garlic,
oregano, tomato and vegetables; or the lighter, simply grilled giant
mediterranean prawns in garlic butter served with salad. Leave room
for the equally good puddings which in winter include some good
steamed varieties. Good wine list and separate vegetarian menu.

DORCHESTER   Mock Turtle

34 High West Street, Dorchester, Dorset DT1 1UP
Telephone: (0305) 264011   **£45**
Open: lunch Tue-Sat, dinner Mon-Sat (closed 26 Dec)
Meals served: lunch 12-2, dinner 7-10

A number of connecting rooms make up this pleasant restaurant situated in a 17th-century town house. Evening specials might include a
choice of cream of Jerusalem artichoke soup, chicken and crab terrine
marbled with salmon or brill, scallop, salmon and basil in pastry followed by ragôut of turbot, scallop and prawn with wild rice, a choice of
whole grilled dover sole, lemon sole, plaice or john dory. You can
choose 2 or 3 courses on the fixed-price menu which might offer rabbit, bacon and mushroom pie with a puff pastry top or a simple grilled
fillet steak and béarnaise sauce. There's something for most people
here.

DORKING   Partners West Street

2-4 West Street, Dorking, Surrey RH4 1BL
Telephone: (0306) 882826   **£45**
Open: lunch Tue-Fri+Sun, dinner Tue-Sat (closed Bank Holidays)
Meals served: lunch 12.30-2, dinner 7.30-9.30   ❖

Very different from the days when it was a fish and chip shop next to a
tea room! Now combined into one enterprise, it is Andrew Thomason
and Tim McEntire's dream restaurant located just off the main street.
Dinner is fixed price and spans a repertoire from boudin noir with
apples to casserole of mullet, squid and tomato with garlic and basil.

The talented team deserve support for their consistently good food.

DORRINGTON   Country Friends

Dorrington, Nr Shrewsbury, Shropshire SY5 7JD
Telephone: (0743) 718707   **£40**
Open: lunch + dinner Tue-Sat (closed Bank Holidays, last 2 wks Jul,
first wk Oct)
Meals served: lunch 12-2, dinner 7-9

This part-timbered building houses a comfortable restaurant and 3
coach-house bedrooms with attractive antiques but no phone or TV
(paradise!). A set dinner menu could be chicken salad with ginger
dressing, fillets of sole with a parmesan soufflé and white wine sauce
and a choice from hot white chocolate soufflé, brandy snaps with dark
and white chocolate cream, lemon flan, poppy seed parfait with plum
sauce or fruit terrine with strawberry sauce. There is also a choice of 6
starters and 6 main courses from the à la carte menu.

DREWSTEIGNTON   Hunts Tor House

Drewsteignton, Devon EX6 6QW
Telephone: (0647) 21228   **£40**
Open: dinner daily (closed Dec-mid Mar)
Meals served: dinner 7.30

Restaurant with 4 rooms situated in the centre of Dartmoor village.
There is no printed menu as they offer a no-choice 4-course dinner
which might include grilled goat's cheese, lemon sole with sorrel and
butter sauce, white chocolate terrine, a choice of Devon cheeses and
coffee. Concise but reasonably priced wine list with no bottle over £16.
The restaurant seats 8, so booking is essential. The overnight accommodation price includes a breakfast of scrambled egg and smoked
salmon.

DULVERTON   Ashwick House

Dulverton, Somerset TA22 9QD
Telephone: (0398) 23868   **£45**
Open: lunch Sun, dinner daily
Meals served: lunch 12.30-1.45, dinner 7.15-8.30

If you want to leave the hurly-burly behind, you can certainly get away
from it all at Ashwick House. Built at the turn of the century for a
wealthy Bristol businessman, it is perched up on top of Exmoor hills
overlooking the wooded Barle Valley. Inside, the proportions of the
hall are baronial with a wide gallery and original William Morris wallpaper! Richard Sherwood runs this quiet hotel as a one-man show, act-
ing as both chef and host, and offering a menu that is concise and simple but well cooked. Dishes such as pork with a sorrel and spinach
stuffing, cream of cauliflower soup and a smoked mackerel hot pot are
typical.

DUNBRIDGE   Mill Arms Inn

Dunbridge, Nr Romsey, Hampshire SO51 0LF
Telephone: (0794) 340401   **£45**
Open: lunch + dinner daily
Meals served: lunch 12-2 (Sun 12-2.30), dinner 7-10 (Fri+Sat 7-10.30)

This free house in the village has had a complete overhaul and a fresh
coat of green paint outside. Inside are Niall Morrow and Sean O'Brien,
offering a menu that far outstrips ordinary pub grub and includes caesar salad, salmon with sweet onion and lemon butter sauce and duck
with port and grape sauce.

DUXFORD   Duxford Lodge

Ickleton Road, Duxford, Nr Cambridge, Cambridgeshire CB2 4RU
Telephone: (0223) 836444 Fax: (0223) 832271   **£30**
Open: lunch Sun-Fri, dinner daily
Meals served: lunch 12-2, dinner 7-9.30

Owners Ron and Sue Craddock formerly ran the Saffron Hotel in
Saffron Walden, and here too there's a relaxed and well-run feel about
the place which immediately helps you unwind. Enjoy traditional cooking from the à la carte and fixed-price 3-course menus which include
some dishes with an exotic touch such as deep-fried croquettes of crab
with lime, mango and chilli.

EAST BOLDON   Forsters

2 St Bedes, Station Road, East Boldon, Tyne & Wear NE36 OLE
Telephone: 091-519 0929   **£50**
Open: lunch Sun, dinner Tue-Sat
Meals served: lunch 12-2, dinner 7-10.30

Gilt frames and clever lighting give the place a spacious feel and make
a setting appropriate for Barry Forster's cooking. While Sue is at front
of house tending to the 7 tables, Barry creates dishes from a concise
menu - toasted muffin with smoked salmon, poached egg and hollandaise sauce, duck with black pudding and olive oil mash, chicken
with mild garlic and sage mousse and a bitter lemon tart with thick
cream or warm sponge pudding with hot toffee sauce. A rare find in
these parts - so be sure to book.

EAST BUCKLAND   Lower Pitt

East Buckland, Barnstaple, Devon EX32 0TD
Telephone: (0598) 760243 Fax: (0598) 760243   **£45**
Open: dinner Tue-Sat (closed 25+26 Dec)
Meals served: dinner 7-8.30

Start with an aperitif in the garden of this 16th-century cottage-style
farmhouse set right on the edge of Exmoor, for it's in this quiet hamlet
that Suzanne and Jerome Lyons have run their restaurant since 1978.
Using fresh produce from their own garden, Suzanne creates an
uncomplicated menu which might include a good home-made soup; a
spinach roulade with smoked salmon and cream cheese, fresh prawns,
mushrooms and cashew nuts all sautéed in garlic butter; or chicken
basquaise. Good puds and a very affordable wine list, all served in the
conservatory dining room. Make a night of it and book into one of the
3 double rooms.

EAST GRINSTEAD   Gravetye Manor

Vowels Lane, East Grinstead, West Sussex RH19 4LJ
Telephone: (0342) 810567 Fax: (0342) 810080   **£70**
Open: lunch + dinner daily (closed dinner Xmas day)
Meals served: lunch 12.30-2, dinner 7.30-9.30 (Sun 7.30-9)

Fish for brown or rainbow trout in the lake, wander through the
English flower and `natural' gardens designed by William Robinson
then return to one of 18 luxurious rooms, each named after a tree or
plant. I wonder whether Peter Herbert ever realised back in the '50s,
when he began quietly and personally to restore this lovely manor, the
extent and potential that his country house would reach? Now
amongst the country's finest, it wins acclaim for hospitality, and for the
cooking of Stephen Morey. The menus are a delightful balance of
reworked traditional and classical dishes, light yet robust. Try quail
and pigeon pâté en croute, steamed skate wings with a delicate caper
and tarragon mousse, wild mushroom timbale and poached Gravetye
hen's eggs with pan-fried foie gras, truffles and madeira sauce. With a
wine list that has been nurtured over time you can't fail to be
impressed.

EASTBOURNE   Grand Hotel

King Edward's Parade, Eastbourne, East Sussex BN21 4EQ
Telephone: (0323) 412345 Fax: (0323) 412233   £60
Open: lunch + dinner Tue-Sat (closed Bank Holidays, 2 wks Jan, 2 wks Aug)
Meals served: lunch 12.30-2.30, dinner 7-10.30
Victorian, whitewashed seaside hotel. Seafront position, 164 bedrooms and high
domed public rooms.

EDBURTON   Tottington Manor

Edburton, Nr Henfield, West Sussex BN5 9LJ
Telephone: (0903) 815757 Fax: (0903) 879331   £35
Open: lunch + dinner daily (closed 25+26 Dec, dinner Jan+Easter)
Meals served: lunch 12-2, dinner 7-9.15
Small hotel and restaurant with 6 bedrooms. Good breakfasts.

EDENBRIDGE   Honours Mill Restaurant

87 High Street, Edenbridge, Kent TN8 5AU
Telephone: (0732) 866757   **£70**
Open: lunch Tue-Fri + Sun, dinner Tue-Sat (closed 1 wk Xmas)
Meals served: lunch 12.15-2, dinner 7.15-10

Owned by the Goodhew boys (Duncan included), this converted mill
is the location for sensible French cooking by Martin Radmall. Fixed-
price menus (cheaper mid-week) include specialities such as terrine of
red mullet lining a salmon mousse with a sharp butter sauce, ragôut of
snails and wild mushrooms, sausage of lamb's sweetbreads and green
peppercorns with lentils or roast duck with orange and Grand Marnier
sauce and exotic fruits. If it's available, try the gigot d'agneau cooked
with just enough garlic and flavoured also with rosemary. A winter
pudding of warm ginger and cinnamon sponge served with pear and a
vanilla crème Anglaise is well worth sampling too.

ELCOT   Elcot Park Resort Hotel

Elcot, Nr Newbury, Berkshire RG16 8NJ
Telephone: (0488) 58100 Fax: (0488) 58288   £33
Open: lunch + dinner daily
Meals served: lunch 12.30-2, dinner 7.30-9.30
Georgian 75-bedroomed hotel between Newbury and Hungerford, surrounded by 16
acres of grounds planted in 1848 by Sir William Paxton, the Royal Gardener. New
leisure facilities.

ELTON   Loch Fyne Oyster Bar

The Old Dairy Building, Elton, Nr Peterborough, Cambridgeshire
PE8 6SG
Telephone: (0832) 280298   **£40**
Open: all day daily (closed 25+26 Dec, 1 Jan)
Meals served: 9-9 (Fri+Sat 9-11)

Opened at the beginning of last year and continuing to follow successfully in the footsteps of the other 3 bar-cum-restaurants, this is the
latest outlet for the Highland crustacea and whisky-barrel-smoked fish
group. There are no deluxe fixtures and fittings - the room is panelled
in Scots pine – but a relaxed informal atmosphere with booths for
those searching privacy over an oyster or two.

ELY   Fen House Restaurant

2 Lynn Road, Littleport, Ely, Cambridgeshire CB6 1QG
Telephone: (0353) 860645   **£50**
Open: dinner Tue-Sat (closed 25+26 Dec)
Meals served: dinner 7-9

Fresh seasonal ingredients go into potted leeks with smoked eel and
lemon dressing, breast of pheasant cooked with dry sherry and toasted
almond sauce, sea trout wrapped in lettuce, and these characterise
David Warne's fresh style of cooking. As owner and chef he works
hard with wife Gaynor at front of house to make your visit as enjoyable
an experience as possible.

ELY — Old Fire Engine House

25 St Mary's Street, Ely, Cambridgeshire CB7 4ER
Telephone: (0353) 662582   **£40**
Open: lunch daily, dinner Mon-Sat (closed Bank Holidays
2 wks Xmas/New Year)
Meals served: lunch 12.30-2, dinner 7.30-9 (light meals 10.30-5.30)

This restaurant-cum-art gallery has been drawing the crowds for many
a year. Uneven tiled floor, simple wooden tables and pew seating all
add to the eccentricity and allure of this restaurant. The cooking is
good, plain and typically English - ham, leek and potato soup, savoury
pies, pork chops in cider and jugged hare to name but a few. Good
wine list with reasonable prices.

EMSWORTH — 36 On The Quay

The Quay, South Street, Emsworth, Hampshire PO10 7EG
Telephone: (0243) 375592   **£65**
Open: lunch Mon-Fri+Sun, dinner Mon-Sat (closed Bank
Holidays, 1 wk Jan, 2 wks Sep)
Meals served: lunch 12-2, dinner 7-10

young, knowledgable staff in Raymond Shortland's

Right on the quay, the decor is yellow and the style upmarket. The fish
may be the finest but the table settings are not to be outdone either -
sparkling silver and elegant china. Chef Frank Eckermann has
brought in a new format with a menu gastronomique which proves
popular with the locals and visitors to these shores, as well as the seasonally changing à la carte. To whet your appetite - local king scallops
with leeks and sauce of lemon and chives, paupiettes of dover sole and
mussels and fillet of veal with sweet braised cabbage and a grain mustard sauce.

→ relaxed restaurant

ERPINGHAM — Ark

The Street, Erpingham, Norfolk NR11 7QB
Telephone: (0263) 761535   £40
Open: lunch Sun, dinner Tue-Sat (closed part of Oct, Tue in winter)
Meals served: lunch 12.30-2, dinner 7-9.30 (Sat 7-10)
Flint cottage with 3 bedrooms. Sheila Kidd's self-taught cooking gathers influences
from all over Europe.

ETON — Antico

42 High Street, Eton, Berkshire SL4 6BD
Telephone: (0753) 863977 Fax: (0628 30045)   **£70**
Open: lunch Mon-Fri, dinner Mon-Sat (closed Bank Holidays)
Meals served: lunch 12.30-2.30, dinner 7-10.30

Don't be misled by the old world atmosphere and the Stable Bar - this
is a place where you'd better book. Ernesto Cassini and Ennio
Morassi's restaurant has been here for 20 years and is as much a part
of everyday Eton life as the school. Authentic Italian food, fiercely popular with the locals.

EVERSHOT   Summer Lodge

Evershot, Dorchester, Dorset DT2 0JR
Telephone: (0935) 83424 Fax: (0935) 83005
Open: lunch + dinner daily
Meals served: lunch 12.30-1.30, dinner 7.30-9

£55

Still, thankfully, refusing bookings from large parties and conferences
to retain intimacy for the other diners, this delightful restaurant owned
by Nigel and Margaret Corbett is in the heart of Thomas Hardy country. The cooking is sound and offers a veritable glory of fixed-price and
à la carte menus. Dishes might include confit of duck with potato
galettes, pan-fried lamb's kidneys, pan-fried fillet of gurnard or tartlet
of tomato and olive. Good selection of local cheeses and puddings to
delight even the most jaded of palates. There's a good wine list and a
generally comfortable, warm feel to the well-tended, Georgian building
which boasts 17 well-designed bedrooms in the main house and stable
block.

EVERSLEY   New Mill Restaurant

New Mill Road, Eversley, Hampshire RG27 0RA
Telephone: (0734) 732277 Fax: (0734) 328780
Open: lunch Tue-Fri (+Sun in Grill), dinner Tue-Sat
 (daily in Grill) (closed 26+27 Dec, 1 Jan)
Meals served: lunch 12-2 (Sun all day 12-8), dinner 7-10

£55

❖

After stints at the Dorchester and Hintlesham Hall, Robert Allen has
come to rest at this most idyllic of settings. It's as pretty as a picture
with little bridges, streams, a working waterwheel and riverside gardens and terraces. All this quickly puts you in the mood for some
equally appealing food in either the Riverside Restaurant with its elegant glazed conservatory looking out over the river, or in the more
informal Grill Room situated in the oldest part of the waterwheel. The
Riverside Restaurant offers favourites such as a trio of home-made
pâtés and terrines or splendid Loch Fyne smoked salmon followed by
a rack of English Lamb with rosemary and roasted garlic or veal kidneys served in a grain mustard sauce; alternatively there are excellent
value fixed price 3-course table d'hoté lunch or dinner menus. The less
formal Grill Room offers simpler hearty bistro fare with dishes such as
mussels marinière, herby sausages with mash and onion gravy, or
hearty stews, casseroles and pies. Try the New Mill mixed grill to
really test your appetite! Alternatively during the week they offer a
recession beating 3-course "Meal for a Tenner" along with a selection
of Wines for a Tenner. Interesting vegetarian dishes are always available in both restaurants. Fine wines selected by manager, Anthony
Finn, and good service make this an admirable place to dine. Well
worth the drive out from London let alone Reading for this country
idyll.

EVESHAM   Riverside Hotel

The Parks, Offenham Road, Evesham, Hereford & Worcester WR11 5JP
Telephone: (0386) 446200 Fax: (0386) 40021   **£50**
Open: lunch Tue-Sun, dinner Tue-Sat
Meals served: lunch 12-2 (Sun 12-1.30), dinner 7.30-9

Check and double check the directions before you set out - it's worth
the trouble since this is a difficult place to find. A white pebble-dash
house, it stands by, and enjoys fine views across the gardens to, the
River Avon. Rosemary Willmott is a professional who pays careful
attention to detail and in her multi-faceted role as owner, keeper and
chef she makes everything cosy and pleasant. Dinner is fixed-price and
offers an extensive choice from local black pudding with Pommery
sauce and a delicious cream of turbot soup with prawns to main
courses cooked in the same homely style, such as young venison with
peppercorn, port and mushroom jus and salmon grilled with lime,
herbs and mangetout. 7 bedrooms.

EXETER   St Olaves Court

Mary Arches Street, Exeter, Devon EX4 3AZ
Telephone: (0392) 217736 Fax: (0392) 413054   £45
Open: lunch + dinner daily (closed 26 Dec-3 Jan)
Meals served: lunch 12-2, dinner 6.30-9.30
1827 town house in its own walled garden near the Cathedral. 15 Georgian-style
bedrooms, 50-seater restaurant.

EXETER   White Hart

South Street, Exeter, Devon EX1 1EE
Telephone: (0392) 79897 Fax: (0392) 50159   £30
Open: lunch Sun-Fri, dinner daily
Meals served: lunch 12-2, dinner 7-9.30
One of the city's most ancient inns, with 61 bedrooms. A must for historians and
travellers alike.

EYTON   Marsh Country Hotel

Eyton, Leominster, Hereford & Worcester HR6 0AG
Telephone: (0568) 613952   **£55**
Open: dinner daily
Meals served: dinner 7.30-9.30

Any qualms that either Martin or Jacqueline Gilleland might have had
when switching careers to run this hotel have been put to rest for the
hotel of their dreams is now very much a reality. In a 14th-century timbered house with only 5 bedrooms, they create a pleasing and cosy
atmosphere. Jacqueline, who was once a home economics teacher,
cooks in a homely style. Dinner at the Marsh could include hot pigeon
breast on a bed of salad leaves, marinated venison with apples and
cranberries and a dessert of Alsace rhubarb tart with ginger meringue
ice cream.

FALMOUTH — Seafood Bar

Lower Quay Hill, Falmouth, Cornwall
Telephone: (0326) 315129   **£40**
Open: dinner daily (closed Sun in winter)
Meals served: dinner 7-11

Down a passageway and a few steps you will find the lively bar that
everyone is talking about. The point of conversation is its fine array of
fresh seafood from stir-fried crab claws and Helford oysters to skate,
squid and lemon sole. Steaks round off the menu, and there is also an
excellent carpetbagger fillet stuffed with oysters - the best of both
worlds.

FARNHAM — Krug's

84 West Street, Farnham, Surrey GU9 7EN
Telephone: (0252) 723277   **£45**
Open: dinner Mon-Sat (closed Bank Holidays)
Meals served: dinner 7-11.30

The hills of Surrey are alive with Austrian fare that is well executed
and somewhat different. This Austrian restaurant might make you
want to pull on the lederhosen and reminisce over *The Sound of Music*.
After saying that, the Tyrolean red tablecloths create a cheerful ambience to this otherwise more rustic, log-burning setting. Tuck into
hearty dishes of fondues and schnitzels and steaks after a starter of
herrings marinated and served with schnapps or a clear soup with liver
dumpling, bacon dumpling or sliced pancake.

FAVERSHAM — Read's

Painter's Forstal, Faversham, Kent ME13 0EE   ⌘
Telephone: (0795) 535344 Fax: (0795) 591200   **£65**
Open: lunch + dinner Tue-Sat (closed Bank Holidays, 2 wks Aug)
Meals served: lunch 12-2, dinner 7-10   ❖

The menu and wine list alone make descriptive and absorbing reading
- Lunedale duckling with armagnac-soaked prunes and a sauce perfumed with fresh, local honeycomb, or brandade of smoked haddock
on a crisp salad of green beans with a virgin olive oil dressing: chef
and owner David Pitchford is indeed master of his subject. In refreshing contrast to so many establishments, David also actively encourages younger bon viveurs with a children's menu in an effort to
encourage young people to eat in restaurants, with the promise of no
fish fingers or burgers. With more people like Rona and David
Pitchford in the business we might be nearer to cracking the
European way of eating en famille. Very good wine list.

FELSTED — Rumbles Cottage

Braintree Road, Felsted, Essex CM6 3DJ
Telephone: (0371) 820996 **£30**
Open: lunch Sun, dinner Tue-Sat (closed Bank Holidays)
Meals served: lunch 12-2, dinner 7-9

The art of discovery continues down Joy's way: her guineapig menus continue to flourish as she tries out new and innovative ideas before allowing them to move, full-time, onto the carte. The reactions to her dishes she finds essential and are offered to adventurous diners on Tuesdays through to Thursdays. Thus Jamaican jerk pork, ackee and smoked cod and a pesto and aubergine roulade have had a recent showing. Such is her success that she has opened a second restaurant in Castle Hedingham.

FLETCHING — The Griffin Inn

Fletching, nr Uckfield, East Sussex TN22 6SS
Telephone: (0825) 722890 **£40**
Open: lunch + dinner daily (closed 25 Dec)
Meals served: lunch 12-2.15, dinner 7.30-10

The long and low main room under a Sussex tiled roof with oak beams, panelling and copper-canopied fireplaces makes this is a typical inn of its time. With Thursday the focal point of the week as fresh fish arrives from Newhaven, likely specials are pan-fried sprats and roast cod with dijon mustard - make sure you book in for that day. The selection of real ales and the local-brewed Harveys of Lewes help make it a very popular place with the locals.

FLITWICK — Flitwick Manor

Church Road, Flitwick, Bedfordshire MK45 1AE
Telephone: (0525) 712242 Fax: (0525) 712242 **£90**
Open: lunch + dinner daily
Meals served: lunch 12-1.30, dinner 7-9.30

Despite another change of management, the second in two years, this charming 17th- and 18th-century house has once again started to deliver the goods. Duncan Poyser has developed a fixed-price menu to peruse while you enjoy canapés, offering a selection of thoroughly modern dishes which make the most of fresh ingredients and read well. Try soup of grilled new season's tomatoes and sweet garlic, grilled pesto bread, or risotto of asparagus dusted with parmesan and lemon, followed by baked supreme of salmon resting on a delicate red bean, smoked bacon and parsley broth or roast chump of lamb with rosemary and olives. Vegetables are used as garnish rather than being served separately. Attention to detail such as making the dining room a non-smoking area and, at the end of the menu, an invitation to see the kitchens, makes this a very pleasant place.

FOLKESTONE · Paul's

2a Bouverie Road West, Folkestone, Kent CT20 2RX
Telephone: (0303) 59697 · £35
Open: lunch + dinner daily (closed Xmas)
Meals served: lunch 12-2.30, dinner 7.30-9.30 (Sat 7-10)

In a warm and friendly pink restaurant, imaginative cooking from Paul Hagger brings a mix of safe options and spicy ones. Paul's uncomplicated cooking uses the freshest of ingredients - a sweet pear stuffed with herb cream cheese pâté, coated with walnut vinaigrette, thin strips of turkey marinated in chillies, cayenne and tossed in butter with mustard seed or, more simply, brill poached gently in fish stock with white burgundy. A bottomless coffee pot and plenty of reasonable wines make this a pleasant and good value place to dine.

FOWEY · Food for Thought

Town Quay, Fowey, Cornwall PL23 1AT
Telephone: (0726) 832221 · £40
Open: dinner daily (closed Jan+Feb)
Meals served: 7-9

A small restaurant run by the Billingsley family, living up to its name. Well presented food, full of flavour with a menu that centres on seafood from scallops griddled simply with garlic and olive oil, to mussels and monkfish topped with crab meat and brioche crumbs and a saffron cream sauce. Meat dishes are available and the service remains friendly.

FRAMPTON-ON-SEVERN · Savery's Restaurant

The Green, Frampton-on-Severn, Gloucestershire GL2 7EA
Telephone: (0452) 740077 · £50
Open: dinner Tue-Sat
Meals served: dinner 7.30-9.15

A small country restaurant minutes from junction 13 off the M5. Owners John Savery and Patricia Carpenter run an evenings-only restaurant with a set menu of £21.95 for 3-courses. John creates a mousse from crab and prawns and serves it with a red pimento sauce or assembles a salad of mixed leaves with black pudding and quails eggs topped with crisp bacon and a light dijon mustard dressing. Main courses give a choice of fish of the day or a mix of beef, game (when in season) through to lamb. All are carefully, rather than elaborately cooked, with attention paid to the right balance of flavours - lamb with piquant sauce and deep-fried leeks and duck with a honey, orange and ginger sauce. Puddings round up all the favourites like prune and armagnac ice cream, chocolate and almond meringue and sticky toffee pudding.

FRESHFORD — Homewood Park

Hinton Charterhouse, Freshford, Avon BA3 6BB
Telephone: (0225) 723731 Fax: (0225) 723820   **£70**
Open: lunch + dinner daily
Meals served: lunch 12-1.45, dinner 7-9.30

Situated in an area of great natural beauty, Homewood Park with its 15 bedrooms is now in the hands of Frank and Sara Gueuning. Tim Ford arrived last year as chef and has brought with him a new stylish menu. Full of interest and flair, it consists of a well-balanced array of dishes - a shellfish bisque with mussels and sauté of yellow and red peppers, an individual pie of pan-fried quail with dumplings and a rich madeira sauce plus pink roasted best end of lamb with a light tarragon sauce and glazed vegetables.

FRESSINGFIELD — Fox and Goose

Fressingfield, Nr Diss, Suffolk IP21 5PB
Telephone: (037 986) 247 Fax: (037 986) 8107   **£55**
Open: lunch + dinner daily (closed 4 days Xmas)
Meals served: lunch 12-2, dinner 7-9.30

Ruth and David Watson moved with the times from Hintlesham Hall to this lovely black and white inn by the church, bringing with them all their knowledge and expertise. Ruth together with chef Brendan Ansbro calls on international elements for their affordable home cooking with bags of variety with even the starters available in main course size - Chinese crispy duck, sashimi of scallop, salmon and pickled ginger, sweet and sour rabbit with prunes and bitter chocolate to homemade sausages, mash, onions and gravy. Cheeses are a highlight featuring Irish, British and French varieties, as far as possibly made from raw milk. The wine list tours France, Italy, Spain, New World and South America, and then comes home to the village (look left of the church and through the graveyard for the vineyard), and good apple juice and cider are also available.

GARSTANG — El Nido

Whinney Brow Lane, Forton, Garstang, Nr Preston, Lancashire PR3 0AE
Telephone: (0524) 791254   £45
Open: lunch Tue-Fri + Sun, dinner daily (closed mid-week lunches
in winter, Bank Holidays)
Meals served: lunch 12-2, dinner 7-10.15
Spanish flavour - plenty of gambas, calamares, tortillas, flambéed steaks and paella.

Homewood Park

GILLINGHAM   Stock Hill House

Stock Hill, Gillingham, Dorset SP8 5NR
Telephone: (0747) 823626 Fax: (0747) 825628
Open: lunch Tue-Sun, dinner Tue-Sat
Meals served: lunch 12.30-1.45, dinner 7.30-9

£70

An enthusiastic couple, Peter and Nita Hauser belong to this 9-bed-roomed house as much as it belongs to them. Having restored it loving-ly and dressed it with antiques and designer fabrics, they have made it a hospitable and peaceful place to stay. The kitchen is the passion and responsibility of Peter who also tends to the kitchen garden, utilising the produce in his menus. His cooking is well practised and presented, the level of skill high and well documented in his menus, but it is his Austrian background that makes him a fine master of desserts. From the set dinner menu of 4 courses with a choice of 6 starters try the deli-cious wild mushroom and lamb sweetbreads lightly sautéed and full of flavour. Then there's a choice of 2 soups, followed by a choice of 5 main courses such as boned quail with an apple and duck liver stuffing, served with Madeira sauce. Peter always has one or two straightfor-ward choices, such as veal escalope, for the less adventurous. Any of the 5 choices of puds makes the journey worthwhile. A good wine list, with some reasonable prices.

GITTISHAM   Combe House

Gittisham, Nr Honiton, Devon EX14 0AD
Telephone: (0404) 42756 Fax: (0404) 46004
Open: dinner daily (closed Mon in Jan+Feb)
Meals served: dinner 7.30-9.30

£55

A family atmosphere still lives on in this stately 15-bedroomed Elizabethan mansion. Enjoy the richness of the rooms by relaxing in a comfy chair with a book or, in the fishing season, enjoy a fruitful after-noon by the River Otter. The feeling of well-being extends both sides of the front door, from the elegant lounges to the ancient cedars in the gardens.

GLASTONBURY   No. 3 Restaurant & Hotel

3 Magdelene Street, Glastonbury, Somerset BA6 9EW
Telephone: (0458) 832129
Open: dinner Tue-Sat (closed Dec+Jan)
Meals served: dinner 7.30-9

£60

A 20-seater restaurant in a neat Georgian town house with 6 stylish en-suite rooms makes this an ideal destination for visitors to this historic town. It's not far from the ruins of Glastonbury abbey. Ann and John Tynan serve a set 4-course menu which includes a choice of 5 starters, and 6 main courses with fresh vegetables, sorbet and dessert - pineap-ple and sunflower salad finished with yoghurt or fillets of smoked trout with a mustard and dill sauce set the scene followed by sautéed guinea fowl with a bouchée of mushrooms and shallots, monkfish provençale or bourguignonne of venison with port and rowan jelly. Desserts encompass red berries soaked in cointreau with chantilly and bite-sized meringues, or try the baked pear frangipane with apricot sauce. Cheese and biscuits are an extra £2.50, coffee and chocs £2.00. Some tables on the terrace in the summer.

GLOUCESTER — **Hatton Court**

Upton Hill, ,Upton St Leonards Gloucester, Gloucestershire GL4 8DE
Telephone: (0452) 617412 Fax: (0452) 612945　　　　**£50**
Open: lunch + dinner daily
Meals served: lunch 12.30-2, dinner 7.30-10 (Sun 7.30-9.30)

A restored 17th-century Cotswold stone house set in 37 acres of gardens and green pastures with views out across the Severn valley to the Malverns. In the dining room you can enjoy starters like confit, tartlette of mussels and leeks and ogen melon with pink champagne sorbet and main courses of chicken kiev with watercress and game chips or chateaubriand. Its main market is business people and tourists.

GOLANT — CORMORANT HOTEL

Golant, Nr Fowey, Cornwall PL23 1LL
Telephone: (0726) 833426 Fax: same　　　　**£50**
Open: lunch + dinner daily
Meals served: lunch 12.30-2, dinner 7-9

This hotel and riverside restaurant is situated above the lovely Fowey estuary in a small fishing village which is a centre for sailing and water-skiing. It's also well placed for travelling to and around the sights of Cornwall - the Poldark Mine, St Michael's Mount and Land's End are all about an hour away. The 11 bedrooms are airy and bright and take in the fabulous views. When the sun is shining take a seat by the swimming pool (the roof opens in fine weather) and relax. French chef Gilles Gaucher and proprietor Geoff Buckle do the cooking for which they are receiving much acclaim. Everything is home-made, from bread, pasta, ice creams, and breakfast marmalade to compôtes. A 4-course dinner and menu gastronomique are available.

GORING-ON-THAMES — **The Leatherne Bottel**

Goring-on-Thames, Berkshire RG8 0HS
Telephone: (0491) 872667　　　　**£60**
Open: lunch + dinner daily (closed 25 Dec)
Meals served: lunch 12.30-2 (Sat+Sun 12.30-2.30), dinner 7-9.30
　(Sun 7.30-9)

Book now for a summers lunch on the lawn - or a winter dinner with log fire blazing.

It's been 4 years since Keith Read came here as chef while Annie Bonnet began a mammoth planting scheme in the garden. In those 4 years the place has become a hit, the good food enhanced by the wonderful location. Clive O'Connor (ex-190 Queensgate) has joined the kitchen and continues the affinity with the char-grill with fillet steak and peppers, salmon with sweet ginger and basil and sun-dried tomatoes and local rabbit with white beans. Such is the industrious nature of this team that the herbs and salads are now all home-grown and bread freshly made. Attention to details to obtain the right supplies of fish, samphire and cheese is considerable and has paid off. A little tranquillity and good taste hidden on the banks of the Thames an hour from London.

GOUDHURST   Hughenden

The Plain, Goudhurst, Kent TN17 1AB
Telephone: (0580) 211771   **£35**
Open: lunch Wed-Sat, dinner Tue-Sat
Meals served: lunch 12-2, dinner 7.30-9.30

Light lunches are now also sometimes available at this village restaurant by the pond. Owner Nick Martin runs the front of house while
James Hooton is the chef. The menu is concise with a set dinner at
£14.95 and a selection of à la carte dishes. Both make imaginative use
of country ingredients - beetroot and bacon salad with caraway and
orange dressing or baked goat's cheese wrapped in sesame seeds.
Main courses from pan-fried lamb glazed with port and provençal
herbs or pigeon with bacon with prunes and red wine.

GRASMERE   Michael's Nook

Grasmere, Nr Ambleside, Cumbria LA22 9RP
Telephone: (053 94) 35496 Fax: (053 94) 35765   **£85**
Open: lunch + dinner daily
Meals served: lunch 12.30 for 1, dinner 7.30 for 8 (booking essential)

Wordsworth's poem inspired the name of this hotel and in terms of
accommodation and service, you couldn't do better. Dedicated hotelier
Reg Gifford has been at the helm since the late '60s when he opened
this house of 14 bedrooms and, with the years, the charm of the place
has grown. Kevin Mangeolles looks happily settled in after his mete-
oric rise from sous chef to the boss of the kitchen. On an extravagant
gourmet menu he serves foie gras with orange and sauternes dressing
and lamb with aubergine and tomato gateau, while dessert is a white
chocolate soup with a dark chocolate soufflé and cherries. If 6 courses
on that scale prove too much, choose the dinner menu which lacks
none of the skill, for example pig's trotter with maxime potatoes and
timbale of spinach and sweetbreads. The interior of this house is full of
interesting antiques and paintings, reflecting Reg Gifford's other passion: antiques.

GRASMERE   White Moss House

Rydal Water, Grasmere, Cumbria LA22 9SE
Telephone: (053 94) 35295   **£55**
Open: dinner Mon-Sat (closed Dec-Feb)
Meals served: dinner 7.30 for 8

Consistency and continuity are watch-words at this small hotel once
owned by William Wordsworth but now tended by the Dixon family.
Susan keeps homely touches in all the rooms while no meal is served
unless Peter is cooking. But rest assured, he doesn't miss a session.
Dinner is served promptly at 8.00 and is a no-choice-until-pudding
affair, typified by carrot, coriander and lentil soup, roast venison with
woodland mushrooms and purée of salsify, celeriac and parsnip with
heather honey. Advocates of British farmhouse cheese, the Dixons'
selection is a beauty, with Sharpham brie, Botton, Cloisters and other
new and not so widely known varieties on show every night. The puddings are good but the cheese must be tried at least once during your
stay.

GRASMERE   Wordsworth Hotel

Grasmere, Nr Ambleside, Cumbria LA22 9SW
Telephone: (053 94) 35592 Fax: (053 94) 35765   **£65**
Open: lunch + dinner daily
Meals served: lunch 12.30-2, dinner 7-9 (Fri+Sat 7-9.30)

Bernard Warne's cooking is a highly complex mix of flavours, such as
a mille feuille of calves' sweetbreads and crisp vermicelli on a hazelnut
jus or tenderloin of pork wrapped in brioche with sage and a coarse
broccoli and raisin sauce. Modern and vibrant, the food is a real highlight, as is the 2-foot high menu! However, the rest of the 37-bed-
roomed hotel is quiet and tranquil, perhaps out of respect to
Wordsworth himself – he's buried in the churchyard next door.

GRAYSHOTT   Woods Place

Headley Road, Grayshott, Nr Hindhead, Surrey GU26 6LB
Telephone: (0428) 605555   **£45**
Open: lunch + dinner Tue-Sat (closed 1 wk Xmas)
Meals served: lunch 12-2.30, dinner 7-11

A useful escape from nearby health farm

The strong similarity to Anna's Place in London comes as no surprise
once you realise that chef/patron Eric Norrgren is Anna's brother.
The dishes also show a distinct resemblance and there's ice-cold aqua-
vit to send a rush and glowing warmth right out to the finger tips and
toes, as well as Swedish mineral water and beer. There is a rustic slant
to the authentic Swedish cooking in the unlikely setting of an old
butcher's shop. Uncomplicated dishes include the ubiquitous gravadlax, marinated baltic herrings, Jansson's temptation – a traditional
bake of potatoes, herring and cream which join other more international main courses such as skate with beurre noisette, salmon in cajun
spices and preserved duck with onions, honey and red wine.

– but watch out, I was caught by matron!

GREAT DUNMOW   The Starr

Market Place, Great Dunmow, Essex CM6 1AX
Telephone: (0371) 874321 Fax: (0371) 876337   **£70**
Open: lunch + dinner Sun-Fri (closed 1 wk Jan)
Meals served: lunch 12-1.30, dinner 7-9.30

English food with a delicate French accent is the best way to describe
Mark Fisher's cooking. Owner Brian Jones has been here since 1979
and enjoys an enviable reputation and much acclaim for his restaurant
with 8 bedrooms. Fresh scallops with bacon, beetroot roulade or vegetable beignets whet your appetite and show an imagination and skill
seen rarely in this part of the world. Calves' kidneys wrapped in bacon
and roasted with a mustard sauce or medallions of beef with aubergine
and port continue the mood. A good showing of wines, mostly French.
This is a reliable and relaxed establishment, much loved and cared for,
and it continues to cater for a loyal and expanding clientèle.

GREAT GONERBY   Harry's Place

17 High Street, Great Gonerby, Grantham, Lincolnshire NG31 8JS
Telephone: (0476) 61780   **£80**
Open: lunch + dinner Tue-Sat (closed Bank Holidays, 1 wk Xmas)
Meals served: lunch 12-2, dinner 7-9.30

The menus, handwritten with care, give an indication of the attention
to detail and skill that Harry Hallam puts into his cooking. With a
choice of 2 dishes at each course, normally one fish and one meat for
main courses, you might be offered a soupe de poisson served with an
unusual saffron and anchovy rouille and, if it's available, try the
Lincolnshire partridge, which he roasts with some tarragon, Parma
ham, coriander, white wine and madeira. A good tangy tarte au citron
to finish. A concise but well chosen wine list. They're prepared to open
on Sundays and Mondays, if you book in advance. Whilst Harry's Place
isn't cheap, it is only a 10 seater restaurant, and you do have the virtually undivided attention of Harry and Caroline, so enjoy the relaxed
atmosphere of this elegant Georgian house.

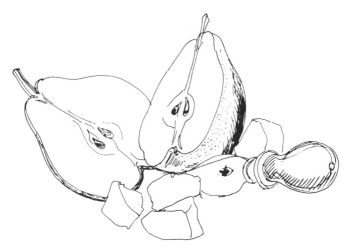

GREAT MILTON   Le Manoir aux Quat'Saisons

Church Road, Great Milton, Oxfordshire OX44 7PD
Telephone: (0844) 278881 Fax: (0844) 278847
Open: lunch + dinner daily
Meals served: lunch 12.15-2.30, dinner 7.15-10.30

£130

The illustrious manor was originally built for a French nobleman: how appropriate then, that it is now home to the cuisine of one of the greatest French chefs of our time. All that you see is the result of dedicated hard work and sheer pleasure. The dining room is an accolade to Raymond Blanc's mastery, his faultless presentation and the dishes of excellence one has come to expect. The production is headed by restaurant director Alain Desenclos, assisted by Etienne Uzureau, cooked by head chef Clive Fretwell and provided for by head gardener Anne-Marie Owens. Warm rolls are a fine vehicle for some Echiré butter and mean that a meal starts as it means to go on. Try morels filled with chicken mousse poached in Arbois wine with asparagus and lamb sweetbreads or clams, oysters, scallops and seaweed lightly poached in lime - these are just some of the hors d'oeuvres. Main courses might include pan-fried beef in a matured Modena vinegar sauce with candied shallots and a herb sabayon, or baby squid roasted with red mullet with sea urchin corals and a meat jus. Cheeses from Britain and France are presented in the traditional way, whereas dessert might be a cider and calvados mousse with crystallines or apple sorbet on an apple and vanilla coulis. Lavish and correct cooking from a brilliant man and a leading team makes this an oasis for the weekend, for the hotel now offers 21 luxury bedrooms.

GREAT MISSENDEN   La Petite Auberge

107 High Street, Great Missenden, Buckinghamshire HP16 0BB
Telephone: (024 06) 5370
Open: dinner Mon-Sat (closed Bank Holidays, Xmas/New Year)
Meals served: dinner 7.30-10.30

£55

A smart local French restaurant with the Martel owners offering everything French, from wine and wording on the menu through to the totally French cheese board. Only open for dinner, they tempt with whole-hearted French cooking - the best. Braised fillets of red mullet with fresh herbs, fricasée of corn-fed chicken in a white vinegar sauce with mushrooms and lardons and fillet of beef with truffles. Caramelized lemon tart and iced nougat with chocolate sauce bring a sensible end to the meal with a glass of 10-year-old pineau des charentes.

GREAT YARMOUTH   Seafood Restaurant

85 North Quay, Great Yarmouth, Norfolk NR30 1JF
Telephone: (0493) 856009   **£55**
Open: lunch Mon-Fri, dinner Mon-Sat (closed Bank Holidays,
3 wks Xmas)
Meals served: lunch 12-1.45, dinner 7-10.30

Choose your own fish from the fridge or a live lobster from a tank
and then leave it up to chefs Chris Kikis and Mark Chrisostomon.
Whichever way it's cooked – grilled, poached, in batter or with a
sauce - the fresh fish arrives daily. Steaks are available for the meat-
eaters. Large selection of white wines and half bottles.

GRIMSTON   Congham Hall

Lynn Road, Grimston, King's Lynn, Norfolk PE32 1AH   ✿
Telephone: (0485) 600250 Fax: (0485) 601191   **£50**
Open: lunch Sun-Fri, dinner daily (closed Bank Holiday lunches)
Meals served: lunch 12.30-2, dinner 7.30-9.30

Congham Hall has already proved to us that it is a place well worth
remembering for both its setting, amiable staff and excellent food. The
standard continues unabated and the gardens continue to flourish,
especially the herb garden which supplements Murray Chapman's
cooking. Owners Christine and Trevor Forecast deserve the praise
that this Georgian country house receives since they care for it meticulously with touches like fresh arrangements of flowers and herbs in
the 14 individually-decorated bedrooms. Peace and quiet reign, with a
cosy fire in winter and well-kept lawns and parklands to enjoy in the
summer. The restaurant is open to residents, their guests and non-residents for breakfast, lunch and dinner.

GUERNSEY   Absolute End

St George's Esplanade, St Peter Port, Guernsey, Channel Islands
Telephone: (0481) 723822 Fax: (0481) 729129   **£45**
Open: lunch + dinner Mon-Sat (closed Jan)
Meals served: lunch 12-2, dinner 7-10

A small cottage-style, sea-front restaurant specialising in fish and shellfish about half a mile from the Elizabeth marina. Assiette de fruits de
mer, grilled sardines, oysters florentine and lobster bisque are complemented by a couple of meat dishes or vegetarian options. A whole host
of fish mains ranging from grilled ray with capers, scallops meuniere,
crab thermidor to monkfish steaks with pepper sauce. Good value
table d'hôte lunch menu at £10.

GUERNSEY   La Frégate

Les Cotils, St Peter Port, Guernsey, Channel Islands
Telephone: (0481) 724624 Fax: (0481) 720443   **£40**
Open: lunch + dinner daily
Meals served: lunch 12.30-2, dinner 7-10

Majoring on scenery, this 13-bedroomed hotel set on a secluded hillside enjoys spectacular south-westerly views of the town and harbour.
The outdoor terrace makes the ideal place to take a long cool drink
and watch the sun go down while the lights of the harbour come up.
Eating in the dining room requires a jacket and tie, and French food is
served in the classic tradition. The table d'hôte menu offers a good
value, 4-course dinner plus coffee for £18.00 and might include fried
goujons of sole with tartare sauce from a choice of 4 starters, followed
by coquilles St Jacques bretonne from the 4 choices of main course.

GUERNSEY   La Grande Mare Hotel

Vazon Bay, Guernsey, Channel Islands
Telephone: (0481) 56577 Fax: (0481) 56532   **£80**
Open: lunch + dinner daily
Meals served: lunch 12-2, dinner 7-9.30

Situated in over 100 acres of private grounds, this golf and country
club hotel offers 27 rooms and a variety of facilities - the bright and
airy dining room actually looks out onto the golf course. Adrian Jones
mans the kitchen and fills the menu with a mix of classical and robust
dishes. The menu gourmand (recommended for the whole table)
might offer a salade de jambon fumé et d'avocat, then saumon grillé à
la Grande Mare, a granité de vin blanc to rest your palate before moving on to filet de boeuf grillé aux champignons du bois. La ballade au
chocolat et poire then café et petits fours bring the proceeding to a
grand finale, all for the equally grand price of £39! His cooking is precise with an eye for detail while the service is masterly. Much attention
is paid to the wine with different bins recommended to accompany
each course.

GUERNSEY   Louisiana

South Esplanade, St Peter Port, Guernsey, Channel Islands
Telephone: (0481) 713157 Fax: (0481) 712191   **£35**
Open: lunch + dinner Wed-Mon (closed Bank Holidays)
Meals served: lunch 12-2.30, dinner 6-10.30

The French and Italian specialities with Cajun overtones offered at dinner will be as pleasant as the panoramic views of Havelet Bay and the
two other closest islands, Herm and Sark. An all-inclusive carte offers
plenty of choice and good value for money.

GUERNSEY · Le Nautique

The Quay Steps, St Peter Port, Guernsey, Channel Islands
Telephone: (0481) 721714 **£45**
Open: lunch + dinner Mon-Sat (closed 1st 2 wks Jan)
Meals served: lunch 12-2, dinner 7-10

Typically French in all aspects, situated right on the harbour, and booking is essential. Fish is what you come here for - monk, scallops, brill, sea bass, turbot, prawns, lobster, each cooked in a variety of ways from grilled and poached to sauced. The vegetables are extra but a great selection is offered.

GUERNSEY · Old Government House

Ann's Place, St Peter Port, Guernsey, Channel Islands
Telephone: (0481) 724921 Fax: (0481) 724429 £55
Open: lunch + dinner daily
Meals served: lunch 12-2, dinner 7-9.15
The original Governor's residence with traditional service and furnishings. Plans in the pipeline for a brasserie and winter garden.

GUERNSEY · St Pierre Park

Rohais, St Peter Port, Guernsey, Channel Islands
Telephone: (0481) 728282 Fax: (0481) 712041 £35
Open: lunch Sun-Fri, dinner Mon-Sat
Meals served: lunch 12-2.30, dinner 7-10.30
135 suites and rooms with balcony or terrace, parklands, ornamental lake and leisure facilities including 9-hole golf course, huge snooker room and indoor pool.

GUIST · Tollbridge

Dereham Road, Guist, Norfolk NR20 5NU
Telephone: (036 284) 359 **£45**
Open: lunch Thu/Fri+Sun (Sun only in winter), dinner Tue-Sat (closed Tue in winter)
Meals served: lunch 12.30-1.30, dinner 7.30-9 (Sat 7-9)

From the terrace of this restaurant, set on the river Wensum, you can watch or hear the wildlife in the rushes - the ideal setting for an aperitif before dinner. The menu is varied with something for just about everyone, from spicy pecan nut and Stilton salad, smoked salmon in filo with lemon sauce, cassoulet to sausage and mash.

GULWORTHY   Horn of Plenty

Gulworthy, Tavistock, Devon PL19 8JD
Telephone: (0822) 832528 Fax: same   **£55**
Open: lunch Tue-Sun, dinner daily (closed 25+26 Dec)
Meals served: lunch 12-2, dinner 7-9.30

Living in the shadow of former owner, Sonia Stevenson, cannot be easy but Elaine and Ian Gatehouse have managed brilliantly, lighting up this 200-year-old house with their own flair and enthusiasm. Overlooking the Tamar valley it is surrounded by gardens and inside is filled with flowers arranged by Elaine. Well-balanced and fixed-price menus are the responsibility of Peter Gorton with dishes such as pan-fried skate with a gazpacho sauce or a warm sausage of rabbit with a mustard sauce. From a selection of 5 main course you might be offered chicken with goats' cheese coated with sesame seeds, or a fillet of venison with nectarines and a pepper sauce. Dessert might be a vanilla bavarois with a passion fruit sauce or selection of sorbets. Good selection of house wines served by the glass, smooth service. Six of the 7 pine-furnished bedrooms are in a separate stable block, each with its own balcony overlooking the Tamar valley.

HALFORD   Sykes House

Queen Street, Halford, Shipston-on-Stour, Warwickshire CV36 5BT
Telephone: (0789) 740976   **£70**
Open: dinner daily (Sun+Tue by arrangement only)
Meals served: dinner 7.30-8.15 (booking essential)

Reservations need to be made 24 hours in advance, and with good reason. David does the cooking while Peggy Cunliffe looks after the front of house at what is called `the home to dine in.' David buys, cooks and serves only daily fresh ingredients (that's why they need the notice) and creates a menu that is set at £32.50 which includes 6 courses, coffee and wine. Guests (for that is what you will feel like) arrive between 7.30 and 8.15 and the evening begins with welcoming appetizers. From then on the dining room becomes a theatre as each successive course is staged - chilled ruby consommé with garden chive cream and smoked buttermilk, fillet of lamb with char-grilled polenta and minted ragôut, Munster cheese with seedless grapes and apricot and pistachio bread. An eating experience.

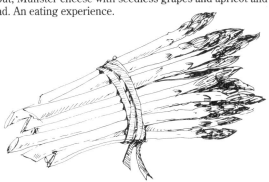

HAMPTON WICK   Le Petit Max

97A High Street, Corner Village Road, Hampton Wick, Middlesex
KT2 5NB
Telephone: 081-977 0236   **£45**
Open: lunch Sun, dinner daily (closed 4 days beginning each month)
Meals served: lunch 12.30 + 3.45, dinner 7-11.15

The Chez Max brothers (that's Max and Marc Renzland), who were
known in Kew for their exalted cooking have turned up here, in a modest abode, sharing shifts with a café by day, so look out for the name
Borzois above the door. They are only on duty at night plus Sunday
lunch and you have to get there early because 7 tables are all they
have and they fill up quickly. Unpretentious food is what you'll get
here, with a set menu that also has extras listed at a supplement. The
manner is chummy; the food is exceptionally good and the pastry chef
certainly knows his stuff. Expect to see a classic, rich, pork pâté with
toast, plenty of seafood with mayonnaise and the likes of guinea fowl
with wilted rocket and a pepper sauce, a generous portion of turbot
with samphire and hollandaise (a £5 surcharge for this) or prime
Aberdeen Angus beef with fleur de sel and sauce béarnaise.

HANCHURCH   Hanchurch Manor
Hanchurch, Nr Stoke-on-Trent, Staffordshire ST4 8JD
Telephone: (0782) 643030 Fax: (0782) 643035   £55
Open: dinner daily (for residents only)
Meals served: dinner 7.30-9.30
Lovely 9-bedroomed hotel in its own grounds – dinner available for residents only.

HARROGATE   Bettys Café & Tea Rooms

1 Parliament Street, Harrogate, North Yorkshire HG1 2QU
Telephone: (0423) 502746 Fax: (0423) 565191   **£30**
Open: all day daily (closed 25+26 Dec, 1 Jan)
Meals served: 9-9

'Fresh and dainty'– this is the original of the tea rooms and cake shops
opened in 1919 by Swiss confectioner Frederick Belmont. Their success has always centred on the excellent home-baked range of breads,
biscuits, scones, muffins and cakes. These days it also stays open in
the evenings with the tinkle of the resident pianist adding to the sense
of occasion. Home-cooked specials include bacon rösti with melted
raclette, Welsh rarebit, croustades, Masham sausages with red cabbage and new potatoes, soups, bakes and salads.

HARROGATE   Café Fleur

3 Royal Parade, Harrogate, North Yorkshire HG1 2SZ
Telephone: (0423) 503034   **£35**
Open: dinner daily (closed 25+26 Dec, 1 Jan)
Meals served: dinner 6-9.30

Right opposite the Crown Hotel is Tim and Kath Burdekin's brasserie-style restaurant. It offers good food - omelettes, baguettes, steak sandwiches and a selection of prix-fixe menus. £14.95 will buy you pâté of venison, hare and pheasant with cumberland sauce, pancakes of asparagus, fennel and broccoli or lemon sole, rounded off with raspberry mousse or crème caramel and with a half bottle of house wine included in the price.

HARROGATE   Drum & Monkey

5 Montpellier Gardens, Harrogate, North Yorkshire HG1 2TF
Telephone: (0423) 502650   **£45**
Open: lunch + dinner Mon-Sat (closed Xmas/New Year)
Meals served: lunch 12-2.30, dinner 7-10.15

The Drum & Monkey continues to be one of the places in Harrogate, from the busy downstairs bar to the slate-topped tables in the upstairs room - full of people enjoying themselves, eating their way through the fish menu. It's the sort of place you can return to time and again to try the different varieties on offer: oysters, langoustines, prawns, crab and lobster cocktail, lobster cooked 4 different ways - my favourite still remains steamed with garlic butter - salmon, trout, monkfish and sea bass, 4 different weights of dover sole and you've probably got the picture by now! A choice of white Burgundy and Loire wines, with a few others to choose from including a couple of reds.

HARROGATE   The Dusty Miller Restaurant

Low-Laithe, Summerbridge, Harrogate, West Yorkshire HG3 4BU
Telephone: (0423) 780837   **£55**
Open: dinner Tue-Sat (closed 25 Dec, 1 Jan, 2 wks Aug)
Meals served: dinner 6.30-11

Chef/proprietor Brian Dennison runs front of house and kitchen with ease and flair. The cooking is simple but not unimaginative - the kind of food he and his wife Elizabeth probably enjoy - escalope of salmon and chives, seafood medley and roast pheasant, prunes and armagnac. 3 menus exist, the first aptly named the proprietors' menu with the dishes of the day and their suggestions for wine; the regular dinner menu; and a special 1-course late dinner menu available after 9.30 (not Saturdays) offering dishes like salmon with spinach hollandaise, stir-fried lamb or fillet of beef au poivre.

HARROGATE   MILLER'S THE BISTRO

1 Montpelier Mews, Harrogate, North Yorkshire HG1 2TG
Telephone: (0423) 530708   £55
Open: lunch Tue-Sun, dinner Tue-Sat
Meals served: lunch 12-2 (Sun 12-3.30), dinner 6.30-10

Some changes have taken place here, with a new oak floor and new cutlery and linen, otherwise service and accomplished cooking remain of a high standard. Simon Gueller is in the kitchen producing good food such as Mediterranean fish soup with rouille and croutons, risotto of saffron, lobster with ginger and spring vegetables or roast rump of lamb with provençale vegetables, and jus of olives.

HARVINGTON   The Mill

Anchor Lane, Harvington, Nr Evesham, Hereford & Worcester WR11 5NR
Telephone: (0386) 870688 Fax: (0386) 870688   £50
Open: lunch + dinner daily (closed 5 days Xmas)
Meals served: lunch 12-1.45, dinner 7-8.45 (Sun 7-8.30)

There is still a place for an old-fashioned dedication to providing hospitality - and it doesn't have to be expensive to be good, as proved at Simon and Jane Greenhalgh's 15-bedroomed hotel. Set in almost 8 acres of wooded parkland with willows on the riverside, herons stalking the shallow waters and woodpeckers, kingfishers and even mink darting about, this is an enchanting place. Menus are frequently changed and every use is made of local Evesham produce. Jane and her small team cook in an admirably simple way. Dinner offers the widest choice and Sunday lunch at £12.95 or £10.95 for 3- or 2-courses respectively includes all the firm favourites with loin of pork with apple sauce, chicken with cider and sage, and lamb with redcurrant and rosemary. A comprehensive wine list includes many half bottles.

HASLEMERE   Morel's

23 Lower Street, Haslemere, Surrey GU27 2NY
Telephone: (0428) 651462   £50
Open: lunch Tue-Fri, dinner Tue-Sat (closed Bank Holidays (open Good Friday, 2 wks Feb, 3 wks Sep/Oct)
Meals served: lunch 12.30-2, dinner 7-10

From a converted row of terraced cottages, this calm, simple restaurant is where Jean-Yves Morel practices his repertoire that is typically French and of an excellent standard. His fixed-price menu includes fish soup, lamb's sweetbreads with quail's eggs, Cornish gurnard with cucumber spaghetti or rabbit cooked with mustard and prunes. This is what his local clientele have come to expect and what he continues to provide. Dessert is sweet perfection with crème Grandmère or lemon tarte.

This is the sort of restaurant that would tempt me to live in Haslemere

HASTINGS   Roser's

4 Eversfield Place, St Leonards on Sea, Nr Hastings, East Sussex
TN37 6DB
Telephone: (0424) 712218   **£45**
Open: lunch Tue-Fri, dinner Tue-Sat (closed Bank Holidays, 1 wk
Jan, 1 wk Aug)
Meals served: lunch 12-2, dinner 7-10

If sun, sand and sea are not the order of the day, head straight for Herr
Röser's seafront restaurant and enjoy the view from there. Undeniably
European it collects together all those influences and amalgamates
them into his short menu, loin of marsh lamb with tapenade, guinea
fowl with lardons and mushrooms, or home-smoked chicken with
orange mustard and whisky sauce. Good wine selection at reasonable
prices.

HATFIELD HEATH   Down Hall

Hatfield Heath, Nr Bishop's Stortford, Hertfordshire CM22 7AS
Telephone: (0279) 731441 Fax: (0279) 730416   £45
Open: lunch + dinner daily (closed New Year)
Meals served: lunch 12.30-2, dinner 7-10
Handsome Italianate mansion set in some 100 acres of parkland with 103 bedrooms,
conference facilities, desks and leisure facilities.

HAVANT   Cockle Warren Cottage

36 Seafront, Hayling Island, Havant, Hampshire PO11 9HL
Telephone: (0705) 464838   **£55**
Open: dinner daily (for residents only)
Meals served: dinner 7.30 for 8

Cockle Warren is a very small hotel on the seafront with only 5 bedrooms, but even so it has much to recommend it, including a large garden and heated swimming pool. Food is also of great importance at
breakfast as well as dinner, and you will find hen and duck eggs as
part of the full English breakfast, all cooked by co-owner Diane
Skelton. Most of the dishes are based on French and traditional
English country cooking with emphasis on the best ingredients. Local
fisherman, Ian, nets the catch each day in his boat the Sole Ventura,
while duck, guinea fowl and bread flour all come from France. This is
cooking for hearty appetites. Plans are well underfoot for a new garden
area which should be finished for 1994.

HAWORTH   Weavers

15 West Lane, Haworth, Nr Bradford, West Yorkshire BD22 8DU
Telephone: (0535) 643822   **£35**
Open: lunch Sun in winter, dinner daily (closed Mon in winter, Bank
Holidays (open 25 Dec), 2 wks Xmas, 2 wks Jul)
Meals served: lunch 12-1.30, dinner 7-9

Good straightforward cooking with no messing about - Yorkshire pud
wi' rich onion gravy, Pennine beefsteak and onion pie with afters that
include Nannie's meringues and old school pud. A restaurant and bar
with 4 guest rooms, it's a zany and informal place with everything
made on the premises and most of the vegetables home-grown.

HAYFIELD BRIDGE END RESTAURANT

7 Church Street, Hayfield, Derbyshire SK12 5JE
Telephone: (0663) 747321   **£45**
Open: lunch Sun, dinner Tue-Sat
Meals served: lunch 12.30-2.30, dinner 7-10

If you've a keen eye for prices, this is the restaurant to come to for reasonable, quality wines and astoundingly good cooking. Jonathan
Holmes cooks up a storm with his good value dishes that are well-pre-
sented - pike tart with chervil cream, sea bass with pickled ginger and
a sesame scented jus or, for vegetarians, aubergines cooked with
tomatoes, coriander, cumin and fennel and finished with Greek
yoghurt. Desserts may include fresh strawberries with sweetened
mascarpone, or apple crumble with cinnamon and raisins. An infec-
tiously friendly mood takes over the evening. There are also 4 bedrooms, and the whole place is well run by Geoffrey and Barbara Tier.

HAYTOR Bel Alp House

Haytor, Nr Bovey Tracey, Devon TQ13 9XX
Telephone: (0364) 661217 Fax: (0364) 661292   £75
Open: dinner daily (closed Dec-Feb)
Meals served: dinner 7.30-8.30
Marvellous location, comfortable and peaceful interior, perfectionism throughout the
lounges and bedrooms. Lovely gardens.

HELFORD Riverside

Helford, Nr Helston, Cornwall TR12 6JU
Telephone: (0326) 231443 Fax: (0326) 231103   **£40**
Open: lunch daily in summer, dinner daily (closed mid Nov-early Feb)
Meals served: lunch 12.15-1.45, dinner 7.30-9.30

If you want to be up the creek without a paddle, then this is where you
should aim to come to rest. The pretty, cottagey retreat is home to 7
bedrooms and Susie Darrell's essentially simple cooking that relies
heavily on local produce, in particular seafood such as mussels with
crab and avocado and a dill dressing, steamed fillet of turbot with pan-
fried scallops with parsley butter sauce. Puddings might include
sliced banana glazed with almond sabayon or layered strawberry
shortbreads. Edward Darrell's expertise can be seen in the extensive
and weighty wine list with a good choice of half bottles and house
wines. Take breakfast on the terrace with home made croissants and
marmalade. Some stunning views and walks can then give you an
appetite for an enjoyable lunch.

HELMSLEY Monet's

19 Bridge Street, Helmsley, North Yorkshire YO6 5BG
Telephone: (0439) 70618   £55
Open: dinner Tue-Sun (closed 24-27 Dec)
Meals served: dinner 7-9.30
Genteel French restaurant with homely dining room and seasonally changing menus,
cooked by owner John Dyson.

HERM   White House

Herm, Channel Islands
Telephone: (0481) 722159 Fax: (0481) 710066   **£35**
Open: lunch + dinner daily (closed Oct-Mar)
Meals served: lunch 12-2, dinner 7-9

Car-free Herm is true escapism for those requiring complete peace
and quiet, and the Woods' 38-bedroomed hotel is a must. A conservatory adds to the brightness and informality of the restaurant, where
the menu offers popular favourites.

HERNE BAY   L'Escargot

22 High Street, Herne Bay, Kent CT6 5LH
Telephone: (0227) 372876   **£35**
Open: lunch + dinner Fri-Wed (closed 2 wks Jan, 2 wks Sep)
Meals served: lunch 12-1.30, dinner 7-9.30

Essentially French food with deep-fried camembert and gooseberry
sauce, assiette de charcuterie and bisque. Main courses of Normandy
pork with apple brandy cream sauce and duck with morello cherry
sauce show Alain Bessemoulin's attitude to cooking - keep it direct and
well executed. He achieves this aim competently, with the help of his
wife and co-partner Joyce.

HERSTMONCEUX   Sundial Restaurant

Gardner Street, Herstmonceux, East Sussex BN27 4LA
Telephone: (0323) 832217   **£60**
Open: lunch Tue-Sun, dinner Tue-Sat (closed 2/3 wks Aug/Sep,
Xmas-mid Jan)
Meals served: lunch 12.30-2.30, dinner 7.30-9.30 (Sat 7.30-10)

Relax in the atmosphere of the 17th-century cottage and garden which
in summer allows alfresco dining. The choice of food is enormous and
it will take time to decide - so let it. Slowly digest hors d'oeuvres, poissons, volailles, gibier and viandes and then take a minute or two to
decide. Do not forget the dishes of the day, which on our latest visit
included asparagus with hollandaise, or smoked salmon, moules
marinières and fettucini with scallops. The table d'hôte du jour takes in
a wider choice with 7 starters from crab and salmon mousse to cannelloni of the house. A passion fruit sorbet breaks the momentum and
then on to a choice between 7 further dishes for main course from
navarin of lamb to pheasant with creole rice. Giuseppe Bertoli and his
young staff run a superb restaurant with a predominantly French wine
list in the upper price bracket.

HETTON   Angel Inn

Hetton, Nr Skipton, North Yorkshire BD23 6LT
Telephone: (0756) 730263   **£45**
Open: lunch + dinner daily (closed 3rd wk Jan)
Meals served: lunch 12-2, dinner 7-9.30 (Bar 12-12 + 6-10,
arlier in winter)

A cut above the rest, Denis Watkins' inn and restaurant sets a high
standard. The brasserie takes on board all the influences of high fashion and high demand from AWT (open sandwich of smoked salmon,
cream cheese, smoked bacon and home-made chutney) and boudin
blanc char-grilled with provençal sauce and mash to Angel's ploughman or salmon fishcake. The dinner menu set at £20.70 for 4 courses
and coffee presents a lively performance with a choice that takes you
on a world tour, from char-grilled lamb on a bed of grilled aubergine,
rocket, sun-dried tomatoes and pesto to oriental- style duck with Thai
spices in a spring roll and a soya and ginger- infused sauce. Puddings
are more firmly based to home with sticky toffee pudding or a creation
of 3 chocolate masterpieces.

HIGH ONGAR   Shoes Restaurant

The Street, High Ongar, Essex CM5 9ND
Telephone: (0277) 363350   **£40**
Open: lunch Sun-Fri, dinner Mon-Sat (closed 1 wk Xmas/New Year)
Meals served: lunch 12-2.30, dinner 7-9.45

Formerly a public house and coaching inn, this was converted into a
restaurant in 1981. Chef Jonathan Siddle had already done a stint here
but went away to France to develop his répertoire and experience further. He has now returned and proprietor Lyndon Wootton is reaping
the benefits with a modern British restaurant loaded with new touches. Look out for confit of duck with compôte of red onions and blackberries with cumberland sauce, or loin of venison served with
caramelised apples and shallot sauce, plus wondrous desserts like
tarte tatin with poached pears, cinnamon and hot caramel sauce or fromage blanc mousse rippled with sour cherry purée.

HINTLESHAM   Hintlesham Hall

Hintlesham, Nr Ipswich, Suffolk IP8 3NS
Telephone: (0473) 652268 Fax: (0473) 652463
Open: lunch Sun-Fri, dinner daily
Meals served: lunch 12-1.45, dinner 7-9.30

£55

Complete with an 18-hole championship golf course and fully equipped country club, Hintlesham is very much the high profile retreat, being only 20 minutes from London by helicopter. There have been many changes in the last couple of years with dining room and bar being moved around to achieve a better use of dramatic space. However, skilled chef Alan Ford is still in situ, offering outstanding dishes like red onion and port soup, sauté of spätzle, marinated leeks and sun-dried tomatoes with a poached egg and parmesan, tournedos of beef with tomato chutney and herb crust and steamed medallions of monkfish with sesame flavoured noodles and hot and sour sauce. A stunning menu from a culinary maestro. This still remains one of my favourite hotels with 33 bedrooms, shared between the main house and the courtyard buildings. Outstanding for architecture, food and service.

HOCKLEY HEATH   Nuthurst Grange

Nuthurst Grange Lane, Hockley Heath, Warwickshire B94 5NL
Telephone: (0564) 783972 Fax: (0564) 783919
Open: lunch Sun-Fri, dinner daily (closed 1 wk Xmas)
Meals served: lunch 12-2.30, dinner 7-9.30

£45

The kitchen is very much the centrepiece at this 15-bedroomed hotel located between Birmingham and Stratford, which you will approach by way of a long avenue drive. Chef/proprietor David Randolph keeps the place fired up with his honest, distinctive cooking including boneless quail in a madeira sauce or ragôut of nuts and mushrooms with pesto. Puddings continue the theme with quenelles of banana, marinated fruits with warm peach sabayon and bitter lemon tart with Kirsch cream. Comfortably furnished and set in landscaped gardens, Nuthurst Grange is a firm local favourite.

HOLBETON   Alston Hall

Alston Cross, Holbeton, Nr Plymouth, Devon PL8 1HN
Telephone: (075 530) 555 Fax: (075 530) 494
Open: lunch + dinner daily
Meals served: lunch 12-2, dinner 7-9.30
An ivy-clad mansion with 20 rooms just outside Plymouth in 4 acres with good views across hills to the sea.

£45

HOLDENBY — Lynton House

Holdenby Road, East Haddon, Holdenby, Northamptonshire NN6 8DJ
Telephone: (0604) 770777   **£45**
Open: lunch Tue-Fri, dinner Mon-Sat (closed Bank Holidays
(open Good Friday), 2 wks Aug, Xmas)
Meals served: lunch 12.30-1.45, dinner 7.30-9.45

At this country restaurant with 5 rooms, Carol and Carlo Bertozzi run a
happy ship, with Carol kept busy in the kitchen while Carlo runs the
front. The menu is an Anglo-Italian affair with ossobuco and poached
scallops with a nutmeg flavoured risotto residing cheerfully alongside
grilled dover sole and salmon in a dill and cream sauce layered in puff
pastry. There is a veritable selection of desserts, with Sicilian cheesecake, semifreddo, tiramisu, walnut roulade and poached strawberries
in amaretto.

HOLT — Yetman's

37 Norwich Road, Holt, Norfolk NR25 6SA
Telephone: (0263) 713320   **£50**
Open: lunch Sat+Sun, dinner Wed-Sun
Meals served: lunch 12.30-2, dinner 7.30-9

Alison and Peter Yetman's daily menus are handwritten and offer a
concise selection. Soups from pea and mint, fennel and apple, fresh
tomato and basil and Jerusalem artichoke confirm that this lady has
her finger on the pulse of current flavours and is a jolly good cook. The
remainder of the menu is a selection of leaf salads topped with tasty
morsels, aubergines prepared in 3 different ways and an unpretentious
mixture of main courses which rely on the best of ingredients with
grilled, marinated quail, steak and kidney with a light butter and herb
crust, confit of duck with blackberry sauce and spiced gnocchi baked
with tomato, cashew and capsicum sauce. Meat eaters and vegetarians
alike will delight in the cooking on offer.

HORNCASTLE — Magpies Restaurant

73-75 East Street, Horncastle, Lincolnshire LN9 6AA
Telephone: (0507) 527004   **£35**
Open: lunch Tue-Sun, dinner Tue-Sat (closed Bank Holidays, 2 wks Sep,
2 wks Jan)
Meals served: lunch 12.30-2.30, dinner 7.30-9.30

The Lee family's restaurant sees Matthew in charge of the kitchen and
Caroline looking after the smooth running of the dining room. The
food and wine are reasonably priced with 3-course lunch and dinner
menus at £8.95 and £13.95 respectively. In the evening the table d'hôte
may offer a filo basket of chicken livers on a leek butter sauce followed
by braised shin of veal with peppers, garlic and tomatoes or medallions
of pork with kumquats and honey and for dessert apple and blueberry
pancakes with maple syrup sauce. Set menus change weekly to take in
the best the local markets can offer, while the à la carte changes
monthly.

HORTON   French Partridge

Horton, Nr Northampton, Northamptonshire NN7 2AP
Telephone: (0604) 870033 Fax: (0604) 870032   **£50**
Open: dinner Tue-Sat (closed 2 wks Xmas+Easter, 3 wks Jul/Aug)
Meals served: dinner only 7-9

This restaurant is situated in a delightful building, set back from the
road, and is somewhat reminiscent of a typical French country-style
restaurant, with a decor which is unpretentious, almost simple in
places - bottle-green walls hung with oil paintings, banquette seating,
and polished tables and chairs. The Partridge family is very much in
evidence in the dining room and in the kitchen, and their strong local
following tuck in with relish to the 4-course fixed-price menu, which
might offer duck terrine with cumberland sauce, warm onion and
roquefort quiche followed by venison steak with gin and juniper sauce
and oeuf à la neige or treacle tart! Coffee is included in the fixed price
of £22. Excellent value, as is the wine.

HORTON-CUM-STUDLEY   Studley Priory

Horton-cum-Studley, Nr Oxford, Oxfordshire OX33 1AZ
Telephone: (0865) 351203 Fax: (0865) 351613   **£50**
Open: lunch + dinner daily (closed Bank Holidays)
Meals served: lunch 12.30-1.45 (Sun 12.30-2), dinner 7.30-9.30 (Sun 7.30-9)

Rich in tapestried history, this magnificent Elizabethan priory has 19
bedrooms. Henry VIII never stayed here but had a hand in its past
when he dissolved its use as a Benedictine nunnery and it became
home to the Croke family, whose presence is still very much in evidence, for instance in the many coats of arms that decorate the stained
glass windows and the cornicing of the hall. Situated in 13 acres of
wooded grounds 7 miles from Oxford it is built on the ridge and enjoys
views of the Cotswolds to the west, to the Chilterns in the east, and
also to the Vale of Aylesbury. Business is considerable so you may find
small conferences in progress during the week. Table d'hôte and à la
carte menus are on offer in the elegant Croke restaurant, perhaps after
an aperitif in the oak-panelled bar warmed in winter by open fires.

HUDDERSFIELD   Paris II

84 Fitzwilliam Street, Huddersfield, West Yorkshire HD1 5BD
Telephone: (0484) 516773   **£35**
Open: lunch Sun, dinner Mon-Sat
Meals served: lunch Sun 12-2, dinner 6-10.30

The early bird catches the worm and in this case the catch is a 3-
course dinner menu at £12.95 which is inclusive of half a bottle of wine
per person. The menu is short but not too restricted and leaves room
for personal choice. You might dine on black pudding with bacon and
mushrooms followed by grilled salmon hollandaise and finish with
peach butterscotch. Good simple cooking.

HULL   Le Bistro

400 Beverley Road, Hull, Humberside HU5 1LW
Telephone: (0482) 43088   **£40**
Open: dinner Mon-Fri (closed Xmas/New Year, 2 wks Aug)
Meals served: dinner 7-10

You can read the menu from blackboards at this jaunty bistro where
small games and quizzes are also on offer. A small and intimate room,
you may dine à deux while playing a game of tiddlywinks, or it could
be Happy Families! A 3-course dinner menu which includes wine in
the price might include felafel with Tabasco mayo, Barnsley lamb
chops with red wine and seed mustard or a more hearty liver
stroganoff with plenty of fresh vegetables. It's well worth knowing that
vegetarians can also play with at least 4 home-made main courses from
butter bean casserole and filo pastry roulade to lentil moussaka.

HULL   Ceruttis

10 Nelson Street, Hull, Humberside HU1 1XE
Telephone: (0482) 28501 Fax: (0482) 587597   **£40**
Open: lunch Mon-Fri, dinner Mon-Sat (closed Bank Holidays, 1 wk Xmas)
Meals served: lunch 12-2, dinner 7-9.30

Ask for the pier if you run into a navigational hitch or just mention the
Ceruttis' name, as after 20 years they are well known in the vicinity.
Whitebait, grilled langoustine, moules provençale or all types of fish
from halibut to plaice are cooked in a variety of ways — dover sole can
arrive on the plate in 8 different guises – all you have to do is choose!
Lamb and steaks creep in on the end of the menu for the dedicated
meat eater.

HUNSTRETE   Hunstrete House

Hunstrete, Chelwood, Nr Bath, Avon BS18 4NS
Telephone: (0761) 490490 Fax: (0761) 490732   **£65**
Open: lunch + dinner daily
Meals served: lunch 12-2, dinner 7.30-9.30

Simple and concise cooking from Darren Bott brings a refreshing air
to the restaurant. He works well with the produce, most of which is
home-grown, and dishes are gutsy in combination and simply prepared. Generous amounts of salmon with various salad leaves and
crisp sautéed mushrooms have a light oil dressing while tender, sweet
lamb comes with a crisp potato cake. The selection of farmhouse
cheese is good and served with home-made chutney, bread, grapes
and biscuits. This 18th-century house and 24 bedrooms overlooks the
Mendip hills and is worth a visit for the mature gardens alone.

HUNTSHAM   Huntsham Court

Huntsham, Bampton, Nr Tiverton, Devon EX16 7NA
Telephone: (039 86) 365 Fax: (039 86) 456   **£65**
Open: dinner daily
Meals served: dinner only 8-10.30

There will never be a dull moment at this very individual 'hotel in the
country' rather than 'country house hotel', with its relaxed and cheerful atmosphere. Each of the bedrooms is named after a musical com-
poser and furnished in an eclectic mix of styles with no television but
an old fashioned wireless, a large fireplace and bathrooms where the
tubs are the old fashioned type with claw feet. In the evening before
dinner, select a record from the vast collection, take a drink from the
honesty bar and enjoy some lively conversation. You are welcome to
wander around the cellar and choose your own wine before sitting
down to a communal supper of traditional dishes such as a fresh
tomato soup, local duck that is cooked twice and has a wonderfully
crisp skin or a tarragon and butter sauce with fish. This is a super
hotel, if not a little eccentric and is perfect for groups of friends, or for
a very jolly and laid-back weekend for two. Book well in advance, since
the demand these days is for house parties that take over the whole
house for the weekend.

HURLEY   Ye Olde Bell Hotel

High Street, Hurley, Nr Maidenhead, Berkshire SL6 5LX
Telephone: (0628) 825881 Fax: (0628) 825939   **£45**
Open: lunch + dinner daily
Meals served: lunch 12.30-2.30, dinner 7.30-9.30 (Sun 7.30-10)

Escape the hurley-burley of life and submerge yourself in the comfort
and ease of reputedly the oldest inn in England (c 1135). 36 bedrooms
with a range of elegant suites and 4-poster rooms provide all the nice
little extras of 20th-century living - TV, radio, hairdryer and trouser
press. Dinner is either from the à la carte or set menu with choices
such as poached quail's eggs with shredded smoked salmon, maize-
fed chicken with celeriac chips or navarin of lamb. The conference
trade has become a fact of life for the hotelier but here at least specific
rooms are set aside (in the adjacent Malt House) so that delegates and
pleasure-seekers needn't mix – unless they want to! Relax with a drink
on the terrace at the rear of the hotel, or take a pleasant stroll through
the gardens.

HURSTBOURNE TARRANT   Esseborne Manor

Hurstbourne Tarrant, Nr Andover, Hampshire SP11 0ER
Telephone: (0264) 76444 Fax: (0264) 76473   **£50**
Open: lunch + dinner daily
Meals served: lunch 12.30-2, dinner 7.30-9.30

Andrew Norman has beat a retreat to this hotel's kitchen but this time with the head chef's hat firmly in position. His menus are combinations of reworked European classics - beetroot and orange soup with sour cream and chives, sautéed herring roes on spinach with light curry sauce and provençal beef stew accompanied by a tossed salad, or a main course of pasta with a tomato and pesto sauce. The 12 bedrooms are shared between the main house and converted stable block, but wherever you stay the standards of upkeep and service are high.

ILKLEY   Bettys

32-34 The Grove, Ilkley, West Yorkshire LS29 9EE
Telephone: (0943) 608029 Fax: (0943) 816723   **£35**
Open: all day daily (closed 25+26 Dec)
Meals served: 9-6 (Fri-Sun 9-6.30)

Run by descendants of Frederick Belmont just as it was in its heyday of the '30s, Bettys is an institution. Its success is founded on the principle `if we want things just right, we have to make them ourselves' - and so the wide range of cakes, snacks and hot dishes continue to be made on the premises or at the Bettys bakery. A pianist plays from 10.30-12.30 on Thursdays.

ILKLEY   Box Tree

29 Church Street, Ilkley, West Yorkshire LS29 9DR
Telephone: (0943) 608484   £75
Open: lunch Wed-Fri + Sun, dinner Wed-Sat (closed 25+26 Dec, 1 Jan)
Meals served: lunch 12.30-2 (Sun 12.30-2.30), dinner 7.30-9.45

The Box Tree still retains its charm continuing under the guidance of owner, local hotelier Mme Avis. The name of the new chef was about to be announced as we went to press. Expectations are high for this long-established restaurant and despite a spate of publicity on the possible involvement of Marco Pierre White in early 1993, the Box Tree has now settled down and I look forward to my next visit. If you eat there and would like to send me your own report, I will send a bottle of Charles Heidsieck champagne for what I consider the best review received.

ILKLEY   Rombalds Hotel

West View, Wells Road, Ilkley, West Yorkshire LS29 9JG
Telephone: (0943) 603201 Fax: (0943) 816586   **£40**
Open: lunch + dinner daily (closed 27-30 Dec)
Meals served: lunch 12-2 (Sun brunch 9-1.30), dinner 7-9.30 (Sun 7-9)

Right on the edge of the moor in a sand- coloured terrace you will find
Jill and Ian Guthrie's 15-bedroomed hotel. Gradual remodelling has
been accelerated by the addition of chef Paul Baxter, from the Chester
Grosvenor, and marks a great step forward for this small hotel. Watch
this space! Typical dishes from the à la carte menu include a trio of
salmon with a yoghurt and chive dressing, roast partridge with chick-
en liver mousse, smoked bacon and lentil broth and a fillet of salmon
poached in court bouillon and served with champagne and cucumber
sauce. Attentive and helpful service. During the weekdays and
evenings a good value table d'hote is offered and on Sundays an
Edwardian breakfast-cum-brunch which includes Manx kippers,
Abroath smokies, bacon, kidneys and black pudding.

IPSWICH   Mortimer's on the Quay

Wherry Quay, Ipswich, Suffolk IP4 1AS
Telephone: (0473) 230225   **£40**
Open: lunch Mon-Fri, dinner Mon-Sat (closed Bank Holidays + following
day, 2 wks Xmas/New Year, 2 wks Aug)
Meals served: lunch 12-2, dinner 7-9, Mon 6.45-8.15

Loch Fyne eel or trout with horseradish, grilled oysters mornay, thick
tuna steaks provençale and breadcrumbed fillet of North Sea plaice
breadcrumbed, pan-fried and served with tartar sauce. As you will have
guessed this is a seafood restaurant offering good quality fresh fish
cooked in various ways and served in a straightforward manner.
Watercolours by the 19th-century artist T. Mortimer hang on the walls
and give the restaurant its name as well as continuing the nautical
theme, as you overlook the boats and yachts of the local community.

IPSWICH   Singing Chef

200 St Helen's Street, Ipswich, Suffolk IP4 2LH
Telephone: (0473) 255236   **£40**
Open: dinner Tue-Sat (closed Bank Holidays)
Meals served: dinner 7-11

Ken Toye must be the one in fine voice while Cynthia his wife leaves
the kitchen for the relative peace but not necessarily quiet of her
restaurant. Small and fun, with a courtyard of 4 tables for better weather, special evenings add spice with jazz music as well as occasional
wine tasting dinners. This is a happening place with a take-out service,
French Food Chez Vous, which brings a European village flavour to
Ipswich – Joe Bloggs turning up with his Le Creuset or Tupperware
tucked under his arm! The greenest take-away service! Plus your
guests will never guess you didn't cook it yourself, that's unless they
catch you en route. Dishes include shellfish and fish baked in a shell
with eastern spice, coq au vin, cassoulet and steak au poivre. Some
interesting as do the reasonably priced wines.

ISLE OF MAN Harbour Bistro

East Street, Ramsey, Isle of Man
Telephone: (0624) 814182   **£40**
Open: lunch + dinner daily (closed Xmas, 2 wks Oct, Tynwald Day)
Meals served: lunch 12.15-2.30, dinner 6.30-10.30

Seafood is the main feature at this bistro down by the quay. Watch the
board for the day's catch or otherwise choose from the menu - plaice
stuffed with crab and avocado, sautéed giant prawns with spice or garlic, the original fisherman's pie or queenies cooked with garlic and
cream, a mornay sauce or more simply with bacon, onion and black
pepper, available as main courses or in starter-sized portions. Roast
and grilled meat and poultry also available.

ISLE OF MAN LA ROSETTE

Main Road, Ballasalla, Isle of Man
Telephone: (0624) 822940   **£55**
Open: lunch Tue-Sun, dinner Tue-Sat (closed 25+26 Dec, last 2 wks Jan)
Meals served: lunch 12-3, dinner 7.30-10.30
French-style restaurant offering local seafood and uncomplicated meat dishes. Close
to the airport.

IXWORTH THEOBALDS

68 High Street, Ixworth, Bury St Edmunds, Suffolk IP31 2HJ
Telephone: (0359) 31707   **£60**
Open: lunch Tue-Fri + Sun, dinner Tue-Sat (closed Bank Holidays)
Meals served: lunch 12-2, dinner 7-9.30 (Sat 7-10)

Simon Theobald's cooking is confident and competent. Oak beams and
log fires make a tremendous setting to enjoy dishes like basil-
flavoured noodles tossed in a cream sauce with crispy bacon and tomatoes, twice-baked goat's cheese soufflé with a crispy cheese top followed by grilled wing of skate with white wine, English mustard and
anchovy sauce or sherry sauce with lamb noisette on a bed of
aubergine, pimento and tomato. Puddings include lemon tart with a
strawberry sauce, chocolate and coffee truffle cake with caramel sauce
or iced mandarin nougat mousse with chocolate sauce. A fine wine
list, well chosen.

JERSEY Château la Chaire

Rozel Bay, Rozel Valley, Rozel, Jersey, Channel Islands
Telephone: (0534) 863354 Fax: (0534) 865137   **£50**
Open: lunch + dinner daily
Meals served: lunch 12-2, dinner 7-10 (Sun + Bank Holidays 7-9.30)

The traditional, wood panelled dining room offers a harmony of
English and French. Local produce is put to good use in dishes such
as spinach and woodland tart with a vermouth sauce, brill with chervil
and orange butter, mussels with braised fennel, cherry tomatoes and
provençal herbs or parcels of home-cured gravadlax filled with dressed
Jersey crab. The 14 bedrooms are well put together and cared for by
friendly staff.

JERSEY   **Hotel Château Valeuse**

Rue de la Valeuse, St Brelade, Jersey, Channel Islands JE3 8EE
Telephone: (0534) 46281 Fax: (0534) 47110   £35
Open: lunch daily, dinner Mon-Sat (closed mid Oct-April)
Meals served: lunch 12.45-1.45, dinner 6.30-8
Quiet, relaxing comfortable rooms. Breakfasts are highly rated. Service good.

JERSEY   Hotel L'Horizon

St Brelade's Bay, Jersey, Channel Islands
Telephone: (0534) 43101 Fax: (0534) 46269   **£55**
Open: lunch + dinner daily
Meals served: lunch 12.30-2, dinner 7.30-10

Right on the golden shores of St Brelade's Bay - plenty of beautiful
scenery, sun and sand castles to view from your balcony. If sand
between the toes is not your pleasure take a day in the hotel's 40-foot
boat and see the island's many secluded bays. Club L'Horizon with
swimming pool and mini gym is available for all year round leisure.
L'Horizon has 107 bedrooms and 3 restaurants to choose from - the
Brasserie, the smaller Star Grill and the Crystal Room.

JERSEY   Jersey Pottery

Gorey, Jersey, Channel Islands
Telephone: (0534) 851119 Fax: (0534) 856403   **£50**
Open: all day Mon-Fri (closed Bank Holidays, 10 days Xmas)
Meals served: 9-5.30

With free admission to the Jersey pottery it is not surprising that the
affiliated restaurant gets packed out. One of Jersey's most popular
tourist attractions pulls the crowds and once here you can choose from
a quick salad or pastry from the self-service café while the restaurant
proper offers relaxed surroundings and platters of fruits de mer, cocktails of prawn or crab or a mixture, pottery prawns with a sweet chilli
dip and seafood vol-au-vent. Meat is on the menu but stick to what
everyone else has come for - beautiful, fresh seafood. It's well worth a
visit, both for the food and the pottery.

JERSEY   The Lobster Pot

L'Etacq, St Ouen, Jersey, Channel Islands
Telephone: (0534) 482888 Fax: (0534) 481574   £35
Open: lunch + dinner daily
Meals served: lunch 12.30-2.15, dinner 7.30-10

With lovely views of the bay and 13 bedrooms, the Lobster Pot is open
all year round. The restaurant offers Continental, English and North
American cooking of fine seafood and a range of grilled and roasted
meats, all executed in fine style. Shellfish dominates the hors d'oeuvres, bisque and soups and then there's a choice from lobster 7 ways,
or well sauced trout, salmon, sole or mussels or even a selection of
grills from chateaubriand through to pheasant.

JERSEY   Longueville Manor

St Saviour, Jersey, Channel Islands JE2 7SA
Telephone: (0534) 25501 Fax: (0534) 31613   **£65**
Open: lunch + dinner daily
Meals served: lunch 12.30-2, dinner 7.30-9.30

This is a very impressive place to stay. The Lewis family are now into
their third generation of ownership, with Malcolm and Ragnhild join-
ing forces with Simon and Sue Dufty. With 40-odd years of impeccable
taste and service invested in this manor it has become the best place to
stay on the island. The cooking, under the auspices of Andrew Baird,
is capable and executed with a good range of imaginative and traditional dishes. The accent is on presentation and flavour, both of which
come up to form. Try the lasagne of salmon and Jersey crab with shellfish sauce and garden leaves, a duck and beetroot consommé with
warm blinis and soured cream and a main-course selection that makes
you want to jump on to the next plane, ferry or yacht to get there —
lamb in a casserole of artichoke, tomato and garden spinach or braised
turbot with tender leeks and lightly poached oysters – tempted? Set in
its own private, wooded valley, complete with lake and swimming pool
(where you can eat in the summer), this beautifully furnished hotel
offers luxury standards and 32 bedrooms.

JERSEY   Old Court House Inn

St Aubin, Jersey, Channel Islands
Telephone: (0534) 46433 Fax: (0534) 45103   £40
Open: lunch + dinner daily (closed 25+26 Dec)
Meals served: lunch 12.30-2.30, dinner 7.30-10.30
Bergerac fans will recognise the bar. Good pub food, decent restaurant with outside
terrace and a few bedrooms overlooking the harbour.

JERSEY   Sea Crest

Petit Port, St Brelade, Jersey, Channel Islands JE3 8HH
Telephone: (0534) 46353 Fax: (0534) 47316   **£45**
Open: lunch + dinner Tues-Sun, dinner Tue-Sat in winter (closed Feb)
Meals served: lunch 12.30-2 (Sun 12.30-3) dinner 7.30-10

The Sea Crest is at the south-west corner of the island and its bright
and airy dining room looks out towards the rocky bay, as do the sun
terrace and cocktail bar. A programme of refurbishment has improved
the kitchen, swimming pool and bedrooms. The menu has also been
re-vamped and includes plenty of fish, as well as a few meat dishes.
Sauces feature strongly. 7 bedrooms complete the picture.

JEVINGTON — Hungry Monk Restaurant

The Street, Jevington, Nr Polegate, East Sussex BN26 5QF
Telephone: (0323) 482178 Fax: (0323) 483989 **£50**
Open: lunch Sun, dinner daily (closed Bank Holidays, 3 days Xmas)
Meals served: lunch 12-2, dinner 7-10

With the ecclesiastical connotations of the name you might expect bread and water and abstinence to be the order of the day. Nothing could be further from the truth, with Claire Burgess and Thai La Roche at the hob roasting rabbit in proscuitto with mustard sauce, putting together a croustade of 3 fish on spinach and ginger with hollandaise and roasting guinea fowl with fresh coriander sauce. The MacKenzies have been managing this popular restaurant for over 26 years – long may they continue, with as interesting and enticing a menu as they have now.

KENDAL — The Moon

129 Highgate, Kendal, Cumbria LA9 4EN
Telephone: (0539) 729254 **£35**
Open: dinner daily (closed 25 Dec, 1 Jan, 4 wks Jan/Feb)
Meals served: dinner 6.30-10 (Fri+Sat 6-10)

This bistro is perfectly located, just opposite the Brewery Arts Centre, which may have influenced the style of menu, half of which is vegetarian. There are interesting combinations such as fennel rice, or mozzarella and sweetcorn filled pancakes with a sour cream topping. Equally artistic are the meat dishes – pork and gooseberry stroganoff, chicken breast in Thai creamed lime, coconut and coriander sauce or fish – haddock fillet with basil, lemon and mushroom stuffing in white wine sauce. A pudding club is hosted here once a month, providing an opportunity to try such treats as ginger and sultana pudding, chocolate glory, or mango and malibu ice cream.

KENILWORTH — Restaurant Bosquet

97a Warwick Road, Kenilworth, Warwickshire CV8 1HP
Telephone: (0926) 52463 **£50**
Open: dinner Tue-Sat (closed 1 wk Xmas, 3 wks Aug)
Meals served: dinner 7-9.30

Bernard Lignier cooks with true class and does great justice to his raw materials and their individual flavours. His resourcefulness enhances seasonal ingredients in a simple way, shown in coarse chicken liver pâté with wild mushrooms or mousse of scallops with lobster sauce. Saddle of lamb with tarragon or calves' liver with mustard sauce are typical main courses. Jane Lignier balances the seriousness of the food with a smiling relaxed manner.

KESWICK   Brundholme Country House Hotel

Brundholme Road, Keswick, Cumbria CA12 4NL
Telephone: (076 87) 74495   **£45**
Open: dinner daily (closed 23 Dec-mid Feb)
Meals served: dinner 7.30-9

Romance and culture are entwined in this house, today the home of
Ian and Lynn Charlton. Set in the heart of the Lakelands, it has drawn
some of the most romantic writers to its cascading, delicious beauty -
William Wordsworth brought Dorothy here in 1794 and on the death
of Raisley Calvert (one of the family of the house at that time) William
was left a bequest that enabled him to pursue his literary career. Stay
in one of the 11 rooms in an oasis of rural tranquillity and let
chef/patron Ian feed your fancy with a cassoulet of west-coast fish with
wild thyme, venison with mustard, madeira and a faggot of its offal followed by Cumbrian cheeses with home-made chutney.

KINGHAM   Mill House

Station Road, Kingham, Oxfordshire OX7 6UH
Telephone: (0608) 658188 Fax: (0608) 658492   **£45**
Open: lunch + dinner daily
Meals served: lunch 12.30-2, dinner 7-9.30

A former flour mill was bought by the Barnetts in 1987 and transformed into this country hotel. The mechanics of the mill have long
gone, but the old proving and baking ovens still exist and add to the
charm of the place. The grounds are full of wild and cultivated flowers
and are bordered by the fast-flowing mill stream where plenty of trout
are to be seen. A fine place to stay for tranquil scenery and from where
to take in the rest of the Cotswolds.

KINGS LYNN   Rococo

11 Saturday Market Place, Kings Lynn, Norfolk PE30 5DQ
Telephone: (0553) 771483   **£55**
Open: lunch Tue-Sun, dinner Mon-Sat
Meals served: lunch 11.30-2.30, dinner 7-10.30

Whenever possible husband-and-wife team Nick and Anne Anderson
use local produce: game, fish, meat, goat's cheese, vegetables, herbs
and wine. Nick's 3-course menu is a repertoire of modern English
cooking peppered with influences that come from as far as the orient:
vegetable tempura with plum sauce, skate gratin with oysters, pan-
fried monkfish with chilli prawn sauce and pan-fried saddle of local
hare with wild mushrooms and port jus. Puddings include grilled
tamarillos with praline ice cream and soufflé omelette with raspberry
sauce. A comprehensive wine list has some good personal recommendations.

KINGSTON — Restaurant Gravier

9 Station Road, Norbiton, Kingston-Upon-Thames, Surrey KT2 7AA
Telephone: 081-547 1121 **£60**
Open: lunch Mon-Fri, dinner Mon-Sat (closed Bank Holidays,
1 wk Jan, 1 wk Aug)
Meals served: lunch 12-2, dinner 7-10

This seafood restaurant is worth a trip out of London down the A3 - but if it's a Friday, leave early or dine late! In an atmosphere of hops, exposed walls and smart table settings, the best of the day's buys from Jean-Philippe Gravier's excursions to Billingsgate are recited at table and extend the choice on an otherwise succinct menu. His wife Joanne cooks in a careful manner and produces dishes that are kind both to the fish and diner, with choucroute of poissons, turbot with wild mushrooms and poached fillet of sea bass with a herb vinaigrette. Oysters come with chicory and scallops with lemon curd and parsley. Lucky old Kingstonites to have such a find on their doorstep!

KINGTON — Penrhos Court

Penrhos, Kington, Hereford & Worcester HR5 3LH
Telephone: (0544) 230720 Fax: (0544) 230754 **£55**
Open: lunch Sun, dinner daily (closed 25+26 Dec)
Meals served: lunch 12.30-3, dinner 7.30-9

Penrhos was falling apart at the seams - a case of anno domini - but in the hands of Martin Griffiths and Daphne Lambert the 13th-century Cruck Hall has been restored complete with beams and flagstones, and renamed. Menus change daily and might offer queen scallops grilled with laverbread, smoked chicken with apricot chutney followed by grilled sea bass with fennel, rabbit with oyster mushrooms, garlic and basil. Desserts are characterised by meringue glacé with greengages or fruit salad with sherry and almond ice cream. Daphne continues to practise and research medieval dishes and runs special evenings and banquets on the old holidays of Midsummer, Michaelmas and so on. There are 19 individually-styled bedrooms, all named after birds.

KINTBURY — Dundas Arms

53 Station Road, Kintbury, Berkshire RG15 0UT
Telephone: (0488) 58263 Fax: (0488) 58568 **£55**
Open: lunch + dinner Mon-Sat (closed 25 Dec)
Meals served: lunch 12-1.30, dinner 7.30-9.15

There's room at this inn, flanked by the Kennet and Avon canal. Here David Dalzell-Piper cooks with a creative approach using the freshest of ingredients. His wild boar pâté and braised rabbit take some beating. His cooking holds nothing back and brings forth plates of good-value traditional country food. 5 rooms are located in a converted stable block which opens onto a canal-side terrace.

KNUTSFORD   La Belle Epoque

60 King Street, Knutsford, Cheshire WA16 2DT
Telephone: (0565) 633060 Fax: (0565) 634150   **£60**
Open: dinner Mon-Sat (closed Bank Holidays, 1 wk Jan)
Meals served: dinner 7.30-10

This is a rather special place and the unusual and interesting 1900s'
architecture only just prepares you for the equally unusual and interesting restaurant, for the imaginative cooking by Graham Codd and
David Mooney only gives you half the picture. Both the dramatic art
nouveau restaurant and the 5 bedrooms have been lovingly restored
by the Mooney family over the last 15 years to re-create the Parisian
Belle Epoque era. Rich exotic drapes and original period pieces create
a mysterious and theatrical atmosphere adequately met by the food.
These are modern interpretations - a pizza of tomato, onion, Cheshire
cheese, herbs, smoked salmon, sour cream and chives; traditional faggots in cider and a casserole of snails. Main courses include lamb's
kidneys and oxtail hot pot, or darne of salmon with hake and wrapped
in spinach with a citrus sauce. A good all-round wine list is enthusiastically described. One to check if you're passing by.

KNUTSFORD   Cottons Hotel

Manchester Road ,Knutsford Cheshire WA16 0SU
Telephone: (0565) 650333 Fax: (0565) 755351   **£45**
Open: lunch Sun-Fri, dinner daily
Meals served: lunch 12-2, dinner 7-10

Built with the corporate customer in mind, this 82-bedroomed hotel is
just off the M6 and only 15 minutes from Manchester airport. The bar
and restaurant areas are themed around the city of New Orleans; find
yourself in the Bourbon Street Bar, choose from the Magnolia
Restaurant, and walk down the corridor called Rue Magnolia, to get
the full flavour. Plenty of parking space, and leisure and conference
facilities.

LACOCK   At the Sign of the Angel

6 Church Street, Lacock, Wiltshire SN15 2LB
Telephone: (0249) 730230 Fax: (0249) 730527   **£55**
Open: lunch Tue-Fri + Sun, dinner Mon-Sat (closed 2 wks Xmas)
Meals served: lunch 1-1.30, dinner 7.30-8.15

A former 15th-century wool merchant's house in this sensational
National Trust village offers the quintessential lunch or candle-lit dinner with a roast and all the trimmings or fish with a tartar or caper
sauce. Starters of Stilton pâté and smoked mackerel with horseradish
are typical and truckles of good Stilton and Cheddar part of the form.
The bedrooms are quaint with tiny windows and low ceilings with the
only concessions to the 20th century being the plumbing. The Angel
has been run by the Levis family since the '50s, and it's good to see
how little changes here, providing a living piece of history.

LANGAR   Langar Hall

Langar, Nottinghamshire NG13 9HG
Telephone: (0949) 60559 Fax: (0949) 61045   **£65**
Open: lunch + dinner Mon-Sat
Meals served: lunch 12.30-2, dinner 7.30-9.30

Hidden behind the village church in the Vale of Belvoir is this delightful 1830 sandstone family home. Imogen Skirving lives here and cooks alongside young chef Jason Timms. Together they produce a veritable feast of good French-influenced cooking, with dishes such as a fish soup of mussels and Venus clams, followed by a char-grilled leg of lamb or poached sea trout with a warm potato salad. The dining room and lounge feature antiques and beautiful views of the garden and moat. Upstairs each of the 12 bedrooms is individually designed according to its character.

LANGHO   Northcote Manor

Northcote Road, Langho, Nr Blackburn, Lancashire BB6 8BE
Telephone: (0254) 240555 Fax: (0254) 246568   **£65**
Open: lunch + dinner daily (closed 1 Jan)
Meals served: lunch 12-1.30, dinner 7-9.30 (Sat 7-10)

After a radical investment programme which doesn't seem to have left a stone unturned, the 13-bedroomed hotel now awaits with open fires and pastel furnishings. The restaurant glows in yellows and golds and offers a menu that is split into simply cooked main courses such as beef with red wine and marrowbone and a sauce of 3 types of peppercorn, or the more adventurous lamb shank glazed in its own juices on Puy lentils. Such is the very good cooking of Nigel Haworth, while co-owner Craig Bancroft is host. A globe trotting wine list has some reasonable prices.

LAVENHAM   Great House

Market Place, Lavenham, Suffolk CO10 9QZ
Telephone: (0787) 247431   **£40**
Open: lunch Tues-Sun, dinner Tues-Sat
Meals served: lunch 12-2.30, dinner 7-9.30

Coq au vin or blanquette de veau are traditional dishes and are well worth choosing. Régis Crépy - French of course - cooks with panache, recently offering a leek gateau served on a bed of chopped tomatoes, prawn and fish cassolette with Pernod and lamb with provençal herbs. This year sees an addition of a conservatory to the 15th-century house, to make the most of the English weather and to launch a bistro menu at lunchtime. A fabulous and lovely house, it also offers 4 bedrooms in cosy surroundings.

LAVENHAM   The Swan

High Street, Lavenham, Nr Sudbury, Suffolk CO10 9QA
Telephone: (0787) 247477 Fax: (0787) 248286   **£45**
Open: lunch + dinner daily
Meals served: lunch 12.30-2, dinner 7-9.30

Beams are everywhere in this 47-bedroomed, 14th-century high street
building, which houses a stunning hotel with fine examples of
Elizabethan carpentry, complete with minstrels' gallery. The staff
serve lunch in a traditional, polished manner, bringing salmon and
asparagus with a champagne sauce, grilled halibut with spring onions
and orange butter or chicken simmered in a cider cream with a hint of
English mustard.

LEAMINGTON SPA   Mallory Court

Harbury Lane, Bishop's Tachbrook, Leamington Spa, Warwickshire
CV33 9QB
Telephone: (0926) 330214 Fax: (0926) 451714   **£75**
Open: lunch + dinner
Meals served: lunch 12.30-2, dinner 7.30-9.45 (Sat 7.30-10 Sun 7.30-9)

Allan Holland obviously feels happy and comfortable about returning
to the kitchen, because a year on he's still there. The panelled dining
room is very much at the heart of this 10-bedroomed hotel and he
maintains his standards at all times. His team help to create menus
that are individual and yet perfectly adjusted to the needs of the
establishment, and might include warm mousseline of crab or
Mediterranean fish soup for first course, followed by fillet of pork with
leeks and glazed apples or pan-fried cod with olive oil, sun-dried tomatoes and creamed potatoes. Thin apple tart with chantilly cream or
kirsch savarin complete the fixed-price menu.

LEDBURY   Hope End

Hope End, Ledbury, Hereford & Worcester HR8 1SQ   ✿
Telephone: (0531) 633613 Fax: (0531) 636366   **£70**
Open: dinner daily (closed 6 wks Feb/Mar)
Meals served: dinner 7.30-8.30

Patricia Hegarty and husband John run a fine house and kitchen garden which provides Patricia with many of her fresh ingredients. Hope
End is not in the usual country house mould of frills and flounces -
expect instead a Scandinavian-style interior with a plain county-style
dining room which matches the cooking and service perfectly - homely
but with some nice touches. The fixed-price menu might include tomato and rosemary soup, local lamb with aubergine and perry gravy, cauliflower, puréed swede and riced potatoes. Pudding brings demerara
meringues with red and blackcurrant sauces, but before it try the
cheese, a first-rate selection of what ever is best that month. In
February it was Lancashire, Blue Wensleydale and Llanboidy. It is the
type of place you are reluctant to leave - tranquillity at its best.

LEEDS   Brasserie Forty Four

44 The Calls, Leeds, West Yorkshire LS2 7EW
Telephone: (0532) 343242 Fax: (0532) 343332   **£45**
Open: lunch Mon-Fri, dinner Mon-Sat (closed Bank Holidays)
Meals served: lunch 12-2.30, dinner 6.30-10.30

Part of the stylish grain warehouse complex converted by Jonathan
Wix, this brasserie has been rushed off its feet since it opened and is
obviously what Leeds has been waiting for. Jeff Baker has taken over
as head chef, rising from within the ranks and creating a contemporary
menu containing all the Californian and Italian influences that have
already proved so popular in London. Dishes include pan-fried garlic
mushrooms on continental toast, aubergine and sweet pepper salad,
mushroom risotto; and main courses of classic coq au vin, char-grilled
Singaporean chicken with pineapple and coconut fried rice and continental sausages with rösti. Desserts include plum and armagnac tart
and classic lemon tart to name but a two. The wine list is sensibly
listed and reasonably priced. Excellent value all round.

It's good to see a children's menu offering some innovative choices, accessibly presented to the junior gourmet.

LEEDS   Bryan's of Headingley

9 Weetwood Lane, Headingley, Leeds, West Yorkshire LS16 5LT
Telephone: (0532) 785679   **£25**
Open: all day daily (closed 25+26 Dec)
Meals served: 11.30-11.30 (Sun 12.30-8)
For the serious fish and chip connoisseur - stacks of chips, fish fried in dripping and
pots of tea to wash it down.

LEEDS   42 The Calls

42 The Calls, Leeds, West Yorkshire LS2 7EW
Telephone: (0532) 440099 Fax: (0532) 344100   **£45**
Open: lunch + dinner daily (closed 5 days at Xmas)
Meals served: lunch 12-2, dinner 6.30-10

Shrewd entrepreneur Jonathan Wix seems to prosper where others
fear to tread. He opened this 39-bedroomed hotel, created from a
derelict riverside grain mill in a redevelopment area, in 1991 - some
must have thought him mad in the cruel bite of the recession, but his
well-researched gamble has paid dividends and he continues to go
from strength to strength. His business acumen is in recognising the
need for excellent standards in decor, food and staff and by perfecting
these he gives the business community exactly what it needs – a good
place to stay. The associated Brasserie 44 next door, where lunch and
dinner are served, is doubling in size to keep up with demands.

LEEDS	Olive Tree

Oaklands, Rodley Lane, Leeds, West Yorkshire LS13 1NG
Telephone: (0532) 569283   **£35**
Open: lunch Sun-Fri (closed Bank Holidays)
Meals served: lunch 12-2 (Sun 12-3), dinner 6.30-11.30

A large Victorian house looking down on a roundabout is about as
unusual a setting as you could possibly imagine for a good Greek
restaurant, but here it is, with some of the best baklava and honeyed
desserts in town. Tuesday evening means music and dancing and for
those interested in such things, it's worth popping into in the hopes of
meeting the aunt of one of the proprietors – she holds the Guinness
Book of Records title for making the world's longest kebab!

LEEDS	Sous le Nez en Ville

Basement, Quebec House, Quebec Street, Leeds, West Yorkshire LS1 2HA
Telephone: (0532) 440108   **£30**
Open: lunch Mon-Fri, dinner Mon-Sat (closed Bank Holidays)
Meals served: lunch 12-2.30, dinner 6-10.30

In this good basement bistro just off the city square, genial staff and
customers make for a pleasant evening. Choose between tapas at the
bar or £11.95 for a 3-course set menu which includes half a bottle of
wine per person. Better-than-average bistro-style food with moules,
fresh fish, steaks and, obviously frites, but also mustardy rabbit and
veal with crème fraîche, gruyère and smoked bacon.

LEICESTER	Welford Place

9 Welford Place, Leicester, Leicestershire LE1 6ZH
Telephone: (0533) 470758 Fax: (0533) 471843   **£45**
Open: all day daily (closed 25 Dec)
Meals served: 8am-midnight

A highlight at this all-day restaurant is a set lunch for under £10.00.
Current specialities include baked cheese soufflé with fresh salmon
and spinach, confit of duck with red cabbage, honey and mint and
calves' liver and kidneys with tarragon mustard. The fresh fish comes
from Brixham market.

LEW	**Farmhouse Hotel & Restaurant**

University Farm, Lew, Oxfordshire OX18 2AU
Telephone: (0993) 850297   **£35**
Open: dinner Mon-Sat (closed Xmas/New Year)
Meals served: dinner 7-9

Pure country, with a warm welcome and cheerful hospitality await you
at this small restaurant with 6 rooms set in a 17th-century Cotswold
stone farmhouse, still part of a working farm. Each of the rooms is full
of homely character with crisp linen, exposed stone walls and some
beams. Nikki Rouse does the cooking with a daily selection of dishes
that might include local trout stuffed with spring onions and mushrooms or blanquette of pork.

LEWDOWN	**Lewtrenchard Manor**

Lewtrenchard, Lewdown, Nr Okehampton, Devon EX20 4PN
Telephone: (056 683) 256 Fax: (056 683) 332   **£55**
Open: lunch Sun, dinner daily
Meals served: lunch 12.30-2, dinner 7.15-9.30

Mussel soup with cardamom and local venison with a tartlet of home-
made apple and mint chutney are examples of Patrick Salvadoris' careful cooking - attractive sounding dishes for attractive surroundings.
Personally run with quiet charm by James and Sue Murray, the former
home of Rev. Sabine Baring Gould (novelist and hymn writer) has
been opened to guests requiring a retreat. The original features of
ornate ceilings, mullioned windows and oak panelling are delightful. 8
rooms are available, and the setting is superb.

LIFTON	**Arundell Arms**

Lifton, Devon PL16 0AA
Telephone: (0566) 784666 Fax: (0566) 784494   **£50**
Open: lunch + dinner daily (closed 3 days Xmas)
Meals served: lunch 12.30-2, dinner 7.30-9

If you feel like escaping to the country with your wellies in the boot of
the car and thoughts of fishing, shooting or riding are on your mind,
this could be the destination for you. 20 miles of fishing rights on the
Tamar belong to Ann Voss-Bark, as does this 29-bedroomed, ivy-clad
hotel, which has therefore been a favourite haunt for anglers for more
than 50 years. Philip Burgess serves up some traditional English and
French dishes in the glowing, chandelier-lit dining room.

LINCOLN   Wig & Mitre

29 Steep Hill, Lincoln, Lincolnshire LN2 1LU
Telephone: (0522) 535190 Fax: (0522) 532402   **£50**
Open: all day daily (closed 25 Dec)
Meals served: 8am-midnight

Sibling to Welford Place in Leicester, and also owned by Valerie and
Michael Hope, the credentials here are the same, except this time the
all-day eating establishment is situated in a 14th-century building in
the centre of Lincoln. Good value food, capably cooked.

LISKEARD   Well House

St Keyne, Liskeard, Cornwall PL14 4RN
Telephone: (0579) 342001   **£70**
Open: lunch + dinner daily
Meals served: lunch 12.30-2, dinner 7.30-9

A pleasant, country house is home for Nick Wainford's smooth- running restaurant with 7 bedrooms. The kitchen remains unchanged
with David Woolfall still very much in charge, creating dishes that
rarely fail to impress. A typical dinner menu may include confit of duck
with braised lentils, mallard with celeriac purée and wild mushrooms
and a hot prune and armagnac soufflé. Advocates of West Country
foods from bottled water down to a fine range of cheese, they are very
proud of local produce and justifiably intent on showing it off.

LITTLE WALSINGHAM   Old Bakehouse

31-33 High Street, Little Walsingham, Norfolk NR22 6BZ
Telephone: (0328) 820454   **£50**
Open: dinner Tue-Sat (closed Tue+Wed in winter, 1 wk Oct, 2 wks Mar)
Meals served: dinner 7-9.30 (earlier in winter)

If you're travelling to north Norfolk, this is an excellent place to stop -
it's a restaurant with just 3 bedrooms. After a supper of terrine of
salmon and smoked halibut served on a tomato coulis followed by local
partridge with cabbage and a chocolate and raspberry vinegar sauce,
followed by summer pudding, you can climb the stairs and sleep it off!
Consistently good food in a warm and friendly atmosphere.

LIVERPOOL   Armadillo

20-22 Mathew Street, Liverpool, Merseyside L2 6RE
Telephone: 051-236 4123   £40
Open: lunch + dinner Tue-Sat
Meals served: lunch 12-3, dinner 6.30-10.30
Decent wine list with good selection of half bottles. Long-established popular local
restaurant.

LIVERPOOL   Jenny's Seafood Restaurant

The Old Ropery, off Fenwick Street, Liverpool, Merseyside L2 7NT
Telephone: 051-236 0332   **£35**
Open: lunch Tue-Fri, dinner Tue-Sat (closed 2 wks Aug, 1 wk
Xmas/New Year, Bank Holidays)
Meals served: lunch 12-2.15, dinner 7-10 (Sat 7-10.30)

Fritto misto - a selection of deep-fried fish with tartare sauce - followed
by poached halibut with prawns and mushrooms or grilled salmon
with a creamed cucumber and white wine sauce might be your choice
from the fixed-price dinner menu at Judy Hinds' well-established
restaurant. There's also plenty for carnivores - roast duckling served in
a port and cherry sauce, or Aberdeen Angus châteaubriand with
béarnaise.

LONG MELFORD   Chimneys

Hall Street, Long Melford, Sudbury, Suffolk CO10 9JR
Telephone: (0787) 379806   **£60**
Open: lunch daily, dinner Mon-Sat
Meals served: lunch 12-2, dinner 7-9

At Sam Chalmers' charming, beamed restaurant the menu changes
every 2 weeks which keeps the locals returning for more. They can try
a plethora of enjoyable country-style cooking with hints of spice now
and then - try spinach and orange soup topped with puff pastry or oyster mushrooms flavoured with basil followed by beef pan-fried with
crisp potato cakes or grilled skate with caper and lemon butter. A fine
wine list and substantial discounts for those belonging to his dining
club. Good local restaurant.

LONGHORSLEY   Linden Hall

Longhorsley, Nr Morpeth, Northumberland NE65 8XF
Telephone: (0670) 516611 Fax: (0670) 88544   £50
Open:lunch + dinner daily
Meals served: lunch 12-2, dinner 7-9.45
Georgian house with 45 bedrooms, ideal for private functions and conferences.

LONGRIDGE   Paul Heathcote's Restaurant

104-106 Higher Road, Longridge, Nr Preston, Lancashire
PR3 3SY
Telephone: (0772) 784969   **£75**
Open: lunch Sun, dinner Tue-Sat
Meals served: lunch 12-2, dinner 7-9.30

This restaurant has continued to grow in stature – recent refurbishment has relocated the kitchen in order to double the size of the
restaurant. The whole enterprise is set in a white-washed cottage and
spreads over 3 levels. Paul is supported by a committed team of young
and enthusiastic staff and a sommelier with a keen eye for a good
wine. The modern and astutely performed menu has reached a consistently high standard and with the assistance of head chef Andrew
Barnes, Paul's attention to the calibre of ingredients is paying off with
each dish perfectly timed, combined and plated. Black pudding on
crushed potatoes with haricot beans and thyme juices, courgette flowers with lobster mousse and mussels with dill juices and casserole of
oxtail, or tongue and shin with red wine, purée of potatoes and root
vegetables. Desserts are outstanding, such as peach, first poached and
then nestled in a tuile with almond ice cream and coulis. Perfection!

LOUTH   Ferns

40 Northgate, Louth, Lincolnshire LN11 0LY
Telephone: (0507) 603209   **£25**
Open:lunch + dinner Tue-Sat
Meals served: lunch 12-2, dinner 7-9.30

You'll need to book to benefit from Nick and Kim Thompson's fixed-
price menu, available at lunch and dinner except on Saturday evening.
They always provide two choices for each course for only £9.90. The à
la carte gives greater choice and excellent value for money all round.

LOWER BEEDING   South Lodge

Brighton Road, Lower Beeding, West Sussex RH13 6PS
Telephone: (0403) 891711 Fax: (0403) 891766   **£60**
Open: lunch + dinner daily
Meals served: lunch 12-2.30, dinner 7.30-10

Flora is abundant at South Lodge with wisteria-framed windows,
arrangements in the rooms and a garden that will captivate amateur
and professional gardeners alike. This hotel was once the home and
garden of explorer and botanist Frederick Duncan Godman. A fine
specimen itself, its 39 bedrooms and its public rooms are all well tended, and the menu brings a traditional yet modern array of dishes to the
table - cutlets of lamb with basil mousse and tomato sauce, strips of
chicken braised in cream with morels and crisp aromatic duck with
creamed potatoes and lentils – to name but a few.

LOWER BRAILES   Feldon House

Lower Brailes, Nr Banbury, Oxfordshire OX15 5HW
Telephone: (060 885) 580   **£55**
Open: lunch daily, dinner Mon-Sat (closed 2 wks Autumn)
Meals served: lunch 12.30-2, dinner 7-8.30

Fennel soup with kummel, quenelles of silver hake and guinea fowl with
sherry sauce are the creations of Allan Witherick who, with his wife
Maggie, has been running this small restaurant with 4 bedrooms for some-
time now. The wine list is well researched with notes and characteristics
for each listing – a great asset for the up-and-coming wine buff.

LOWER SLAUGHTER Lower Slaughter Manor

Lower Slaughter, Nr Bourton-on-the-Water, Gloucestershire
GL54 2HP
Telephone: (0451) 20456 Fax: (0451) 22150   **£65**
Open: lunch + dinner daily
Meals served: lunch 12-2 (Sun 12.30-2.30), dinner 7-9 (Fri+Sat 7-9.45)

Formerly owners of Rookery Hall before they tried retirement and
found they couldn't get on with it, Audrey and Peter Marks have found
themselves the next best thing - a peaceful manor close to a village
church deep in the Cotswolds. Top-notch housekeeping and an interi-
or that gently insists on relaxation make this a wonderful place to stay.
Refined offerings come out of Julian Ehler's kitchen with an outstanding parsley and shallot ravioli and hot sweet soufflé. Enchanting hotel,
outstanding food and easy-to-use wine list with plenty of choice - long
may it continue. Well decorated bedrooms in the main house and
coach house, all set in wonderful gardens.

LUDLOW   Feathers Hotel

Bull Ring, Ludlow, Shropshire SY8 1AA
Telephone: (0584) 875261 Fax: (0584) 876030   **£45**
Open: lunch + dinner daily
Meals served: lunch 12-2.30, dinner 7.30-9.30

Built in 1603 and described by Pevsner as 'that prodigy of timer-
framed houses', the Feathers, with its impressive timbered and gabled
façade, still offers old-style charm. From the ornate plaster ceilings and
log fires to the bright floral fabrics and wood panelled rooms, you can
find comfort and traditional hospitality. There are 40 suitably furnished
bedrooms, some with 4-poster beds.

LUPTON	Lupton Tower

Lupton, Carnforth, Nr Kirkby Lonsdale, Cumbria LA6 2PR
Telephone: (053 95) 67400   **£40**
Open: dinner daily
Meals served: dinner 7.30 for 8

A great rarity, a totally vegetarian hotel. Set in an 18th-century country house, it offers a relaxed and friendly atmosphere with 6 bedrooms. The set dinner menu of 4 courses might start with fresh herb tartlets with tomato and red pepper sauce followed by a soup of parsnip and turnip, and then cheese mousse dumplings served with saffron sauce and plenty of vegetables, and finally apple and almond galette. The restaurant is open to non-residents and it has received much acclaim for innovative cooking which doesn't resemble the brown-on-brown image much vegetarian cooking has earned.

LYMINGTON	Gordleton Mill

Silver Street, Hordle, Nr Lymington, Hampshire SO41 6DJ
Telephone: (0590) 682219 Fax: (0590) 683073   **£55**
Open: lunch Wed-Mon, dinner Wed-Sat + Mon (closed 1-3 Jan)
Meals served: lunch 12.30-2, dinner 7.30-10

This old mill with 7 bedrooms, makes a wonderful setting for a hotel. Set in its own grounds, it was completely restored in 1992. It has already played host to 2 chefs of immense creative talent, so let's hope that new chef Didier Heil can emulate their success.

LYMINGTON	Stanwell House

High Street, Lymington, Hampshire SO41 9AA
Telephone: (0590) 677123 Fax: (0590) 677756   **£45**
Open: lunch + dinner daily
Meals served: lunch 12.30-2, dinner 7.30-9.30

Slices of parma ham served with artichoke bottoms and pink grapefruit segments and oven-baked halibut stuffed with smoked mussels and glazed with a lime sabayon are typical dishes from the à la carte menu and represent Mark Hewitt's fresh style of cooking. The hotel with its 35 bedrooms has been carefully modernised with a smart cocktail bar and chintzy drawing room.

LYMPSTONE	River House

The Strand, Lympstone, Devon EX8 5EY
Telephone: (0395) 265147   £65
Open: lunch + dinner Tue-Sun (closed Bank Holidays)
Meals served: lunch 12-1.30, dinner 7-9.30 (Sat 7-10.30)
Beautifully situated restaurant with 14 rooms, views over the River Exe and some very good cooking from Shirley Wilkes.

MAIDEN NEWTON   Maiden Newton House

Maiden Newton, Nr Dorchester, Dorset DT2 0AA
Telephone: (0300) 20336 Fax: (0300) 21021   **£50**
Open: dinner daily (closed 1st 3 wks Dec)
Meals served: dinner at 8

A unique blend of British and the best of French cooking make dining at the restaurant within Elizabeth and Brian Ferriss' 6-bedroomed hotel, an elegant affair, but one that is certainly not locked into tradition. Dinner is fixed and served all guests sitting together around one large, well polished dining room table. A typical menu could include hot salmon mousse with tarragon sauce, venison goulash followed by a bruléed banana and coconut cheesecake. With wines chosen to match the food another decision is taken out of your hands but rest assured, Brian's choices will be well thought out and correct.

MAIDEN NEWTON   Le Petit Canard

Dorchester Road, Maiden Newton, Dorset DT2 0BE
Telephone: (0300) 20536   **£45**
Open: dinner Tue-Sat
Meals served: dinner 7-9

Geoff and Lin Chapman migrated here from Vancouver quite some time ago bringing with them an insider's knowledge of the West Coast cooking of America and the Orient. So do not be surprised to find roast gigot of lamb brushed with hoisin sauce on a nest of beansprouts, a mango and lime sorbet with Christmas cookies, fricassée of roast pheasant with bacon and sweet-roasted garlic and fresh mussels steamed with white wine and a sun-dried tomato pesto. A novel and inspired mix of dishes offsets the East with the West and is well received by the locals of the surrounding villages.

MAIDENHEAD   Fredrick's

Shoppenhangers Road, Maidenhead, Berkshire SL6 2PZ
Telephone: (0628) 35934 Fax: (0628) 771054   **£65**
Open: lunch Sun-Fri, dinner daily (closed Dec 24-30)
Meals served: lunch 12-2, dinner 7-9.45

Rich on glitz and style, this hotel caters for a large executive clientele and while modern in interior the standards are luxurious with glasses of champagne offered as you arrive. Brian Cutler is in charge in the kitchen with a traditional French à la carte and 4-course menu which might include duck liver parfait on cumberland sauce followed by chicken and asparagus with chervil sauce and bread and butter pudding. 37 luxury bedrooms.

MALVERN — Cottage in the Wood

Holywell Road, Malvern Wells, Hereford & Worcester WR14 4LG
Telephone: (0684) 573487 Fax: (0684) 560662   **£55**
Open: lunch + dinner daily
Meals served: lunch 12.30-2, dinner 7-9 (Sun 7-8.30)

High up in the Malvern hills, in a rare and unspoilt part of England, is the Pattins' leisurely and secluded 20-bedroomed hotel. In fact it is 3 buildings huddled close together above the village of Malvern Wells on a thickly wooded hillside, enjoying far views of the Severn valley from cosy lounges with stacks of books. The cooking, by Kathryn Young, is equally colourful with a few traditional flavours in dishes such as squid cooked with red pepper, spring onions and celery with a hint of ginger or sherry, slices of veal with an apple and fresh kumquat sauce or slices of lamb grilled and topped with Stilton and mint. Puddings `so yummy they are guaranteed to be bad for you' reads the menu, which includes crunchy custard orange pie and hazelnut caramel ice cream. An extensive wine list selected by John Pattin, who encourages his customers to at least try an English wine on offer - if you don't like it he will refund the money and drink it himself!

MALVERN — Croque-en-Bouche

221 Wells Road, Malvern Wells, Hereford & Worcester   ✿
WR14 4HF
Telephone: (0684) 565612   **£75**
Open: dinner Wed-Sat (closed Xmas/New Year)
Meals served: dinner 7.30-9.15

Another successful husband-and-wife team lies behind this small restaurant with Marion Jones cooking while Robin runs front of house and tends to his outstanding wine cellar. He's a wizard with wine, so do listen to him, he's not just trying to sell the bottle but wants you to really enjoy it too. Marion will cook an excellent fixed-price 6-course menu with dishes such as guinea fowl roasted with fresh coriander pushed under the skin and lamb marinated with a parsley pesto and stuffed with bulgar wheat, spinach and mint or a soup made from a purée of smoked haddock, tomato and celery and flavoured with basil.

MANCHESTER — Market Restaurant

104 High Street, Smithfield City Centre, Manchester, M4 1HQ
Telephone: 061-834 3743 **£45**
Open: dinner Tue-Sat (closed 1 wk Xmas, 1 wk Easter, Aug)
Meals served: dinner 6-9.30 (Sat 7-9.30)

First there was the Pudding Club held in the Elizabeth Raffald room, where those hooked on puddings could sample a light main course of trout followed successively by 5 equally delicious puddings. Now Tuesday evenings have been joined at the other end of the spectrum by the Starters Society. The same concept but in reverse! Downstairs the restaurant continues in a more familiar manner with antique crockery, house wine served from '30s milk bottles and a menu with far-reaching influences - Israeli mixed salad, felafels with tahini, chicken fritters with mint and coriander and lemon sole with a sauce of turmeric, nut and lemon grass, all accompanied by 1940's music.

MANCHESTER — Victoria & Albert Hotel

Water Street, Manchester M60 9EA
Telephone: (061) 832 1188   Fax: (061) 834 2484 **£55**
Open: lunch + dinner Mon-Sat
Meals served: lunch 12-2, dinner 7-10.30

This hotel, which was built in the 19th Century as a warehouse on the banks of the river Irwell, became Granada Television's prop store but with the popularity of the Studios' Tour came the brainwave to re-utilize the building as a hotel. It's a place for serious TV addicts, for an engraved name plate depicting one of their programmes graces each of the 132 bedroom doors and inside the theme is continued with furnishings, props or little extras in keeping with each production. As for room service, just press the button on the TV remote control and up pops the menu. The hotel is complete with Sherlock Holmes Restaurant, Watson's Bar and Café Maigret. Thankfully the menu remains unthemed but is still characterised by toad-in-the-hole with onion gravy, cottage pie and crisp battered haddock with chips and fresh tomato sauce. Don't be put off by the overly themed names of the restaurant and café - there is some good food here, and good standard of service.

MANCHESTER — Woodlands

33 Shepley Road, Audenshaw, Manchester, Greater Manchester
M34 5DJ
Telephone: 061-336 4241 **£40**
Open: lunch Tue-Fri, dinner Tue-Sat (closed Xmas/New Year,
1 wk Easter, 2 wks Aug)
Meals served: lunch 12-2, dinner 7-9.30 (Sat 7-10)

Plaice with parsley butter, turbot layered with a light mousse and then wrapped in pastry, medallion of venison deglazed in brandy and red wine with roasted chestnuts echo Mark Jackson's classic past with the Savoy and Claridge's. But it is not all tradition and rich sauces in the melting pot at this suburban restaurant, there are also a few more recent elements such as filo pastry, spring onions and a dab of spice.

MANCHESTER AIRPORT — Moss Nook

Ringway Road, Moss Nook, Manchester, Greater Manchester M22 5NA
Telephone: 061-437 4778   **£70**
Open: lunch Tue-Fri, dinner Tue-Sat (closed Bank Holidays, 2 wks Xmas)
Meals served: lunch 12-1.30, dinner 7-9.30

Mancunians have long beaten a trail to this door to sample the
Harrisons' hospitality, with a menu and atmosphere that is larger than
life and full of surprises with pleurottes, shiitake and girolles accompanying a fillet of beef, filo parcel of cooked duck and a baked rack of
lamb with garlic, rosemary and honey. A well-respected and opulent
restaurant echoing Kevin Lofthouse's formal cooking – well polished
and heavily draped.

MANNINGTREE — Stour Bay Café

39-41 High Street, Manningtree, Nr Colchester, Essex
Telephone: (0206) 396687   **£40**
Open: lunch Tue-Sun, dinner Tue-Sat (closed Bank Holidays)
Meals served: lunch 12-2.45, dinner 7-10

Don't be misguided by the café connotation, for the menu here doesn't
mention sandwiches and doughnuts. Lunchtime will find a fine array of
Italian-style snacks with baked mozzarella on olive toast and steamed
mussels with fennel or spicier options of grilled Mongolian lamb chops
and cajun-spiced prawns. More of the same in the evening but at a different pace - char-grilled pigeon breast on mixed salad with blood
oranges and beetroot, sautéed crab cakes and cioppino – a spicy
Californian seafood stew trailed by toasted hazelnut waffle with vanilla
ice cream and drunken bananas. Note that all meat and poultry is
hormone-free and free-range.

MARSTON MORETEYNE — Moreteyne Manor

Woburn Road, Marston Moreteyne, Bedfordshire MK43 0NG
Telephone: (0234) 767003 Fax: (0234) 765382   **£50**
Open: lunch Tue-Sun, dinner Tues-Sat (closed 4 days Jan)
Meals served: lunch 12.15-2, dinner 7.15-10   ❖

Jeremy Blake O'Connor's Tudor manor house has been reborn since it
was savaged by fire last year, an event that has not in any way damp-
ened his enthusiasm or spirit. By leaving the choice to him you'll get a
well-balanced enjoyable repast in the 3-course dinner menu which
might include one of his embellished concoctions of velouté of haddock with celery followed by pot roasted topside with red wine and
herbs, and hot 'light' apple tart with vanilla ice cream and an apple and
honey sauce. Uncomplicated enough to be savoured and enjoyed -
welcome back, Jeremy!

MARY TAVY — The Stannary

Mary Tavy, Devon PL19 9QB
Telephone: (0822) 810897 **£60**
Open: dinner Tue-Sat
Meals served: dinner 7-9.30

If ever you were to succumb to a food allergy (horror of horrors for those that love it all) you will be relieved to find this vegetarian restaurant and guesthouse that has a mission to please and feed well regardless of such constraints. Every bit a mainstream restaurant, it uses semi-skimmed or soya milk if you prefer, alcohol or garlic only where it says and rice cakes and sunflower margarine if you want them. The menu consists of starters of parcels of laver seaweed with a centre of sweetcorn, stuffed figs with cream cheese chopped nuts and grapes and a truffle pâté, the main courses which might be peppery – a soft bake of sweet peppers layered with an onion relish and a fiery hot pepper sauce or vine leaves with black olives, seeds and tomato or palm hearts in a creamy sauce with pink peppercorns and fragrant rice.

MASHAM — Floodlite Restaurant

7 Silver Street, Masham, Nr Ripon, North Yorkshire HG4 4DX
Telephone: (0765) 689000 **£25**
Open: lunch Fri-Sun, dinner Tue-Sun (closed 2-3 wks Jan)
Meals served: lunch 12-2.30, dinner 7-9.30

Flexibility is the name of the game at Charles and Christine Flood's small restaurant where the menu is a collection of straightforward dishes, well cooked, with the minimum of fuss. The most novel dish on the à la carte is loin of roe deer with black peppercorn sauce, otherwise there are generous portions of well-cooked king prawns and squid with ginger and garlic, saddle of hare with wild mushrooms and duck with apple and mustard seed.

MATLOCK — The Peacock

Rowsley, Matlock, Derbyshire DE4 2EB
Telephone: (0629) 733518 Fax: (0629) 732671 **£50**
Open: lunch + dinner daily
Meals served: lunch 12-2, dinner 7-9

This stone-built, 17th-century Dower House with oak-beams and plenty of antiques is set on the banks of the River Derwent and makes an ideal place for a leisurely weekend. The beautiful gardens sweep down to the river bank, from where the avid angler can fish for trout which the chef will prepare and cook! With just 15 bedrooms, a comfortable lounge, Peacock bar and restaurant this hotel has a relaxed and homely atmosphere. Dinner is served in the Garden Restaurant and if personally-netted trout is not your choice, the fixed price dinner menu offers 3 or 4 courses of well-cooked dishes such as whiting with a Provence herb and chive butter, an oven-baked Barnsley chop with a garden herb and Stilton crust, or a light casserole of chicken with seafood, white wine and basil. The final course offers a sweet or savoury dilemma with a choice between a slice of caramel mousse with bitter chocolate sauce, fruit strudel with icing sugar and a summer fruit sauce or a croque monsieur on a bed of lightly dressed leaves.

MATLOCK — Riber Hall

Matlock, Derbyshire DE4 5JU
Telephone: (0629) 582795 Fax: (0629) 580475 £60
Open: lunch + dinner daily
Meals served: lunch 12-1.30, dinner 7-9.30

In this characterful Elizabethan manor saved from dereliction in the '70s, old beams and 4-poster beds give the bedrooms lots of added charm, while the public rooms are no less attractive with fine period furniture and fireplaces. Peace, quiet and seclusion with extensive views and walks will sooth you. Food in the dining room is modern French and English with leanings towards game and fish cooked with infusions, purées, mousses and jus. It proves popular, so book.

MAWNAN SMITH — Meudon Hotel

Mawnan Smith, Nr Falmouth, Cornwall TR11 5HT
Telephone: (0326) 250541 Fax: (0326) 250543 £40
Open: lunch + dinner daily (closed Dec-Feb)
Meals served: lunch 12.30-2, dinner 7.30-9
Family-run hotel with 32 bedrooms overlooking the spectacular 'Capability' Brown sub-tropical gardens.

MAWNAN SMITH — Nansidwell

Mawnan Smith, Nr Falmouth, Cornwall TR11 5HU
Telephone: (0326) 250340 Fax: (0326) 250440 £50
Open: lunch + dinner daily (closed Jan) (booking advisable)
Meals served: lunch 12.30-1.45, dinner 7-9 (Sun 7-8.30)

Make the most of the location of Jamie and Felicity Fletcher's 12 bedroom hotel by enjoying oysters, lobsters, mussells and fresh seafood in abundance. Wellies (roller skates and an outboard motor) meet you in the porch and inside the door, a friendly puppy and roaring fire! This is the type of wonderful and peaceful location anyone living in the centre of a town or city yearns for, with wisteria around the door and 5 acres of gardens surrounded by National Trust land, between the Hereford river and the sea. Yellow-ragged walls and views over the terraced garden greet you in the dining room as well as a sophisticated menu that might include hot pigeon salad, steamed salmon with local scallops and garden sorrel and hot apple and almond tart (puddings are a particular strength) with apricot and ginger sauce. Short but well chosen wine list.

MEDMENHAM   Danesfield House

Medmenham, Marlow, Buckinghamshire SL7 3ES
Telephone: (0628) 891010 Fax: (0628) 890408   **£70**
Open:lunch + dinner daily
Meals served: lunch 12-2.30, dinner 7-10

Big on scenery and surroundings, this hotel is crammed full of artefacts from minstrels' gallery, sun-filled atrium, baronial Grand Hall
with tapestry wall hangings to views across formal gardens to the
Thames. It displays a myriad of styles with Elizabethan chimneys,
square towers and Jacobean windows. This place isn't for the indecisive, with 2 restaurants, the Italian-inspired Loggia for more relaxed
dining, or the more typical and formal Oak Room with a menu that
might read rillettes of salmon, Cornish fish with lemon grass and
coriander cooked in paper and a light blackcurrant mousse with vanilla
sauce and seasonal berries.

MELBOURN   Pink Geranium

Station Road, Melbourn, Nr Royston, Hertfordshire SG8 6DV
Telephone: (0763) 260215   **£55**
Open: lunch Tue-Fri + Sun, dinner Tue-Sat
Meals served: lunch 12-2, dinner 7-10 (Sat 7-10.30)

As you would expect from the name, Steven and Sally Saunders'
restaurant is pretty in pink from the pale walls to the flowers in the fabrics. A thatched 16th-century cottage it was refurbished in '91 after a
fire and has chef David Whiffen (ex-Connaught) in the kitchen. A cosy
and homely place, the cooking is sophisticated and well-executed. The
fixed-price dinner menu offers baked goat's cheese salad with balsamic vinegar or venison terrine followed by rack of lamb with crisp rösti
or supreme of salmon with spaghetti of vegetables and a fresh herbed
beurre blanc. Dessert brings a choice between white peach délice with
white chocolate mousse or profiteroles with hot chocolate sauce.
There is a chauffeur-driven car to take home those who want to
indulge in the reasonably priced and comprehensive wine list.

MELKSHAM   Beechfield House

Beanacre, Nr Melksham, Wiltshire SN12 7PU
Telephone: (0225) 703700 Fax: (0225) 790118   **£55**
Open: lunch + dinner daily
Meals served: lunch 12-2, dinner 7-9.30

A mellow, Bathstone building dating back to 1878 stands in well
tended gardens. High ceilings, fine marble fireplaces and stylish
furnishings make this an elegant and relaxing place to stay. It offers
traditional leisure pursuits with a swimming pool, tennis, croquet and
fishing. A sedate restaurant overlooks the fountain and walled garden
from where the kitchen collects much of the fruit and vegetables used
in the menus which offer classic style cooking. This 24-bedroomed
hotel is situated just a few miles from the National Trust village of
Laycock.

MELKSHAM — Toxique

187 Woodrow Road, Melksham, Wiltshire SN12 7AY
Telephone: (0225) 702129   £50
Open: lunch Sun, dinner Tue-Sat (closed 2 wks Jan/Feb)
Meals served: lunch 12.30-2, dinner 7-10

A somewhat unusual personalised farmhouse is the setting for Helen Bartlett's menu of dishes such as baked baby aubergines with red peppers and a piquant sauce, pan-fried trio of fish with lime and sweet pepper oil and poussin served whole, roasted with garlic and tarragon. Co-owner Peter Jukes is strong on service and the restaurant, with its abstract mural and unusual mixture of decor, makes for an interesting venue. There are 4 bedrooms if you wish to stay over.

MELMERBY — Village Bakery

Melmerby, Penrith, Cumbria CA10 1HE
Telephone: (0768) 881515 Fax: (0768) 881848   £25
Open: all day daily (closed 25+26 Dec, 1 Jan)
Meals served: 8.30-5 (Sun 9.30-5)

Committed to organic methods with free-range eggs, organic flour and home-reared pork, the Village's breakfast couldn't be better. It's also open all day for breakfast, snacks, lunch or tea with wonderful bread, croissants, scones and cakes, all baked in their notorious `Scotch' brick ovens. People will travel from far and wide for a chunk of their bread and North Country cheese and on tasting them you can understand why (PS. Lucky Southerners can now purchase their breads in branches of Waitrose). Small array of lagers and wines with Soil Association or similar credentials are listed. The tea garden is being prepared and should be ready this year.

MELTON MOWBRAY Olde Stocks Restaurant

Grimston, nr Melton Mowbray, Leicestershire LE14 3BZ
Telephone: (0664) 812255   £55
Open: dinner Tue-Sat
Meals served: dinner 7-10

In the shadow of the old chestnut tree are both the original Grimston stocks and this aptly-named restaurant, run by Jack and Penni Harrison. The hand-written menu includes a wide choice of novel dishes from leg of lamb baked in hay with a mint and redcurrant gravy, pan-fried organic-reared beef with a light horseradish cream sauce garnished with roasted garlic to a trio of salmon, monkfish and king prawns on a bed of fried `seaweed' and a spring onion sauce. Starters are no less extensive or inspired with a trio of poached, smoked and cured salmon with soured cream, lemon mayonnaise and dill mustard or sautéed duck livers with cream and brandy in choux pastry.

MIDDLE WALLOP   Fifehead Manor

Middle Wallop, Nr Stockbridge, Hampshire SO20 8EG
Telephone: (0264) 781565 Fax: (0264) 781400   £60
Open: lunch + dinner daily (closed 2 wks Xmas/New Year)
Meals served: lunch 12-2.30, dinner 7.30-9.30
16-bedroomed manor house with medieval dining hall and mullioned windows. Foundations date back to the 11th Century.

MIDHURST   Maxine's

Elizabeth House, Red Lion Street, Midhurst, West Sussex GU29 9PB
Telephone: (0730) 816271   **£25**
Open: lunch Wed-Sun, dinner Wed-Sat (closed 3 wks Jan)
Meals served: lunch 12-2, dinner 7-11

In Robert and Marti de Jäger's cottagey dining room you will be served
good old home-cooking. Well-prepared and with prices encompassing
all extras, including service, the menu is a bargain. A 3-course dinner
(except Saturdays) offers creamy liver pâté with a ginger sauce and
rabbit in mustard or alternatively lamb's kidneys and sweetbreads with
mushrooms and brandy followed by the day's desserts, all for £11.95.

MILFORD-ON-SEA   Rocher's

69-71 High Street, Milford-on-Sea, Hampshire SO41 0QG
Telephone: (0590) 642340   **£40**
Open: lunch Sun, dinner Mon-Sat (closed 2 wks Jun)
Meals served: lunch 12.15-1.30, dinner 7-9.30

Spick-and-span and ready for action since its major redecoration, this
French restaurant is now resplendent in its new chic decor of green
carpet and tones of burgundy red and blue used in linen and curtains.
Alain Rocher and his wife Rebecca have created a charming restaurant
where Alain's cooking is best described as cuisine bourgeoise with the
emphasis on simple presentation and maximising on taste and
saucing. Choose from a variety of table d'hote, gastronomic and à la
carte menus with typical dishes such as a feuilleté of spinach and shallot, turbot with beurre blanc or duck with a blackcurrant sauce.
Dessert might be a hazelnut parfait with a vanilla and armagnac sauce.

MINSTER LOVELL   Old Swan

Minster Lovell, Nr Witney, Oxfordshire OX8 5RN
Telephone: (0993) 774441 Fax: (0993) 702002   £45
Open: lunch + dinner daily
Meals served: lunch 12-2, dinner 7-10
Quintessential village setting for traditional pub with restaurant.

MONTACUTE   Milk House

The Borough, Montacute, Nr Yeovil, Somerset TA15 6XB
Telephone: (0935) 823823   **£45**
Open: lunch Sun, dinner Wed-Sat
Meals served: lunch 12.30-2, dinner 7.30-9

Sugar and spice and all things nice are included in the dishes you will
find on Lee and Bill Dufton's menu – smoked Dorset ham served with
saupignet (onion and sour cream sauce), sorrel crêpe with asparagus
and spiced mushrooms and brown sugar meringues with cream and
fruit. Wherever possible they use organic produce and unadulterated
vegetable oils, so it's not just good to eat, but better for you. Phone to
find out what's cooking or to discuss your special favourites. The wine
list has organic wines amongst others. Two double rooms are
available.

MORETON-IN-MARSH   Annie's

3 Oxford Street, Moreton-in-Marsh, Gloucestershire GL56 0LA
Telephone: (0608) 651981   **£50**
Open: lunch Sun, dinner Mon-Sat (closed 2 wks Jan)
Meals served: lunch 12-2, dinner 7-10

David Ellis' self-styled English and French cooking is a joy: smoked
haddock feuillété with creamy Stilton sauce, butter-roasted corn-fed
poussin with a lemon and rosemary sauce with pistachio nuts, or
guinea fowl with a red wine sauce which includes grapes and raisins
steeped in armagnac. Puddings continue the hedonism with individual
toffee puddings with butterscotch and pecan sauce and iced ratafia.
Wife Anne adds her own radiant touch along with a warm welcome to
her small restaurant, candlelit at night with flagstone floors and
exposed Cotswold stone walls.

MORETON-IN-MARSH   Marsh Goose

High Street, Moreton-in-Marsh, Gloucestershire GL56 0AX
Telephone: (0608) 52111   **£50**
Open: lunch Tue-Sun, dinner Tue-Sat
Meals served: lunch 12.15-2.30, dinner 7.30-9.45

Quietly building on a reputation that is set to grow and grow, Sonya
Kidney continues to cook in her modern mode: salmon with ginger,
sultanas and spring onions, warm marinated mushrooms with mixed
leaves, poached quail's eggs and toasted pine kernels and breast of
guinea fowl with bacon-wrapped prunes and lentils. Desserts are dramatic productions with iced strawberry and ginger terrine with fruit
sauce or chocolate torte and caramelized walnuts served with white
and dark chocolate sauces. Fixed-price daily menus offer an excellent
and colourful choice. Good selection of wines and half bottles available
– even for cava and champagne.

MORPETH   Embleton Hall

Longframlington, Morpeth, Northumberland NE65 8DT
Telephone: (0665) 570249   **£45**
Open: lunch + dinner daily
Meals served: lunch 12-2, dinner 7-9.30

The traditional stone building breathes the history and charm of the
border region. A small, friendly, family-run hotel housed in an 18th-
century building with 19th-century additions, Embleton is typical of the
region. 10 personalized bedrooms, each named after members of the
former household, are tastefully decorated. Chef Ian Mixon creates a
daily menu with vegetables and fruits from the walled garden, some
from their home farm and the rest from local merchants.

MORSTON — Morston Hall

Morston, Holt, Norfolk NR25 7AA
Telephone: (0263) 741041 Fax: (0263) 741041   **£50**
Open: lunch Sun, dinner daily (closed Jan 2- early Mar)
Meals served: lunch 12.30, dinner 7.30

A new country house hotel joins the ranks, but owners Tracey and
Galton Blackiston and their partner Justin Fraser are already known to
the trade. All 3 met at Miller Howe where Galton rose through the
ranks to become head chef. After their first year alone, they are busy
concentrating on the overall standard with food remaining at the top of
their list of priorities. A light and delicate touch is at work in the
kitchen, shown in potato pancake with smoked salmon and lemon
crème fraîche followed by chicken stuffed with hazelnuts, apricots and
dolcelatte and a masala sauce and a selection of 3 puddings or a platter
of cheese with biscuits, chutney and quince cheese to complete a typical set menu.

MOTTRAM ST ANDREW — Mottram Hall

Mottram St Andrew, Prestbury, Cheshire SK10 4QT
Telephone: (0625) 828135 Fax: (0625) 829284   **£50**
Open: lunch Sun-Fri, dinner daily
Meals served: lunch 12.30-2, dinner 7-9.45 (Sat 7-10)

This 133-bedroomed hotel featuring an Adam ceiling and fine panelling
has all the mod cons you'd expect from De Vere, despite it being an
original Georgian mansion. Dinner is à la carte or from the fixed-price
market menus, produced by Ian Myers and his brigade, combining traditional dishes with healthy options and seasonal specialities. Friday
and Saturday will set your toes tapping with music and dancing included in the evening's enjoyment. The set menu of £30 gives extensive
choice and all the favourites from salmon to duck and lamb.

MOULSFORD-ON-THAMES — Beetle & Wedge

Moulsford-on-Thames, Oxfordshire OX10 9JF
Telephone: (0491) 651381 Fax: (0491) 651376   **£30**
Open: lunch Tue-Sun, dinner Tue-Sat (closed 25 Dec)
Meals served: lunch 12.30-2, dinner 7.30-10 (Brasserie same times)

Richard Smith arranges the kitchen while Kate conducts front of
house. Following on from where he left off at the Royal Oak in
Yattendon, Richard seeks only the best. Terse and to-the-point descriptions introduce roast lamb with herb crust and braised endive for 2,
whole baked sea bass with noodles, fennel and pastis and grilled
medallions of venison with onions, figs and port sauce. The Boathouse
on the water's edge with its own terrace couldn't be more endearing
and offers food that belongs to the Elizabeth David school of good
cooking: brown shrimps with garlic mayonnaise, hare casserole with
creamy potatoes and a really good down-to-earth ploughman's with a
fine array of unusual cheeses. If I had my way it would be dinner and
lunch here every day for a month just to try it all, as it's the sort of
menu that requires iron will to make a decision. The 10 bedrooms add
up to a relaxed and pleasant visit.

MOULTON   Black Bull

Moulton, Nr Richmond, North Yorkshire DL10 6QJ
Telephone: (0325) 377289   **£50**
Open: lunch + dinner Mon-Sat (closed 24-26 Dec)
Meals served: lunch 12-2, dinner 7-10.15

Sample a fish soup with croutons and rouille, spicy skewered prawns
with garlic bread, brochette of scallops and bacon accompanied by
spinach and new potatoes or lobster thermidor, and you'll realise why
the Black Bull has built such a reputation for the quality of its fresh
fish. There is also a selection of meats with steaks playing a major role,
but lamb and roast quail too. Choose your dining area to match your
mood – either the conservatory with its huge grapevine or an original
Pullman carriage c. 1932 from the Brighton Belle. Decent wines at
good prices make for a satisfying meal in an enjoyable ambience.

NANTWICH   Rookery Hall

Worleston, Nr Nantwich, Cheshire CW5 6DQ
Telephone: (0270) 610016 Fax: (0270) 626027   **£55**
Open: lunch + dinner daily
Meals served: lunch 12-1.45, dinner 7-9.30 (Sat 7-10)

After a multi-million pound refurbishment this hotel offers 45 bedrooms and extensive conference facilities. New chef David Alton offers
modern British cooking in decent-sized portions and with a European
influence that Baron Von Schroder, the Bavarian owner who converted
the Georgian country house, would have approved of. The menu could
include sirloin of beef with choucroûte and smoked bacon, fillets of red
mullet with a fennel salsa and provençale vegetables or duck cooked
pink on a potato galette with a rich fig and sherry vinegar sauce.
Dominique Schikele produces the outstanding desserts which include
a spectacular orange marmalade soufflé with a sharp lemon ice cream,
a hot puff pastry filled with sliced poached pear and served with a rich
raspberry sauce or hot strudel of apple and cinnamon on a rhubarb
and ginger sauce. Very good wine list with some reasonable prices.

NAYLAND   Martha's Vineyard

18 High Street, Nayland, Suffolk CO6 4JF
Telephone: (0206) 262888   **£45**
Open: dinner Tue-Sat (closed 2 wks summer, 2 wks winter)
Meals served: dinner 7-9.30

Chef Larkin Rogers has adopted a Californian style, with a hand-written menu that offers 5-spiced pasta with smoked chicken and sage
cream or salad of mixed mushrooms with jarlsberg, potatoes and winter lettuces. Main courses offer gutsy home cooking: pumpkin calzone
stuffed with mozzarella or pan-seared chicken breast with black olive
herb butter. Puddings offer lemon pudding cake with blueberry sauce
and chocolate crêpes with hot chocolate sauce. The wine list includes
45 predominantly New World wines with a few South African and
Italian for good measure.

NEW ALRESFORD   Hunters

32 Broad Street, New Alresford, Hampshire SO24 9AQ
Telephone: (0962) 732468   **£30**
Open: lunch daily, dinner Mon-Sat (closed 24-27 Dec)
Meals served: lunch 12-2, dinner 7-10

This wine-bar-cum-brasserie is candle-lit at night and filled with promise - worth remembering for lunch too. The young chef Michael Greenhalgh creates distinctive well-sauced dishes like a salad of home-smoked duck on a bed of sliced potatoes flavoured with basil and dressed with a shallot and port vinaigrette or fresh salmon rillettes with a cucumber salad and a lemon and chive dressing. Main courses show as much enthusiasm with grilled halibut served with a sauce of creamy leeks, tomatoes and chives or a roast fillet of beef with a herbal crust and finished with thyme and cream sauce. Good value all round, especially the 3-course set menu. Three guest rooms are available for visitors.

NEW MILTON   Chewton Glen

Christchurch Road, New Milton, Hampshire BH25 6QS
Telephone: (0425) 275341 Fax: (0425) 272310   **£90**
Open: lunch + dinner daily
Meals served: lunch 12.30-2 (Sun 12.30-2.30), dinner 7.30-9.30

Opulent, exclusive, immaculate and dramatic immediately come to mind when thinking of this sanctuary for the body and soul, and in reality it lives up to every expectation. 90 miles south-west of London between the New Forest and the sea, Martin and Brigitte Skan's hotel has a worldwide reputation for polite staff, elegance and exquisite antiques - most certainly a place to treasure. But all of this doesn't just happen by chance, the Skans' work hard with their meticulously cho-sen team to maintain these standards. The personal touch is the hall-mark of Chewton Glen - nothing is ever overlooked from the `hello' when you arrive to the abundance of flowers in the hotel all year round. Chef Pierre Chevillard's soft meld of classical cuisine with a bent for the lighter and healthier ingredients is awe-inspiring. Both lunch and dinner see fixed-price and à la carte menus offered although you could have 2 lighter starters if you prefer - scallops finely sliced and marinated in coconut milk and exotic fruit and terrine of pheasant and pistachio nuts with onion jam and plum chutney, for example. Be guided by Gérard Basset, a masterly sommelier, when selecting from a truly superb cellar. A pricy and flamboyant hotel all round but in a decidedly agreeable English way.

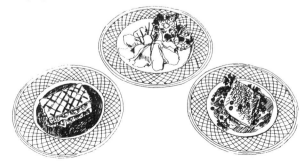

NEWARK — Gannets Cafe-Bistrot

35 Castlegate, Newark, Nottinghamshire NG24 1AZ
Telephone: (0636) 702066   **£40**
Open: lunch + dinner Wed-Sat (closed 25+26 Dec)
Meals served: lunch 12-2.30, dinner 6.30-9.30 (light meals ground floor café
10-4.30, 7 days)

This bistro offers the food that Hilary Bower herself really enjoys and
therefore cooks - an archetypal range of dishes such as lamb's liver,
prime steak and breast of chicken all sauced imaginatively or a cod
and prawn gratin, seafood pancakes with parsley sauce or good old
beef bourguignon eaten by candle-light with atmospheric background
music. A casual place to dine, upstairs or down.

NEWBURY — Millwaters

London Road, Newbury, Berkshire RG13 2BY
Telephone: (0635) 528838 Fax: (0635) 523406   £30
Open: lunch + dinner daily
Meals served: lunch 12-2, dinner 7-9.30
Impressive 32-bedroomed Georgian house set by the River Lambourn, surrounded by
8 acres of beautiful and lush gardens. Conference and function facilities.

NEWBURY — Regency Park Hotel

Bowling Green Road, Thatcham, Newbury, Berkshire RG13 3RP
Telephone: (0635) 871555 Fax: (0635) 871571   £55
Open: lunch + dinner daily
Meals served: lunch 12.30-2.30, dinner 6.30-10.30 (Sun 7-9.30)
Original Edwardian house with modern extensions to accommodate 50 bedrooms.
Keen, and helpful staff. Separate purpose-built conference centre.

NEWCASTLE-UPON-TYNE — Blackgate Restaurant

Milburn House, The Side, Newcastle-upon-Tyne, Tyne & Wear
NE1 3JE
Telephone: 091-261 7356   **£55**
Open: lunch Mon-Fri, dinner Tue-Sat (closed Bank Holidays)
Meals served: lunch 12-2, dinner 6.30-10

Situated in an old office block, the restaurant was originally the staff
dining-room (c. 1905). There's still a Victorian feel about the place,
complemented by a distinctly English menu that chef Douglas Jordan
describes as first-class British and modern cuisine. It's good to see the
restaurant (one of the longest-established in Newcastle) being
restored to its standing of long ago. The set menu (£15.10 for 3 courses including coffee) might offer a celestine of spiced chicken on a fine
bean salad with tomato dressing, baked paupiettes of plaice filled with
shellfish mousse, and a brown bread trifle, while the à la carte menu
features dishes such as a velouté of fresh salmon flavoured with fennel
served under a light and flaky pastry lid, and venison (cooked perfectly) sautéed in walnut oil with cinnamon and brandied black
cherries.

NEWCASTLE-UPON-TYNE   The Café Procope

35 The Side, Newcastle-upon-Tyne, Tyne & Wear NE1 3JE
Telephone: 091-232 3848   £35
Open: all day daily (closed Bank Holiday Mon)
Meals served: 11-10.30
Eclectic mix of different cuisines (Greek, Mexican, Indian subcontinent for a start)
served in informal surroundings with daily blackboard specials.

NEWCASTLE-UPON-TYNE   Courtney's

5-7 The Side, Quayside, Newcastle-upon-Tyne, Tyne & Wear NE1 3JE
Telephone: 091-232 5537   **£45**
Open: lunch Mon-Fri, dinner Mon-Sat (closed Bank Holidays
except Good Friday)
Meals served: lunch 12-2, dinner 7-10.30

Behind a dark green and white facade, this restaurant (in Newcastle's
prime gastronomic area) is fast gaining a reputation as one of the city's
best. Simply decorated yet elegant, with pleasant and helpful staff, the
menu (with a good vegetarian section) offers sound cooking with an
English bent - starters such as scallop mousse with a lemon and basil
vinaigrette, or goat's cheese and leek filo with a walnut salad, followed
by main courses - perhaps a tomato and aubergine gratin, or suprême
of salmon in a herb crust with a lemon butter sauce. Desserts will not
disappoint - try the Lindisfarne mead posset (a sort of runny syllabub!)
or the raspberry crème brûlée.

NEWCASTLE-UPON-TYNE Fisherman's Lodge

7 Jesmond Dene, Jesmond, Newcastle-upon-Tyne, Tyne & Wear
NE7 7BQ
Telephone: 091-281 3281 Fax: 091-281 6410   **£65**
Open: lunch Mon-Fri, dinner Mon-Sat (closed Bank Holidays)
Meals served: lunch 12-2, dinner 7-11

The decor is dazzling and heavily patterned and the menu leaves little
room for criticism. It is the fish that you come here for and believe me,
after 2 courses you'll hardly be able to contemplate a third, yet knowing dessert will be as good as what came before, you'll soldier on. The
menu is simply and directly worded so you might be surprised by the
plates that actually arrive - artistically arranged as well as cooked. A
fish and shellfish soup flavoured with fennel and pernod, a trio of
flavours of salmon (smoked, gravadlax and tartare), salmon soufflé
served with mussels and saffron sauce flavoured with dill and supreme
of turbot with fennel and mushrooms cooked in its own juices.

NEWCASTLE-UPON-TYNE 21 Queen Street

21 Queen Street, Princes Wharf, Quayside, Newcastle-Upon-Tyne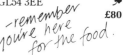
NE1 3UG
Telephone: 091-222 0755 Fax: 091-230 5875 **£65**
Open: lunch Mon-Fri, dinner Mon-Sat
Meals served: lunch 12-2, dinner 7-10.45

This smart and sophisticated restaurant in pale pastel colours is owned
by Terence Laybourne. He's also the chef, and has an affinity for well-
matched combinations such as shellfish risotto with a hint of crisp ginger, griddled scallops, cured salmon and aromatic vegetables and main
courses of pigeon with broad beans and polenta, and oxtail boned and
stuffed with root vegetables and red wine – time-consuming preparation that pays dividends on the plate. Reasonably priced wine list.

NORTHALLERTON Bettys

188 High Street, Northallerton, North Yorkshire DL7 8LF
Telephone: (0609) 775154 Fax: (0609) 777552 **£35**
Open: all day daily (closed 25+26 Dec, 1 Jan)
Meals served: 9-5.30 (Sun 10-5.30)

The Bettys name is synonymous with the best of baking. Not much
has changed here since those early days of the '20s and '30s, with
some of the best bakes and range of teas in Yorkshire. Snacks and hot
dishes and a brunch menu add to the day's production. For `Betty-ites'
miles away and hooked on their fruit cake or croissants, don't forget
the mail order service on (0423) 531211.

NORTHLEACH Old Woolhouse

Market Place, Northleach, Gloucestershire GL54 3EE
Telephone: (0451) 860366 **£80**
Open: dinner Tue-Sat (closed 1 wk Xmas)
Meals served: dinner only 8.15-9.30

*remember
you're here
for the food.*

You could be lucky and be the only 2 customers, but this is rare. Such
is the popularity of one of my favourite small restaurants that it's more
likely that you will be joined to capacity by the other 3 tables.
Everything about Jacques and Jenny Astic's 2 rooms, with their low-
beamed ceilings is comforting – the first is where you have an apéritif
before dinner. The rumbling might be from the refrigerator, but more
often than not it is the stomachs of the waiting guests, as tempting aromas drift through from the kitchen. The lack of frills' and sophistication are more than just charming - this is honest cooking and that's the
beauty of it. A short fixed-price menu brings you the best of the day,
read to you by Jenny while Jacques creates his dishes – highlights
include wild mushrooms and mussels in a creamy sauce followed by
sweetbread and kidneys in cassis.

NORTHLEACH   Wickens

Market Place, Northleach, Gloucestershire GL54 3EJ
Telephone: (0451) 860421   **£50**
Open: lunch + dinner Tue-Sat (closed Bank Holidays)
Meals served: lunch 12.15-1.45, dinner 7.20-8.45

Tradition in the modern English manner is typical of Christopher
Wickens' restaurant set on the side of the village square. Expect to
choose from the likes of a 3-course menu which starts with platters of
crudités, olives and pastries with drinks and then on to a cream of
Jerusalem artichoke soup, lamb with home-made apple jelly and white
onion sauce and Joanna's selection of puddings. Good team work and a
well compiled wine list.

NORWICH   Adlard's

79 Upper St Giles Street, Norwich, Norfolk NR2 1AB
Telephone: (0603) 633522   **£70**
Open: Tue-Fri, dinner Tue-Sat
Meals served: lunch 12.30-1.45, dinner 7.30-10.30

Celebrating its 10th year, of which 3 have been at this city centre location, this restaurant remains popular with David Adlard keeping standards as high as ever. A stylish and serious atmosphere, it is classical
in atmosphere yet cosy and welcoming. The set price lunch is remarkable – a well-thought-out balance of dishes making choice difficult yet
pleasurable. With simplicity of form, yet complexity of content, each
dish he creates is a display of intelligence and research. You may sample Norfolk asparagus and fried pasta with tomato coulis and fresh
parmesan, softly boiled quail's egg on brioche with spinach and
smoked salmon, fricassée of chicken with a tomato and balsamic vinegar sauce or spiced venison sausage rolled in sesame seeds with
braised red cabbage and gratin potatoes. Puddings are undoubtedly
award-winning with a crisp tulip-shaped basket studded with nuts and
filled with an excellent creamy and tart rhubarb fool, or a hot brioche
with a compôte of prunes steeped in armagnac and orange and served
with a pistachio ice cream. David Adlard is a dedicated virtuoso who
sources his produce from far and near with passionate zeal. He has a
nose for the best cheese, quality ingredients and an eye for the perfect
dish.

NORWICH   Brasted's

8-10 St Andrew's Hill, Norwich, Norfolk NR2 1DS
Telephone: (0603) 625949   **£55**
Open: lunch + dinner Mon-Sat (closed Bank Holidays)
Meals served: lunch 12-2, dinner 7-10

Inspiration has reached this cosy restaurant tucked away in the old
part of the city in the guise of new chef Adrian Clarke. He arrived this
year and has added to this familiar candy-striped restaurant some
reflective combinations – terrine of fishes (wrapped in salmon and
scented with herbs), fresh tomato tart in an individual cheese-
flavoured flan with tomatoes, chives and pesto sauce, and navarin of
lamb finished with flageolet beans.

NORWICH Greens Seafood Restaurant

82 Upper St Giles Street, Norwich, Norfolk NR2 1LT
Telephone: (0603) 623733 Fax: (0603) 615268 **£50**
Open: lunch Tue-Fri, dinner Mon-Sat (closed Bank Holidays,
1 wk Xmas)
Meals served: lunch 12.15-2.15, dinner 7-10.45

Pop into the bar and take a light snack from the new menu or move
into the main restaurant and enjoy a choice from the new set menus
and specials such as salmon baked in filo with seasoned spinach and
chive beurre blanc, monkfish with a confit of braised onions and peppers with red wine sauce and an olive mash or a platter of seafood,
lightly grilled and glazed with herb butter. Lunch offers lighter alternatives and options from the blackboard, and all of the fresh fish can be
served unsauced and simply prepared on request. A rich decor is
emphasised by Henry Ford Jenkin's sepia prints of the Lowestoft fishing industry when it was at its peak – docks, fishing fleet and herring
packers.

NORWICH Marco's

17 Pottergate, Norwich, Norfolk NR2 1DS
Telephone: (0603) 624044 **£50**
Open: lunch + dinner Tue-Sat (closed Bank Holidays)
Meals served: lunch 12.30-2, dinner 7.30-10

An advocate of how things should be done, Marco Vessalio greets you
in the same way he has been greeting his guests for the last 24 years —
from the door of his kitchen. Then he leaves it to the staff and nips
back to the stove to rustle up a glorious selection of provincial Italian
food. A colourful character with an equally vibrant restaurant. Skilfully
cooked food might include gnocchi with mushrooms, garlic and parsley, crespoline of seafood and saltimbocca of chicken. `I love and
respect all good wines.. but as I am offering Italian food, and Italy is
one of the greatest producers, I thought it appropriate to offer you only
Italian wine.' – who can argue!

NORWICH St Benedict's Grill

9 St Benedicts Street, Norwich, Norfolk NR2 4PE
Telephone: (0603) 765377 **£40**
Open: lunch + dinner Tue-Sat (closed Dec 25, Jan 1)
Meals served: lunch 12-2, dinner 7-10 (Fri+Sat 7-10.30)

Nigel and Jayne Raffles have been involved in this concern from its
very beginning in 1991, but this year they became the proud, sole owners. Still very much part of the everyday running of the brasserie-cum-
restaurant, Nigel continues in the kitchen while Jayne is at front of
house. The menu is short with main courses ranging from leek and
blue cheese sausages on a bed of mixed pulses, roast wing of skate
with dijon mustard sauce, a sandwich of potato rösti with breast and
leg meat of duck, to a best-end of lamb with herb juices and a mound
of saffron mash. Friendly prices are matched by the friendly service.

NOTTINGHAM   Loch Fyne Oyster Bar

17 King Street, Nottingham, Nottinghamshire
Telephone: (0602) 508481   £45
Open: all day Mon-Sat (closed Bank Holidays)
Meals served: 9-8.30 (Thu-Sat 9-10.30)

The world is your oyster and here you can dine on them from morning
to night. In fact there is nothing like the slap of a dozen creamy oysters
instead of a pot of tea at 4.00, after a busy afternoon's shopping – try it.
Other seafood platters, salads and soups are available, and a selection
of wines and beers is also offered.

NOTTINGHAM   Sonny's

3 Carlton Street, Hockley, Nottingham, Nottinghamshire NG1 1NL
Telephone: (0602) 473041   **£45**
Open: lunch + dinner daily (closed Bank Holidays)
Meals served: lunch 12-2.30, dinner 7-10.30 (Sat 7-11)
(light meals in café Mon-Sat)

Ian Broadbent's cooking at this establishment makes a refreshing
change in this neck of the woods. The offspring of the London proto-
type it has now taken to opening on Sundays and also has a café
offering focaccia, baguettes, soups, pasta and salads in a similar big
gutsy way. The main menu has Mediterranean touches and a char-
grill, producing effective dishes of salmon and chervil butter, calves'
liver, bacon and caramelised apple and aubergine and courgette with
mint and pistachio pesto. Unquestionably popular with the young and
chummy.

OAKHAM   Hambleton Hall

Hambleton, Nr Oakham, Leicestershire LE15 8TH
Telephone: (0572) 756991 Fax: (0572) 724721   **£60**
Open: lunch + dinner daily
Meals served: lunch 12-1.45, dinner 7-9.30

A house in such a setting as this is on to a winner. Created by Tim and
Stefa Hart, it is an elegant and stately house, filled with magnificent
blooms from the gardens and a Nina Campbell interior served by con-
genial staff. The Hambleton tradition is continued in the kitchen by the
energy and aptitude of young chef Aaron Patterson who cooks through
the seasons with deft ability and taste, with dishes such as pressed
layers of tomatoes and fresh crab with Mediterranean vegetables and
saffron vinaigrette and braised fillet of brill with shellfish and own
juices completed by caramelised lemon tart with pears and red wine
sauce.

OAKHAM   Whipper-In Hotel

Market Place, Oakham, Rutland, Leicestershire LE15 6DT
Telephone: (0572) 756971 Fax: (0572) 757759   **£35**
Open: lunch daily, dinner Mon-Sat
Meals served: lunch 12.30-2, dinner 7.30-9.30

At this flagstoned 17th-century coaching inn, you can eat in the bar at
lunchtime or the restaurant in the evening. Room service is available
for all meals, but who would want to be cooped up inside when you
could be out enjoying the surrounding countryside and the spectacular
Rutland Water? 25 bedrooms, some with 4-posters and antiques.

OLD BURGHCLERE   Dew Pond

Old Burghclere, Newbury, Berkshire RG15 9LH
Telephone: (0635) 278408   **£55**
Open: lunch Tue-Fri, dinner Tue-Sat (closed 2 wks Jan, 2 wks Aug)
Meals served: lunch 12-2, dinner 7-10

This creeper-clad, 16th-century country house at the foot of Watership
Down specialises in fresh game and local produce which I suspect
occasionally means rabbit! A warm, family-run hotel, it has co-owner
Keith Marshall residing over the cooking and creating well-priced set
menus from which gastronomes will enjoy his 6-courser of salad of
quail with quail's eggs, sweetbreads and pine kernels followed by
steamed salmon with mousseline of scallop before a sorbet of champagne, lamb with dijon mustard accompanied by a confit of garlic and
then farmhouse cheese and a grand finale of desserts. The vegetarian
will be delighted by his millefeuille creation of creamed wild mushrooms with a glaze of Stilton crumble.

ORFORD   Butley-Orford Oysterage

Market Square, Orford, Woodbridge, Suffolk IP12 2LH
Telephone: (0394) 450277   **£35**
Open: lunch + dinner daily (closed 25+26Dec)
Meals served: lunch 12-2.15, dinner 6-8.30

With a busy coffee shop decor this is the place to come and have plates
of oysters straight from local beds, smoked eel on toast, angels-on-
horseback (grilled bacon and oysters on toast) with a few slabs of
brown bread, together with an oyster cocktail of fresh oysters in
tomato juice. Bring some friends, for that way you will get to sample all
the goodies, including their home-smoked fish which includes wild
Irish salmon. If there are only 2 of you opt for a mixed platter.

OSWESTRY — Restaurant Sebastian

45 Willow Street, Oswestry, Shropshire SY11 1AQ
Telephone: (0691) 655444   **£35**
Open: dinner Tue-Sat (closed 25+26 Dec, 1 Jan)
Meals served: dinner 6.30-10.30

Seafood is the speciality here with the fish menu changing every week in high season - coquilles St Jacques with green chartreuse and caramelized apples and a 1lb dover sole, pan-fried and served with parsley butter make a pleasant change from steak frites or hâché – there are plenty of classical-style meat dishes to choose from. Mark Sebastian Fisher does the cooking while wife Michelle runs front of house at this provincial French restaurant. Some affordable wines on the list.

OXFORD — Bath Place Hotel & Restaurant

4 & 5 Bath Place, Holywell Street, Oxford, Oxfordshire OX1 3SU
Telephone: (0865) 791812 Fax: (0865) 791834   **£55**
Open: lunch Wed-Sun, dinner Tue-Sat
Meals served: lunch 12-2, dinner 7-10 (Fri+Sat 7-10.30)

A restaurant with 8 pristine rooms makes a good destination for a weekend in Oxford. Peter Cherrill continues to hold court in the kitchen with his light style of cooking, presented in a modest manner. A leek soup with carrot julienne and goujons of sole or thinly sliced salt-cured duck with artichoke heart, then pot-roast savoy cabbage in cinnamon juices typify what you might find on the 3- or 2- course menu. A good restaurant, tucked down a cobbled lane, it is proving popular for lunch on Sundays. The bedrooms are individually decorated, some with 4-posters.

OXFORD — Browns

5-11 Woodstock Road, Oxford, Oxfordshire OX2 6HA
Telephone: (0865) 511995 Fax: (0865) 52347   **£30**
Open: all day daily (closed 25+26 Dec)
Meals served: 11am-11.30pm (Sun 12-11.30)

An Oxford institution, this triple-fronted brasserie-style restaurant and bar remains popular with all ages. Bustling during the week with shoppers, families and students it is frequented for the good-value menu which offers dishes in good-sized portions, always freshly prepared. Spaghetti comes with a choice of 4 sauces, there are 6 salads and a variety of main courses from leg of lamb with rosemary, char-grilled venison steak and a fisherman's pie with a Cheddar cheese crust. The pressure on busy Sundays will be relieved by this year's refurbishment that has increased the size of the bar and improved the seating.

OXFORD   Cherwell Boathouse

Bardwell Road, Oxford, Oxfordshire OX2 6SR
Telephone: (0865) 52746 Fax: (0865) 391459   **£40**
Open: lunch daily in summer, dinner Tue-Sat (closed
Bank Holidays, Xmas)
Meals served: lunch 12-2, dinner 7-10 (Sat 7-10.30)

You have to be in the know to find this place, let alone pronounce it.
Look out for the Dragon School playing field and you will be just about
there. Improvements are on the horizon, for extensive all-round use.
Owner Anthony Verdin is enthusiastic about the use of special home-
grown vegetable varieties – so be prepared for some unusual and
adventurous creations over the next year. Current options include
lentil salad with fresh sage, roasted peppers and feta cheese, followed
by sea trout in a creamy anchovy sauce finishing with chocolate and
orange roulade. The wine list has been overhauled and gives good
value throughout. An idyllic venue for lunch or dinner by the river.

OXFORD   15 North Parade

15 North Parade Avenue, Oxford, Oxfordshire OX2 6LX
Telephone: (0865) 513773   **£45**
Open: lunch daily, dinner Mon-Sat (closed some Bank Holidays)
Meals served: lunch 12-2, dinner 7-10.30   _local loyal following_

In a narrow street with a good local pub and antique shops leading to
St Anthony's College, new chef Colin Gilbert is at work bringing the
flavours of Provence and a hint of the orient to primarily English cooking. His daily menus offer strong flavour combinations: pork marinated
in cider and coriander and served with apples and lemon balm, potted
fresh rainbow trout with a sauce of tomatoes and a cucumber chutney,
lamb with provençal vegetables and a port wine sauce and pan-fried
pigeon with celeriac and walnut salad scented with soy sauce. This talented patissierer's tart of lemon and limes should not be missed. The
wines take a lap of the world from the Lebanon to France and then on
to Australia.

OXFORD   Gee's

61a Banbury Road, Oxford, Oxfordshire OX2 6PE
Telephone: (0865) 53540   **£45**
Open: lunch + dinner daily (closed 25+26 Dec)
Meals served: lunch 12-2.30, dinner 6-11

Herbs, spices and the char-grill are chef Graham Corbett's signatures
on a menu that reworks so many favourites including the beefburger.
Graham gives it a new twist by serving his chopped steak on ciabatta
bread with Swiss cheese, while the baby chicken is steeped in garlic
and lemon and served with a garlic mayonnaise. There's also good
pasta and imaginative salads. This delightful, tiled conservatory is full
of plants and flowers, is simply lit and is an oasis of good modern food–
with young, informal staff who work hard to help you enjoy yourself.

OXFORD   Restaurant Elizabeth

82 St Aldate's, Oxford, Oxfordshire OX1 1RA
Telephone: (0865) 242230   £55
Open: lunch + dinner Tue-Sun (closed Good Friday, 24-31 Dec)
Meals served: lunch 12.30-2.30, dinner 6.30-11 (Sun 7-10.30)

Things won't have changed much since the last time you were here,
for happily, trends have come and gone but have never been taken
seriously here, nor allowed to creep on to the menu, which is predominantly French with the occasional dash to Spain and Greece. Owner
Antonio Lopez has been in charge for the last 30 years while chef
Salvador Rodriguez has been here since the late '70s cooking the specialities of the house - prawns with rice and aiöli, pipérade, entrecôte
and pan-fried salmon. Very good wine list. A relaxed atmosphere and a
warm welcome awaits.

PADSTOW   Seafood Restaurant

Riverside, Padstow, Cornwall PL28 8BY
Telephone: (0841) 532485 Fax: (0841) 533344   *Great for food & atmosphere*   £70
Open: lunch + dinner Mon-Sat (closed late Dec-end Jan)
Meals served: lunch 12.30-2.15, dinner 7-9.30

At possibly one of the most enthusiastic fish restaurants to be found on
this temperate isle, Rick Stein, it goes without saying, is an authority
on sea bass and salmon, and it is difficult to judge which is the more
superb - the bustling, informal, quayside location or the depth of his
menu. The restaurant is light and bright and very unfussy, just like his
style of cooking, but do not underestimate the work that will have
gone into the most simple dish on the carte. Beauty is in the eye of the
beholder and here it looks back at you in unadulterated freshness with
razor-shell clams, mussels, velvets and langoustine, to name a few of
the varieties that come in a hot garlic and lemon oil. Dover sole takes
well to a seasoning of sea salt and can never taste better than when
cooked until the skin is crisp but the flesh still succulent, whereas sea
bass is better with a piquant salsa verde and deep fried potato. His fish
are the freshest, his cooking the kindest and the wine keenly priced. 8
bedrooms above the restaurant make it worth staying for a couple of
days to sample more than one meal.

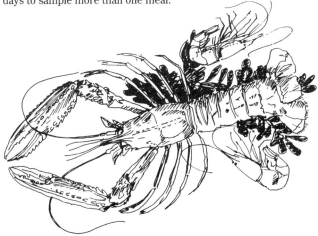

PAINSWICK — Painswick Hotel

Kemps Lane, Painswick GL6 6YB
Telephone: (0452) 812160 Fax: (0452) 812059   **£55**
Open: lunch + dinner daily
Meals served: lunch 12-2, dinner 7-9.30

A Palladian-style house that was built in 1790, Painswick has been restored to create a fine hotel with 20 luxury bedrooms. Elegant and stylishly put together with antiques, portraits and 4-poster beds, it is run in a welcome and relaxed manner by the Moore family. Friendly staff and good breakfasts make this a great place to stay overnight. Light luncheons and 5-course dinner menus use locally-reared Cotswold meat and Vale of Evesham vegetables. Expect to see dishes such as lobster with lemon mayonnaise, beef with watercress mousse and horseradish and parsley sauce and lamb with glazed shallots and a redcurrant and orange sauce.

PAULERSPURY — Vine House

High Street, Paulerspury, Northamptonshire NN12 7NA
Telephone: (032 733) 267 Fax: (032 733) 609   **£50**
Open: lunch Mon-Fri + Sun, dinner Mon-Sat (closed 26 Dec, 1 Jan)
Meals served: lunch 12-2.30, dinner 7-10

Self-taught and extremely enthusiastic, Marcus Springett has kept up with the house's reputation for fine dining. He uses the freshest ingredients possible and is a firm believer in home-made bread, compotes and sweetmeats - the dedication has paid off. The menus change every day but might include a brandade of smoked cod's roe and prawns served with bacon and leeks, pheasant and garlic sausage terrine with home-made apricot chutney and main courses of fresh salmon with a ginger and green peppercorn sauce. Puddings include plum and Cointreau sorbet and a crème brulée made with Jersey cream and Calvados. After all of that you will be glad that you have booked into one of the 6 bedrooms!

PENKRIDGE — William Harding's House

Mill Street, Penkridge, Stafford, Staffordshire ST19 5AY
Telephone: (078 571) 2955   **£38**
Open: lunch Sun, dinner Tue-Sat (closed Bank Holidays)
Meals served: lunch 12.30-1.45, dinner 7.30-9.30

Chronicled as a `house with a stable' and home to one William Harding, groom to the local landowner, the house today is better known as `rooms for licensed dining'. Owned by the Bickleys, it still has an old-fashioned ring about it, as demonstrated by pheasant terrine with cumberland sauce, Cornish crab soup, and puddings plus British regional cheeses served from the sideboard.

PENZANCE   Abbey Hotel

Abbey Street, Penzance, Cornwall TR18 4AR
Telephone: (0736) 66906 Fax: (0736) 51163   *A charming,*
Open: dinner daily   *welcoming hotel.* **£50**
Meals served: dinner 7.30-8.30

Telephone and ask for one of their brochures if you're thinking of staying here and you'll find that for once, the reality lives up to the marketing. The building, formerly an Abbey, dates back to 1660 and has been lovingly restored and decorated in an informal, relaxed style, now offering 7 bedrooms. It's also worth eating in the intimate candle-lit dining room. The handwritten menu changes daily and offers 3 choices for each course with vegetarian alternatives always available. Dinner might be salad of spicy chickpeas, avocado and smoked salmon followed by roast quail stuffed with crab apples and cumin or king prawns flambéed in brandy. Puddings are always good and might be butterscotch pudding or a chestnut and chocolate slice.

PLUMTREE   Perkins Bar Bistro

Old Railway Station, Station Road, Plumtree, Nottinghamshire NG12 5NA
Telephone: (0602) 373695   **£40**
Open: lunch + dinner Tue-Sat (closed 25+26 Dec, 1 Jan, Easter Mon+Tue)
Meals served: lunch 12-2, dinner 6.45-9.45

An unusual setting for a French influenced bistro: Tony and Wendy Perkins bought the train station in the early '80s and converted it to this informal restaurant with impressionist prints and posters of food and wine from the Victorian era. The food is mainly French with as much of Tony's attention spent on the vegetables as the main courses. Typical blackboard offerings include mousseline of spiced lentils with tomato coulis, warm salad of scallops, bacon and mushrooms, skewers of vegetables and fruits with herb omelette and hollandaise sauce and banana and rum raisin tart. Some reasonably priced wines by the bottle and by the glass.

Abbey Hotel, Penzance

PLYMOUTH Chez Nous

13 Frankfort Gate, Plymouth, Devon PL1 1QA
Telephone: (0752) 266793 £65
Open: lunch + dinner Tue-Sat (closed Bank Holidays, 3 wks
Feb, 3 wks Sep)
Meals served: lunch 12.30-2, dinner 7-10.30

Cuisine Spontanée sets the mood here and this is the type of restaurant in which you immediately feel at home. Owners Jacques and Suzanne Marchal come a chat to you and offer you a drink. Suzanne runs through the list of specials from the blackboard, and then Jacques saunters back to the kitchen to rustle up some delightful dishes. Don't underestimate the immense talent of the man – he has been doing this for 12 years – and his confidence lies in the knowledge that the morning's shopping is the top of the crop. His specials could include medallions of venison with black pepper, veal with shiitake, chateaubriand with béarnaise or a casserole of snails with mushrooms. Decent house wine and collection of half bottles offer good value. Although set in a parade of shops, once you're inside you will forget you're in Plymouth: in the twinkling of an eye you're back in the bistro you ate at during your last visit to provincial France – blackboard menu, wall posters and paintings and genial hosts.

PLYMOUTH Piermasters Restaurant

33 Southside Street, The Barbican, Plymouth, Devon PL1 2LE
Telephone: (0752) 229345 £50
Open: lunch + dinner Mon-Sat (closed Dec 24-Jan 2)
Meals served: lunch 12-2, dinner 7-10

Down by the quayside in the Barbican complex you will find this bustling restaurant that specialises in good fish dishes and traditional but well-cooked main courses of lamb with tarragon and fillet of beef with wild mushroom sauce. But what you mainly come here for is the fish - hot oysters hollandaise, monkfish with pesto, sea bass with chive sauce, scallops in a saffron consommé and Med-style seafood ragoût all deftly cooked and presented by the French chef. A good restaurant, not too formal where the service is exact but not overbearing. On Fridays and Saturdays there is a fixed-price menu as well as choice from the à la carte. It seems incredible that a city of this size has so few good places to eat – but this certainly helps fills the gap.

POLPERRO   Kitchen at Polperro

The Coombs, Polperro, Cornwall PL13 2RQ
Telephone: (0503) 72780   **£35**
Open: dinner Mon-Sun in summer, Fri+Sat in winter
 (closed 25+26 Dec, Jan)
Meals served: dinner only 7-9.30

You will have to park in the village car park and take a stroll down to
the harbour and this little restaurant, lovingly cared for by Ian and
Vanessa Bateson. The cooking is enjoyable and seafood is the focus:
garlic mussels, Fowey sea trout baked simply with lemon and herb
butter, prawns in filo with coconut and coriander sauce, lobster, crab
and lemon sole when in season but other Cornish delights are also on
offer such as char-grilled Cornish sausages with an onion marmalade
and duck with blueberry and Drambuie sauce.

POOL-IN-WHARFDALE   Pool Court

Pool Bank, Pool in Wharfedale, West Yorkshire LS21 1EH   🎗
Telephone: (0532) 842288 Fax: (0532) 843115   **£80**
Open: dinner Tue-Sat (2 wks July/Aug, 2 wks from 24 Dec)
Meals served: dinner 6.30-10

Formal and elegant and under the long-standing proprietorship of
Michael and Hanni Gill, this hotel is hard to fault. David Watson, a talented Yorkshireman, directs a kitchen full of talent with excellent
results. Specialities include sweetbreads and scallops, set between
crisp sesame layers, with a warm, mild curry and vanilla dressing; a
main course of fresh Scottish salmon poached in a light stock with fennel, leeks and tomatoes, enriched with butter; and a dessert of layered
raspberry parfait, laced with vodka, between brandy snaps and a sharp
rhubarb sauce. An excellent selection of interesting wines. 6 bedrooms
make this a worthwhile place to stay.

POOLE   Haven Hotel

Banks Road, Sandbanks, Poole, Dorset BH13 7QL
Telephone: (0202) 707333 Fax: (0202) 708796   **£65**
Open: lunch + dinner daily (La Roche Restaurant: dinner Tue-Sat)
Meals served: lunch 12.30-2, dinner 7-9.30 (La Roche: 7-10.30)   ❖

With almost the eighth and ninth wonders of the world here - the second largest natural harbour and the place from where Marconi made
his first wireless telegraphy broadcast - it is a location well worth noting. Right on the water's edge at the entrance to the harbour, the
Haven is immaculately kept and constantly updated – it now has 92
bedrooms and exclusive leisure facilities. Chef Karl Heinz Nagler,
comes here with an excellent record including time at Michael Nook's
in the Lake District. In La Roche restaurant is where you will now find
his dishes ranging from terrine of chicken and lobster served in a tarragon jelly or a salad of wood pigeon as starters, followed perhaps by a
Pernod and saffron flavoured papillote of sea bass or a steamed
supreme of maize-fed chicken served with ravioli in a saffron fondue.

POOLE — Mansion House

11 Thames Street, Poole, Dorset BH15 1JN
Telephone: (0202) 685666 Fax: (0202) 665709 **£45**
Open: lunch Sun-Fri, dinner daily (closed 1 Jan, Easter Mon)
Meals served: lunch 12.30-2.15, dinner 7.30-9.30 (Sun 7.30-9)

In this dining club-style restaurant, the main course sets the price of your meal (except pudding) - the starter, soup or sorbet and coffee all come included. So go to the main course first and work from there. Breast of duckling on a sage and port sauce with a compôte of spiced apricots could be coupled with warm salad of king prawn tails with black beans or sweet and sour poached pear with Denhay ham and tarragon sauce, or pan-fried sweetbreads with seed mustard sauce — an unusual way of working out your meal! But novelty aside, Tony Parsons' cooking is recommended and the service is good. The Mansion House is a sophisticated and stylish setting for lunch or dinner.

PORLOCK — Oaks Hotel

Porlock, Somerset TA24 8ES
Telephone: (0643) 862265 **£45**
Open: dinner daily
Meals served: dinner 7-8.30

A homely setting in an Edwardian house with a sense of well being, the Oaks Hotel is made even more desirable and cosy by the aromas of Anne Riley's cooking in the early evening air - sauté of mushrooms with herbs and white wine, leg of local roast lamb with rosemary and garlic and a chocolate brownie with vanilla ice cream and a hot chocolate fudge sauce. 10 rooms with views of Porlock Bay and the village itself.

POWBURN — Breamish House

Powburn, Alnwick, Northumberland NE66 4LL
Telephone: (066 578) 266 Fax: (066 578) 500 **£50**
Open: lunch Sun, dinner daily (closed Jan)
Meals served: lunch 12.30 for 1, dinner 7.30 for 8

This Georgian hotel and its small restaurant rely on the expertise of Cordon Bleu cooks - poached egg on toasted muffin with watercress sauce, pâté of local, smoked, wild brown trout and poached fillet of monkfish with chervil sauce being some of the options. On a scenic note, the gardens in spring are carpeted with bluebells and daffodils while inside the house the 11 bedrooms continue the country theme, being named after trees from the surrounding woodlands.

PUCKRUP   Puckrup Hall

Puckrup, Tewkesbury, Gloucestershire GL20 6EL
Telephone: (0684) 296200 Fax: (0684) 850788   **£50**
Open: lunch + dinner daily
Meals served: lunch 12.30-2, dinner 7-9.30 (Fri+Sat 7-10)

Fast becoming a leisure-oriented hotel, with an 18-hole golf course and
new additions to the complex at the end of '93, Puckrup now has more
bedrooms than can be named after just months and seasons, as they
originally were. Geoff Balharrie continues with his modern British
cooking, offering deep-fried Cheddar with celery relish and a hazelnut
salad, potato gnocchi with gorgonzola, aubergines, tomatoes and roasted garlic or fillet of beef with a marrow crust and a tomato and rosemary reduction, but health and the heart are nowadays obviously a pri-
mary concern, so the menu makes allowances for this and highlights
the dishes most suitable for those on a low cholesterol diet.

PULBOROUGH   Stane Street Hollow

Codmore Hill, Pulborough, West Sussex RH20 1BG
Telephone: (0798) 872819   **£50**
Open: lunch Wed-Fri + Sun, dinner Wed-Sat (closed 1 wk Xmas,
1 wk May, 2 wks Oct)
Meals served: lunch 12.30-1.15, dinner 7.30-9.15   *Homely & cottagey setting*

René Kaiser has been cooking here for nearly two decades and much
is pleasantly still the same - the enthusiasm, the good solid cooking
with overtones of his Swiss background and a keenly priced wine list.
The menus keep abreast with the seasons but the quality of the food is
always notably consistent. Recent dishes have included fish knödels
(little fish dumplings flavoured with a hint of curry served with a
soured cream and mayo sauce) and prawns cooked in a light batter.
Game is prevalent with a jaegertopf - casseroled rabbit and venison
cooked in wine and served with delectable apples filled with quince
paste, and guinea fowl cooked in white wine with mushrooms, bacon
and fresh thyme. This year sees a welcome change to opening hours
with René and Ann opening for lunch on Sundays with a 3-and 2-
course set menu - a bonus to those who don't often get the chance to
dine like a king. With an affordable wine list, friendly service and good
cooking, it must be on the list of everyone who lives in a 20 mile
radius.

PURTON   Pear Tree

Church End, Purton, Nr Swindon, Wiltshire SN5 9ED
Telephone: (0793) 772100 Fax: (0793) 772369   **£55**
Open: lunch Sun-Fri, dinner daily
Meals served: lunch 12-2, dinner 7-9.30

Set in a most traditional Victorian garden nestled in the Vale of the
White Horse, this elegant 18-bedroomed country house should whim-
sically be named Floribunda rather than Pear Tree as a tribute to Anne
Young's dedication to the blooms that bedeck the rooms and well man-
icured gardens. Janet Pichel-Juan takes charge of the kitchen with
French expertise applied to typically British recipes - pea and
Bromham ham soup or grilled Grimsby sardines with coarse grain
mustard glaze, breaded lamb chops pan-fried with a spicy tomato
sauce and pot roasted oxtail in a rich burgundy and orange peel sauce.
Don't miss the larger-than-life puddings, amongst which that pear
eventually puts in an appearance, filled with blackberry mousse on a
vanilla sauce or, if even richer creations are required, sample the
chocolate ice cream, here served with an apple sauce. The Pear Tree
apparently was moved stone by stone in the early 1900s from its original location close to the village church. This, together with Paris
House in Woburn, which was moved to the Great Exhibition in Paris
and back again, makes me wonder if there are any more travelling
hotels and restaurants in Great Britain? I'll send a bottle of Charles
Heidsieck for the most entertaining and original story, preferably - but
not compulsory - based on fact!

QUORN   Quorn Grange

Wood Lane, Quorn, Leicestershire LE12 8DB
Telephone: (0509) 412167 Fax: (0509) 415621   **£55**
Open: lunch Sun-Fri, dinner daily
Meals served: lunch 12-2.30, dinner 7-9.30 (Sat 7-10 Sun 7-9)

Crunch up the short drive and a pleasant rambling, ivy-clad Victorian
house greets you - Agatha Christie-style thrillers and weekend house
parties immediately spring to mind. But under all this foliage is a serious restaurant with chef Gordon Lang's flair very much in the fore,
doing justice to Jeremy Lord's endeavours to create an elegant and
peaceful place to stay. 17 bedrooms are available for visitors but the
restaurant is also open to non-residents who enjoy the likes of sole and
lobster mousse with lobster sauce, soup of leek, coriander and saffron
and fillets of sea bass with saffron noodles and Provence-style sauce.

RAMSBOTTOM   The Village

16 Market Place, Ramsbottom, nr Bury, Greater Manchester BL0 9HT
Telephone: (0706) 825070   **£60**
Restaurant:
Open: dinner Sat (closed 1 Jan)
Meals served: 8 for 8.30
Coffee Shop & Supper Room:
Open: lunch + dinner Tue-Sat (closed 1 Jan)
Meals served: lunch 12-2.30, dinner 6.30-9

All change! Re-shuffling to keep abreast of changing trends has meant
alteration to a Coffee Shop and Supper Room during the week and
keeping the more formal restaurant purely for Saturday nights and
special occasions. The Chris Johnson and Ros Hunter team remains
the same, the attitude confident and Ros' cooking just as good, the
only modification being the format. Rest assured that the standards
remain high even in the more accessible, lighter menu options of inexpensive lunches and bistro-style suppers. The food served is organic
wherever possible, meat is non-intensively reared, and there's always
something for the vegetarian. In the restaurant the wine list is
daunting, with over 1200 bins! A typical Saturday menu might include
a red pepper salad with anchovy sauce, brill with a tomato sauce or
beef with organically grown vegetables. British farmhouse cheese
precede dessert, coffee and Valrhona chocolates.

REIGATE   La Barbe

71 Bell Street, Reigate, Surrey RH2 7AN
Telephone: (0737) 241966   £50
Open: lunch Mon-Fri, dinner Mon-Sat (closed Bank Holidays, 25-27 Dec
but open Good Friday)
Meals served: lunch 12-2, dinner 7-10
Classic and provincial French cuisine from a fixed-price 2- or 3-course menu. A 2-
course daily menu marked on a blackboard offers very good value. Cross referencing
of wines with dishes helps the uninitiated.

REMENHAM   The Little Angel

Remenham, Henley-on-Thames, Oxfordshire RG9 2LS
Telephone: (0491) 574165   **£55**
Open: lunch + dinner daily (closed 25+26 Dec)
Meals served: lunch 12-3, dinner 6-10

Right by the bridge just south of Henley, the Little Angel is a very popular pub and restaurant. It offers an extensive range of bar snacks and
hugely generous full meals in either the garden, the bar area (even at
the bar when it's exceptionally crowded) or the restaurant proper.
Although it really comes into its own in July when Henley is on everyone's lips, either for the Regatta or the subsequent festival, the Angel
is rightly popular all year round, being as cosy and enticing in winter
as it is outgoing and welcoming in summer.

RICHMOND — Café Flo

149 Kew Road, Richmond, Surrey
Telephone: 081-940 8298 Fax: 081-332 2598   £30
Open: lunch + dinner daily (closed 2-3 days Xmas)
Meals served: lunch 12-3, dinner 6-11.30

One of the many Cafés Flo, opened by Russel and Juliette Joffe over six years ago. Now considered a flagship, it continues the theme of offering good quality French-style food, reasonably priced and with no pretentions. There's plenty to get your teeth into in the way of steaks, fish, or saucisses and pastas and the ubiquitous frites. Outside terrace for the summer and a friendly welcome from the staff led by Dawn Painter.

RICHMOND — Petersham Hotel

Nightingale Lane, Richmond, Surrey TW10 6UZ
Telephone: 081-940 7471 Fax: 081-940 9998   £45
Open: lunch + dinner daily (closed 25+26 Dec)
Meals served: lunch 12.15-2.15, dinner 7-9.45

Standing proudly on Richmond Hill surveying the Royal parklands and meandering curves of the River Thames, this 60-bedroomed hotel enjoys some of the most exceptional and breath-taking scenery - exactly the views that inspired Turner and Reynolds. Architecturally impressive, this house is just 8 miles from the centre of London and is an excellent place for those fanatical about sport with Twickenham and Wimbledon close by. The kitchens and menu have had their share of attention and both return redesigned this year with some new interpretations and some old favourites, but with food cooked in a lighter and healthier way, in keeping with today's lifestyle.

RICHMOND — Howe Villa

Whitcliffe Mill, Richmond, North Yorkshire DL10 4TJ
Telephone: (0748) 850055   £40
Open: dinner daily (closed Dec+Jan)
Meals served: dinner 7.30 for 8

A comparatively rare opportunity for you to take your own wine, for this is an unlicensed premises - a bonus since it is cheaper this way but also for those fanatical about the stuff, the specific vineyard, bin number etc, it's an opportunity to take along exactly what you enjoy and want to drink. The beautiful house has 5 bedrooms, and in the tranquil dining room you can view the River Swale as you savour chef and co-owner Anita Berry's home cooking — sole and salmon mousseline, noisettes of lamb and fruits marinated in Cointreau. The menu changes daily so ring before you go if you want to check that you have a suitable wine, and also to obtain directions since this is so well hidden away you are unlikely to find it otherwise!

RICHMOND   Kings Head

Market Place, Richmond, North Yorkshire DL10 4HS
Telephone: (0748) 850220 Fax: (0748) 850635   £35
Open: lunch Sun, dinner daily
Meals served: lunch Sun 12-2, dinner 7-9.15

Look no further than the bar of this 28-bedroomed hotel for a pint of
the best - Theakstons, the local beer, that is - and it won't be ringing
that you will hear in you ears but the chiming of the collection of
clocks in the nearby room. This hotel dominates the cobbled market
square with its Georgian façade, and was originally built as an elegant
town house. The town itself nestles in a wide curve of the River Swale
and is characterised by winding streets and small shops.

RIDGEWAY   Old Vicarage

Ridgeway Moor, Ridgeway. Nr. Sheffield, Derbyshire S12 3XW   ❀
Telephone: (0742) 475814 Fax: (0742) 477079   £85
Open: lunch Tue-Sun, dinner Tue-Sat (closed Bank Holiday
Mon, 27-30 Dec)
Meals served: lunch 12.30-3, dinner 7-11

Be careful not to miss this comparatively well-hidden house, set back
from the road and surrounded by trees, with only a hint of a nameplate
on the gate. A family-run concern, the welcome is warm from Andrew
Bramley who runs front of house while mother Tessa leads a fine team
in the kitchen, supported by fellow head chef Rupert Staniforth. Much
care goes into the preparation and presentation, evident in dishes such
as the thinly sliced, sautéed scallops with golden marjoram and a lime
dressing, accompanied by asparagus spears and herb flavoured cream.
Many ingredients are home-grown, even small edible flowers which
lend a myriad of taste sensations to the dishes. Main courses include
braised oxtail with mashed potato and roast parsnip, filo parcels of
ratatouille and pissaladière on a bed of polenta. No compromises in the
desserts with hot strawberry soufflé and a tuile basket of home-made
ice creams and fresh fruit - delicious! A recent addition is the Bistro,
which opened in February 199, and offers gutsy food for a reasonable
price from a frequently changing menu with a blend of Eastern,
French, Italian and British rural influences.

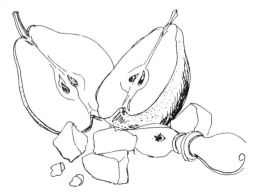

RIPLEY   Michels

13 High Street, Ripley, Surrey GU23 6AQ
Telephone: (0483) 224777   £90
Open: lunch Tue-Fri + Sun, dinner Tue-Sat (closed 25+26 Dec, 1 Jan)
Meals served: lunch 12.30-1.45, dinner 7.30-9

Elegant and stylish just about sum up this Georgian-fronted restaurant
and Erik Michel's cooking merely heightens the impression. The
clever juxtaposition of ingredients creates dishes such as chicken liver
parfait served with sliced artichoke heart in crayfish dressing, smoked
eel ravioli with a light sauce scented with Gewürtztraminer, lemon sole
fillets steamed with crab soufflé and nettle sauce, served with a salad
of vegetables. Since only the freshest produce is used, the menu
changes constantly. They use their home-grown herbs and collect wild
mushrooms, so watch out for these on the menu. The ingredients
sound exciting on the menu and tickle the tastebuds too.

RIPPONDEN   Over the Bridge Restaurant

Millfold, Ripponden, Sowerby Bridge, West Yorkshire HX6 4DL
Telephone: (0422) 823722   £50
Open: dinner Mon-Sat (closed Bank Holidays)
Meals served: dinner 7-9.30

At the bridge near the centre of this village you will find a small but
well-established restaurant that only opens for dinner. The menu is set
and in the hands of Sue Tyas who cooks up a positive feast with a
selection of starters and main courses from garlic noodles with mushrooms and pesto, or gravadlax with apple and horseradish to poached
chicken with prawn mousse and citrus sauce. Puddings are traditional
and the cheeses only British with Cotherstone, Lancashire, Blue Vinny
and Ribblesdale goat's as likely candidates. A friendly and relaxed
restaurant with a good ambience.

ROADE   Roadhouse

16 High Street, Roade, Northamptonshire NN7 2NW
Telephone: (0604) 863372   £45
Open: lunch Tue-Fri + Sun, dinner daily (closed Bank Holidays,
2 wks Jul/Aug)
Meals served: lunch 12.30-1.45, dinner 7-10

Without fuss or frills Chris Kewley continues to cook a concise but
very satisfying menu with 6 options to each course. Inviting and well
sourced - or is it sauced! Salmon and crab with mussel and saffron
sauce, duck with confit of its leg meat with ginger and kumquat sauce
and sautéed calves' liver served on sweetcorn and pulses with warmed
sherry vinegar and walnut oil are typical. Puddings are also good, in
particular the strawberries baked on brioche with vanilla ice cream. It
is just as well that they have increased the capacity of the restaurant to
45 covers!

ROCHFORD — Hotel Renouf & Renouf's Restaurant

Bradley Way, Rochford, Essex SS4 1BU
Tel: (0702) 541334 Fax: (0702) 549563Z   £60
Open: lunch daily, dinner Mon-Sat (closed 26-30 Dec)
Meals served: lunch 12-1.45, dinner 7-9.45
Hotel with 24 bedrooms run by Derek Renouf.

ROMSEY — Old Manor House

21 Palmerston Street, Romsey, Hampshire SO51 8GF
Telephone: (0794) 517353   **£80**
Open: lunch Tue-Sun, dinner Tue-Sat (closed 1 wk Xmas)
Meals served: lunch 12-2, dinner 7-9.30

This Tudor town house and its intriguing menu are what one now
expects from Mauro Bregoli, and he is never known to fail, offering
modern Italian dishes that are long in flavour and live on in the memory.
Expect to find risotto with cream of mushrooms and truffles, his own
smoked bresaola or home-made piping-hot cotechino with lentils, grilled
sea bass with fennel and thyme and duck with a honey and lime sauce,
all simple and appropriately dressed. A 3-course fixed price menu is
available from Tuesday to Thursday. Good wine list, reasonably priced.
With log fires in winter and an outside area for drinks in summer, the
Old Manor House is well worth a visit.

ROTHERWICK — Tylney Hall

Rotherwick, Nr Hook, Hampshire RG27 9AJ
Telephone: (0256) 764881 Fax: (0256) 768141   **£65**
Open: lunch + dinner daily
Meals served: lunch 12.30-2, dinner 7.30-9.30

Sir Lionel Phillip's home in the 19th Century, a hospital during the First
World War, base for a shipping line during the second, then a local
school, Rotherwick has finally come suitably to rest as a hotel with 91
bedrooms and appropriate baronial halls. A tapestry of life and its changing pace, but let's hope it has found its true vocation in the experienced
hands of manager Rita Mooney, who has nurtured this transition into a
well-run hotel with mature grounds and formal lakes. It's set in 60-odd
acres of woodland with formal gardens designed by Gertrude Jekyll.
Stephen Hine matches the splendour of the surroundings with a menu
of traditional English fare – a roast joint of the evening with all the trimmings, beef medallions with a sauté of mushrooms, strips of venison
with gin and juniper sauce.

ROWDE — George & Dragon

High Street, Rowde, Wiltshire SN10 2PN
Telephone:(0380) 723053   **£35**
Open: lunch Tue-Sun, dinner Tue-Sat (closed 25+26 Dec, 1 Jan)
Meals served: lunch 12-2, dinner 7-10

Some of the finest and most inventive cooking can be sampled in this little village pub - food you wish you could find in every local. Tim Withers
is the wizard in the kitchen - he learnt his trade at the Hole in the Wall in
Bath and the Carved Angel in Dartmouth. Inspired by Elizabeth David,
the cooking has a definite hint of the Mediterranean about it.

RUSHLAKE GREEN   Stone House

Rushlake Green, Heathfield, East Sussex TN21 9QJ
Telephone: (0435) 830553 Fax: (0825) 764673   **£55**
Open: lunch + dinner daily (residents only) (closed 24 Dec-16
Jan, 2 wks Sep)
Meals served: lunch 12.30-2, dinner 7.30-9

Be sure to pack your wellies so you can fish for trout or shoot pheasant
to your heart's content; or if that isn't your pleasure, take leisurely
walks through the woods and fields. Then return at the end of an
autumn day to crackling log fires in the old manor house and plenty of
Jane Dunn's good wholesome cooking - local wild duck and orange
terrine with onion marmalade, lamb with ratatouille with rosemary and
garlic sauce, poussin stuffed with pine kernels, apricots and herbs.
Eight rooms are available, but the restaurant is not licensed for non-
residents.

RUSPER   Ghyll Manor

High Street, Rusper, Nr Horsham, West Sussex RH12 4PX
Telephone: (0293) 871571 Fax: (0293) 871419   **£75**
Open: lunch + dinner daily
Meals served: lunch 12.30-2.30, dinner 7-10

One of Forte's more graceful country hotels this Elizabethan manor,
comprising 2 cottages and converted stables mews, is set deep in
stockbroker country. It makes a rambling setting with the 22 rooms
shared between the buildings all centred around the cobbled courtyard which is in turn surrounded by 40 acres of gardens. Possible
change of ownership as we went to press.

RUSTICHOME   Kiddington Manor

Rustichome, Nottoo-Far-From-The-Sea
Telephone: 0891 334 329   - see page 14

This restaurant is based on a French-style restaurant avec chambres
and is twinned with On The Town, a lively London restaurant. The
menu, which changes with the seasons, is prepared by celebrated
chefs: The Spring menu from Anton Mossiman includes the likes of
carpachio of salmon painted on to the plate or English lamb stuffed
with a duxelle of truffle and mushrooms, served with roast potatoes.
On the summer menu, Michel Roux offers noisettes of lamb with a
herb mousse topping, garnished with lamb sweetbreads and served
with baby vegetables and a tarragon juice followed by a dessert of
warm soufflé flavoured with raspberry eau de vie and served with raspberry coulis. Shaun Hill's Autumn menu lists such delights as saffron
risotto with steamed vegetables followed by roast corn-fed pigeon with
gnocchi and sage and Franco Taruschio's winter menu contains old
favourites such as bollito misto or a cotechino with lentils. The
impeccable service is under the watchful eyes of Silvano Giraldin and
Joseph Lanser on alternate nights.

In the summer season don't miss their Fri. & Sat. nig
concer by the lake (orangery when wet) When Mich
Roux serves the 1st course before the concert & ma
course in the interval. Enjoy a glass of Charles
Heidsieck champagne during the concert.

RYE   Landgate Bistro

5/6 Landgate, Rye, East Sussex TN31 7LH
Telephone: (0797) 222829   **£35**
Open: dinner Tue-Sat (closed Xmas, 1 wk Jun, 1 wk Oct)
Meals served: lunch , dinner only 7-9.30 (Sat 7-10)

This admirable restaurant is much favoured by locals. Toni Ferguson-Lee is a polished cook, while partner Nick Parkins creates a very relaxed and friendly atmosphere to the quaint and plastic table-clothed restaurant. The cooking is seasonal, contemporary and uncomplicated and it is a pleasure to be there and eat there. The hand-written menu might include leek and roquefort tart, salad of chicken and duck livers with parsley sauce, local squid braised with white wine, tomatoes and garlic and main courses of cod with ginger and spring onions and lamb with flageolet beans, tomatoes and garlic.

RYE   Mermaid Inn

Mermaid Street, Rye, East Sussex TN31 7EU
Telephone: (0797) 223065 Fax: (0797) 226995   £45
Open: lunch + dinner daily
Meals served: lunch 12.30-2.15, dinner 7-9.15
The Mermaid Inn is rich with smuggling history. Rooms are in keeping with the style of the building. Under new management in 1993.

ST AUSTELL   Boscundle Manor

Tregrehan, St Austell, Cornwall PL25 3RL
Telephone: (0726) 813557 Fax: (0726) 814997   **£50**
Open: dinner daily (closed mid Oct-Easter)
Meals served: dinner 7.30-8.30 (Sun 7.30-8)

Andrew and Mary Flint have lovingly nurtured and cared for their 18th-century manor house and in doing so have created a fabulous hotel where the secluded grounds and 7 bedrooms are greatly sought after during the six months of the year that they are open. Mary cooks some pleasing dishes which further enhance the feelings of wellbeing engendered here.

ST AUSTELL   Clarets Restaurant

Trethowel House, Bodmin Road, St Austell, Cornwall PL25 5RR
Telephone: (0726) 67435   **£45**
Open: lunch Tue-Fri, dinner Mon-Sat (closed 25+26 Dec)
Meals served: lunch 12-2, dinner 7-10

Popular for lunch and dinner, this provincial and traditional French restaurant cooks a good selection of favourites from frog's legs to lightly sautéed snails in a bordelaise sauce, magret of duck with port and black cherry sauce and scampi à la crème cooked and flambéed at your table.

ST IVES   Pig'n'Fish

Norway Lane, St Ives, Cornwall TR26 1LZ
Telephone: (0736) 794204   **£45**
Open: dinner Tue-Sat (closed Xmas-mid Feb)
Meals served: dinner 7-9.30

There is an undeniable similarity between this small, informal restaurant and Rick Stein's Seafood Restaurant in Padstow, both serving fresh fish cooked boldly with plenty of herbs, olive oil and tomatoes such as cod with a basil crust and haricot beans in a tomato and olive oil and sole with chicory and Noilly Prat. First courses could be fish soup, crab cakes and smoked sausages with a warm potato salad and Puy lentils. The influence might well be Rick's since chef/patron Paul Sellars did spend many years working with him, but the expertise here is entirely Paul's.

ST MARGARET'S   Wallett's Court

West Cliffe, St Margaret's, Dover, Kent CT15 6EW
Telephone: (0304) 852424   **£45**
Open: dinner Mon-Sat (closed Xmas, 1 wk Jan, 1 wk Nov)
Meals served: dinner 7-9

Chris Oakley still does the cooking at this old manor house, also home to the Oakleys themselves. As keen as ever in the kitchen, Chris creates an array of specials from leek and potato potage with chives and cream, kipper pâté with toasted almonds and lemon and then on to fillet of English pork sautéed in butter and laid on old-fashioned Tewkesbury mustard sauce with oyster mushrooms. Prime beef is braised in red wine provençal-style and salmon is baked more simply with lemon and herbs. This is good cooking, not over-done or puffed up but genuine and enjoyable.

ST MAWES   Idle Rocks Hotel

Tredenham Road, St Mawes, Cornwall TR2 5AN
Telephone: (0326) 270771 Fax: (0326) 270062   **£45**
Open: dinner daily
Meals served: dinner 7-9.15 (light meals 10am-9.15pm)

A picture postcard couldn't have as delightful a view as the one you will enjoy from the terrace of this hotel, as you gaze across the harbour at sunset or through the large windows of the dining room whilst sampling Alan Vickops' sound cooking. Alan, previously at Alverton Manor, has settled in well after his first year and his cooking has benefitted - seafood is always going to be a good choice, as is the duck. It's worth noting that twice a week, weather permitting, trips are available on the hotel's own 55-foot ketch. This is a delightful harbourside hotel with 24 rooms.

SALCOMBE   Spinnakers

Fore Street, Salcombe, Devon TQ8 8JG
Telephone: (0548) 843408   **£40**
Open: lunch Tue-Sun, dinner Tue-Sat (lunch + dinner Mon Aug only)
(closed Dec+Jan, Tue in winter)
Meals served: lunch 12-2, dinner 7-9

Spinnakers enjoys waterside views of the comings-and-goings on the
estuary, while in the kitchen David May cooks up a storm of informal
bar meals and lunchtime menus, whistling on to a more sedate selection in the evening with a carte offering cured English sirloin beef with
Waldorf salad, spiced grilled chicken with a coconut and turmeric
sauce, grilled rib of beef steak with candied shallots and a tajine of
lamb with chickpeas and spices. The daily fish special is chalked up on
the blackboard menu.

SANDIWAY   Nunsmere Hall

Tarporley Road, Sandiway, Cheshire CW8 2ES
Telephone: (0606) 889100 Fax: (0606) 889055   **£55**
Open: lunch + dinner daily
Meals served: lunch 12.30-2 (Sun 1.30-2.30), dinner 7.30-10 (Sat 7.30-10.30)

Built in 1900 with the same eye to design that was later to create the
Queen Mary and later the QE2, Nunsmere was originally the home of
the Brocklebanks of Cunard fame. The Victorian (now extended) hall
is set against a secluded backdrop of trees surrounded by a 60-acre
lake and is run today as a 32-bedroomed hotel by Julie McHardy. A
plush interior and spacious bedrooms make it ideal for the business
end of the hotel trade with luxury standards and smart boardroom and
conference facilities.

SARK   Aval du Creux

Sark, Channel Islands
Telephone: (0481) 832036 Fax: (0481) 832368   **£35**
Open: lunch + dinner daily (closed Oct-Apr)
Meals served: lunch 12-2, dinner 7-8

A good rendezvous for international sailors who come here for terra-
firma and the fine seafood. Peter and Cheryl Tonks run an open house
for guests who come for their cooking, 12 bedrooms and the natural,
unspoilt beauty of the island. A good place to head for when out at sea
in a force 9 gale, but tie up your boat securely as travel is slow-moving
on this otherwise traffic-free island.

SARK	Dixcart Hotel

Sark, Channel Islands
Telephone: (0481) 832015 Fax: (0481) 832164   **£30**
Open: dinner daily
Meals served: dinner 7-9.30

Good value eating at the island's longest established hotel. After extensive refurbishment the rooms are appealing with most of the original
features preserved. The view is best from the dining room where the
gardens can be appreciated, together with Sark scallops in bacon, rainbow trout with capers and shrimps and sauté of beef stroganoff. 50
acres of land surround this 18-bedroomed hotel and the grounds offer
private access to Dixcart Bay beach.

SARK	La Sablonnerie

Sark, Channel Islands
Telephone: (0481) 832061 Fax: (0481) 832408   **£45**
Open: lunch + dinner daily (closed Oct-Easter)
Meals served: lunch 12.30-2.30, dinner 7.30-9.30

On Little Sark - the more southern of the 2 islands - is Elizabeth
Perrée's hotel where self-sufficiency is the norm and the dairy is just
down the lane. As bicycle, tractor or horses are the only modes of
transport available here, this is the sort of place you come to for relaxation and simple pursuits. The dining room is small and simple with
wooden tables and wheelback chairs and the food delicious. The 5-
course meal includes canapés perhaps followed by conger eel soup
with marigold petals, honey-roast home-cured ham with fresh peaches
steeped in old cognac or lemon sole with lobster and a white wine
sauce.

SARK	Stocks Hotel

Sark, Channel Islands
Telephone: (0481) 832001 Fax: (0481) 832130   **£40**
Open: lunch + dinner daily (closed mid Oct-Easter)
Meals served: lunch 12-2.30, dinner 7.30-9 (Sun 7.30-9)

The island may seem untouched by 20th-century values but this hotel
has kept abreast with continual up-grading - this year the greenhouse
is disappearing to be replaced by a conservatory. Stocks has been a
haven for artists and celebrities since it first opened its doors almost
100 years ago with *Salad Days* and *Free as Air* both written here. For
those relishing anonymity and freedom of spirit the craving couldn't be
stronger than for the cooking itself - Sark crab and smoked bacon
soup, stuffed aubergine fritters with apple and mussels poached in
white Rioja, garlic, chives and cream. The hotel is approximately 20
minutes walk from the harbour. You can eat in either the Cider Press
Restaurant or the Courtyard Bistro, or in fine weather on the Patio
next to the swimming pool. There are 25 bedrooms.

SEAFORD   Quincy's

42 High Street, Seaford, East Sussex BN25 1PL
Telephone: (0323) 895490   **£45**
Open: lunch Sun, dinner Tue-Sat (closed 25+26 Dec)
Meals served: lunch 12-2, dinner 7-10

Sound, robust cooking by owner and chef Ian Dowding offers warm
salads and tarts, terrines and gravadlax with a potato pancake followed
by main courses from steamed suet pudding with beef and kidney,
mussels or a rack of lamb with leeks and lentils to loin of pork with
chestnuts and wild mushrooms. Dawn, Ian's wife, takes care of the
business and front of house while Ian enjoys free rein in the kitchen.

SEAVIEW   Seaview Hotel

High Street, Seaview, Isle of Wight PO34 5EX
Telephone: (0983) 612711 Fax: (0983) 613729   **£45**
Open: lunch daily, dinner Mon-Sat (closed 25 Dec)
Meals served: lunch 12-2, dinner 7.30-9.30 (Sat at 7.15 + 9.15)

The Haywards have been running this 16-bedroomed hotel for quite
some years, its snug lounges, nautical bar and bedrooms with views
across the Solent making it a popular destination. The bar snacks are
good and make ideal Sunday night eating while the restaurant offers a
3-course set menu at lunch and dinner. With a choice of 6 starters and
12 main courses you shouldn't be disappointed. As you might imagine
dover sole and lobster feature on the menu in this pleasant candle-lit
dining room.

SETTLE   Blue Goose

Market Square, Settle, North Yorkshire BD24 9EJ
Telephone: (0729) 822901   **£40**
Open: lunch Tue-Sat, dinner Mon-Sat
Meals served: lunch 12-2, dinner 7-9.30

A small personally-owned restaurant that offers a wine bar menu plus
an à la carte menu on which everything down to the bread is home-
made. Simple, clean tasting dishes include a mousse of lemon sole
with a pinch of saffron and a tomato cream sauce, buckwheat crêpes
filled with spinach, mushrooms and goat's cheese and halibut with
mushrooms wrapped in spinach and steamed and served with a light
tarragon cream.

SEVENOAKS   Royal Oak

High Street, Sevenoaks, Kent TN13 1HY
Telephone: (0732) 451109 Fax: (0732) 740187   **£50**
Open: lunch Sun-Fri, dinner daily
Meals served: lunch 12.30-2, dinner 7.30-10.30

The 17th-century building is in the garden of England and thus has the
pick of the crops to use in its menus. Maybe that is why the overall
colour scheme is a lush green? James Butterfill continues cooking for
a welcome audience, serving dishes like fillet of pork en croûte with
fresh sage, duck with pan-fried savoy cabbage and noodles or fried
skate served on a generous potato and fennel salad. Pudding could be
a huge portion of sticky toffee pudding with dates. The bar offers a
good range of wines by the glass, and you can eat some interesting
modern style food here, cooked with care and attention to flavours and
served in a candle-lit section of the bar with scrubbed pine tables and
comfortable, well-upholstered seats.

SHAFTESBURY   La Fleur de Lys

25 Salisbury Street, Shaftesbury, Dorset SP7 8EL
Telephone: (0747) 53717   **£45**
Open: lunch Tue-Sat, dinner Mon-Sat
Meals served: lunch 12-2.30, dinner 7-10

The trio of Shepherd, Griffin and Preston, originally from
Lewtrenchard Manor, are making impact on the locals here with their
good-value decisive French cooking. Choose from the à la carte or the
reasonably priced (£18.50) set dinner menu. One choice out of 3 main
courses on offer might be fillet of salmon, poached and served with
home-made noodles, savoy cabbage and red peppers in a light basil
sauce.

SHANKLIN OLD VILLAGE   The Cottage

8 Eastcliff Road, Shanklin Old Village, Isle of Wight PO37 6AA
Telephone: (0983) 862504   **£44**
Open: lunch Tue-Sun, dinner Tue-Sat (closed 26 Dec, 4 wks Feb/Mar, Oct)
Meals served: lunch 12-2, dinner 7.30-9.45

A trusted formula: Neil Graham in the kitchen and Alan Priddle out
front taking care of things and, most importantly, you. They have
found the locals relish the traditional 'Britain greets France' menu and
thankfully have had no reason to deviate to trendier dishes - that's
good to know. You'll find them in the town side of the old village, a row
of 3 old cottages in a cul-de-sac.

SHEFFIELD — Charnwood Hotel

10 Sharrow Lane, Sheffield, South Yorkshire S11 8AA
Telephone: (0742) 589411 Fax: (0742) 555107 **£45**
Open: dinner Tue-Sat (closed Bank Holidays)
Meals served: dinner 7-10

Val and Chris King opened their 28-bedroomed hotel in 1985 and have now created a special niche in the market, aided by new chef Stephen Hall who arrived last year to take over from Kevin Hensby. The menu offers supremes of salmon with spinach cream and pork with a confit of apples. Eat in either Henfrey's Restaurant or Brasserie Leo.

SHEFFIELD — Harley, The Hotel

334 Glossop Road, Sheffield, South Yorkshire S10 2HW
Telephone: (0742) 752288 Fax: (0742) 722383 **£40**
Open: lunch Mon-Fri, dinner Mon-Sat (closed Bank Holidays)
Meals served: lunch 12-3, dinner 7-10

Harley gets its name because of the number of London medical practitioners who lodged there when attending the hospitals of the town and University. No longer a lodging house, it's now a reputable 22-bedroomed hotel. Dining here ranges from the good-value table d'hote menu to the usual heights of the à la carte. Chef Ian Morton has risen through the ranks of the kitchen and took over in 1991, since when the menu has turned a corner and dishes like lightly roasted lamb with lamb's kidneys finished with a rosemary-scented sauce on pan-fried turnip deserve a mention.

SHEPTON MALLET — Blostin's Restaurant

29 Waterloo Road, Shepton Mallet, Somerset BA4 5HH
Telephone: (0749) 343648 **£35**
Open: dinner Tue-Sat (closed 2 wks Jan, 1 wk Jun, 1 wk Nov)
Meals served: dinner 7-9.30

Hidden behind an ordinary façade is this small, evocative and successful candle-lit bistro. Good, dependable cooking by Nick Reed is complemented by the charming front-of-house service of his wife Lynne, who welcomes you into the tiny bar. Meals here are always enjoyable and care is taken in the presentation of dishes, making much use of fresh herbs and seasonal produce. Fish soup with rouille, a substantial warm salad of smoked bacon and chicken. Guinea-fowl roasted with apples, Somerset cider brandy and cream, a delicious sea bass with fennel and hollandaise are typical. Puddings are good and the home-made ice creams excellent, while home-made chocolate fudge with the cafetière coffee will fill up any corners you may have missed!

SHERBORNE — Eastbury Hotel

Long Street, Sherborne, Dorset DT9 3BY
Telephone: (0935) 813131 Fax: (0935) 817296 **£45**
Open: lunch + dinner daily
Meals served: lunch 12.30-2, dinner 7.30-10

Set in Hardy country, this friendly 15-bedroomed town house is full of 18th-century character with a library full of antiquarian books. Each of the rooms is named after English garden flowers, and all are well furnished with polished wood pieces and pleasant fabrics. The conservatory dining room gives chef Denise Sullivan the opportunity to serve some more unusual dishes amongst the standard favourites, such as Dorset black pudding with home-made apple chutney or a main course of escalope of salmon served with watercress sauce.

SHIFNAL — Weston Park

Weston Park, Shifnal, Shropshire TF11 8LE
Telephone: (095 276) 201 Fax: (095 276) 430 **£60**
Open: by arrangement (closed 25 Dec)
Meals served: by arrangement

Get your butler to find out about their next Gourmet Evening to give them a call

Exclusive accommodation and dining facilities ideal for corporate or private entertaining are available on the Earl of Bradford's estate. Special weekend house parties can be arranged for 20 people or more with clay pigeon shooting, rally driving, treasure hunts and hovercrafting to choose from. It is primarily only open for use for residential stays, but on some occasions gourmet dinner evenings are open to anyone who books dinner or accommodation. 19 sumptuous bedrooms, decorated in the same style as the rest of the gracious but friendly 17th-century stately home, are available. As a restaurateur and keen cook (President of the Master Chefs of Great Britain) His Lordship takes a keen interest in making sure that standards are kept up, not just in the house and grounds, but in the dining room as well.

SHINFIELD L'Ortolan

Old Vicarage, Church Lane, Shinfield, Nr Reading, Berkshire
RG2 9BY
Telephone: (0734) 883783 Fax: (0734) 885391   **£100**
Open: lunch Tue-Sun, dinner Tue-Sat (closed last 2 wks
Aug, last 2 wks Feb)
Meals served: lunch 12.15-2.15, dinner 7.15-10.30

John Burton-Race is a well documented culinary saint, for the dishes
he creates are pure magic and appropriately find sanctuary in this
18th-century former vicarage. The menu excites, stimulates and
rewards, as demonstrated by new potatoes filled with snails and
cooked in red wine, garlic and herbs, the sauce enriched with beef
marrow, or fillet of lamb sealed in olive oil, rolled in herbs and breadcrumbs and wrapped in a salt crust. On to his desserts, by which he is
further distinguished - slices of apple dipped in an almond batter, fried
until crisp and eaten with a damson coulis and almond ice cream. This
is the measure of a man dedicated to exquisite food and impeccable,
smooth service, which is happily maintained by his wife Christine and
her staff. A wine list of the calibre is rarely seen, and the decor is a
relief to the eye, deservedly making this one of the best restaurants in
Britain.

SILVERTON Silverton Inn & Restaurant

Silverton, Devon BX5 4HP
Telephone: (0392) 860196   **£50**
Open: lunch Sun, dinner Thu-Sat
Meals served: lunch 12-3, dinner 7-10.30

An informal place on the first floor of the inn, the restaurant is only
open 3 evenings a week, plus Sunday lunch. The simple surroundings
may mislead you but you will be pleasantly surprised. Chef Matthew
Mason's cooking is enjoyable - he spent a few years in the kitchen with
Shaun Hill at Gidleigh Park. Old beams, candles and lots of fresh flowers set an intimate scene, and the menu (read from a blackboard)
might include pigeon with basil potato purée (a Shaun legacy), rack of
lamb with ratatouille and salmon hollandaise. Puddings are particularly good.

SISSINGHURST   Rankins

The Street, Sissinghurst, Kent TN17 2JH
Telephone: (0580) 713964   **£50**
Open: lunch Sun, dinner Wed-Sat (closed Bank Holidays,
1 wk Oct, 1 wk May)
Meals served: lunch 12.30-1.30, dinner 7.30-9

Steamed fillet of brill and prawns with a ginger butter sauce and fresh
coriander, roast duck with braised red cabbage and cumberland sauce
and pan-fried lamb with curry butter and compote of lentils are the sort
of dishes you will find on Hugh Rankin's menu. A country restaurant, it
keeps its menus short in length but not on imagination with a good use
of aromatic ingredients, spices and vegetables. Puddings are typically
English and cheese comes in a finger-serving or a slice. Reasonably
priced wine list.

SIX MILE BOTTOM   Swynford Paddocks

Six Mile Bottom, Nr Newmarket, Cambridgeshire CB8 0UE
Telephone: (063 870) 234 Fax: (063 870) 283   **£45**
Open: lunch Sun-Fri, dinner daily (closed between Xmas/New Year)
Meals served: lunch 12.30-2, dinner 7-9.30 (Sun 7-8.30)

Sir Thomas Beecham is credited as having said 'Try anything once,
except incest and folk dancing'. As it points out in Swynford Paddocks'
brochure, it is not known if Byron ever tried folk dancing, but the illicit
affair between poet Lord Byron and half-sister Augusta is rumoured to
have taken place here. It's now an elegant, luxury hotel with 15 bedrooms, standing in 60 acres or so of a stud farm. The menu might offer
a seasonal roast haunch of Scottish deer in a juniper sauce or King
Edward's steak - a sirloin stuffed with pâté and braised in a Burgundy
sauce.

SLOUGH   Tummies

5 Station Road, Cippenham, Slough, Berkshire SL1 6JJ   **£40**
Tel: 0628 668486 Fax: (Sandwich Shop) 0628 663106
Open: lunch Sun-Fri, dinner daily (closed 25+26 Dec, lunch
New Years Day)
Meals served: lunch 11.30-3 (12-3.30 Sun), dinner 5.30-11 (7-10 Sun)

Friendly, local neighbourhood bistro, handy for the Slough Industrial
Park, and busy with locals. Some rather unusual dishes are available at
this down-to-earth, informal place offering a good variety of dishes and
blackboard specialities marked up. They have their own take-away
and sandwich shop next door, called you've guessed it, Yummies!

SOLIHULL   The George

The Square, Solihull, West Midlands, B91 3RF
Telephone: (021) 711 2121 Fax: (021) 711 337   **£40**
Open: lunch + dinner daily
Meals served: lunch 12.30-2, dinner 7-9.45

Once a coaching inn, this 16th-century building has matured into a
129-bedroomed hotel with a sophisticated style of service. Set beside
the village bowling green with its 600 year-old yew tree, the George is
still very much the focal point of Solihull with the Club Bar proving
extremely popular with residents and locals. Thursday evening means
dinner and live jazz. For a quieter option, choose the Restaurant On
the Green with its international selection of dishes including prawns
with lemon grass and garlic butter, asparagus pancake with hollandaise, or duck with a black cherry and honey sauce. The Rôtisserie
(carvery) menu offers a selection of roasts and fish. The 10
Townhouse suites added during this year's refurbishment programme
offer a unique style of accommodation with duplex rooms connected
by a spiral staircase and a 'secret' service – a hatch next to the front
door that indicates when a delivery has been made be it lunch, dinner,
a message or newspaper – the ultimate in absolute privacy. Rooms also
come with a TV, radio, hairdryer and choice of hot beverages.

SOURTON   Collaven Manor

Sourton, Nr Okehampton, Devon EX20 4HH
Telephone: (083 786) 522 Fax: (083 786) 570   **£40**
Open: lunch + dinner daily
Meals served: lunch 12-1.30, dinner 7.30-9 (Fri+Sat 7.30-9.30)

The homely aura remains untouched and the creeper has grown at
least another couple of inches but there is more to report from the
kitchen over the last year than the interior and colours of the walls.
Jacky Rae has gone to pastures new and her accomplished sous Emma
Streeter has slipped into her clogs and taken over the running of the
kitchen and 2 dining rooms. The good value (£16.50) set dinner gives
a choice of 5 starters and 6 main courses including a fish of the day
when available. Some dishes carry supplements but I would be happy
with peppers sautéed with garlic and thyme, followed by breast of
duck with a fumet of cèpes and ending with their bread and butter
pud, (don't mention the clotted cream)! 7 bedrooms complete the
picture.

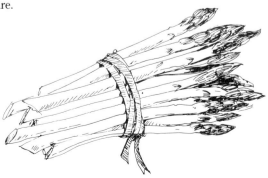

SOUTH GODSTONE   La Bonne Auberge

Tilburstow Hill, South Godstone, Surrey RH9 8JY
Telephone: (0342 893184 Fax: (0342) 893435   **£75**
Open: lunch Tue-Sun, dinner Tue-Sat (closed Bank Holidays)
Meals served: lunch 12-2, dinner 7-10

Crunch up the drive, take in the view out towards the lake, and then
slip under the wisteria to the bar. A popular place on Sundays, you will
need to book. A preferred table is in the smaller second bow window
by the bar, slightly higher than the rest of the dining room. From it
you can watch the goings-on and yet be relatively aloof from the rest of
the clièntele - very pleasant when dining intimately or with clients! The
service is attentive, the menu regional French with a modern bent -
salmis of game braised in wine and covered with pastry or a pot pourri
or red mullet, salmon and monkfish cooked in 3 different ways and
served with a lime butter sauce or slices of lamb with beetroot tagliatelle and a creamy mustard sauce. Cheese are selectively French, and
puddings as dramatically presented as the preceding courses. Run skilfully by the Jalley family since 1962 - let's hope it continues to flourish!

SOUTH MOLTON   Whitechapel Manor

South Molton, Devon EX36 3EG
Telephone: (0769) 573377 Fax: (0769) 573797   **£60**
Open: lunch + dinner daily
Meals served: lunch 12.30-2, dinner 7-8.45

In the foothills of Exmoor there's a truly special place, an Elizabethan
manor house surrounded by wooded valleys and rolling hills, a quin-
tessentially English country house. Owners John and Patricia
Shapland contribute to the calm and solitude with their careful choice
of colours and furnishings. Choose one of the larger rooms overlooking the garden. Breakfast starts the day on a high note with lightly
smoked bacon and herb sausages. Patricia's cooking is very classy,
whatever the meal, and the dishes whet the appetite just reading them!
From the 3-course dinner menu try terrine of duck leg confit with celeriac and walnut oil and braised shoulder of lamb with garlic.
Presentation, service and flavour all score top marks.

SOUTHAMPTON   Browns Brasserie

Frobisher House, Nelson Gate, Commercial Road, Southampton,
Hampshire SO1 0GX
Telephone: (0703) 332615   **£35**
Open: lunch + dinner Mon-Sat (closed 25+26 Dec, 1 Jan)
Meals served: lunch 12-2.30, dinner 7-11 (Sat 7-11.30)

`Our aim is simple – to serve you exquisite food at sensible prices',
reads Richard and Patricia Brown's menu, and they try hard to achieve
it offering goat's cheese coated in hazelnuts and quickly baked, or king
scallops, prawns, lobster and clams cooked briskly and served in a
shrimp sauce with asparagus. The meat dishes include their own variation of zampone – pig's trotter stuffed with forcemeat and served in a
beef sauce, or pot-roasted squab served with lentil and herb
dumplings.

SOUTHEND-ON-SEA · Slassor's

145 Eastern Esplanade, Southend-on-Sea, Essex SS1 2YD
Telephone: (0702) 614880   **£30**
Open: lunch Tue-Fri, dinner Mon-Sat (closed Bank Holidays in summer)
Meals served: lunch 12-2, dinner 7-9.30

Bring your own bottle and they'll open it for 75p. A whimsical restaurant that serves 'foods of the world', with a menu set out as follows - Surprise Openings, Chef's Specialities, Today's Fish 'Sometimes Limited', In the Mood for a Great Steak and Salad Ways - there is something here for everyone. PS. Slassor's promise no corkage on a bottle of Charles Heidsieck!

SOUTHSEA · Bistro Montparnasse

103 Palmerston Road, Southsea, Hampshire PO5 3PS
Telephone: (0705) 816754   **£45**
Open: dinner Tue-Sat (closed Bank Holidays, 3 wks Jan)
Meals served: dinner 7-10

Hot lemon rice pudding with caramelised oranges, black bottom pie with nutmeg sauce or rhubarb cobbler make resounding finales to the 3-course £12.50 dinner menu. At such sensible prices it is possible to come here on a regular basis and never tire of the menu with such choices as a warm gougère with a spinach and pine nut filling, duck liver pâté with honey-vinegar pickled vegetables and pan-roast guinea fowl with cornbread stuffing and onion sauce.

SOUTHWOLD · The Crown

90 High Street, Southwold, Suffolk IP18 6DP
Telephone: (0502) 722275 Fax: (0502) 724805   *Delightful*
Open: lunch + dinner daily (closed 1 wk Jan)   *pub/restaurant* **£40**
Meals served: lunch 12.30-1.45, dinner 7.30-9.30 *with rooms*

Owned by wine merchants and brewers Adnams, it goes without saying that the wine list at this Georgian hotel is well above average, and it also serves as a watering hole to the locals. The staff are young and friendly and serve a good pint of beer along with borscht with sour cream or baked cod with garlic and parsley sauce from the bar menu. The restaurant menu is shorter with main courses of red mullet with ginger, lime and garlic and roast beef with Yorkshire puddings. 12 bedrooms make this a good place to stay if you want to explore the area. See also the Swan, on next page.

SOUTHWOLD — The Swan

Market Place, Southwold, Suffolk IP18 6EG
Telephone: (0502) 722186 Fax: (0502) 724800
Another Adnams success story **£45**
Open: lunch + dinner daily (closed dinner 3rd Sun in Jan)
Meals served: lunch 12.15-1.45 (Sun 12.15-1.30), dinner 7-9.30 (Sun 7-9)

Backing onto the Adnams brewery, the old inn stands on the market place adjacent to the town hall. There are 27 bedrooms in the main building and another 18 are clustered around the old bowling green in the garden, and from almost every window you can glance down narrow streets or across to the sea. Competent cooking, the perfect pint of Adnams, one of the best wine lists and a walk along the seashore – what more could you want from a sleepy town hotel? Absolutely right for a winter weekend break with a slight air of genteel eccentricity. The comfortable restaurant offers a good variety of dishes, such as saddle of English lamb with a black pudding farce or a grilled halibut steak served on white cabbage with smoked bacon. I have to admit to being a bit of a Southwold groupie summer or winter, and the Swan, along with the Crown (previous page) provide most of what I need for the perfect weekend. They are very obliging at the Swan and will even provide you with a bucket of ice to take to your beach hut (a must) to cool your lunch-time or evening bottle of champagne.

SPARK BRIDGE — Bridgefield House

Spark Bridge, Ulverston, Cumbria LA12 8DA
Telephone: (0229) 885239 Fax: (0229) 885379 **£55**
Open: dinner daily
Meals served: dinner 7.30 for 8

Free fishing on the river, stupendous views, country cooking and genuine hospitality are the reasons guests return here. Modesty in decor makes a refreshing change, and David and Rosemary Glister's good-sense values reign at this 5-bedroomed country house. Dinner cooked by Rosemary is candle-lit and set at £24 for 6-courses which is a miracle of value when you consider what is involved from course to course - goat's cheese, fennel and red apple salad with a hazelnut oil dressing, tomato and basil soup with Cheddar bannocks, boned pigeon cooked in red wine with damson tartlets with a variety of vegetables such as kohlrabi with coriander, glazed onions with pumpkin seeds and red cabbage with juniper berries followed swiftly by elderflower water ice. Pudding brings a choice, of which whisky mac and crystallised stem ginger syllabub must be a favourite and then finally, as if you really needed any more, sautéed lamb's sweetbreads in madeira on toast and pear with blue Stilton and walnuts.

| SPEEN | **The Old Plow Inn at Speen** |

Flowers Bottom Lane, Speen, Nr Princes Risborough,
Buckinghamshire HP27 0PZ
Telephone: (0494) 488300
Open: lunch Tue-Sun, dinner Tue-Sat (closed Bank Holidays)
Meals served: lunch 12-2, dinner 7-9

there is something here for everyone
£55
— well worth a visit.

In the dip before the village you will find Malcolm and Olivia Cowan's place. Since the early 1990s they have conscientiously been developing the bistro-style menu in what used to be the bar. It runs alongside the longer standing à la carte and still meets their high standards. The bistro is extremely popular and it is wise to book. Mixed Provence olives are available at the bar and when Malcolm has time a nice line in `amazing nibbles' such as half-pint prawns, toasted almonds and dim sum will appear. In the restaurant the specials remain true to his style - Tuscan vegetable soup with basil, roasted local pheasant and baby turbot. If available, try the Aberdeen Angus rib steak, char-grilled and served with a shallot and red wine sauce.

| STADDLE BRIDGE | McCoy's |

The Tontine, Staddle Bridge, nr Northallerton, North Yorkshire
DL6 3JB Telephone: (0609 882) 671
Restaurant: **£70**
Open: dinner Tue-Sat (closed Bank Holidays except Good Friday)
Meals served: 7-10
Bistro: **£50**
Open: lunch + dinner daily (closed Bank Holidays except Good Friday)
Meals served: lunch 12-2, dinner 7-10

The cooking is brilliant but don't go expecting this to be a traditional restaurant in terms of food or decor. The paper umbrellas might have gone and a new glossy burgundy paint changes the tone of the restaurant while a bright green carpet adds a new element to the bar, but the eccentric and laid back '30s ambience remains. The cooking is in the hands of Tom, one of the trio of McCoy brothers. Main courses from the hand-written menu include a wild French mushroom tart and muscadet sauce, king-sized scallops with parsley, capers and an olive oil dressing, chicken Jo Jo (a breast of chicken with crème fraîche, vermouth and mushrooms) and sea bass with lemon sauce and brown rice. An imaginative repertoire, superbly cooked.

STAMFORD — The George of Stamford

71 St Martins, Stamford, Lincolnshire PE9 2LB
Telephone: (0780) 55171 Fax: (0780) 57070 **£65**
Open: lunch + dinner daily
Meals served: lunch 12.30-2.30, dinner 7-10.30

Once an old coaching inn and now part of Poste Hotels, The George has retained its 'olde worlde' charm. On the approach, a gallows sign indicates the entrance, while inside flagstone floors strewn with rugs, dark panelling, beams, exposed stone walls and a bright lounge area create a lasting impression. The restaurant is somewhat more civilised than it may have been in the days of old, with soup of the day, king prawns, tortellini and other pasta dishes featuring on the decidedly more modern menu, though there's still a roast sirloin of beef from the silver carving wagon, followed by dessert or cheese. All this can be enjoyed while sitting in an oak panelled dining room at polished tables with gleaming silverware and imbibing from one of the best wine lists in the country, masterminded by managing director Lawrence Hoskins.

STANDON — No. 28

28 High Street, Standon, Nr Ware, Hertfordshire SG11 1LA
Telephone: (0920) 821035 Fax: (0920) 822630 **£60**
Open: lunch + dinner Tue-Sat (closed 2 wks Aug)
Meals served: lunch 12-2, dinner 7-9.30

Menus change daily at the Balls' small restaurant but what they lack in length they make up for in composition - scallops with fromage frais and fresh herbs in filo pastry followed by roulade of smoked salmon and fresh plaice with basil beurre blanc and a finale of Drambuie cream served with home-made shortbread and a rich chocolate sauce, or bananas flambéed in brown sugar and brandy and served with coffee and nut parfait. A very comprehensive range of British farmhouse and organic cheese completes the picture.

STAPLECROSS — Olivers

Cripps Corner, Staplecross, Nr Robertsbridge, East Sussex TN32 5RY
Telephone: (0580) 830387 **£50**
Open: lunch Thu-Sun, dinner Thu-Sat (closed Bank Holidays, 2 wks Jan)
Meals served: lunch 12-1.30, dinner 7-9.30 (Sun 7-9)

The recession has been at its most cruel in these parts and the main aim for any restaurant is to weather the storm but without giving in to cheap produce and pre-cooked foods. Endeavouring to keep this banner flying the Olivers have returned to the open but short à la carte which changes with the markets and uses mostly local produce – home-made seafood and chervil noodles, smoked pork and raisin pâté, salmon torte with sorrel, tomato and leek and braised rabbit and bacon with coarse grain mustard. We wish them all the best.

STAPLEFORD   Stapleford Park

Stapleford, Nr Melton Mowbray, Leicestershire LE14 2EF
Telephone: (057 284) 522 Fax: (057 284) 651   **£60**
Open: lunch + dinner daily
Meals served: lunch 12-3 (Sun 12-3.30), dinner 7-9.30 (Fri+Sat 7-10)

Larger-than-life character Bob Payton created this larger-than-reality
country house in the late '80s, heralding a newcomer to the fold with
some typical Payton hype! 35 bedrooms, designed by the likes of
David Hicks, Lindka Cierach, Crabtree & Evelyn, Liberty and Nina
Campbell, amongst others, are sumptuous if not a little unusual, and
that is what the place is all about. The house itself is a masterpiece of
architecture, on a stately mansion scale, with gardens and parkland
designed by Capability Brown. The restaurant is light-hearted in
approach with a mixture of Payton-style grills, salads and pastas which
would be just at home in one of his London establishments. But one
sure thing is the ingenuity of the place - it has bags of style, with laid-
back but professional staff.

STOKE-BY-NAYLAND   Angel Inn

Stoke-by-Nayland, Suffolk CO6 4SA
Telephone: (0206) 263245 Fax: (0206) 37324   **£40**
Open: lunch Wed-Sun, dinner Tue-Sat (closed 25+26 Dec, 1 Jan)
Meals served: lunch 12-2, dinner 6.30-9 (bar meals all week)

This restaurant with 6 bedrooms stands at the crossroads of the
ancient Suffolk town, its ecclesiastical name being a knock-on effect of
Henry VIII's dissolution of monasteries. Beamed ceilings, rafters and a
52-foot-deep well make for a characterful dining room. Chef Mark
Johnson strikes a balance between the adventurous and the traditional
with his emphasis on flavour – baked tartlet of fresh mushrooms,
baked fillet of salmon en croûte with hollandaise, rack of lamb with
honey and mint glaze and chicken filled with brie, rolled in hazelnuts
and served with a light herb butter sauce.

STOKESLEY   Chapters

27 High Street, Stokesley, North Yorkshire TS9 5AD
Telephone: (0642) 711888 Fax: same (+ ext 223)   **£55**
Open: dinner Mon-Sat
Meals served: dinner 7-9.30 (Sat 7-10)

Restaurant and hotel with 13 rooms and a new bistro and a daily
changing menu from the blackboard. I was unable to get to Chapters
before we went to press, but judging by their menus I don't think I'd
be disappointed. Drop me a line when you've been and I'll send a bottle of Charles Heidsieck champagne for the most accurate review.

STON EASTON
Ston Easton Park

Ston Easton, Nr Bath, Avon BA3 4DF
Telephone: (0761) 241631 Fax: (0761) 241377 £90
Open: lunch + dinner daily
Meals served: lunch 12.30-2, dinner 7.30-9.30 (Fri+Sat 7.30-10) ❖

Take to the terraces for lunch when the weather is fine but even inside
the flowers are used in great arrangements throughout. This splendid
imposing listed grade I Palladian mansion offers a glimpse of the
'upstairs-downstairs' style of life with much of the downstairs left as it
is and the upstairs renovated by Jan Monro, an authority on 18th-cen-
tury decor. Your bedroom with fine period antiques will overlook
romantic parklands created by Humphrey Repton in 1793 - it's all here,
exceptional architecture, ornate plaster work and trompe l'oeil murals.
For the dining room, Mark Harrington uses the produce from the
restored walled kitchen garden to produce a 4-course menu combining
traditional and modern choices. The cooking is serious stuff with
poached quenelles of pink trout with roasted scallops and fried leek,
salad of smoked goose breast and poached blueberries and main
courses of guinea fowl with braised butter beans, or the traditional and
more simple dishes of charcoal-grilled dover sole on or off the bone or
fan of melon with fresh fruits. There's a welcome emphasis on half bottles of wine.

STONEHOUSE
STONEHOUSE COURT

Bristol Road, Stonehouse, Gloucestershire GL10 3RA
Telephone: (0453) 825155 Fax: (0453) 824611 £50
Open: lunch + dinner daily
Meals served: lunch 12.30-2, dinner 7.30-10

This imposing 17th-century listed building is set in its own 6 acres of
secluded gardens and parklands overlooking Stroud Water and the
local wildlife. Mellow oak panelling, soft lighting and open stone fireplaces set the character and add to the appeal of the place.

STONHAM
Mr Underhill's

Stonham, Nr Stowmarket, Suffolk IP14 5DW
Telephone: (0449) 711206 £55
Open: dinner Tue-Sat (closed Bank Holidays (open 25+26 Dec))
Meals served: dinner 7.30-9

Short and sweet are the choices on Chris and Judy Bradley's fixed-
price menus but as cooked by Chris, they are reliable dishes with
flavour, in keeping with the tone of the place. A modern French style
brings unpretentious combinations like warm salad of asparagus followed by wild salmon with sorrel, a choice of whatever cheese is at its
best that day and dessert which might well be apple or pecan tart.
Interesting wine list with some reasonable prices in this intimate
restaurant.

STONOR   **Stonor Arms**

Stonor, Nr Henley-on-Thames, Oxfordshire RG9 6HE
Telephone: (0491) 63345 Fax: (0491) 638863   **£65**
Open: dinner Mon-Sat
Meals served: dinner 7-9.30 (light meals Blades: 11.45-1.45, 6.45-9.30
(Sun 6.45-9)

A fine country hotel in the Thames valley. Once a pub, it has become
an address to remember for the pleasurable setting, but it is the cooking by Stephen Frost that is the main pull. This year the bar has been
replaced by a lounge in which to take a snack at lunch-time, while the
brasserie remains interesting and bold with grills of fish and meat,
haddock fishcakes with creamed leeks and rillettes of venison or pan-
fried herring roes with granary toast. The Restaurant, with its polished
tables and chairs, moves up a notch or two, offering a terrine of rabbit
and juniper served with lentil salad, scallops and mussels with a cream
and saffron sauce and a casserole of lamb, sweetbreads and kidneys
with trumpet mushrooms. Good and fairly priced wine list, 9 bedrooms.

STORRINGTON   **Abingworth Hall**

Thakeham Road, Storrington, West Sussex RH20 3EF
Telephone: (0798) 813636 Fax: (0798) 813914   **£50**
Open: lunch + dinner daily
Meals served: lunch 12.30-1.45, dinner 7.15-9

Relax in the oak-panelled drawing room or in one of the rattan chairs
in the conservatory and look out across the lawns to the lake. This
hotel, built in the early 1900s, is run by the Bulmans and has 20 bedrooms, each carefully furnished. Chef Peter Cannon produces well
conceived dishes - top-notch traditional cooking with modern interpretations such as lamb cutlets in sherry vinegar, salmon with brandy and
crab sauce and roast lamb with garlic and rosemary. Suitable attire is
requested for dinner, which means a jacket and tie.

STORRINGTON   **Little Thakeham**

Merrywood Lane, Storrington, Little Thakham, West Sussex RH20 3HE
Telephone: (0903) 744416 Fax: (0903) 745022   **£75**
Open: lunch daily, dinner Mon-Sat (closed 2 wks Xmas/New Year)
Meals served: lunch 12.30-2, dinner 7.30-9

This Edward Lutyens manor house was converted with minimum alter-
ations into a luxurious country house hotel and is run by Tim and
Pauline Ractliff. The superb gardens with paved walks, flowering
shrubs and trees, were created in the style of Gertrude Jekyll. Interior
restoration and redecoration have been carried out with aplomb, with
original stone fireplaces, mullioned windows, polished floors of wood
and flagstones and massive oak doors lovingly cared for. Enjoy the
haute cuisine in the small, intimate dining room, with short fixed
menus of straightforward cooking, such as carrot and coriander soup,
fillet of brill with a prawn sauce, or Southdown lamb with redcurrant
sauce. The wine list is reasonably priced.

STORRINGTON   Manley's

Manleys Hill, Storrington, West Sussex RH20 4BT   ✿
Telephone: (0903) 742331   **£65**
Open: lunch Tue-Sun, dinner Tue-Sat (closed Bank Holidays
(open Good Friday), 1st 2 wks Jan)
Meals served: lunch 12-2, dinner 7-9.30

Layers of artichoke with tomato concassé, artichoke purée and basil-
flavoured hollandaise or the sole filled with crab, scallops, ginger and
topped with a soufflé and baked quickly, show the skill and precision
of owner and chef Karl Löderer, and they are only for starters. Main
courses entail strips of veal in a piquant cream sauce with gruyère
cheese and served with spinach spätzli or pan-fried turbot with a thin
crust of shellfish and potatoes with langoustine sauce. This might be a
cottagey restaurant but cooking of this nature is rare and gifted. Leave
room for pudding and the delectable strawberry crêpe cooked in eau-
de-vie. A good wine list and efficient and friendly staff make this a
handsome and enjoyable place to pass the evening. If hooked, an
overnight stay is possible in the one suite overlooking the Downs.

STORRINGTON   Old Forge

6a Church Street, Storrington, West Sussex RH20 4LA
Telephone: (0903) 743402   **£50**
Open: lunch Tue-Fri + Sun, dinner Tue-Sat (closed Bank Holidays,
3 wks Oct)
Meals served: lunch 12.30-1.30, dinner 7.30-9

Clive Roberts' cooking acquires from many continents the right
degree of spice or essential ingredient that makes his cooking stand
out from the crowd - baked magret of duck stuffed with salami, orange
and walnuts and served with Italian vermouth sauce, freshly grilled
shrimp set round a scallop pudding with a coriander sauce and lentil
and mushroom pâté flavoured with garlic and thyme. While Clive
enjoys exploring the possibilities of other countries he also appreciates
the necessity of handing on knowledge to the punter, and runs food
and wine evenings 6 times a year for his customers.

STOW BRIDGE   Swinton House

Stow Bridge, King's Lynn, Norfolk PE34 3PP
Telephone: (0366) 383151   **£40**
Open: lunch Sun, dinner Tue-Sat (closed 1 wk Xmas)
Meals served: lunch 12-2, dinner 7-9

Chicken with a sauce of woodland mushrooms and deep-fried breaded
pheasant with cranberry chutney and a pecan and maple syrup tart are
typical of Graham Kitch's fixed-price menu. A small and informal
restaurant with the emphasis on good, simply prepared food, friendliness and value for money, including the reasonably priced wine list.

STOW-ON-THE-WOLD — Fosse Manor

Fosse Way, Stow-on-the-Wold, Cheltenham, Gloucestershire GL54 1JX
Telephone: (0451) 30354 Fax: (0451) 32486 £40
Open: lunch + dinner daily (closed Dec 22-30)
Meals served: lunch 12.30-2, dinner 7.30-10
Traditional English cooking. Bob and Yvonne Johnston have run this hotel for 21 years.

STOW-ON-THE-WOLD — Grapevine Hotel

Sheep Street, Stow-on-the-Wold, Gloucestershire GL54 1AU
Telephone: (0451) 830344 Fax: (0451) 832278 **£40**
Open: lunch + dinner daily (closed Bank Holidays, 24 Dec-6 Jan)
Meals served: lunch 12-2, dinner 7-9.30

This is a charming and very welcoming hotel run by Sam Elliott. Each of the 23 bedrooms is well decorated and furnished but for a romantic weekend, plump for one of the canopied or 4-poster bedrooms. A highlight is the conservatory restaurant with romanesque vine that covers the ceiling and bestows a relaxed continental quality. An apt setting for Audrey Williams' light style of cooking – tossed salad of parma ham and spiced salami with apple and walnut dressing or a terrine of salmon and monkfish wrapped in tender leeks and an escalope of salmon served on a tomato and chive sauce. The housekeeping is immaculate and the service enthusiastic and well trained. A lovely place to stay and from which to enjoy the Cotswolds.

STOW-ON-THE-WOLD — Wyck Hill House

Burford Road, Stow-on-the-Wold, Gloucestershire GL54 1HY
Telephone: (0451) 831936 Fax: (0451) 832243 **£80**
Open: lunch + dinner daily
Meals served: lunch 12.30-2, dinner 7.30-9.30 (Sat 7.30-10)

Former home to the feudal Lord of Rissington, the house fell on hard times and decay until 3 Texans bought their little bit of England and nursed it back to life. Now, years on and a couple of owners hence, the 18th-century stone house is a substantial hotel complete with lived-in feel and attentive, friendly staff. The contrasting styles meet in the restaurant: the opulence of the room and the contemporary style of Ian Smith's cooking. Hot Stilton and walnut beignets served on a grape, celery and apple salad, terrine of marinated goat's cheese, aubergine and pimento for starters and then on to Cornish monkfish rolled in aromatic herbs and surrounded by a warm fennel, tomato and olive oil dressing are typical. Finish with dessert, or British farmhouse cheeses served with warm chive and onion bread. The wine list, like the house, has been strengthened. 31 rooms in the main house, Orangery and Coach House.

STRATFORD-UPON-AVON   Billesley Manor

Billesley, Alcester, Nr Stratford-upon-Avon
Warwickshire B49 6NF
Telephone: (0789) 400888 Fax: (0789) 764145   **£55**
Open: lunch + dinner daily
Meals served: lunch 12.30-2, dinner 7.30-9.30

The smell of wood polish and leather pervades over the public rooms of this old stone house. With the log fire crackling in the winter this is just the place to curl up in an armchair with tea, scones and toasted muffins after a day visiting the heart of Shakespeare country.

STRATFORD-UPON-AVON   Ettington Park

Alderminster, Stratford-upon-Avon, Warwickshire CV37 8BS
Telephone: (0789) 450123 Fax: (0789) 450472   **£60**
Open: lunch + dinner daily
Meals served: lunch 12.30-2, dinner 7-9.30 (Fri+Sat 7-9.45)   ❖

The 48-bedroomed hotel lives up to the promise of the setting with finely refurbished drawing and dining rooms, and no less impressive bedrooms with well-chosen antiques. The large rooms with vaulted ceilings, private dining room (this room was a 14th-century chapel), leisure facilities and helipad make it a tasteful addition to the midweek conference and business market, as well as a weekend retreat.

STREATLEY-ON-THAMES   Swan Diplomat

High Street, Streatley-on-Thames, Berkshire RG8 9HR
Telephone: (0491) 873737 Fax: (0491) 872554   **£55**
Open: lunch Sun-Fri, dinner daily
Meals served: lunch 12.30-2, dinner 7.30-9.30 (Sat 7-9.30 Sun 7.30-9)

Down by the Thames is this much refurbished hotel, complete with boats, country flowers and bridge. Relish the view and make sure you book one of the rooms with a balcony over the river. An exceptional location, it would make an ideal place to stay during the Henley Regatta. The Riverside restaurant takes maximum advantage of the setting with Christopher Cleveland's cooking being light and bright but never far from traditional, with à la carte and set dinner menus that might include green pea soup or potted crab followed by fresh tuna marinated in lime and served grilled with a lime butter, or fillet of veal with woodland mushrooms and ravioli.

STRETTON   Ram Jam Inn

Great North Road, Stretton, Nr Oakham, Rutland, Leicestershire LE15 7QX
Telephone: (0780) 410776 Fax: (0780) 410361   **£40**
Open: lunch + dinner daily (closed 25 Dec)
Meals served: lunch 12-2.30, dinner 7-10 (light meals 7am-10pm)

With a name which the Harts evolved from a special drink that Charles Blake, the 16th-century publican, produced for in-house or take-away consumption, the inn lives on thought the recipe is sadly lost. Before hurtling past on the A1, if you need refreshment, be it bed, breakfast, lunch or supper – rest assured that none of the usual horrors of English roadside fare awaits. Here you can be confident that the food is going to be some of the best you have sampled, even though the place sits incongruously on the edge of a major thoroughfare. On the main menu (there are 3 menus from breakfast through to dinner) there is an invigorating selection such as falafel with tabbouleh and minted Greek yoghurt, fresh linguini with cherry tomatoes, basil and parmesan or confit of duck. For main courses there are sautéed and char-grilled meats with spicy fried potatoes, or a Mediterranean platter of stuffed vine leaves, hummus, olives, grilled aubergine and warm pitta bread. Warm treacle tart with praline ice cream, summer pudding or a French-style lemon tart with a blackcurrant coulis mean you might have to break your diet - but then, only you and the rest of the travellers on the A1 will ever know. 10 neat and comfortable bedrooms.

STROUD   Oakes

169 Slad Road, Stroud, Gloucestershire GL5 1RG   🏵
Telephone: (0453) 759950   **£80**
Open: lunch Tue-Sun, dinner Tue-Sat (closed Bank Holidays)
Meals served: lunch 12.30-1.45, dinner 7.30-9.30

Chris Oakes concentrates on the best of local ingredients and creates an interesting combination of flavours. A former school house is the setting for this striking cooking, with typical dishes such as home-made Gloucestershire Old Spot pork sausages with mixed lettuces, poached egg, bacon and a shallot vinaigrette, tiger prawns served with spinach flavoured garlic butter and lemon sole poached with a white wine and cream sauce. Cheeses come from Abergavenny and are served with home-made biscuits, while pudding could be a warm sultana and almond brioche served with chocolate sauce and vanilla ice cream. A good, reliable standard of cooking in this simply decorated restaurant guarantees an enjoyable meal.

STUCKTON — The Three Lions

Stuckton, Nr Fordingbridge, Hampshire SP6 2HF
Telephone: (0425) 652489 Fax: (0425) 656144
Open: lunch + dinner Tue-Sat (closed Bank Holidays)
Meals served: lunch 12.15-1.30, dinner 7.15-9 (Sat 7.15-9.30)

£50

New Forest game soup or a trilogy of Swedish marinated herrings are on the starters and snack menu that typifies Karl Wadsack's spring collection. This moves up-beat to main courses consisting of fricassée of gambas, scallops and sea fish in an aromatic coriander curry or fillets of john dory with warm sun-dried tomatoes and olive oil dressing. This is confident cooking with a reputation and atmosphere to match. An excellent wine list with Australian, Alsace and German selections worth noting.

STURMINSTER NEWTON — Plumber Manor

Hazelbury Bryan Road, Sturminster Newton, Dorset DT10 2AT
Telephone: (0258) 72507 Fax: (0258) 73370
Open: dinner daily (closed Feb)
Meals served: dinner 7-9.30

£55

Built in the early 17th-century for the forefathers of present owners Richard, Alison and Brian Prideaux-Brune, Plumber Manor was turned into a restaurant with rooms 10 years ago. Set in the midst of Hardy's Dorset, it is a good place to stay for those exploring the surrounding countryside. Brian is the chef and is well known for his traditional and classic French cooking which is supported by a good wine list. The dining area is split between 3 rooms and serves 3- and 4-course menus. The 16 bedrooms are shared between the main house, stable block and converted stone barn. Free stabling available if you wish to hack or hunt!

SUDBURY — Mabey's Brasserie

47 Gainsborough Street, Sudbury, Suffolk CO10 7SS
Telephone: (0787) 374298
Open: lunch + dinner Tue-Sat (closed Bank Holidays)
Meals served: lunch 12-2, dinner 7-10

£45

This brasserie would be welcome in any town.

A split level brasserie with an open kitchen may seem a bit of a change for Robert Mabey (ex-Hintlesham Hall) but he is in his element, with wife Johanna running things out in front. Pew seating, pine tables and a sea of blue walls set the scene at this restaurant which offers a short menu of crab and prawn filo parcels, Japanese-style tempura chicken and crisp mackerel fish cakes. Salmon comes on a bed of saffron rice with champagne sauce and grilled chicken with mashed potatoes and a red wine sauce.

Some seriously good cooking & a light, homely approach.

SURBITON   Chez Max

85 Maple Road, Surbiton, Surrey KT6 4AW
Telephone: 081-399 2365   **£50**
Open: lunch + dinner Tue-Sat (closed Bank Holidays, open
Mothering Sunday)
Meals served: lunch 12.30-2, dinner 7.30-10

In a conservatory-roofed restaurant Max Markarian cooks a menu of
well-executed French classics with a few new touches added to the
repertoire. Strong, decisive flavours are combined with game, meat
and poultry. On the set price menu with supplements expect to see
dishes such as pigeon with red wine and prunes, lamb with shallots
and white wine and a smoked trout mousse with smoked salmon and
an avocado purée. Puddings delight with a chocolate truffle cake with
orange and Grand Marnier and home-made sorbets. The wine list is
comprehensive and offers a good selection of half bottles.

SUTTON   Partners Brasserie

23 Stonecot Hill, Sutton, Surrey SM3 9HB
Telephone: 081-644 7743   **£30**
Open: lunch Tue-Fri + Sun, dinner Tue-Sat (closed Bank Holidays)
Meals served: lunch 12-2, dinner 7-9.30

In a busy parade of shops on the A24 is this up-market brasserie with
green ragged walls and hand-written menus. Tim Franklin continues
in the kitchen with a characteristic menu of casserole of fish and shellfish, cassoulet of crisp duck legs with white beans and tartlet of goat's
cheese.

SUTTON COLDFIELD   New Hall

Walmley Road, Sutton Coldfield, West Midlands B76 8QX
Telephone: 021-378 2442 Fax: 021-378 4637   **£60**
Open: lunch Mon-Sun, dinner daily
Meals served: lunch 12.30-2 (Sun 12.30-2.15), dinner 7-10 (Sun 7-9.30)

Set in 26 acres of lush private gardens and surrounded by (reputedly)
the oldest lily-filled moat, Ian and Caroline Parkes continue to lavish
time and care on this restored luxury hotel. The panelled dining room
is in the oldest part of the house and is an elegant setting for Glenn
Purcell's cooking. Attractive in both composition and presentation, he
cooks in a classic style but with new touches - grilled monkfish served
on a niçoise and crisp bacon salad, lamb stuffed with apricots and
black pudding farci or corn-fed chicken marinated in saffron with a
warm gazpacho vinaigrette. A millefeuille of hot caramelised bananas
with a mandarin cream or iced apple and raspberry parfait complete
the day nicely. And so to bed in one of the 60 elaborate bedrooms.

SWANAGE   Galley

9 High Street, Swanage, Dorset BH19 2LN
Telephone: (0929) 427299   £35
Open: dinner daily (closed Jan+Feb)
Meals served: dinner 6.45-9.30 (Sat 6.45-10)

Daily baked bread marks a big change to this restaurant as Nick Storer
improves an already popular local restaurant. Healthy, elegant and exciting fish, game, poultry, meat and vegetarian dishes are their market.
The operation continues to improve as each year passes and at present
they are moving over to a fixed-price 3-course menu with a fair choice of
dishes. The Galley is now totally self-sufficient in herbs which are used
more often – all steps in the right direction.

TADWORTH   Gemini Restaurant

Station Approach, Tadworth, Surrey KT20 5AH
Telephone: (0737) 812179   £50
Open: lunch Tue-Sun, dinner Tue-Sat (closed 1 wk Xmas, 2 wks Jun)
Meals served: lunch 12-2, dinner 7-9.30

Robert Foster will tempt you into his uncomplicated surroundings and
offer you a menu that has been simply conceived yet well executed.
Starters may include fettucini of mussels and prawns bound with crème
fraîche and scented with fresh coriander, or Gemini chinese spoons
filled with fish delicacies of the day. These could be followed by breast
of chicken in an oyster mushroom café au lait sauce flavoured with ginger or roast rack of English lamb served with a red wine, rosemary and
pimento jus. Stick to the simpler dishes for an enjoyable meal.

TAPLOW   Cliveden

Taplow, Nr Maidenhead, Berkshire SL6 0JF
Telephone: (0628) 668561 Fax: (0628) 661837   £100
Open: lunch + dinner daily
Meals served: lunch 12.30-2.30, dinner 7.30-10

The majestic drive sets the tone for a very special occasion and it's
worth arriving in plenty of time to take in the magnificent views of the
Thames and landscapes from the terrace. One of our best pieces of heritage and once home of the Astors, it opened its doors as a hotel on the
grandest scale in 1984 with opulent and finely furnished public rooms.
The service is exactly as you would expect, the bedrooms beautiful and
for those who wish to be energetic, there are swimming pools inside and
out, squash courts and a gym. The Terrace and the private French
Dining Room escape none of the sumptuousness and employ the finest
Spode china and table settings. Here, a classical English approach to
cooking is lifted by contemporary thinking, with dishes such as oxtail
with olives and roast seasonal vegetables, while Waldo's, the second
restaurant, allows Ron Maxfield to give full rein to his inspiration and
create à la carte and 6-course menus including red mullet with saffron
and olive oil, morrels and asparagus, char-grilled lamb with sorrel and
mint sauce followed by warm tartlet of camembert matured in calvados
with apples and a rocket salad, before an iced pistachio parfait dipped in
chocolate. The wine list is notable and the coffee is some of the best, so
after dinner, take to the terrace in the evening air and soak up the
atmosphere. With its majestic dimensions and supremely fine architecture this might be the closest you will ever come to staying in a palace.

TAUNTON	Castle Hotel

Castle Green, Taunton, Somerset TA1 1NF
Telephone: (0823) 272671 Fax: (0823) 336066
Open: lunch + dinner daily
Meals served: lunch 12.30-2, dinner 7.30-9

£55

With beef cooked in a salt crust and Yorkshire pudding, it is not surprising this place is favoured on Sundays. Phil Vickery continues where his forerunners left off with a menu that stimulates and lives up to expectations. Introduced with a list of faithful suppliers, the ingredients are top notch and the cooking gifted and special. If you were to be sensible about these things, steamed lobster sausage with couscous and lobster and caviar wouldn't be followed by roasted scallops with saffron noodles and braised onions but with both on the same menu it is impossible not to be tempted! On another week it might be different: braised duck with lentils and creamed potatoes or braised ham hocks with onions and seed mustard. Desserts are just as good as is the selection of Jeroboam's and Montgomery cheeses. Baked egg custard tart with nutmeg ice cream is a must, as is the almond blancmange with lemon grass syrup and candied lemon. The wisteria-draped 35-bedroomed hotel remains, as in former years, Kit Chapman's illustrious castle.

TAUNTON	Nightingales Restaurant

Bath House Farm, Lower West Hatch, Nr Taunton, Somerset TA3 5RH
Telephone: (0823) 480806
Open: dinner Tue-Sat
Meals served: dinner 7.30-9.30

£50

The menu is short with only 6 dishes at each course, but is based on the best local produce and everything is made from scratch in the kitchen by chef Sally Edwards - mousseline of smoked haddock with tomato and fennel vinaigrette followed by roast breast of chicken with a guinea fowl sausage, creamed leeks and madeira sauce. Puddings are good with sticky gingerbread sponge served with crème anglaise and poached rhubarb or meringues layered with praline cream and a warm butterscotch sauce.

TAUNTON	Porters Wine Bar

49 East Reach, Taunton, Somerset TA1 3EX
Telephone: (0823) 256688
Open: lunch Mon-Fri, dinner Mon-Sat (closed Bank Holidays)
Meals served: lunch 12.30-2, dinner 7.30-10

£35

Daily changing menus mean that chef Clive Arthur needs several new ideas up his sleeve. These he has in plenty, which means he helps owners, the Porters, indulge clients with cosmopolitan lunches and suppers of spiced apple soup, grilled plaice in a champagne sauce or strips of beef with wholegrain mustard and brandy. The cooking is simple but uses fresh ingredients and vegetarians are well catered for - a good local place to eat with about 20 wines available by the glass.

TEDDINGTON — Spaghetti Junction

20/22 High Street, Teddington, Middlesex TW11 8EW
Telephone: 081-977 6756 Fax: 081-977 8890   £40
Open: lunch + dinner daily (closed mid-July- mid-August, 4 days
Xmas + Easter)
Meals served: lunch 12-2.30, dinner 6-11.15

A splash of paint spruces up this stylish Italian restaurant, which offers
good seafood, pasta and calves' liver. If it's available, try the Sardinian
fish casserole, or the very good risotto crema tartufata. Don't be fooled
by the name, this is a smart restaurant, with a full-blown Italian wine
list.

TEFFONT EVIAS — Howard's House

Teffont Evias, Dinton, nr Salisbury, Wiltshire SP3 5RJ
Telephone: (0722) 716392 Fax: (0722) 716820   £60
Open: lunch Sun, dinner daily (closed)
Meals served: lunch 12.30-2, dinner 7.30-10

Paul Firmin is owner and chef at this small family-run hotel (originally
a Tudor stone farmhouse) with 8 charming and well-furnished bedrooms. Paul's excellent country cooking has a modern twist. His menu
offers a selection of 7 starters and main courses - you may start with
chilled pea and mint soup or scallops with lentils and coriander,
perhaps followed by lamb and steamed spinach with an infusion of
redcurrants and rosemary, or snapper and seabass with provençale
vegetables. A good place to dine and stay.

TEIGNMOUTH — Thomas Luny House

Teign Street, Teignmouth, Devon TQ14 8EG
Telephone: (0626) 772976   £35
Open: dinner daily (for residents and their guests only)
(closed mid Dec-mid Jan)
Meals served: dinner at 7.30

Go through the archway to this attractive Georgian town house - truly
a home from home. Ring the bell for admission and owners Alison and
John Allan will greet you and, without the formalities of reception
desks and form-filling, will whisk you upstairs and show you to your
room. The atmosphere of this town house with only 5 bedrooms
makes you feel more like a house guest than client, and you all gather
round one highly polished dining room table for dinner. A set menu
make the best use of local produce – avocado salad with tomato and
mozzarella, roast loin of lamb with watercress sauce and spicy butter
apple tart.

TETBURY   Calcot Manor

Tetbury, Gloucestershire GL8 8YJ
Telephone: (0666) 890391 Fax: (0666) 890394   **£60**
Open: lunch daily, dinner Mon-Sat
Meals served: lunch 12.30-2, dinner 7.30-9.30

Rolling hills, fields of flower-filled hedgerows and open log fires are all
in store at this hotel, originally a stone farmhouse complete with 14th-
century tithe barns and stables. From the 16 bedrooms, some
canopied or with 4-posters, the early morning views are both relaxing
and breathtaking as you look out over the undulating Cotswolds.
Richard and Catherine Ball have taken over where his parents left off
and aim to continue the family traditions. New chef Ben Davies has
brought a less complex and better value approach to the menu with
the likes of a warm salad of smoked salmon and wild mushrooms with
tomato and shallot vinaigrette, pan-fried English lamb on a stew of
lentils with beetroot and vegetable sauce followed by a gratin of fresh
fruit with a Grand Marnier sabayon and apricot sauce. Happy
retirement, Brian and Barbara – it looks like you have left Calcot in
extremely capable hands.

TETBURY   The Close

8 Long Street, Tetbury, Gloucestershire GL8 8AQ
Telephone: (0666) 502272 Fax: (0666) 504401   **£55**
Open: lunch + dinner daily (closed 1 wk Jan)
Meals served: lunch 12.30-2, dinner 7.30-10 (Sun 7.30-9)

The Close was built over 400 years ago on the site of a Cistercian
monastery, around a central courtyard. The elegant gabled house now
boasts a walled garden and 15 bedrooms each designed with rich fabrics - the Tower and Doves are the largest 4-poster rooms. Everything
is just as it should be at this refined, relaxed town house with a special
feel and atmosphere. There's a young and enthusiastic team both in
front of and behind the scenes. Choose from the carte or the set menu
which offers a choice of 3 starters such as ribbons of home-made pasta
with spears of asparagus and red pesto, or a warm salad of chicken livers with glazed apples. Out of the 4 main courses you might find
breaded medallions of pork tenderloin with couscous on a peppercorn
sauce. Save room for desserts – perhaps iced muesli parfait with pears
poached in Barolo.

THAME   Spread Eagle

Cornmarket, Thame, Oxfordshire OX9 2BW
Telephone: (0844) 213661 Fax: (0844) 261380   **£40**
Open: lunch Sun-Fri (Sat bar lunch only), dinner daily (closed 29+30 Dec)
Meals served: lunch 12.30-2, dinner 7-10 (Sun 7-9)

This place was once run by John Fothergill, chum of Oscar Wilde, who
brought notoriety to the inn with his good cooking and social connec-
tions - famous politicians, Oxford dons, writers and artists – they all
happily travelled to Thame. Today, the menu includes delicacies to tan-
talize the eye as well as the palate with whimsical drawings from a col-
lector's edition of *An Innkeepers Diary* by Fothergill. A praline, apple
and cream cigar or rhubarb and thyme fool are some of the tempting
desserts. Other specials include green pea soup with lardons, trout
and cottage cheese tart, steak Bocuse and mignons of veal with wild
mushrooms and a spinach roulade. The Barringtons now run this hotel
with much care and dedication.

THORNBURY   Thornbury Castle

Thornbury, Avon BS12 1HH   ✸
Telephone: (0454) 281182 Fax: (0454) 416188   **£50**
Open: lunch + dinner daily (closed 2 days early Jan)
Meals served: lunch 12-2, dinner 7-9.30

Henry VIII, who confiscated property on a whim, acquired this castle
after beheading the Duke of Buckingham. He stayed here for a couple
of days with Anne Boleyn before it was her untimely turn to visit the
Tower. Now it's owned by the Baron and Baroness of Portlethen, and
the main apartments have been restored to provide 18 chambers,
some with the original large Tudor fireplaces and 4-poster beds.
Surrounded by its vineyard, gardens and high walls, it affords views
over the Severn into Gloucestershire and Wales much the same as
those Mary Tudor would have appreciated during the years she
resided here. This is a very special place to stay and the young team
do their best to make you feel at home. A very good wine list has some
reasonable prices. Competent service in the restaurant, where the
simpler dishes are best. Very good cheese board selection.

THORNTON CLEVELEYS   Victorian House

Trunnah Road, Thornton Cleveleys, Lancashire FY5 4HF
Telephone: (0253) 860619 Fax: (0253) 865350   **£45**
Open: lunch + dinner Mon-Sat (closed 2 wks Jan)
Meals served: lunch 12-1.30, dinner 7-9.30

At this French restaurant with 3 bedrooms, chef Didier Guerin creates
a fixed-price 4-course menu with salads of goat's cheese or smoked
halibut on a wholemeal pancake, mussels or clam chowder. Main
courses might include braised pheasant with apples and cider cream
sauce, casserole of lamb, tomato and haricot beans or roulade of
chicken stuffed with spinach and wrapped in pastry. Good wine list,
and service by staff dressed in Victorian costume.

THORNTON-LE-FYLDE   River House

Skippool Creek, Thornton-le-Fylde, Nr Blackpool, Lancashire FY5 5LF
Telephone: (0253) 883497 Fax: (0253) 892083   **£45**
Open: lunch Sun by arrangement, dinner Mon-Sat (closed
some Bank Holidays)
Meals served: lunch 12.30 for 1, dinner 7.30-9.30

When it comes to looking after you Bill and Carole Scott have never
been known to do things by half. The motto at their restaurant with
rooms says that `to invite a person into your house is to take charge of
their happiness for as long as they are under your roof'. They fulfil
that obligation perfectly, creating a harmonious atmosphere all round
even when they're both working in the kitchen. Bill takes care of the
fish and meat while Carole takes charge of the starters and sauces.
Fish from Fleetwood is always well represented on a menu that might
include goujons of salmon, scallops in a creamy wine and herb sauce,
chateaubriand, or grouse with redcurrant sauce. Spirited yet unfussy
cooking with great puds.

THUNDRIDGE   Hanbury Manor

You can also eat in the Vardon Bar & Grill style in the delightful or in the conservatory.

Thundridge, Nr Ware, Hertfordshire SG12 0SD
Telephone: (0920) 487722 Fax: (0920) 487692   **£65**
Open: lunch daily, dinner Mon-Sat
Meals served: lunch 12-3, dinner 7-10

Much money and time has been lavished on Hanbury Manor and
whilst it is well equipped for banqueting, such potentially large groups
do not intrude upon the individual guest. A perfect environment for
working, entertaining, celebrating and relaxing, this is the retreat for
the executive business and conference market. A Jacobean mansion
set in over 200 acres of rural countryside, it provides 96 bedrooms that
are historic and handsomely furnished but with all the up-to-date
extras. An 18-hole golf course and health club provide plenty of activities to wind down after a hard day brain-storming. Thus in a relaxed
frame of mind, you can take dinner in the Zodiac room complete with
cloche-covered plates and an à la carte menu masterminded by Albert
Roux but executed by Rory Kennedy. Try nage of sole and oysters in
chardonnay, duck with olives and braised shallots and pigeon with cauliflower and star anise. An all-round reasonable wine list.

TINTAGEL   Trebrea Lodge

Trenale, Nr Tintagel, Cornwall PL34 0HR
Telephone: (0840) 770410   £35
Open: dinner daily
Meals served: dinner at 8

An old Cornish manor set in over 4 acres of wooded hillside, Trebrea
is furnished throughout with antiques. In the drawing room a log fire
burns for most of the year and an 'honesty bar' welcomes those who
have been experiencing the fine countryside at first hand. Dinner is a
simple no-choice affair with hand-written menus featuring smoked
haddock and prawn au gratin, mustard and paprika baked chicken followed by meringue and then Yarg and Stilton cheese. There are only
12 wines to choose, but there is bound to be something to suit, otherwise good house wines are served by the glass. 8 bedrooms in the
same elegant style as the rest of the lodge.

TORQUAY   Mulberry House

1 Scarborough Road, Torquay, Devon TQ2 5UJ
Telephone: (0803) 213639   £35
Open: lunch Wed-Sun, dinner Fri+Sat
Meals served: lunch 12.15-2.30, dinner 7.30-9.30 (light meals all day)

Just up from the seafront, turn right and you'll find Lesley Cooper's
small, individually-run guest house. A one-woman band, she offers personal attention to just a handful of guests (only 3 rooms) before heading towards the kitchen to start preparing dinner - wild rabbit stew
with saffron and cucumber, fresh local sole with herb butter and a luscious array of desserts like a terrine of prunes, port and chocolate with
crème anglaise or Normandy apple flan perhaps.

TORQUAY   Remy's

3 Croft Road, Torquay, Devon TQ2 5UN
Telephone: (0803) 292359   £35
Open: dinner Tue-Sat (closed 2 wks Xmas/New Year)
Meals served: dinner 7.30-9.30

Good service, good food and good value have always been Remy Bopp
and his wife Dolene's intentions for their small French restaurant.
Until now they have managed admirably and there seems no reason
why that shouldn't continue. A fixed-price 3-course menu keeps the
customers happy and loyal, and offers tremendous choice and value
with old faithfuls such as snails wrapped in pastry with cream and garlic sauce, chicken in basil and tomato sauce, venison with cranberry or
sirloin with green peppercorn.

TORQUAY — Table Restaurant

135 Babbacombe Road, Babbacombe, Torquay, Devon TQ1 3SR
Telephone: (0803) 324292 **£55**
Open: dinner Tue-Sun (closed Bank Holidays, 2 wks Feb, 2 wks Sept)
Meals served: dinner 7.30-10 (Sun 7.30-9.30)

The fresh delights of Brixham fish market find their way to Trevor Brooks and Jane Corrigan's tiny restaurant on the outskirts of Torquay. Dinner is a fixed 3-course menu - sausage of free-range chicken with lemon pasta and black beans, sesame seed crêpe with home smoked salmon and a horseradish and lime fondue followed by breast of duck served with tarragon jus and fried polenta. Desserts are good with poached pears with saffron ice cream and bread and butter pudding with ginger marmalade. Trevor shows a spark of ingenuity in the way he combines ingredients and is undoubtedly a good cook. This is a good local restaurant and well worth a visit. Among its devotees are Paul and Kay Henderson of Gidleigh Park, who rate it highly, and so do I.

TRURO — Alverton Manor

Tregolls Road, Truro, Cornwall TR1 1XQ
Telephone: (0872) 76633 Fax: (0872) 222989 £65
Open: lunch + dinner daily
Meals served: lunch 12-1.45, dinner 7.15-9.45
A former convent with 25 spacious bedrooms on the edge of the town.

TRURO — Pennypots Restaurant

Blackwater, Truro, Cornwall TR4 8EY
Telephone: (0209) 820347 £55
Open: dinner only Tues-Sat (closed 3 wks in winter)
Meals served: dinner 7.30-10
Welcoming, small à la carte restaurant with interesting variety. Selection of fish, seafood and meat dishes on a frequently changed menu.

TUNBRIDGE WELLS — Cheevers

56 High Street, Tunbridge Wells, Kent TN1 1XF
Telephone: (0892) 545524 **£55**
Open: lunch + dinner Tue-Sat (closed Bank Holidays, 2 wks Jan)
Meals served: lunch 12.30-2 (Sat 12.30-1.45), dinner 7.30-10.30

As adept with a pen as a filleting knife, Tim Cheevers keeps his clients up-to-date with his newsletter of up-coming events. His restaurant is cool, crisp and restful with ingenious food showing plenty of imagination. A la carte at lunchtime, and fixed-price in the evening, expect dishes such as mousse of crab wrapped in spinach, lamb in an almond and mint crust, brill baked in flaky pastry with dill. Some reasonable prices on the concise wine list.

TUNBRIDGE WELLS — Thackeray's House

85 London Road, Tunbridge Wells, Kent TN11 1EA
Telephone: (0892) 511921
Restaurant **£50**
Open: lunch Tue-Sun, dinner Tue-Sat (closed Bank Holidays, 1 wk Xmas)
Meals served: lunch 12.30-2.30, dinner 7-10
Bistro: **£45**
Open: lunch + dinner Tue-Sat (closed Bank Holidays, 1 wk Xmas)
Meals served: lunch 12.30-2.30, dinner 7.30-9.30

Once the novelist's abode, Thackeray's House has been home to the cooking of chef/patron Bruce Wass for the last 10 years. A classical array of dishes make up the carte, and a good-value midweek menu may include croustade of smokies, a curried parsnip soup with coriander and orange and main courses of wood pigeon with blackcurrants or grey mullet with tomato and olive oil. Desserts are a pudding lover's ecstasy, such as walnut and ginger pudding with toffee sauce, chocolate armagnac loaf and apricot compote with marscapone. Downstairs is Bruce's cosy bistro, run with ease and flair with the help of head chef Peter Lucas. A popular contemporary menu might offer you zampone with Puy lentils, braised ham with prunes in red wine, pork with seed mustard and cod with dijon mustard. With its own courtyard entrance and new wine bar, Thackeray's has become quite a happening place.

TURNERS HILL — Alexander House

East Street, Turners Hill, West Sussex RH10 4QD   *A place to*
Telephone: (0342) 714914 Fax: (0342) 717328   *dress up for &* **£80**
Open: lunch + dinner daily   *enjoy*
Meals served: lunch 12.30-2, dinner 7.30-9.30 (Sun 7.30-9)

Glamour and gloss jump out of the pages of the brochure, for the pictures would look as much at home in the pages of *Tatler* or *Hello*. Home of the present Earl Alexander, who with the Countess, still hosts many events here, this 17th-century house is one of the few remaining private mansions of this calibre. To eat and sleep in such luxurious surroundings is most certainly a treat with numerous grand rooms and 14 bedrooms adorned with antiques and original paintings. The staff (some in tail-coats) add a touch of class and distinction - the like of which few probably have ever, nor will ever, see again. The cooking by Alan Pierce is as smooth and polished as the place itself - asparagus mousse with truffles, ragoût of poached lobster, crayfish and red mullet or pan-fried beef with celeriac and foie gras.

TWICKENHAM — Cezanne's Restaurant

68 Richmond Road, Twickenham, Middlesex TW1 3BE
Telephone: 081-892 3526   **£45**
Open: lunch Mon-Fri, dinner Mon-Sat (closed Bank Holidays)
Meals served: lunch 12.30-2, dinner 7-10.30 (Fri+Sat 7-11)

Cezanne is now more of a restaurant than a café, and the menu has grown up to include roast breast of duck with orange glazed sweet potatoes and grilled fillet of cod with a hot balsamic vinaigrette. With new chef Steven Whitney (ex-Savoy) the repertoire has broadened and includes dishes of a more robust nature. First courses include crab, ginger and sweetcorn filled samosas and poached figs with parma ham and a goat's cheese tartlet.

TWICKENHAM — Hamiltons

43 Crown Road, St Margarets, Twickenham, Middlesex TW1 3EJ
Telephone: 081-892 3949   **£40**
Open: lunch Tue-Fri + Sun, dinner Tue-Sat (closed 1 wk New Year)
Meals served: lunch 12-2.30, dinner 7-11

Anglo-French cooking's on offer here, with live jazz during family lunch on Sundays when there will be 2 roasts, a vegetarian and a fish dish. The interior is best described as artistic - walls adorned with French impressionist pictures, large walnut-framed mirrors, stained glass windows and a gold ceiling. During the week there is no minimum charge, so you are quite welcome to have a starter followed by dessert from the à la carte, or even just a main course, or you can opt for the fixed-price 3-course menu. This 40-seater restaurant is very popular with the Twickies.

TWICKENHAM — McClements

12 The Green, Twickenham, Middlesex TW2 5AA   ✿
Telephone: 081-755 0176 Fax: 081-890 1372   **£60**
Open: lunch Mon-Fri, dinner Mon-Sat
Meals served: lunch 12.30-2.30, dinner 7-10 (Sat 7-10.30)

Squeezed into a row of houses opposite Twickenham Green is this pretty little French restaurant, run by chef/patron John McClements. It's well-established and popular, and he works on his own to create a small menu of French cuisine. Each and every dish reads superbly – confit of rabbit with a stuffing of ham and foie gras, a salad of fresh crab with a basil dressing, scallops straight from the grill with roasted endive and a sauternes sauce and main courses of guinea fowl with olive oil and wild mushrooms. A really good local restaurant. As we went to press John was opening a brasserie at 2 Whitton Road - lucky Twickenham.

good value

UCKFIELD HOOKE HALL

250 High Street, Uckfield, East Sussex TN22 1EN
Telephone: (0825) 761578 Fax: (0825) 768025 **£55**
Open: dinner Tue-Sat (closed Xmas/New Year)
Meals served: dinner 7.30-9

Good cooking comes from the kitchen of owner and chef, Cordon Bleu trained, Juliet Percy. Together with husband Alister she runs this Queen Anne town house with comfortable drawing room and 9 bedrooms, each named after famous mistresses and lovers! It's sumptuous and relaxing.

UCKFIELD Horsted Place

Little Horsted, Uckfield, East Sussex TN22 5TS
Telephone: (0825) 750581 Fax: (0835) 750459 *very special* ❀
Open: lunch Sun-Fri, dinner daily *& relaxed hotel* **£65**
Meals served: lunch 12.30-2, dinner 7.30-9.30

If Pugin's works are a favourite, then this is the place for you. He wasn't the architect but he certainly had a great influence on the final look of the place, with its striking oak staircase (one of his works). High Victoriana, it makes a striking impression with distinctive checkerboard brickwork and grounds laid out by Geoffrey Jellicoe. Glyndebourne and the East Sussex National golf course (the home of the European Open Championship) are just around the corner, so it is ideally placed for the socialite and fanatic golfer. Sparkling silver, fine porcelain and crisp linen match Allan Garth's sensible short menu of well judged and balanced dishes - steamed panaché of fish with tomato and tarragon sauce and beef on a potato rosti with a red wine sauce, or perhaps a squab pigeon served with brown lentils and a Port wine sauce with confit of garlic. Rich in history, this house has a wine list to match. The team here includes the Hon John Sinclair (ex-Cliveden), Jonathon Ritchie (ex-Chester Grosvenor), and Allan Garth, who has had stints at Le Gavroche and Gravetye Manor – quite a pedigree!

ULLINGSWICK Steppes Country House

Ullingswick, nr Hereford, Hereford & Worcester HR1 3JG
Telephone: (0432) 820424 **£45**
Open: dinner daily (closed 2 wks before + after Xmas)
Meals served: dinner 7.30-9

A small country hotel created within a 17th-century farmstead. The lounge, dining room and bar are rich in heavy oak beams, inglenook fireplaces, cobbled floors and antique furniture. The bedrooms are converted traditional timber-framed barns and are warmly decorated.

ULLSWATER   Leeming House

Watermillock, Ullswater, Cumbria CA11 0JJ
Telephone: (076 84) 86622 Fax: (076 84) 86443   **£60**
Open: lunch + dinner daily
Meals served: lunch 12.30-1.45, dinner 7.30-8.45

On the shores of Lake Ullswater and set in its own 20 or so acres of
woodland and garden, this 40-bedroomed hotel is now a Forte Grand.
The bedrooms at the front of the house enjoy the best views of the
lake and the backdrop of the fells beyond. A pillared entrance hall
welcomes you inside this classically designed house complete with
conservatory. The dining room relishes similar views and a traditional
3- or 6-course dinner menu.

ULLSWATER   Old Church Hotel

Watermillock, Ullswater, Cumbria CA11 0JN
Telephone: (076 84) 86204 Fax: (076 84) 86368 *staggeringly* **£50**
Open: dinner daily (closed Nov-Mar)   *beautiful location*
Meals served: dinner 7.30 for 8

You're treated as house guests rather than visitors at the Whitemores'
hotel. Superb views of the mountains and lake can be relished, even
from the confines of a comfy chair in the lounge, where magazines and
board games are also provided for your entertainment. Breakfasts
here are an added bonus, and Kevin's good Lakeland cooking might
include local yoghurts, creamy porridge with whisky and demerara,
compote of armagnac-soaked prunes and home-made muesli plus
hearty plates of Cumberland sausages with black pudding and smoky
bacon, apple and cinnamon compôte and a pair of Manx kippers with
butter, lemon and parsley. The dinner menu is equally as tempting but
sadly, with restricted space, only a few non-resident diners can be
accommodated.

ULLSWATER Rampsbeck Country House Hotel

Watermillock, Ullswater, Cumbria CA11 0LP
Tel + Fax: (076 84) 86442   **£50**
Open: lunch + dinner daily (closed 6 wks Jan/Feb)
Meals served: lunch 12-1.45, dinner 7-8.45

With its lakeside garden and backdrop of the fells, the Gibbs have a
distinctive 20-bedroomed hotel with log fires and a bar that opens onto
the patio, making this an enchanting place to stay, winter or summer.
Andrew McGeorge cooks the 4-course menu and experiments with
combinations such as brill lasagna served with a mussel cream sauce
flavoured with lemon grass and ginger. Reasonable wine list.

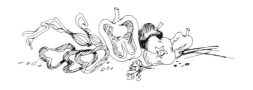

ULLSWATER   Sharrow Bay

Ullswater, Howton, nr Penrith, Cumbria CA10 2LZ
Telephone: (076 84) 86301 Fax: (076 84) 86349   **£90**
Open: lunch + dinner daily (closed Dec-Feb)
Meals served: lunch 1-1.45, dinner 8-8.45

`Cooking is an art and all art is patience', notes the top of each menu, which paraphrases all that has been written or said of this place. Nestling on the lakes, this is one of the most outstanding locations in which you could ever wish to find yourself. With the waves lapping on the shore beneath the terrace, the setting couldn't be more perfect for these views are legendary in any season. The dining room is always packed, for such is the might of the cooking of Johnnie Martin (the style set by owners Francis Coulson and Brian Sack) that the hotel has continued to pull in a pot-pourri of visitors even in these days of down-turn spending, The food is rich, steadfastly traditional and service helpful. You will be spoilt for choice, but at least only 3 times during the 6 courses. Even so, they may well be the most difficult decisions of your day. Should it be duck foie gras on a bed of Sharrow noodles with a pancake of summer vegetables and a champagne and herb sauce, then a main course of fried calves' liver with lardons of smoked bacon, sautéed onions wrapped in pastry and lime flavoured sauce, and finally a Regency syllabub for pudding? The wine list is traditional and good for wines by the glass too. The 28 bedrooms are all decorated and furnished to the owners' taste.

ULVERSTON   Bay Horse Inn & Bistro

Canal Foot, Ulverston, Cumbria LA12 9EL
Telephone: (0229) 53972   **£50**
Open: lunch Tue-Sun, dinner daily
Meals served: lunch 12-2, dinner 7.30 for 8

A real find - once you've found it! Look out for the Glaxo plant and if you think you're driving into it you're on the right path! Don't let that put you off, for on the contrary, once you have reached this charming inn, the views, food and service make it worthwhile. After many years at Miller Howe, Robert Lyons opened this bistro with help from his friend and employer, and created from an old pub 6 bedrooms, a bar and conservatory restaurant. Set on the side of the Leven estuary you can sample simple bar food from home-made soups, pies and the like but it is the restaurant that most come here for, with a menu that offers more sophisticated Tovey-style choices of chilled pea, lemon and mint soup with cream and almonds and pan-fried fillet of beef stuffed with duck livers wrapped in smoked bacon.

UPPER SLAUGHTER   Lords of the Manor

Upper Slaughter, Nr Bourton-on-the-Water, Gloucestershire GL54 2JD
Telephone: (0451) 820243 Fax: (0451) 820696   **£75**
Open: lunch + dinner daily
Meals served: lunch 12.30-2, dinner 7.30-9.30

This creeper-clad, 17th-century rectory is a cluster of buildings, for bits
have been added at various times over the years. It is typically English
with a traditional atmosphere and service, with nice little extras like
Penhaligon toiletries in the 29 bedrooms. Clive Dixon in the kitchen
shows no hesitation with a freshness of cooking and a good use of
herbs in his pleasing fixed-price and à la carte menu, which might
include langoustine soup with coriander and Pernod with rouille and
croutons and well-prepared terrine of salmon and brill layered with
spinach and soft herbs. Set in its own grounds, the Manor is an ideal
base for touring the Cotswolds.

UPPINGHAM   The Lake Isle

16 High Street East, Uppingham, Leicestershire LE15 9PZ
Telephone: (0572) 822951 Fax: (0572) 822951   **£45**
Open: lunch Tue-Sun, dinner Mon-Sat
Meals served: lunch 12.30-1.45 (Sun 12.30-2), dinner 7.30-9.30 (Sat 7-10 Sun
7.30-8.30)

This 10-bedroomed restaurant, cascading with flowers, is set in a
market town and offers the personal touches. It's owned by the
Whitfields - David prepares food which is strong on flavours and imaginative combinations, cooked in a French farmhouse-style and served
in the wood-panelled restaurant, with its collection of different wooden
chairs. The weekly changing dinner menu might include a parsnip and
chestnut soup and a main course of wild boar cooked with Guinness
and port. The wine list is outstanding and shows great attention to
research and tasting. Claire looks after front of house.

WALKINGTON   Manor House

Northlands, Walkington, Beverley, Humberside HU17 8RT
Telephone: (0482) 881645 Fax: (0482) 866501   **£45**
Open: lunch Wed-Sat, dinner Mon-Sat
Meals served: lunch 12.15-1.30, dinner 7.30-9.30

Surrounded by the Yorkshire Wolds is this late 19th-century house run
by Derek and Lee Baugh. The cooking is classical with new-wave
touches. Derek is an accomplished cook and has shaken off the over-
fussy and long-worded dishes that he formerly employed and is moving in the right direction with sauté of kidneys with sausage and courgette in a white onion sauce or panaché of North Sea fish, served in
the dining room or conservatory. There are 6 bedrooms in the friendly
and welcoming Manor House.

WALTERSTONE   Allt-Yr-Ynys Hotel

Walterstone, Hereford & Worcester HK2 0DU
Telephone: (0873) 890307   **£45**
Open: dinner daily (closed 25+26 Dec)
Meals served: dinner 7.30-9.30

Pronounced `Allt-er-Innis', this hotel stands on the banks of the river
Monnow. The conversion from farmhouse to elegant country-house
hotel with 8 bedrooms, has been very successful. None of the original,
historic appeal has been lost - nor is it lacking character. A good warm
atmosphere.

WANSFORD-IN-ENGLAND   Haycock Hotel

Wansford-in-England, Peterborough, Cambridgeshire PE8 6JA
Telephone: (0780) 782223 Fax: (0780) 783031   **£60**
Open: lunch + dinner daily
Meals served: lunch 12-2.30, dinner 7-10.30

A celebrated 17th-century coaching inn, it was the last port of call for
Mary, Queen of Scots, before prison; a stop-over for Queen Victoria, a
racing stable and an ammunition factory in the war! The checkered
history adds to the attraction, and with 51 bedrooms all full of character and designed with great flair by Julia Vanocci, it is worthy of a stay.
The restaurant is traditional in style and Richard Brandrick's cooking
is traditional too with jugged hare, roast pheasant, rack of lamb and
fillet of beef (allow an extra £3.95 for vegetables).

WAREHAM   Priory Hotel

Church Green, Wareham, Dorset BH20 4ND
Telephone: (0929) 551666 Fax: (0929) 554519   **£50**
Open: lunch + dinner daily
Meals served: lunch 12.30-2, dinner 7.30-10 (Teas 3-6)

Enjoy the quality furnishings, service and food in the historic surroundings of this 16th-century priory with 19 bedrooms. The 4 acres of
gardens slope gently down to the River Frome, which runs down to
the sea at Poole harbour. Breakfast and lunch are taken in the pastel
Greenwood Room, while dinner is more romantic, by candlelight in
the flagstoned Cellar Room.

WARMINSTER   Bishopstrow House

Boreham Road, Warminster, Wiltshire BA12 9HH
Telephone: (0985) 212312 Fax: (0985) 216769
Open: lunch + dinner daily
Meals served: lunch 12.30-2, dinner 7.30-9 (Fri+Sat 7.30-9.30)

£75

The cooking at this illustrious house is well known for being in the
safe hands of Chris Suter. Ingenuity is at work throughout his cooking
which is refined yet gutsy. Lamb shank with potatoes, garlic and rosemary, terrine of chicken livers wrapped in bacon and served with a
grape and kumquat chutney and warm winter salad of smoked duck
and black pudding show the depth of his imagination. He continues to
cook with consistency and maturity and his weekly chef's menu is
good value, and might comprise risotto marinara with saffron, wild
boar sausages with mashed potatoes and onion gravy followed by a
grape-flavoured crème brulée with a Granny Smith sorbet. The hotel,
complete with 32 bedrooms, is immaculate with extensive leisure facilities both inside and outside, with swimming pools, tennis courts and
fly fishing on the river Wylye.

WATERHOUSES   Old Beams

Leek Road, Waterhouses, Staffordshire ST10 3HW
Telephone: (0538) 308254 Fax: (0538) 308157
Open: lunch Tue-Fri+Sun, dinner Tue-Sat (closed Bank Holidays,
2 wks Jan)
Meals served: lunch 12-2, dinner 7-10

£70

The conservatory at the rear, with its murals, is a relaxing place in the
summer months for lunch or dinner. As you would expect from its
name this restaurant is characterised by beams, but also fresh flowers
and good quality linen and china. The menu is well balanced, suggest-
ing dishes that are minus all the frills but not missing out on the most
important point - flavour. Nigel Wallis cooks a fine selection, from
spring rolls of salmon to a breast of duck with horseradish potatoes
and a madeira sauce. Diners are well looked after by wife Ann and her
team. The 6 bedrooms are just across the road and include some 4-
posters. The whole place has a rural French feel to it and is a relaxing
place to eat and stay.

I gave Nigel Wallis a white clover, some years ago in the Guide, & I'm glad to see he's now getting the recognition he deserves in other Guides as well.

WATH-IN-NIDDERDALE   Sportsman's Arms

Wath-in-Nidderdale, Pateley Bridge, Nr Harrogate, North Yorkshire
HG3 5PP
Telephone: (0423) 711306   **£45**
Open: lunch + dinner daily (closed 25 Dec)
Meals served: lunch 12-2, dinner 7-9.30

Locally-made black pudding in a creamed apple and cider sauce, loin
of pork with ginger, prune and orange, and duck with redcurrants,
olives and oranges with a tarragon sauce sum up the imagination of
Ray Carter, who as chef and owner with wife Jane has created a popular restaurant in this former 17th-century inn. Continental overtones to
otherwise English cooking make it a place worth the visit. A reasonably priced and well selected wine list. There are 7 rooms for an
overnight stay.

WATLINGTON   Well House

34-40 High Street, Watlington, Oxfordshire OX9 5PY
Telephone: (0491) 613333   **£45**
Open: lunch Tue-Fri + Sun, dinner Tue-Sat (closed most
Bank Holidays, open 25 Dec)
Meals served: lunch 12.30-2, dinner 7-9.15 (Sat 7-9.30)

With such attentive service and unfussy English food Alan and Patricia
Crawford cannot fail to impress you in their delightful beamed restaurant with well-spaced tables. Patricia is the master of the stove and
cooks a 2- or 3-course menu which might include deep-fried cauliflower with red pepper sauce or gratin of seafood followed by lamb's
liver with apple and rosemary or stir-fried beef with ginger. It is the
type of place where you will instantly feel at home and want to visit
again, so the 11 bedrooms may well come in handy.

WELLS   Ritcher's

5 Sadler Street, Wells, Somerset BA5 2RR
Telephone: (0749) 679085   **£40**
Open: lunch + dinner daily (closed 26 Dec)
Meals served: lunch 11.30-2.30, dinner 7-9.30

The choice is yours as to whether you would like to eat steaks or
salmon with hollandaise in the relaxed atmosphere of the ground floor
bistro and bar and outside courtyard, or climb the stairs to a more formal setting with rattan chairs and crisp linen and a menu that steps up
to quail with a citrus and tarragon butter or chateaubriand.

WELLS-NEXT-THE-SEA — The Moorings

6 Freeman Street, Wells-Next-The-Sea, Norfolk NR23 1BA
Telephone: (0328) 710949   **£35**
Open: lunch Fri-Mon, dinner daily (closed 24-26 Dec, 2 wks Dec,
 2 wks Jun)
Meals served: lunch 12.30-2, dinner 7.30-9

Just off the quay is a quaint restaurant run by Carla and Bernard
Phillips. Daily set menus offer an enormous selection of dishes with a
good range of locally landed seafood, attentively cooked with just the
right amount of fennel or herbs. Cockle pie might interest you, or
Louisiana-style crabs. Good selection of wine at very affordable prices.

WEOBLEY — Jules Café

Portland Street, Weobley, Hereford & Worcester HR4 8SB
Telephone: (0544) 318206   **£40**
Open: lunch + dinner daily (closed some Mons in winter, 25 Dec)
Meals served: lunch 12-2.30, dinner 7.15-10.30

A restaurant and café bar with 3 bedrooms, this is really not a hotel but
more like a diminutive guest house with owner Juliet Whitmarsh running the show including the kitchen, which produces breakfast for
those lucky enough to be staying. The restaurant offers mainly organic
cooking with a tempting and honest menu - fresh pineapple stuffed
with prawns, deep-fried butterfly prawns with aiöli and fresh tomato,
gratin of Cornish scallops and Herefordshire pippin pie.

WEST AUCKLAND — Old Manor House

1 Front Street, The Green, West Auckland, Durham DL14 9HW
Telephone: (0388) 834834 Fax: (0388) 833566   £30
Open: lunch daily (booking essential), dinner Mon-Sat (closed 24+26 Dec)
Meals served: lunch 12-2, dinner 7-9.15
17th-century manor house with 30 bedrooms, extends northern hospitality.

WEST MERSEA — Le Champenois Restaurant

Blackwater Hotel, 20-22 Church Road, West Mersea, Essex CO5 8QH
Telephone: (0206) 383338   **£55**
Open: lunch Wed-Mon, dinner Mon-Sat (closed 3 wks Jan)
Meals served: lunch 12-2, dinner 7-10

Near the church, in the heart of the town you will find this traditional
French restaurant and small 7-bedroomed hotel. A short menu with
simple no-nonsense cooking – pâtés, snails, moules, a rack of lamb
(carved at the table) and steak au poivre.

WEYMOUTH   Perry's

4 Trinity Road, Old Harbour, Weymouth, Dorset DT4 8TJ
Telephone: (0305) 785799   £45
Open: lunch Tue-Fri + Sun, dinner daily (Mon-Sat in winter)
Meals served: lunch 12-2, dinner 7-10

Right beside the harbour you will find the Hodders' friendly restaurant. Chef Andy Pike cooks a resourceful and modern collection of
dishes - mushroom and basil lasagna, salmon and Cumbrian air-dried
ham pizza, salmon en papillote, and gruyère cheese tart. Don't forget
to sample the pear and apple crumble tart!

WHIMPLE   Woodhayes Hotel

Whimple, Nr Exeter, Devon EX5 2TD
Telephone: (0404) 822237   £55
Open: dinner daily
Meals served: dinner 7-9.30

You will be guaranteed personal attention at this small, 6-bedroomed
hotel. A charming Georgian house, it is set in its own garden,
surrounded by apple orchards and is only a short walk away from the
Devon coastline. Owners Katherine and Michael Rendle might offer,
on a typical 6-course evening menu, hot asparagus tartlet, chilled
cucumber and mint soup, fillet of red mullet with herbs and olive oil,
and roasted duck with a plum sauce followed by crème brulée and
local cheese with oatcakes and walnuts. But if there is something you
would particularly like one evening, tell them in advance and they will
do their utmost to accommodate you. Bright and welcoming is how
they like the place to stay and look, and there is no doubt that this is
how it always is.

WHITBY   Magpie Café

14 Pier Road, Whitby, North Yorkshire YO21 3PU
Telephone: (0947) 602058   £40
Open: all day daily (closed late Nov-Mar)
Meals served: 11.30-6.30

With so much fish fresh on the doorstep it will come as no surprise
that the fish dishes here are excellent. There are always at least 5 varieties which are either grilled, poached or baked in a range of dishes.
But the favourites of the house are undoubtedly deep-fried, with a slice
of bread and butter – choose from cod, haddock, woof, plaice, lemon
sole, skate, monk and halibut or even opt for a mixed platter, but you
might have to queue or share a table in high season.

WHITBY   Trenchers

New Quay Road, Whitby, North Yorkshire YO21 1DH
Telephone: (0947) 603212   £25
Open: all day daily (closed mid Nov-mid Mar)
Meals served: 11-9
No-nonsense, bright and breezy, mainly seafood restaurant (with some alternatives),
taking advantage of the fresh supplies of fish from the market.

WHITSTABLE   Whitstable Oyster Fishery Co

Royal Native Oyster Stores, Horse Bridge Beach, Whitstable,
Kent CT5 1BU
Telephone: (0227) 276856   **£40**
Open: lunch + dinner Tue-Sat
Meals served: lunch 12-2.30, dinner 7-9.30

A real fish restaurant with only fresh fish and seafood served - and not
a chip in sight! The menu is short and chalked on a board and depends
on the day's catch. This was once the store for the oyster company of
the same name and still has tidal holding tanks containing live shellfish. Otherwise it's simple in decoration with bare wooden floors. The
direct link to the producer means you couldn't be eating fresher fare
and so this place is to be strongly recommended for its basic simplicity
and unfailing quality.

WICKHAM   Old House Hotel

The Square, Wickham, Hampshire PO17 5JG
Telephone: (0329) 833049 Fax: (0329) 833672   **£35**
Open: lunch Tue-Fri, dinner Mon-Sat (closed Bank Holidays,
2 wks Xmas, 2 wks Aug)
Meals served: lunch 12.30-1.45, dinner 7.30-9.45

It's almost strange to find such a French feel within the walls of an old,
12-bedroomed house hotel that appears so English, but within this
Georgian house, listed for its architectural interest, is served a fine
French regional menu. Filet de porc à l'orange, le magret de canard
grillé à la vinaigrette chaude aux fines herbes are examples of main
courses, with soup de lentilles aux épices or a pâté de foie de volaille à
la mangue fraîche preceding. The rooms are well decorated, furnished
with period furniture and antiques. A real marriage of French and
English styles that works well.

WILLITON   White House

Williton, Nr Taunton, Somerset TA4 4QW
Telephone: (0984) 632306   **£55**
Open: dinner daily (closed Nov-May)
Meals served: dinner 7.30-8.30

It's a long drive from London to this Somerset village but once you
arrive your patience will be rewarded. Dick and Kay Smith are wonderful hosts and welcome you into their home as if you're long-time family
friends – which some long standing visitors virtually are. From the
kitchen there is a lot of good food to be tried with a wine list well worth
perusing for the interesting selection, plus the good collection of half
bottles.

WILMSLOW   Stanneylands

Stanneylands Road, Wilmslow, Cheshire SK9 4EY
Telephone: (0625) 525225 Fax: (0625) 537282   **£55**
Open: lunch daily, dinner Mon-Sat (closed 1 Jan, Good Friday)
Meals served: lunch 12.30-2, dinner 7-10

With easy access to Manchester airport, 33 bedrooms and high standards of interior and service, this has become a popular business
hotel, set in picturesque gardens. The well-decorated rooms in this
red-bricked Edwardian hotel are cosy and traditional. Steven Kitchen's
menu includes an à la carte and a gourmet set menu, with dishes such
as Swiss spätzli noodles with a ragout of wild mushrooms and garlic or
chilled aubergine and leek soufflé with provençale vegetables with
main courses of seared scallops on finely sliced aromatic vegetables,
or baked dover sole with a pickle and herb mayonnaise.

WINCHESTER   Lainston House

Sparsholt, Winchester, Hampshire SO21 2LJ
Telephone: (0962) 863588 Fax: (0962) 72672   **£75**
Open: lunch + dinner daily
Meals served: lunch 12-2.30, dinner 7-10   ❖

Fine Delft tiles, bowls of flowers and parquet flooring greet the guest
then beyond is a large homely lounge and carved cedar bar.
Surrounded by fabulous parkland, this grand William-and-Mary house
has 38 fine and luxurious bedrooms, a 12th-century chapel and a
converted barn for conference and business facilities. The standard of
decor and service make this a charming place to stay.

WINDERMERE   Holbeck Ghyll

Holbeck Lane, Windermere, Cumbria LA23 1LU
Telephone: (053 94) 32375 Fax: (053 94) 34743   **£50**
Open: dinner daily
Meals served: dinner 7-8.45

Looking over Lake Windermere, with all the comforts of a country
house hotel, you can see why Lord Lonsdale of boxing-belt fame and
original president of the AA made this his home. Oak panelling, the
scent of polish and lots of traditional country character still remain.
Attention to detail is thorough, with decanters of sherry to sip on a
chill winter's evening, carefully placed in each of the 14 bedrooms
along with fresh flowers. The menu combines old-style English dishes
with touches of new and are cooked on the Aga in traditional fashion.

WINDERMERE   Miller Howe

Rayrigg Road, Windermere, Cumbria LA23 1EY
Telephone: (053 94) 42536 Fax: (053 94) 45664
Open: dinner daily (closed early Dec-early Mar)
Meals served: dinner at 8.30 (Sat at 7, Bank Holidays at 7 + 9.30)
(light meals Conservatory: 10-11.30, 3.30-5.30 (30 seats))

£80

Drinks on the terrace or in the conservatory, and it's bring on the food, which has always been pure theatre, with the lights dimmed as the dishes emerge in procession from the kitchen. John Tovey is the mastermind and is always in evidence, but these days it is Ian Dutton who is in charge of the kitchen and he produces dishes like cream of sage and onion soup with puréed apple, toasted pine kernels and herbs; and salmon marinated in soy, orange and garlic; and roast sirloin of beef with caramelised onion marmalade and horseradish pudding. The hotel is quaint with characterful rooms that the Americans lap up. Great attention to detail and comfort doesn't spoil the homely appeal of the place. 13 bedrooms and wonderful views over Windermere and the surrounding hills.

WINDERMERE   Roger's Restaurant

4 High Street, Windermere, Cumbria LA23 1AF
Telephone: (053 94) 44954
Open: dinner Mon-Sat (closed 1 wk Xmas)
Meals served: dinner 7-9.30

£35

None of the fads and trends of recent cooking are to be found at Roger Pergl-Wilson's French restaurant. At his most brilliant when in the kitchen, it will be his wife Alena who cordially greets you and shows you to your table. Choose the set price dinner menu and relax, for it is not very often that you can enjoy such good value. You will start with canapés and then possibly move on to a hot tart of aubergine with tomato followed by a game pie in flaky pastry with fresh vegetables and finally apple and almond tart. Powerful traditional cooking.

WINDSOR   Oakley Court

Windsor Road, Water Oakley, Nr Windsor, Berkshire SL4 5UR
Telephone: (0628) 74141 Fax: (0628) 37011   **£60**
Open: lunch + dinner daily
Meals served: lunch 12.30-2, dinner 7.30-10   ❖ 🍾

You might recognise the setting - was it in *St Trinians* or *The Rocky Horror Show*? You won't be mistaken since it was featured in both, and about 200 other films from those dejected days before it was restored to its former glory and became this impressive hotel. Situated on a stretch of the River Thames, it has its own jetty for cruises up and down the river. After an afternoon spent messing about in boats, what could be better than dinner in the elegant Oak Leaf restaurant cooked by Murdo MacSween? Try a mousseline of cèpes or sauté of scallop followed by monkfish with black olive tapenade and basil, or lamb with his remarkable garlic fritters. For the more enthusiastic and younger set this turreted Victorian Gothic manor house has opened a new brasserie called Boaters with a choice from the blackboard and some set dishes.

WINKLEIGH   Pophams

Castle Street, Winkleigh, Devon EX19 8HQ
Telephone: (0837) 83767   **£30**
Open: all day Mon-Sat (closed 25 Dec, all Feb)
Meals served: 9-3

Bring your own bottle to this the tiniest of restaurants – it looks like a little corner shop, so don't walk by. There are only 2 tables and a couple of stools. Melvyn Popham creates his short blackboard menu daily with the likes of watercress soup, fish terrine with chilled hollandaise, duck with plum sauce or vegetable goulash.

WINTERINGHAM   Winteringham Fields

Winteringham, Humberside DN15 9PF   🦐
Telephone: (0724) 733096 Fax: (0724) 733898   **£70**
Open: dinner Mon-Sat (closed Bank Holidays, 2 wks Xmas, 1 wk Aug)
Meals served: dinner 7-9.30

Chef and proprietor Germain Schwab adds his touch of individuality to the old classics and creates a rousing menu for comparatively isolated area. A typical menu might include brochettes of North Sea fish with risotto, salmon with pistou and tomato sauce, turbot enclosed in savoy cabbage with foie gras, sherry and tomato and hake fillet on a pasta cake with spinach and a vermouth sauce. There are 6 bedrooms and some splendid furniture in this comfortable, 16th-century house.

WITHERSLACK — Old Vicarage

Church Road, Witherslack, Cumbria LA11 6RS
Telephone: (053 95) 52381 Fax: (053 95) 52373 **£45**
Open: dinner daily
Meals served: dinner 7.30 for 8

The advent of a small specialist selection of top quality British beers complements the patriotism and quest for quality by the Burrington-Browns and Reeves, who together run this 15-bedroomed Georgian house hotel. The cooking by Stanley Reeve is good honest English stuff with excellent roasts with all the trimmings; or a roulade of chicken and pigeon with fresh cumberland sauce; or a lakeland lamb casserole with dumplings made with rosemary from the garden. The desserts include hot ginger and rhubarb brown betty or perhaps a chocolate and chestnut roulade. The wine list is extensive, with some reasonably priced wines. The style is not casual, neither is it over-formal but you will enjoy the evening and afterwards it's about all you can do to climb the stairs and make for your room.

WIVELISCOMBE — Langley House

Langley Marsh, Wiveliscombe, Nr Taunton, Somerset TA4 2UF
Telephone: (0984) 23318 Fax: (0984) 24573 **£50**
Open: dinner daily (closed Feb)
Meals served: dinner 7.30-8.30 (Sat only at 8.30)

In a stretch of rural and unspoilt Somerset, at the foot of the Brendon Hills, you will come across Peter and Anne Wilson's Georgian house. Very much active in the everyday life of the hotel, Peter masterminds the 5-course evening menu while Anne tends to the house and 8 bedrooms. A recent dinner exemplified his cooking – chilled mangetout soufflé with tomato coulis, carrot and orange soup with coriander, grilled Brixham turbot with a crab crust followed by lamb fillet with a tartlet of onion and cassis purée. It was only the dessert course that offered a difficult choice, of which elderflower and elderberry syllabub must have been the right one. Sheer perfection.

WOBURN — Paris House

Woburn Park, Woburn, Bedfordshire MK17 9QP
Telephone: (0525) 290692 Fax: (0525) 290471 **£80**
Open: lunch Tue-Sun, dinner Tue-Sat (closed Bank Holidays)
Meals served: lunch 12-2, dinner 7-10

Up among the favourites, Peter Chandler (now in his 10th year) has a steady and loyal following. A grand entrance awaits you: a distinguished gateway takes you through to the deer park, and as you sweep up the drive towards the part-timbered house you must know from the bottom of your stomach that you also are about to dine at one of the best. Peter's cooking is a mix of robust cooking and clever saucing. Recent sampling of dishes have seen salad of pig's trotters in a ravigotte sauce followed by gigolette of lamb with a saffron sauce. Whilst Peter has valued the knowledge gained while working with the Rouxs, he continues to develop his own style of dishes in this delightful setting.

WOODSTOCK   Bear Hotel

Park Street, Woodstock, Oxfordshire OX7 1SZ
Telephone: (0993) 811511 Fax: (0993) 813380   **£55**
Open: lunch + dinner daily
Meals served: lunch 12.30-2.30 (Sun 12-2.30), dinner 7-10 (Sun 7-9.30)

Chef Ian Morgan, a recent acquisition from the Randolph Hotel in
Oxford, seems to fit his new hat well, as his menu demonstrates - slivers of goose livers between crisp layers of potato or poached king
prawns and scallops with braised rice. Main courses continue with
semi-cured grilled salmon with vegetable and caper sauce and fillet of
veal wrapped in cured ham on a bed of lentils, tomato and basil butter.
The coaching inn is full of charm and the rooms are full of antiques.

WOODSTOCK   Feathers Hotel

Market Street, Woodstock, Oxfordshire OX7 1SX
Telephone: (0993) 812291 Fax: (0993) 813158   **£60**
Open: lunch + dinner daily
Meals served: lunch 12.30-2.30, dinner 7.30-9.30 (light meals
Whinchat Bar: 12.30-10.30)

The Feathers is undoubtedly one of the best places to stay in a village
almost entirely constructed from Cotswold stone. Visitors come for the
history of the area and the quaintness of the shops and lanes. The
hotel is welcoming with polite staff and comfortable public rooms, an
upstairs drawing room and, at the rear, a flagstoned bar with log fires
in winter. The restaurant is hushed but with a bright modern approach
and a good use of vegetables - smoked salmon torte with a dill and
brandy sauce and a spinach mousse with marinated wild mushrooms.
Tuna is accompanied by scallops and Mediterranean vegetables with
crisp leeks, and beef by deep fried vegetables. Good house wines and
17 individually decorated bedrooms.

WOOLTON HILL   Hollington House

nr Newbury, Woolton Hill, Berkshire RG15 9XR
Telephone: (0635) 255100 Fax: (0635) 255075   **£55**
Open: lunch + dinner daily
Meals served: lunch 12-2.30, dinner 7-9.30

This 20-bedroomed Edwardian hotel has been carefully and lovingly
furnished by proprietors John and Penny Guy, has some delightful
reception rooms and an elegantly appointed dining room. Everything
combines to makes this an English country house hotel that looks as if
it's here to stay. As we went to press, a new chef was about to be
appointed.

WORCESTER   Brown's

24 Quay Street, Worcester, Hereford & Worcester WR1 2JJ
Telephone: (0905) 26263   **£60**
Open: lunch Sun-Fri, dinner Mon-Sat (closed Bank Holidays, 1 wk Xmas)
Meals served: lunch 12.30-1.45, dinner 7.30-9.45 (Sat 7.30-10)

The Tansleys are on to a winner with their riverside warehouse
restaurant and its fully inclusive fixed-price menus at both dinner and
lunch. Lunch is available at half the cost of dinner and includes main
courses such as char-grilled quail with risotto or tarte tartin of leeks
and onion, whereas in the evening similar honest rustic dishes appear
with roast rack of lamb with flageolet beans and rosemary and sauté of
calves' liver with avocado and sage. First courses also include lentils
but this time with confit of duck whereas crab cakes are served with a
mild curry sauce. The mouth tingles with the anticipation of the tang
of rhubarb ice cream with ginger sauce (and I am not the greatest
devoté of ice cream, but this does the trick) and rice pudding soufflé
with winter fruit compôte.

WORFIELD   Old Vicarage

Worfield, Bridgnorth, Shropshire WV15 5JZ
Telephone: (074 64) 497 Fax: (074 64) 552   **£50**
Open: lunch + dinner daily
Meals served: lunch 12-2, dinner 7-9 (Sun at 7)

Peter and Christine Iles have created a charming hotel overlooking
fields and farmland. Daily set menus combine the usual with the
adventurous and offer a good selection of New World and other wines.
Dinner could be curried parsnip and apple broth or escalope of
smoked codling topped with Welsh rarebit followed by maize-fed
guinea fowl with rioja and port glaze or baked salmon with herb and
brioche crust and a sun-dried tomato and basil sauce. Not to ignore the
vegetarians, John Williams cooks a baked yellow tomato with tapenade, a tartlet of roasted shallots and a light carrot gateau and serves
them all together. Outstanding cheese selection.

WYLAM   Laburnum House

Main Street, Wylam, Northumberland NE41 8AJ
Telephone: (0661) 852185   **£55**
Open: dinner Mon-Sat (closed Bank Holidays (open Good Friday),
 2 wks Feb)
Meals served: dinner only 6.30-9.30 (Sat 6.30-10)

This small restaurant with 4 bedrooms is situated in the main street,
opposite the Ship Inn. Originally an 18th-century house, it was also
formerly a general store and still has a shop-like façade with two box
windows either side of the door. But don't let that deter you for inside,
Kenn Elliott's straightforward country-style cooking is a treat and best
typified by loin of lamb with rosemary and lavender jelly, wild boar cutlet with garlic and herb mushrooms, and game pie with red wine and
mushrooms.

WYMONDHAM	**Number Twenty Four**

24 Middleton Street, Wymondham, Norfolk
Telephone: (0953) 607750   **£35**
Open: lunch daily, dinner Wed-Sat (closed 25+26 Dec)
Meals served: lunch 12-2.30 (Sun 12-2), dinner 7.30-9.30
(light meals 10am-3pm)

In these exacting times it is enlightening to hear of dedication reaping benefits, and for Richard and Sue Hughes this is exactly what 1993 has brought. Richard has not allowed himself to take a back seat in the 2 years the restaurant has been open and has lost no time in establishing a growing reputation for his modern and classical English cooking. But the demand from hungry customers has been so great that he has rekindled the former South Walsham Hall team and retrieved young star Nigel Crane from Oz and the Four Seasons in Alice Springs. You would have thought that after closing the deli side of the business in 1992 to give extra room for the hordes, the space would have been sufficient but it isn't, so at present they are hoping to expand into the premises next door. Sunday lunch has been added to the hours of opening and proves popular with families.

YATTENDON	**Royal Oak**

The Square, Yattendon, Nr Newbury, Berkshire RG16 0UF
Telephone: (0635) 201325 Fax: (0635) 201926   **£80**
Open: lunch + dinner daily (closed 25 Dec)
Meals served: lunch 12-2, dinner 7-10

An important change in the kitchen has brought Graham Newbould (once at Inverlochy Castle) to this village inn with rooms, just as we went to press. He'll bring a broadening of style, and his recruitment is quite a scoop. Alan Campbell stays on at front of house.

YEOVIL	**Little Barwick House**

Barwick Village, Nr Yeovil, Somerset BA22 9TD
Telephone: (0935) 23902 Fax: (0935) 20908   **£50**
Open: dinner Mon-Sat (closed 2 wks Jan)
Meals served: dinner 7-9 (Sat 7-9.30)

Very good price for winter breaks

A country retreat with 6 bedrooms and restaurant attached in a charming setting makes you relax immediately. This old listed Georgian dower house is 2 miles from Yeovil. Veronica and Christopher Colley make great hosts chatting and passing the time with you as if you were old friends. Veronica's cooking is straightforward and uses the best ingredients she can buy. Small private parties can be accommodated.

— and a charming idea of Folly Hunting! telephone & ask, I'm going to try it.

YORK   Grange Hotel

Clifton, York, North Yorkshire YO3 6AA
Telephone: (0904) 644744 Fax: (0904) 612453   **£50**
Open: lunch + dinner daily
Meals served: lunch 12.30-2.30, dinner 7-10

A super, classical Regency town house the Grange has been richly
restored to its former glory. The visitor immediately succumbs to
warmth, care and devotion, kept topped up by the young management
and friendly staff. A brasserie proves lively outside the hours of the
more formal Ivy restaurant where the accomplished hands of Cara
Baird are still creating an admirable and unpretentious collection of
dishes. Good price set lunch. Very good puddings. Open fires in winter
and some nice decorative touches.

YORK   Melton's

7 Scarcroft Road, York, North Yorkshire YO2 1ND
Telephone: (0904) 634341   **£50**
Open: lunch Tue-Sun, dinner Mon-Sat (closed 3 wks Xmas/New Year,
 1 wk Aug)
Meals served: lunch 12-2, dinner 7-10

Michael Hjort's seasonally-changing menu is what you would expect
from a scholar of the Roux brothers' stable. Formative years at Le
Poulbot and Paris House have left their touch, but don't underestimate
his own imagination, with an intriguing mix of traditional and reworked recipes – lasagna of fennel and black olives, peppered roast rib
of beef with beetroot pasta and wild mushrooms and fillet of brill with
lobster sauce. Since our last visit the restaurant has received a
warming coat of paint, relieving the deep chill of winter. You can buy
pictures by local artists off the wall. Good selection of wines by the
glass.

YORK — Middlethorpe Hall

Bishopthorpe Road, York, North Yorkshire YO2 1QB
Telephone: (0904) 641241 Fax: (0904) 620176
Open: lunch + dinner daily
Meals served: lunch 12.30-2.30, dinner 7.30-9.45

£70

The hall, with its wonderfully elegant façade, stands in 26 acres of parkland peace and quiet with York racecourse only a stone's throw away. With ha-ha, white garden, walled garden, small lake and collection of specimen trees the inherent beauty of the place is stunning. First impressions count, and on stepping into the William III house with its black-and-white tessellated floor, the sense of well-being and anticipation cannot be solely described in words. Attention to detail is apparent throughout, no more so than in the panelled dining room where Kevin Franksen's cooking shines. Distinct in composition yet soft in texture and enticement the sauces are well defined, the flavours are clean and the choice unconfined. The daily changing menu leaves enough room to move around freely, with 5 choices to each course. Recent samples are a sauté of wild mushrooms with a bone marrow sauce flavoured gently with distinctive bay, a fillet of red snapper with celeriac purée, a boudin noir ravioli with soy sauce and a breast of pigeon with a confit of walnuts, chestnuts, fennel and button onions. With the fish dishes came new potatoes while the meat enjoyed a bordelaise sauce. Creamed leeks in mustard, and glazed parsnips in herbs complete an inventive dish while the whole meal could be rounded off by a pancake, tart and ice cream all of lemon.

YORK — 19 Grape Lane

19 Grape Lane, York, North Yorkshire YO1 2HU
Telephone: (0904) 636366
Open: lunch + dinner Tue-Sat (closed 3 days Xmas, 3 days New Year, 2 wks Feb, 2 wks Sep)
Meals served: lunch 12-1.45, dinner 7.30-10.30 (Sat 7-10.30)

£50

Around the corner from York Minster and down a narrow lane is Gordon Alexander's restaurant offering contemporary English cooking, a traditional place where Michael Fraser creates light yet significant lunches supplemented by the specials of the day. Options in the evening include a good value 3-course set menu or choices from the carte. Standard dishes include gravadlax with lime dressing, duck and lentil terrine and beef wrapped in bacon and herbs with madeira sauce. The set menu offers some adventurous dishes and represents good value. Wine list with some affordable prices, including the trusty Georges Blanc house wines.

YORK   Ristorante Bari

15 The Shambles, York, North Yorkshire YO1 2LZ
Telephone: (0904) 633807   **£35**
Open: lunch + dinner daily (closed 25+26 Dec, 1 Jan)
Meals served: lunch 10.30-2.30, dinner 6-11

Set on one of the town's most picturesque streets, this is York's oldest established Italian restaurant. A favourite with locals and visitors for over 15 years it serves a selection of pasta, pizza, risottos and daily specialities.

YORK   Taylor's Tea Rooms & Coffee Shop

46 Stonegate, York, North Yorkshire YO1 2AS
Telephone: (0904) 622865 Fax: (0904) 640348   **£25**
Open: all day daily (closed 25+26 Dec, 1 Jan)
Meals served: 9-5.30

For the connoisseur, or anyone who enjoys a good cuppa, this is a must. The family business was founded in 1886, importing teas and coffees from all over the world and blending them on the premises. The selection of both is as comprehensive as many a good wine list and varies from China rose petal to special estate tippy Assam teas and speciality coffees that require descriptions like 'smooth body', 'light acidity' and 'finely balanced light taste'. A good selection of salads, sandwiches and hot dishes are available between elevenses and teatime.

Scotland Establishment Reviews

ABERDEEN   Silver Darling

Pocra Quay, North Pier, Aberdeen Grampian AB2 1DQ
Telephone: (0224) 576229 Fax: (0224) 626558   **£55**
Open: lunch Mon-Fri, dinner Mon-Sat (closed 2 wks Xmas)
Meals served: lunch 12-2, dinner 7-10

The self-styled, barbecue seafood restaurant offers far more than the
very good char-grilled salmon on the menu. Besides 3 or 4 other fish
dishes – lotte et langoustine, sea trout and turbot – you might be
offered a char-grilled marinated rib of beef. Prices for the meal are
determined by the main course. There's some good food on offer here,
served in the old customs house by the quay.

ABERFELDY   Farleyer House

Weem, Aberfeldy, Tayside PH15 2JE
Telephone: (0887) 820332 Fax: (0887) 829430   **£65**
Open: dinner daily
Meals served: dinner 7.30-8.30 (Bistro 10-2 + 6-9.30)

Richard Lyth is a new name to this kitchen and he offers a fixed 5-
course menu starting with an appetizer and then moving on perhaps to
a warm salad of duck, wood pigeon and oyster mushrooms. A fresh
flavoured cream of asparagus soup follows and then a main course of
pan-fried turbot with spinach and courgettes enhanced with tomatoes,
finishing with a dessert of macerated oranges and grapefruit with a
light orange mousse. Richard's cooking is well judged. Originally built
as a croft in the 16th-century, the white painted hotel is situated in the
grounds of the old ancient castle on the Menzies estate and offers 11
rooms.

ABERFOYLE   Braeval Old Mill

Braeval, By Aberfoyle, Central FK8 3UY
Telephone: (087 72) 711   **£55**
Open: lunch Sun, dinner Tue-Sat (closed Bank Holidays, 2 wks Nov)
Meals served: lunch 12.30-1.30, dinner 7-9.30

With standards set high by owner and chef Nick Nairn the menu has
moved away from multiple choices to a fixed-price no option menu
(except for pudding where there are 3 or 4). But that's not a bad thing
since it means Nick will cook for you what is best in the market that
day - a solid and sound practice. He always offers soup first and then
moves on to starter, main course and cheese or pudding. He leaves the
wine choice to the guest — there are some very good bottles for under
£20.

ONE OF the differences between greatness and mere eccentricity, is an ability in the truly great *to draw out the genius* in another.

So it was with some smacking of the lips that we heard of a recent tasting organized by Decanter Magazine.

Three of Scotland's *Most Lauded* malt whiskies were to be rated in terms of 'partnership appeal' with that other great Scottish contribution to world gastronomy~ *Smoked Speyside Salmon.*

And which one emerged with commendations such as 'a real corker...', 'full, strong, dry *grippy flavours*' and 'the perfect partner'?

Yes, you have *smoked it out.* ' I love it and would recommend it.'

The **MACALLAN.** *The* **MALT.**

ACHILTIBUIE   Summer Isles

Achiltibuie by Ullapool, Highland IV26 2YG
Telephone: (085 482) 282 Fax: (085 482) 251   **£65**
Open: dinner daily (closed mid Oct-Easter.)
Meals served: dinner at 8

With its relaxed atmosphere and beautiful scenery this 11- bedroomed
family hotel offers comfort in an informal, homely style, and good food.
The speciality is fish, wonderfully fresh and innovatively cooked. The
menus are changed with the seasons and may include Summer Isles
lobster with a fillet of cod roasted with a herb crust in two sauces;
steamed broccoli, with leeks and anchovy and new potatoes tossed in
Italian parsley; Summer Isles prawns - caught, landed and cooked the
same day, with hollandaise sauce; and a cheeseboard offering 15
cheeses every night (mainly Scottish). The wine list is extensive and
imaginative with a good selection of half bottles. Vegetarians will also
be catered for with advance notice.

ALYTH   Drumnacree House

St Ninians Road, Alyth, Tayside PH11 8AP
Telephone: (082 83) 2194   £40
Open: dinner Tue-Sat (closed 25+26 Dec, Jan+Feb)
Meals served: dinner 7-10
After four years in the business, Allan Cull has now proved his worth in the kitchen of
this hotel and restaurant offering a well cooked, fixed-price menu. 5 bedrooms.

ANSTRUTHER   Cellar

24 East Green, Anstruther, Fife KY10 3AA
Telephone: (0333) 310378   **£60**
Open: lunch Tue-Sat, dinner Mon-Sat
Meals served: lunch 12.30-1.30, dinner 7.30-9

A small popular place where people come to enjoy Peter Jukes' fine
quality fish dishes cooked in a straightforward manner, sensitively
with light saucing. A simple setting with only about 8 tables, so book
for lunch and dinner. Excellent wine list with a few New World wines
but more position given to France.

APPIN   Invercreran Country House Hotel

Appin, Glen Creran, Highland PA38 4BJ
Telephone: (063 173) 414 Fax: (063 173) 532   **£60**
Open: lunch + dinner daily (closed 16 Nov-28 Feb, (open 29 Dec-3 Jan))
Meals served: lunch 12-2, dinner 7-8

This family-run hotel is set in mature gardens and woodland, and overlooks Glen Creran. It's an unusual modern building (1970s) with bal-
conied terracing that houses the lounge and dining areas. The 9 bedrooms are luxurious! The food is simple and well executed and has
Mallaig-landed crab mousse on a pool of watercress sauce, pheasant
laced with brandy served with hot poppy-seed toast, and pan-fried
breast of wild wood-pigeon with a rowan and red Burgundy sauce.

ARISAIG   Arisaig House

Beasdale, Arisaig, Highland PH39 4NR
Telephone: (068 75) 622 Fax: (068 75) 626   **£80**
Open: lunch + dinner daily (closed end Oct-early Apr)
Meals served: lunch 12.30-2, dinner 7.30-8.30

The Bonnie Prince would surely have stopped here, had it been built when he passed by nearly a quarter of a millenium ago! The hotel's welcoming and cheerfully decorated, with 15 bedrooms. The grounds are carefully nurtured and offer a variety of beautiful walks. You can stroll amongst the rhododendrons, roses and azaleas to work up an appetite before dinner (well worth doing). Two choices of 4-course menus are available as well as a totally vegetarian 4-course menu, put together by head chef David Wilkinson, who has been demonstrating his culinary skills since March 1993. Alternatives include Mallaig scallops quickly fried with red wine and shallot sauce, asparagus feuilléte, or grilled tranche of west coast halibut with a sesame crust, finishing with iced Drambuie soufflé or warm lemon curd tartlet.

AUCHTERARDER   Gleneagles Hotel

Auchterarder, Tayside PH3 1NF
Telephone: (07646) 62231 Fax: (07646) 62134   **£85**
Open: lunch + dinner daily
Meals served: lunch 12.30-2.30, dinner 7.30-10

A name synonymous with hunting, shooting, fishing and of course golf, Gleneagles offers almost every sporting and leisure facility. The sports offered are linked to many top professionals. It has become virtually a monument as well as a hotel, revered by many and definitely a Scottish landmark. The rooms - dining, 236 bedrooms, bars and lounges - are grandiose yet comfortable. There is a choice of restaurants: the Conservatory where you may be served soup of watercress, lime and smoked mussels and fennel, main courses of duck with honey, lime and herb spätzli or beef with goose liver and madeira; or the Dormy Grill with its specialities of prime Aberdeen Angus beef, spit-roasted grouse or guinea fowl, grilled halibut with parsley butter or haggis with neeps and champit tatties; and finally the more formal Strathearn Restaurant, which offers an à la carte with dishes such as roast of the evening, grills of fish and meat and flambéed dishes such as scampi tails with Pernod followed by morello cherries with eau de vie and heather honey ice cream. Peter Lederer heads a dedicated and capable young team.

Farleyer House - page 368

AUCHTERHOUSE — Old Mansion House

Auchterhouse, By Dundee, Tayside DD3 0QN
Telephone: (082 626) 366 Fax: (082 626) 400   **£60**
Open: lunch + dinner daily (closed Xmas, 1 wk Jan)
Meals served: lunch 12-2, dinner 7-9.30 (Sun 7-9)

A fine example of a successful conversion from splendid baronial
house to comfortable hotel, offering 6 bedrooms and an outdoor swimming pool. Many features still remain such as the vaulted entrance and
splendid Jacobean fireplace. Sit in high-backed chairs and enjoy
smoked salmon and smoked trout mousse served with Marie Rose
sauce, collops in a pan with a rich sherry and pickled walnut sauce, or
prawn tails in a curried apple and cucumber cream sauce served with
braised rice. Desserts might include raspberry crème brulée, fresh
fruit pavlova with a strawberry coulis or a selection of cheese from the
trolley. A vegetarian menu is also available.

AYR — Fouters Bistro

2a Academy Street, Ayr, Strathclyde KA7 1HS
Telephone: (0292) 261391   **£25**
Open: lunch Tue-Sat, dinner Tue-Sun (closed 25+26 Dec, 1-3 Jan)
Meals served: lunch 12-2, dinner 6.30-10.30 (Sun 7-10).

Be sure not to miss the narrow doorway along this little cobbled lane –
Fouters is worth a visit. Down the stairs the walls are attractively decorated with flower stencils and the menu is equally tempting, pricewise.
You may opt for the house pâté of chicken livers and cognac, or the
'Taste of Scotland Platter' including smoked salmon, smoked venison,
pâté, shrimps, smoked chicken and gravlax. Save room for the main
courses of steaks or scallops with tarragon, and of course desserts:
cloutie dumpling – a traditionally-made, rich fruit dumpling served hot
with double cream.

AYR — The Stables

Queen's Court, 41 Sandgate, Ayr, Strathclyde KA7 1BD
Telephone: (0292) 283704   **£40**
Open: all day daily (closed 25+26 Dec, 1+2 Jan)
Meals served: 10-5 (Sun 1-5)

Part of the Stables Coffee House at night transforms into a thriving
restaurant with owner Edward Bairns adding to the entertainment.
The menu makes good reading for the history you will glean from it.
Have you ever wondered what haggis really was? Why pies are always
featured in nursery rhymes? Try ham and haddie pie, the Real McCoy
(an 18th-century recipe of beef, mussels and pickled walnuts) and
cranachan. Steaks are cut from only the best local Scottish beef with
the natural fat left in place to give flavour, so if you are watching those
saturated fats tell Ed when ordering!

BALLATER   Balgonie Country House

Braemar Place, Ballater, Grampian AB35 5RQ
Telephone: (033 97) 55482 Fax: (033 97) 55482   **£60**
Open: lunch + dinner daily
Meals served: lunch 12.30-2, dinner 7-9

An Edwardian 9-bedroomed hotel with sprawling lawns, Balgonie offers very good Scottish cuisine using the best local produce. Fresh salmon from the River Dee is accompanied by a chive mayonnaise, local venison medallions come garnished with a chestnut croquette, poached pears and redcurrants finished with a port wine game jus, and Aberdeen Angus beef is presented on a duo of white onion cream and rich madeira sauces. A good selection of local cheeses and good wines complement the seasonal menu. John and Cilla Finnie work hard to make your stay an enjoyable one.

BALLATER   Craigendarroch Hotel

Braemar Road, Ballater, Aberdeenshire AB3 5XA
Telephone: (033 97) 55858 Fax: (033 97) 55447   **£40**
Open: lunch + dinner daily (closed 5-10 Jan)
Meals served: lunch 12.30-2.30, dinner 7.30-10 (Sun 7.30-9.30)

Craigendarroch offers comfort and has 50 bright, modern bedrooms and excellent facilities for children including a crèche. It also has its own country club, which offers an all-weather tennis court, a 55-ft lagoon and a fun pool for children, squash courts and beauty salon. Two restaurants are open, the Café Jardin for lighter fare, or the Oaks Restaurant for more sophisticated tastes. The latter features game terrine with an orange and grapefruit salad finished with a yoghurt and Arran mustard sauce, cullen skink (a delicate fish soup with flakes of smoked haddock) or a mille feuille of mushrooms in a white wine sauce, edged with seasonal leaves.

BALLATER   Tullich Lodge

Ballater, Grampian AB35 5SB
Telephone: (03397) 55406 Fax: (03397) 55397   **£50**
Open: lunch + dinner daily (closed Dec-Mar)
Meals served: lunch at 1, dinner 7.30-8.30

This rather imposing pink granite, baronial mansion, complete with turret and towers and 10 handsomely furnished bedrooms, overlooks the River Dee. The dining room is oak panelled with furnishings in keeping with the historic feel of the place. The menu, which is fixed and presented on a handwritten card, is cooked by Neil Bannister and provides good value 4-course meals with a Scottish and seasonal note. Perhaps try marinated salmon in lime juice served with guacamole, then mushroom soup, followed by grilled spring lamb cutlets served with spinach, ratatouille and potatoes. Scottish cheeses will almost certainly follow, or lemon and raspberry tart. This is certainly a hotel of real character.

BANCHORY	Invery House

Bridge of Feugh, Banchory, Grampian AB31 3NJ
Telephone: (033 02) 4782 Fax: (033 02) 4712 £75
Open: lunch + dinner daily
Meals served: lunch 12.30-2.15, dinner 7.30-10 (Sun 7.30-9)
Georgian mansion set on west bank of river Feugh. Croquet lawn, walled garden and 14 bedrooms. Good country cooking.

BANCHORY Raemoir House

Raemoir, Banchory, Grampian AB31 4ED
Telephone: (033 02) 4884 Fax: (033 02) 2171 **£55**
Open: lunch Sun + dinner daily (closed 1 week in Jan)
Meals served: lunch 12.30-2, dinner 7.30-9

Sixteen miles south-west of Aberdeen, this 18th century mansion is set in a beautiful area renowned for its scenery, castles and hill-walking. The hotel offers 28 bedrooms, with good views and self-catering apartments. Tapestried walls and traditional log fires feature in public rooms. The restaurant offers an extensive menu, simple rather than elaborate, featuring creamed Arbroath smokies, game pâté, deep-fried Camembert cheese with cranberry sauce for starters; main courses like roast haunch of venison, pan-fried medallions of beef with a rich burgundy jus, or poached Dee salmon served with a lemon and dill reduction followed by a tempting and adventurous sweet selection: tuile basket filled with fruits of the forest, resting on a coulis of summer fruits, chocolate teardrop filled with a raspberry cream, a timbale of lemon soufflé and cheeseboard. Vegetarians will not be disappointed as their menu is equally extensive.

BEARSDEN Fifty Five BC

128 Drymen Road, Bearsden, Glasgow, Strathclyde G61 3RB
Telephone: 041-942 7272 Fax: 041-942 9650 **£50**
Open: lunch + dinner daily
Meals served: lunch 12-2.30, dinner 7-11

All change! This was the October Restaurant. However, with new owner Hamish McLean comes a new style of smart designer bar and small restaurant. Char-grilled red spiced chicken, their own special-recipe burger and spare ribs, Oban mussels, a warm scallop and potato salad with pine nuts and walnut dressing, or roast Yorkshire pudding with chicken, field mushrooms and a light onion gravy. A separate children's menu includes corn on the cob and cheese and bean toastie.

BLAIRGOWRIE — Kinloch House

Kinloch, by Blairgowrie, Tayside PH10 6SG
Telephone: (0250) 884237 Fax: (0250) 884333   **£50**
Open: lunch + dinner daily (closed 2 wks Dec)
Meals served: lunch 12.30-2, dinner 7-9.15

This ivy-clad hotel, built in 1840, extended in 1911 and in the same
ownership of David and Sarah Shentall since 1981, is a fine example of
a Scottish country house, with an oak-panelled hall, first floor galleries
and 21 bedrooms. It is set in 25 acres of parkland with plenty of
grazing Highland cattle to add to the atmosphere. The dining room
brings Scottish produce to the fore with Highland salmon, best beef,
game, fish and shellfish but assembled with an international flavour on
a fixed-price menu which might include marinated herring, chick pea,
spring onion and avocado salad, Arbroath scampi with Pernod butter
or breast of pigeon cooked in red wine with strips of bacon, mushroom
and sultanas. A quenelle of rainbow trout or a sorbet gives a respite
between courses. Good, fairly priced wine list.

CAIRNDOW — Loch Fyne Oyster Bar

Clachan Farm, Cairndow, Strathclyde PA26 8BH
Telephone: (049 96) 264 Fax: (049 96) 234   **£35**
Open: all day daily
Meals served: 9-9

As the name suggests the speciality is seafood, so stop for a plate of
fresh oysters or splash out on the platter of fresh oysters, crab, mussels, langoustines and queen scallops (£10.95) and a well-matched
glass of wine or champagne, and look out at the spectacular views over
the Loch. All the items on the menu are of local origin, the oysters
from their own fishery and the fish from the Loch Fyne smokehouse.
There's no set menu, or any particular dishes for starters or main
courses so mix and match to suit your appetite and budget. A simply
furnished dining room, service by pleasant local ladies and the smokehouse is just next door. Well worth a visit.

CANONBIE — Riverside Inn

Canonbie, Dumfries & Galloway DG14 0UX
Telephone: (038 73) 71512   **£45**
Open: lunch Mon-Sat, dinner daily (closed 2 days Xmas,
2 days New Year, 2 wks Nov, 2 wks Feb)
Meals served: lunch 12-2, dinner 7.30-8.30

Well situated for those special Northern sights - Hadrian's Wall, the
Northern Lakes and the Solway Coast - it's well worth stopping off
here to take in the view over the River Esk and enjoy this colourful,
welcoming inn. It's also an excuse to sample some of the traditional
country cooking.

CASTLE DOUGLAS — Collin House

Auchencairn, Castle Douglas, Fife DG7 1QN
Telephone: (055 664) 292 Fax: (055 665) 292   **£55**
Open: dinner daily (closed 8 Jan-10 Mar)
Meals served: dinner 7.30-8.30

A small hotel, pink washed with 6 en-suite bedrooms, set within 20 acres of grounds with superb views across Achencairn Bay. The 5-course menu, made up of seasonal game and seafood, changes daily to make the most of fresh local produce. A typical menu may include spicy parsnip or carrot, apple and ginger soups, medallions of wild roe deer with pink and green peppercorn sauce, escalope of sea bass with red butter and shallot sauce, poached pears with chocolate mousse and ginger cream or avocado ice cream with a strawberry coulis. The wine list includes some rare and unusual wines.

COLBOST — Three Chimneys Restaurant

Colbost, By Dunvegan, Isle of Skye, Highland IV55 8ZT
Telephone: (047 081) 258   **£65**
Open: lunch + dinner Mon-Sat, + Sun before Bank Holidays
(closed Nov-Easter)
Meals served: lunch 12-2, dinner 7-9

The emphasis here is on the Isle of Skye's fine seafood and the fishing boats bring it fresh to the doorstep every day, at Eddie and Shirley Spear's converted crofting cottages. Expect to see a platter of warm shellfish with garlic and lemon butter, a flummery of smoked salmon with white port and strawberries and jumbo prawns with a herb and lemon mayonnaise. Halibut comes roasted with a hot leek and hazelnut sauce and scallop and monkfish brochette with a warm citrus vinaigrette.

CONTIN — Coul House Hotel

Contin, by Strathpeffer, Highland 1V14 9EY
Telephone: (0997) 421487 Fax: (0997) 421945   **£50**
Open: lunch + dinner daily
Meals served: lunch 12-2, dinner 7-9

Formerly a stately home, this country house hotel offers both relaxation and a range of activities. The menu successfully combines wholesome Scottish fare and Continental cuisines, but it's the 'Taste of Scotland' menu that really provides food for thought: home-made game pâté or Summer Isles beer-cured smoked ham with fresh melon slices for starters, and as a main course, fillet steak Balmoral flamed in malt whisky and finished with cream or sirloin steak Rob Roy filled with haggis and served with pan juices, followed by a Scottish maiden's kiss(!) - ice cream with toasted oatmeal, honey and Drambuie. This 21-bedroomed hotel also caters for the conference market.

CRINAN   Crinan Hotel

Crinan, by Lochgilphead, Strathclyde PA31 8SR
Telephone: (054 683) 261 Fax: (054 683) 292
Lock 16 Restaurant: **£75**
Open: Tue-Sat dinner (closed Oct-Mar)
Meals served: dinner at 8
Westward Room: **£60**
Open: dinner daily (closed 3 days Xmas)
Meals served: dinner 7-9

On the canal connecting Loch Fyne with the Atlantic stands the Ryans' hotel with every room enjoying at least a glimpse of the water. The decoration is attributed to Frances MacDonald, the local well known artist (actually Mrs Ryan) with varnished pine bedrooms, some with balconies. The top floor is the Lock 16 seafood restaurant - menu decisions wait until the local boats return at 4pm, so that chef/patron Nick Ryan has the best possible choice - it couldn't be fresher than that! The menu is set and will depend on the day's catch but could include split fresh Sound of Jura lobster or Loch Fyne princess clams on the half shell and jumbo prawns or mussels marinières. Nick oversees this and the Westward restaurant, where dining is more formal.

CUMBERNAULD   Westerwood Hotel

St Andrew's Drive, Westerwood, Cumbernauld, Strathclyde G68 OEW
Telephone: (0236) 457171 Fax: (0236) 738478   **£40**
Open: lunch Mon-Fri, dinner Mon-Sat
Meals served: lunch 12-2.30, dinner 7-9.45

A relatively new hotel and country club, the Westerwood's claim to fame is that their 18-hole golf course was designed by Severiano Ballesteros. The rest of the hotel is also run by experts in their own field. More informal food is served in the Clubhouse but for dinner the Old Masters Restaurant is the place to go! In the kitchen, chef Tom Robertson produces skilled, sophisticated dishes including, as a sample starter, a chilled roulade of lemon sole enhanced with saffron and centred with langoustine presented on a fennel and sweet pepper vinaigrette. Intermediate courses of crayfish bisque or light watercress and lime soup finished with cream and toasted almonds are follwed by breast of Gressingham duck accompanied with a mille feuille of the braised leg served on a rich blackcurrant sauce, or Scottish venison accompanied by a delicate Arran mustard cream, presented on a liquorice and juniper perfumed sauce.

CUPAR   Ostlers Close

25 Bonnygate, Cupar, Fife KY15 4BU
Telephone: (0334) 55574   **£55**
Open: lunch + dinner Tue-Sat (closed 25+26 Dec, 1+2 Jan, 1 wk Jun)
Meals served: lunch 12.15-2, dinner 7-9.30 (Sat 7-10)

Jimmy Graham can be found foraging in the surrounding forests for
mushrooms to add to his pot. An unassuming restaurant situated in a
side alley belies the skill and judgement of this chef who grows his
own salads and herbs and uses organic produce whenever possible.
His menu is handwritten and short but each dish is inviting, from
starters such as seafood soup or lobster ravioli to main courses like
roe venison served with woodland mushrooms or a gamekeepers bag -
a selection of roast local game, served with a game sauce.

DALGUISE   Kinnaird

Kinnaird Estate, Dalguise, By Dunkeld, Tayside PH8 0LB
Telephone: (0796) 482440 Fax: (0796) 482289   **£75**
Open: lunch + dinner daily (closed Feb)
Meals served: lunch 12.30-1.45, dinner 7.15-9.30

This expensively furnished and decorated 18th-century country house
surrounded by a vast estate and a wonderful view of the Tay, is the
pride and joy of Constance Ward, upon which she has lavished a great
sense of style. Antiques, flower arrangements and 9 wonderfully styled
bedrooms with their own fires for winter make this a grand family
home. John Webber continues as chef with careful, gentle cooking of
dishes like cassoulet of salt water fish, lobster and monkfish terrine,
breast of wood pigeon with an essence of wild mushrooms and
smoked bacon, and noisettes of local lamb with onion and coriander
tartlet. Puddings continue to demonstrate his expertise, as in sugar-
glazed orange mousseline set in a buttered syrup of oranges and
Grand Marnier, or a hot banana and Galliano soufflé. Service in a
stylish dining room is by young, smiling staff.

DRUMNADROCHIT   Polmaily House

Drumnadrochit, Highland IV3 6XT
Telephone: (0456) 450343   £55
Open: dinner daily
Meals served: dinner 7.30-9.30
18 acres of unspoilt grounds and 9 bedrooms. Cooking is based on local ingredients.

DRYBRIDGE — Old Monastery Restaurant

Drybridge, Buckie, Grampian AB56 2JB
Telephone: (0542) 32660 **£60**
Open: lunch + dinner Tue-Sat (closed Bank Holidays, 3 wks
Jan, 2 wks Nov)
Meals served: lunch 12-1.45, dinner 7-9.30 (Sat 7-10)

For those of you old enough to remember, listen out for Ronnie
Ronalde as you walk through the gardens! This former monastery has
some spectacular views of the sea and the Grampian mountains
beyond. It's family run: Maureen Gray heads the front of house while
Douglas, in the kitchen, combines French and Scottish cuisine. The
menu may feature fish from the Spey and seasonal game, smoked venison waldorf - thin slices of smoked venison garnished with a salad of
walnuts, celery and apples. Popular choices include scampi and
salmon thermidor and pan-fried Aberdeen Angus sirloin steak.
Candlelight softens the restaurant at night, while Maureen and her
team out front make you feel welcome.

DRYBURGH — Dryburgh Abbey

St Boswells, Dryburgh, Borders TD6 0RQ
Telephone: (0835) 22261 Fax: (0835) 23945 £50
Open: lunch + dinner daily
Meals served: lunch 12.30-2.15, dinner 7.30-9.15
Set on the Tweed, alongside Dryburgh's abbey ruins, this Edwardian sandstone
house offers good shooting and fishing, and 3- and 4-course dinner menus.

DULNAIN BRIDGE — Auchendean Lodge

Dulnain Bridge, Grantown-on-Sprey, Highland PH26 3LU
Telephone: (047 985) 347 **£55**
Open: dinner daily (closed 2 wks Nov)
Meals served: dinner 7.30-9

This is a 7-bedroomed hotel for all seasons, with spectacular views. A
range of activities is available at this converted hunting and fishing
lodge, including canoeing, fishing, skiing, shooting and hiking. The
less energetic, however, will find comfort inside. The menu reflects
chef Eric Hart's hobby – mycology. Over 20 varieties of wild mushroom are on offer in various guises such as cep and mushroom soufflé,
spicy steak pieces in oatmeal with mushroom cream, or baked
haddock with chanterelle cream. Guests are also invited on fungal for-
ays in the Autumn. Desserts include crème brulée and pavlova with
kiwi fruit. (New Zealand owner Ian Kirk's choice perhaps?) The wine
list also reflects the owner's origins, with a good selection of New
World wines.

DULNAIN BRIDGE   Muckrach Lodge

Dulnain Bridge, Nr Grantown-on-Spey PH26 3LY
Telephone: (047 985) 257 Fax: (047 985) 325   **£50**
Open: lunch + dinner daily (closed Nov)
Meals served: lunch 12-2, dinner 7.30-9

A 19th-century hunting lodge set in 10 acres in the Dulnain Valley, this
is the place to come to if you enjoy outdoor activities. All 10 bedrooms
in the main house and 2 suites in the annex are individually furnished.
Captain Roy Watson and wife Pat do not stint on Highland hospitality,
while dinner is a 5-course affair with home-cured herrings, wild Spey
salmon, haggis 'n' neeps and medallions of Aberdeen Angus beef with
a spicy tomato sauce, served in the conservatory-style restaurant.

DUNBLANE   Cromlix House

Kinbuck, Dunblane, Central FK15 9JT
Telephone: (0786) 822125 Fax: (0786) 825450   **£70**
Open: lunch + dinner daily (closed mid Jan-end Feb)
Meals served: lunch 12.30-1.30, dinner 7-9

Leave the hustle and bustle of town life behind and enjoy the many
pleasures and wonderful fresh air at this 14-bedroomed country house
hotel. For complete exclusivity some of the rooms have private sitting
rooms; and on Sundays there's a service in an 1874 chapel. Chef
Stephen Robertson came with the new owners David and Ailsa Assenti
at the beginning of the year and has created a fine fixed-price menu
with a few choices - broccoli and courgette soup, terrine of salmon
with tomato and pimento dressing followed by pan-fried duck with
pear and shallot or lemon sole with asparagus and prawns. Puddings
require no cream, as the hot apple and rhubarb pie comes with
lashings of good home-made custard.

DUNDONNELL   Dundonnell Hotel

Dundonnel, By Garve, Highland IV23 2QR
Telephone: (085 483) 204 Fax: (085 483) 366   **£45**
Open: dinner daily (closed Dec-Xmas, New Year-Easter)
Meals served: dinner 7-8.30

A family owned and run 24-bedroomed hotel. The restaurant is the
heart of the hotel and chef Mark Sage takes advantage of local
produce - salmon, seafood and Scotch beef feature strongly on the set
and à la carte menus. Try the home-made leek and potato soup
followed by roast leg of Highland lamb, or baked cod topped with a
cheese and prawn glaze, and for dessert passion fruit ice cream or
chocolate hazelnut meringue are typical choices.

DUNOON   Chatters

58 John Street, Dunoon, Strathclyde PA23 8BJ
Telephone: (0369) 6402   **£55**
Open: lunch + dinner Mon-Sat (closed Jan)
Meals served: lunch 10-4, dinner 6-10

A terrine of guinea fowl and rabbit on a tomato and basil coulis or a hot roulade of red pepper and wild mushrooms with a Stilton and spinach sauce are some of the well cooked starters you might find at Rosemary MacInnes' small restaurant that specialises in good home cooking. The menu changes every month but you might sample lamb chartreuse - cooked in its own juice with a timbale of cream and parsley - or salmon with tiger prawns and spiced pear and blackberries, or medallions of venison with pickled walnuts and claret. Between lunch and dinner they are open for coffee and afternoon tea.

EDINBURGH   Alp-Horn

167 Rose Street, Edinburgh, Lothian EH1 4LS
Telephone: 031-225 4787   **£45**
Open: lunch + dinner Mon-Sat (closed 25+26 Dec, 1st week Jan)
Meals served: lunch 12-2, dinner 6.30-10

A good restaurant to visit if you feel like a little escapism. Inside this Swiss restaurant, the Alpine scenes and cowbells lend an authentic air, as does the menu featuring fondues, rösti and apfel strudel. The wine list also includes Swiss wines, which, although more expensive than others on the list, are worth a try.

EDINBURGH   The Atrium

Saltire Court, 10 Cambridge Street, Edinburgh, Lothian
Telephone: 031-228 8882   **£50**
Open: lunch Mon-Fri, dinner Mon-Sat (closed 2 wks Xmas)
Meals served: lunch 12-3, dinner 6-10.30

Andrew Radford returns to the kitchen but this time under his own roof. The chef from the acclaimed Waterloo Place has started his own restaurant with the team he assembled last time round. With distressed textured walls in an ochre tone and dark, wood floor, the image is modern and arty and this is also reflected in the style of cooking. Choices include wood pigeon with lentils and leek and olive oil mash, roast loin of venison with lentils and roast cod with garlic and asparagus. Dessert could be a baked apple with chantilly cream or tart of summer fruit with fruit caramel.

EDINBURGH   L'Auberge

56 St Mary Street, Edinburgh, Lothian EH1 1SX   *very good*
Telephone: 031-556 5888   *food to* **£40**
Open: lunch + dinner daily (closed 25+26 Dec, 1st 2 wks Jan) *had*
Meals served: lunch 12.15-2 dinner 6.30-9.30 (Sat 6.30-10) *be here.*

A winning Anglo-French combination with French chef Fabrice
Bresculier and owner/manager Daniel Wencker producing what it
takes. The menu's written in French and simply explained. Entrées
could include a panaché of rillettes, mousse and gravadlax - marinated
salmon with a sour-cream and hints of vodka, or sauté of snails and
mushrooms à la provençale parcelled in ravioli with a delicate garlic
and white wine cream sauce. Main courses or `les plats de résistance'
are mostly meat, usually with a vegetarian choice and a fish dish, but
save room for some real French desserts – les crêpes suzettes, crème
brulée and the house speciality, la tarte aux poires Bourdaloue – and
cheese.

EDINBURGH   The Balmoral

Princes Street, Edinburgh, Lothian EH2 2EQ
Telephone: 031-556 2414 Fax: 031-557 3747
Grill No. 1:   £75
Open: lunch Mon-Fri, dinner daily
Meals served: lunch 12-2, dinner 7-10.30
Bridges Brasserie: £35
Open: all day daily
Meals served: 7am-11pm

One of the great railway hotels of its time, the Balmoral has been
restored to full glamour. A kilted doorman will greet you and luxury
awaits inside, where `ornate, glittering and plush' sums up the scene,
all in keeping with the niceties of yesteryear but underneath it all bang
up-to-date, with even a TV in the sauna! The cooking at the renamed
Grill No. 1 is in the hands of Ralph Porciani who remains patriotic, a
thistle symbol on the menu highlighting the best of local produce –
compote of Western Isles seafood set in a vegetable nage or a baked
torte of Crathie pigeon filled with spinach and woodland mushrooms
and a loganberry vinaigrette. Main courses include soufflé of Western
Isle scallops wrapped in lemon sole and Angus beef with Arran mustard and soft herb crust. Bridges Brasserie is an informal continental-
style restaurant for guests and non-residents. Take lunch or a bite to
eat in the evening with fish and chips, cullen skink, bang-bang chicken
and minute steak on sour dough from an all-day menu that moves
through breakfast, club sandwiches, to lunchtime light snacks, then
cakes and pastries at around 3.30. Good place to stop before boarding
the train at Waverley station, or for meeting those getting off.

EDINBURGH   Caledonian Hotel

Princes Street, Edinburgh, Lothian EH1 2AB
Telephone: 031-225 2433 Fax: 031-225 6632
The Pompadour Room: **£70**
Open: lunch Mon-Fri, dinner daily (except Sun Nov-Mar)
Meals served: lunch 12.30-2, dinner 7.30-10.30
Carriages Restaurant: **£45**
Open: lunch + dinner daily
Meals served: lunch 12.30-2.30, dinner 6.30-10

One of the top hotels in Edinburgh both for the accommodation and
the food. Of the two restaurants, the Pompadour Room offers elegance
and formality in contrast to the less formal and homely atmosphere of
Carriages Restaurant. Chef Tony Binks pulls out all the stops out when
serving Scottish specialities, haggis, neeps 'n' tatties, or marinated
venison fillet with a salad of artichoke and raspberry vinaigrette, and
turns his hand well to modern French cooking in the evenings. Good
French and Scottish cheeses, and an admirable list of half bottles on a
well selected wine list. The 240 bedrooms make the Caledonian a destination for tourists from all over the world, and whilst it's in the grand
hotel tradition, the staff and management work hard to offer Scottish
hospitality at its best.

EDINBURGH   Channings Hotel

South Learmouth Gardens, Edinburgh, Lothian EH4 1EZ
Telephone: 031-315 2226 Fax: 031-332 9631   £70
Open: lunch + dinner daily
Meals served: lunch 12.30-2, dinner 6.30-9.30
Popular business and tourist hotel, 48 bedrooms and a brasserie style restaurant.

EDINBURGH   Denzlers 121

121 Constitution Street, Leith, Edinburgh, Lothian EH6 7AE
Telephone: 031-554 3268   **£45**
Open: lunch Tue-Fri, dinner Tue-Sat (closed Bank Holidays,
1st wk Jan, 2 wks Jul)
Meals served: lunch 12-2, dinner 6.30-10

For Swiss cuisine in the heart of Leith visit this restaurant, which was
once a bank and is entered via an imposing pillared doorway. Inside it
is welcoming and not at all foreboding. Sister restaurant to the
Alp-Horn, Denzlers offers a selection of bundnerplatti (wafer-thin
slices of air-dried Swiss beef and ham), salmon tossed in oatmeal and
served with mild horseradish, guinea fowl with a sweet and sour honey
sauce with spätzle and choice of fondues. And of course don't forget
the apple strüdel or coupe nesselrode – a fresh chestnut purée piped
over vanilla ice cream and meringue, topped with cream.

EDINBURGH	Howard Hotel

36 Great King Street, Edinburgh, Lothian EH3 6QH
Telephone: 031-557 3500 Fax: 031-557 6515   **£55**
Open: lunch Sun-Fri, dinner daily
Meals served: lunch 12-2.30, dinner 7.30-9.30

Gillian Thompson took over this elegant Georgian city house at the
end of last year and is adamant that the standard of service is to be
first class and the atmosphere warm. The menu is competently cooked
by Gordon Inglis, with wild pigeon marinated in claret and served on a
crouton as just a taster! Main courses unfold with fillet of veal with
Lanark blue sauce, venison with a burgundy and thyme jus and fillet of
turbot with scallop mousse wrapped in spinach. The Howard is small
and intimate with a memorable style in its 16 well-thought-out and
designed bedrooms and relaxing lounges.

EDINBURGH	Kelly's

46 West Richmond Street, Edinburgh, Lothian EH8 9DZ
Telephone: 031-668 3847   **£55**
Open: dinner Tue-Sat (closed 1st week Jan, 1st 3 wks Oct)
Meals served: dinner 6.45-9.45

Named after the owners (Jeff and Jacquie) this restaurant, once a bak-
ers shop, is set in a Georgian block. The restaurant is small and simple
in style, the cooking modern British and the menu full of temptation:
turbot parcel with seafood mousse and a leek and lemon timbale with a
dill beurre blanc and the more meaty galantine of duck with
Cumberland sauce; lemon tart with crème anglaise to finish.

EDINBURGH	Le Marché Noir

2/4 Eyre Place, Edinburgh, Lothian EH3 5EP
Telephone: 031-558 1608   **£40**
:Open: lunch Mon-Sat, dinner daily (closed 25+26 Dec, 1+2 Jan)
Meals served: lunch 12.30-2.30, dinner 7-10 (Fri+Sat 7-10.30, Sun 6.30-9.30)

A popular restaurant and an inspiring menu, occasionally exchanged
for regional food and wine evenings on Thursdays and Sundays. The
menu has French overtones, although the best local produce features
strongly. Peppered smoked mackerel salad with pink peppercorns and
lavender, black pudding in a red wine and garlic sauce, breast of
guinea fowl with garlic and hazelnuts and baked breast of chicken with
squid noodles and a tomato coulis are among the specialities, followed
by simple desserts. The wine list is extensive and includes a few
surprises and some reasonable prices.

EDINBURGH   Martin's

70 Rose Street, North Lane, Edinburgh, Lothian EH2 3DX   ✿
Telephone: 031-225 3106   **£60**
Open: lunch Tue-Fri, dinner Tue-Sat (closed 4 wks Dec/Jan,
1 wk Oct)
Meals served: lunch 12-2, dinner 7-10

Down a cobbled back lane there is a surprise in store for anyone who
doesn't know the whereabouts of one of the city's best restaurants.
Martin and Gay Irons give a heart-felt welcome to a simple room
jazzed up with flowers. It is for the characterful cooking of Forbes
Scott that you come here, and he rarely fails to please with menus that
might include grilled rabbit served with red cabbage, sea bream with
watercress and mint, boned quail stuffed with wild rice, peppers and
apricots and sautéed langoustine with lentils and chilies. A smashing
place that celebrates its 10th birthday this year. Reasonably priced
wines and cheerful service.

EDINBURGH   Round Table

31 Jeffrey Street, Edinburgh, Lothian EH1 1DR
Telephone: (031) 557 3032   **£30**
Open: all day Mon-Sat (closed some Bank Holidays, 25+26 Dec, 1+2 Jan)
Meals served: 10-10

This is a bistro-style Scottish restaurant with a limited, but no less
interesting, menu that's reasonably priced especially for a quick snack,
light lunch or a non-extravagant dinner. Auld Reekies fowl, a supreme
of chicken with spinach in a malt whisky cream sauce and gigot lamb
steak sautéed in butter with Drambuie liqueur and mint head the meat
main courses. But there are also 3 or 4 vegetarian dishes and 3 or 4
fish dishes that offer lighter and less alcoholic options!

EDINBURGH   The Shore

3/4 The Shore, Leith, Edinburgh, Lothian EH6 6QW
Telephone: 031-553 5080   **£40**
Open: lunch + dinner daily
Meals served: lunch 12-2.30 (Sun 12.30-2.30), dinner 6.30-10
(light meals 11am-midnight)

As the name suggests, The Shore lies on the Leith waterfront, approximately a mile from the city centre. With such positioning it's only apt
that they specialise in fish. A small selection of alternative dishes are
available, but to resist mussels with saffron and garlic, pan-fried cod's
roe with lime dressing, or roast monkfish with garlic, anchovy and
avocado sauce may prove too much for some.

EDINBURGH — Vintners Room

The Vaults, 87 Giles Street, Leith, Edinburgh, Lothian EH6 6BZ
Telephone: 031-554 6767 £55
Open: lunch + dinner Mon-Sat (closed 2 wks Xmas)
Meals served: lunch 12-2.30, dinner 7-10.30

It's rather a novel experience to dine in the old sale rooms of the Vintners' Guild, with its ornate plasterwork and burning candles that light the way to a wonderful menu. Tim Cumming's cooking is gutsy, some dishes are obviously Mediterranean-influenced and all are well cooked. Start, perhaps, with a fish soup à la provençale, or an asparagus cheese tartlet, then move to steamed halibut with sweet pepper sauces, or rare roast entrecôte with red wine, shallot and herb sauce. Don't forget the puds which include apple and calvados soufflé, hot pear and almond tart or a brandy snap basket with brown bread ice cream. Comprehensive wine list with some reasonable prices.

The wine bar & old sale room (candle-lit) are delightful & full of atmosphere - good food & wine in this historic setting.

ERISKA — Isle of Eriska

Eriska, Ledaig, By Oban, Strathclyde PA37 1SD
Telephone: (063 172) 371 Fax: (063 172) 531 £80
Open: dinner daily (closed Nov-Mar)
Meals served: dinner 8-9

This is a very special place to visit, especially if you really want to get away from it all. The island is virtually a nature reserve and you can walk in this unspoilt countryside for hours without meeting another person, or choose from the many activities on offer here such as tennis, riding and windsurfing. The house was built towards the end of the Scottish Baronial period but depite its grand exterior and oak panelled interior, it's warm and comfortable. Mrs Buchanan-Smith cooks up a feast of 5 courses served in the Edwardian dining room. This may consist of deep-fried brie with a spicy tomato sauce, fillet of plaice with chive butter, or a real roast - beef perhaps with Yorkshire pudding, horseradish sauce and gravy - desserts from the trolley and a fine selection of Scottish cheeses.

A Buchanan-Smith quote
'a sanctuary for seabirds, seals & humans

FORT WILLIAM Crannog Seafood Restaurant

Town Pier, Fort William, Highland PS33 7NG
Telephone: (0397) 705589 **£40**
Open: lunch + dinner daily
Meals served: lunch 12-2.30, dinner 6-10.30

A quayside restaurant, once a ticket office and bait store, specialising
in fish. The langoustines are a speciality, caught from the restaurant's
own fishing boats. In the smokehouse attached to the restaurant, they
also smoke salmon, trout and mussels. With that in mind you might
choose langoustines with mayonnaise or smoked mussels and aioli to
start, followed by the Crannog selection of trout, mackerel,
langoustines, squat lobster, herring and haddock with a garlic mayonnaise dip. A simple setting for some good fresh fish.

FORT WILLIAM The Factor's House

Torlundy, Fort William, Highland PH33 6SN
Telephone: (0397) 705767 Fax: (0397) 702953 **£45**
Open: dinner Tue-Sun (closed mid Nov-mid Mar)
Meals served: dinner 7-9

Part of the Inverlochy estate, this was once the estate manager's
house. Nestling at the bottom of Ben Nevis it offers 7 bedrooms and
good warm Scottish hospitality. Take to the loch in the hotel's sailing
boat Diggity, go fishing or pony trekking, or take a walk through the
unspoilt countryside.

FORT WILLIAM Inverlochy Castle

Torlundy, Fort William, Highland PH33 6SN
Telephone: (0397) 702177/8 Fax: (0397) 702953 **£90**
Open: lunch + dinner daily (closed Dec-Feb)
Meals served: lunch 12.30-1.45, dinner 7.15-9.30

Built by Lord Abinger in 1863 this is a very grand, Victorian house,
rather than a drafty castle, surrounded by the foothills of Ben Nevis
and an abundance of blazing rhododendrons in summer. Secluded and
beautiful with frescoed ceiling it even inspired Queen Victoria, who
wrote in her diaries 'I have never seen a lovelier or more romantic
spot.' Michael Leonard manages his staff in a way that ensures the
place is run with precision without being obsequious – highly polished
and genuine. Comfort and endless antiques fill the rooms and in the
two dining rooms Simon Haigh creates a civilised menu appropriate
for such impressive surroundings. No gimmickry here but well-balanced fine cooking which loses nothing in translation from the menu
to the plate - salad of roasted scallops with olive oil dressing, ballotine
of foie gras with a sauternes jelly and French bean salad, or a lobster
bisque and then braised fillet of turbot with shiitake mushrooms and
leeks or roast loin of roe deer with pear and walnuts. Afterwards, relax
over cheese with oat biscuits or sample a hot chocolate tart with
orange sauce, or raspberry crème brulée. 16 suites, all styled in the
grand country house manner.

GAIRLOCH	Creag Mor

Charleston, Gairloch, Highland, IV21 2AH
Telephone: (0445) 2068 Fax: (0445) 2044   £85
Open: dinner daily
Meals served: dinner 6.30-10
All year round hospitality; 17 bedrooms and 100 whiskies on offer. Marvellous views.

GLAMIS   Castleton House

Glamis, By Forfar, Angus, Tayside DD8 1SJ
Telephone: (0307) 840340 Fax: (0307) 840506   **£50**
Open: lunch + dinner daily
Meals served: lunch 12-2.30, dinner 7-9.30 (Conservatory: 8am-10pm)

Surrounded by moors and mountains, this 6-bedroomed hotel makes a
good base from which to travel. Good friendly service accompany a
menu on which salmon and game vie strongly for position alongside
game terrine, wood pigeon with pine kernels, wild salmon in a 'hot
cushion' with salad niçoise, seafood risotto and West Coast mussels
with garlic. The best Angus beef comes simply unadorned and juicy.

GLASGOW   Brasserie on West Regent Street

176 West Regent Street, Glasgow, Strathclyde G2 8HF
Telephone: 041-248 3801   **£45**
Open: all day Mon-Fri, Sat lunch + dinner only (closed Bank Holidays)
Meals served: 12-11, (Sat lunch 12-3, dinner 6-12)

Apart from the tartan carpet, the flavour is French in this Scottish
brasserie. The food is simply prepared and features grilled sardines
with black butter, lentil soup, oysters, baked salmon in filo pastry, and
steak tartare with french fries or rack of lamb with ginger jus. There
are also the 'something lighter' and 'post-theatre' menus offering wild
mushrooms in pastry, goujons of sole or beef stroganoff. Friendly,
white-aproned staff.

GLASGOW   Buttery

652 Argyle Street, Glasgow, Strathclyde G3 8UF
Telephone: 041-221 8188 Fax: 041-204 4639   **£70**
Open: lunch Mon-Fri, dinner Mon-Sat (closed Bank Holidays)
Meals served: lunch 12-2.30, dinner 7-10.30

A real treasure trove, from the objets d'art that decorate this old converted pub to the beautifully handwritten menus. Options of equally
well-cooked dishes include pasta in a wild mushroom and thyme
sauce, shallow-fried mignons of venison with julienne of leek on a
yellow split pea jus, fillets of lemon sole on an apple, pear and raisin
pancake with a light lemon sauce. And some masterpiece desserts —
crème brulée with a mixed-nut praline glaze, and the Buttery Grand
Dessert. It's worth seeking out this restaurant, where you will almost
certainly be well looked after and made to feel welcome – forget the
setting, with its urban Glasgow landscape of bridges and tower blocks,
and step back in time.

GLASGOW   D'Arcy's

Basement Courtyard, Princes Square, Glasgow, Strathclyde G1 3JN
Telephone: 041-226 4309   £25
Open: all day daily (closed 25+26 Dec, 1+2 Jan)
Meals served: 9.30am-12 midnight (Sun 11-6)
Fixed-price, good value dinner in the back room - from brasserie-style langoustines in
garlic butter through to steaks.

GLASGOW   Glasgow Hilton

1 William Street, Glasgow, Strathclyde G3 8HT
Telephone: 041-204 5555 Fax: 041-204 5004   **£80**
Open: lunch Mon-Fri, dinner daily
Meals served: lunch 12-2.30, dinner 7-11

While the 320 bedrooms might be standard Hilton, the ground floor is
given over to a wide open atrium, fitted with a modern bar that leads
through to the American deli-style Minsky's. The dining room,
Camerons, with its tartan chairs and plush fittings, quite makes you
forget you are in a modern hotel, with service and atmosphere more
like that of a country house. Ferrier Richardson is at the stove and his
own style comes into play in dishes with a Scottish flavour - Loch Fyne
oysters and langoustines, mussels or supreme of salmon, grilled
Angus steaks or roast saddle of venison. After dinner, it's into the
colonial-style Raffles Bar for a nightcap.

GLASGOW   One Devonshire Gardens

1 Devonshire Gardens, Glasgow, Strathclyde G12 0UX

Telephone: 041-339 2001 Fax: 041-337 1663   **£80**

Open: lunch Sun-Fri, dinner daily

Meals served: lunch 12.30-2, dinner 7-10

Knock at the door and they will welcome you in, such is the homely atmosphere of this stylish town house (in fact 3 knocked into one) that its reputation has carried far. Each of the 27 rooms are individually designed in deep colours and sumptuous fabric. The drawing rooms complete with sofas that you sink into have hushed lighting and restful colours and are an experience of style and comfort. Ladies in pinafores serve a menu that changes each evening, and might include escabèche of red mullet in a saffron marinade with warm langoustine, or wild salmon in coriander and sweet pepper vinaigrette followed by corn-fed chicken with mushroom galette or a turbot with a crab and brioche crust with compote of spinach and fennel. This place is an experience and one not to be missed. It rates in my top 10, worldwide, of small intimate hotels.

GLASGOW   Ristorante Caprese

217 Buchanan Street, Glasgow, Strathclyde G1 2JZ

Telephone: 041-332 3070   £45

Open: lunch Mon-Fri, dinner Mon-Sat (closed Bank Holidays)

Meals served: lunch 12-2.30, dinner 5.30-11

An inexpensive old-style Italian restaurant, situated in a basement, with bustling service and traditional Italian food. Still remains a favourite with locals and visitors alike.

GLASGOW   Rogano

11 Exchange Place, Glasgow, Strathclyde G1 3AN

Telephone: 041-248 4055   **£75**

Open: lunch Mon-Sat + dinner daily (closed Bank Holidays)

Meals served: lunch 12-2.30, dinner 6.30-10.30 (Sun 7-10.30)

(café 12-11, Fri+Sat 12-12)

A cornucopia of Art Deco for 1930s' fans, this ground-floor restaurant and basement café has remained virtually unchanged since 1935. Fish features strongly, continuing the ocean-liner theme indicated by the decor - a wonderful place with wonderful food. Dishes include clam chowder, smoked mackerel mousse with warm toast, herrings in oatmeal with mustard sauce, grilled swordfish with lime mayonnaise, although there are also some meat and some totally vegetarian dishes.

This deserves a visit for its amazing decor, food & service.

GLASGOW Two Fat Ladies

88 Dumbarton Road, Glasgow, Strathclyde G11 6NX
Telephone: 041-339 1944 £50
Open: dinner Tue-Sat (closed 2 wks Xmas/New Year)
Meals served: dinner 6.30-10.30
Restaurant specialising in fresh fish and vegetables.

GLASGOW Ubiquitous Chip

12 Ashton Lane, Glasgow, Strathclyde G12 8SJ
Telephone: 041-334 5007 **£50**
Open: lunch + dinner daily (closed 25 Dec, 31 Dec-2 Jan)
Meals served: lunch 12.30-2.30, dinner 5.30-11

It's been called a legend in its own lunchtime and is affectionately referred to by Glaswegians as The Chip. Ronnie Clydesdale decided 20-odd years ago to open a restaurant with an allegiance to traditional Scottish cooking and since you couldn't eat any where at the time without chips appearing, the name seemed only fitting. A warehouse conversion, on different levels, it bustles at lunchtime and resounds at night. The menu incorporates fine Scottish ingredients in a contemporary fashion, such as fillets of Ayr landed cod on a bed of clapshot with roasted and chillied red peppers to Perthshire wood pigeon with a wild mushroom and game sauce included among some more traditional dishes. Comprehensive wine list, covering most countries and price ranges.

GLENELG Glenelg Inn

Glenelg, by Kyle of Lochalsh, Highland IV40 8AG
Telephone: (059 982) 273 **£40**
Open: all day daily (closed Nov-Easter)
Meals served: 8.30-9

For those of you who wish to explore the sea lochs and unspoilt beaches, this 6-bedroomed inn should be your resting point. Owned and run by Christopher Main it is genial, friendly and hospitable, with a self-styled 'home-from-home' atmosphere overlooking the Glenelg Bay and Isle of Skye. Wholesome, traditional fare makes up the set menu for dinner, with seafood always a speciality. Try monkfish topped with baby scallops and finished with a fresh orange, ginger and pepper sauce or entrecôte with Dijon mustard, horseradish and mushroom sauce.

GULLANE — Greywalls Hotel

Muirfield, Gullane, Lothian EH31 2EG
Telephone: (0620) 842144 Fax: (0620) 842241   £75
Open: lunch + dinner daily (closed Nov-Mar)
Meals served: lunch 12.30-2, dinner 7.30-9.30

A fine house and an example of Lutyens' architecture, appropriately placed for some, next to the Muirfield golf course. From a menu that begins with a potted history of the house's past characters you will be ready for a quick choice when you get to the dishes themselves, helped already by Paul Baron's condensed set menu. The visual reward is in the presentation of your choice, whether it be casserole of seafood poached in the oven with a light puff pastry case and herb sauce or loin of venison with beetroot purée with juniper sauce. Desserts may include a pressed terrine of chilled fruits with strawberry sauce, and a tangy lemon tart. *Note — the gardens are by Gertrude Jekyll.*

GULLANE — La Potinière

Main Street, Gullane, Lothian EH31 2AA
Telephone: (0620) 843214   £65
Open: lunch Sun-Tue + Thu, dinner Thu-Sat (closed 25+25 Dec,
1+2 Jan, 1 wk June, 1 wk Oct)
Meals served: lunch at 1, dinner at 8

Bowls of flowers and sweet scent welcome the diner to this delightful restaurant, brilliantly run by an acclaimed husband and wife team. Hilary will be in the kitchen perfecting her French-inspired cooking, which is light and well presented, while David Brown is in the dining room and will talk you through the menu. Listen to his sound advice on wine for he is an expert with an outstanding cellar - with some good affordable bottles too! Hilary is a perfectionist and never ceases to amaze, with her cooking improving year on year – surely the margin must be well narrowed by now! Book plenty of time ahead, as this 30-seater restaurant is very busy and quite rightly so.

INGLISTON   Norton House

Ingliston, Nr Edinburgh, Lothian EH28 8LX
Telephone: 031-333 1275 Fax: 031-333 5305   £60
Open: lunch Sun-Fri, dinner daily
Meals served: lunch 12-2, dinner 7-9.30
Scottish hospitality on the outskirts of Edinburgh. Fine rooms and conservatory-style
dining with 46 bedrooms.

INVERNESS   Culloden House

Culloden, Inverness, Highlands IV1 2NZ
Telephone: (0463) 790461 Fax: (0463) 792181   **£70**
Open: lunch + dinner daily
Meals served: lunch 12.30-2, dinner 7-9

This grand and distinctive Adam-style Georgian house is constantly
cared for by the McKenzies and in 1993 they had their work cut out,
with bathrooms and some of the suites to redesign and decorate. In
the kitchen, everything remains calm and Michael Simpson's cooking
persists strongly with the best of Scottish beef, game, fish and lamb
put to good use. Try venison coated in a honey and red wine sauce
with wild mushrooms, or duck stuffed with orange and raisins and
served with a juniper sauce. Good wine list with some reasonable
prices. There are 23 individually designed and decorated bedrooms,
including some non-smoking suites in the Garden Mansion.

INVERNESS   Dunain Park

Inverness, Highlands IV3 6NJ
Telephone: (0463) 230512 Fax: (0463) 224532   **£50**
Open: dinner daily (closed 2 wks Feb)
Meals served: dinner 7-9

Lunch is available by arrangement, otherwise Ann Nicoll spends that
time tending to the house and guests with husband Edward. Her cooking is proudly Scottish using seasonal and local produce, but you will
see hints of French influence in the saucing - game terrine with
chutney vinaigrette, saddle of venison cooked pink and rolled in oatmeal, and whole boned pigeon stuffed with prunes, apple and pecans
with a brandy and apple sauce. Set in its own grounds and surrounded
by woodlands, this Georgian country house offers comfort in its 14
bedrooms and suites.

KENTALLEN OF APPIN — Ardsheal House

Kentallen of Appin, Highland PA38 4BX
Telephone: (063 174) 227 Fax: (063 174) 342   **£75**
Open: lunch + dinner daily (closed 3 wks Jan)
Meals served: lunch 12-2, dinner at 8.15

A private drive will take you a mile along the edge of Loch Linnhe and mass-planted rhododendrons, holly trees and ancient sycamores. A tranquil place, the house is big on location with the Morvern mountains ending behind the house and the Loch at the front. Owners Robert and Jane Taylor keep a good house and with George Kelso cooking, dinner is country-house style with a carrot and swede soup between the courses which could start with fillet of john dory with spaghetti of cucumber, going on to venison with onion marmalade and a pear and spring onion salad to refresh. The Taylors are surrounded by fresh produce from the Loch and local farms, and whenever possible, these items appear on the menu.

A friendly, homely house where you made to feel welcome.

KILCHRENAN — Ardanaiseig

Kilchrenan, By Taynuilt, Strathclyde PA35 1JG
Telephone: (08663) 333 Fax: (08663) 222   **£70**
Open: lunch + dinner daily (closed Nov-Easter)
Meals served: lunch 12.30-2, dinner 7.30-9

James and Julia Smith have recently taken on this baronial-style mansion with azalea-filled woodland on the edge of Loch Awe. Mark Taylor has been with the house for a couple of years but has only just inherited the chef's hat and meets his challenge with a 5-course dinner which might include roast pheasant with bread sauce and game chips, or monkfish tails with a mussel stew.

KILCHRENAN — Taychreggan Hotel

Kilchrenan, By Taynuilt, Strathclyde PA35 1HQ
Telephone: (086 63) 211 Fax: (086 63) 244   **£55**
Open: lunch + dinner daily
Meals served: lunch 12.30-2 dinner 7.30-9

A change of ownership at Taychreggan during 1993 has brought a central heating system, refurbishment of some of the lounges, with similar plans for the bedrooms. One thing they wouldn't wish to change though, is the splendid view across Loch Awe. Head chef Hugh Cocker offers a 5-course set menu that changes each day, and draws on the best of local ingredients to receive his individual treatment, which pays homage to France and the Med.

KILDRUMMY — Kildrummy Castle

Kildrummy, Alford, Grampian AB3 8RA
Telephone: (097 55) 71288 Fax: (097 55) 71345   **£55**
Open: lunch + dinner daily (closed 3 wks Jan)
Meals served: lunch 12.30-1.45 (Sun 12.30-1.15), dinner 7-9

This is a actually a grand, 17-bedroomed, country house hotel which overlooks the ruins of the 13th-century castle. From elegant public rooms to the charm of the sloping ceilings in some of the attic bedrooms, this is a place of impressive beauty which has undergone a couple of years' extensive refurbishment by long-time owner Thomas Hanna. Choose dinner from the 4-course set menu with feuillété of lamb with a mint and wild rowanberry sauce or pan-fried venison with grape and herb sauce, served by young and helpful staff. Many sporting pursuits on offer and the area is a golfer's paradise.

KILFINAN — Kilfinan Hotel

Kilfinan, By Tighnabruaich, Strathclyde PA21 2AP
Telephone: (070 082) 201 Fax: (070 082) 205   **£45**
Open: dinner daily
Meals served: dinner 7.30-9.30

Set next to the ancient church of Saint Finan this 11-bedroomed, old white coaching inn attracts clients that take to the great outdoors for deer-stalking, fishing and shooting. The candle-lit restaurant offers well-cooked dishes of salmon, venison, pheasant and the best Scottish beef, and in winter is warmed by a real log fire.

KILLIECRANKIE — Killiecrankie Hotel

Killiecrankie, By Pitlochry, Tayside PH16 5LG
Telephone: (0796) 473220 Fax: (0796) 472451   **£50**
Open: lunch + dinner daily (closed Jan+Feb)
Meals served: lunch 12.30-2, dinner 6.30-9.30

Set in 4 acres of wooded grounds this former dower house overlooks the River Garry. Red squirrel and roe deer are to be found in the surrounding countryside which makes it a favourite spot for nature lovers. The house has a cosy atmosphere with a small panelled bar.

KILMORE — Glenfeochan House

Kilmore, Oban, Strathclyde PA34 4QR
Telephone: (063 177) 273 Fax: (063 177) 624   **£70**
Open: dinner daily (closed Nov-early Mar)
Meals served: dinner at 8

This house lies at the head of Loch Feochan, 5 miles south of Oban. Lots of relaxing pursuits on offer, whether it be a wander around the beautifully kept gardens, fishing during the season, or birdwatching. The interior has been tastefully restored with beautiful fabrics and family antiques, while in your room you will find fresh flowers and bowls of fruit. Patricia Baber, who taught at the Cordon Bleu in London, cooks up delicious dinners each night mainly with food from the estate. Sea trout served fresh or smoked traditionally on the premises is a speciality.

KILMUN   Fern Grove

Kilmun, Argyll, Strathclyde PA23 88B
Telephone: (036 984) 334 Fax:(036 984) 424   **£40**
Open: dinner daily
Meals served: dinner 7.30-9.30

Overlooking the Holy Loch is this restaurant with 2 rooms, run by Ian
and Elizabeth Murray. The cooking is cordon bleu-style, and includes
a semi-set menu with leek and potato soup, smoked trout pâté with oat
cakes and main courses of lamb with mint and orange butter or
smoked haddock with salmon and trout under puff pastry.

KINCLAVEN   Ballathie House

Kinclaven by Stanley, Tayside PH1 4QN
Telephone: (0250) 883268 Fax: (0250) 883396   **£55**
Open: lunch + dinner daily (closed 2 wks Feb)
Meals served: lunch 12-2, dinner 7-9

There's a new team here, Christopher Longden heading the front of
house while Kevin MacGillivray tends to the stove. The menu is set
and offers a relaxing evening while each course is laid before you –
charcuterie with marinated peppers with basil and olive oil, leek and
mussel soup with chives, roast venison with glazed apples and root
ginger sauce and a choice between apple pie or cheese. Choose one of
the 27 bedrooms with a view of the River Tay from this turreted, baronial-style house, set in its own gently sloping grounds and woodlands.

KINGUSSIE   The Cross

Tweed Mill Brae, Ardbroilach Road, Kingussie, Highland PH21 1TC 🏵
Telephone: (0540) 661166 Fax: (0540) 661080   **£60**
Open: lunch Thu-Mon, dinner Wed-Mon (closed Dec-Feb)
Meals served: lunch 12.30-2, dinner 7-9

A moveable feast: the restaurant moved lock, stock and barrel to this
renovated tweed mill, a superb setting for Ruth Hadley's gutsy yet
refined cooking. White-painted rough walls and beamed ceiling
enhance the true character of the building while pristine tablecloths
and fine table settings making an appropriate setting for Ruth's fixed-
price menus (at the weekend they become gastronomic in length).
The cooking and choice of wines remain perfectly in tune, with dishes
that range from sausage of teal, venison and pigeon with red cabbage,
a mushroom flan of wild and cultivated mushrooms with a parsley and
tomato vinaigrette, to guineafowl with rosemary and crème fraîche and
Shetland salmon highlighted with pesto. Dessert is typified by chocolate whisky laird or strawberry and hazelnut shortbread. A very good
wine list offers a comprehensive range at reasonable prices. The
Cross, with its 9 individually-styled bedrooms, is now situated in its
own grounds complete with mill-stream.

KIRKNEWTON   Dalmahoy Hotel, Golf and Country Club

Kirknewtown, Lothian EH27 8EB
Telephone: 031-333 1845 Fax: 031-335 3203   **£50**
Open: lunch Sun-Fri, dinner daily
Meals served: lunch 12-2, dinner 7-10

For the golf and leisure connoisseur, this is a dream come true; surrounded by 2 golf courses, with a leisure centre and pool, the 115-bedroomed hotel is what you'd expect from a country house hotel. Armchair golfers will also be pleased to hear that the restaurant over-looks the 2 courses. In fact, there are 2 restaurants (they obviously don't do things by halves here) - the Pentland Restaurant and the Terrace Restaurant. The first, being the more formal of the two, serves tradition-al Scottish fare: cullen skink, terrine of Highland game, fillet of trout in oatmeal with a Drambuie and chive sauce and desserts from the trolley.

LINLITHGOW   Champany Inn

Champany, Linlithgow, Lothian EH49 7LU
Telephone: (050 683) 4532   *Good food & wine* ✽   **£65**
Open: lunch Mon-Fri, dinner Mon-Sat (closed 1 wk Xmas). *with an*
Meals served: lunch 12.30-2, dinner 7-10   *enthusiastic welcome.*

With a reputation as great as an Aberdeen bull, this restaurant devotes the majority of its menu to the best prime angus beef (vegetarians be warned) but seafood specialities are also available. Rib, sirloin on the bone, rib-eye, T-bone and porterhouse can all be cut to order and are weighed and charged (by the ounce) before being charcoal grilled and served with a choice of accompaniments. Clive and Anne Davidson buy beef that is hung on the bone for a minimum of 3 weeks - undoubt-edly some of the best quality available, delicious and juicy. Other spe-cialities include carpetbagger fillet, chateaubriand, or a variety of steaks with sauces. The wine cellar is just as impressive and deserves a good read.

LINLITHGOW   Champany Chop & Ale House

Champany, Linlithgow, Lothian EH49 7LU
Telephone: (050 683) 4532   **£40**
Open: lunch + dinner daily (closed 2 wks Xmas)
Meals served: lunch 12-2.30 (Sat 12-2.15, Sun 12.30-2.30), dinner 6.30-10

A scaled-down version of the Champany Inn, with the same outstand-ing beef but in smaller portions. Beef, sausages and burgers draw the greatest attention.

MARKINCH   Balbirnie House Hotel

Balbirnie Park, Markinch, Glenrothes, Fife KY7 6NE
Telephone: (0592) 610066 Fax: (0592) 610529   **£45**
Open: lunch + dinner daily
Meals served: lunch 12-2, dinner 7.30-9.30 (Sat 7-10)

A grand, classical 18th-century house, Balbirnie has grace and grandeur with a long gallery, elegant and cosy drawing room and library. Nicholas Russell has joined as manager after a stint at the Savoy and Bibendum and, together with long standing chef George McKay, is strengthening the team. The dining room has undergone a change with the re-styling of the menu. Some busy months are obviously ahead.

MARYCULTER   Maryculter House

South Deeside Road, Maryculter, Grampian AB1 OBB
Telephone: (0224) 732124 Fax: (0224) 733510   **£55**
Open: lunch daily, dinner Mon-Sat
Meals served: lunch 12-2, dinner 7-9.30

Traditional hospitality is enjoyed at this house on the banks of the Dee which provides a wide range of sporting activities, obviously including some inspiring angling. The cooking here is unmistakably country-style with plenty of game and seafood appearing on the set menu – pheasant baked with bacon, saddle of lamb with black pudding and a woodland mushroom sauce, platter of seafood and prawns and a dish of oysters cooked with creamy parsley sauce.

MAYBOLE   Ladyburn

Maybole, Strathclyde KA19 7SG
Telephone: (065 54) 585 Fax: (065 54) 580   **£50**
Open: dinner Mon-Sat (closed few wks Jan/Feb)
Meals served: dinner 7.30-8.45

Family memorabilia and fresh flowers grace the rooms and make this 8-bedroomed house a pleasant place to stay. Dinner cooked by Jane Hepburn is a simple home-cooked affair with the benefit of plenty of fresh produce from their own garden and meat and free-range eggs purchased locally. Expect an unfussy menu with the likes of fresh melon with cassis or ginger wine or pears with tarragon sauce, followed by roast beef or pork chop with mushrooms and sherry sauce, and plenty of fresh vegetables.

MELROSE   Burts Hotel

Market Square, Melrose, Borders TD6 9PN
Telephone: (089 682) 2285 Fax: (089 682) 2870   £50
Open: lunch + dinner daily (closed Dec 26)
Meals served: lunch 12-2, dinner 7-9.30 (Sun 7-9)
This 21 bedroom hotel is right on the side of the market square.

MOFFAT — Well View Hotel

Ballplay Road, Moffat, Dumfries & Gallway DG10 9JU
Telephone: (0683) 20184 **£50**
Open: lunch Sun-Fri, dinner daily (closed 1st wk Jan, 1 wk Nov) 26 Dec)
Meals served: lunch 12.15-1.15, dinner 6.30-8.30

This is a small, 6-bedroomed hotel, with pretty gardens and relaxing ambience. The husband and wife team works well, for while Janet Schuckardt cooks, John (who has been elected to the Academy of Wine Service) recommends wines to match the food. The menu includes venison turnovers with a little salad and apple relish, l'escargot with warm toast, pan-fried fillet of turbot with scallops and a dill sauce with cheese and desserts to follow.

MUIR-OF-ORD — Dower House

Highfield, Muir-of-Ord, Highland IV6 7XN
Telephone & Fax: (0463) 870090 **£60**
Open: dinner daily (closed Xmas, 2 wks Feb, 1 wk Oct)
Meals served: dinner 7.30-8.30

More of a private house than a hotel, this is the home of Robyn and Mena Aitchison. Robyn is responsible for the kitchen and offers a set menu of strong country cooking, maybe including warm marinated quail salad or skate with black butter and toasted hazelnuts, a mussel soup and then roast grouse with a heather honey sauce and apple and calvados crêpes to finish. The wine list is small with some well-priced French and New World bottles.

NAIRN — Clifton Hotel

Viewfield Street, Nairn, Highland IV12 4HW
Telephone: (0667) 53119 Fax: (0667) 52836 **£50**
Open: dinner daily (closed Nov-Mar)
Meals served: dinner 7-9.30

Home of the present owner for about 60 years, it's no wonder this 12-bedroomed hotel has built up such a reputation and more than a handful of regulars. J Gordon Macintyre has filled the house with antiques and objets d'art while at the same time creating a relaxing, theatrical atmosphere. Classical music can be heard – a nice finishing touch. Although the menu's in French, the owner enjoys taking you through it and translating, if necessary, such delights as melon aux fraises et au gingembre, langoustines et coquilles en phyllo, carré d'agneau à la touraine and sole meunière. Allez, vite!

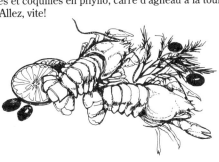

NEWTOWNMORE — Ard-na-Coille Hotel

Viewfield Street, Nairn, Highland IV12 4HW
Telephone: (0540) 673214 Fax: (0540) 673453   **£55**
Open: dinner daily (closed, 1 wk Apr, 1 wk Sep, 6 wks Nov/Dec)
Meals served: dinner 7.45

Translated from the Gaelic, this literally means 'high in the woods' and
that's where you'll find it – nestled amongst the pine trees, with views of
the Cairngorm Mountains and the Spey Valley. Most of the hotel bedrooms face south, and each is tastefully and individually furnished. The
restaurant menu makes the most of local produce, beautifully prepared.
A typical menu would be fresh Loch Linnhe scallops, lightly spiced,
char-grilled and garnished with salad, asparagus and lemongrass soup,
breast of wild duck with madeira sauce, cheeseboard and delicious
desserts.

NORTH BERWICK — Harding's Restaurant

2 Station Road, North Berwick, Lothian EH39 4AU
Telephone: (0620) 4737   **£45**
Open: lunch + dinner Wed-Sat (closed 4 wks Jan/Feb, 1 wk Oct)
Meals served: lunch 12-2, dinner 7-9

Memorable for its extensive Australian wine list, only one page of French
wines competing with 15 of Australians! So maybe it's more a case of
choosing a meal to go with the wine rather than the other way round. The
selection includes cream of tomato and carrot soup with chives, smoked
salmon served on a crisp salad with lemon yoghurt dressing, medallions of
roast duck breast with a red wine (presumably from down under) and
shallot sauce, a fine selection of British, Irish and French cheeses and
desserts.

NORTH MIDDLETON   Borthwick Castle

North Middleton, Gorebridge, Lothian EH23 4QY
Telephone: (0875) 20514 Fax: (0875) 21702 £65   *Romantic, real castle!*
Open: dinner daily
Meals served: dinner 7-9

Stay just outside Edinburgh in one of 10 bedrooms in this 15th-century building, rich
in history. Traditional Scottish cooking by chef Martin Russell, served in the candle-lit
Great Hall.

OBAN   Knipoch Hotel

by Oban, Strathclyde PA34 4QT
Telephone: (085 26) 251 Fax: (085 26) 249   **£65**
Open: dinner daily (closed mid Nov-mid Feb)
Meals served: dinner 7.30-9

This hotel, owned and run by the Craig family and enjoying a waterside setting, offers 3- or 4-course dinner menus, sympathetically
cooked by Jenny and Colin. A modest menu such as Highland potato
soup served with home-made bread followed by poached Loch Creran
salmon with a light hollandaise, then by crèpes with an orange caramel
and Cointreau is simple and allows the flavour of the ingredients to
come through, using only the best of ingredients and their own garden
produce.

ONICH — Allt-nan-Ros Hotel

Onich, by Fort William, Highland PH33 6RY
Telephone: (085 53)250/210 Fax: (085 53) 462   **£40**
Open: lunch + dinner daily (closed mid Nov-mid Dec)
Meals served: lunch 12.30-2, dinner 7-8.30

Grilled cod with mangoes in a ginger, orange and spring onion sauce, pan-fried sirloin with tomato and grain mustard and leg of lamb filled with onion and a sage stuffing in a rosemary sauce jostle for position on a typical evening fixed-price menu offering 3 choices at each course. Desserts could include hot flambéed strawberries and pineapple in a Tia Maria sauce, or chocolate mousse with Grand Marnier - the third option is cheese with fruit and oat cakes. It appears that chef Stewart Robertson has settled in comfortably at this 16-bedroomed family-run hotel situated between Glencoe and Ben Nevis.

PEAT INN — Peat Inn

Peat Inn, By Cupar, Fife KY15 5LH
Telephone: (033 484) 206 Fax: (033 484) 530   **£65**
Open: lunch + dinner Tue-Sat
Meals served: lunch at 1, dinner 7-9.30

It's the chicken-and-egg syndrome - which came first, the village or the inn? Whichever it was, the cooking and hospitality at David and Patricia Wilson's inn have certainly helped put this small village on the map. The Auld Alliance comes to the fore - the best available produce is served in the dining room as a mixture of Scotland and provincial France. The menu might include such favourites as their fish soup, best spring lamb, lobster and pigeon breast in a beef broth with pulses. Puddings continue to demonstrate the excellence of the kitchen with a trio of caramel desserts or a small but exceedingly rich pot of chocolate, flavoured with rosemary. The wine list includes something for most people's palates and has some very fair prices. The 8 bedroom suites are luxuriously designed in French style, again with some Scottish touches.

PEEBLES — Cringletie House

Peebles, Borders EH45 8PL
Telephone: (0721) 730233 Fax: (0721) 730244   **£55**
Open: lunch + dinner daily (closed 2nd wk Jan-1st wk Mar)
Meals served: lunch 1-1.45, dinner 7.30-8.30

Redecorating the drawing room and opening a new all-weather tennis court has kept the Maguire family busy over the last year, and lightened the feel of the place. A mid 19th-century baronial mansion with 13 bedrooms, it is well served by Aileen's good wholesome cooking, using fruit and vegetables fresh from the garden.

PERTH   Number Thirty Three

33 George Street, Perth, Tayside PH1 5LA
Telephone: (0738) 33771   **£45**
Open: lunch + dinner Tue-Sat (closed 10 days Xmas/New Year)
Meals served: lunch 12.30-2.30, dinner 6.30-9.30

The Billingshursts' seafood restaurant is the place to head in Perth.
For theatre goers or those in a hurry, there is the oyster bar with
lighter choices of whitebait or platters of seafood, whereas the restaurant is a more formal affair, offering a selection of fresh fish grilled,
poached and baked, with various accompaniments or just left plain.

PORT APPIN   Airds Hotel

Port Appin, Appin, Strathclyde PA38 4DF
Telephone: (063 173) 236 Fax: (063 173) 535   **£75**
Open: lunch + dinner daily (closed early Jan-early Mar)
Meals served: lunch 12.30-1.30, dinner 8-8.30

Upgrading the bedrooms is an ongoing task and one that is not taken
lightly. No less rewarding is the attention and care taken in the restaurant, where Betty Allen has a set menu which offers an inspiring and
unfussy selection at each course. To start, choose lightly-cooked oysters with smoked salmon served with a champagne jelly, followed by a
warm cream of tomato and basil soup. Main course could be roe deer
with a potato cake or halibut on a bed of honeyed aubergines. If available try the poached pear shortcake with caramel and lime sauce. All
the tables enjoy a view of the loch.

PORTPATRICK   Knockinaam Lodge

Portpatrick, Nr Stranraer, Dumfries & Galloway DG9 9AD
Telephone: (077 681) 471 Fax: (077 681) 435   **£65**
Open: dinner daily (closed Jan-mid Mar)
Meals served: dinner 7.30-9

So secluded is this location that Churchill used the house for a secret
rendezvous with Eisenhower during the war. Surrounded on 3 sides
by cliffs, with stunning views out across the Irish Sea, the dramatic
scenery makes it a unique place for a hotel. With the house safely in
the hands of Marcel and Corinna Frichot, it is today a popular place for
those interested in wildlife and walking. The newest recruit to the
team is chef Stuart Muir, who creates and cooks the French-influenced
menus with plenty of seafood and game in season. Dishes like langoustine with a herb dressing and grouse with wild mushrooms and a
tarragon jus are typical.

QUOTHQUAN   Shieldhill

Quothquan, Biggar, Strathclyde ML12 6NA
Telephone: (0899) 20035 Fax: (0899) 21092   **£55**
Open: lunch + dinner daily
Meals served: lunch 12-2, dinner 7-9 (Sat 7-9.30)

Jack Greenwald owns this country house, where each bedroom is individually styled in muted tones with king, queen or 4-poster beds, overlooking beautiful lawns and woodlands. New chefs Nicola and Keith
Braidwood bring their own style to duck with a ragout of onion and
lentils and a pink and green peppercorn sauce, steamed roulade of sole
and smoked salmon with a centre of langoustine served with green
herb fondue, and venison on a bed of mushrooms and mustard.

ST ANDREWS   Old Course Hotel

St Andrews, Fife KY16 9SP
Telephone: (0334) 74371 Fax: (0334) 77668   **£75**
Open: lunch + dinner daily
Meals served: lunch 12-3, dinner 7-10

Golf fanatics will be in seventh heaven at this hotel, which is pitched
on the 17th hole of the Old Course, enjoying views across the city to St
Andrews Bay and then on to the Highlands. The weekend can be
relaxing yet moderately healthy, with a swim before a good Scottish
breakfast of Finnan haddock, porridge with cream or heather honey,
an Aberdeen butterie with smoked bacon and cheese or French toast
crusted with oatmeal. With some 30 courses in the area to choose from
and expert coaching, the remainder of the day can be taken up with
outdoor pursuits. Standards are high throughout this luxurious hotel,
where every attention is paid to detail with oriental rugs and fine
antiques adorning the 125 rooms, and an extensive leisure complex.

SCARISTA   Scarista House

Scarista, Isle of Harris, Highland PA85 3HX
Telephone: (0859 550) 238 Fax: (0859 550) 277   **£55**
Open: dinner daily (closed Oct-Mar)
Meals served: dinner at 8

This is one of the most remote hotels in Great Britain and as such is
ruggedly beautiful. Take advantage of the location by staying in one of
the 8 bedrooms overlooking a 3-mile, shell-sand beach - perfect for
birdwatchers, walkers and fishermen. The drawing room on the first
floor attracts a wonderful light in the sun. Sit and read the many books
that line the walls or choose from the collection of baroque and
classical music records provided for guests. The food is home-grown
or procured locally, and particular care is taken not to use the products
of inhumane systems of livestock husbandry. Eggs are free-range, so
is the meat, and no farmed fish or shellfish appear on the menu - very
refreshing. The wine list also features a small selection of organically
grown and produced wines.

SCONE   Murrayshall House

Scone, Tayside PH2 7PH
Telephone: (0738) 51171 Fax: (0738) 52595   **£45**
Open: lunch + dinner daily
Meals served: lunch 12-2, dinner 6.30-9.30

Changes have not bypassed this 19-bedroomed country house hotel,
restaurant and golf course. Prices have been reduced somewhat and
so have personnel in the kitchen. Entered via an arched doorway, this
elegantly designed house is a pleasant mix of modern fabrics and soft
furnishings, punctuated by Dutch 16th- and 17th-century oil paintings
in the Old Masters Restaurant. A lighter lunch menu offers home-
made soups or pancakes filled with whisky flavoured haggis, topped
with melted cheese, and main courses of grilled marinated chicken
breast with salad leaves and a minty yoghurt dip or goujons of plaice,
rolled in breadcrumbs and sesame seeds, served with French fries and
a herb dip. The à la carte menu in the evening is more accomplished
however, with a hot pot of both smoked and fresh fish and shellfish,
cooked in a saffron sauce with a herb crust, or roast breast of guinea
fowl garnished with medallions of local black pudding with a port and
lentil sauce.

SLEAT   Kinloch Lodge

Sleat, Isle of Skye, Highland IV43 8QY
Telephone: (047 13) 214 Fax: (047 13) 277   **£65**
Open: dinner daily (closed Dec-mid Mar)
Meals served: dinner at 8 (or by arrangement)

This is more of a family home than a hotel. The rooms vary consider-
ably in size, as do the views (some of the sea), but they've been decorated and equipped to ensure a comfortable stay. Lord and Lady
Macdonald are good hosts and Lady Macdonald's cooking is definitely
worth sampling. So after a bracing walk in the surrounding beautiful
countryside, come back and enjoy a spinach, cheese and garlic terrine
with tomato salad and basil dressing, a mushroom and garlic soup,
baked fillet of cod with julienne vegetables and a creamy lemony
sauce, and save room for the cinnamon pavolva with blackcurrant
cream or perhaps just fresh fruit, cheese and biscuits. Digest in the
drawing room with a little coffee and fudge.

STEWARTON   Chapeltoun House

Stewarton-Irvine Road, Stewarton, Strathclyde KA3 3ED
Telephone: (0560) 482696 Fax: (0560) 485100   £53
Open: lunch + dinner daily (closed 1st 2 wks Jan)
Meals served: lunch 12-2, dinner 7-9
Well-executed, light modern cooking. An 8-bedroomed hotel with good fishing.

STRACHUR — Creggans Inn

Strachur, Strathclyde PA27 8BX
Telephone: (036 986) 279 Fax: (036 986) 637   £45
Open: lunch + dinner daily
Meals served: lunch 12-3.30, dinner 7.30-9

New chef Jean-Pierre Puech brings an added French flavour to this
white painted, 21-roomed inn on the edge of Loch Fyne. Creggans is
owned by Sir Fitzroy and Lady Maclean, who is famous in this neck of
the woods for her cookery books. People come here expecting good
food and will find some of her recipes on the menu - mussel and onion
stew, lamb with créme de cassis and duck à l'orange. Sir Fitzroy
chooses the wines and also has a wide range of rare old malt whiskies -
a dram or two wouldn't go amiss while enjoying the views from the
peaceful sitting room.

TIRORAN — Tiroran House

Tiroran, Isle of Mull, Strathclyde PA69 6ES
Telephone: (068 15) 232 Fax: (068 15) 232   **£65**
Open: dinner daily (closed early Oct-mid May)
Meals served: dinner at 7.45

This is more like visiting friends than staying at a hotel, for Sue and
Robin Blockey create a warm welcome on arrival and a dinner party
atmosphere in the dining room. It's set in picturesque gardens and
woodlands on the Isle of Mull, and the most is made of the dramatic
views from the rooms which have large windows. Sue is in charge of
the kitchen and her food is imaginative, making the most of local
produce. A menu may feature toasted almond and watercress soup
with deep-fried pastry croûtons, fresh Mull prawns with a garlic
mayonnaise, or noisettes of venison with a red wine and pink peppercorn sauce. Desserts include old-fashioned treacle tart with ginger and
pear ice cream and chocolate marquise with a Drambuie sauce. Set on
the shores of Loch Scridain, this antique-filled, 6-bedroomed house
provides an ideal location for getting away from it all.

TROON — Highgrove House

Old Loans Road, Troon, Strathclyde KA10 7HL
Telephone: (0292) 312511 Fax: (0292) 318228   **£40**
Open: lunch + dinner daily
Meals served: lunch 12-2.30, dinner 6.30-9.30

Bill Costley is something of a culinary celebrity in the area having
competed at the International Food Olympics and won a gold medal
for Scotland. Together with his wife Cathy, he runs this hotel overlooking the Firth of Clyde, where you can sample his cooking. Try beef
with a Stilton mousseline, chicken stuffed with almonds and wrapped
in pastry or a rich fish stew with dry vermouth and crusty aioli croutons. Bread and butter pudding with fresh custard would round the
meal off nicely. Simpler dishes are on offer, as are supper grills, for the
less hungry.

TURNBERRY — Turnberry Hotel

Turnberry, Strathclyde KA26 9LT
Telephone: (0655) 31000 Fax: (0655) 31706
Open: lunch Sun, dinner daily
Meals served: lunch 1-2.30, dinner 7.30-10

£75

Turnberry is, without doubt, an international hotel, with facilities the pampered and well-travelled expect. The decor and style of the rooms are sumptuous, yet refined, and standards of housekeeping are first class. To make your stay worth while book into one of the suites and check out on which evening the bagpipes will be played outside your window. One of the foremost sporting hotels at the turn of the century, it has kept up standards to the present day with an extensive leisure complex linked to the hotel, complemented by a trio of restaurants each designed for a different style of eating. The main restaurant offers formal cooking in French style, luxurious and well presented; while at The Bay the surroundings are less formal and the menu lighter, with a healthy slant. Newest to the repertoire is the Clubhouse, which opened in early 1993 and is relaxed and casual. With a wide variety of dishes, salads and a roast, it is open all day to refresh either the keen golfer or the more leisurely guest who simply needs a light snack at any time of day.

UIG — Baile-Na-Cille

Timsgarry, Uig, Isle of Lewis, Highland PA86 9JD
Telephone: (085 175) 242
Open: dinner daily (closed Oct-Mar)
Meals served: dinner 7.30-8.30

£40

Do you want to stay in a secluded area of great beauty, with mountains, sandy beaches, birds and flowers on your doorstep? Then this is the place. Joanna Gollin's 18th-century manse and stables offer 12 bedrooms. Each day bread - from walnut to banana - is baked fresh and sticky buns as well. In the evening a menu is cooked using the best available ingredients which, more often than not, means fish and shellfish, but it could just as well be duck stuffed with ham, walnuts and black pudding. Lots of cakes and puddings to be had! Breakfast means the Stornoway black pudding, kippers and oatmeal.

ULLAPOOL   Altnaharrie Inn

Ullapool, Highland IV26 2SS
Telephone: (085 483) 230   **£100**
Open: dinner daily (closed early Nov-Easter)
Meals served: dinner at 8

Make sure you have some change for the phone otherwise you could
be left stranded on the wrong side of Loch Broom. The hotel launch
will take you on a 10-minute journey across the loch to the enchantment of Fred Brown and Gunn Eriksen's restaurant with rooms. Many
people come here just to relax in the simple surroundings, enjoying
the stunning views and the sounds of the water, but for all visitors, a
major highlight is Gunn's cooking. Though she plays down her ability
she is obviously passionate about what she creates. She cooks what is
available from the fresh fish and vegetable supplies brought in by boat,
enhances by what grows - wild or cultivated - around Altnaharrie. Her
intensity is as rare and precious as the wildlife around these shores. A
real treat to visit and, for many, a pilgrimage.

ULLAPOOL   Ceilidh Place

14 West Argyle Street, Ullapool, Highland IV26 2TY
Telephone: (0854) 612103 Fax: (0854) 612886   £45
Open: all day daily (closed 2 wks Jan)
Meals served: 9.30-9
A 13-bedroomed hotel with a coffee shop open all day for light dishes and a dining
room open in the evening.

WHITEBRIDGE   Knockie Lodge

Whitebridge, Highland IV1 2UP
Telephone: (0456) 486276 Fax: (0456) 486389   **£65**
Open: dinner daily (closed Nov-Apr)
Meals served: dinner 7.30 for 8

Off the beaten track, surrounded by wildlife and close to Loch Ness,
is this rare treat of a hotel run by the Milwards. There is plenty of
countryside to cover in a day's outing and when you return, a 5-
course dinner will be waiting for you. A typical menu might start with
chicken liver and leek terrine with a ratatouille and herb dressing,
then courgette and lemon soup to warm before a main course of
salmon baked with herbs then coated with saffron mayonnaise and
grilled until just brown. Finish with apple tatin with plenty of cream
and cheese with home-made walnut bread. Booking is essential for
non-residents.

Wales Establishment Reviews

ABERCYNON   **Llechwen Hall**

Abercynon, Nr Llanfabon, Mid-Glamorgan CF37 4HP
Telephone: (0443) 742050 Fax: (0443) 742189   £30
Open: lunch + dinner daily
Meals served: lunch 12-2.30, dinner 7-10
Situated high on the hill, this originally 17th century farmhouse enjoys spectacular
views of the valley. 11 bedrooms.

ABERGAVENNY   **Walnut Tree Inn**

Llandewi Skirrid, Abergavenny, Gwent NP7 8AW
Telephone: (0873) 852797 Fax: (0873) 859764   £60
Open: lunch + dinner Mon-Fri (closed Xmas, 2wks Feb)
Meals served: lunch 12-3, dinner 7.15-10

Franco Taruschio is a star. I don't know which pulls in more guests,
the man himself or his cooking. The Walnut Tree has the look of a
country inn with plenty of flowers as well as Anne and Franco to greet
you - it's a place you will want to visit more than once for you are certain of a warm welcome. Franco draws inspiration from many sources -
a bit of the Orient, fragments from Wales - but in essence, the cooking
is unmistakably Italian, and some of the finest at that. Try crostini of
cotechino with home-made onion and tomato chutney, warm salad of
fennel, dried tomatoes and crisp globe artichoke with focaccia, carpaccio of warm salmon, his famous bresaola; or main courses of roast
monkfish with laverbread and orange sauce, lamb sweetbreads with
mushrooms and marsala, or an escalope of salmon with rhubarb and
ginger. Homely and sophisticated, this is a place to go out of your way
for, just to experience it. *Stylish country restaurant with no pretensions!*

ABERSOCH	Porth Tocyn Hotel

Bwlchtocyn, Abersoch, Gwynedd LL53 7BU
Telephone: (0758) 713303 Fax: (0758) 713538 £55
Open: lunch + dinner daily (closed mid-Nov-wk before Easter)
Meals served: lunch 12.30-2, dinner 7.30-9.30
High above Cardigan Bay is a row of former lead-miners' cottages, now run as a family hotel by the Fletcher-Brewers. Homely atmosphere and food.

ABERSOCH   Riverside Hotel

Abersoch, Gwynedd LL53 7HW
Telephone: (0758 81) 2419 Fax: (0758 71) 2671 **£50**
Open: dinner daily (closed Dec-Feb)
Meals served: dinner 7.30-9.00

A *Swallows and Amazons* location with canoe and rowing boat available in which to potter about on the water. Situated on the harbour with the River Soch running behind the house, John and Wendy Bakewell's no-frills, 14- bedroom hotel wins acclaim for the food and friendly service. Special evening meals for children between 5.30-6.00. Coffee by the pool is served complete with home-made biscuits after a meal consisting of young salted herrings in an onion marinade, or cream of carrot and orange soup, followed by escalope of turkey with gruyère cheese and Westphalian ham served with balsamic vinegar sauce.

ABERYSTWYTH	Conrah Country Hotel

Chancery, Aberystwyth, Dyfed SY23 4DF
Telephone: (0970) 617941 Fax: (0970) 624546 £50
Open: lunch & dinner daily (closed 1 wk Xmas)
Meals served: lunch 12-2, dinner 7-9
Fine views, good food and an old-fashioned style of service make for a well deserved weekend break in this 20-bedroomed Welsh country mansion.

BARRY   Bunbury's

---

14 High Street, Barry, South Glamorgan CF6 8EA
Telephone: (0446) 732075 **£45**
Open: lunch + dinner Tues-Sat (closed Bank Holidays)
Meals served: lunch 10.30-2.30, dinner 7.30-10 (Sat 7-10.30)

Not much has changed at this exuberant '30s-style restaurant, driven by two-man band John Gosset and Chris Hogg. John still does the entertaining front of house, while Chris continues to cook an imaginative collection of dishes which change every 4 weeks. Lunchtime alternatives are on offer from the blackboard.

BEAUMARIS	Ye Olde Bulls Head Inn

Castle Street, Beaumaris, Anglesey, Gwynedd LL58 8AP
Telephone: (0248) 810329. Fax: (0248) 811294 £45
Open: lunch + dinner daily (closed 25+26 Dec, 1 Jan)
Meals served: lunch 12-2.30 (Sun 12-1.30), dinner 7.30-9.30
Dickens left his mark on this Grade II listed post-house dating back to 1472, with each of the 11 bedrooms named after a character from one of his novels. Located in the south east of the Isle.

BUILTH WELLS	Caer Beris Manor

Builth Wells, Powys LD2 3NP
Telephone: (0982) 552601 Fax: (0982) 552586 £45
Open: lunch + dinner daily
Meals served: lunch 12.30-2.30, dinner 7.30-10
Twenty-two bedroomed Elizabethan manor set in 27 acres of parkland beside the
River Irfon.

CARDIFF — Armless Dragon

97 Wyeverne Road, Cathays, Cardiff, South Glamorgan CF2 4BG
Telephone: (0222) 382357 **£45**
Open: lunch Tue-Fri, dinner Tue-Sat (closed Bank Holidays, except Good
Friday, 24 Dec-1 Jan)
Meals served: lunch 12.30-2.15, dinner 7.30-10.30 (Sat 7.30-11.00)

Catering for the adventurous end of an otherwise staid market, David
Richards offers fresh, seasonal dishes with a flair for the unusual.
'French inspiration, spiced by the Orient and brought home to Wales',
would describe both the menu and David's career. Scallops come with
a sorrel sauce, while fish can be cooked Barbados style (spicy tomato
sauce), bonne femme or just simply grilled. Fried cod's soft roe with
chive vinaigrette, or home-made brawn with parsley and green peppercorns complete the choices in this bistro-style, relaxing restaurant.

CARDIFF	La Brasserie

60 St Mary Street, Cardiff, South Glamorgan CF1
Telephone: (0222) 372164 £40
Open: lunch + dinner Mon-Sat (closed 25+26 Dec)
Meals served: lunch 12-2.30, dinner 7-12.15
French menu and wines. The same owners as Champers and Le Monde.

CARDIFF — Le Cassoulet

5 Romilly Crescent, Canton, Cardiff, South Glamorgan CF1 9NP
Telephone: (0222) 221905 **£50**
Open: lunch Tue-Fri, dinner Tue-Sat (closed Aug, 2 wks Dec)
Meals served: lunch 12-2, dinner 7-10

The Vianders run their French restaurant with a menu that offers a
selection of typical dishes such as cassoulet, saucisse and crêpes.
Originally from Toulouse and a patriotic supporter of his rugby team,
Mr Viander has decorated the restaurant in the Toulouse team colours
of black and red, with a white and black ceramic floor. Post-theatre
bookings by arrangement.

CARDIFF   Champers

61 St Mary Street, Cardiff, South Glamorgan CF1 1FE
Telephone: (0222) 373363   **£50**
Open: lunch Mon-Sat, dinner daily (closed 25+26 Dec)
Meals served: lunch 12-2.30, dinner 7-12

A busy, Spanish themed-bar and restaurant which offers tapas and a sizable selection of red and white riojas. Otherwise take a seat in the restaurant and decide between grilled steaks and chicken or a few fish specialities. Unlike its sibling restaurants this remains open on Sunday evening.

CARDIFF   LE MONDE

60 St Mary Street, Cardiff, South Glamorgan CF1 1FE
Telephone: (0222) 387376   £40
Open: lunch + dinner Mon-Sat (closed 25+26 Dec)
Meals served: lunch 12-2.30, dinner 7-12
The seafood version of the chain-of-three. Fine array of wet fish and shellfish. Recently expanded.

CARDIFF   New House Country Hotel

Thornhill Road, Cardiff, South Glamorgan CF4 5UA
Telephone: (0222) 520280 Fax: (0222) 520324   £45
Open: lunch + dinner daily
Meals served: lunch 12-2, dinner 7-11
Fine old 12-bedroomed house situated on the fringes of Cardiff. Boasts unrivalled views over the city and valley.

CARDIFF   Quayles

6/8 Romilly Crescent, Cardiff, South Glamorgan CF1 9NR
Telephone: (0222) 341264   **£40**
Open: lunch Wed-Mon, dinner Mon + Wed-Sat
 (closed Bank Holidays, 26 Dec, Easter Mon)
Meals served: lunch 12-2.30 (Sun 11.30-3.30), dinner 7.30-10.30

Fun and very successful. An enterprising venture for the Canning family, who, 2 years down the line, are keeping abreast of trends. The brasserie reflects the mood for Mediterranean-style cooking, and on certain evenings of the week, there is also live music. In the kitchen, Matthew and Irene bake their own bread, ranging from tomato and olive, or walnut, to olive oil, and utilize home-grown herbs in making their own sausages and gravadlax. Set menus change daily as they will not use any frozen or bought in goods.

CHEPSTOW — Beckfords

15-16 Upper Church Street, Chepstow, Gwent NP6 5EX
Telephone: (0291) 626547   £50
Open: lunch Tue-Sun, dinner Mon-Sat (closed Bank Holidays)
Meals served: lunch 12.30-1.45 (Sun 12.30-2.30), dinner 7.30-10

An elegant restaurant, with cooking by proprietor Jeremy Hector, whose lunchtime menu is chalked on a board. In the evening the choice is small but imaginatively put together, such as stuffed quail salad with bacon and croutons, or scallops with mushrooms and ginger followed by rack of lamb with pink peppercorn sauce or a supreme of chicken with Stilton and walnuts. The cooking is straightforward and good, the puddings a prospect worth waiting for.

CHIRK — Starlings Castle

Bron Y Garth, Oswestry, Shropshire SY10 7NU
Telephone: (0691) 718464   £40
Open: lunch Sun, dinner daily (closed 2 wks end of Feb)
Meals served: lunch 12-2.30, dinner 7-10

The address is English, but the location is actually in Wales for this well hidden, sandstone farmhouse within sight of Offa's Dyke and the plain of Shropshire. Relaxed and informal, it has 8 bedrooms, each overlooking the garden. The kitchen is the heart of the house with a small but interesting menu. Down-to-earth cooking, centring on Mediterranean influences, with plentiful fresh produce and abundant flavours – fillet of halibut with oysters and dill, casserole of pigeon provençale and steamed monkfish with spiced prawn balls.

COLWYN BAY — Café Niçoise

124 Abergele Road, Colwyn Bay, Clwyd LL29 7PS
Telephone: (0492) 531555   £45
Open: lunch Tue-Sat, dinner Mon-Sat (closed 1 wk Jan, 1 wk Nov)
Meals served: lunch 12-2, dinner 7-10

This local French-style restaurant, candle-lit at night, is decorated in dusty pinks with French navy napkins and fresh flowers. Friendly and popular, it has some good value wines and serves more than 6 Welsh and French cheese.

CONWY — Sychnant Pass Hotel

Sychnant Pass Road, Conwy, Gwynedd LL32 8BJ
Telephone: (0492) 596868 Fax: (0492) 870009   £45
Open: lunch + dinner daily
Meals served: lunch 12.30-2, dinner 7-9
Hotel with 14 bedrooms, comfortable public rooms and lovely views.

| COYCHURCH | Coed-y-Mwstwr Hotel |

Coychurch, Bridgend, Mid Glamorgan CF35 6AF
Telephone: (0656) 860621 Fax: (0656) 863122   £55
Open: lunch + dinner daily
Meals served: lunch 12-2.30, dinner 7.30-10.15 (Sat-10.30, Sun-9.30)
Set in mature woodland, this 24-bedroomed hotel has high beamed ceilings, wood-panelled walls and chandeliers. It offers elegant and homely charm to both restaurant and hotel visitor. Welsh specialities.

CRICKHOWELL   Bear Hotel

High Street, Crickhowell, Powys NP8 1BW
Telephone: (0873) 810408 Fax: (0873) 811696   **£45**
Open: lunch (bookings only), + dinner Mon-Sat (closed 25 Dec)
Meals served: lunch 12-2, dinner 7-9.30

A quaint and individually furnished hotel-cum-pub. The hub of the market town, it has won great acclaim for its food. Welsh lamb and salmon from the Usk and Wye are favourites. Complete re-furbishment and upgrading now brings the number of bedrooms to 28.

| CRICKHOWELL | Gliffaes Country House Hotel |

Crickhowell, Powys NP8 1RH
Telephone: (0874) 730371 Fax: (0874) 730463   £40
Open: lunch + dinner daily (closed 31 Dec-25 Feb)
Meals served: lunch 1-2.30 (Sun 12.30-2.30), dinner 7.30-9.15
This late-Victorian, 22-bedroomed house stands in the valley of the River Usk in the National Park. Improvements have taken place during the winter months, telephone for further details.

| DOLGELLAU | Dolmelynllyn Hall |

Ganllwyd, Dolgellau, Gwynedd LL40 2HP
Telephone: (0341 40) 273 Fax: (0341 40) 273   £45
Open: dinner daily (closed Jan+Feb)
Meals served: dinner 7.30-9
'Meadow of the yellow lake,' this 11-bedroomed country house hotel is as tranquil as its name suggests. Surrounded by terraced formal gardens and swiftly running streams.

DOLGELLAU   Dylanwad Da

2 Smithfield Street, Dolgellau, Gwynedd LL40 1BS
Telephone: (0341) 422870   **£35**
Open: dinner daily Jul-Sep, Thu-Sat in winter (closed Feb)
Meals served: dinner 7-9.30

A lamb, plum and ginger pie or steak with a pommery mustard sauce are the popular mainstays for this small restaurant. Starters have an international flavour, such as stir-fried beef with a dark Chinese sauce, or mushroom and smoked bacon filling, for a herb pancake. Generous portions.

EGLWYSFACH   Ynyshir Hall

Eglwysfach, Machynlleth, Powys SY20 8TA
Telephone: (0654) 781209 Fax: (0654) 781366   **£55**
Open: lunch Sun, dinner daily
Meals served: lunch 12.30-1.30, dinner 7-8.30

It's not often that you stay in a house that has been owned by royalty. Rob and Joan Reen's Georgian hotel was once Queen Victoria's and stands in 12 acres of picturesque gardens. There are 8 bedrooms for visitors, each decorated with an artist's eye. Rob himself is more than a dab hand with a brush, and you will see some of his own works of art adorning the dining room walls. Traditional meets modern in the cooking with a hot radicchio salad accompanying a rabbit and calvados pie, or a purée of potato and carrot and a red onion marmalade served with lamb.

EWLOE   St David's Park Hotel

St David's Park, Ewloe, Clwyd CH5 3YB
Telephone: (0244) 520800 Fax: (0244) 520930   £40
Open: lunch + dinner daily
Meals served: lunch 12.30-2, dinner 7-10
Purpose-built neo-Georgian hotel with 121 bedrooms catering for the business and conference market. Nearby sister hotel, Northop Country Park, opens mid-1994 offering extensive leisure facilities to both hotels.

FISHGUARD   Three Main Street

3 Main Street, Fishguard, Dyfed SA65 9HG
Telephone: (0348) 874275   **£45**
Open: lunch + dinner Mon-Sat in summer, Tue-Sat in winter (closed Feb)
Meals served: lunch 12-2.30, dinner 7-9.30

Coffee house open during day for cakes and pastries, and a restaurant that serves a good selection of interesting dishes, ranging from main courses of roast leg of Welsh lamb to sea bass baked with a herb crust. Limited accommodation available in this Georgian house.

GLANWYDDEN   The Queen's Head

Glanwydden, Llandudno Junction, Llandudno, Gwynedd LL31 9JP
Telephone: (0492) 546570 Fax: (0492) 546487   £35
Open: lunch + dinner daily (closed 25 Dec)
Meals served: lunch 12-2.15, dinner 6.30-9 (Sat 6-9)
Good pub-grub, all the usuals to choose from plus house specials, such as Arbroath smokies or green lipped mussels and anchovy butter. Finish with spotted dick and custard or a fruit crumble.

GOWERTON   Cefn Goleu Park

Cefn Stylle Road, Gowerton, West Glamorgan SA4 3QS
Telephone: (0792) 873099   **£55**
Open: lunch Sun, dinner Tue-Sat (closed Jan)
Meals served: lunch 12.30-2, dinner 7.30-9.30

A distinguished 19th-century manor house. With 48 acres of gardens,
Emma and Claude Rossi have plenty to occupy them. They call it a
love affair, and it is fair to say this is one that has blossomed. In fact
they saved the house from extinction in 1987 and restored it to the
style of its former glory. It greets you with a magnificent entrance hall
complete with minstrels' gallery and ceiling of rafters. In 1991 they
were rewarded by the Prince of Wales Trust, who acknowledged their
restoration workmanship and achievement for the environment. The
cooking is hearty and full of flavour – stuffed mussels and snails,
chicken with walnuts or a sherry and mustard sauce and steaks
cooked in a variety of ways.

HARLECH   The Cemlyn

High Street, Harlech, Gwynedd LL46 2YA
Telephone: (0766) 780425   **£40**
Open: dinner daily (closed Nov-mid Mar)
Meals served: dinner 7-9 (Sat 7-9.30)

Ken Goody's unpretentious restaurant is a great find, with its 2- or 4-
course fixed-price menus. Local produce including seafood feature
marinated and grilled venison with baked pear and redcurrant jelly,
rabbit with shallots and mustard, Hereford duck with brandy and
orange sauce, fresh crab with mayonnaise. There's one twin-bedded
room, with the same great views as the restaurant and a spectacular
breakfast. Some good wines on offer at reasonable prices. Phone for
details of Ken's speciality evenings.

LAKE VYRNWY   Lake Vyrnwy Hotel

Lake Vyrnwy, (via Oswestry), Llanwyddyn, Powys SY10 0LY
Telephone: (069 173) 692 Fax: (069 173) 289   **£50**
Open: lunch + dinner daily
Meals served: lunch 12.30-1.45, dinner 7.30-9.30

A popular sporting hotel with 24,000 acres of shooting rights and fly
fishing. Miles of splendid walks over the Berwyn mountains, and country pursuits which can include helicopter safaris, laser shooting and
white-water rafting. Faring equally well in the garden are the herbs,
fruits and vegetables which during the summer make up three-
quarters of the produce required by the kitchen. The menu offers well-
cooked dishes such as potted rabbit with sloe gin sauce and toasted
Guinness bread, or salad of pigeon with avocado fritters followed by
pan-fried guinea fowl, roast saddle of lamb or baked monkfish with a
herb crust. A well-packaged hotel with 38 bedrooms, discreet yet
friendly.

LLANBEDR — Llew Glas Brasserie

Llanbedr, Gwynedd LL45 2LD
Telephone: (034123) 555   **£30**
Open: lunch daily (summer only), dinner daily (Thu-Sat only in winter, closed 26 Dec)
Meals served: lunch 11-4, dinner 6-10 (winter 7-10)

This restaurant relocated here from Harlech in early '93. Vegetarians and gluten-free customers are well catered for. Welsh lamb and local produce are used whenever possible, plus a good selection of Welsh cheese. The simpler dishes are the better ones, chosen from a menu which offers a wide selection that would suit most palates. Some organic wines available on a reasonably priced list.

LLANDRILLO — Tyddyn Llan

Llandrillo, nr Corwen, Clwyd LL21 0ST
Telephone: (049 084) 264 Fax: (049 084) 264   **£45**
Open: lunch + dinner daily (closed 1 wk Feb)
Meals served: lunch 12.30-2, dinner 7.30-9.30

Midway between Bala and Corwen on the B4401 is Peter and Bridget Kindred's delightful country house, well placed from which to explore Snowdonia. All 10 rooms enjoy restful views of the gardens and Berwyn mountains. On the lawn there is croquet, and tea on fine days. Dominic Gilbert matches the outdoor pursuits with a 3- or 4-course, fixed-price menu with a good range, from fillet steak with potato rösti, or trio of Welsh lamb, to escalopes of monkfish with Welsh mussels. Amongst the desserts you might find Snowdonia pudding with madeira sauce, mixed fruit crumble and iced chestnut parfait with chocolate sauce. The hotel enjoys rights to 4 miles of salmon, trout and grayling fishing on the River Dee. This year sees falconry courses added to the pursuits available to residents.

LLANDUDNO — BODYSGALLEN HALL

Llandudno, Gwynedd LL30 1RS
Telephone: (0492) 584466 Fax: (0492) 582519   **£65**
Open: lunch + dinner daily
Meals served: lunch 12.30-2, dinner 7.30-9.45

There are some outstanding views from this jewel in the Historic House Hotel chain - a grand, 17th-century hall with bedrooms shared spread between the main house and 9 cottages set around a courtyard. Young chef Mair Lewis confidently cooks British dishes, taking advantage of the local produce, offering a roast of the day or a 3-course menu which might include a veal, bacon and herb terrine with hot toasted brioche, or quenelles of smoked trout followed by veal with puréed onion and tarragon jus or pot roast guinea-fowl with red currants and a lime jus. Many historic features to note, including a knot garden of box hedges.

LLANDUDNO   Richard's Bistro Restaurant

7 Church Walks, Llandudno, Gwynedd LL30 2HD
Telephone: (0492) 877924/875315   **£40**
Open: dinner daily
Meals served: dinner 6.30-10

Richard Hendey has merged his bistro and restaurant into one, result-
ing in a more relaxed and informal atmosphere and a good choice on
the menu that might include sweet-cured herring fillets, char-grilled
swordfish or pigeon char-grilled and served with plum sauce. Finish
with treacle tart.

LLANDUDNO   St Tudno Hotel

The Promenade, Llandudno, Gwynedd LL30 2LP
Telephone: (0492) 874411 Fax: (0492) 860407   **£55**
Open: lunch + dinner daily
Meals served: lunch 12.30-2, dinner 7-9.30

The Blands' 21-bedroomed, seafront hotel has been welcoming guests
for the past 21 years and such is the friendliness of the hoteliers that
they are willing to share a glass or two of wine with you - you will find a
small bottle in your room when you arrive. A fixed-price menu of 5
courses or choices from the à la carte could include smoked haddock
and leek tart, tomato and basil soup, poached halibut and of course
Welsh lamb, but here it is served with plum and port sauce.

LLANGAMMARCH WELLS   Lake Country House

Llangammarch Wells, Powys LD4 4BS
Telephone: (059 12) 202 Fax: (059 12) 457   **£60**
Open: lunch (non-residents by arrangement only), dinner daily
Meals served: lunch 1-2, dinner 7.30-8.45

Peaceful and restful, this rather splendid 19-bedroomed hotel is run
efficiently and enthusiastically by Jean-Pierre and Jan Mifsud. Standing
in 50 acres of parkland, it is a fisherman's paradise with salmon and
trout from the rivers Wye and Ithon. Refurbishment of many of the
rooms and a new practice golf course complete the upgrading. In the
restaurant the fixed-price, 5-course menu is good value for money with
a cream of celery and apple soup, duck terrine served with plum compote, roulade of chicken with pistachio and sweet peppers and orange
and cardamom ice cream on a cinnamon sauce. Extensive wine list and
friendly service complete an enjoyable experience in the candle-lit
dining room.

LLANGEFNI   Tre-Ysgawen Hall

Capel Coch, nr Llangefni, Anglesey, Gwynedd LL77 7UR
Telephone: (0248) 750750 Fax: (0248) 750035   **£45**
Open: lunch + dinner daily
Meals served: lunch 12-2.30 (Sat 12.30-2.30), dinner 7.30-9.30

A fine Victorian mansion just off the B5111, owned by the Craighead
family. The friendly atmosphere and high standards have won them
great acclaim, and put this hotel into a class of its own. Well furnished,
its public rooms are handsome but not fussy, and the 19 good-sized
bedrooms have beautiful en-suite bathrooms. The restaurant is in the
large conservatory extension and is elegant and formal. Steven Morris
continues to turn out a well-cooked and presented menu. 3000 acres of
private shooting.

LLANGYBI   Cwrt Bleddyn Hotel

Tredunnock, nr Usk, Gwent NP5 1PG
Telephone: (0633) 49521 Fax: (0633) 49220   £50
Open: lunch + dinner daily   ❖
Meals served: lunch 12-3, dinner 7-10.30
Thirty-six bedroom hotel, standing in 17 acres of countryside. New library addition
and some redecoration during '93.

LLANRUG   Seiont Manor

Llanrug, Caernarfon, Gwynedd LL55 2AQ
Telephone: (0286) 673366 Fax: (0286) 672840   **£40**
Open: lunch Sun-Fri, dinner daily
Meals served: lunch 12-2.30, dinner 7-9.45

Set in its own 150 acres of parkland, a Welsh country mansion with
country club facilities. Pleasant walks are on the doorstep and the
delights of Snowdonia National Park and the Isle of Anglesey are
within a short drive. Seiont's 28 bedrooms are all en-suite. Sport and
leisure can be found along the banks of its salmon and trout filled river
or in the 'Welsh Chapel' style swimming pool. Improvements to the
on-site leisure club include an enlarged gym and new sauna.

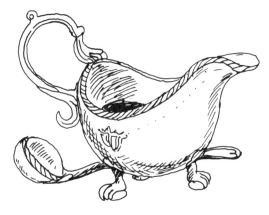

LLANSANFFRAID GLAN CONWY   Old Rectory

Llanrwst Road, Llansanffraid Glan Conwy, Gwynedd LL28 5LF
Telephone: (0492) 580611 Fax: (0492) 584555   **£60**
Open: dinner daily (closed 20 Dec-1 Feb)
Meals served: dinner at 8

Set in the heart of the beautiful Conwy estuary, here you will find some
of the best of Wales. The cooking is outstanding, the cellar acclaimed
and the ingredients only Welsh with black beef and Mountain lamb followed by an array of Celtic cheese. It's run by talented husband and
wife team Michael and Wendy Vaughan, past masters at entertaining,
and dinner might be served at individual tables or with everyone
grouped together around one large table as if at a dinner party. There
is no doubt that the food will be the height of conversation. Wendy is a
splendid cook and each night prepares a 4-course menu using the best
of local produce. The first and main courses are set and could be escalope of sea bass with asparagus and a saffron sauce followed by
poached fillet of lamb wrapped in leek with roasted shallots and a tarragon jus. Desserts are also Wendy's forte - try a chocolate velvet slice
or a glazed lemon tart. Michael is a wealth of information on wine.

LLYSWEN   LLANGOED HALL

Llyswen, Brecon, Powys LD3 0YP
Telephone: (0874) 754525 Fax: (0874) 754545   **£80**
Open: lunch + dinner daily
Meals served: lunch 12.15-2.30, dinner 7.15-9.30

Beetroot consommé with poached squab and fresh thyme gives an
insight into what awaits at this 23-bedroomed, Jacobean mansion. A
gracious house, it fulfils the dream and aims of Sir Bernard Ashley, as
a hotel of exacting quality. The set menu of 5-courses might include
baked fillet of Cornish cod with a herb crust and a chive butter sauce
followed by pan-fried duck with potato wafer and a ginger scented
sauce. The appropriate pudding is a warm champagne sabayon over
fresh fruit and vanilla ice cream. Very good wine list with some reasonably priced wines.

MATHRY   Ann Fitzgerald's Farmhouse Kitchen

Mabws Fawr, Mathry, Haverfordwest, Dyfed SA62 5JB
Telephone: (0348) 831347   £50
Open: all day daily
Meals served: lunch 12-2, dinner 7-9
Good country cooking: roasted and braised rabbit, duck or pheasant, as well as a
touch of the Italian and Orient with tempura, risotto or gnocchi in. Popular local
restaurant.

MISKIN   Miskin Manor

Penddylan Road, Pontyclun, Miskin, Mid-Glamorgan CF7 8ND
Telephone: (0443) 224204 Fax: (0443) 237606   £50
Open: lunch + dinner daily
Meals served: lunch 12-2 (Sun 12-1.45), dinner 7-9.45 (Sun 7-9)
A handsome stone mansion (c.1858), with 32 extremely spacious bedrooms.
Tastefully luxurious. Hotel undergoing extensive refurbishment as we went to press.

MUMBLES   **Norton House**

17 Norton Road, Mumbles, Swansea, West Glamorgan SA3 5TQ
Telephone: (0792) 404891 Fax: (0792) 403210   £55
Open: dinner Mon-Sat (closed 25-26 Dec)
Meals served: dinner 7.15-9.30
Charming 15-bedroomed Georgian hotel, personally run by Jan and John Powers.
Rooms vary from four-poster bed with beamed ceiling to smaller rooms in new wing.
2-or 3-course set menus with some interesting, modern, Welsh-style dishes.

NEWPORT   Celtic Manor

Coldra Woods, Newport, Gwent NP6 2YA
Telephone: (0633) 413000 Fax: (0633) 412910   **£50**
Open: lunch Mon-Fri, dinner Mon-Sat
Meals served: lunch 12-2.30, dinner 7-10.30

Built in 1865 and set in 300 acres of beautiful Welsh hillside and woodlands, this manor house offers 73 good-sized bedrooms and extensive
conference facilities, without losing any of its elegance and charm. The
two restaurants offer differing styles of menu. Hedleys, the à la carte
restaurant, is an elegant room with oak-panelled walls and stained
glass windows that takes on a romantic atmosphere at dinner with
flickering candlelight. The Patio Grill is in a tinted glass conservatory,
popular at lunchtime for its grill-style menu.

NEWPORT   Cnapan Country House

East Street, Newport, nr Fishguard, Dyfed, SA42 0SY
Telephone: (0239) 820575 Fax: (0239) 820878   **£35**
Open: lunch + dinner daily, Wed-Mon in summer (closed Xmas, Feb)
Meals served: lunch 12-2, dinner 7-9

The Lloyds and Coopers run this listed, personalised, 5-bedroomed
hotel, situated close to the National Park coastline where the birdwatching is notable. Further amenities include golf, fishing and pony
trekking. Light lunches and à la carte dinner menus available with
novel use of Welsh ingredients. Vegetarians well catered for with separate menu.

NORTHOP — Soughton Hall

Northop, nr Mold, Clwyd CH7 6AB
Telephone: (0352) 840811 Fax: (0352) 840382   **£55**
Open: lunch Sun (Mon-Sat by arrangement), dinner daily (closed 1st 2 wks
Jan)
Meals served: lunch 12-2, dinner 7-9.30 (Sat 7-10, Sun 7-7.30)

Not much has changed, nor have standards dropped, since Soughton
Hall opened in 1987. Set in 150 acres of parkland, just fifteen minutes
outside Chester, this magnificent and grand house stands in a world of
its own. Once a bishop's palace, it has a charm and elegance rarely
seen. Now the home of the Rodenhurst family, it offers 12 bedrooms
with period furniture and plenty of extras. The splendid State Dining
Room has highly polished tables, crystal glass and fine china. The
fixed-price menu incorporates old classics and traditional dishes –
black pudding with mustard and white wine sauce, terrine of pork with
parsley-spiced aspic, darne of River Dee salmon with prawns and julienne vegetables brushed with tarragon butter, and a variety of seafood
on a bed of noodles and a butter sauce. The wine list offers some reasonably priced wines.

*Breakfast in the original servant's hall
— complete with old kitchen range.*

PORTHKERRY — Egerton Grey

Porthkerry, Nr Cardiff, South Glamorgan CF6 9BZ
Telephone: (0446) 711666 Fax: (0446) 711690   **£50**
Open: lunch + dinner daily
Meals served: lunch 12-2, dinner 7-9.30

Anthony and Magda Pitkin's 17th-century rectory set in a wooded
valley, makes an ideal bolt-hole for anyone wishing to write all the let-
ters they have meant to over the year, finish that book or get out and
enjoy the fresh air. If the latter is your preference, then head for the
coastline and take in the views out across the channel to Devon and
Cornwall, but return by 7.00 and take up your chair by the fireside for
a leisurely glass of champagne followed by a set dinner of 3 courses.

PORTMEIRION — Hotel Portmeirion

Portmeirion, Gwynedd LL48 6ER
Telephone: (0766) 770228 Fax: (0766) 771331
Open: lunch + dinner daily (closed 4 wks Jan/Feb)
Meals served: lunch 12.30-2.30, dinner 7-9.30

£55

Unique fairytale setting — charming service

The village of which this dream-like hotel is an integral part, was created by Sir Clough Williams-Ellis, an eminent architect who used his savings to buy the site in the late '20s. On a secluded peninsula of the Traeth Bach estuary, 50 buildings group around a central piazza. Coming to stay here is always an experience to treasure. The hotel is an early Victorian villa built by the shore and has exquisite rooms in the main house, enjoying the best sea views. Other rooms are spread through the village in cottages. The cooking is as carefully crafted as the walls and marbled pillars of the setting and centres on a continental flavour, under the trained eye of chef Craig Hindley. A year after his arrival he has settled in well, offering a menu perhaps consisting of crab with tomato and a citrus vinaigrette, salad of avocado with apple, celery and trout, or terrine of vegetables with endive and olive oil, followed by Welsh lamb with tagliatelle of leeks and roast garlic, or roast duck with oyster mushrooms, lentils and a white parsley sauce.

PWLLHELI — Plas Bodegroes

Nefyn Road, Pwllheli, Gwynedd LL53 5TH
Telephone: (0758) 612363 Fax: (0758) 701247
Open: dinner Tue-Sun (closed Jan-Feb)
Meals served: dinner 7-9.30 (Sun 7-9)

£65

Cutlet of free-range pork with apple, marjoram and garlic is an example of the work of Chris Chown who came to cooking slightly late in life, but like those who wake up with a mission, he is inspired. Herbs and spices are his friends and he knows how to use them: grilled guinea fowl with mango and celeriac and green peppercorn sauce, roast fillet of seabass with fennel and red pepper and tarragon sauce. His saffron, Gewürztraminer and shredded duck risotto breaks with tradition while a tartare of salmon with avocado and cucumber pickle makes an unusual starter. Puddings leave nothing to chance. Choose from cinnamon biscuit of rhubarb and apple with elderflower custard, or a barabrith and buttermilk pudding with orange and hazelnut ice cream. Set in a Georgian manor house with its own gardens, this restaurant with 8 rooms is undeniably one of the places to stay in Wales.

REYNOLDSTON   Fairyhill

Reynoldston, Gower, Swansea, West Glamorgan SA3 1BS
Telephone: (0792) 390139 Fax: (0792) 391358   £45
Open: lunch Sun, dinner daily (closed Nov-Jan)
Meals served: lunch 12.30-1.15, dinner 7.30-9
Peaceful, 15-bedroomed hotel in a woodland setting. French cooking with overtones of Welsh and some interesting and unusual dishes on offer – the puddings are worth trying.

ROSSETT   Llyndir Hall

Llyndir Lane, Rossett, Nr Wrexham, Clwyd LL12 0AY
Telephone: (0244) 571648 Fax: (0244) 571258   £40
Open: lunch + dinner daily
Meals served: lunch 12-2, dinner 7-10
Surrounded by beautiful gardens and furnished with great taste, this 38-bedroomed hotel offers the finest ingredients for a pleasurable stay, including spa bath and indoor swimming pool.

SWANSEA   Annie's Restaurant

56 St Helens Road, Swansea, West Glamorgan SA1 4BE
Telephone: (0792) 655603   £35
Open: dinner Mon-Sat (closed Bank Holidays, Mon in winter)
Meals served: dinner 7-10

Informal dining in a relaxed setting are the keywords here. Fixed-price and à la carte menus offer a good variation of dishes, including Normandy- style mussels or grilled escalope of salmon with bacon and laverbread for the starters, while from the main courses I would choose the braised shank of lamb cooked in white wine and garlic. French wines.

SWANSEA   Number One

1 Wind Street, Swansea, West Glamorgan SA1 1DE
Telephone: (0792) 456996   £45
Open: lunch Mon-Sat, dinner Wed-Sat (closed 25-30 Dec)
Meals served: lunch 12-2.30, dinner 7-9.30

You will need to book into Kate Taylor's bistro, since seating is limited. Fish and shellfish are popular - hot oysters with laverbread and Stilton or quenelles of pike with prawn sauce to start. Monkfish in ricard or grilled john dory with dill and mustard sauce are main courses but there is also a choice of duck, woodpigeon and hare in season. Good selection of Welsh cheese. Small choice, but value for money all round and fun.

TALSARNAU — Maes-y-Neaudd

Talsarnau, Nr Harlech, Gwynedd LL47 6YA
Telephone: (0766) 780200 Fax: (0766) 780211   **£60**
Open: lunch Sun, dinner daily
Meals served: lunch 12-2, dinner 7-9

You're unlikely to leave here without feeling well rested and extremely well fed. Set on a wooded mountainside across from the Snowdonia National Park this Welsh granite and stone manor plays host to travellers from all over the globe. Peter Jackson (ex-Colonial in Glasgow) takes charge of the kitchen and brings an authoritative skill to the menu, shown in collops of venison on a bed of calvados and onion jam, or a medley of asparagus and oyster mushrooms with a basil essence. Welsh cheese is served with carrot and walnut bread baked fresh daily. Weekly specials plus 2 other main dishes feature on the menu which means Monday always offers steak and kidney pie, Wednesday chicken casserole and there's no need to tell you what comes on Friday!

TINTERN ABBEY — Royal George

Tintern Abbey, nr Chepstow, Gwent NP6 6SF
Telephone: (0291) 689205 Fax: (0291) 689448   £40
Open: lunch + dinner daily
Meals served: lunch 12-2, dinner 7-10
Convenient for the ruins of Tintern Abbey, 19-bedroomed, 17th-century hotel set at the foot of a wooded hillside.

TRELLECH — Village Green

Trellech, Nr Monmouth, Gwent NP5 4PA
Telephone: (0600) 860119   **£50**
Open: lunch Tue-Sun, dinner Tue-Sat (closed Bank Holidays, 1 wk Jan)
Meals served: lunch 12-2, dinner 7-9.45

Bob Evans' food displays many influences with a brasserie-style menu chosen from the blackboard that turns to international flavours with fritto misto, marrow stuffed with spicy chicken or king prawns with garlic butter. Alternatively, try salmon with orange and basil butter, guinea fowl with madeira and pasta, or pan-fried beef with port sauce topped with foie gras, then finish with a sweet brioche of fresh fruit and iced nougat. Two double bedrooms are available in what was formerly a priory and then a coaching inn.

WELSH HOOK   Stone Hall

Welsh Hook, Wolfscastle, nr Haverfordwest, Dyfed SA62 5NS
Telephone: (0348) 840212 Fax: (0348) 840815   £35
Open: dinner Tue-Sun (closed Dec-Mar)
Meals served: dinner 7.30-9.30

10 miles west of the A40, halfway between Haverfordwest and
Fishguard, you will find this charming flagstone-floored and oak-
beamed 14th-century manor house. Request directions before you set
off, since it is well hidden in the lanes near Wolfscastle. A limited number of simply furnished rooms is available. With Martine Watson in
overall charge of the kitchen, a French à la carte menu offers you
sautéed salad of chicken livers and grapes, brill with a cucumber
sauce, confit de canard or pork with mushroom, apples and calvados
sauce.

WHITEBROOK   Crown at Whitebrook

Whitebrook, Monmouth, Gwent NP5 4TX
Telephone: (0600) 860254 Fax: (0600) 860607   **£55**
Open: lunch Tue-Sun, dinner Mon-Sat (closed 2 wks Jan, 25+26 Dec)
Meals served: lunch 12-2, dinner 7-9 (Sat 7-9.30)

On the edge of the Tintern forest and deep in the Wye Valley is this
restaurant with rooms. It is not dissimilar to the French-style auberge
where you will dine well on good food and fine wines and then enjoy a
good night's sleep before moving on again the next day. Sandra Bates'
cooking has all the right credentials: French-influenced, finely
prepared with an imaginative selection of dishes on the fixed-price
menu – try gravadlax with scallops and a honey and lime dressing, or
marinated pigeon breast roasted in filo pastry, duck cooked pink with
caramelised apples and a duck liver pastry served alongside and
finished with calvados sauce, or juicy pan-fried calves' liver with grilled
polenta on a bed of onions and a piquant sherry sauce.

Northern Ireland Establishment Reviews

BELFAST	La Belle Epoque

61-63 Dublin Road, Belfast, Co Antrim
Telephone: (0232) 323244   £55
Open: all day Mon-Sat (closed 25+26 Dec, 12+13 July)
Meals served: 12-11

The restaurant has just relocated to this new address but continues to serve good French cooking. Entrées might be smoked salmon with horseradish cream or pan-fried pigeon breast with a honey and ginger dressing and main courses feature lamb, duck and veal.

BELFAST	Crown Liquor Saloon

46 Great Victoria Street, Belfast, Co Antrim BT2 7BA
Tel: (0232) 249476   £45
Open: lunch daily (closed 25 Dec, 12 Jul)
Meals served: lunch 12-3
Victorian pub dating back to the 1800s, serving lunch and light bar snacks in the afternoon.

BELFAST	Dukes Hotel

65 University Street, Belfast, Co Antrim BT7 1HL
Telephone: (0232) 236666 Fax: (0232) 237177   £95
Open: lunch Sun-Fri, dinner Mon-Sat
Meals served: lunch 12.30-2.30 (Sun 1-2.30), dinner 6.30-10.15 (Sat 6.30-10.45)
The Victorian façade belies a modern interior. Style and comfort are nicely combined here. 21 spacious rooms. Situated close to Queen's University, and the Botanical Gardens.

BELFAST	Nick's Warehouse

35-39 Hill Street, Belfast, Co Antrim BT1 2LB
Telephone: (0232) 439690   £50
Open: lunch + dinner Mon-Fri (closed Bank Holidays)
Meals served: lunch 12-3, dinner 6-9

Set in a converted warehouse, Nick and Kathy Price's restaurant is lively and busy, with an uncomplicated menu including some contemporary dishes. The operation is two-tier with a wine bar at night in the basement, while the restaurant is on the first floor. It's informal and fun with T-shirted staff offering menus of Italian salami and olives, game terrine with rhubarb, and blackened swordfish with a garlic mayonnaise. Basil and pistachio pesto come with monkfish and a pot luck of seafood. Comprehensive wine list.

BELFAST   Roscoff

Lesley House, Shaftesbury Square, Belfast, Co Antrim BT2 7DB
Telephone: (0232) 331532   **£75**
Open: lunch Mon-Fri, dinner Mon-Sat (closed 11+12 Jul, 26 Dec, 1 Jan)
Meals served: lunch 12.15-2.15, dinner 6.30-10.30

With a style that speaks of time spent in London – Paul Rankin worked at Le Gavroche with Albert Roux – the decor here is high chrome and minimalistic. Now Paul has returned to his roots and is treating his clients to sophisticated cooking and a reputation for good value dining. His Californian influences are helped along by his wife Jeanne (his pastry chef) who also takes care of service and the customers with ease and a smile. The results are set menus of a contemporary manner - a ragôut of seafood with a spiced basil cream, crisp duck confit with soft polenta and mushrooms and bourbon pecan tart with caramelised bananas, followed by a selection of Irish, French and English cheeses. Good wine list with some reasonable prices.

BELFAST   Strand Restaurant

12 Stranmillis Road, Belfast, Co Antrim BT9 5AA
Telephone: (0232) 682266   **£25**
Open: all day Mon-Sat, lunch + dinner Sun (closed 25+26 Dec, 12+13 July)
Meals served: Mon-Sat 12-12 (lunch Sun 12-3, dinner Sun 5-10)

Anne Turkington makes an excellent hostess and her restaurant proves a favourite, with its café-style operation on the ground floor and the conservatory-style restaurant and bar upstairs. Anne has been here for over 10 years and her formula has been influential in starting a pattern of similar restaurants across the city. Food is served throughout the day and includes curried pancakes or a steak with a choice of sauces. This is straightforward cooking, reasonably priced and popular.

CRAWFORDSBURN   Old Inn

15 Main Street, Crawfordsburn, Co Down BT19 1JH
Telephone: (0247) 853255 Fax: (0247) 852775   **£80**
Open: lunch + dinner daily (closed 25+26 Dec)
Meals served: lunch 12.30-2.30, dinner 7-9.30 (Sun 5-7.30)
Dates back to the 16th Century, with oak beams, antiques and four-posters in its 32 bedrooms. Close to airport.

DUNADRY   Dunadry Inn

2 Islandreagh Drive, Dunadry, Co Antrim BT41 2HA
Telephone: (084 94) 32474 Fax: (084 94) 33389   **£40**
Open: lunch Sun-Fri, dinner daily (closed 24-26 Dec)
Meals served: lunch 12.30-1.45, dinner 7.30-9.45 (Sun 5.30-9.45)

This attractive inn, formerly a linen mill, has become well known for its
riverside setting, and has 67 bedrooms centred around a courtyard.
The panelled restaurant overlooks Six Mile Water and a mill stream,
and makes a breathtaking location. The à la carte and set menus offer
a classic array of dishes from fillet of char poached and then finished
with a vermouth and dill sauce, to pork loin filled with figs and served
with a light barbecue sauce. Pleasant gardens and a well-equipped
country club with indoor pool and jacuzzi are included among its
amenities.

GARVAGH   Blackheath House & MacDuff's

112 Killeague Road, Blackhill, Garvagh, Co Londonderry BT51 4HH
Telephone + Fax: (0265) 868433   **£45**
Open: dinner Tue-Sat (closed 25+26 Dec, 12 Jul)
Meals served: dinner 7-9.30

A restaurant with rooms, run by Joseph and Margaret Erwin, set in a
former rectory. With rivers famed for trout and salmon and plenty of
game in season, both make regular appearances on Margaret's
inspired country menu. A typical list of recent dishes includes Stilton
puffs with a hot and sweet and sour sauce, scallops of veal with
vermouth, and a symphony of seafood. The dining room is located in
the former cellars, with an appropriately good wine list. 5 spacious
bedrooms are adorned with fresh flowers and fruit. Blackheath House
has some lovely landscaped gardens and an indoor swimming pool.

HOLYWOOD   Culloden Hotel

142 Bangor Road, Craigavad, Holywood, Co Down BT18 0EX
Telephone: (0232) 425223 Fax: (0232) 426777   £40
Open: lunch Sun-Fri, dinner daily (closed 24+25 Dec)
Meals served: lunch 12.30-2.30, dinner 7-9.45 (Sun 7-8.30)
A local landmark set in lovely gardens with views of Belfast Loch. Good business and
conference location. 50 bedrooms, health club, pool and inn.

PORTAFERRY   Portaferry Hotel

10 The Strand, Portaferry, Co Down BT22 1PE
Telephone: (024 77) 28231   £40
Open: lunch + dinner daily (closed 24+25 Dec)
Meals served: lunch 12.30-2.30, dinner 7-9
This waterside village inn with 14 bedrooms, overlooks Strangford Lough. Renowned
for its seafood dishes, the restaurant also uses local Ulster beef, Mourne lamb and
game.

PORTRUSH — Ramore

The Harbour, Portrush, Co Antrim BT56 8VM
Telephone: (0265) 824313
Open: dinner Tue-Sat (closed 2 wks Feb, Xmas/New Year)
Meals served: dinner 7-10.30

£50

A modern style of cooking has brought a new flavour and look to this restaurant, and a restyled kitchen means guests can now watch George McAlpin at work. Bigger now and brighter, the restaurant offers a wider choice of food but there's more informal seating at the bar for those who would rather eat just a one-course meal. Seafood is still part of the menu but the emphasis is now on dishes like Tuscan style chicken, sliced pork fillet with truffles and Irish lamb shank with grilled courgettes and garlic mash. Puddings might include a crème brulée on a bed of crushed meringues in a Drambuie cream, or a traditional bread and butter pudding with lots of whipped cream. A sensibly priced wine list.

TEMPLEPATRICK — TEMPLETON HOTEL

882 Antrim Road, Templepatrick, Ballyclare, Co Antrim
Telephone: (084 94) 32984 Fax: (084 94) 33406
Restaurant:
Open: dinner daily (closed 24-26 Dec)
Meals served: dinner 7-9.45
Grill:
Open: lunch + dinner Mon-Sat
Meals served: lunch 12-12.30, dinner 5-9 Mon-Thu, 5-10 Fri+Sat

£40

£35

A 20-bedroomed, modern hotel that endeavours to combine the old with the new and ends up as a rich tapestry of colours and styles. Each contrasting room brings a surprise from the swanky, black and gold cocktail bar with its cathedral pews and ecclesiastical wooden figures, to futuristic chrome staircases and highly polished floors. Scandinavian-style banqueting halls make for an intriguing if unusual interior. The food is more straightforward – breast of barbary duck, or fillet of salmon on a saffron cream as main courses. Convenient for Belfast International Airport.

Republic of Ireland Establishment Reviews

ADARE   Adare Manor

Adare, Co Limerick
Telephone: (061) 396566 Fax: (061) 396124
Open: lunch + dinner daily
Meals served: lunch 12.30-2.30 (Sun 12.30-3), dinner 7.30-10

£70

Set on the banks of the River Maigue, this neo-Gothic manor is famous for its formal gardens, fashioned and designed in a box pattern. The grandeur of the interior public rooms is highlighted by chandeliers and fine ornate work, an impressive oak stairway and a gallery whose design was based on that at the Palace of Versailles. The rooms are full of mahogany furniture and fine fireplaces are to be found in many of the 64 luxury bedrooms. A rich and historic place to spend the weekend and a favoured spot for golf fanatics, with a new Robert Trent Jones course. The dining room sees a new talent in Gerard Costelloe, whose menu is classic with overtones of modern Irish and European - char-grilled duck on a tomato and garlic sauce and steaks with béarnaise sauce are some examples of his cooking. The wine list is French-based with a good New World section.

ADARE   Dunraven Arms

Adare, Co Limerick
Telephone: (061) 396209 Fax: (061) 396541
Open: lunch + dinner daily
Meals served: lunch 12.30-2 (Sun 12.30-2.15), dinner 7.30-9.30 (Sat 7.30-10)

£50

This rather special hotel is situated in a pretty, Irish village renowned for its sporting activities. Equestrian holidays are a particular speciality here, and some of the modern rooms provide plenty of space to hang your riding tack. Bryan Murphy is a keen huntsman himself and you can arrange to gallop alongside the County Limerick, the Black and Tan or the Galway Blazer packs. But if a round of golf or an afternoon's fishing for pike, salmon or trout is more your style, then these are here too. A good business and conference venue, 45 well-furnished bedrooms.

ADARE — Mustard Seed

Main Street, Adare, Co Limerick
Telephone: (061) 396451   **£50**
Open: dinner Tue-Sat (closed 25+26 Dec, Feb)
Meals served: dinner 7-10

This setting consists of several cottagey rooms and a cuisine that looks to France for its foundations and Ireland for the produce and modern interpretation. The menu will depend on what the chef has found at the market that day, but a recent 4-course dinner menu included terrine of game on a quince vinaigrette followed by a winter salad with garlic and scallion and pan-roasted breast of pheasant with cranberry jus, followed by a light chocolate truffle cake with a brandy chocolate anglaise.

AHAKISTA — Shiro

Ahakista, Nr Bantry, Co Cork
Telephone: (027) 67030   **£65**
Open: dinner daily
Meals served: dinner 7-9

In such a remote setting you might not believe your eyes when you see sake-mushi (steamed salmon with capers and a garlic mayonnaise dip), teriyaki (beef roasted with a sake blend) and yaki-niku (pork filet roasted in spicy onion-based ginger sauce). Here in Kitchen Cove on the Sheep's Head peninsula overlooking Dunmanus Bay, Kei Pilz, an artist in her own right, paints a beautiful scene with some exquisite Japanese cooking. Her German husband Werner tends to the front of this Japanese Dinner House and together they make an exceedingly rare team. Delicately and deftly prepared, the choice is both inspiring and wondrous, with a daily changing menu that includes a selection for vegetarians. A cottage is available if you wish to stay over.

ATHY — Tonlegee House

Athy, Co Kildare
Telephone: (0507) 31473 Fax: (0507) 31473   £50
Open: dinner Mon-Sat (closed 25+26 Dec, Good Friday)
Meals served: dinner 7-9.30 (Fri+Sat 7-10.30)
Mark and Marjorie Molloy have a talent for welcoming and caring for their guests in this Georgian restaurant with rooms.

AUGHRIM — Aughrim Schoolhouse Restaurant

Aughrim, Nr Ballinasloe, Co Galway
Telephone: (0905) 73936   **£35**
Open: lunch Sun, dinner Mon-Sat, Tue-Sat in winter (closed 24-26 Dec)
Meals served: lunch 12-3, dinner 6.30-11

A labour of love has turned an old school house into the enjoyable restaurant it has become today. Michael and Geraldine Harrison have achieved much in their first year and have settled in well. The word is out about their good country cooking, and customers are travelling from afar to taste and experience their creations. Free of gimmicks but with plenty of flavour and taste, their dishes are the likes of warm crab tart with a saffron and chive sauce and chicken stuffed with cheese and basil with a seed mustard sauce. Sundays prove popular with even more good traditional cooking.

BALLDEHOB   Annie's

Main Street, Ballydehob, Co Cork
Telephone: (028) 37292   £50
Open: lunch + dinner Tue-Sat (closed 25+26 Dec, 3 wks Oct)
Meals served: lunch 12.30-2.30, dinner 6.30-9.30

While you wait in the pub across the road, Anne Ferguson Barry will
take your order and get your meal under way. Choose from a short
handwritten menu of liver and bacon pâté, baked avocado with crab
and main courses of either scallops pan-fried or cooked in a white wine
sauce or fillet of beef with a peppercorn sauce. Husband David
conducts matters in the kitchen.

BALLINA   Mount Falcon Castle

Ballina, Co Mayo
Telephone: (096) 21172 Fax: (096) 21172   £40
Open: dinner daily (closed Xmas, Feb+Mar)
Meals served: dinner at 8

Constance Aldridge is as much a part of the attraction as the house
and surrounding area. After 50 years of welcoming guests into her 10-
bedroomed home, she has quite a list of old clients who return to sample her country house cooking. All gathered around one table, you can
enjoy the speciality of the house which is gravadlax and some of the
best butter and cream which is supplied by the out-of-house guests - 2
Jersey cows. The vegetables come from the garden and there are
always fine Irish cheeses to sample.

BALLYLICKEY   Ballylickey Manor House

Ballylickey, Bantry Bay, Co Cork
Telephone: (027) 50071 Fax: (027) 50124   £50
Open: lunch + dinner Thu-Tue (closed Nov-Mar)
Meals served: lunch 12.30-2, dinner 7.30-9.30
17th-century manor house and gardens overlooking Bantry Bay. 12 bedrooms,
salmon and trout fishing.

BALLYVAUGHAN   Gregans Castle Hotel

Ballyvaughan, Co Clare
Telephone: (065) 77005 Fax: (065) 77111   £60
Open: lunch + dinner daily (closed Nov-Mar)
Meals served: lunch 12-3 in bar, dinner 7-8.30

The aim of a quiet and relaxed atmosphere is achieved here with a setting of great beauty, surrounded by meadows full of flowers - the
alpine and arctic varieties will delight botanists - and who can help but
be transfixed by the views of the Galway. Take a chair in the
Corkscrew Room or leaf through a book in the library and look for the
famous mural painting by Raymond Piper of Burren flora. All the
rooms, including the 22 bedrooms, are well designed and decorated.
Each evening Peter Haden offers a 5-course menu with fish from the
local seas and Burren lamb being specialities.

BALTIMORE   Chez Youen

The Pier, Baltimore, Co Cork
Telephone: (028) 20136   **£50**
Open: all day daily (closed lunch in winter, mid Nov-mid Feb)
Meals served: 12.30-midnight

Simple rustic restaurant overlooking the harbour. The lobster here is
good all year really and is the show-stopper. Youen Jacob has been
cooking in a simple Breton manner for some years and has become
quite an attraction. Dinner is set and includes a choice between a good
onion soup, or melon with port then steak with green peppercorns, but
it is the likes of platefuls of prawns, crab mayonnaise and main courses
of poached turbot, hake or wild salmon with fennel sauce or poached
lobster with lemon and butter that you should opt for. If you don't have
the lobster you can have a platter of seafood of crab, tiny velvet crabs,
prawns and Baltimore shrimps instead for the same price as the 3-
course menu - definitely worth it.

BIRR   Tullanisk

Birr, Co Offaly
Telephone: (0509) 20572 Fax: (0509) 20572   **£40**
Open: dinner daily (closed 1 wk Xmas)
Meals served: dinner at 8.30

Since 1989 this 18th-century dower house has been run as a private
country house hotel by George and Susie Gossip. It makes a lovely
place to stay with its well-manicured gardens stocked with plants,
plenty of wildlife, and public rooms furnished and decorated with care.
It is George who masterminds the kitchen, creating dishes according
to what fresh, local produce is available with plenty of vegetables
picked from their own gardens. To round off the evening, try home-
made biscuits with farmhouse cheese. With slumber only a couple of
steps away in one of the 7 bedrooms, you will be able to sample an
excellent breakfast next morning.

BLACKLION   MacNean Bistro

Blacklion, Co Cavan
Telephone: (072) 53022   **£40**
Open: lunch + dinner Tue-Sun (closed 25+26 Dec, Good Friday)
Meals served: lunch 12.30-3, dinner 6-9.30 (light meals 3-6)

An ideal partnership has been struck between Vera Maguire and her
son Nevan. Together they run a tiny, blue and pink restaurant on the
main street where Vera's traditions and Nevan's sense for new trends
results in a powerful mix that creates menus that are high on imagination, with dishes served on large black plates. Good cooking and
presentation.

BOYLE   Cromleach Lodge

Ballindoon, Castlebaldwin, Nr Boyle, Co Sligo
Telephone: (071) 65155 Fax: (071) 65455   **£60**
Open: dinner daily (closed 3 days Xmas, 3 wks Jan)
Meals served: dinner 7-9 (Sun 6.30-8)

For a relatively young and modern restaurant, this is a corker. The spectacular views look out across the quiet hills above Lough Arrow with the Carrowkeel Cairns in the background. Moira Tighe, owner and self-taught cook, works with a lightness of touch to create tartlet of organic leeks and smoked bacon, Irish smoked salmon and smoked trout roulade, and main courses of chicken with spring onion sauce or wild salmon served with lemon sole. Puddings are exemplified by an iced chocolate and passion fruit gateaux. A good value wine list. Take advantage of one of the 10 bedrooms for a stopover.

Modern building takes advantage of the incredibly beautiful scenery.

BUNRATTY   MacCloskey's

Bunratty House Mews, Bunratty, Co Clare
Telephone: (061) 364082   **£55**
Open: dinner Tue-Sat (closed Jan, Good Friday)
Meals served: dinner 7-10

In the basement of this 17th-century house, situated alongside Bunratty Castle itself, is this well-established restaurant. Originally the wine cellar, it has white-washed walls, plenty of flowers and is candle-lit at night. Gerry MacCloskey cooks a 5-course menu of dishes such as baked snails, mussels in a sabayon sauce, shark steak or free range chicken, followed by hot raspberries with vanilla ice cream and a warm chocolate sauce. Farmhouse cheese is always available.

CAHERDANIEL   Loaves & Fishes

Caherdaniel, Nr Derrynane, Co Kerry
Telephone: (066) 75273   **£40**
Open: dinner daily (closed Mon Jun-Aug + Tue Sep (closed Oct-Easter))
Meals served: dinner 6-9.30

Fun and lively, this restaurant has built up an excellent reputation for its well cooked food, and even in a remote area it proves popular. The decor is cottagey with a collection of plates, appealing country furniture and low ceilings. Cooking is by co-owner Helen Mullane, whose recent dishes have been a country terrine of pork and garlic with a tomato and mustard-seed relish, or wild Irish salmon with a creamed Noilly Prat sauce. All are served with a plate of vegetables.

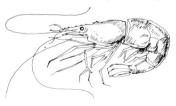

CARLINGFORD   Jordan's Bar & Restaurant

Carlingford, Co Louth
Telephone: (042) 73223   **£40**
Open: lunch Sun in summer, dinner daily (closed 25+26 Dec, 2 wks Jan)
Meals served: lunch 12.30-3.30, dinner 7-10

Each day the restaurant is filled with the glorious smell of fresh
baking, as Harry and Marian Jordan prepare the baskets of rolls and
soda bread. At this warm and friendly restaurant, offering a menu of
modern and traditional dishes, local lamb and seafood feature strongly.
Desserts are very good, with a selection of home-made ices and a duo
of white and dark chocolate mousse.

CASHEL   Cashel House

Cashel, Co Galway
Telephone: (095) 31001 Fax: (095) 31077   **£60**
Open: lunch + dinner daily (closed 10-31 Jan)
Meals served: lunch 1-2, dinner 7.30-8.30 (Sun 7.30-9)

Cashel House, with its 32 bedrooms, is set in 50 acres of dramatic
grounds including a private beach and prize-winning gardens. The dining room, pride and joy of Dermot and Kay McEvilly, is a fine operation with menus that use good quality local produce. Split-level, with a
conservatory extension, it offers a fixed-price, 4-course dinner menu
which places a great emphasis on local fish, with dishes that range
from terrines to poached lobster and scallops in a white wine sauce, or
roast Connemara lamb with garlic and rosemary. At breakfast you
must try the Cashel Bay smoked salmon with scrambled eggs - a
delight all round.

CASHEL   Chez Hans

Rockside, Cashel, Co Tipperary
Telephone: (062) 61177   **£45**
Open: dinner Tue-Sat (closed Bank Holidays, 3 wks Jan)
Meals served: dinner 6.30-10

A former Wesleyan chapel at the foot of the Rock of Cashel is an
unlikely venue for Hans-Peter Matthiä's cooking. He cooks a superb
range of fish and shellfish dishes ranging from quenelles of brill and
turbot to a cassoulet of fresh seafood. Kinsale lobster becomes a
bisque or receives a basting of hot butter. The wine list is mainly
French.

CASTLEDERMOT — Doyle's School House

Main Street, Castledermot, Co Kildare
Telephone: (0503) 44282   **£50**
Open: lunch Sun, dinner Tue-Sat (closed mid Jan-mid Feb)
Meals served: lunch 12.30-2, dinner Nov-Mar 7.30-10.30 (Apr-Oct 6.30-
10.30)

Good country cooking from John Doyle - dishes such as poached
young eel, fillet of lamb with a wild rowan sauce, pigeon salad with
plum and vinegar sauce, or a parfait of chicken livers. A reasonable
wine list is also on offer in this antique-furnished restaurant, which
remains a favourite with locals and guests staying in the 12 bedrooms.

CASTLEDERMOT — Kilkea Castle

Kilkea, Castledermot, Co Kildare
Telephone: (0503) 45156 Fax: (0503) 45187   **£55**
Open: lunch + dinner daily (closed 25 Dec)
Meals served: lunch 12.30-2.30, dinner 7-9.30

The oldest inhabited castle in Ireland, Kilkea was built in 1180 by
Hugh de Lacy. If staying the night in one of the 45 bedrooms, keep a
look out for the ghost! In the restaurant, aptly named after the original
architect, the menu is cooked by Scottish chef George Smith who has
a light touch and an interesting array of recipes, his speciality dish
being a mixture of West Coast scallops and crayfish flamed in an Irish
Mist sauce. Other dishes include a terrine of shellfish with a spiced
tomato sauce, quenelles of chicken liver pâté and a breast of duck with
garlic and basil. The menu tends to be elaborate, and sometimes the
simpler dishes are best. Breakfasts are good and include a potato
scone with poached eggs which, can be worked off by a game of golf, a
canter in the surrounding countryside or a morning's fishing - or, for
the less energetic, a gentle stroll.

CASTLETOWNSHEND — Mary Ann's

Castletownshend, Nr Skibbereen, Co Cork
Telephone: (028) 36146   **£50**
Open: lunch daily, dinner Mon-Sat (closed Mon in winter)
Meals served: lunch 12.30-2.30, dinner 6.30-10

Patricia O'Mahony's good home cooking is making her name, in a
restaurant within in a grand old pub. She provides a menu that
specialises in local lamb, seafood and beef. The seafood platter is well
worth choosing with piles of prawns, crab claws, oysters and poached
and smoked salmon all jostling for position, or instead try chicken
stuffed with salmon and served with a prawn sauce. The potatoes are
beautiful and just freshly boiled while vegetables are cooked to just the
right degree. Dessert might be a strawberry shortcake or good lemon
meringue pie, or instead opt for the selection of farmhouse cheese.

CLIFDEN O'Grady's Seafood Restaurant

Market Street, Clifden, Co Galway
Telephone: (095) 21450   **£50**
Open: lunch + dinner daily (closed mid Nov-end Feb)
Meals served: lunch 12.30-3.30, dinner 6.30-10

The popularity of this neat, seafood restaurant has been thriving since its opening in the '60s. Scallops receive a ginger cream while brill takes a more luxurious coating of champagne sauce. It's predominantly a seafood restaurant but there are also chicken and beef dishes. Tables are well spaced with some set into alcoves, while for a more informal lunch, the new piano bistro offers a simpler style with one-plate specialities.

CONG Ashford Castle

Cong, Co Mayo
Telephone: (092) 46003 Fax: (092) 46260
George V   **£75**
Open: lunch + dinner daily
Meals served: lunch 1-2, dinner 7.30-9.30
Connaught Room   **£80**
Open: lunch + dinner daily
Meals served: lunch 12.45-2.30, dinner 7-9.30

Set in vast parklands, this French-style chateau incorporated into the 13th-century castle overlooks the lakes of western Ireland. The public rooms are grand and richly adorned with panelling, carved balustrades, suits of armour and fine paintings, while the 83 well-appointed bedrooms and luxurious suites contain more antiques. The George V restaurant is also panelled and has large windows looking out over the formal gardens. The menus offer a wide choice of traditional and continental dishes. The Taste of Ireland menu offers the best variety from traditional Irish stew to Clew Bay scallops. The Connaught Room offers a different but equally opulent setting and a menu that specialises in French cooking – dishes such as local snails, wild nettles, spinach and mushrooms in puff pasty, Jerusalem artichoke and almond soup, pan-fried duck with a hazelnut and duck confit brandade, or a ginger and white port sauce.

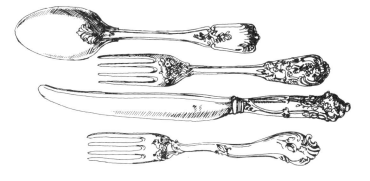

CORK — Arbutus Lodge

Montenotte, Cork, Co Cork
Telephone: (021) 501237 Fax: (021) 502893   £70
Open: lunch + dinner Mon-Sat (closed 1 wk Xmas)
Meals served: lunch 1-2, dinner 7-9.30

Works of art belonging to Ireland's modern painters adorn the walls of
this former Lord Mayor's house. And from its lofty position, the restaurant is the talk of Ireland for its mixture of Irish and French cooking
with an imaginative and well cooked collection of dishes - warm duck
salad with Puy lentils, cassoulet of fresh prawns, mussels with saffron
and orange and perhaps a main course of turbot with a herb crust.
There is a good selection of Irish cheese and an interesting wine list;
19 well-furnished bedrooms.

CORK — Bully's

40 Paul Street, Cork, Co Cork
Telephone: (021) 273555   £75
Open: all day daily (closed 25+26 Dec, Good Friday)
Meals served: 12-11.30

Eugene Buckley cooks brilliant pizzas in an oven fuelled by the teak
and beech off-cuts from the local furniture maker, which is possibly
what gives his pizzas that little added extra and makes them stand
head and shoulders above the rest. Light and crisp, they are delicious,
although the quality of the other choices on the menu is no less noteworthy - pastas, fresh fish, omelettes and grills. This is far more than
just a pizza parlour and is incredibly popular so arrive early, or you
may not get a table.

CORK — Clifford's

18 Dyke Parade, Cork, Co Cork
Telephone: (021) 275333   £60
Open: lunch Tue-Fri , dinner Mon-Sat (closed Bank Holidays, 2 wks Aug)
Meals served: lunch 12.30-2.30, dinner 7.30-10.30

This magnificent building was once a library and has been converted
into Michael and Deirdre Clifford's first-class restaurant - its decor is
now more artistic than literary! Take a drink in the first floor bar
before supper and then enter the dining room with its immaculate
tables laid with simple linen and minimalistic extras. Michael's fixed-
price menu is highly inventive and includes reworked classics such as
Clonakilty black pudding with puréed mushrooms, a burger of free
range duck Clifford-style, and rabbit with a purée of spring vegetables.
The puddings are luscious - there's a warm almond and apricot gateau
you simply can't afford to miss. Well worth a visit if you're ever near
Cork.

CORK   Crawford Gallery Café

Emmet Place, Cork, Co Cork
Telephone: (021) 274415   **£35**
Open: lunch Mon-Sat, dinner Wed-Fri (closed Bank Holidays, 2 wks Xmas)
Meals served: lunch 12-2.30, dinner 6.30-9.30

In a 1724 building next to the Opera House, lunch could be a tartine
(open brown and white bread sandwich) of roasted red peppers and
grilled farmhouse cheese, or a Ballymaloe bacon chop with an Irish
whiskey sauce. Vegetarians need not feel left out either, for there is
always a dish for them on the menu - a delicious spinach and mushroom pancake is well worth sampling. In the evening matters are more
concise, with a set menu or quick snacks along the lines of oysters in a
champagne sauce or fresh pasta with olive oil and spring herbs.
Inspiration, skills and staff drawn from Myrtle Allen's Ballymaloe
ensure good standards here.

CORK   Flemings

Silver Grange House, Tivoli, Cork, Co Cork
Telephone: (021) 821621 Fax: (021) 821800   **£45**
Open: lunch + dinner daily (closed 24-26 Dec, Good Friday)
Meals served: lunch 12.30-2.30, dinner 6.30-11

Michael Fleming's classically French restaurant is decorated in shades
of yellow and green with light coloured furniture. Flemings is set in a
large Georgian house with 4 spacious bedrooms and 5 acres of garden,
where Michael grows many of the herbs and vegetables that he uses
in his French dishes. The à la carte menu offers an imaginative selection of dishes such as crab with prawns and a sour cream, chive and
lemon sauce, guinea fowl with prune, liver and herb stuffing, or pan-
fried lamb with foie gras and a sweetbread tartlet and tarragon sauce.
Desserts include a strawberry and raspberry strudel and peaches
poached in champagne. The fixed-price menu is excellent value.

CORK   Huguenot

French Church Street, Cork, Co Cork
Telephone: (021) 273357   **£35**
Open: lunch Mon-Sat, dinner daily, (closed 25+26 Dec, Sun in winter)
Meals served: lunch 10.30-2.30, dinner 6-10.30 (Sun Jun-Aug 6-10) (light
meals Sat Jun-Aug 12.30-11)

Crab cakes with caper sauce and a Mediterranean fish stew, chicken
cooked 4 ways as well as pancakes with fillings of chicken and mushroom or smoked haddock are some of the options at Michael
Callaghan's bistro-style restaurant. Exceedingly good value, it updates
its menus regularly and offers an early evening menu that is ideal for
the theatre-goer, and, at under £7, a very good bargain.

CORK   Isaacs

48 MacCurtain Street, Cork, Co Cork
Telephone: (021) 503805   **£40**
Open: lunch Mon-Sat, dinner daily (closed 3 days Xmas)
Meals served: lunch 12-2.30, dinner 6.30-10.30 (Sun 6.30-9)

The Ryan family from Arbutus Lodge have put their heads together
with chef Carnice Sharkey to create a modern eclectic restaurant. An
18th-century warehouse, it is a mix of terracotta brick work and
vibrant modern art with an equally dazzling menu: blackeye bean stew
with mushrooms, buffalo chips with burgers, colonial lamb curry and
fried squid with tomatoes. Puddings are simple but are a breath of
fresh air, yoghurt with honey and hazelnuts, summer compote and
baklava being good examples.

CORK   Jacques

9 Phoenix Street, Cork, Co Cork
Telephone: (021) 277387 Fax: (021) 270634   **£55**
Open: lunch Mon-Sat, dinner Tue-Sat (closed Bank Holidays,
10 days Xmas)
Meals served: lunch 12-4, dinner 6-10.30

Modern influences pepper the menu at this intimate and informal
restaurant. Chicken accompanies Irish asparagus in a crisp salad with
an oriental sesame dressing, whereas sun-dried tomatoes come with
hot bruschetta, before a typical main course of pork parmigiani,
Tuscan chicken and monkfish with a garlic and tomato vinaigrette
which is topped with shavings of fresh parmesan and a parsley pesto.
It is the early bird that will enjoy the evening special of a choice of 2
starters and main courses for a very reasonable price.

CORK   Morrisons Island Hotel

Morrisons Quay, Cork, Co Cork
Telephone: (021) 275858 Fax: (021) 275833   **£50**
Open: lunch + dinner daily
Meals served: lunch 12.30-2, dinner 6-9.30

The first hotel in Cork to have only suites instead of single rooms, this
is ideal for the business executive or family who are staying longer
than a night or two. Set on the river bank, the view is arresting and the
rooms well designed. The decor of the foyer is completed by rich
colours and oriental rugs.

CORK   O'Keeffe's

23 Washington Street West, Cork, Co Cork
Telephone: (021) 275645   **£55**
Open: dinner Mon-Sat (closed Bank Holidays, 1 wk Xmas)
Meals served: dinner 6.30-10.30

Marie O'Keefe rattles the pans while husband Tony is responsible for
the smooth running of this small restaurant. It is nice to see that their
hard work is reaping the benefits of a loyal following, and with dishes
that are cooked to order they deserve all the praise they get. An imaginative repertoire includes crubeens (pig's trotter), boned, and stuffed
with a mix of chicken mousse and Clonakilty white pudding, kassler
with colcannon cake and a mustard sauce, or chicken on tomato and
onion slices with wild mushroom sauce. Puds are good too.

CORK   Rochestown Park Hotel

Cork, Co Cork
Telephone: (021) 892233 Fax: (021) 892178   £45
Open: lunch + dinner daily (closed 25 Dec)
Meals served: lunch 12.30-2.30, dinner 7-10
Lovely gardens, 63 rooms and 5 luxury suites make this a good hotel for business
executives; leisure facilities.

DALKEY   Il Ristorante

108 Coliemore Road, Dalkey, Co Dublin
Telephone: (01) 284 0800   **£50**
Open: dinner Tue-Sun (closed Bank Holidays (open Good Friday),
wk Xmas, 2 wks Feb)
Meals served: dinner 7.30-10.30

This small, friendly restaurant above the pub has just a few tables, so
you had better be quick off the mark to reserve one. Ragged walls and
Italian cooking with modern presentation by Roberto Pons is what you
will find here: spaghettini with garlic and olive oil, ravioli with lobster,
and turbot with lemon and basil. All the usuals are here too with veal,
liver and onions, saltimbocca, beef with pesto sauce and rack of lamb
with garlic sauce. Plenty of sun-dried tomatoes.

DINGLE   Beginish Restaurant

Green Street, Dingle, Co Kerry
Telephone: (066) 51588 Fax: (066) 51591   **£50**
Open: lunch + dinner Tue-Sun (closed mid Nov-Mar)
Meals served: lunch 12.30-2.15, dinner 6-9.30

With a series of connecting rooms, a small bar, a conservatory and garden to the back, this is a popular place, especially when Americans are
in town. The decor is soft and gentle and the restaurant is run by Pat
and John Moore. Pat is the talent in the kitchen, cooking turbot perfectly, with olive oil scented potato purée and chive sauce and pan-fried
monkfish with fennel confit and a tomato and basil sauce. Desserts
include an excellent rhubarb soufflé tart with crème anglaise and
assorted ice creams in a tuile biscuit. Expect a good cup of coffee.

DINGLE   Doyle's Seafood Bar

4 John Street, Dingle, Co Kerry
Telephone: (066) 51174 Fax: (066) 51816   **£45**
Open: dinner Mon-Sat (closed mid Nov-mid Mar)
Meals served: dinner 6-9

John and Stella Doyle's well established seafood restaurant with rooms offers chowder, hot trout smokies and main courses of black sole with orange beurre blanc. Cooked in generous portions, and in a straightforward manner, you can hardly get fish fresher than this, unless you catch it yourself! Choose your own lobster from the tank and it will be cooked to perfection. The restaurant has flagstone floors and pine furniture and the 8 bedrooms are decorated in a splendid manner with stylish fabrics and well designed bathrooms.

DINGLE   Half Door

John Street, Dingle, Co Kerry
Telephone: (066) 51600 Fax: (066) 51206   **£50**
Open: lunch + dinner Wed-Sun (daily in Jul+Aug) (closed Jan-Easter)
Meals served: lunch 12.30-2.30, dinner 6-10

There are no half measures at the O'Connors' seafood restaurant. Opt for Denis' shellfish selection of lobster, mussels and crab with a tangy marie-rose sauce for your first course and then decide between paupiettes of sole stuffed with a smoked salmon mousse with a prawn sauce or baked salmon in pastry with Grand Marnier. Desserts are good and might be a fresh fruit pavlova or strawberry millefeuille. Some reasonably priced wines on offer.

DINGLE   Lord Baker's Bar & Restaurant

Main Street, Dingle, Co Kerry
Telephone: (066) 51277   **£45**
Open: lunch + dinner daily (closed 25 Dec)
Meals served: lunch 12.30-2.30, dinner 6-10

A good local that serves some very good food. A bar-cum-restaurant, the menu offers fresh fish from turbot and sole dressed simply, to traditional entrées of lamb with rosemary butter or duck with orange. Dinner is set with a choice of 7 starters and main courses and might bring stuffed loin of pork with apple sauce or a good lamb kebab and pilaf rice. Informal and characterful - it's a pity there are not more places like this.

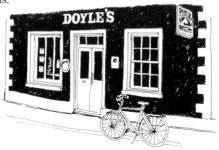

DUBLIN   Blooms Hotel

Anglesea Street, Dublin 2
Telephone: (01) 671 5622 Fax: (01) 671 5997   **£55**
Open: lunch Mon-Fri, dinner daily (closed 25+26 Dec)
Meals served: lunch 12.30-2, dinner 5-9.45

Named after Leopold Bloom, the hero from James Joyce's Dublin-inspired novel Ulysses, this hotel is situated close to Trinity College and Dublin Castle in an area known as Temple Bar (similar in concept to London's Covent Garden). After extensive refurbishment, this 86-bedroomed hotel now boasts a new restaurant called Bia (meaning food in Irish), a bar called the Anglesea and a nightclub – Club M. Lunch and dinner cater as much for passing customers as for residents and offer adventurous menus to complement the mood of the area. Well-priced dishes include a terrine of pork with courgette chutney, chicken with crab meat, apple and Calvados, best Irish heifer steaks from Mullingar which are grilled or pan-fried to order and served with a range of sauces, salmon poached with saffron and toasted almonds or a veal cutlet with Irish honey and fresh rosemary.

DUBLIN   Chapter One

18/19 Pannell Square, Dublin, Co Dublin
Telephone: (01) 873 2266 Fax: (01) 873 2281   **£65**
Open: lunch Tue-Fri + Sun, dinner Tue-Sat (closed Bank Holidays,
1 wk Xmas)
Meals served: lunch 12.30-2.30, dinner 7-11

This well established restaurant, now under new ownership, has a rustic and Scandinavian influence, offering such dishes as blini, lime and ginger-marinated salmon with cucumber accompanied by angel hair pasta, or a hearty coriander and lentil broth with plenty of mussels. Sister to the Old Dublin, its more modern contemporary menu could also include baked fillet of turbot with a soya and sesame seed coating served with a lemon and chive sauce, or beef cooked with honey and served with soya-roasted shallots and a red wine sauce.

DUBLIN   Cooke's Café

14 South William Street, Dublin, Co Dublin
Telephone: (01) 679 0536 Fax: (01) 679 0546   **£55**
Open: lunch + dinner daily (closed Bank Holidays)
Meals served: lunch 12-2.30, dinner 6-12 (light meals 12-12)

A small and fun café-cum-restaurant belonging to John Cooke (ex-Polo One). With a modern contemporary style of cooking, it serves an international menu in rather elegant surroundings, with dishes varying from rigatoni with gorgonzola cream, Mexican quesadillas, to fried columbaria with arrabiatta sauce. Chicken comes flavoured with olive oil, lemon juice and roasted garlic, while duck receives a balsamic butter sauce and wilted endive. Puddings include honey chocolate cake, fresh plum cake, and chocolate pecan tart.

DUBLIN · Commons Restaurant

Newman House, 85-86 St Stephen's Green, Dublin, Co Dublin 2
Telephone: (01) 475 2597 Fax: (01) 478 0551 £65
Open: lunch Mon-Fri, dinner Mon-Sat (closed Bank Holidays)
Meals served: lunch 12.30-2.15, dinner 7-10.15

Looking out on to a large courtyard and 5 acres of gardens beyond, this modern restaurant in shades of blues and creams is an elegant setting for Gerard Kirwan's cooking. He takes as a starting point some excellent local produce and builds it into a colourful and lively array of dishes such as sautéed lamb with cucumber, mint and yoghurt and steamed turbot set in a slightly spiced butter. Desserts look the picture with blackcurrant and vanilla bavarois. The cheese, Java coffee and petits fours are all good.

DUBLIN · Le Coq Hardi

35 Pembroke Road, Ballsbridge, Dublin 4, Co Dublin
Telephone: (01) 689070 Fax: (01) 689887 £60
Open: lunch Mon-Fri, dinner Mon-Sat (closed Bank Holidays,
1 wk Xmas, 2 wks Aug)
Meals served: lunch 12-2.30, dinner 7-11

Good classic cooking using Irish ingredients.

High ceilings, immaculate table settings and fine French cuisine with a few modern influences are the characteristics of John and Catherine Howard's enthusiastically run restaurant. In an end-of-terrace Georgian house they offer à la carte and set menu on which you can expect to see dishes such as terrine of young rabbit with apricot chutney, salmon and hake fish cakes with herb butter, lamb's kidney and veal sausages in a red wine sauce or the speciality of the house Le Coq Hardi - corn fed chicken filled with potato, wild mushrooms and special herbs wrapped in bacon and oven roasted with Irish whiskey! The wine list is a good one and reads like a connoisseur's handbook.

DUBLIN · The Davenport Hotel

Merrion Square, Dublin 2
Telephone: (01) 661 6799 Fax: (01) 661 5663 £35

If you want to stay in the heart of Dublin, this hotel is well worth a visit. Surrounded by Trinity College, the National History Museum and National Gallery, and hidden as it is behind the façade of a church that dates back to 1863, you would hardly guess that the hotel is in fact a new one. Blending perfectly with the Merrion Square, an impressive marble pillared lobby draws you into an atrium soaring 6 storeys to a doomed roof. This 90-bedroomed hotel is a beauty, and has colour schemes that are bold, a bar that is clubby and masculine and a variety of styles of rooms.

DUBLIN   Grey Door

22 Upper Pembroke Street, Dublin, Co Dublin
Telephone: (01) 676 3286 Fax: (01) 676 3287   **£40**
Open: lunch Mon-Fri, dinner Mon-Sat (closed 1 wk Xmas)
Meals served: lunch 12.30-2.30, dinner 6-11

Ring the bell to gain entrance to this well-respected town house, set in
a Georgian terrace. There are 7 bedrooms here and 2 well-established
restaurants. The Grey Door restaurant is famous for its fine cooking of
fish, shellfish and game whereas Blushes offers a more informal setting. Both have set menus and are furnished in a charming, homely
way, making this an enjoyable place to dine and sleep.

DUBLIN   Hibernian Hotel

Eastmoreland Place, Ballsbridge, Dublin, Co Dublin
Telephone: (01) 668 7666 Fax: (01) 660 2655   **£45**
Open: lunch Sun-Fri, dinner daily (closed Xmas, Good Friday)
Meals served: lunch 12.30-2.30, dinner 6.30-10.30

Even though this 30-bedroomed hotel is small it lacks no grace or
style. A Victorian building, it has well designed public rooms and a
quiet and peaceful library furnished with Chesterfield sofas, where you
can relax before dinner with a glass of champagne whilst musing over
the next day's agenda. The dining room, complete with conservatory,
serves an equally sedate menu, typical examples being warm roast
quail with grapes, medallions of chateaubriand with mushrooms and
garlic, or a grilled tuna steak with black peppers and walnut oil.

DUBLIN   Kapriol

45 Lower Camden Street, Dublin, Co Dublin 2
Telephone: (01) 475 1235   **£60**
Open: dinner Mon-Sat (closed Bank Holidays, 3 wks Aug)
Meals served: dinner 7.30-12

At this small and quaint restaurant run by Giuseppe and Egidia
Peruzzi, you can enjoy good traditional Italian cooking - dishes such as
chicken stuffed with ham and mushrooms and a white wine sauce, or
sole with prawns and veal with garlic and cream. A mainly Italian wine
list, reasonably priced.

DUBLIN   Longfield's Hotel

Fitzwilliam Street Lower, Dublin, Co Dublin
Telephone: (01) 761367 Fax: (01) 761542   £55
Open: lunch Mon-Fri, dinner daily (closed lunch Bank Holidays)
Meals served: lunch 12.30-2.30, dinner 6.30-10 (Fri+Sun 6.30-11)
Georgian style, 28-bedroomed, town hotel furnished with antiques - quiet, with
friendly service.

DUBLIN   Old Dublin Restaurant

90-91 Francis Street, Dublin, Co Dublin 8
Telephone: (01) 542028 Fax: (01) 541406   **£50**
Open: lunch Mon-Fri, dinner Mon-Sat (closed Bank Holidays)
Meals served: lunch 12.30-2.30, dinner 7.15-11

Eamonn Walsh's ground floor restaurant, complete with smiling doorman, borrows from Scandinavian and Russian cooking. In a comfortable setting of interconnecting rooms, each warmly decorated and
with soft lighting, the menu offers authentic versions of borscht,
gravadlax, beef stroganoff and chicken kiev. Specialities of the house
include planked sirloin hussar in which the meal is baked between 2
planks then served on an oak platter with sweet pickle; and a salmon
kulebjaka (for 2) which is a filo pastry creation with salmon, dill, rice,
eggs and mushrooms, served with a dill butter and soured cream. A
good selection of Irish farmhouse cheese brings the menu to a superb
close.

DUBLIN   Patrick Guilbaud

46 James Place, Off Lower Baggot Street, Dublin 2,Co Dublin   ❀
Telephone: (01) 676 4192 Fax: (01) 660 1546   **£60**
Open: lunch + dinner Tue-Sat (closed Bank Holidays)
Meals served: lunch 12.30-2, dinner 7.30-10.15

After 10 years Patrick Guilbaud remains supreme in its class, and both
cooking and service here are of a consistently high standard.
Guillaume Lebrun's cooking is light and imaginative - breast of duck
with white turnips and coriander, grilled breast of chicken with dried
grapes and beef served with baked celery and hazelnut cream are
some examples. The restaurant has an elegant decor with abstract
paintings on the wall and a plant-filled atrium. If choosing proves to be
a problem let the kitchen take the decision out of your hands with a
menu surprise of 6-courses that are all based on what was best in the
market that day. In my opinion, still the restaurant in Ireland.

DUBLIN   Roly's Bistro

7 Ballsbridge Terrace, Dublin, Co Dublin 4
Telephone: (01) 668 2611   **£45**
Open: lunch Sun-Fri, dinner daily (closed 25+26 Dec, Good Friday)
Meals served: lunch 12-3, dinner 6-10 (Sun 6-9)

This two-tier French-style bistro has become the fashionable eating
place of Dublin. Buzzing with life, it has lots of little booths and corners furnished with cheap and cheerful furniture and a menu that
includes game tartlets, seafood sausages with a red pepper sauce,
beignets of brie with an apple and mint chutney and main courses of
pan-fried fish, rabbit and pigeon pie or roast guinea fowl with grapes.
Finish with a good crème brûlée. The wine list is short and friendly.

DUBLIN   Shelbourne Hotel

St Stephen's Green, Dublin 2, Co Dublin
Telephone: (01) 676 6471 Fax: (01) 661 6006   **£45**
Open: lunch + dinner daily
Meals served: lunch 12.30-2.30, dinner 6-10.30 (Sun 6-10)

Well worth a visit even if it's just for lunch. This 18th-century red-brick
hotel was where the Irish Constitution was drafted and has played host
to many great and famous people since then. A wonderful hotel, it has
no fewer than 164 bedrooms and a welcome and friendly atmosphere.
This year a new bar has been added which serves food throughout the
day; otherwise a selection of roast and grills from the restaurant
proves to be good value. There is always a vegetarian option on offer,
and desserts are from the trolley. Saturday evenings in the summer
months also offer music and entertainment.

DUBLIN   La Stampa

35 Dawson Street, Dublin 2, Co Dublin
Telephone: (01) 677 8611 Fax: (01 677 3336   **£35**
Open: lunch + dinner Mon-Sat (closed 3 days Xmas, Good Friday)
Meals served: lunch 12-2.30, dinner 6-11.30 (Fri+Sat 6-12)

Louis Murray enticed Michael Martin back from London, after his
stints at Le Gavroche and La Tante Claire, to take up the post of chef at
his restaurant. The decor of the interior, including pre-Raphaelite etch-
ings, granite horse heads and large displays of fruit and flowers, gives
the restaurant a warm, Renaissance feel. The menus have been
revised, and include starters of roast quail with bacon and pine nuts
and grilled red mullet with a salad of feta cheese, salt cod poached and
served with a mussel, cockle and crab cream sauce, and roast supreme
of chicken with bacon and tarragon. Desserts bring no end to the
abundance - a sharp lemon tart with a raspberry sauce, or a perfect
apple tart with caramel sauce may set your taste buds tingling.

One of Dublin's most stylish restaurants.

DUBLIN — Stephen's Hall Hotel

14-17 Lower Leeson Street, Dublin, Co Dublin 2
Telephone: (01) 661 0585 Fax: (01) 661 0606
The Terrace Bistro: **£35**
Open: lunch Mon-Fri, dinner Mon-Sat (closed 1 wk Xmas)
Meals served: lunch 12.15-2.30, dinner 6.15-9.30
The Terrace Restaurant: **£60**
Open: lunch Mon-Fri, dinner Mon-Sat (closed 1 wk Xmas)
Meals served: lunch 12.15-2.30, dinner 6.15-9.30

As this hotel is situated right in the heart of the town the art galleries, shops and business city are on the doorstep and make this the ideal venue for business executives. Set in Sir Arthur Guinness' magnificent square, the verdant lawns, trees and flowers in the centre make an arresting display when seen from this luxury townhouse. This is not a hotel of rooms but rather a collection of suites, each having its own sitting room, lobby and kitchen with shopping and cleaning services available. The Terrace bistro offers a short menu of accessible dishes such as seafood terrine, baked salmon with sun-dried tomatoes and char-grilled fillet steak with shallots and red wine. Although linked to the hotel, there's also a separate entrance to The Terrace restaurant, which overlooks a courtyard where chef Giles O'Reilly grows his herbs. His imaginative menu is proving popular, with dishes that might include bamboo-steamed plaice with a lime butter sauce, eel terrine flavoured with beer and herbs or salmon and turbot baked in butter and coriander.

DUN LAOGHAIRE — De Selby's

17/18 Patrick Street, Dun Laoghaire, Co Dublin
Telephone: (01) 284 1761 Fax: (01) 284 1762   **£30**
Open: dinner daily, all day Sat+Sun (closed 24+26 Dec, Good Friday)
Meals served: dinner 5.30-11, (Sat 12-11 Sun 12-10)

A relaxed and well-priced restaurant decorated in a nautical theme, with wooden tables and chairs and a stone floor. Good selection of lamb, steaks and chicken, plus a variety of fresh fish dishes every night. Very popular with families.

DUNDALK — Cellars

Backhouse Centre, Clanbrassil Street, Dundalk, Co Louth
Telephone: (042) 33745   £15
Open: lunch Mon-Fri (closed Bank Holidays)
Meals served: lunch 12.15-2
Daily changing menus depend upon the market that day; vegetarians well catered for.

DUNDERRY   Dunderry Lodge Restaurant

Dunderry, Navan, Co Meath
Telephone: (046) 31671   **£50**
Open: lunch Sun (+ Sat May-Aug), dinner Tue-Sat. (closed Bank Holidays)
Meals served: lunch 1-2, dinner 7-9.30

A well-known, characterful house of old stone has been restored lovingly by Paul and Fiona Groves and decorated with country style furniture. The dining room is immaculately set with fine crisp linen and glass. Paul's cooking is a well-balanced menu of rustic cooking with free range poultry and pork, and herbs and vegetables from the garden, all put to the best use in dishes that include creamy scrambled eggs with mushrooms, herb and a cèpe butter sauce and game pâté with an elderberry dressing. Breasts of mallard come with creamed lentils and chicken is cooked with aromatic herbs and garlic. The saucing is excellent and the dessert trolley shouldn't be missed. Interesting wine list with some fair prices.

DUNWORLEY   Dunworley Cottage

Butlerstown, Clonakilty, Dunworley, Co Cork
Telephone: (023) 40314   **£40**
Open: lunch + dinner Wed-Sun (closed Nov, Jan+Feb)
Meals served: lunch 1-5, dinner 6.30-10

The cottage is typically Scandinavian with bare floors and a roaring fire in winter, and is home to Swedish owner Katherine Noren and her passion for good wholesome food. Bread is baked every day, salami is made from her own pigs and she sources her ingredients through the Organic Growers of Ireland Association. The menu is a mix of whatever the local catch brings in, steaks from local cattle, soups made from vegetables or nettles and the local specialities of white and black pudding. She takes her food extremely seriously and wants her guests to recognise good cooking but is quite happy to cater for special dietary needs and her menu goes so far as to highlight low cholesterol, gluten free and vegan dishes.

DURRUS   Blairs Cove House Restaurant

Blairs Cove, Durrus, Nr Bantry, Co Cork
Telephone: (027) 61127   **£55**
Open: dinner Mon-Sat (closed Nov-Feb, Mon Sep-Jun)
Meals served: dinner 7.30-9.30

Another great husband and wife team, Sabine and Philippe de Mey run this restaurant with 5 rooms overlooking Dunmanus Bay. Sabine supervises the kitchen with a menu of straightforward cooking which allows all the natural flavours to come through: try smoked fillet of cod, salmon with a horseradish crust, grilled dover sole and grilled steaks all cooked on an open wood fire. Appetizers are selected from a buffet and cheese is the centrepiece with the desserts laid out on the top of the grand piano.

ENNISKERRY   Enniscree Lodge

Glencree Valley, Enniskerry, Co Wicklow
Telephone: (01) 286 3542 Fax: (01) 286 6037   **£40**
Open: lunch + dinner daily (Fri-Sun only in Jan+Feb)
Meals served: lunch 12.30-2.30, dinner 7.30-9.30 (Sat 7.30-10 Sun 7.30-9)

You will feel like you are on top of the world when overlooking the
Djouce, Tonduff, Kippure and Sugarloaf mountains. Here the friendly
old inn has a cosy bar and good all day food while in the Terrace
Restaurant the menu is more imaginative but still served in an unpretentious and informal manner. The 10 bedrooms allow you to stay a little longer and soak up the special scenery.

FURBO   Connemara Coast Hotel

Furbo, Nr Galway, Co Galway
Telephone: (091) 92108 Fax: (091) 92065   **£50**
Open: dinner daily
Meals served: dinner 6.30-10

Overlooking the Galway Bay this 120-bedroomed hotel, with a modern
and well-finished interior, offers accommodation from standard to
executive suites. The hotel grounds sweep down to the shores of the
bay and look to the west to the Aran Islands. The à la carte and set
menus offer fine fish and thick soups from chowder to bisques with
main courses that are the pride of Ireland's finest quality ingredients.

GALWAY   Casey's Westwood Restaurant

Dangan, Upper Newcastle, Galway, Co Galway
Telephone: (091) 21442   **£40**
Open: lunch + dinner daily (closed 3 days Xmas, Good Friday)
Meals served: lunch 12.30-2.15, dinner 6.30-10

This restaurant is housed in a long low building run by the Casey
family and provides a selection of different rooms. John Casey cooks
for the Westwood Restaurant with a repertoire of dishes including
daily specials, à la carte and his 5-course set dinner menu. In all cases
the cooking is good with dishes such as tartlet of mussels with
smoked bacon and leeks and a saffron sauce, breast of chicken with a
fresh fig sauce and a ratatouille and basil butter sauce. Take time first
to relax in the cocktail bar where your order will be taken. Low cholesterol and vegetarian dishes are available.

Marlfield House —see opposite

GOREY	Marlfield House

Gorey, Co Wexford Gorey
Telephone: (055) 21124 Fax: (055) 21572   **£60**
Open: lunch + dinner daily (closed Dec+Jan)
Meals served: lunch 12.30-2, dinner 7-9.30

A luxurious country house hotel in Regency style is the setting for Rose Brannock's cooking. She continues to produce a menu with an emphasis on modern interpretations of traditional dishes highlighted by country overtones. In the conservatory dining room you will enjoy dishes such as pan-fried lamb's kidneys on an oatmeal potato cake with a mustard grain sauce, turbot with asparagus, baby spinach and garlic scented butter, or lamb with oyster mushrooms and a rosemary jus. Rhubarb sorbet refreshes the palate, followed by chilled honey parfait with armagnac-soaked prunes, or a summer pudding with champagne sabayon and raspberry coulis to make a fine finale to a splendid and well-cooked menu. With views over the landscaped gardens and fine furniture, this house makes a restful place to stay.

GREYSTONES	The Hungry Monk

Greystones, Co Wicklow
Telephone: (01) 287 5759   **£50**
Open: lunch Sat+Sun, dinner Tue-Sat
Meals served: lunch 12.30-3, dinner 7-11

Set over the Irish Building Society in the main street, this first-floor restaurant does indeed have a monastic air, with its monks' gallery adorning the walls and candles lit on every table even during lunch. This is an informal place with a light-hearted French menu offering moules normande (Galway mussels steamed over cider), faisan rôti (roasted off the bone with chestnuts and a traditional game sauce) and filet de boeuf madère (beef wrapped in bacon with a herb crust). The wine list is good value, extensive and takes pride of place with owner Pat Keown.

HOWTH	King Sitric

East Pier, Harbour Road Howth, Co Dublin
Telephone: (01) 326729 Fax: (01) 392442   **£50**
Open: (lunch Seafood Bar May-Sep only), dinner Mon-Sat
(closed Bank Holidays, 1 wk Jan, 1 wk Easter)
Meals served: (lunch 12-3), dinner 6.30-11

Sole cooked on the bone and Howth crab and lobster are the specialities of the house at this harbourside restaurant in a wonderful location with one of the biggest fishing fleets in the whole of Ireland right on the doorstep. At the east of the pier is Aidan MacManus' restaurant resplendent in patriotic green with sea views to be enjoyed from the lounge upstairs. Also on the first floor is the seafood bar that is open for lunch and offers good value bisques and fishermen's platters and lobster. In the evening the restaurant is in full swing with haddock, cod, ray, turbot and salmon all cooked with appropriate saucing. Good selection of wines by the half bottle and glass.

KANTURK	Assolas Country House

Kanturk, Co Cork
Telephone: (029) 50015 Fax: (029) 50795   **£60**
Open: dinner daily (closed Nov-Mar)
Meals served: dinner 7-8.30 (Sun 7-8)

You'll find none of the stuffiness of a formal hotel in the Bourkes' 9-bedroomed manor. They run it like their home (which it is!), with a laid back and welcome attitude that is a pleasure to experience. Beautifully situated and furnished, the dining room offers a daily changing menu mainly featuring local fish. Hazel is the cook, producing dishes with modest saucing that allow the true flavours of the ingredients to come through and speak for themselves. A typical dinner menu might include twice-baked cheddar soufflé, loin of venison served with a wild rowanberry jelly or loin of lamb with a rosemary-scented jus.

KENMARE	The Old Bank House

Main Street, Kenmare, Co Kerry
Telephone: (064) 41589 Fax: (064) 41589   **£55**
Open: dinner daily in summer (Wed-Sat in winter) (closed 2 wks Feb)
Meals served: dinner 7-9 (5-9 in summer)

The old bank and its vault make an unusual setting for Matthew d'Arcy's restaurant, which he runs with his wife Aileen. It's into its second season and presents a cosy and welcoming place to dine. The menu begins with some very good bread and reflects Matthew's foundations in classical food preparation: warm ravioli of prawn mousse with a sweet pepper scented butter and a soup of parsnip and apple, followed by main courses of baked sea trout and smoked salmon in pastry, pan-fried scallops with leeks and grapes and crumbed veal with capers and butter. His careful selection of ingredients pays off and there's a keen wine list too. There are 5 neat bedrooms and good breakfasts are available for overnighters.

KENMARE	Packies

Henry Street, Kenmare, Co Kerry
Telephone: (064) 41508   **£40**
Open: dinner Mon-Sat (closed Nov-Easter)
Meals served: dinner 5.30-10

With a style that gathers ideas from around the world and carefully moulds them together, Tom and Maura Foley have created a well frequented restaurant that is up-to-date with trends in food. This lively menu might easily be found in some of the more popular restaurants of London's West End, offering dishes such as crumbed scallops with olive oil, pesto or garlic butter, gnocchi with tomato and basil, casserole of braised beef with Guinness and desserts of warm rhubarb crumble with nuts and sunflower seeds, or pears in marsala with mascarpone ice cream. If this place is closed, then a couple of doors down is Maura's sister's pub, the Purple Heather, where you can enjoy an excellent and informal lunch. Packies offers a relaxed place to eat with its simple decor, bare wooden tables and paper napkins.

KENMARE   Park Hotel

Kenmare, Co Kerry
Telephone: (064) 41200 Fax: (064) 41402   **£80**
Open: lunch + dinner daily (closed mid Nov-Xmas, 4 Jan-Easter)
Meals served: lunch 1-1.45, dinner 7-8.45

An enchanting place to visit, The Park has wonderful views over the
Kenmare estuary to the mountains, offset by the fine furnishing of the
public rooms with marble fireplaces and plenty of fresh flowers. There
are 50 bedrooms, each quite luxurious, and the service prompt and
pleasant. The restaurant offers an immaculately-served dinner with
every attention paid to detail. The chef is proud of his local produce
and presents a menu which might include pan-fried chicken with a
tomato and mushroom sauce or veal with mustard and starters of roast
duck with a raspberry vinaigrette or fresh asparagus with a light
orange sauce. The desserts are classical but the most interesting is a
mix of fresh and poached fruits in a lime syrup with a champagne
sorbet.

KENMARE   Sheen Falls Lodge

Kenmare, Co Kerry
Telephone: (064) 41600 Fax: (064) 41386   **£90**
Open: lunch Sun, dinner daily (closed Jan-mid Mar)   *40 rooms & suites*
Meals served: lunch 1-2, dinner 7.30-9.30

Floodlit at night and as bright as a canary by day, painted in a distinctive yellow, this hotel is surrounded by the Sheen Falls and Kenmare
Bay. Relax in the well-decorated public rooms or leaf through the large
library before dinner. In the Cascade Restaurant the menu shows
imaginative dishes including starters of langoustine tails with tomato
and red onion or thinly sliced smoked salmon with sour cream and
herbs and main courses of oven-roasted chicken with potato rosti and
lightly grilled salmon with lemon grass. Desserts bring out a gratin of
fresh strawberries with ice cream and quenelles of chocolate mousse
with rolled cinnamon biscuits. One early summer evening take a stroll
along the Queen's Walk, through the exotic gardens and lush woodlands that surround the lodge and plan the next day's game of golf or
afternoon's fishing.

Park Hotel

KILKENNY   Lacken House

Dublin Road, Kilkenny, Co Kilkenny
Telephone: (056) 61085   **£55**
Open: dinner Tue-Sat (closed 1 wk Xmas)
Meals served: dinner 7-10.30

Eugene McSweeney's cooking has been described as progressive
Irish, and he uses local produce well. The dining room may be tightly
packed but the cooking makes up for it, with a seafood soup full of
flavour and a medallion of venison, ample in size and rich and tender.
Eugene's wife Breda with a professional manner and welcoming smile
is responsible for front of house. A first class sommelier, she also
manages the good wine list. Take to the drawing room after dinner,
which with its raging fire in winter makes a cosy place to relax and
enjoy your coffee. The 8 bedrooms are elementary and neat but it is
the breakfast that is the star and really shouldn't be missed.

KILLARNEY   Aghadoe Heights Hotel

Aghadoe, Killarney, Co Kerry
Telephone: (064) 31766 Fax: (064) 31345   **£70**
Open: lunch + dinner daily
Meals served: lunch 12.15-2, dinner 7-9.30

A modern, yet elegant and stylish hotel, which benefits from fine views
of the mountains and islands of Lake Killarney. Expansion has
increased the leisure facilities. Seafood is a speciality, as is local lamb,
with fixed-price menus offering choice. Good desserts and reasonable
wine list.

KILLARNEY   Gaby's Seafood Restaurant

27 High Street, Killarney, Co Kerry
Telephone: (064) 32519 Fax: (064) 32747   **£65**
Open: lunch Tue-Sat, dinner Mon-Sat (closed Feb)
Meals served: lunch 12.30-2.30, dinner 6-10

The minute the fish has been landed by the Kerry fishing fleet it
makes its way to Gert Maes' restaurant and is served up on his menu -
grilled wild salmon, black sole, lobster, turbot, brill. At lunchtime a
more concise menu offers cold plates of seafood, salmon pâté and hot
plates of Kenmare Bay mussels and seafood vol-au-vent - good, light
alternatives. Very good wine list with some reasonable prices.

KILLORGLIN   Nick's Restaurant

Lower Bridge Street, Killorglin, Co Kerry
Telephone: (066) 61219 Fax: (066) 61233   **£60**
Open: lunch + dinner daily (closed Nov, 25+26 Dec, Mon+Tue Jan-Easter)
Meals served: lunch 12.30-3, dinner 6.30-10

A steak and seafood restaurant that relies on local supplies of both,
supplemented by organically grown vegetables. The style of the menu
is mainly French and traditional with grilled mushrooms and cream,
cockle and mussel soup, salmon and prawns in champagne sauce and
duck with orange or simply grilled cutlets of Kerry lamb. All come
with a selection of freshly steamed vegetables and potatoes. Home-
made desserts include a warm caramelised pineapple, cheesecake and
crème brulée.

KINSALE   Blue Haven Hotel

3 Pearse Street, Kinsale, Co Cork
Telephone: (021) 772209 Fax: (021) 774268   **£55**
Open: dinner daily (closed 25 Dec, 2 days mid-week in winter)
Meals served: dinner 7-10.30

The restaurant is as well-run and maintained as the rest of the hotel. It
is a characterful place with a courtyard garden and a menu that is
straightforward with a bias towards fish. Clonakilty black and white
puddings with apple and calvados join baked oysters glazed with hollandaise or in the raw as starters. Main courses include house specialities of hot, wood-smoked salmon, fresh hake with Pernod batter and
sole cooked on the bone. Choose the more simple dishes, although
the seafood kashmiri is well balanced and comes with all the right
accompaniments. Excellent vegetables and cheeses are local.
Reasonably priced wine list.

KINSALE   Chez Jean-Marc

Lower O'Connell Street, Kinsale, Co Cork
Telephone: (021) 774625 Fax: (021) 774680   **£50**
Open: lunch Mon-Sat in summer (Sun only, in winter), dinner
Mon-Sat in summer (Tue-Sat in winter) (closed Xmas, mid Feb-mid Mar)
Meals served: lunch 12.30-3, dinner 6.45-10.30 (winter 7-10)

Resplendent in its new colours of deep blue and yellow, the external
paint work of this cottage-style restaurant has received a new lease of
life. Inside the tones are docile with green and deep peony red creating a warm atmosphere complementing beams and exposed brickwork. The service is welcoming and chef-owner Jean-Marc Tsai cooks
classical French dishes with overtones of the orient. A typical menu
might offer a mille feuille of crisp vegetables with Chinese drumsticks,
fettucini with clams, mussels and salmon and a soufflé for dessert. The
presentation is paramount and the flavours assertive. Very good house
wines.

KINSALE   Man Friday

Scilly, Kinsale, Co Cork
Telephone: (021) 772260   **£60**
Open: dinner daily (closed Sun in winter)
Meals served: dinner 7-10

Owner/chef Philip Horgan's popular restaurant offers a variety of dishes that use local seafood and other ingredients, from croquettes of West Coast crab with a plum and port sauce, hot Kinsale platter of seafood, escalopes of monkfish with a light chive and mustard sauce and rack of lamb with a red wine and rosemary sauce. An eclectic and highly imaginative menu that pulls in the crowds.

KINSALE   Max's Wine Bar

Main Street, Kinsale, Co Cork
Telephone: (021) 772443   **£35**
Open: lunch + dinner daily (closed Nov-Feb)
Meals served: lunch 1-3, dinner 7-10.30

A charming small restaurant with simple decor and plain tables with varnished tops, serving a creative menu with the emphasis on starters such as deep-fried mozzarella with tomato and basil and a spinach pasta with fresh salmon. Salads include chopped raw vegetables and fruit with a yoghurt dressing topped with seeds and nuts and is ample for a main course, whereas main courses are divided into seafood, vegetarian and meat with plenty of choice, and simple saucing. Service is good and cooking sympathetic. Good home-made bread.

KINSALE   Old Presbytery

Cork Street, Kinsale, Co Cork
Telephone: (021) 772027   **£35**
Open: dinner Mon-Sat (closed 1 wk Xmas)
Meals served: dinner 7.30-8.30

Set in the middle of this fishing village is this quaint restaurant with 6 bedrooms, each with big comfortable beds and crisp linen. The restaurant is charming with a short, daily changing menu of good home cooking, fish being a speciality. Several good puddings.

Longueville House
Mallow.

LETTERFRACK   Rosleague Manor

Letterfrack, Connemara, Co Galway
Telephone: (095) 41101 Fax: (095) 41168   **£50**
Open: lunch + dinner daily (closed Nov-Easter)
Meals served: lunch 1-2.30, dinner 8-9.30 (Sun 8-9)

Owned and managed by the Foyle family, this 20-bedroomed,
Georgian house plays hosts to visitors who come here to relax in the
secluded landscapes and to dine on seafood and home-grown vegetables. Set in the middle of a wooded area by the coast and in the centre
of the Connemara National Park the 200-year-old house is a real haven.
The dining room is decorated with a great sense of comfort and style,
with antique tables and chandeliers. Cooking is by brother-in-law Nigel
Rush who keeps his menus short and interesting with smoked trout
mousse and medallions of monkfish with garlic and pine nuts. The
good Irish cheeses and whiskey trifle are a must.

MALAHIDE   Bon Appetit

9 St James Terrace, Malahide, Dublin, Co Dublin
Telephone: (01) 845 0314 Fax: £45
Open: lunch Mon-Fri, dinner Mon-Sat (closed Bank Holidays, 1 wk Xmas)
Meals served: lunch 12.30-2, dinner 7-11
Intimate French-style restaurant, classical international food. Front bar enjoys fine
views of the estuary.

MALAHIDE   Roches Bistro

12 New Street, ,Malahide, Co Dublin
Telephone: (01) 845 2777   £45
Open: lunch Mon-Sat, dinner Thu-Sat (closed Mon Jan-Jun, Bank Holidays, 2 wks Jan)
Meals served: lunch 12-2.30, dinner 7-10.30
French country-style cooking, large menu, some good seafood dishes.

MALLOW   Longueville House

Mallow, Co Cork
Telephone: (022) 47156 Fax: (022) 47459   **£55**
Open: lunch + dinner daily (closed 20 Dec-28 Feb)
Meals served: lunch 12.30-2, dinner 7-9

The ancestral home of the Callaghan family plays host to visitors who
come to enjoy well-proportioned rooms that contain many antiques
and family treasures. In the dining room a gallery of Irish presidents
looks down as you dine under the chandelier on food that the talented
William Callaghan cooks using ingredients from the family farm and
garden. The à la carte menu offers suckling pig with applè and truffle
sauce, but it is the set menu that offers the best value, a recent menu
offering a hot slice of salmon with a vegetable terrine followed by
poussin with a basil-scented sauce. Bread and butter pudding with
poached pears and almonds brings a fine end to the menu. Relax in the
drawing room or, for the smokers, in the library and take in the old-
world charm of the house before climbing the stairs to bed in one of
the 16 rooms.

MOYCULLEN   Drimcong House Restaurant

Moycullen, Co Galway
Telephone: (091) 85115   **£40**
Open: dinner Tue-Sat (closed Jan+Feb)
Meals served: dinner 7-10.30

The Georgian, lakeland home of Gerry and Marie Galvin is a happy
place offering some talented and well presented cooking that has a
modern ring with Italian and oriental touches to an otherwise French
menu. The menus are devised and cooked by Gerry who grills oysters
with garlic and gruyère to make a delicious savoury to enjoy with a
glass of champagne! The flavours of the orient punctuate his menu
with a sesame dressing for smoked salmon and a Chinese chicken
broth before main courses of open ravioli with lamb's kidneys and
devil sauce and beef with polenta and mushroom sauce. Desserts hit
back with jelly and ice cream and a hot steamed lemon and raspberry
pudding. A fixed-price dinner menu gives excellent value.

NAVAN   Ardboyne Hotel

Dublin Road, Navan, Co Meath
Telephone: (046) 23119 Fax: (046) 22355   £40
Open: lunch + dinner daily (closed 24-27 Dec)
Meals served: lunch 12.30-2.30, dinner 5-10 (Sun 5-9)
Good, modern one. Simple, straightforward menus plus a carvery. Popular for confer-
ences and with business executives.

NEWBAY   Newbay Country House

Newbay, Nr Wexford, Co Wexford
Telephone: (053) 42779 Fax: (053) 46318   **£55**
Open: dinner Tue-Sat (closed mid Nov-mid Mar)
Meals served: dinner at 7.30

In an early 19th-century house, the tall hall and elegant staircase greet
and welcome you before you enter equally impressive drawing and
dining rooms. All of the rooms are decorated and furnished in sympa-
thy with the period of the house, which is still very much the home of
the Drums. Dinner is taken by everyone altogether, around one table,
with the no-choice menu prepared by owner Paul Drum depending on
what is in season or best from the markets that day - a unique and very
pleasant experience. Coffee and petits fours are taken later in the
drawing room. The 6 bedrooms make it feel like staying with friends,
rather than in a hotel.

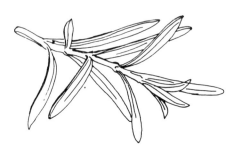

NEWMARKET-ON-FERGUS   Dromoland Castle

Newmarket-on-Fergus, Co Clare
Telephone: (061) 368144 Fax: (061) 363355   **£75**
Open: lunch + dinner daily
Meals served: lunch 12.30-2, dinner 7-9.30

Complete with 18-hole golf course, this castle is rich with family portraits that adorn the walls, Gothic cornicing and chandeliers. But there
is a comfortable air with roaring wood fires and cosy public rooms. A
new wing was built last year and includes the Brian Boru Hall with
banqueting and conference facilities. The cooking and menu are
French, created by Jean-Baptiste Molinari who has managed to keep
both in tune with the majestic dining room. A harpist and fiddler play
as you dine on a 5-course affair of Kinavara Irish oak-smoked salmon,
fish soup, salmon with sorrel or monkfish braised in the oven with a
light champagne and saffron sauce. Desserts are classical or there's an
excellent cheeseboard. Good petits fours and coffee conclude.

NEWPORT   Newport House

Newport, Co Mayo
Telephone: (098) 41222 Fax: (098) 41613   **£70**
Open: dinner daily (closed 7 Oct-18 Mar)
Meals served: dinner 7.30-9.30

An impressive creeper-clad house whose chandeliered dining room
with damask curtains and marble fireplace offers an elegance in keeping with the remainder of the house - sweeping staircases and
galleried landing. The menu relies on the good flavours of the food and
is not over-fussy. A typical dinner menu might include baked fillet of
hake with a lemon butter sauce, cream of vegetable soup followed by
monkfish with a wild sorrel sauce or spring lamb with a red wine and
rosemary sauce. Puddings remain strictly traditional with French
lemon tart and poached pears with orange. 20 individually styled bedrooms, with antiques and good furnishings. Good, friendly hospitality.

OUGHTERARD   Currarevagh House

Oughterard, Connemara, Co Galway
Telephone: (091) 82312 Fax: (091) 82731   **£40**
Open: dinner daily (closed Nov-Mar)
Meals served: dinner at 8

An early Victorian, 15-bedroomed house with parkland and woodlands
provides a relaxing and private place to stay. Run by the Hodgson family the house still remains a home, which is what makes it so charming.
Old fashioned Irish hospitality speaks volumes here with cosy rooms
and friendly service. June Hodgson is in charge of the kitchen and
cooks in a simple manner. Dinner is a 5-course set menu with a grapefruit soufflé and roulade of pork with calvados sauce being typical and
always followed by dessert and cheese. Good breakfasts and wonderful views.

| OYSTERHAVEN | The Oystercatcher |

Oysterhaven, Nr Kinsale, Co Cork
Telephone: (021) 770821   **£55**
Open: dinner daily (closed Jan)
Meals served: dinner 7-9.30 (bookings only, in winter)

A flower-clad cottage beside a creek is the setting for Bill and Sylvia Patterson's restaurant where the menu is bright and modern in contrast to the old-fashioned style of the building. Bill manages to blend reworked traditional dishes with new creations and comes up with an enticing menu, offering dishes like roast partridge with a wild mushroom sauce or snails with ham and garlic perfumed with Pernod. The sweet things in life are typified by prunes in armagnac and drunken bananas flambéed with dark rum.

| RATHMULLAN | Rathmullan House |

Rathmullan, Nr Letterkenny, Co Donegal
Telephone: (074) 58188 Fax: (074) 58200   **£45**
Open: lunch Sun, dinner daily (closed Nov-mid Mar)
Meals served: lunch 1-2, dinner 7.30-8.45

This gracious mansion is set amidst ancient oak trees in the heart of the Donegal countryside and makes a fine setting for Bob and Robin Wheeler's hotel. The dining room is decorated with silks in an Arabian tent design, and has a menu that is French and Irish based - loin of Cranford pork with a prune and apple stuffing, poached fillet of brill with crab meat or lamb with a minted pear sauce. The 23 bedrooms are elegant and beautiful and the Egyptian baths with an indoor ionised salt-water pool, sauna and steam room are worth a visit.

| RATHNEW | Tinakilly House |

Rathnew, Wicklow, Co Wicklow
Telephone: (0404) 69274 Fax: (0404) 67806   **£60**
Open: lunch + dinner daily
Meals served: lunch 12.30-2, dinner 7.30-9

A putting green has been added to the Victorian gardens where there was already a croquet lawn. A mid-19th-century mansion with 29 rooms, it boasts a well-stocked garden, overlooking the flats of Wicklow harbour and is of great interest to wildlife fanatics. John Moloney continues to cook his mix of Irish cooking with dishes like traditional Irish stew with garden vegetables, warm escalope of salmon on a dill sauce and loin of pork with a port and rosemary sauce. Puddings are of strength including tipsy pudding with mulled wine, honey and cream cheese and raspberry and Grand Marnier parfait with a mint cream. Fine local produce is put to the best use with many of the vegetables and fruit home grown.

ROUNDWOOD	Roundwood Inn

Roundwood, Co Wicklow
Telephone: (01) 281 8107 £50
Open: lunch Tue-Sun, dinner Tue-Sat (closed 25 Dec, Good Friday)
Meals served: lunch 1-2.30, dinner 7.30-9.30 (Sat 7.30-10)
Good local cooking (using seasonal produce) - more mainstream than bar food.

SCOTSHOUSE	Hilton Park

Scotshouse, Nr Clones, Co Monaghan
Telephone: (047) 56007 Fax: (047) 56033 £50
Open: dinner daily (closed Oct-Easter)
Meals served: dinner 8-9.30
Owned by the 8th generation of the Madden family, classic porticoed house with an old world interior, 5 bedrooms and fine views.

SHANAGARRY — Ballymaloe House

Shanagarry, Co Cork
Telephone: (021) 652531 Fax: (021) 652021 £70
Open: lunch Sun, dinner daily (closed 24-26 Dec)
Meals served: lunch at 1, dinner 7-9.30 (Sun buffet only at 7.30)

If ever asked how a country house should be, Ballymaloe always springs to mind, with its informal air and welcoming tone, and I defy anyone not to feel relaxed here. The countryside is lush and green, the house still very much Ivan and Myrtle Allen's home. A mish-mash of pottery, watercolours and plentiful vases of country flowers imparts an Irish tone and a quiet and simple sophistication, with the dining room a cosy series of 4 rooms. Meal times are more than just a delight, with a mixture of family and locals serving. Dinner is not flash but shows an excellence of Irish cooking rarely experienced anywhere else. Local ingredients work their ways into terrines, soups, desserts of sweet poached rhubarb and plenty of home-made ices. A typical evening's meal could run thus - shellfish from the nearby fishing village of Ballycotton with a tarragon coulis, lamb with ratatouille and water chestnuts, sirloin of beef with marrow, veal with wild mushrooms or duck with soy and ginger sauce. Puddings include pink grapefruit and melon sauternes and lime sabayon, clafoutis of plums and a terrine of chocolate and pistachio. The 29 bedrooms are quaint and neat, looking out into the green countryside. The enticing smell of breakfast wafts up the stairs as you wake, and proves as much of an impressive spread as that of the night before. A wonderful location that has to be seen and experienced.

SPIDDAL   Boluisce Seafood Bar

Spiddal Village, Connemara, Co Galway
Telephone: (091) 83286 Fax: (091) 83285   **£35**
Open: all day daily (closed 24-26 Dec)
Meals served: 12-10 (Sun 4-10)

A family-run restaurant that serves simple seafood snacks from a
downstairs bar, together with a separate menu in the friendly first-floor
restaurant designed by family member and cook John Glanville. He
offers excellent lobster, mussels in a cream sauce or crab claws with
lots of garlic butter, along with some meat alternatives. Excellent
range of Irish cheeses.

STRAFFAN   Kildare Hotel

Straffan, Co Kildare
Telephone: (01) 6273333 Fax: (01) 6273312   **£70**
Open: lunch Sun-Fri, dinner daily
Meals served: lunch 12.30-2, dinner 7-10

This legacy of the Barton wine family, who lived here in the 19th
Century, is set in lush countryside and overlooks its own golf course,
designed by Arnold Palmer. A 45-bedroomed hotel, it is furnished with
splendid pieces and also holds a magnificent collection of paintings by
well-known artists, with a whole room devoted to Jack B T. Yeats.
Expansion has been necessary, but not to the detriment of the building. The dining room is a fine example of this - with its elegant drapes,
marble columns and tones of deep terracotta, cream and green, it
effectively blends new with old. It makes a striking room in which to
enjoy French classical cooking, offset by crested china and mono-
grammed white linen. With a well presented and detailed menu you
can dine on poached truffled egg with globe artichoke and foie gras
butter, roast petal of monkfish with cream of lobster, and pan-fried silver bream with vegetables in a basil dressing. Dessert brings out
rhubarb torte with an allspice ice cream and a selection of Irish and
French cheeses.

SWORDS   The Old Schoolhouse

Coolbanagher, Swords, Co Dublin
Telephone: (01) 840 4160 Fax: (01) 840 5060   **£45**
Open: lunch Mon-Fri, dinner Mon-Sat
Meals served: lunch 12.30-2.30, dinner 6.30-10.30

In a quiet haven off the beaten track is an old stone building, lovingly
restored by Brian and Ann Sinclair and transformed into this delightful
restaurant. With a new chef in the kitchen the menu is also transformed, and features fish from nearby Skerries and Howth harbours.
The cooking is straightforward and hearty with soups so substantial
that they're a meal in themselves.

THOMASTOWN   Mount Juliet Hotel

Mount Juliet, Thomastown, Co Kilkenny
Telephone: (056) 24455 Fax: (056) 24522   £65
Open: lunch + dinner daily (closed 2 wks Jan)
Meals served: lunch 12.30-2, dinner 7-9

Complete with the Jack Nicklaus Signature Golf Course and 3-hole
Golf Academy, this hotel stands in 1500 acres of parkland and formal
gardens through which the Kings and Nore rivers flow. In this 18th-
century house you'll be staying in the lap of luxury, surrounded by
Adam fireplaces, solid oak furniture and deep-cushioned sofas. The
Lady Helen McCalmont restaurant is airy, with delicate pastel work
and sweeping views across gentle greens and rolling countryside.
Chris Farrell's menu is colourful and flavoursome with specialities of
beef and wild salmon from the Nore. The wine list is extensive.

WATERFORD   Dwyer's Restaurant

8 Mary Street, Waterford, Co Waterford
Telephone: (051) 77478 Fax: **£40**
Open: dinner Mon-Sat (closed Xmas, Easter, 2 wks Jul)
Meals served: dinner 6-10 (set dinner 6-7.30)

There's some good cooking to be found here in chef/patron Martin
Dwyer's restaurant. A modern European menu is served in this former
barracks, now decorated in pastels with classical music to add a
genteel air. The cooking is unfussy and well executed with a contrast
of texture and flavour - profiteroles of crab, smoked salmon pirozhki,
followed by main courses of guinea fowl with chive sauce and medallions of pork with lemon and thyme. Puddings include pear and
almond tart, or rhubarb and orange fool.

WATERFORD   Waterford Castle

The Island, Ballinakill, Waterford, Co Waterford
Telephone: (051) 78203 Fax: (051) 79316   **£65**
Open: lunch + dinner daily
Meals served: lunch 12.30-2, dinner 7-10 (Sun 7-9)

Set on an island with an 18-hole golf course, Waterford Castle makes
for an enjoyable weekend in a dramatic setting: gargoyles, towers and
studded oak doors without, Regency-style furnishing and plenty of
wood panelling within. The 19 bedrooms are fittingly grand, with
4-poster beds in some and lots of wood furnishings. In the characterful
dining room, fixed-price dinner menus are offered with a hint of an
international flavour, maybe including seafood pancake with stir-fried
vegetables or roast leg of lamb with coriander and garlic, along with
the more traditional roast rib of beef with red wine sauce and horseradish cream.

WICKLOW   Old Rectory

Wicklow, Co Wicklow
Telephone: (0404) 67048 Fax: (0404) 69181   **£55**
Open: dinner daily (closed Nov-Easter)
Meals served: dinner at 8

A pink-washed country house greets you with pillared doorway and
flowers in every corner. Linda and Paul Saunders are your hosts and
will make your stay pleasurable and warm. Linda takes to the kitchen
and cooks à la carte and 6-course gourmet dinner menus, with fresh
flowers often making an appearance in salads or stuffed with mousseline. Breakfast comes in 3 styles - Scottish with porridge and kippers,
Swiss with muesli and fresh fruit and Irish with a full cooked plate
which includes white and black puddings.

YOUGHAL   Aherne's Seafood Restaurant

163 North Main Street, Youghal, Co Cork
Telephone: (024) 92424   **£50**
Open: lunch + dinner daily (closed 5 dys Xmas)
Meals served: lunch 12.30-2 (Sun 12.30-1.45), dinner 6.30-9.30

Found in the old historic port (pronounced Yawl), this used to be a
pub but is now into its third generation of Fitzgibbon owners and has
been transformed into a seafood restaurant with rooms. The seafood
comes from local fishermen, and an average day's catch can bring into
the restaurant lobster, prawns, salmon, turbot and sole. Take a quick
snack at the bar on Rossmore natives or gratin of hot potato and
smoked salmon. In the restaurant full à la carte and set menus bring
more adventurous main courses with pan-fried monkfish with Pernod
and fennel, or sole, salmon and prawns in a chablis sauce.

1. SOUTH-WEST ENGLAND & WALES

The maps show only those
villages, towns and cities
where recommended
hotels and restaurants
may be found.

MERSEY-
Liverpool
SIDE

Llandudno   Glanwydden
Beaumaris   Colwyn Bay
Llangefni   Conwy   Llansanffraid
             Glan Conwy
        Llanrug   Northop   Ewloe
                                    CLWYD
                         Ruthin
                         Rossett
GWYNEDD   Chirk
Pwllheli   Portmeirion   Llandrillo
    Talsarnau   Oswestry
Abersoch   Lake Vyrnwy
Llanbedr   Harlech   SHROP-
           Dolgellau   Shifnal
                                    Dorrington
                                    SHIRE
        Eglwysfach
                                    Ludlow
Aberystwyth   Brimfield   Abberley
                         POWYS   Weobley   HEREFORD
                                    Kington   Eyton
                                    AND
                    Llangammarch   Builth   WORCESTER
                    Wells   Wells   Malvern Wells
                         Llyswen   Ledbury
Mathry   Newport   DYFED   Walterstone
Fishguard
Welsh
Hook   Crickhowell
                    Abergavenny
                         Trellech   Whitebrook
                    GWENT   Tintern Abbe
        Gowerton   WEST   Llangybi
        Swansea   GLAMORGAN   Abercynon
Reynoldston   GLAMORGAN   MID   Chepstow
                    GLAMORGAN   Miskin   Newport   Thornbury
        Mumbles   Coychurch   AVON
                    STH   Cardiff   Bristol
                    GLAMORGAN   Clevedon
            Porthkerry   Barry   Hunstrete
                                    Chelwood   Bath
                                    Ston Easton
                                    Wells
                                    Shepton Mallet
                    Porlock   Bruton
            Bishop's   Williton   Glastonbury
Barnstaple   Tawton   Dulverton   SOMERSET   Castle
        East   Wiveliscombe   Cary
        Buckland   South   Taunton   Montacute
                    Molton   Huntsham   Yeovil
        Winkleigh   Chedington   Evershot
                    Broadhembury   DORSET
            Silverton   Gittisham   Maiden Newton
        DEVON   Whimple   Dorchester
Tintagel   Drewsteignton   Exeter   Bridport
        Lewdown   Chagford   Lympstone
Padstow   Lifton   Sourton   Teignmouth
        Mary Tavy   Teignmouth
    Liskeard   Gulworthy   Ashburton   Torquay
    Calstock
CORNWALL   Plymouth
St Austell   Golant   Holbeton
    Fowey   Dartmouth
Truro   Polperro   Bigbury-
ves   on-Sea   Salcombe
Falmouth   St. Mawes
Penzance   Mawnan Smith
        Helford

Alderney

Sark

Guernsey   Jersey

CHANNEL
ISLANDS

Liverpool
Altrincham
Sheffield   SOUTH
Hayfield   YORKSHIRE
Knutsford   Wilmslow   Ridgeway
Alderley Edge   Mottram St. Andrew
Bollington
Chester   Baslow   Linc
Sandiway
CHESHIRE   DERBY-   NOTTINGHAM-
Matlock   SHIRE   Becking
Nantwich   Waterhouses   Newark
Ashbourne   Great
Gonerby
STAFFORD-   Nottingham
SHIRE   Langar
Plumtree
Penkridge   Melton   Str
Mowbray
SHROPSHIRE   Quorn   Stapleford
Shifnal   LEICESTERSHIRE   Oak
Dorrington   Leicester
Worfield   Wolverhampton   Uppingham
WEST   Sutton
MIDLANDS   Coldfield
Ludlow   Birmingham   NORTHAMPTON-
Chaddesley   Solihull   SHIRE
Corbett   Holdenby
Harvington   Hockley   Kenilworth   Horton
Bromsgrove   Heath   Leamington   Roade
Brimfield   Abberley   Spa
Eyton   HEREFORD   WARWICKSHIRE
Weobley   Stratford-upon-Avon   Horton
Ullingswick   Worcester   Roade
AND WORCESTER   Halford   Paulerspury   Marsto
Malvern Wells   Lower Brailes   Morteyn
Ledbury   Broadway   Charingworth   Aspley Guise
Puckrup   Buckland   Chipping Camden   Woburn
Corse   Moreton-in-Marsh   Fli
Lawn   Upper   Stow-on-the-Wold
Cheltenham   Slaughter   Kingham
Gloucester   Lower   Chadlington   Aylesbury
GLOUCESTER-   Slaughter   Charlbury   Dinton   Aston C
GWENT   Birdlip   Woodstock   OXFORD-   Horton-cum-   BUCKINGHAM-
Trellech   SHIRE   Northleach   Minster   Studley   Thame   SHIRE
Whitebrook   Painswick   Burford   Lovell   Oxford   Great
Tintern   Bibury   Lew   Milton   Speen   Great
Abbey   Stroud   Clanfield   Watlington   Misse
Devauden   Frampton-   Stonehouse   Abingdon
Llangybi   on-Severn   Tetbury   Moulsford-   Stonor
Chepstow   on-Thames   Medmenham   Hurley   S
Purton   Remenham   Tap
Goring-on-Thames   Maidenhead
Castle Combe   Yattendon   Bray-on-Thames
Colerne   Corsham   Elcot   Windsor   Han
Avebury   BERKSHIRE   Ascot
Lacock   Rowde   Kintbury   Shinfield   Bagshot
Freshford   Newbury   Old Burghclere   Ch
Bradford-   Melksham   Woolton Hill   Eversley   R
on-Avon   Rotherwick
WILTSHIRE   Hurstbourne   Basingstoke
Tarrant   Farnham
Warminster   Bramley
Crar
HAMPSHIRE   Grayshott   Hasl
Teffont Evias   New Alresford
Gillingham   Dunbridge   Winchester   Midhurst
Shaftesbury   Romsey   Chilgrove   Pulboro
Stuckton   Southampton   Botley   Amber
Sherborne   Sturminster   Storr
Newton   Wickham   Havant
Evershot   Blandford Forum   Brockenhurst   Cosham   Emsworth   Chichester
Chedington   DORSET   Beaulieu
Maiden Newton   New Milton
Bridport   Christchurch   Lymington   Southsea
Wareham   Poole   Milford-   Seaview
Corfe Castle   Bournemouth   on-Sea   Isle of Wight   Shanklin
Weymouth   Swanage   Bonchurch
W

Louth
Horncastle
Burgh le Marsh
NCOLNSHIRE

Wells-next-
the-Sea
Morston
Holt
Little Walsingham
Erpingham
Grimston
Guist
King's Lynn
NORFOLK
Stow Bridge
Norwich
Wymondham
Great
Yarmouth

Stamford
ford-in-England
lton

Ely
CAMBRIDGE-
SHIRE
Diss
Fressingfield
Ixworth
Southwold
Bury St Edmunds
SUFFOLK
Cambridge
Bradfield
Combust
Stonham
Campsea
Ashe
Six Mile
Bottom
Long Melford
Lavenham
Orford
Duxford
Melbourn
Hintlesham
Ipswich
Sudbury
Stoke-by-
Nayland
Broxted
Nayland
Dedham
Manningtree
Standon
Great Dunmow
Coggeshall
Colchester
HERTFORD-
Thundridge
Hatfield
Heath
Felstead
SHIRE
ESSEX
West Mersea
High Ongar

on-
es
GREATER
London
Southend-on-Sea
vickenham
LONDON
ddington
Surbiton
Herne
Bay
Claygate
Sutton
Croydon
Faversham
Whitstable
Tadworth
Canterbury
ate
South Godstone
Sevenoaks
Boughton
Monchelsea
KENT
Chartham
Barham
ng
SURREY
Edenbridge
St. Margaret's
Rusper
East
Grinstead
Goudhurst
Ashford
Lower
Beeding
Turner's Hill
Tunbridge
Wells
Sissinghurst
Folkestone
ckfield
Uckfield
Staple
Cross
SEX
EAST
Brightling
gton
Rushlake Green
SUSSEX
Rye
dburton
Fletching
Herstmonceux
Battle
Brighton
Jevington
Hastings
Seaford
Eastbourne

2. SOUTH & CENTRAL ENGLAND

3. NORTH OF ENGLAND

Berwick-on-Tweed

Powburn
Alnwick

Longhorsley
Morpeth

NORTHUMBERLAND

TYNE AND WEAR
Newcastle-upon-Tyne
East Boldon

Wylam
Shotley
Bridge

Brampton
Crosby-on-Eden

Alston

Melmerby

Appleby-
in-Westmorland

CUMBRIA

Bassenthwaite
Cockermouth
Keswick ● Applethwaite
Braithwaite ● Ullswater

Grasmere ● Ambleside
Bowness- ● Windermere
on-Windermere
Spark Bridge ● Kendal
Witherslack ● Lupton
Ulverston ● Cartmel

Thornton-le-Fylde
Thornton Cleveleys
Blackpool ● Broughton

Garstang

LANCASHIRE
Longridge ● Langho
Ramsbottom
**GREATER
MANCHESTER**
Bury

Durham

DURHAM
West Auckland

Darlington

Richmond ● Moulton

Cowan Bridge

Austwick ● Settle
Clitheroe

Bolton Abbey
Hetton

Masham

Northallerton

Staddlebridge

Stokesley

CLEVELAND

Whitby

Kilburn ● Helmsley

Wath-in-Nidderdale
Markington
Harrogate

NORTH YORKSHIRE

York

Pool-in-
Wharfedale ● Bibrough

Ilkley
Haworth ● Leeds
Bradford ● **WEST
YORKSHIRE**
Ripponden
Huddersfield

Barnsley
Bury ● **SOUTH**

HUMBERSIDE
Walkington
Hull
Winteringham

Isle of Man

4. SCOTLAND

Walls

ORKNEY
ISLANDS

Isle of Lewis

Scarista

Colbost

Uig

Isle of
Skye

Sleat

Arisaig

Isle of Iona

Tiroran
Isle
of
Mull

Achiltibuie

Ullapool
Dundonnel

Gairloch

Contin

Muir-of-Ord
Inverness

Nairn

Drybridge

Drumnadrochit

HIGHLAND

Whitebridge

Dulnain
Bridge

GRAMPIAN

Kildrummy

Aberdee

Kingussie

Newtonmore

Ballater

Maryculter
Banchory

Fort
William

Onich
Kentallen

Kilchrenan

Port Appin
Eriska

Oban

Kilmore

Cairndow

Strachur

Crinan

Kilmun

Kilfinan

Dunoon

Killiecrankie

TAYSIDE

Aberfeldy

Dalguise

Alyth

Blairgowrie

Glamis

Kinclaven

Perth

Scone

Auchterarder

Peat Inn

Cupar

Markinch

St Andrews

FIFE

Anstruther

Aberfoyle

Dunblane

CENTRAL

Bearsden

Linlithgow

North Berwick

Cumbernauld

Ingliston

Edinburgh

Gullane

Glasgow

LOTHIAN

Kirknewton

Stewarton

North Middleton

Isle of Islay

STRATHCLYDE

Quothquan

Troon

Ayr

Peebles

Melrose

BORDERS

Dryburgh

Maybole

Turnberry

Moffat

DUMFRIES
AND
GALLOWAY

Canonbie

Castle
Douglas

Portpatrick

Glenelg

5. IRELAND

Index